*Blood and Ink*

# Blood and Ink

Ignacio Ellacuría, Jon Sobrino,
and the Jesuit Martyrs of
the University of Central America

Robert Lassalle-Klein

*with a Foreword by*
*Jon Sobrino*

ORBIS BOOKS

Maryknoll, New York 10545

 ORBIS BOOKS
Maryknoll, New York 10545

 Fathers and Brothers
MARYKNOLL™

Founded in 1970, Orbis Books endeavors to publish works that enlighten the mind, nourish the spirit, and challenge the conscience. The publishing arm of the Maryknoll Fathers and Brothers, Orbis seeks to explore the global dimensions of the Christian faith and mission, to invite dialogue with diverse cultures and religious traditions, and to serve the cause of reconciliation and peace. The books published reflect the views of their authors and do not represent the official position of the Maryknoll Society. To learn more about Maryknoll and Orbis Books, please visit our website at www.maryknollsociety.org.

---

---

*Library of Congress Cataloging-in-Publication Data*

Lassalle-Klein, Robert Anthony.
    Blood and ink : Ignacio Ellacuría, Jon Sobrino, and the Jesuit martyrs of the University of Central America / Robert Lassalle-Klein.
        pages cm
    Includes bibliographical references and index.
    ISBN 978-1-62698-063-1 (pbk.)
    1. Ellacuría, Ignacio. 2. Sobrino, Jon. 3. El Salvador—Politics and government—1979-1992. 4. El Salvador—Politics and government—1944-1979. 5. Jesuits—Political activity—El Salvador—History—20th century. 6. Victims of state sponsored terrorism—El Salvador—Biography. 7. Martyrs—El Salvador—Biography. 8. Universidad Centroamericana José Simeón Cañas—History—20th century. 9. Liberation theology—El Salvador—History—20th century. 10. Poverty—El Salvador—Religious aspects—History—20th century. I. Title.
    F1488.3.L37   2014
    972.8405'2—dc23
                                                                2013049379

*For Kate, Rosie, and Peter, who grew up with this story;*
*for Lynn, who embraced its meaning for our lives together;*
*and for the UCA martyrs,*
*whose faith, hope, and love for the crucified people of El Salvador*
*are a blessing for those who receive it*

# Presentation

## Rodolfo Cardenal, S.J.

*Blood and Ink* is the story of the martyrs of the University of Central America "José Simeón Cañas" of San Salvador (UCA) interpreted as a sign of the mysterious presence of God in human history. In Robert Lassalle-Klein's telling, God has visited El Salvador in the UCA martyrs, Monseñor Romero, and various other martyrs. The memory of the UCA martyrs finally confronts the American reader with God's appearance there.

This is a complex story whose point of departure is the historical reality of El Salvador, which includes Washington's military intervention in Central America, the role of the church in Latin America, the theology of liberation, and the Society of Jesus. As the reader delves into this rich historical material he or she discovers why the UCA martyrs were killed and what they died for.

This is the story of six Jesuits and two Salvadoran women, mother and daughter, told with respect and admiration, inspired by lives willingly dedicated to the liberation of a people. The fact that this occurred at a Jesuit university raises interesting questions. For how could a university, without ceasing to be what it is, be inserted at the historical crossroads of the Salvadoran people and, led by its commitment to justice, help to realize salvation in history?

The spirituality of the Society of Jesus and the theology of Jon Sobrino and Ignacio Ellacuría offer answers to these questions. But going beyond these theoretical formulations Lassalle-Klein emphasizes the encounter of these six Jesuits with the suffering of the Salvadoran people and with the Risen One. These encounters, which in reality comprise a single encounter with the crucified people of El Salvador, marked the lives and thought of these Jesuits. This is not a depressing story, however, for beyond the tragedy the reader perceives the hope of the resurrection of the Christ of God, which alone provides a nonillusory meaning to history. In the end, then, the question arises as to whether the follower of Jesus today is not also called to help take down from their crosses the crucified peoples of history.

---

Rodolfo Cardenal, S.J. is the former vice-rector for social outreach at the University of Central America in San Salvador. He and Jon Sobrino, S.J., were the two surviving members of the UCA Jesuit community.

# Contents

*Foreword: With Hope and Gratitude*
by Jon Sobrino     xiii

*Acknowledgments*     xv

*Introduction: "It's Them or Us!"*     xvii

### PART I

AWAKENING TO GOD IN THE HISTORICAL REALITY
OF THE PEOPLE OF EL SALVADOR:
ARCHBISHOP ROMERO'S PROPHECY AND
THE BIRTH OF A NEW KIND OF UNIVERSITY

1. *Grasping the Historical Reality of El Salvador (1965-1969):*
   *From Development to the Option for the Poor*     3
   Discontent with the Unfulfilled Promises of Development     4
   The Latin American Church Charts Its Own Path:
       A Deafening Cry     14
   The Conversion of the Central American Jesuits to
       the Preferential Option for the Poor     23

2. *Taking Responsibility for the Historical Reality*
   *of El Salvador (1969-1979): From the Option*
   *for the Poor to the UCA Coup*     53
   Toward a University That Serves Its People: The Presidency
       of Fr. Luis Achaerandio (1969-1974) and the Speech
       to the Inter-American Bank     56
   Consolidating the New Idea of the University: The Presidency
       of Dr. Román Mayorga (1975-1979)     85
   The Church in Defense of Civil Society     101

3. *Transforming the Historical Reality of El Salvador*
   *(1979-1989): From the Agency of the Elite to the Heart*
   *of the People*     121
   Battle for the Soul of Civil Society: State-Sponsored Violence
       versus the Voice of Prophecy     121
   Gradual Emergence of a New Kind of Christian University     157
   Role of the UCA in the Life, Death, and Resurrection
       of Salvadoran Civil Society     167
   Conclusion     180

## PART II

**DOING THEOLOGY WITH THE CRUCIFIED PEOPLE
AND THOSE WHO LOVE THEM:
IGNACIO ELLACURÍA'S FUNDAMENTAL THEOLOGY**

**Introduction**                                                      185

**4. *The Spiritual Exercises of St. Ignatius: Latin America's***
   ***Retreat Master, Miguel Elizondo, S.J.***                        188
   A Daring Challenge                                                 190
   Theologian of the *Spiritual Exercises* of St. Ignatius            195

**5. *Ellacuría's Philosophy of Historical Reality:***
   ***Xavier Zubiri's Sentient Intelligence and Neuroscience***       201
   Mentor and Student                                                 201
   Zubiri's Critique of the Evasion of Reality in the West            204
   Free to Get Real: Sentient Intelligence and the Primacy of Reality 212
   Ellacuría's Christian (or Theological) Historical Realism:
      Innovations                                                     219

**6. *Gloria Dei, Vivens Pauper: Archbishop Oscar Romero***           228
   "In Santiago de María I Ran into Suffering" (1970-1977)            230
   Monseñor Romero: Sent by God to Save His People (1977-1980)        243

**7. *Mysterium Salutis: Karl Rahner***                               253
   Studies with the Great Theologian of the Council                  254
   Historical Reality and Holy Mystery                                257
   The Crucified People: Scandal and Sign of Salvation                273
   Conclusion                                                         284

## PART III

**BEARING THE SPIRIT TO A SUFFERING WORLD:
THE CONTEXTUAL CHRISTOLOGY
OF JON SOBRINO AND IGNACIO ELLACURÍA**

**Introduction**                                                      285

**8. *Mysterium Liberationis: The Christian Historical Realism***
   ***of Ignacio Ellacuría***                                         289
   Introduction: Liberation and the Historicity of Salvation          289
   History and Salvation: Two Aspects of a Larger Whole               291
   Salvation History Is a Salvation in History                        293
   The Historical Reality of Jesus                                    301
   Historical Soteriology and the Crucified People                    303

**9. Analogatum Princeps of the Historical Reality of Jesus:**
   **The Crucified People of El Salvador**                                        309
   Introduction                                                                         309
   The Historical Reality of Jesus as Starting Point for
      Latin American "Saving History" Christology                             313
   "Rising Up" from the Historical Reality of Jesus to
      the Christ of Faith                                                            324
   "Raising Up" Living Signs to the Resurrection: "An Act Proper
      to God Himself"                                                               333
   Conclusion                                                                          335

CONCLUSION:

LIVING SIGNS OF THE RESURRECTION:
THE TRINITARIAN SPIRITUALITY OF THE UCA MARTYRS

Where Have We Been?                                                                337
Whom Did They See?                                                                  340
Their Christological Spirituality: Recognizing Jesus
   in the Crucified People ·                                                        342
Companions of Jesus: Bearers of Jesus' Holy Spirit
   to the People of El Salvador                                                   346
An Easter Event: Sacrament of the Mystery of God
   Transforming the Historical Reality of the Americas                  354

*Index*                                                                                    358

# Foreword

# *With Hope and Gratitude*

## Jon Sobrino

This brief foreword will not attempt to introduce the contents of this book, which I think is magnificent. It is rather a word to encourage the reader, especially those who are younger, to live in a way that humanizes us all.

We have more than enough expectations and false promises today, but hope is not plentiful. In my humble experience hope has always flowered in the presence of great love; from people who have given what they have and what they are; from their time, their knowledge, and their lives. For this reason martyrs are not just witnesses, but rather witnesses of a very special kind. They are witnesses who have given their lives so that the victims and the poor might finally have life.

In the early 1980s while writing my doctoral dissertation on Jürgen Moltmann I read his *Theology of Hope*. Paradoxically, however, it was his book *The Crucified God* that gave me more hope. As he later wrote in a similar vein, "Not every life is an occasion of hope, but the life of Jesus is, who for love took upon himself the cross and death."

In El Salvador I have been given the grace of meeting thousands of people like this Jesus of Nazareth. In March we recall Rutilio Grande and Monseñor Romero. In November we always remember the UCA Jesuits, with Julia Elba and Celina. In December we honor the four North American women, Ita, Maura, Dorothy, and Jean, as well as many hundreds of lay people and campesino men and women like Ticha and Polín.

This book gives testimony to the lives of these people who give us hope, and each person who reads it will find their own way to respond. My hope is that we all might be moved to a desire for conversion, compassion for the victims, and a determination to work for justice and to take the crucified peoples down from the cross. Hopefully, and what is most humanizing of all, we will be grateful to them.

This gratitude (like hope) is not plentiful in our world, and perhaps that is because it does not even occur to us that we need to thank the poor and the victims. Nonetheless, as Monseñor Romero and Father Ellacuría used to say, it is the poor and victims who save us.

In the terms used here, then, they have the power to humanize us. They are sources of living water, given so that this world might overcome its insensitivity and triviality. They are living water that strengthens us in the struggle against injustice and lies.

What we have spoken about here is utopia. But without utopia there is no life. My hope is that this book will help to promote both utopia and life so that, in a word, we might be human.

March 12, 2014
Anniversary of Fr. Rutilio Grande, S.J., martyr

# Acknowledgments

Four years after the assassinations of his brothers and friends, Jon Sobrino, S.J., answered my request to write a dissertation on his Christology with an invitation. He agreed to serve on the committee if I would tell the story of the martyrs, and especially Ellacuría. What I did not understand was that my *yes* to this life-changing invitation would open the door to a remarkable community of scholars, friends, saints, and martyrs who would be there to help. Thus, much of what is best in this book has been given to me by others, including the martyrs themselves, while its defects must be considered solely my own.

First and foremost I am grateful to Jon Sobrino, who in directing me to Ellacuría's writings patiently explained that it was the historical reality of the people of El Salvador and their encounter with God, most especially in the presence of Monseñor Romero, where the grace of the martyrs' conversion was to be found. Dean Brackley, S.J., warmly embraced the role of spiritual godfather for this journey, providing housing in the Jesuit community, friendship, and a wry warning on a weekend bus to Jayaque (where he carried on the ministry of Ignacio Martín-Baró, S.J.) that I should plan to get to know Ellacuría's mentor, Xavier Zubiri.

Rodolfo Cardenal, S.J., generously read the historical sections (Part I) and provided invaluable feedback and insights without which the book would be much poorer. Charles Beirne, S.J., improved the history and provided direction to important archival materials located in the offices of the president at the University of Central America and the provincial headquarters of the Central American Jesuits. Román Mayorga and Juan Hernández-Pico, S.J., provided crucial interview material and shared unpublished materials; Francisco Estrada, S.J., generously agreed to be interviewed about his time as provincial; and I will always remember traveling with Jon Cortina, S.J. to the parish at Aquilares, where he replaced Rutilio Grande, S.J., after his death.

The treatment of each major figure owes much to communities of scholars without whose expertise and support such an ambitious book would have been impossible. The sections on Ellacuría owe much to the groundbreaking work of Antonio González, Kevin Burke, S.J., Martin Maier, S.J., Michael Lee, José Sols, Matt Ashley, José Mora Galiana, and opportunities to discuss early drafts at the International Colloquium on Ignacio Ellacuría, the Catholic Theological Society of America, and the Academy of Catholic Hispanic Theologians in the United States. The treatment of Karl Rahner's influence on Ellacuría and Jon Sobrino builds on the pioneering work of Martin Maier, S.J.; it benefitted from the generous suggestions of Peter Fritz, Ann Riggs, and Paul Crowley, S.J.;

and is indebted to Mark Fisher and the Karl Rahner Society, who allowed me to present and refine this work, and to Michael Buckley, S.J., who introduced me to Rahner and first encouraged me go on for doctoral studies. I am grateful to Antonio González and the Fundación Xavier Zubiri, who introduced me to Zubiri scholars from Europe and Latin America, for the opportunity discuss this work at meetings of the International Congress on Xavier Zubiri; to Javier Montserrat, S.J., who first introduced me to Zubiri and the significance of his work on sentient intelligence for cognitive neuroscience; and to Joel Nigg, who helped me to advance this work. Jon Sobrino, Dean Brackley, and the Centro Monseñor Romero provided crucial insights and support for the work on Archbishop Romero, including finding lost editorials from *Orientación*, the diocesan newspaper. Bernie Bush, S.J., provided spiritual support and important scholarship on the mystical foundations of the *Spiritual Exercises* of St. Ignatius. Gene Palumbo provided perspective and an inexhaustable source of personal recollections regarding key historical events and protagonists; Raúl Fornet-Betancourt helped me to see the intercultural implications of the philosophical writings of Ellacuría and Zubiri; Francisco Mena provided important information on his father; José Antonio and Rosa Marina Zavala provided crucial testimony; and Dick Howard, Peter Hinde, O.Carm., and Cathy Cornell carefully reviewed the historical sections.

Grants, fellowships and other forms of financial support were generously provided at various times by the Santa Clara University; Holy Names University; DePaul University; the Wabash Center for Teaching and Learning in Theology; the Ignatian Center for Jesuit Education (Santa Clara University); the University of Notre Dame; Berchmanskolleg, Hochschule für Philosophie, Munich; Universitat Ramon Llul, Barcelona, Spain; the International Congress on Intercultural Philosophy; the Universidad Centroamericana José Simeón Cañas; the Center for Liberation Theology, University of Louvain; Institut Catholique, Paris; and the Jesuit School of Theology at Berkeley.

Special thanks are due to Fr. Virgilio Elizondo and Fr. Gustavo Gutiérrez, O.P., whose constant support and wise counsel opened many doors and helped to shape the project; to the John Courtney Murray Group, whose members generously read most of the book; to Sophia Park, S.N.J.M., and our colleagues at Holy Names University; to the community of the Oakland Catholic Worker, where much of this started; and to Tom Smolich, S.J., Bill O'Neill, S.J., Steve Kelly, S.J., and Francisco Herrera, whose friendship and faith helped sustain the project.

Finally, I am grateful to my wife, Lynn, and to our wonderful children, Kate, Rose, and Peter. I thank God for the chance to love you and to share life's great adventures with each of you. Love is a gift, which grows and multiplies like the tiny mustard seed when it is freely given in the Reign of God.

# Introduction

## *"It's Them or Us!"*

[The 1993 Commission on the Truth for El Salvador produced] a chilling Report which . . . reveals how violence and state terrorism were used mercilessly against civil society. . . . Two [cases], in particular, shook the conscience of the world: the assassination of Archbishop Romero, committed by a death squad under the command of the founder of the ARENA party [Roberto D'Aubuisson], and the assassination of the Jesuit fathers and their domestic employees, ordered by the military high command.

> Pedro Nikken, President of the Inter-American
> Court of Human Rights[1]

It's Them or Us!

> Words of Colonel Guillermo Benavides to
> Jesuit high school graduate, Lieutenant Ricardo Espinoza,
> ordering him to assassinate Fr. Ignacio Ellacuría, S.J.,
> President of the University of Central America[2]

A few minutes after 8:00 p.m. on November 11, 1989, rebel forces of the National Liberation Party (FMLN) launched the largest urban offensive of its eight-year civil war against El Salvador's repressive right-wing government.[3] The country's

---

1. Pedro Nikken, *El manejo del pasado y la cuestión de la impunidad en la solución de los conflictos armados de El Salvador y Guatemala*, published in "Liber Amicorum—Héctor Fix-Zamudio," Volume I, Secretariat of the Inter-American Court of Human Rights, San José, Costa Rica, 1998, 149. Nikken was designated the United Nations independent expert on El Salvador by Resolution 1992/62 of March 3, 1992, of the U.N. Commission on Human Rights, and submitted his report in 1993 (see UN, E/CN.4/1993/11, February 15, 1993). With respect to the extrajudicial execution of the Jesuit priests and two domestic employees, committed in November 1989, see Inter-American Court of Human Rights, Annual Report 1999, Report No. 136/99, December 22, 1999.

2. Extrajudicial statements of Lt. José Ricardo Espinoza Guerra and Lt. Yusshy René Mendoza Vallecillos, cited in Martha Doggett, *Death Foretold: The Jesuit Murders in El Salvador* (Washington, DC: Georgetown University Press, Lawyers Committee for Human Rights, 1993), 65.

3. A CIA analysis of the offensive states, "The rebel's principal focus was the capital, but they also initiated heavy fighting throughout much of the country, including the departments of Santa Ana, San Miguel, and Usulután." *U.S. Declassified Documents I*, CIA, Directorate

military and its U.S. sponsors were stunned by the strength and scope of the attack. The noise of fierce gun battles erupted throughout the capital city of San Salvador, and military flares illuminated the night sky. Two thousand rebel troops occupied entire neighborhoods until aerial bombing of the civilian population by the Salvadoran Air Force forced them to retreat. From there the rebels entered the wealthy Escalón district, home of government and business elites,[4] attacking the official and private residences of the president and the head of the Legislative Assembly and the barracks of three separate Infantry Brigades and the Infantry Police.[5] Nearby, they provoked a standoff at the iconic Sheraton Hotel with U.S. Green Berets, who beat a hasty retreat unharmed into awaiting helicopters. Analyzing the rebels' ability to hold portions of the capital for three weeks, the *Los Angeles Times* reported that "the intensity and duration of the offensive" had the "right-wing government reeling," threatened to "make the country ungovernable," and "undermined" the central claims of "a decade of U.S. counterinsurgency policy."[6] Embarrassed by early losses and worried about continued U.S. support for its nine-year civil war against the rebels, on November 12 the government declared a state of emergency and established combat zones throughout the capital under the command of Colonel René Emilio Ponce, chief of staff of the Salvadoran Armed Forces.

At 6:30 p.m. on November 15, the fifth day of the occupation, with no end in sight, the United Nations Commission on the Truth for El Salvador says that Colonel Ponce convened "a meeting of the General Staff with military heads and commanders to adopt new measures to deal with the offensive."[7] The meeting took place at military headquarters (the *Estado Major*), and one participant described the mood as FMLN guerrillas roamed the capital just blocks away as "the most tense and desperate gathering of the country's top military commanders since the war . . . began a decade ago."[8] Colonel Ponce states that some twenty-four officers attended the meeting "to analyze the positions we had lost since November 11 [and to determine] . . . what we needed to do to regain them," adding ominously, "We understood that we needed to take stronger measures."[9]

---

of Intelligence, "El Salvador: The FMLN after the November 1989 Offensive," January 26, 1990. Cited in Hugh Byrne, *El Salvador's Civil War: A Study of Revolution* (Boulder, CO: Lynne Rienner, 1996), 171.

4. The preceding details are from Byrne, *El Salvador's Civil War*, 152–53.

5. United Nations, *Report of the Commission on the Truth for El Salvador, From Madness to Hope: The 12-Year War in El Salvador*, March 15, 1993, 49.

6. Richard Boudreaux and Marjorie Miller, "Offensive Pushed Salvador War to New, Bloodier Level," *Los Angeles Times*, November 30, 1989, 1. Cited in Byrne, *El Salvador's Civil War*, 152–53.

7. United Nations, *Report of the Commission on the Truth for El Salvador*, 50.

8. *San Francisco Examiner*, February 5, 1990. Cited in Doggett, *Death Foretold*, 56; and Inter-American Commission on Human Rights, Organization of American States, Report No. 136/99, "*Ignacio Ellacuría, et al*," December 22, 1999, 128.

9. Lawyers Committee interview with Col. René Emilio Ponce, Estado Mayor, February 14, 1990. Cited in Doggett, *Death Foretold*, 55.

This was evidently a euphemism for Ponce's decision to start dropping 500 to 700-pound bombs on occupied civilian neighborhoods[10] and to implement long-held plans to begin murdering civilian political opponents. What followed evokes more recent images of dictators ordering troops to fire on unarmed civilians in desperate attempts to hold onto power during the "Arab Spring," which began in 2011. The United Nations states,

> Colonel Ponce authorized the elimination of ringleaders, trade unionists and known leaders of the FMLN and a decision was taken to step up bombing [of civilian neighborhoods] by the Air Force and to use artillery and armored vehicles to dislodge the FMLN from the areas it controlled. The Minister of Defense, General Rafael Humberto Larios López, asked whether anyone objected. No hand was raised. It was agreed that President Cristiani would be consulted.[11]

Emboldened by this *carte blanche* to attack civilians, Colonel Guillermo Benavides turned to General Rafael Bustillo, seated next to him, and said, according to a source who attended the meeting, "This is a chance to go after" civilian groups considered supporters of the FMLN, adding, "I have the UCA [University of Central America] in my sector." General Bustillo replied, "Well then, you know what you have to do."[12]

General Larios López states that the session broke up around 10:00 p.m.,[13] and the United Nations says, "After the meeting, the officers stayed in the room talking in groups."[14] Colonel Ponce gathered with several top-ranking officers, including General Bustillo (chief of the Air Force), Colonel Francisco Elena Fuentes (commander of the First Infantry Brigade), Colonel Juan Orlando Zepeda (vice minister of defense), and Colonel Inocente Orlando Montano (vice minister of public security). The report then asserts, "Colonel Ponce called over Colonel Guillermo Alfredo Benavides [director of the Military Academy] and, in front of the four other officers, ordered him to eliminate Father Ellacuría and to leave no witnesses," adding that he was "to use the unit from the U.S.-trained Atlacatl Battalion."[15]

Within the hour, around 11:00 p.m., Colonel Benavides summoned Lieutenant Ricardo Espinoza, a young graduate of the Jesuit high school in San Salvador,[16] and ordered him to assassinate Fr. Ignacio Ellacuría, S.J., president

---

10. This detail is from Doggett, *Death Foretold*, 56.

11. United Nations, *Report of the Commission on the Truth for El Salvador*, 50.

12. Lawyers Committee interview, May 25, 1991, anonymity requested. Reported in Doggett, *Death Foretold*, 10.

13. Written statement of General Humberto Larios, Fourth Criminal Court, August 29, 1990; INTERJUST, Sistema Informativo de la Corte Suprema de Justícia, September 4, 1990. Cited in Doggett, *Death Foretold*, 57.

14. United Nations, *Report of the Commission on the Truth for El Salvador*, 50.

15. Ibid.

16. Martha Doggett states that this detail was provided by "the extrajudicial confessions of the suspects." Doggett, *Death Foretold*, 65.

of the Jesuit-run UCA, and to leave no witnesses. This implied the murder of Ellacuría's housemates, including Fr. Segundo Montes, S.J., the young man's former high school principal and teacher. Espinoza protested, saying, "this is a serious problem."[17] But Benavides insisted and ordered Lieutenant Yusshy Mendoza, who had been sent to fetch his former Military Academy classmate, that he must participate in the action "in order to overcome any reluctance on . . . [Espinoza's] part."[18] Knowing he might face Fr. Montes, Espinoza took a bar of black camouflage grease with which to disguise himself and a little over three hours later "gave the order to kill the priests."[19] Espinoza later testified that his eyes filled with tears as he hurriedly left the Jesuit university residence while his troops riddled the helpless victims with bullets.[20]

General Larios reports that he called President Cristiani, who arrived at the military headquarters at 11:00 p.m. and stayed until about 2:00 a.m.[21] The U.N. report confirms that President Cristiani was indeed present at the Military Academy and that he met with the high command during most of the operation on November 16.[22] The report by the Lawyer's Committee on Human Rights, an official plaintiff in the case, asserts that the assassinations took place around 2:30 a.m., at which point it suggests that President Cristiani may have left the grounds of the military headquarters.[23] Thus, the Jesuit murders were ordered by the highest levels of the Salvadoran military, with possible approval by the president of the country, and were in the process of being carried out while he was closeted with the military leadership about a mile from the scene of the crime.[24] At the time of this writing, the Spanish National Court has reserved the right to indict former President Cristiani for involvement in the killings.[25]

The question remains, however, why implicate virtually the entire command structure of the Salvadoran military, and possibly the president, in order to kill one priest and a handful of associates? The easy answer is that Colonel Ponce and the others understood that their ability to avoid prosecution as the intellectual authors of the assassinations would depend upon implicating all of their

---

17. Ibid., 65. Cited from "Narración de los hechos," prepared by the Jesuits of Central America, which appeared in *Estudios centroamericanos* (*ECA*) nos. 493-494 (November-December 1989): at 1125-32.

18. United Nations, *Report of the Commission on the Truth for El Salvador*, 48.

19. Ibid., 47. Also Doggett, *Death Foretold*, 65.

20. Extrajudicial confession of José Ricardo Espinoza Guerra, *ECA* nos. 493-494 (November-December 1989): 1162.

21. Written statement of General Humberto Larios, Fourth Criminal Court, August 29, 1990; INTERJUST, Sistema Informativo de la Corte Suprema de Justícia, September 9, 1990. Cited in Doggett, *Death Foretold*, 57; see n. 162.

22. The U.N. report offers a slightly different timetable, stating, "From 12 to 1:30 a.m. . . . , 16 November, President Cristiani met with the High Command." United Nations, *Report of the Commission on the Truth for El Salvador*, 50.

23. Doggett, *Death Foretold*, 282.

24. United Nations, *Report of the Commission on the Truth for El Salvador*, 45-54.

25. The Center for Justice and Accountability, "El Salvador: The Jesuits' Massacre Case"; http://cja.org/article.php?list=type&type=84; accessed July 31, 2011.

peers. Clearly, the decision to murder Ellacuría was by no means a last-minute decision taken in a state of near panic in the face of FMLN control of parts of the capital.[26] Indeed, a variety of historical, ideological, and personal factors fueled the deep-seated animosity of El Salvador's extreme right for Ignacio Ellacuría. But the most important irritant may have been the threat posed by the work of Ignacio Ellacuría and his UCA colleagues to continued U.S. support for the government of El Salvador and its suppression of Salvadoran civil society with its demands for economic, political, and social change.

Martha Doggett, in her exhaustive report on the UCA murders, explains that in light of such factors, "Some observers believe that these officers have in retrospect exaggerated the severity of the FMLN challenge as well as their despair at the time in an attempt to rationalize the Jesuit murders and extensive aerial bombardment."[27] Her report on behalf of the Central American Jesuits and the Lawyers Committee for Human Rights, the official plaintiffs in the case before the Inter-American Commission on Human Rights, charges, "An examination of events during the year preceding the UCA murders suggests that the decision to move against the Jesuits may have been taken months earlier."[28] Confirming this view, the Inter-American Commission on Human Rights cites a pattern of slanders and "attacks by government officials and members of the Armed Forces" against the Jesuits going back "three years before the extra-judicial executions."[29]

Thus, Doggett concludes, "While the guerrilla offensive provided a last-minute impetus and suitable cover, hard-liners within the Army had long before resolved finally to act on their 10-year wish to silence Fr. Ignacio Ellacuría." Indeed, she says, "The decision to kill Father Ellacuría was consistent with a long-standing pattern of attacks against the Jesuits [and] . . . increasing attempts to link the Jesuits to FMLN violence and to portray the priests as apologists for guerrilla actions."[30]

In the pages that follow we shall trace the roots of this long-held antipathy and its role in the decision to carry out the assassinations in the epoch-changing religious and political events that rocked Latin America and the Catholic Church in the decades after World War II.

Those who died included Fr. Ignacio Ellacuría, S.J., university president and the country's leading public intellectual; Fr. Martín-Baró, S.J., university vice president for academic affairs and director of the University Institute of Public Opinion (IUDOP), El Salvador's only functioning public opinion poll; Fr. Segundo Montes, S.J., director of the Human Rights Institute of the UCA (IDHUCA) and superior of the Jesuit community; Fr. Amando López, S.J., professor of theology and philosophy, and ex-president of the UCA in Managua;

---

26. See Lawyers Committee interview with Col. René Emilio Ponce, Estado Mayor, February 14, 1990. Cited and described in Doggett, *Death Foretold*, 55.

27. Doggett, *Death Foretold*, 55.

28. Ibid., 4.

29. Inter-American Commission on Human Rights, Report 136/99, 13-14.

30. Doggett, *Death Foretold*, 4.

Fr. Joaquin López y López, S.J., national director of *Fe y Alegría*, an education and direct service program for children in poverty; Fr. Juan Ramón Moreno, S.J., assistant director of the newly constructed Oscar Romero Pastoral Center, campus home of the Center for Theological Reflection and part of the Jesuit community; Elba Ramos, cook for one of the seminary communities; and her sixteen-year-old daughter, Celina.

Jürgen Moltmann's famous book, *The Crucified God*, was found soaked in blood by the body of Fr. Juan Ramón Moreno and is preserved in the university's museum of the martyrs, just feet from where they died. It is a visceral sign of the cost of this ultimately unsuccessful attempt to silence the voice of a university that, for almost two decades, scrupulously documented the need to take the "crucified people" of El Salvador down from their cross. The blood and ink mingled on its pages serves as a fitting symbol of the faith, hope, and love that animated them and their vision of a Christian university grounded in God's preferential option for the poor.

* * *

Part I of this book, then, tells the story of the UCA martyrs, focusing on their awakening to God's self-offer in the crucified people of El Salvador and to Medellín's call to take them down from the cross. We will follow the journey that led to the crossroads above, exploring the martyrs' vision of the Christian university and their efforts "to do in our university way what [Oscar Romero] did in his pastoral way"[31] as archbishop of San Salvador. I will discuss a variety of factors and events, both sacred and profane, including the conversion of Archbishop Romero; relevant aspects of the social, economic, political, and indigenous history of El Salvador; the influence on the thinking and spirituality of the martyrs of the *Spiritual Exercises* of St. Ignatius, Vatican II, and the Latin American bishops at Medellín; the post–World War II promise of development and the role of the United Nations in Latin America; U.S. Cold War counterinsurgency doctrine and foreign policy; and many other factors.

Part II treats the Latin American fundamental theology of Ignacio Ellacuría and the underlying Christian historical realism that informs it. Here I will critically explore the transformations produced by Ellacuría's dialogue with Ignatian spirituality, Xavier Zubiri's neuroscientifically informed model of intelligence and his philosophy of God, the face of Christ revealed by Archbishop Romero in El Salvador's suffering people, and Rahner's christocentric and trinitarian fundamental theology.

Part III analyzes Ellacuría's fundamental theology and Sobrino's Christology as a collaborative theological reflection on God's gracious self-offer in the life, death, and resurrection of Jesus Christ and its *analogatum princeps* in the crucified people of the planet. I will examine why they consider the poor and

---

31. Ignacio Ellacuría, "La UCA ante el doctorado concedido a Monseñor Romero," *Escritos teológicos*, III (San Salvador: UCA Editores, 2002), 104.

oppressed to be the defining sign of the times and a privileged *locus theologicus* for the encounter with God.

Finally, I will conclude by exploring the God revealed to the UCA martyrs and their companions by the suffering people of El Salvador.

This is a story of blood and ink; of writers, books, teaching, service projects, and learning dedicated to uncovering the truth about El Salvador's state-sponsored persecution of civil society funded by U.S. tax dollars. But most of all it is the tale of a university's efforts to help take El Salvador's "crucified people" down from the cross by supporting their efforts to construct a society in which all would have a chance to share a future where dignity, love, compassion, and sanity might prevail.

# Part I

## *Awakening to God in the Historical Reality of the People of El Salvador*

### Archbishop Romero's Prophecy and the Birth of a New Kind of University

# 1

# Grasping the Historical Reality of El Salvador (1965-1969)

## From Development to the Option for the Poor

When I came back in 1972 I heard what had been going on in the Central American Jesuit Province at the end of the sixties . . . there had been a conversion. But what does that mean, conversion? Well, I would say it meant discovering the reality that had always been in front of us. We had it in front of our eyes, and had not seen it. . . . But all of a sudden you see things the way they are, or at least . . . a little more the way they are. And that changes everything. It is, at least, the beginning of a process of change.

Jon Sobrino, S.J.[1]

The movement into a new horizon involves an about-face; it comes out of the old by repudiating characteristic features; it begins a new sequence that can keep revealing ever greater depth and breadth and wealth. Such an about-face and new beginning is what is meant by a conversion. . . . [But] conversion involves more than a change of horizon. It can mean that one begins to belong to a different social group, or, if one's group remains the same, that one begins to belong to it in a new way.

Bernard Lonergan, S.J.[2]

This is the story of the Jesuit martyrs and their companions at the University of Central America (UCA). Fr. Jon Sobrino, S.J., is the most important living witness to the events that form the core of our story, a survivor of the assassinations and Ignacio Ellacuría's closest friend. Looking back on forty years of teaching,

---

1. Robert Lassalle-Klein interview with Jon Sobrino, July 5, 1994, 2, 5.

2. Bernard Lonergan, *Method in Theology* (New York: Crossroad/Herder & Herder, 1972; Seabury, 1979), 237-38, 269.

writing, and ministry in El Salvador since Medellín, Sobrino believes that the Central American Jesuits and their colleagues at the UCA experienced a conversion to God's preferential option for the poor brought about by their engagement with the historical reality of the people of El Salvador. The trailhead of the path that brought them face to face with this reality and the change of horizon it provoked surely begins with the renewal of the Catholic Church initiated by the worldwide meeting of Catholic bishops at Vatican II (1962-1965). Its signature document, *Gaudium et spes* (GS), the Pastoral Constitution on the Church in the Modern World, presented the leadership of churches on every continent with the challenge "of reading the signs of the times and of interpreting them in light of the Gospel" (GS 4). Just three years later the Second General Conference of Latin American Bishops at Medellín, Colombia, August 26-September 6, 1968, took up the Council's call, declaring, "A deafening cry pours from the throats of millions of men and women asking their pastors for a liberation that reaches them from nowhere else."[3] The bishops' response to this *cri de coeur* from 1968 to the present has been their watershed discernment that God is calling the Latin American church to live out what Catholic Social Teaching calls a "preferential option for the poor."[4]

### Discontent with the Unfulfilled Promises of Development

In what follows I will show that the embrace by the leadership of the church in Latin America of what they saw as God's preferential option for the poor coincided with a growing conviction that the promises of the U.N. Decade of Development had failed to adequately address the suffering and poverty of its people. I will argue that these and other factors led the bishops to subordinate the concept of *development* to a *preferential option for the poor* as the proper horizon or framework for the work of the church in Latin America. The bishops did not abandon the term "development," but tried to build on the use of "integral development" by Pope Paul VI in order to critique uses of the term "development" and developmentalist strategies that changed little and legitimated an oppressive status quo. Thus, Medellín asserts, "If development is the new name for peace, Latin American underdevelopment, with its own characteristics in the different countries, is an unjust situation which promotes tensions that conspire against peace."[5] This criticism is further concretized in Medellín's use of

---

3. Second General Conference of Latin American Bishops, "Document on Poverty in the Church" (2), in *The Church in the Present-Day Transformation of Latin America in the Light of the Council: II Conclusions* (Washington, DC: Division for Latin America–United States Catholic Conference, 1973).

4. Pope John Paul II *Sollicitudo rei socialis*, December 30, 1987, §42; and Pope Benedict XVI *Address of His Holiness Benedict XVI to the Bishops of Latin America and the Caribbean*, Shrine of Aparecida, May 13, 2007, no. 3.

5. "Document on Peace" (1), in *The Church in the Present-Day Transformation of Latin America*.

the word "liberation"[6] to highlight and clarify its claim that fundamental social and structural "change will be essential in order to liberate the authentic process of Latin American development and integration."[7] Accordingly, the document insists that God's call to live out a preferential option for the poor implies real, and sometimes drastic, economic, social, political, and cultural changes designed to promote and defend human dignity, the church's ultimate criterion for all forms of development.

In this chapter I will tell the story of how the term *development*, which dominated the international discussion about material aid to those living in poverty and subject to marginalization, became subordinated in the Latin American church to *the preferential option for the poor*, and to the struggle for *liberation* and justice, which that commitment implies. I will also describe how these two concepts began to function as an effective historical framework or horizon that would lead the UCA Jesuits and their lay collaborators to become aware of, to take responsibility for, and finally to help transform and be transformed by the historical reality of the poor majorities of El Salvador.

In what follows, I will focus on the emergence of the development regime after World War II and its subordination to the option for the poor by the Latin American bishops and Latin American liberation theology because it is directly relevant to the response of the UCA martyrs to the "irruption of the poor" in the last third of the twentieth century. It is worth noting, however, that our approach will focus on only one aspect of the many forms of oppression to which Christian communities and churches around the globe (including Latin America) have responded during this period with critiques and prophetic calls for liberation from military rule, and serious social, cultural, and political change.[8]

### President Truman, the Cold War, and Development

The end of World War II in 1945 brought a dramatic shift in the balance of power from the European countries and their colonial empires to two new competing super-states, the United States and the Soviet Union. In this new context, "development" and military aid (punctuated by occasional military interven-

---

6. Examples include "Document on Justice" (3-4); "Document on Education" (2, 9); "Document on Youth" (15); "Document on Catechesis" (6); "Document on Lay Movements" (2, 4, 9, 13); "Document on the Poverty of the Church" (2, 7) in *The Church in the Present-Day Transformation of Latin America*.

7. "Document on Justice" (3), in *The Church in the Present-Day Transformation of Latin America*.

8. While the following list is by no means comprehensive, one has only to think of the lasting contributions of Black theologies from Africa and the United States and Dalit theologies from India on the theme of race, the contributions of U.S. Latino/a theologies on the importance of culture, the contributions of Asian Christians on interreligious dialogue, the contributions of any number of groups calling for a global ethic, and the global contributions of women on the importance of gender, and of indigenous theologies on respect for the planet in fleshing out our understanding of how God has acted, stirring faith, hope, and love among followers of Jesus around the planet.

tion) would replace European colonialism as the principle tools for projecting and maintaining power abroad in the respective "spheres of influence" of the two emerging superpowers.

The stage for this post-war Cold War drama was set with the close of the Battle of Berlin, when the German General, Helmuth Weidling, surrendered to the Soviet army on May 2, 1945, while the armies north of Berlin surrendered to the Western Allies. It soon became clear that the Soviet leader, Joseph Stalin, who envisioned a communist Bloc allied with Russia that would provide a buffer zone in Eastern Europe against centuries of European imperialism, was not going to withdraw his armies from Berlin and Eastern Germany. Working to establish a post-war Soviet sphere of influence, Stalin soon provided Soviet support to the military wing of the Greek Communist Party in its civil war (1946-49) against the right-wing Greek government and the monarchy, and used Soviet troops to threaten Turkey in the strait linking the Black Sea with the Mediterranean Sea. The United States, however, had a radically different vision for a worldwide democratic and capitalist alliance rooted in a united Europe (the North American Treaty Organization or NATO), and supported by overwhelming U.S. military might. The latter was epitomized by U.S. possession of the atomic bomb, which it used three months later against civilian populations in Hiroshima (August 6, 1945) and Nagasaki (August 9, 1945) ostensibly in order to induce the August 15, 1945, "unconditional surrender" of Japan, the remaining Axis power.

A little over two years later, on March 12, 1947, President Harry S. Truman outlined before a joint session of Congress his plan to provide economic and military aid to Turkey and Greece in order to prevent their falling into the emerging Eastern Bloc. Truman requested $400 million in military and economic aid for Greece and Turkey,[9] and "American civilian and military personnel"[10] in order to assist those countries in defeating what he saw as the proxy forces of Soviet expansionism in post-war Europe. The underlying logic became known as the *Truman Doctrine*, and it would shape U.S. foreign policy for the next forty years. The Cold War was on!

Shortly thereafter, on June 5, 1947, Secretary of State George C. Marshall outlined at Harvard University what became known as the *Marshall Plan*, which many considered the economic corollary of the Truman Doctrine. The United States would create a program for post-war reconstruction and economic recovery funded by U.S. aid for European countries threatened with Soviet expansion. Barely a month later, George F. Kennan, head of policy planning at the State Department, framed U.S. post-war foreign policy in the larger context of "firm and vigilant *containment* of Russian expansive tendencies."[11] In this way

---

9. Harry S. Truman, "Recommendation for Assistance to Greece and Turkey," 5, in "Address of the President to Congress, Recommending Assistance to Greece and Turkey, March 12, 1947," http://www.trumanlibrary.org; accessed June 1, 2011.

10. Ibid.

11. George F. Kennan (identified only as "X"), "The Sources of Soviet Conduct," *Foreign*

the Truman Doctrine, which was focused on U.S. military aid and Soviet containment, and the Marshall Plan, which was focused on post-war reconstruction and economic *development*, came to be seen as two sides of a single coin, providing the foundation of U.S. foreign policy at the beginning of the Cold War. The policy achieved apparent success over the next twenty years in Europe and Japan. But the often contradictory imperatives of war and economic development would undermine U.S. foreign policy and counter-insurgency efforts in Latin America, Africa, and Asia, sometimes contributing to the suffering of the poor majorities in those parts of the world.[12]

Gilbert Rist notes that two years later President Truman's January 20, 1949, Inaugural Address formally "inaugurated the 'development age.'"[13] The speech lists four policies that would dominate Truman's second term and define U.S. foreign policy until the collapse of the Soviet Union in 1991. The first three points essentially summarized the existing policy of U.S. support for the New United Nations, European reconstruction through the Marshall Plan, and Soviet containment through NATO. But the fourth point, which Rist says was "taken on board as a public relations gimmick," proposed "a bold new program . . . for the improvement and growth of underdeveloped areas."[14]

## From "Colonization" to "Underdevelopment"

Rist explains in *The History of Development* that Truman's use of the adjective "underdeveloped" marked "the first time the term had been used in a text intended for such wide circulation as a synonym for 'economically backward' areas."[15] U.S. policy makers embraced the term as the embodiment of "a new way of conceiving international relations"[16] that fit nicely with the goals of U.S. post-war foreign policy. North-South relations, which before World War II had been largely cast in terms of the troubled relationships between European colonizers and their restless clients in the South and the East, soon faced national liberation struggles. With Truman's speech, however, the hierarchical subordination of colonized to colonizer was being reframed. "'*Underdeveloped*' and '*developed*' were [recast as] *members of a single family*: the one might be lagging a little behind the other, but they could always hope to catch up—rather as a 'deputy manager' can always dream of becoming a manager himself . . . so

---

*Affairs* 25 (July 1947): 566-82. Reprinted in Paul F. Boller, Jr., and Ronald Story, eds., *A More Perfect Union: Documents in U.S. History*, Vol. II: *Since 1865* (3rd ed.; Boston: Houghton Mifflin 1992), 186.

12. Gilbert Rist, *The History of Development: From Western Origins to Global Faith* (new rev. and expanded ed.; New York: Zed Books, 2002), 71.

13. Ibid., 69-79.

14. Ibid., 71.

15. Ibid., 72.

16. Ibid.

long as he continues to play the same game and his conception of managing is not too different."[17]

Rist argues, however, that there was a darker side to the aforementioned shift.

> From 1949 onwards, often without realizing it, more than two billion inhabitants of the planet found themselves changing their name, being "officially" regarded as they appeared in the eyes of others, called upon to deepen their Westernization by repudiating their own values. No longer African, Latin American or Asian . . . they were now simply "underdeveloped." . . . Whereas the world of colonization had been seen mainly as a political space to encompass ever larger empires, the "development age" was the period when economic space spread everywhere, with the raising of GNP as the number one imperative.[18]

Development soon became a major focus of United Nations activities and remained so throughout the Cold War to the present. This was true in part because of strong international support for the lofty goals stated above, and in part because Cold War politics led the permanent members of the U.N. Security Council to use their veto power to block the majority of U.N. initiatives "with respect to threats . . . , breaches of the peace, and acts of aggression."[19]

### Decolonization and Post-Colonial Critiques

Outside Europe, the United States, and the Soviet Union, however, the post-war collapse of the overseas colonial empires of the Western powers constituted nothing short of a turning point in world history in the eyes of many. Between 1945 and 2000 approximately ninety countries gained independence from colonial rule, including India, Pakistan, China, Vietnam, Cuba, Malaysia, Nigeria, Congo, Angola, South Africa, and virtually the entire African continent, which saw the birth of over fifty nations between 1950 and 1980 alone. On December 14, 1960, the United Nations passed the *Declaration on the Granting of Independence to Colonial Countries and Peoples*, with eighty-nine nations in favor, and abstentions by nine colonial powers (Australia, Belgium, Dominican Republic, France, Portugal, Spain, Union of South Africa, United Kingdom, and United States).

Julius K. Nyerere, president of Tanzania evocatively described the spirit of decolonization as "a worldwide movement . . . to put an end to the exploitation of man by man [so that] imperialism and racialism will become . . . a chapter in the history of man we shall hear about . . . in museums."[20] In this connection, Prasenjit Duara explains, "Decolonization represented not only the transfer-

---

17. Ibid., 74.

18. Ibid., 79.

19. Ibid., 81.

20. Julius. K Nyerere, *Freedom and Development/Uhuru Na Maen-Deleo: A Selection of Writings and Speeches, 1968-1973* (Dar es Salaam: Oxford University Press, 1973).

ence of legal sovereignty but a movement," with an "emancipatory ideology" driven by the emerging "national historical consciousness" of liberation movements outside Europe, and articulated in literature *written by the colonized*.[21] This literature analyzed imperialism and decolonization from the perspective of the former colonies, allowing, in the words of reviewer Richard Gunde, those "who live in the West, in the former colonial powers—to witness the process from the other side, so to speak," and to understand that "despite the variety of colonialisms and decolonizations, the history of decolonization in the twentieth century presents a coherent, interconnected phenomenon."[22]

It should come as no surprise, then, that political, economic, and cultural commentators from Africa, Asia, and Latin America raised increasingly serious concerns in the ensuing years about the misuse of development aid as a tool for promoting Euro-American and Soviet geo-political interests (some would say imperialism), undermining political self-determination and development among its supposed beneficiaries. While these writings are too diverse and complex to summarize here, post-colonial writers from Africa and Asia, and Latin American "dependency" theorists emblemize these trends. In this section I will briefly mention the seminal contributions of Frantz Fanon and Edward Said to post-colonial thought, and later in the chapter I will address dependency theory in association with Latin America critiques of development. My purpose is to bring forward important voices from outside the circle of the United States and its close allies, critical of what they saw as culturally and economically exploitative aspects of development.

Frantz Fanon, a black Martinican psychiatrist who devoted himself to the Algerian revolution against the French, synthesized nationalist and anticolonial reservations about post-war imperialism in *Black Skins, White Masks* (1952) and *The Wretched of the Earth* (1962). While continuing to insist on the importance of national struggles for liberation from European colonial rule, Fanon was a ferocious critic of the metamorphosis of anti-colonial African leaders after independence in the late 1950s into what he saw as a regressive neocolonial force "that serves to immobilize the people."[23] Rejecting all forms of neocolonialism, Fanon also argued against the Marxists that race had ultimately trumped class in African colonialism, insisting, "When you examine . . . the colonial context, it is evident that . . . you are rich because you are white, you are white because you are rich."[24] Writing during the transition "between colonial-

---

21. Prasenjit Duara, *Decolonization: Perspectives from Now and Then* (Routledge, 2003); cited by Richard Gunde, "Decolonization: A Postcolonial Perspective," UCLA International Institute (February 2, 1994); http://www.international.ucla.edu/article.asp?parentid=7158; accessed May 10, 2011.

22. Ibid.

23. Franz Fanon, "The Pitfalls of National Consciousness" (1963), 171; cited in Neil Larsen, "Imperialism, Colonialism, Postcolonialism," in Henry Schwarz and Sangeeta Ray, eds., *A Companion to Postcolonial Studies* (Malden, MA: Blackwell, 2005), 35.

24. Franz Fanon, "Concerning Violence" (1963), 40; cited in Larsen, "Imperialism, Colonialism, Postcolonialism," 36.

ism and the establishment of the postcolonial (or, more accurately, neocolonial) national state,"[25] Fanon argued that race had become just another Cold War ideology, uniting former colonizers with the new African elites in a common effort to protect ill-gotten privilege.

Shawn Copeland, a contemporary African American Catholic theologian interested in the psychological trauma inflicted by racism, observes, "Perhaps no thinker exceeds Fanon's ability to signify racial alienation, to explicate its crushing objectification, to diagnose its ruthless hurt, and to evoke its shock and shame."[26] Speaking from within the racialized identity imposed on him as a child in a racist society, Fanon chillingly writes,

> My body was given back to me sprawled out, distorted, recolored, clad in mourning in that white winter day. The Negro is an animal, the Negro is bad, the Negro is mean, the Negro is ugly; look, a nigger, it's cold, the nigger is shivering . . . shivering because he is cold, the little boy is trembling because he is afraid of the nigger . . . I sit down at the fire and I become aware of my uniform. I had not seen it. It is indeed ugly. I stop there, for who can tell me what beauty is.[27]

Here and elsewhere Fanon gives eloquent voice to the dehumanizing consequences of internalized racism for its colonialized victims.

The defining work of post-colonial thought, however, is widely considered to be *Orientalism*, written by Edward Said in 1978. The book unites literary and cultural criticism with Cold War political analysis, demonstrating how cultural specialists on "the Orient" functioned as sometimes innocent collaborators with European colonialism, and later with U.S.–Soviet Cold War politics. The book begins with a famous quote from Karl Marx, "They cannot represent themselves; they must be represented,"[28] which the author uses to critique both Soviet and Western cultural imperialism. Said shows how centuries of *Orientalists* from Europe and elsewhere constructed the "Orient" (or East) in opposition to the *Occident* (or West) as an object of study and fascination for consumption at home, thereby defining and controlling its meaning, and silencing Asian voices in whose name they claimed to speak. The Orient was said to be premodern, irrational, and traditional in opposition to the superior West, which was typically portrayed as modern, rational, and civilized. Interestingly enough, the post-colonial critiques of Marxism by Fanon and Said helped them to gain exposure among scholars in the United

25. Anthony C. Alessandrini, "Humanism in Question: Fanon and Said," in Henry Schwarz and Sangeeta Ray, eds., *A Companion to Postcolonial Studies* (Malden, MA: Blackwell, 2005), 435.

26. Shawn N. Copeland, *Enfleshing Freedom: Body, Race, and Being* (Minneapolis: Fortress Press, 2009), 15.

27. Franz Fanon, *Black Skin, White Masks* (New York: Grove, 1967), 113-14; cited in Copeland, *Enfleshing Freedom*, 16.

28. Edward Said, *Orientalism* (New York: Random House, Vintage Books, 1979), xiii.

States and the Europe during the Cold War, allowing them to become part of the canon for those studying post-colonial and liberation movements in Western universities.

## The Non-Aligned Nations Endorse Development

Despite the importance of decolonization and various theoretical critiques of development as a vehicle for Western imperialism, however, international relations in the 1950s continued to be dominated by Cold War politics. Indeed, national liberation movements throughout the "developing world" became political and ideological battlegrounds for influence among the major powers. For the United States, General MacArthur led American and U.N. member troops in a "police action" when Soviet-supported North Korean forces invaded South Korea on June 25, 1950 (Korean War 1950-53). In Russia, Joseph Stalin died on March 5, 1953, and was replaced by Nikita Khrushchev, under whom the Soviets invaded Hungary and Poland in 1956 in order to consolidate control over the "Eastern Bloc," which included East Germany, Bulgaria, Czechoslovakia, Rumania, Albania, and Yugoslavia. France was faced with the Algerian War of Independence (1954-1962), and its efforts to hold on to Vietnam were defeated in 1954 at Dien Bien Phu under president Ho Chi Minh. In July 1955 the Geneva Accords divided independent Vietnam at the 17th parallel into the communist North, and the U.S.-supported Diem government in the South. U.S. troops began combat operations in Vietnam shortly thereafter, on November 1, 1955, and the Vietnam War lasted until the fall of Saigon and the South to communist North Vietnam on April 30, 1975. When Gamal Abdel Nasser nationalized the Suez Canal on July 26, 1956, the Franco-British-Israeli Suez military operation ensued, which succeeded militarily and reopened the canal to Israeli shipping, but ultimately failed to regain control of the precious waterway for the former colonial power, England, because of U.N. intervention.

In this dynamic and rapidly evolving post-colonial context, the governments of Burma, Ceylon, India, Indonesia, and Pakistan called a conference of twenty-nine new African and Asian nations, April 18-24, 1955, in Bandung, Indonesia. Its stated aims were to promote Afro-Asian economic and cultural cooperation, and to oppose colonialism and neocolonialism by the United States, the Soviet Union, and other imperial powers. The final communiqué outlined ten principles found in the U.N. Charter condemning colonialism as "a denial of the fundamental rights of man" and "a means of cultural suppression," and promoting economic, technical, and cultural cooperation among the new states.[29]

The meeting also famously initiated the "non-aligned nations" movement, voicing the demands of the developing or "Third World" nations to the emerging post-war international order. Rist notes, however, that the final communiqué also offered powerful legitimation for the goal of economic development being promoted by the United States and the United Nations.[30] Indeed, it called

---

29. Rist, *The History of Development*, 82-83, 86.
30. Ibid., 86.

for the creation of institutions and key elements included in the economic and political agenda already agreed upon at the U.N. Monetary and Financial Conference attended by the forty-four Allied Nations at Bretton Woods, New Hampshire, July 1-22, 1944, laying out rules for the post-war monetary system. Thus, from one perspective, Bandung can be said to symbolize what might be called the "critical" embrace of Truman's notion of development by the non-aligned nations of the Third World outside of Europe, the United States, the Soviet Union, and their allies.

### The Catholic Church Critically Embraces Development

> In every age, the church carries the responsibility of reading the signs of the times and of interpreting them in the light of the Gospel. . . . We must be aware of and understand the aspirations, the yearnings, and the often dramatic features of the world in which we live (Vatican II, *Gaudium et spes,* Pastoral Constitution on the Church in the Modern World (§4).

If there was any doubt that the concept of development would play a key role in international relations for the rest of the century, it was erased in December 1961 when the U.N. General Assembly launched its first Decade of Development. The document called on all member states "to mobilize support for measures required to accelerate progress toward self-sustaining economic growth and social advancement," with a goal of at least 5 percent GNP growth in the developing countries.[31] In response, the Catholic Church under the leadership of Pope John XXIII (1958-1963), his successor Paul VI (1963-1978), and Vatican II (1962-1965) embraced the notion of development, integrating it into the rich tradition of Catholic Social Teaching.

The term received its first extended treatment, outside a brief mention by Pius XII (1939-1958),[32] in *Mater et magistra* (1961) by John XXIII under headings such as "Balancing Economic Development and Social Progress" (§§73-81), "Aid to Less Developed Areas" (§§150-152), "Requirements of Justice as Between Nations Differing in Economic Development" (§§157-184), "Population Increase and Economic Development" (§§185-199), etc. The term appears twenty-four times John's *Pacem in terris* (1963), issued during the Council, with a section explicitly dedicated to the United Nations (§§142-145) and treatments associated with human rights and duties (§§11, 13, 19, 36), the status of women (§41), participation in public life (§§73, 74), truth (§86), the rights and duties of states (§§64, 86, 92), the treatment of minorities (§97), race relations

---

31. United Nations, "Economic and Social Development—First UN Development Decade," *Encyclopedia of the Nations,* http://www.nationsencyclopedia.com/United-Nations/Economic-and-Social-Development-FIRST-UN-DEVELOPMENT-DECADE.html#ixzz0wVhwjTip; accessed March 27, 2014.

32. Pius XII, Radio Message, August 24, 1939. *Acta apostolicae sedis* 34 (1942), 16-17. Quoted in John XXIII, *Pacem in terris* §124.

(§100), the arms race (§109), underdevelopment (§§121-124), and salvation and justice (§162).[33] The term also runs through a variety of documents issued by the Council, including *Lumen gentium* (the Dogmatic Constitution on the Church, 1964), which emphasizes how gospel values complement the "genuine development of human persons" (§46); *Gaudium et spes* (the Pastoral Constitution on the Church in the Modern World, 1965), which offers norms on how to avoid the imposition of Western-style development on the Third World (§86);[34] and thirty-eight occurrences in *Gravissimum educationis* (the Declaration on Christian Education, 1965).

By the late 1960s, however, the optimistic tone of these earlier documents had been replaced by a more critical attitude embodied in Paul VI's addition of the qualifier "integral" (§14) to his treatment of development, the central theme of his 1967 encyclical, "On the Development of Peoples" (*Populorum progressio*). In a famous passage summarizing the meaning of this term the Pope wrote, "The fullness of authentic development . . . is for each and all the transition from less human conditions to those which are more human." He says that humanizing development involves

> the passage from misery towards the possession of necessities, victory over social scourges, the growth of knowledge, the acquisition of culture . . . , increased esteem for the dignity of others, the turning toward the spirit of poverty, cooperation for the common good, the will and desire for peace . . . [, and] the acknowledgement by human beings of supreme values, and of God as their source and their finality. Conditions that, finally and above all, are more human. . . . (§§20-21)

In passages such as these, therefore, the term "integral development" began to function in Catholic Social Teaching as a way to criticize "developmentalist" schemes benefitting the superpowers, but doing little to seriously advance the quality of life and the standard of living for peoples in the "underdeveloped" or "developing" world.

Such reservations were soon confirmed by events on the ground. As the United Nations itself later observed, "Throughout the . . . 1960s . . . the growth rate in the economically advanced market economies accelerated, [while] . . . the gap between the per capita incomes of the developing countries and those of the developed countries widened."[35] The net result was that by the end of the decade, "Two-thirds of the world's population living in the less developed regions . . . still had less than one-sixth of the world's income."

The first U.N. Development Decade ended in 1970 with its major goal unattained, and little improvement from 1962 when "annual per capita income in those regions averaged $136, while that of the economically advanced market

---

33. John XXIII, *Pacem in terris* §§64, 121-25, 131.

34. Vatican II, *Gaudium et spes* §§35, 44, 53-56, 60, 64-72, 85-86.

35. United Nations, "Economic and Social Development—First UN Development Decade."

economies in North America and Western Europe averaged $2,845 and $1,033." Even during its most productive years, 1960-1967, "the increase in their per capita gross product was only about 2%." Such results did little to discourage growing suspicion that Truman's program of "development" was nothing more than a tool of Cold War Soviet containment, ultimately designed to advance the economic self-interests of the United States in emerging markets, and to reduce hostility and promote further economic and political dependency on the United States and other "First World" economic institutions and nations.

### The Latin American Church Charts Its Own Path:
### A Deafening Cry

Inspired in part by liberation movements in Africa and Asia and post-colonial critiques of development as an instrument of continued imperialism, pressures continued to grow throughout Latin America during the 1950s and '60s for governmental and economic reforms of U.S.-supported military dictatorships controlled by local elites. Indeed, U.S. policy makers were shocked by the broad popular support in Latin America for the successful Cuban revolution of 1959. For this and other reasons, the United States turned from blatant military subversion and support for military dictatorships toward a new approach, President Kennedy's Alliance for Progress, built on promises associated with international development. The Alliance adopted the earlier two-pronged strategy of the Truman Doctrine and the Marshall Plan, hoping to counter Cuba's revolutionary influence by coupling intensive military subversion with civilian economic development and political reform. However, while U.S. policy makers and their partners promoted gradual change through *development*, the word *liberation* gained currency in Latin America as a euphemism for the immediate end to military rule and rapid transition to large-scale political and economic reform, whether by voluntary elections or by coup.

### *Latin American Critics of Development*

Most Latin American nations gained formal independence from Spain and Portugal during the nineteenth century, so twentieth century struggles to end military rule and oppression by local elites did not follow the pattern of independence movements in Africa and Asia. However, the spirit of decolonization nonetheless infused the thinking of movements mobilizing literally millions of people in Latin American civil society behind demands for elections and economic reform. Frequently chaotic, driven by nationalistic concerns, and sometimes backed by armed rebellions, these movements nonetheless eventually succeeded in bringing an end to military rule in Argentina in 1983, Bolivia in 1982, Brazil in 1985, Chile in 1990, El Salvador in 1984, Guatemala in 1986, Haiti in 1990 and 1994, Honduras in 1982, Nicaragua in 1979, Panama in 1989, Paraguay in 1993, Peru in 1980, and Uruguay in 1985. In this context, the emergence of a powerful critique of U.S.-sponsored development regimes known as "dependency theory" provided an important argument delegitimating Latin American military regimes by characterizing their economic policies as systematically distorted by neo-colonial U.S. interests imposed on its military clients. In what follows I will briefly describe these theories and their role in our story.

Latin American dependency theory had its origin in the U.N. Economic Commission for Latin America (CEPAL), founded in Chile in the 1950s and headed by Paul Prebisch, who became first secretary-general of the United Nations Conference on Trade and Development (UNCTAD) in 1964.[36] Fernando Henrique Cardoso, a professor of political science and sociology at the University of São Paolo, who taught abroad following the right-wing-backed military coup of 1964 (and who later became two-term president of Brazil, 1995-2003), developed his own version of "dependency theory," which proved to be very influential in Catholic circles pressing for change. In 1967 Cardoso published an influential text proposing corrections to the model for "development" guiding U.S. projects in Latin America through the Alliance for Progress based on the theory of dependency.[37]

Commentators distinguish Cardoso's relatively more "nuanced form of dependency analysis," which informed the work of Fr. Gustavo Gutiérrez and the Latin American bishops, from the more Marxist analysis of Andre Gunder Frank, who argued that "Europe and the United States financed their own development by exploiting poor nations and draining off profits (surplus value)," thus keeping "Latin America . . . from developing, by drawing off the capital needed for development, and imposing their own technology and controls."[38] Cardoso accepted the influence of foreign investors, but also paid attention to the autonomy of economic and socio-political forces operating within Latin America itself. Later, as the Cold War drew to a close, Cardoso contributed important reflections on the role of civil society in the Latin American transition from military to civilian rule, which fit well with the role played by the church.[39] Commentators on Cardoso's many contributions to Latin American political and economic theory during his long career as a scholar, finance minister, and later president of Brazil note that he consistently advocated economic and political movement toward globalized social democracy over other, more

36. Gilbert Rist, "The Latin American *Dependentistas*," *The History of Development*, 113-18.

37. Fernando Henrique Cardoso and Enzo Faletto, *Dependencia y desarrollo en América Latina* (mimeo, Santiago de Chile: ILPES, 1967; Mexico, D.F.: Siglo Veintiuno, 1969); translated as *Dependency and Development in Latin America* (Berkeley, CA: University of California Press, 1979).

38. Arthur McGovern, S.J., "Dependency Theory, Marxist Analysis, and Liberation Theology," in Marc H. Ellis and Otto Maduro, eds., *The Future of Liberation Theology* (Maryknoll, NY: Orbis Books, 1989), 274.

39. F. H. Cardoso, "Associated Dependent Development and Democratic Theory," in Alfred Stepan, ed., *Democratizing Brazil* (New York: Oxford University Press, 1989).

isolationist, anti-globalization approaches, though always in a form designed to protect and promote Latin American interests.[40]

Cardoso eventually became very critical of dependency theorists, proponents of the very school of thought he had helped to create. He argued that they tended to take "refuge in affirmations of the principle of Revolution without managing to light up the way towards it . . . [insisting] there can only be a radical way out, even though the class or classes that might deal a final blow to the existing order are never really delineated."[41] Cardoso's point was that dependency theorists (himself included) offered few solutions to the problem they posed, substituting an unsubstantiated belief that a "revolutionary explosion" was about to take place. Many Latin American church leaders who were influenced by Cardoso's version of dependency theory in these early years, eventually abandoned it for this and other reasons, but his contributions were significant. Cardoso won the John W. Kluge Prize for Lifetime Achievement in the Humanities and Social Sciences in July 2012 (considered by some the Nobel Prize for the humanities), and was described by James H. Billington, the Librarian of Congress, as "the outstanding political scientist in late-twentieth-century Latin America."[42] His influential 1969 book is still well regarded for detecting new possibilities for growth among the "periphery" countries in the early glimmerings of globalization. As president of Brazil from 1995 to 2002 he is regarded as the primary architect of Brazil's rise past Britain and Italy to become the sixth largest economy in the world.

### The Latin American Bishops Change the Conversation at Medellín, Colombia, 1968: God's Preferential Option for the Poor

Just as such critiques were gaining greater traction, the Latin American bishops (CELAM) met in Medellín, Colombia, August 26-September 6, 1968, the first episcopal conference to respond to the call of Vatican II (1962-1965) to read the signs of the times in light of the gospel. CELAM held its first general meeting in 1955, and reconvened thirteen years later for the express purpose of promoting the conversion and renewal (*aggiornamento*) of *The Church in the Present-Day Transformation of Latin America in the Light of the Council*. The bishops chose an anguished phrase to capture their reading of pastoral situation of the church in Latin America in 1968, stating, "A deafening cry pours from the throats of millions of men and women asking their pastors for a liberation that reaches them from nowhere else."[43] Linking this cry to the ongoing debate about

---

40. Gerardo L. Munck, "Democracy and Development in a Globalized World: Thinking about Latin America from Within," *Studies in Comparative International Development (SCID)* 44, no. 4 (December 2009): 337-58.

41. F. H. Cardoso, "Les idées á leur place" (Paris: Presses universitaires de France, 1984), 179; cited in Rist, *The History of Development*, 117-18.

42. Larry Rohter, "Brazil's Ex-Leader Honored as Scholar," *New York Times*, May 14, 2012, C1-2.

43. Second General Conference of Latin American Bishops, "Document on Poverty in the Church" (2), *The Church in the Present-Day Transformation of Latin America in the*

development outlined above, the bishops asserted, "Latin America appears to live beneath the tragic sign of underdevelopment." In response, the bishops sought to formulate "a global vision of humanity, and the integral vision of Latin America's development" that "does not pretend to compete with the attempts for solution made by other national, Latin American, and world bodies," but rather tries "to encourage these efforts, accelerate their results, deepen their content, and permeate all the process of change with the values of the gospel."[44]

It would take us too far afield to review the renewal of the Latin American church outlined in Medellín's sixteen documents. What is important is that here and elsewhere the bishops insisted on the priority of *liberating* development, and in their own words a decade later, sought to "affirm the need for conversion on the part of the whole Church to a preferential option for the poor, an option aimed at their integral liberation."[45] With this epoch-changing discernment the Latin American bishops at Medellín became the first episcopal conference, three years after the close of Vatican II, to officially respond to the call to read the signs of the times in light of the gospel. Their prayerful conclusion was that the growing aspirations of the continent's poor majorities for liberation was a sign that God was calling the Latin American church to embrace a "preferential option for the poor" as an appropriate horizon for its renewal after Vatican II.

Years of controversy, debate, and clarification followed these statements at Medellín (1968) and Puebla (1979), but Pope John Paul II eventually incorporated the preferential option for the poor into the heart of Catholic Social Teaching during his long pontificate (1978-2005). In his 1991 encyclical *Centesimus annus*, the pope unambiguously affirms what he describes as "the continuity within the Church of the so-called 'preferential option for the poor,' . . . which I defined [in *Sollicitudo rei socialis*, §42] as a 'special form of primacy in the exercise of Christian charity'" (John Paul II, Encyclical Letter *Centesimus annus* §11).

Further, in his encyclicals *Sollicitudo rei socialis* (1987) and *Redemptoris missio* (1990) Pope John Paul II explicitly ties the salvation brought by Jesus to action for liberation when he asserts, "Jesus came to bring integral liberation," and "the liberation and salvation brought by the Kingdom of God come to human persons in [both] their physical and spiritual dimensions" (*Redemptoris missio* 14). Assessing the teaching of John Paul II, the Irish social ethicist Donal Dorr writes, "there is no 'backtracking' [in the writings of John Paul II] from the position of Paul VI or John XXIII. Indeed, on this issue he has taken much stronger stands against injustice and in defense of human rights [and] . . . on the

---

*Light of the Council: II Conclusions* (2nd ed.; Washington, DC: Vision for Latin America—United States Catholic Conference, 1973), in Alfred T. Hennelly, ed., *Liberation Theology: A Documentary History* (Maryknoll, NY: Orbis Books, 1992), 114.

44. Latin American Bishops, "Message to the Peoples of Latin America," in Hennelly, ed., *Liberation Theology*, 91.

45. Third General Conference of Latin American Bishops, *Puebla: Evangelization at Present and in the Future of Latin America: Conclusions* (London: St. Paul and CIIR, 1980); cited in Donal Dorr, *Option for the Poor: A Hundred Years of Vatican Social Teaching* (rev. and enlarged ed.; Maryknoll, NY: Orbis Books, 1983), 210.

two key issues of liberation and the 'option for the poor.'"[46] While not all would agree with this assessment, there is no question that the preferential option for the poor has become official Catholic Social Teaching, and been continually affirmed by the Latin American church. Likewise, it was explicitly and energetically affirmed at the most recent meeting of the Conference of Latin American and Caribbean Bishops in Aparecida, Brazil, in May 2007, some forty years after Medellín. Indeed, Pope Benedict XVI insisted in his opening address at the Conference that "the preferential option for the poor is implicit in the Christological faith in the God who became poor for us, so as to enrich us with his poverty (cf. 2 Cor 8:9)."[47]

But what sort of action and what sort of society does Medellín envision? Some find evidence of "two conflicting models of restructuring Latin American society . . . in the Medellín documents."[48] On the one hand, the bishops criticize "neocolonialism" in the *Document on Peace* (§§8-10) and explicitly concede that "revolutionary insurrection can be legitimate in the case of evident and prolonged 'tyranny,'" while cautioning with Paul VI that "'armed revolution' generally 'generates new injustices, introduces new imbalances, and causes new disasters" (*Document on Peace* §19, citing Paul VI, *Populorum progressio* §31). On the other hand, the *Document on Justice* outlines what one author calls a *quasi-corporatist* approach to development[49] that includes an appeal to "business leaders, to their organizations and to the political authorities" (*Justice* §10). It envisions a network of "intermediary structures" between the individual and the state (*Justice* §7) that play an essential role in mediating participation from all sectors of society in the process of development (*Justice* §§7-15). Thus, the development and mobilization of a vigorous and flourishing Latin American "civil society" emerges as the key to the bishops' vision for the promotion of peace and justice on the continent.

Rather than interpreting these divergent views as representing contradictory models, however, I would suggest that the bishops are struggling to integrate long-standing themes in Catholic Social Teaching that stand in creative tension (i.e., rights based vs. corporatist approaches). The bishops offer principles for a flourishing civil society, envisioning a path toward real change that avoids the extremes of both laissez-faire capitalism and Marxism, which they seek to avoid (*Justice* §10), while at the same time lending support to processes of social change with liberating effects on the "downtrodden of every social class" (*Justice* §20). Thus, they write,

---

46. Dorr, *Option for the Poor*, 361.

47. Pope Benedict XVI, Address of His Holiness Benedict XVI to the Bishops of Latin America and the Caribbean, Shrine of Aparecida, May 13, 2007, no. 3, http://www.vatican. va/holy_father/benedict_xvi/speeches/2007/may/documents/hf_ben-xvi_spe_20070513_ conference-aparecida_en.html; accessed March 24, 2009.

48. William T. Cavanaugh, "The Ecclesiologies of Medellín and the Lessons of the Base Communities," *Cross Currents* (Spring 1994): 71.

49. Ibid., 72.

> The system of liberal capitalism and the temptation of the Marxist system . . . both . . . militate against the dignity of the human person. One takes for granted the primacy of capital, its power and its discriminatory utilization in the function of profit-making. The other, although it ideologically supports a kind of humanism, is more concerned with collective humanity, and in practice becomes a totalitarian concentration of state power. Thus, we must denounce the fact that Latin America sees itself caught between these two options and remains dependent on one or another of the centers of power which control its economy. (*Justice* §10)

Drawing on the church-sect theory of Max Weber, the prelates explicitly opt for an inclusive understanding of the church and its membership, stating, "The Church is faced with the dilemma of either continuing to be a universal Church or, if it fails to attract and vitally incorporate such groups, of becoming a sect." Rejecting the latter path, the bishops insist that "because she is a Church rather than a sect, she must offer her message of salvation to all men . . ." ("Pastoral Care for the Masses," §3).

This leads the bishops to argue that salvation entails the "authentic liberation" of all peoples, communities, families, and persons from death-dealing oppression (whether Christian or not). They say this entails the creation of "new human beings who know how to be truly free and responsible" in the modern world (*Justice* 3), and are the artisans of their own destiny. This in turn requires that the church's religious commitment to God's preferential option for the poor be realized through responsible participation in secular struggles for liberation from economic, political, and cultural oppression. Thus, on the one hand, the church is obliged to take sides on the issue of the poor, and cannot stand apart from the world in this regard. On the other hand, however, the church must find ways to live out and to explain how its preferential option for the poor functions as a part of God's plan of the salvation, not just for some, but for all.

### Fr. Gustavo Gutiérrez, Latin American Liberation Theology, and the Irruption of the Poor

No figure is more closely identified with the emergence of a theology of liberation and its defining concept, the preferential option for the poor, than Fr. Gustavo Gutiérrez, O.P. Born June 8, 1928, and raised amid genuine poverty in a loving mestizo family (part Hispanic and Quechua Indian) in Lima, Peru, Gutiérrez was bedridden by osteomyelitis from age twelve to eighteen. After three years as a medical student at the University of San Marcos, he entered the local seminary and was ordained a priest in 1959 by the Archdiocese of Lima after studies (1951-1959) in philosophy and psychology at the Catholic University of Louvain (Belgium), and in theology at the University of Lyon in France and the Gregorian University in Rome. Gutiérrez returned to Peru in 1959 as advisor to the National Union of Catholic Students and a professor of theology at the Pontifical Catholic University of Peru. There he observed the growing unrest and dissatisfaction with the first U.N. Decade of Development (1961-1969), fueled in part by the emphasis on justice and the modern world at Vatican II (1962-1965), which he attended in its fourth and final session as theological assistant to Bishop Manuel Larraín of Chile.

As a close observer of the powerful transformations reshaping Latin American society and the church, Gutiérrez concluded they were being driven by what he would later call the "irruption of the poor" from the status of non-actors to agents of their own history.[50] Reflecting on this "new presence" of the poor and oppressed as significant actors in liberation movements across Latin America and around the globe, Gutiérrez offered what many consider the first proposal for a "theology of liberation" at a gathering of priests and lay people in Chimbote, Peru, in July 1968, one month before Medellín. Three years later in 1971 he published *A Theology of Liberation*. In the revised Introduction to this book Gutiérrez identifies three "basic" or "primary" claims of Latin American liberation theology: (1) human history is being reshaped by the irruption of the poor as agents of their own liberation, and by the "option for the poor" of Christians living their faith through solidarity and support for those liberation struggles; (2) liberation theology is critical reflection on this Christian praxis of a "preferential option for the poor" in light of the word of God, which constitutes a "new stage" in the history of Christian theology;[51] and (3) the irruption of the poor as actors for their own liberation, and the church's option for the poor expressed in Christian solidarity with their struggles for liberation, constitute an authentic proclamation of the Kingdom of God to the modern world.

Building on what we have discussed, we can locate Fr. Gutiérrez as part of an influential and growing number of Catholic leaders in Latin America who had concluded by the end of the 1960s that President Truman's "developmentalist approach has proven to be unsound and incapable of interpreting the economic, social and political evolution of the Latin American continent."[52] As noted earlier, Gutiérrez was careful to endorse the use of "integral development"[53] by Paul VI in *Populorum progressio* as capturing how "the term 'development' has synthesized the aspirations of poor peoples during the last few decades," while simultaneously critiquing "developmentalism,"[54] which Gutiérrez understands as an "ideology of modernization" that has "sanctioned timid and in the long run deceitful efforts."

Instead of focusing on development, however, Gutiérrez emphasizes what he

---

50. Gustavo Gutiérrez, *The Power of the Poor in History*, trans. Robert R. Barr (Maryknoll, NY: Orbis Books, 1983), 191; Spanish, *La fuerza histórica de los pobres* (Lima, Peru: Centro de Estudios y Publicaciónes, 1979).

51. Gustavo Gutiérrez, "Introduction to the Revised Edition: Expanding the View," in *A Theology of Liberation: History, Politics, and Salvation* (rev. ed. with new intro.; Maryknoll, NY: Orbis Books, 1988), xliv.

52. Ibid., 51.

53. Paul VI, *Populorum progressio*, §14.

54. Gutiérrez, *Theology of Liberation*, 16.

sees as the more fundamental phenomenon of the "irruption" or "new presence" of the poor and oppressed as actors on the stage of history. He asserts, "The most important instance of this presence in our times, especially in underdeveloped and oppressed countries, is the struggle to construct a just and fraternal society, where persons can live with dignity and be the agents of their own destiny." He concludes, "Therefore, it is my opinion that the term *development* does not well express these profound aspirations. *Liberation*, on the other hand, seems to express them better."[55]

But liberation from whom or what? Gutiérrez asserts, "The building of a just society . . . in Latin America . . . revolves around the *oppression-liberation axis*." Thus, on the one hand, the demands from poor or otherwise marginated groups for structural change "may seem difficult or disturbing to those who wish to achieve—or maintain—a low-cost conciliation" in order "to keep living off the poverty of the many."[56] On the other hand, however, he asserts "that the Latin American peoples will not emerge from their present status except by means of a profound transformation, *a social revolution*, which will radically and qualitatively change the conditions in which they now live."[57] This observation would be confirmed over the next twenty years by a series of painful, but largely successful, campaigns to bring an end to military rule in various countries in Latin America, and by less successful efforts to promote political and economic reforms.

Gutiérrez, however, eventually revised his early position that "dependence and liberation are correlative terms,"[58] which he said implies "that there can be authentic development for Latin America only if there is liberation from the domination exercised by the great capitalist countries, especially by the most powerful, the United States of America."[59] He changed this position in 1988 when he stated, "It is clear . . . that the theory of dependence . . . is now an inadequate tool, because it does not take sufficient account of the internal dynamics of each country or of the vast dimensions of the world of the poor," and because "the world economy has evolved."[60]

What has remained consistent, however, is his position that "the social praxis of contemporary humankind has begun to reach maturity. It is the behavior of a humankind ever more conscious of being an active subject of history, . . . determined to participate both in the transformation of social structures and in effective political action."[61] Thus, in the *Theology of Liberation* Gutiérrez goes on to cite Max Weber's claim that "nothing lies outside the political sphere"[62] for the modern person, arguing that this now includes the poor, once they have irrupted into the modern world as agents of their own history. And he insists

---

55. Ibid., xiv.
56. Ibid., 31.
57. Ibid., 54.
58. Ibid., 49.
59. Ibid., 54.
60. Ibid., xxiv.
61. Ibid., 30.
62. Ibid., 30-31.

that this irruption constitutes an epoch-changing reality, for it is precisely as a responsible agent in the political sphere "that a person emerges as a free and responsible being, as a person in relationship with other persons, as someone who takes on a historical task."[63]

It should not surprise us, then, that Gutiérrez believes that the preferential option for the poor is the source and the driving insight of Latin American liberation theology, as well as its primary contribution to the universal church. He writes,

> The vision of Christian life manifested in this statement [of the pref-
> erential option for the poor] and in the practice of this commitment is,
> in fact, the most substantial part of the contribution from the life and
> theological reflection of the Church in Latin America to the universal
> church. The option for the poor took its first steps in the years before
> Medellín, was affirmed in the period after that conference, and was
> invoked in subsequent episcopal conferences and in the recent teach-
> ings of Benedict XVI and [the bishops' conference in 2007 at] Apare-
> cida, which have given it an impact and a place it would not have had
> without them.[64]

He argues, therefore, that action for liberation is a secondary or derivative contextual commitment that makes the disciple's embrace of God's preferential option for the poor historically effective. Thus, from the perspective of the theologian most often considered the founder of Latin American liberation theology, the emphasis on the religious and social significance of the "irruption of the poor" as actors on the stage of world history and the church's "preferential option for the poor," first stated at Medellín in 1968, are the principle contributions of Latin American liberation theology to the universal church.

Despite this insistence on the priority of the option for the poor, however, Gutiérrez is probably best known for having formulated the basic methodology of Latin American liberation theology, which has served as a paradigm for a global family of theological approaches inspired by the mandate from *Gaudium et spes* "of reading the signs of the times and of interpreting them in light of the Gospel" (*Gaudium et spes* §4). As Gutiérrez himself notes, "One of the first statements of my way of understanding the theological task was that liberation theology is 'a critical reflection on Christian praxis in light of the word of God.'"[65]

The key to this definition was that it shifted the focus of reflection from ambiguous "signs of the times" to the actual faith-based solidarity of Christian disciples with the liberating struggles of the poor. Gutiérrez says this better reflects the message of the Bible, which "shows us that the doing of God's will is the main demand placed on believers," and fulfills the prophetic tradition in

---

63. Ibid.

64. Gustavo Gutiérrez, "The Option for the Poor Arises from Faith in Christ," *Theological Studies* 70, no. 2 (Spring 2009): 318.

65. Gutiérrez, *Theology of Liberation*, xxix.

twentieth-century theology that originates with "Karl Barth . . . when he said that 'the true hearer of the word is the one who puts it into practice.'"[66] Gutiérrez argues that this generates a "hermeneutical circle"[67] that moves between two poles: the living word of God and the present historical reality of its interpreters, which he says should involve solidarity with the irruption of the poor into history as actors on their own behalf.

Thus, Gutiérrez concludes, "The historical womb from which liberation theology has emerged is the life of the poor and . . . the Christian communities that have arisen within the bosom of the present-day Latin American church." For its part, this "theology tries to read the word of God and be alert to the challenges that faith issues to the historical process in which that people is engaged."[68] For Gutiérrez, this approach amounts to an updating of the famous definition of theology by St. Anselm of Canterbury (1033-1109) as "faith seeking understanding" (*fides quaerens intellectum*).[69] In the hands of Gutiérrez, Anselm's definition refers both to the faith of the poor and to that of the church, which makes the preferential option for the poor that theology seeks to articulate and understand.

### The Conversion of the Central American Jesuits to the Preferential Option for the Poor

Reflecting some of the same sensitivities discussed above, in El Salvador Archbishop Luis Chávez y González brought a consistent concern with poverty to the diocese of San Salvador over which he presided from 1939 to 1977, when he was replaced by Archbishop Oscar Arnulfo Romero. In the early 1950s Archbishop Chávez encouraged the peasant-based cooperative movement, sending priests to Canada to learn how to form cooperatives, and setting up the Pius XII Institute to impart these skills in the context of Catholic Social Teaching.[70] As noted above, the Catholic Church of the early 1960s under the leadership of John XXIII (1958-1963), Paul VI (1963-1978), and Vatican II (1962-1965), embraced the concept of development being promoted by the United Nations and other secular organizations, integrating it into the rich tradition of Catholic Social Teaching. Archbishop Arturo Rivera Damas (archbishop 1983-1994) remembers that Archbishop Chávez was very "anxious to put into practice the social doctrines that came out of the Council and to have them diffused and practiced."[71]

---

66. Ibid.

67. Ibid., xxxiii.

68. Ibid.

69. Ibid., xxxiii-xxxiv.

70. Interviews with José Inocencio Alas (January 1982) and Hector Dada (February 1982) by Phillip Berryman, summarized in Berryman, *The Religious Roots of Rebellion: Christians in Central American Revolutions* (Maryknoll, NY: Orbis Books, 1984), 100.

71. Interview with then Bishop Arturo Rivera Damas by Tommie Sue Montgomery; cited

### Development, the Church in El Salvador, and the Founding of the UCA

On August 6, 1966, Archbishop Chávez issued a pastoral letter, "The Responsibility of the Laity in the Ordering of Temporal Life," which attempted to relate some of the teachings of the Council to the need for economic and political development in El Salvador. Rivera Damas recalled that the letter aroused the animosity of both the government and the oligarchy for its perceived "criticism of capitalism" and its possibilities for encouraging the potential threats embodied in the nascent Christian Democratic Party and the organization of voluntary grassroots movements.[72] Through these and other activities, during the 1960s the notion of development began to guide the application of the church's social teaching to the historical realities of El Salvador. Not surprisingly, development also framed the documents and ecclesial perspectives that shaped the founding of the University of Central America (UCA).

On August 24, 1964, the six bishops of El Salvador officially petitioned the papal secretary of state for permission to open a Catholic university in their country.[73] The letter presents the Catholic university as a much-needed alternative to the perspective of the National University of El Salvador, which they believed was characterized by a "position and focus that was friendly to Marxism."[74] Later that year the Jesuits of Central America put their own stamp on the proposed university, subordinating the bishops' anti-communism to a commitment to development as a horizon more consonant with the church's social teaching and adequate to the project of a Christian university. Indeed, the document makes Third World development a founding premise for the work of the university, suggesting, "All academic faculties should be set up with a

---

in Tommie Sue Montgomery, *Revolution in El Salvador: From Civil Strife to Civil Peace* (Boulder, CO: Westview Press, 1995), 86.

72. Ibid.

73. This section draws on the following studies of the founding of the Universidad Centroamericana José Simeón Cañas (in order of publication): Román Mayorga Quirós, *La Universidad para el cambio social* (San Salvador: UCA Editores, 1976); Ignacio Ellacuría, "Sobre la fundación de la Universidad 'José Simeón Cañas,'" September 30, 1982, appendix to Minutes of the Meeting of the Board of Directors of the University of Central America, October 11, 1982 (San Salvador: Archives of the University of Central America); Charles Beirne, *Jesuit Education and Social Change in El Salvador* (New York: Garland Publishing, 1996), 47-87.

74. Letter from the bishops of El Salvador to Cardinal Amleto Cicognani, August 24, 1964 (San Salvador: Archives of the Society of Jesus of Central America). Copy in the UCA El Salvador file. Cited in Beirne, *Jesuit Education and Social Change*, 73. Note that the Jesuit curial staff of the Central American Province of the Society of Jesus has decided that sensitive correspondence in its archives dating from this period shall remain confidential until an undetermined future date. Fr. Beirne was a high-ranking official of the university shortly after the assassinations, and before the province's decision to close these files, and therefore had a unique opportunity to study this correspondence. Where I must rely on his description of a document, it is cited in the form above.

sense of absolute priority on university graduates with a development mentality not only in the economic arena but also in the social realm. This priority is presented not only because of the evident danger from communism but also in the light of social justice."[75]

Thus, on September 15, 1965, Fr. Florentino Idoate, S.J., the UCA's first president,[76] would inaugurate the University of Central America José Simeón Cañas with a speech celebrating the university's role in forming professionals who would contribute to El Salvador's future "socio-economic development."[77] And five years later in a speech written by Ignacio Ellacuría and Román Mayorga celebrating the signing of the first loan from the Inter-American Development Bank, university treasurer Fr. José María Gondra, S.J., recalled, "When our university began its foundational labors in 1965, it believed its service should be focused around the concept of development."[78] As we have seen, however, by 1970 a decade of experience with the concept of development had brought the Latin American Conference of Bishops, together with many other important leadership and grassroots groups, to seriously question the adequacy of this horizon as a framework within which to interpret and respond to the historical realities of Latin America.

As a result, the decades of the 1970s and '80s would find the Jesuits of Central America and the UCA at the center of a deadly serious national struggle to define a new horizon for a national vision including the hopes and aspirations of the majority of El Salvadorans. The UCA and many others would insist with Archbishop Romero and the Latin American bishops that development should be subordinated to the preferential option for the poor and the struggle for liberation it implies, metaphors chosen to capture the social-political-economic transformations considered necessary to achieve truly "integral" development.

### The Early Years of the UCA: 1965-1969

Fr. Charles Beirne, S.J., describes 1965 to 1969 as "the founding years" of the UCA.[79] The aforementioned "development mentality" favored by the UCA team

---

75. "Estudio preliminar para la creación de una universidad privada en El Salvador" (San Salvador: Archives of the Society of Jesus of Central America, 1964), 38. Cited in Beirne, *Jesuit Education and Social Change,* 75.

76. Though the UCA uses the term "rector" to refer to its legal and titular head, I will translate this with the more familiar term "president" throughout this chapter.

77. Florentino Idoate, S.J., "Discurso del rector de la Universidad Centroamericana José Simeón Cañas, Forentino Idoate, con motivo de la inauguración de la Universidad," *Planteamiento universitario 1989* (San Salvador: UCA, 1989), 136.

78. José María Gondra, S.J., "Discurso de la Universidad Centroamericana José Simeón Cañas en la firma del contrato con el BID," *Planteamiento universitario 1989* (San Salvador: UCA, 1989), 10.

79. My description of the Universidad Centroamericana during these years again draws on the following studies: Román Mayorga Quirós, *La Universidad para el cambio social,* esp. 21-37; Ellacuría, "Sobre la fundación de la Universidad 'José Simeón Cañas'"; Beirne, *Jesuit Education and Social Change,* esp. pp. 71-87.

in El Salvador would characterize their work until Medellín, a 1968 meeting of the Jesuit provincials of Latin America in Rio, Brazil, and the emerging theology of liberation shook the Central American Jesuits to their roots at the province retreat in December 1969. In the meantime, however, the structural foundations for a truly modern, if conventional, Catholic university were being laid.

Drawing on research from the Jesuit archives, Fr. Beirne has traced the development and implementation of the idea for a Jesuit Central American university from the original proposal by Jesuit General Fr. John B. Janssens to Central American provincial Fr. Miguel Elizondo on April 21, 1958 through 1994. Fr. Beirne highlights two key structural decisions taken while the university was "still on the drawing boards."[80] First was the implementation of the recommendation by Fr. Janssens,[81] based on the advice of his education consultant, Fr. Paolo Dezza, S.J., to establish one university with campuses in Managua (Nicaragua), Guatemala City, and San Salvador (this was added later) so that "cooperation and help from various nations would be made easier, and cultural and economic bonds encouraged."[82] Fr. Beirne notes, "Although the Roman Jesuit curia would raise the issue from time to time, and consider each of the universities as 'branches,' the one UCA never came into existence. Separate institutions developed in El Salvador, Nicaragua, and Guatemala."[83]

Second, and more significant, is the unanticipated singular importance of the Private School Law passed by the Salvadoran legislature on March 24, 1965.[84] This law essentially pre-empted seven years of sometimes difficult negotiations among Jesuit, diocesan, and Vatican officials by mandating "a legally separate entity, a special kind of not-for-profit corporation (*corporación de utilidad pública*)," in which "neither the church nor the Society of Jesus would be its owner," but rather "its Board of Directors, who were to administer it according to its 'public' or 'societal' purposes."[85]

Fr. Beirne says the new arrangement "essentially changed . . . [the UCA] from the type of university envisioned at the meetings with the hierarchy . . . when a 'Catholic' university was being planned," to a structure that "would protect the university from intervention by the Salvadoran and Vatican hierarchy."[86] Fr. Luis Achaerandio could not have imagined how the new university's legal autonomy would protect its implementation of the Central American Jesuits' option for the poor from being crippled by those very forces during the 1970s

---

80. Beirne, *Jesuit Education and Social Change*, 71.

81. Letter from John B. Janssens to Miguel Elizondo, April 21, 1958 (San Salvador: Archives of the Society of Jesus of Central America, 1958). Cited in Beirne, *Jesuit Education and Social Change*, 87-88.

82. Letter from John B. Janssens to Miguel Elizondo, October 11, 1958 (San Salvador: Archives of the Society of Jesus of Central America, 1958). Cited in Beirne, *Jesuit Education and Social Change*, 71-72.

83. Ibid., 74-75.

84. Ibid., 76.

85. Ibid., 76-77.

86. Ibid.

and 1980s. But it seems clear that he intended to create a truly modern Catholic university; one with sufficient religious and secular autonomy to fully engage the new Latin America emerging during the 1960s.[87] As Fr. Beirne notes, after Medellín and the Central American Jesuits' option for the poor, everything would look different.

> Luis Achaerandio and his team built independence and autonomy into the model: a special kind of "public," not an official Catholic, university. In 1965 the Salvadoran bishops and the oligarchy wanted a Catholic haven within which their charges could be protected from noxious influences outside. If the UCA had been an official Catholic university from the beginning, it is not hard to imagine how the bishops might have intervened, even dramatically and as early as 1970, when the university began to define itself as an agent for social change, and as a creative and critical conscience for the nation.[88]

Thus, exactly one month after the initial August 15, 1965, meeting of the all-Jesuit Board of Directors,[89] Fr. Idoate would officially inaugurate the university's efforts in "the preparation of citizens well equipped to lead the intense development which is coming."[90] The issues that would arise in the remaining years of the decade are appropriately described by Fr. Ibisate (who joined the Board with Fr. Ignacio Ellacuría at the beginning of the second academic year) as focused on the process of the UCA's "being born,"[91] and by Fr. Beirne as "growing pains,"[92] terms that connote a period of establishing foundations in continuity with the founders' development-oriented original vision.

During the university's first few months, deans of engineering and economics were appointed, and negotiations were completed with the Salesians to establish the campus temporarily on their Don Rua property. Jon Sobrino, then a Jesuit seminarian (who would describe his apostolic vision in 1966 as "helping the people to . . . become a little bit more like Spaniards, Europeans, or North Americans"[93]), was assigned to teach engineering.[94] And Fr. Idoate took

---

87. Fr. Luis Achaerandio has indicated to Fr. Beirne that "UCA staff members had a major role in formulating the law in the first place." See Charles J. Beirne, "Conversations with Luis Achaerandio, S.J., December, 1990." Cited in Beirne, *Jesuit Education and Social Change*, 192.

88. Ibid., 233.

89. The first Board included Florentino Idoate (president), Segundo Azcue (vice president), Joaquin López y López (secretary), José Ignacio Scheifler (pro-secretary), and Jesús de Esnaola (member). See Beirne, *Jesuit Education and Social Change*, 77.

90. Idoate, "Discurso del rector de la Universidad Centroamericana José Simeón Cañas," 135.

91. Interview with Francisco Javier Ibisate, S.J., by Charles J. Beirne, November 1992. Cited in Beirne, *Jesuit Education and Social Change*, 79.

92. Ibid.

93. Interview with Jon Sobrino, S.J., by Robert Lassalle-Klein, July 5, 1994, 2.

94. Minutes of the meeting of the Board of Directors of the University of Central America

a 50 percent pay cut to cover still unfunded scholarships. Shortly thereafter President Julio Rivera came to the rescue with thirty scholarships worth $52 a month.[95]

The San Salvador UCA opened its doors in 1966 with 309 students (136 in engineering and 173 in economics) and ended the year with 14 professors having taught 367 pupils.[96] Later that year the School of Business Administration was approved.[97] Fr. Beirne endorses the belief of Román Mayorga, university president from 1975 to 1979, that "the school got off the ground . . . because of three factors: the international prestige of the Jesuits as educators, negative impressions of the National University's quality and atmosphere, and the initial academic programs of engineering and business [which were] in great demand during this era of 'developmentalistic optimism.'"[98]

In 1967 the UCA grew to 541 students taught by 26 teachers (mostly part time). And on May 12 the Board obtained a $240,000 loan to purchase land for a campus. But shortages of Jesuit personnel and fund-raising problems led its president, Fr. Idoate, to tell his provincial that if the Jesuits were going to continue to staff the seminary, "I do not see the university as viable." Though twenty donors had promised to help purchase a campus site, Fr. Idoate reports that "the project is moving desperately slowly, and some have put on the brakes because of nervousness at the publication of certain church social documents."[99] One can see why the paradigm shift from development to the option for the poor, which was about to take place at Medellín, would take several years to arrive at the UCA.

In the meantime, the UCA had more immediate and mundane concerns. On July 28, 1967, the university was evicted from the Salesian property. The Salesian superior, Fr. José C. Di Pietro, wrote with equal parts of disgust and irony to the Jesuit provincial:

> I have nothing to say about the music, dancing and happiness of the students at their parties, but what surprises me is that on these occasions they are given total freedom in our house to get drunk with barrels of beer at their disposal. . . . After my complaints . . . they suspended the

José Simeón Cañas, November 15, 1965 (San Salvador: Archives of the University of Central America).

95. Minutes of the meeting of the Board of Directors of the University of Central America José Simeón Cañas, November 25, 1966 (San Salvador: Archives of the University of Central America).

96. *Plan Quinquenal, 1977-81*, Vols. I-III (San Salvador: UCA Editores, 1976), 6.

97. Minutes of the meeting of the Board of Directors of the University of Central America José Simeón Cañas, September 28, 1966 (San Salvador: Archives of the University of Central America).

98. Mayorga Quirós, *La Universidad para el cambio social*, 27, 28; and Beirne, *Jesuit Education and Social Change*, 79.

99. Letter from Florentino Idoate, S.J., to Segundo Azcue, S.J., April 21, 1967 (San Salvador: Archives of the Society of Jesus in Central America). Cited in Beirne, *Jesuit Education and Social Change*, 81.

distribution of beer for a time, but the students continued with their supply of rum, and threw the empty bottles from the second floor to the street. . . . I am sure that such orgies are not the usual custom in your high schools and universities.[100]

Fortunately, the UCA was able to move with its now 719 students and 42 instructors to a temporary home at the Jesuit high school where they stayed until finally moving to a permanent campus in February 1969. Yet, despite these setbacks, by 1968 the UCA would begin sending faculty for Fulbright-sponsored graduate studies in the United States,[101] and establish a third faculty or division (in addition to business/economics and engineering) in the area of philosophy, letters, and human sciences. The year 1969 ended with 57 UCA faculty having educated 1,039 students, and the appointment of Fr. Luis Achaerandio, S.J., the recently retired provincial superior of the Central American Jesuits, as university president. Like the rest of the Latin American Church, the UCA was about to be rocked by the impact of Medellín.

### The 1968 Jesuit Meeting in Rio, Brazil

The documentary history of liberation theology compiled by Alfred T. Hennelly, S.J., bears eloquent testimony to the fact that the preferential option for the poor, and the struggle for liberation and justice it implies, only gradually came to supplant development as an overarching horizon for many Latin American church leaders, including the Jesuits. Hennelly traces this outcome to the church's disenchantment with the failure of the First Decade of Development to address what Medellín would eventually call the "institutionalized violence" of "international monopolies and [the] international imperialism of money" directed against the poor (citing Pius XI in *Quadragesimo anno* and Paul VI in *Populorum progressio*).[102] He also cites the effect of events like the March 31, 1964, military coup in Brazil, and the subsequent adoption of Brazil's "totalitarian ideology" of the National Security State by other Latin American regimes.[103] But Hennelly suggests that the crucial break occurred when the Latin American church began to attend to its own experience that "unlike the United States and Europe, Latin America constituted an enormous ocean of poverty."[104] This

---

100. Idoate correspondence folder (San Salvador: Archives of the Society of Jesus in Central America). Cited in Beirne, *Jesuit Education and Social Change*.

101. Fr. Beirne notes that through 1994 the UCA would have sponsored fifty-two faculty members for Fulbright scholarships for U.S. graduate studies. Of these twenty-nine were no longer teaching at the UCA, twelve were still on the staff, two had died, and nine were still in studies. See Beirne, *Jesuit Education and Social Change*, 82.

102. Second Conference of Latin American Bishops, "Document on Peace" (9e), in Hennelly, ed., *Liberation Theology*, 108.

103. Second Conference of Latin American Bishops, in Hennelly, ed., *Liberation Theology*, 41.

104. Ibid., 2.

experience became an important "source"[105] for the church's pastoral and theological reflection, a move that was further stimulated by Vatican II's call for
ecclesial renewal and inculturation.

While it would take until 1971 for Gustavo Gutiérrez to elaborate his "theology of liberation,"[106] what was clearly understood by the bishops at Medellín
in 1968 was that the church was giving apostolic "preference to the poorest
and most needy," and "pre-eminence" to "our duty of solidarity with the poor."
Indeed, the bishops went out of their way to point out that "this solidarity means
that we make ours their problems and their struggles," through "criticism of
injustice and oppression" and participation in "the struggle against the intolerable situation that a poor person often has to tolerate."[107] Thus, as I have already
noted, the church's discernment that God was calling it to a preferential option
for the poor would lead some to see the church as an important participant in
civil movements for social change and liberation from military rule and other
forms of oppression.

It is important to distinguish the meaning and history of the church's disenchantment with developmentalism and its subordination of integral development to the option for the poor as the horizon for its apostolic activity during the
1960s, from the history of the formal consideration of these concepts by theologians and church leaders. For while the latter history must address the work of
Gustavo Gutiérrez, who dedicated himself to this task, the former more encompassing paradigm shift involved a broad cross-section of individual believers,
pastoral agents, and church leaders throughout the Latin America. This larger
history would include the church's adaptation of Paulo Freire's development of
methods of literacy training designed to "conscienticize" Latin America's poor,
Brazilian experiments with basic Christian communities, and the meeting of
the Jesuit provincials of Latin America with their General, Fr. Pedro Arrupe,
S.J., in Rio de Janeiro, Brazil, May 6-14, 1968. The dramatic results of this meeting (yet another important meeting in the months before Medellín) would play a
crucial role in the history of the Central American Jesuits and the University of
Central America by inspiring the province retreat of December 1969.[108]

---

105. Ibid.

106. Gutiérrez, *Theology of Liberation*.

107. Second Conference of Latin American Bishops, "Document on Poverty in the
Church" (9, 10), in Hennelly, ed., *Liberation Theology*, 116.

108. In order to avoid confusion, I will not use the terms "vice-province," "vice-provincial,"
etc., substituting "province," "provincial," etc., throughout this work. The only exception is that
printed works will retain their original titles in the footnotes. Miguel Elizondo, "El sentido
teológico y espiritual de una reunión comunitaria de la viceprovincia" [The Theological and
Spiritual Meaning of a Community Meeting of the Vice-Province], in "Reunión Ejercicios."
The prefix "vice" is inherently confusing since it is also used in English to mean *assistant*. At
the time referred to in the text the Society of Jesus in Central America was still formally a
vice-province of the Spanish Province of Castile. Fr. Juan Hernández-Pico explains that after
having been elevated from the status of a "mission" on February 7, 1937, it would remain
a vice-province until August 5, 1976, when Jesuit general Pedro Arrupe officially elevated
its status and appointed Fr. César Jerez the first provincial of the new province. See Juan

The final document represents an official statement of the vision of the highest levels of governance of the Society of Jesus in Latin America for the post–Vatican II renewal of its membership. In their analysis of "the social problem of Latin America" the Jesuit leaders "propose to give this problem absolute priority in our apostolic strategy; indeed we intend to orient our whole apostolate around it."[109] Leaving no doubt that their option for the poor has a political dimension they state, "We hope to participate, as best we can, in the common quest of all peoples . . . for a freer, more just, and more peaceful society." Emphasizing that this implies a commitment to critically reexamine their various works in light of the struggle for liberation from military rule and other forms of oppression in Latin American they assert, "In all our activities, our goal should be the liberation of humankind from every sort of servitude that oppresses it." And "aware of the profound transformation this presupposes," including a "break with some of our attitudes in the past," the provincials assert with some prescience that though these changes "will almost certainly arouse reactions," still "we promise to work for bold reforms that will radically transform existing structures (*Populorum progressio* §32) . . . as the only way to promote social peace."[110] The document (written two-and-one-half months before Gutiérrez's speech in Chimbote, Peru) is an unusually clear exemplar of the significance and depth of the shift in the Latin American church before Medellín in 1968 from development to the option for the poor and the efforts to promote liberation it implies.

The Jesuit provincials are quintessentially Ignatian in their preoccupation with exploring the practical apostolic implications of this paradigm shift for Jesuit works in Latin America. First, they propose to "prepare priests and lay persons for their apostate in the world of today."[111] Second, the document proposes all Latin American provincials "allocate a part of our apostolic resources to the growing mass of those who are most neglected." Examples given include "Centers of Research and Social Action," "rural parishes," and "pastoral work among grassroots communities" of the poor.[112] Third, the provincials ask that all Jesuit "schools and universities accept their role as active agents of national integration and social justice in Latin America."[113] Fourth, "adults in every walk of life" are to be supported as "active promoters of social change."[114] Fifth, the Jesuit leadership asks that "communications media" be given "decisive importance in inculcating human values . . . that will help to create the new order we seek."[115] Sixth, the superiors propose that "our participation in the creation of

Hernández-Pico, S.J., *Historia reciente de la Provincia de Centroamérica (1976-1986)* (San Salvador: Ediciones Cardoner, 1991), 17.

109. Provincials of the Society of Jesus, "The Jesuits in Latin America," in Hennelly, ed., *Liberation Theology*, 77-83 at 78.

110. Ibid., 78, 79.

111. Ibid., 79.

112. Ibid., 80.

113. Ibid., 80, 81.

114. Ibid., 81.

115. Ibid., 82.

a new social order presuppose[s] a deep, inner conversion within each one of us."[116] And seventh, the Jesuit provincials state, "We also realize that . . . [this] presupposes changes in our decision-making process as provincials. . . . But we are pledged to carry it through as quickly as possible."[117]

Within one year the Jesuits of Central America would begin a planning process to reevaluate all of their existing works in light of the decrees of Vatican II, Medellín, the Rio letter, and the commitment of the Central American Jesuits themselves to solidarity with the poor. It was this process as much as any other that served to translate the paradigm shift from developmentalism to the option for the poor stated by their leaders at Rio and Medellín into a reality for the Jesuits in El Salvador.

### *The Call for Renewal: Ellacuría and the Voice of Jesuit Formation*

Jesuit students immersed in a course of studies far removed geographically and thematically from the realities of Central America were among the first members of the Central American province to embrace the "profound conversion"[118] called for by the bishops of Latin America, and the Latin American provincials at Rio. Fr. Juan Hernández-Pico notes in his *Recent History of the Central American Province (1976-1986)* that thirty-nine of the Province's seventy-two Jesuits doing studies gathered in Madrid, June 26-29, 1968, with Fr. Segundo Azcue, provincial of Central America, in order to discuss "the crisis hitting religious life."[119] The students complained of the "inertia" and lack of "new proposals and planning" from the Central American Jesuits in response to the challenges of secularization, the suffering of "the Third World," and the 1968 Rio letter signed by Fr. Azcue calling Latin American Jesuits to an option for the poor. Fr. Hernández-Pico reports that Ignacio Ellacuría, who was at the meeting, proposed that Fr. Azcue convene "a representative meeting of the Province in order to create a shared consciousness and sense of co-responsibility for the necessary changes" mandated by Medellín and Rio.[120] The author adds that the elderly provincial "demonstrated an admirable openness of heart to the new challenges," and "decided to convoke the [requested] meeting of the Province during December 1969."[121] A decade later Fr. Azcue would serve as confessor for Archbishop Romero.[122]

---

116. Ibid.

117. Ibid., 82.

118. Second General Conference of Latin American Bishops, "Document on Justice," in Hennelly, ed. *Liberation Theology*, 98.

119. Hernández-Pico, *Historia reciente*, 4-5.

120. Ibid., 5. Fr. Hernández-Pico identifies Ellacuría as the source of the proposal in personal correspondence with Fr. Charles Beirne, S.J., July 1993. See Beirne, *Jesuit Education and Social Change*, 84 n. 45.

121. Hernández-Pico, *Historia reciente*, 6.

122. James R. Brockman, *Romero: A Life* (Maryknoll, NY: Orbis Books, 1989), 46.

Hernández-Pico says Azcue "entrusted the preparation to Frs. Llasera and Ellacuría." Fr. Javier Llasera, assistant to the provincial, was named general secretary for the meeting, and the young Ellacuría recruited his former novice master to the team, Fr. Miguel Elizondo, now retreat master and director of the final stage of Jesuit formation in Medellín, Colombia. The group also invited two other Spaniards to give presentations, Fr. Florentino Idoate, S.J., the UCA's first rector, and Fr. Ricardo Falla, S.J., a young anthropologist ordained in 1964 and in training for assignment to one of the new Centers for Research and Social Action (CIAS). Elizondo and Ellacuría, still only thirty-eight years old and ordained in 1961 just before Vatican II, would play a critical role in turning Azcue's request into an epoch-defining moment for the Central American Jesuits.

The leaders of the retreat were all Spaniards, which is not surprising in light of the still official subordination in 1969 of the Central American Province to Spain. It is important to understand this relationship and its impact on Ellacuría and Elizondo as leaders of this crucial retreat. The Spanish Jesuits first arrived in Guatemala in 1579,[123] seven years after coming to Mexico on September 28, 1572,[124] and three decades after the first New World Jesuits arrived in Brazil on March 29, 1549. However, the worldwide suppression of the Society of Jesus by Pope Clement XIV on August 16, 1773,[125] and the expulsion of all Jesuits from El Salvador in 1872,[126] meant that no Jesuits returned to El Salvador until the arrival in 1914 of a group of Jesuits fleeing religious persecution from the Mexican revolution. A little over twenty years later, on February 7, 1937, the Jesuit "mission" in Central America was elevated to the status of a vice-province under the care and supervision of the Spanish Province of Castille.

As part of this mission in 1949 six young Jesuits were sent to San Salvador from Spain under the direction of novice master Miguel Elizondo in order to help found a Jesuit novitiate for Central America. One can imagine tears running down the face of Ignacio Ellacuría's worried parents, his father an oculist

---

123. See the historical study written by the Central American Jesuit provincial Jesús M. Sariego, S.J., *Tradición jesuita en Guatemala: Una aproximación histórica* (Guatemala: Universidad Rafael Landívar, 2010), 3; http://www.url.edu.gt/PortalURL/Archivos/24/Archivos/Trad_jesuita_en_Guatemala.pdf, accessed March 26, 2011.

124. The dates for Mexico, Brazil, and the worldwide suppression of the Jesuits are provided by William V. Bangert, S.J., *A History of the Society of Jesus* (St. Louis, MO: Institute of Jesuit Sources, 1972), 95, 37.

125. The Jesuit order was restored worldwide on August 7, 1814. See Bangert, *History*, 428.

126. This date and the information through the following sentence are from Teresa Whitfield, *Paying the Price: Ignacio Ellacuría and the Murdered Jesuits of El Salvador* (Philadelphia: Temple University Press, 1994), 20-21, following two historical articles published in the UCA journal *Estudios centroamericanos* (*ECA*). See Judex (pseudonym), "Cincuentenario de la llegada de los jesuitas a El Salvador," *ECA* no. 198 (October 1964): 289-91; Césareo García del Cerro, S.J., "Aportación de los jesuitas españoles a Iberoamérica," *ECA* no. 214 (April 1966): 64-68. Sariego says, "The second Jesuit epoch in Guatemala, the modern period occurs . . . with the missionary group sent from Spain and New Granada (Colombia) in 1850." See Sariego, *Tradición jesuita en Guatemala*, 5.

from outside of town, as they bid goodbye with other heartsick parents to their sons leaving Bilbao, Spain, by train on their way to El Salvador. Like the others, "Ellacu" had entered the Jesuit novitiate in Loyola, the home of St. Ignatius, only a year before. But there he was, a firmly solicited (yet willing) eighteen-year-old "volunteer" about to begin what he would later call his "American" life.[127]

The true "Central-Americanization" of the province only became a reality with the wave of native-born sons who entered the Jesuit novitiate during the 1970s and '80s, making it possible to end the legal dependency on the Province of Castille on August 5, 1976.[128] But Ellacuría and the other Spaniards who came as teenagers felt that, unlike Spaniards who came later in formation as priests, they had adopted the reality of Central America as their own.[129]

Looking back on the challenge of forming mainly Spanish novices to serve in the Americas, Elizondo recalls being guided by Ignatius's motto, *Ad majorem Dei gloriam* (for the greater glory of God), and says, "I felt totally free of my past, of my antecedents as a Jesuit and as a novice master, although I was a 'novice' in that myself."[130] Not suprisingly, Elizondo sought to instill freedom in his novices as well. He encouraged them to interiorize the spirituality of their yearly retreat encounter with the *Spiritual Exercises* of St. Ignatius by studying the founding history and documents of the Society of Jesus, and by learning to use their own judgment in adapting to their new reality. This seemed better than depending on Spanish convention regarding "the many things they were supposed to do in order to be a good Jesuit—the many rules to obey, virtues to practice, devotions to keep and so on in order to reach what one can consider essential in the vocation of the Society."[131] Elizondo admits that he sometimes struggled to live with the "somewhat adolescent" exuberant energy of his young charges, such as Segundo Montes (one of the martyrs), who arrived from Valladolid, Spain, in 1951. But as Fr. César Jerez, S.J. (the native-born provincial who would lead the

---

127. "El volcán jesuita: entrevista con el Padre Ellacuría, rector de la Universidad Centroamericana," *ABC* (March 28, 1982). Cited in Whitfield, *Paying the Price*, 17, and Rodolfo Cardenal, S.J., "De Portugalete a San Salvador: de la mano de cinco maestros," in J. Sobrino and R. Alvarado, eds., *Ignacio Ellacuría, 'Aquella libertad esclarecida'* (San Salvador: UCA Editores, 1999), 42-58 at 44.

128. Hernández-Pico, *Historia reciente*, 17. This date is provided in the "Recent History of the Central American Province" by Fr. Hernández-Pico, which mentions "central-americanization" as a central challenge (*Historia reciente*, 3). It was also the subject of a difficult meeting of the province's men in formation with their superiors in 1994. The younger men, who are overwhelmingly from Central America, complained of the overemphasis on Spanish culture and customs and the lack of attention to inculturation by Spanish-born Jesuits. Interview of Central American Jesuits in formation by Robert Lassalle-Klein, San Salvador, July 1994.

129. Based on a comment by a Jesuit who came as a teenager from Spain to Central America. Interview with Salvador Carranza by Teresa Whitfield (Santa Tecla, El Salvador, January 25, 1991). Cited in Whitfield, *Paying the Price*, 21 n. 20.

130. Interview with Fr. Miguel Elizondo, S.J., by Teresa Whitfield (Guadalajara, Mexico, December 31, 1990). Cited in Whitfield, *Paying the Price*, 21.

131. Ibid., 22.

province through its first persecutions and the martyrdoms of Rutilio Grande, S.J., and Archbishop Romero) would later recall, Elizondo "taught us not to be afraid."[132]

It was this generation, especially Ellacuría and his old novice master, Elizondo, who would set the stage during these days for a thorough renewal of Jesuit formation in light of the historical realities of Central America. The two helped create an epoch-changing moment of conversion by confronting the faith of the province gathered for the Christmas 1969 retreat with the historical reality of the suffering people of Central America. Jon Sobrino believes that the question that faced the Society of Jesus during these years after Medellín (1968) and the call of Vatican II (1962-1965) to read the signs of the times in light of the gospel was, "So, how do you react in the midst of [Central America's] reality?" In trying to explain what prepared Ellacuría for his leading role in helping the UCA and the Central American Jesuit province to answer this question, Sobrino recalls,

> Ellacuría used to say he was impressed by four people during his life: his novice master, Fr. Elizondo, at the human, spiritual level; Espinosa Pólit, his humanities professor in Ecuador; Karl Rahner as a theologian at Innsbruck; and Xavier Zubiri in Spain, the subject of his doctoral dissertation in philosophy. What I think Ellacuría appreciated from Zubiri was the critical realism. Zubiri taught him to ask, "What is the university in the midst of reality? And what is the reality of the University?"[133]

The enthusiasm for reality inspired by these men, and the aforementioned freedom grounded in the tradition of the *Spiritual Exercises* of St. Ignatius nurtured by Elizondo,[134] helped prepare Ellacuría not only to embrace the younger Jesuits' criticism in Madrid of their far-flung formation, but to be converted himself by the historical reality of Central America they so missed. Sobrino adds that for the rest of his life (1967-1989) "Ellacuría was pioneering that; taking risks, not being afraid—we were, of course—but not being stopped by problems, persecution, bumps."[135] This process was about to take a massive leap forward with the Christmas 1969 province retreat.

---

132. Interview with César Jerez by Teresa Whitfield (Managua, Nicaragua, February 18, 1991). Cited in Whitfield, *Paying the Price*, 24.

133. Interview with Jon Sobrino by Robert Lassalle-Klein and Barry Stenger (San Salvador: UCA, January 29, 1992), 4.

134. Jon Sobrino believes that "Ellacuría was strongly affected by the realism of the *Exercises* of St. Ignatius." He suggests that the deep-seated realism of the *Exercises* is embodied in the centrality they give to the following: (a) the examination of the present historical moment; (b) the notion of imitation [of Christ]; (c) the doctrine of the incarnation; and (d) the meditation on the two standards. Note from Jon Sobrino to Robert Lassalle-Klein, July 24, 1995.

135. Interview with Jon Sobrino by Robert Lassalle-Klein (San Salvador: UCA, July 5, 1994), 6.

Looking back, Fr. Hernández-Pico, secretary for the gathering, recalls,

> The predictions were realized that there would be "large disputes" in this "*Spiritual Exercises*–conference." The Province experienced a powerful and conflictive cleansing, whose effects, redoubled during the year 1970, would be present during all of the years Fr. Miguel F. Estrada was provincial. The meeting itself was seen by some as the time when the foundations were able to be established to sketch a new navigational map for the Central American Jesuits. Others saw it as an assembly vitiated by the emotionality of new positions, and more like a meeting of fundamentalist fanatics than a time of calm discernment. [However, w]ith quite a few directives put there to try to avoid a serious rupture in the union of hearts among the Jesuits of the Province, Fr. Arrupe substantially approved the practical conclusions of the meeting.[136]

The perspective provided by the distance of almost a quarter of a century gives us a broader appreciation of the seminal importance of this gathering. It is now clear that a shift in horizons, comparable to that experienced by the bishops at Medellín, occurred during the days of December 24-31, 1969, for the majority of Jesuits gathered at the diocesan Seminary in San Salvador. The importance of later decisions and events inspired by the meeting would tend to overshadow the open-ended and properly affective character of this attempt by a group of Central American Jesuits to update their own grasp of Ignatian spirituality. They began by returning to the spirituality of their founder embodied in the *Spiritual Exercises* of St. Ignatius to prepare themselves to respond to the epoch-making challenges of Medellín and Rio. Fortunately we are able to ground the living memory of the event in documents that provide an in-process record of the meeting itself.[137]

### Conversion of Heart and the Option for the Poor of the Central American Jesuits: The December 1969 Retreat

Ellacuría and Elizondo used a truly "radical" approach for the retreat in returning to the long-neglected tradition of group discernment described in *Deliberatio primorum patrum*,[138] the official account of the 1539[139] discern-

---

136. Hernández-Pico,*História reciente*, 9.

137. "Reunión-Ejercicios de la viceprovincia Jesuitica de Centroamérica, Diciembre 1969," in *Reflexión teologico-espiritual de la Compañía de Jésus en Centroamérica, II* (San Salvador: Archives of the Society of Jesus, Central American Province, Survey S.J. de Centroamérica).

138. *Constitutiones societatis Iesu* I, 1-7; in *Monumenta Historica Societatis Jesu, Monumenta Ignatiana*, Series III. See Jules J. Toner, S.J., "The Deliberation That Started the Jesuits: A Commentary on the *Deliberatio primorum patrum*, Newly Translated with a Historical Introduction," *Studies in the Spirituality of the Jesuits* 6, no. 4 (June 1974).

139. Ignatius and his early companions deliberated for several months during 1539 on

ment by Ignatius of Loyola and his companions to found the Society of Jesus. Yet the meeting's central theme of "renewal"[140] (*renovación*), like Vatican II's *aggiornamiento* (bringing up to date) of church traditions, made this admittedly bold recovery of Jesuit foundations seem truly traditional in the hands of the province's former novice master and the soon-to-be director of Jesuit formation (Ellacuría). "Following the parameters of the *Spiritual Exercises* of St. Ignatius,"[141] the two sought to renew the whole province by constituting it as single subject united "in communal reflection and prayer."[142] The object of prayer and reflection was to be "the image of the Jesuit and the Society [of Jesus] . . . in the circumstances of Central America today."[143]

## Principles and Foundations

Ellacuría's first talk summarized the "goal and meaning" of the gathering in three points: (1) to create a moment of communal reflection for the Central American Jesuits about the present historical situation of Central America guided by their shared tradition of the *Spiritual Exercises* of St. Ignatius; (2) to offer the Jesuits an opportunity to come to prayerful agreement about the fundamental principles for the renewal of their members and apostolic works; and (3) to prepare the hearts (affections) of those gathered by seeking an attitude of openness and "indifference" through the *Spiritual Exercises* as the principle and foundation for the personal and structural renewal of the province.[144] The approach was effective, though, as we shall see in the next section, not without its risks.

The first morning was filled out by the Fr. Azcue's provincial welcome, a communal rendition of "Veni Creator," and Elizondo's introductory reflection on "The Theological and Spiritual Meaning of a Community Meeting of the Province."[145] This talk emphasized the christological depth of Ignatius's principle that "we should make ourselves indifferent to all created things, insofar as we are allowed free choice and are not under any prohibition."[146] Elizondo

---

whether to formally constitute themselves as a religious order. This decision was confirmed during communion of a Mass celebrated for the group by Pierre Favre on April 15, 1539.

140. Ignacio Ellacuría, "Finalidad y sentido de la reunión" (Goal and Meaning of the Meeting), 1, in "Reunión-Ejercicios," 37.

141. "Presentación," in "Reunión-Ejercicios," 1.

142. "Documento final de la reunión de El Salvador," 1, in "Reunión-Ejercicios," 183.

143. "Presentación," 1. Juan Hernández-Pico links the reflection on this theme and the postulate developed at the Province Congregation of 1970 to the historical development of Decree Two ("The Jesuits Today") of the 32nd General Congregation of the Society of Jesus, December 2, 1974–March 7, 1975 (see Hernández-Pico, *Historia reciente*), 9, 10.

144. Ellacuría, "Finalidad y sentido de la reunion," 4.

145. See note 108, above.

146. *The Spiritual Exercises of St. Ignatius Loyola*, trans. Elisabeth Meier Tetlow (Lanham, MD: University Press of America, 1987), 11. The complete text reads: "Human persons are created to praise, reverence, and serve God the Lord and by this means to attain salvation. The other things on the face of the earth are created for us, to help us in attaining

asserts, "If we have to renew ourselves, we won't begin by renewing 'things,' nor will we begin by renewing ourselves, as persons; rather we will begin by renewing our . . . [experience] of the God who has communicated himself to us" in the *Spiritual Exercises*."[147] Many were no doubt surprised by the depth of humility and feeling with which this elder Jesuit invited his brothers to put aside their doubts and fears and to embrace a spirit of communal conversion in meeting the challenge of Medellín.

> I have a lot of people here who have been my novices, to whom I have given the *Exercises*, and have tried to explain what the Society is. I was superior of this province, which meant I had to look after the majority of those who are here. [And] you may have an image which could become an obstacle to the correct interpretation of what, in reality, the *Exercises* are, identifying this spirituality with what you received from me. I always think that the third class of humility [see note] for me is to have been master of novices twenty years before the present epoch, because it was impossible that one could have prepared people for such a different era from the one in which we lived and those things which used to condition our life. Thus it is that I am beginning to be converted myself and to acknowledge the sins . . . which I may have had in a thing so essential as the transmission of that which the Society of Jesus should be. I have tried to change [*convertirme*] and to be open-mindedly indifferent, without worrying about anything but what the truth is, whatever it may be, even though it might be very different from what I have lived. I have tried to adjust a bit to the rhythm of the times and the voice of the call of God which manifests itself there.[148]

---

the purpose for which we are created. Therefore, we are to make use of them insofar as they help us to attain our purpose, and we should rid ourselves of them insofar as they hinder us from attaining it. Thus we should make ourselves indifferent to all created things, insofar as we are allowed free choice and are not under any prohibition. Consequently, as far as we are concerned, we should not prefer health to sickness, riches to poverty, honor to dishonor, a long life to a short life. The same holds for all other things. Our one desire and choice should be what will best help us attain the purpose for which we are created."

147. Elizondo, "Sentido teológico," 1.

148. Ibid., 3. In his *Spiritual Exercises* St. Ignatius elevates the "third degree of humility" above the others in the following words: "By grace, I find myself so moved to follow Jesus Christ in the most intimate union possible, that his experiences are reflected in my own." This is reflected in "a love and a desire for poverty in order to be with the poor Christ; a love and desire for insults in order to be closer to Christ in his own rejection by people; a love and a desire to be considered worthless and a fool for Christ, rather than to be esteemed as wise and prudent according to the standards of the world. See David L. Fleming, S.J., *A Contemporary Reading of the Spiritual Exercises* (St. Louis: Institute of Jesuit Sources, 1976; 2nd ed. rev. 1980, 1987), 40, 41; §167.

Elizondo then forcefully asserts that what is at stake is nothing short of a "dia-logical encounter of the whole province . . . with the Christ of today, with his church of today, and with the Christ located here, in this province."[149]

Looking back, we can see that this historical encounter with the Christ of Medellín, Rio, and the region's suffering people had the effect of actualizing the radical freedom inspired by the *Spiritual Exercises*, which Elizondo had tried to instill in his recently immigrated charges in 1949. While he could not have known his efforts would bear fruit in the birth of a prophetic vision for the church in Latin America, Elizondo later recalled: "I [had] wanted to prepare in them the openness that is necessary for what the future will bring, without ever knowing what the future may be."[150]

### The "First Week" of the *Spiritual Exercises:*
### The Province Examines Its Conscience

The first day ended with a presentation summarizing the results of the June 1968 student meeting in Madrid, a review of the various Jesuit works in the nations of the province (Honduras, Guatemala, Nicaragua, El Salvador, and Costa Rica), a Christmas-eve dinner, and a large concelebrated mass. Christmas morning was dedicated to a beginning of the small group process. After lunch Elizondo gave the first of two talks on the first week of the *Exercises*, emphasiz-ing how unjust and hurtful patterns of behavior among the Jesuits of Central America might inhibit a free response to God's call to a preferential option for the poor discerned by the bishops at Medellín.

In "The First Week as Indispensable Beginning for Conversion,"[151] Elizondo argues that it was Ignatius's tangible experience "that the Reign of God has already come,"[152] which made the saint aware of sin and brought about the two stages of his conversion. The initial conversion was provoked by an experience of the reality of the Kingdom in the lives of the saints, which Ignatius read while recuperating at Loyola from a serious injury sustained in a military cam-paign. The second, more profound, conversion was provoked by a deeply mysti-cal experience years later while writing the *Spiritual Exercises* in Manresa of God's "salvific design" through the work of the Trinity in the world.[153] As a son of Ignatius, Elizondo similarly argues that if "we speak of a conversion at the level of the province," then "we all have to face, or confront ourselves with the Reign of God." But he adds a crucial point. He says, "There can be sin without guilt—that is, situations which are sinful . . . [simply] because they impede" the

---

149. Elizondo, "Sentido teológico," 5.

150. Interview with Miguel Elizondo by Teresa Whitfield, December 31, 1990. Cited in Whitfield, *Paying the Price*, 24.

151. Miguel Elizondo, "La primera semana como indispensable de conversión" (The First Week as Indispensable Beginning for Conversion), 1-8, in "Reunión-Ejercicios," 46-53.

152. Ibid., 1.

153. Ibid., 2.

Reign of God. On the other, however, he says we must take responsibility for "our faults," which include "my judgments or ideas, my positions or situations, which may be the cause of these sins."[154] Elizondo then calls each Jesuit, and the province as a whole, to do a traditional Ignatian examination of conscience regarding how their individual and social sins may have become obstacles to "our encounter with Christ . . . which is our apostolic vocation."[155]

Having dealt with the preliminaries, Latin America's Jesuit retreat master then invited his colleagues to accept what he sees as the fundamental grace of the Ignatian charism:

> The Ignatian vocational experience consists in a Trinitarian experience, of the Trinity present and operative in this world, in all things . . . realizing its plan for the salvation of the whole world. In this experience Ignatius sees that all things are born from God and return to God through the presence and operation of God's self. And not only by means of the presence and operation of God, but through the insertion of humanity in history. Into this history of salvation comes the human "par excellence," Christ, and with him all persons chosen to actively cooperate in the operation of the Trinity, to realize the salvific plan of God.
>
> When St. Ignatius feels that this is the call, that the one calling him . . . is . . . the God of salvation, he emerges from his solitude and . . . engages the world. [Thus,] . . . the definitive God of Ignatius is going to be the God of this world, . . . the world is the location for the encounter with God. . . . [Consequently,] action becomes a totally different category. . . . Love will not be principally affective or contemplative, but a love which is realized in works, which translates into service, which is realized in this cooperation with God. And, in this way, *action will be for St. Ignatius the response to this Trinitarian God, and the sign of the active presence of the Trinity in Ignatius and the life of his Society*[156] [my emphasis].

The talk ends by relating this profoundly Ignatian understanding of human action to a recent interview with the Jesuit superior general, Fr. Pedro Arrupe, pointedly subtitled "The Society of Jesus has decided to dedicate itself to the world of the poor and recognizes the necessity for structural change."[157] The retreatants spent Christmas afternoon in small group reflection on Elizondo's points, followed by a eucharistic celebration, and a free evening to visit local friends and family.

---

154. Ibid.
155. Ibid.
156. Ibid., 3, 4.
157. Ibid., 7, 8.

## Tensions and Challenges

Ellacuría began the following morning with a fraternal correction intended to preserve the unity of minds and hearts, which the Jesuit general, Fr. Pedro Arrupe, considered essential to the success of the retreat.

> Yesterday, unfortunately in my opinion, the young people said little about their sins, as if it was not intended here to look at what is sinful in the lives of all of us. However, it is necessary to confront not only our works, but our lives. It is easy to criticize our works. But it is not so easy to examine our lives, and the young people have lives as well. . . .
>
> I want to say from this moment, to avoid misunderstandings, that this schema is not designed to attack anybody. . . . So then, I would ask that neither the older people nor those who are in authority think that this . . . has been prepared as a weapon to attack them. Nor, equally, should the younger people think that it is a weapon with which they can attack and which frees them from all [self]reflection.[158]

He then offered a challenging meditation on "Our Collective Situation as Seen from the Perspective of the First Week."[159]

Here Ellacuría argues (perhaps surprisingly for 1969) that any Christian anthropology "without essential and constant reference to sin" is "deformed."[160] With Elizondo, he distinguishes "personal" from "collective" sin, noting that in the Christian tradition "human self-destruction is due to . . . personal sin."[161] He asserts that, while the traditional understanding of "original sin goes beyond personal liberty," it nonetheless includes the notion that "in one way or another we are all responsible" for the evils of this world.[162] Thus, he concludes, "the collective evil of social injustice, which is in the teachings of Vatican II, . . . Medellín, and . . . Rio, the great sin of our time, the 'mystery of evil' of our day, is itself . . . caused by sin, the sin of not attending to the other as a human being, . . . as a person."[163]

Juan Hernández-Pico recalls the remarkable impact of Ellacuría's words.

> All were powerfully struck by the consideration of sin as "collective sin," a biblical interpretation of the crystallization of evil in history. Attention was called to the fact that Vatican II, Medellín, and the Rio Letter were pointing to, for our present history, social injustice as the great collective sin. The compliance with this great sin in our lifestyles

---

158. Ibid., 1.
159. Ellacuría, "Nuestra situación colectiva vista desde la perspectiva de la primera semana," 1-14, in "Reunión-Ejercicios," 58-71.
160. Ibid., 3.
161. Ibid., 7.
162. Ibid., 5.
163. Ibid., 7.

(individualism, adoption of bourgeois values, worldliness) and in the way of structuring our works (preference given to the upper classes, economic commitments to the rich, collaboration with oppressive forces) pointed out our co-responsibility for this collective sin.[164]

Ellacuría's challenging reflection echoed throughout the morning dedicated to time for personal reflection, an hour for small group discussion, and a general assembly for reports and discussion. The official record of the meeting[165] documents the electric effect of the presentations, and the strong mood for change building in the province. While noting the "terror" felt by many in the face of the unknown, one group called for "hope" and "faith in the continuing presence of the Spirit in . . . our epoch."[166]

After lunch, small groups discussed the results of a questionnaire that had been distributed asking all to assess the current state of the province. The survey revealed a general feeling of satisfaction with the renewal of religious life,[167] with the notable exception of the vow of poverty.[168] However, strong majorities felt the province favored the rich and neglected the poor in its apostolic works.[169] And there was virtual unanimity in the opinion that "the great renewal documents of the church" were still little known and lacked implementation in the province.[170]

The general assembly that followed became a profound and surprisingly detailed communal reflection on the individual and collective shortcomings of the Central American Jesuits when examined in the spirit of Medellín and Rio. Group seven, which included the next provincial, Fr. Miguel Estrada, and a current member of the provincial staff, Brother Francisco Azurza,[171] suggested:

> Upon analyzing the causes of the shortcomings in the changes, we believe that sufficient practical respect for the aforementioned documents does not exist. There has been a lack of decision and courage in the superiors, including both the consultors [the Executive Board of the province], and the subjects as well, . . . and a lack of planning at the provincial level. There is no concrete plan of action and the principal cause of this is the magnitude of the change to be realized.[172]

---

164. Hernández-Pico, *Historia reciente*, 8.

165. "Nuestra situación colectiva desde la perspectiva de la primera semana" (Dia. 26:3, 4), 1-4, in "Reunión-Ejercicios," 72-75.

166. Ibid., 2.

167. "Primera encuesta o examen practica. Resultados," 1-5, in "Reunión-Ejercicios," 156-60.

168. Ibid., 2, questions 6.1, 6.2, 6.3.

169. Ibid., 3-4, subsection on "Sobre el sendido de nuestras obras colectivas."

170. Ibid., 4, subsection on "Sobre la renovación de nuestras obras de acuerdo a las directivas de la Iglesia y la compañía."

171. For a list of the members of each discussion group, see "Reunión provincial: Grupos de trabajo," in "Reunión-Ejercicios," 12.

172. "Resumen de la discusión por grupos y la asamblea general" (Dia 26. 5:1, 2), 3, in "Reunión-Ejercicios," 154.

The group proposed the creation of a structure for province planning that would carry out a process of discernment regarding the works of the province guided by the conclusions of the retreat. This process would play a powerful role in helping to transform the Central American province in a few short years, but as Ellacuría prophetically warned, "You have to die to sin [to follow this path], and death is not without pain."[173]

### The "Second Week" of the *Spiritual Exercises*: The Reign of God Preached by Jesus

The following day, December 27, Miguel Elizondo gave two talks exploring a key theme from the second week of the *Exercises*: "The Ignatian Vision for the Following of Christ."[174] The first presentation[175] claims that Ignatius, Jerome Nadal, and their companions understood the Jesuit and Christian vocation as an active collaboration with the Trinity in bringing about the Reign of God. Indeed,

> This call from Christ to the whole world and to each one in particular is, not only to enter into the Reign, but rather to collaborate with it. And so the importance of apostolic action will take on a sharp relief in Saint Ignatius. *In this concept of the Trinitarian experience, the world is not going to be saved only through prayer or only through penance, but rather, in this Ignatian view, through apostolic action which is, at the same time, prayer*[176] [my emphasis].

After time for personal reflection and small group sharing, the retreatants gathered for a general assembly.

The discussion had clearly gained considerable momentum by this point. There were apparently contradictory calls for serious change, strong criticisms of the current province leadership, complaints of an overemphasis on social themes, an appeal for the importance of priesthood, a discussion on how to sort out the various images of Christ present in the province, and an urgent plea for practical models to integrate religious life with work for social change in the service of the poor. Perhaps the question of a recently ordained Jesuit from the Jesuit high school in Panama captured the moment best: "It seems that a certain fear still exists that this meeting is being guided toward the social. But is it certain people who are guiding us, or is it the contemporary situation itself? If it is the latter, we have to go in this direction and come up with real solutions."[177]

---

173. Ellacuría, "Nuestra situación colectiva," 14.

174. "Temario, distribución de los días y horario" (List of Topics, Daily Plan and Schedule), 3, "Reunión-Ejercicios," 5.

175. Miguel Elizondo, "La visión Ignaciana del seguimiento de Cristo" (Dia 27:1), 1-8, in "Reunión-Ejercicios," 76-83.

176. Ibid., 3.

177. Br. Luis Tadeo Ardila, S.J., quoted in "Resumen de la discusiones de grupo y las intervenciones en la asamblea" (Dia 27: 3,4), 4, in "Reunión-Ejercicios," 87.

After lunch Elizondo's second talk, on "Prayer in the Society of Jesus,"[178] again highlighted Ignatius's Trinitarian experience of God as creating, acting in, and sanctifying history in order to explain Nadal's famous description of Ignatius as a "contemplative in action."[179] Elizondo suggests this is why action became the *locus classicus* for the Ignatian encounter with God. And he says this is the reason that Ignatius, even though he prays two hours a day, puts no legislation in his *Constitutions*[180] requiring a specific duration for daily prayer. Elizondo's argument is that,

> The spirituality of Saint Ignatius is a spirituality of action in this double sense: in that all prayer should translate into apostolic service, and that action and apostolic service are in themselves prayer, which is characteristically Ignatian. Speaking in clearer terms, they are union with God.[181]

His point is that, while "Medellín . . . is urging [Latin American Christians] to find a theology for the person of action . . . the Ignatian experience gave it to us four hundred years ago."[182]

Elizondo's talk was then followed by a general assembly in which Luis Achaerandio, president of the UCA, charged that "some young people are trying to justify not explicitly praying."[183] While this intervention would be read by some as representing the growing split between the "gradualists" and the "liberationists,"[184] it is only fair to Fr. Achaerandio to point out that the intervention was about the role of prayer in the renewal of religious life. And here it is crucial to recall that the monumental shift of the Central American province toward the option for the poor at the 1969 retreat emerged from an honest discernment about the proper path for religious renewal. It was not a strategic

---

178. Miguel Elizondo, "La oración en la Compañía of Jesus" (Prayer in the Society of Jesus) (Dia 27:5), 1-8, in "Reunión-Ejercicios," 88-95.

179. Jesuit historian Joséph de Guibert, S.J., notes: "Jeronimo Nadal, one of the men who knew Ignatius most intimately, thinks that his special grace was 'to see and contemplate in all things, actions, and conversations the presence of God and the love of spiritual things, to remain a contemplative even in the midst of action' (*simul in actione contemplativus*)." See *The Jesuits: Their Spiritual Doctrine and Practice,* trans. William J. Young, S.J., ed. George E. Ganss, S.J. (St. Louis: Institute of Jesuit Sources, [1953], 1964, 1972), 45.

180. On this point, see St. Ignatius of Loyola, *The Constitutions of the Society of Jesus,* trans. George E. Ganss, S.J. (St. Louis: Institute of Jesuit Sources, 1970), §§582-84, 259-61. Footnote 2 (p. 260) maintains, "With respect to the length, Ignatius assigned for the scholastics still in formation one hour of prayer daily, which could be divided into different periods (342). But he steadily refused to prescribe one universal rule obliging all the formed members to one specified duration of daily prayer (582-83)."

181. Elizondo, "La oración," 3.

182. Ibid., 90.

183. "Preguntas a los padres Elizondo y Ellacuría" (Dia 27, 5), 1, in "Reunión-Ejercicios," 96-98.

184. Beirne, *Jesuit Education and Social Change,* 84.

referendum on politics, the Alliance for Progress, or liberation theology. No doubt, however, many struggled to hold such strategic concerns at bay as the province gathered to celebrate Mass at the day's end.

### Following the Christ of the San Salvador Retreat: Discernment and Decision

Achaerandio's admonition on the importance of prayer is important to keep in mind as we turn to the two talks by Ignacio Ellacuría built around what many regard as the key moment in the *Spiritual Exercises*, "making a choice [election] of a state or way of life."[185] Significantly, the retreat's final document places these talks under the critical heading, "The election, and the reform of our works."[186] The first presentation, on "The Problem of the Translation of the Spirit of the *Exercises* to the Province,"[187] offers the Christ of the San Salvador retreat as the norm for that reform. Ellacuría argues,

> The province should be the efficacious sign of [the] Christ experienced in the *Exercises*. Because if it is [part of the] church, it should be a sign, and it should be an efficacious sign; an efficacious sign of Christ. And which Christ? Of the Christ experienced in the *Exercises*, in the historical situation in which we are living. Saint Ignatius made his Society the historical objectification of the charism of the *Exercises*. That is to say: . . . he thought, . . . that the Society is the great outcome of the *Exercises*, the great objectification of the *Exercises*, the great body animated by the spirit of the *Exercises*.[188]

Ellacuría's challenge was to apply this experiential-Christological norm to the present historical reality of the province. Recognizing that each work of the province inevitably reflects the worldly dynamics of its historical situation, he warns, "If the high school or the university or the work in which I am engaged competes against, due to its own dynamics, what each one of us personally thinks or has experienced is the dynamic of the *Exercises*, then there is a problem to be solved."[189]

The rest of the day was given to two more rounds of personal reflection, small group discussion, and a general assembly. The record bears eloquent testimony to the almost irresistible momentum building to confront a question posed from the floor by Miguel Elizondo himself: "the Society will have to see concretely

---

185. This translation is from Fleming, *Contemporary Reading of the Spiritual Exercises*, 103.

186. "Documento final de la reunión de San Salvador" (Final Document for the San Salvador Meeting), 2, in "Reunión-Ejercicios," 184.

187. "El problema del traslado del Espíritu de los Ejercicios a la vice" (The problem of the Translation of the Spirit of the *Exercises* to the Vice-province) (Dia 28:1), 1-12, in "Reunión-Ejercicios," 104-15.

188. Ibid., 6.

189. Ibid., 11.

if these high schools and universities are a sign, in the higher and transcendent sense of Christ, for serving and loving others."[190]

It was in this atmosphere that Ellacuría delivered his most powerful, and potentially explosive, talk on the penultimate day of the retreat—an all-out effort to confront the faith of his fellow Jesuits with the scandalous historical reality of Central America as part of the Third World. In a daring and very Ignatian move, he turned what many already knew to be a dangerous confrontation with this seemingly hopeless reality into the ultimate apostolic challenge, recommending "The Third World as the Optimal Place for the Christian to Live the *Exercises*."[191] It is interesting to note that he portrays the talk as a "small attempt" to go beyond the work of his teacher, Karl Rahner, by focusing on the "worldly reality [of Central America], and conceiving of it in theological terms."[192]

Noting that the overwhelming majority of the world's population lives in the Third World, Ellacuría argues that if "Christ is in the poor," then "it is not us who have to save the poor, but rather it is the poor who are going to save us."[193] He then offers a prophetic reflection on what would prove to be his own fate.

> A minimal solidarity with the Third World elicits a turn to the road to redemption and the march to the resurrection. . . . Imagine the day on which a professor at the university turns his whole orientation toward prophetic denunciations of the allies of the . . . [First and Second] Worlds in this Third World. . . . The day in which a university professor dedicates himself categorically and thematically to prophetically denouncing that reality, be assured on that day one of two things [will happen]: either those outside, or those inside, will end up removing him, . . . and they will start taking away his posts. And [likewise] be assured that if the Society puts itself wholly on this valiant road of protest, the Society will not have to renounce [its posts], they will be taken away.[194]

Ellacuría then proceeds with his stunning argument that the *Spiritual Exercises* of St. Ignatius is leading the Jesuits of Central America to serve, and therefore to share, the fate of the crucified Christ of the poor. Laying out a rationale for Jesus' death on the cross, he asserts on the one hand, "It is not true . . . that Christ loved the cross, and that he went looking for pain, poverty, and the rest. Christ was only seeking to fulfill his mission. On the other hand, however, he did know that his mission would carry him in the end to the cross; and conse-

---

190. "Resumen de las discusiones de grupo e intervenciones en la Asamblea General" (Dia 28: 3,4), 8, in "Reunión-Ejercicios," 120.

191. Ignacio Ellacuría, "El tercer mundo como lugar optimo de la vivencia Cristiana de los Ejercicios" (The Third World as the Optimal Place for the Christian to Live the Exercises) (Dia 29:1), 1-12, in "Reunión-Ejercicios," 127-38.

192. Ibid., 2.

193. Ibid., 4.

194. Ibid., 6.

quently what he did was say, 'I will fulfill my mission even though I know I am going to die.'"[195] Ellacuría then argues that a similar dynamic is at work in the Jesuit vocation to apostolic action, which requires them to confront the inherently anti-evangelical dynamics of the Third World. And he suggests it places the Society of Jesus in the Third World on the same road that Christ walked:

> We are in the same situation [as he was]. . . . [And] what is it they will say to us priests or Jesuits when we dedicate ourselves to this task? First of all [they will say] . . . "these priests are communists or Marxists, we can't help them anymore. Let's find other priests, because there is always a need for priests that support us in our situation, since these Jesuits are not helping us." . . . [But] we must stay with the mission of the Old Testament prophets, not because we are seeking that, . . . but rather because of our understanding of the secular mission that we have to fulfill, and everything else will be given to us besides: the pain we spoke of yesterday and the beatitude which this pain gives.[196]

Ellacuría's words would prove eerily prophetic. In the early hours of November 16, 1989, following the Jesuit assassinations, a military sound truck from the First Infantry Brigade circulated in the neighborhood of the bishop's headquarters announcing triumphantly, "Ellacuría and Martín-Baró have fallen. We are going to continue killing communists!"[197]

Following this talk and time for personal and small group reflection, the general assembly strongly endorsed "the creation of a Central Planning Commission which will work until Holy Week looking for a practical manner in which to realize these ideals."[198] The strongly supported proposal would be implemented. But the voice of Fr. Noel Garcia from the Managua UCA ended the session with a poignant challenge to his fellow Jesuits, adding a sobering reminder that the outside world was rapidly changing even as their prayerful deliberations drew to a close.

> I have been working for nine years in social questions, having been trained for that. [And] I see that we are confronted with a social revolution in Latin America. For that reason I believe that, rather than discussing whether the high schools or the universities should abolish themselves as such, we should see if they are fulfilling their end of forming agents of change, so that this social revolution which has to have an ideology—Marxist or Christian—becomes Christian. This is our great responsibility.[199]

---

195. Ibid., 8, 9.

196. Ibid.

197. Martha Doggett, *Death Foretold: The Jesuit Murders in El Salvador* (Washington, DC: Georgetown University Press, Lawyers Committee for Human Rights, 1993), 309, 71.

198. "Resume de la discusión por grupos y la Asamblea General" (Dia 29: 3.4), 2, in "Reunión-Ejercicios," 140.

199. Ibid., 3.

The final document would recall Ellacuría's talk, and the discussions that followed, as a critical turning point toward the decision "[t]o put ourselves efficaciously at the service of this Third World with the power of the gospel and the resources of our human preparation."[200]

### The Third and Fourth "Weeks" of the *Spiritual Exercises:*
### Coming to Conclusion

After lunch the survey team reported that an overwhelming proportion of the gathered Jesuits had written that they were now "ready to leave everything" in order to "undertake an honest search for what we should do."[201] Thus, December 29 1969, ended with the formation of working groups to prepare a discussion for the following day "regarding the accommodation of our works to the spirit . . . of these days."[202] Afterward they gathered for the Eucharist, celebrating the "apostolic mission"[203] of the Jesuits in Central America.

On the final morning, thirty-seven-year-old Ricardo Falla predicted that "death and resurrection" would inevitably accompany the Society's option for the poor in Central America. But he identified this with "The Sacrificial and Resurrectional Meaning of Religious Life,"[204] and reminded his brothers that, after Ignatius's insight at the River Cardoner into the role of the Trinity in the world, the saint reported beginning "to see everything with another set of eyes, and to discern and test the good and the bad spirits."[205] The sixty-three-year-old ex-president of the El Salvador UCA, Florentino Idoate, then responded to Falla's challenge by summoning the province "to see God in all the concrete urgency of today for us in the Third World," and to begin a process of apostolic discernment in the ecclesial spirit "concretized by the documents [of] the Council, Medellín, [and] Rio. . . ."[206] Fr. Idoate's fusion of the horizons of Jesuit renewal with Medellín's call to the option for the poor in his interpretation of "The Contemplation to Attain [Divine] Love in a Secularized World"[207] shows how far things had progressed since his 1965 speech inaugurating of the UCA in the name of "development."[208]

---

200. "Documento final de la reunión de El Salvador," 3.

201. "Resultados de la segunda encuesta o cuestionario" (29:5), 4, in "Reunión-Ejercicios," 168 (results: 84 respondents, 5 = very strongly agree; 5=56, 4=16, 3=6, 2=1, 1=4; abstain=1; 86 percent responded 5 or 4, "very strongly agree" or "strongly agree").

202. "Temario, distribución de los días, y horario," 6, in "Reunión-Ejercicios," 7.

203. Ibid.

204. Ricardo Falla, S.J., "El sentido sacrificial y resurreccional de la vida religiosa," (30.1), 1-2, in "Reunión-Ejercicios," 142-43.

205. Ibid., 2.

206. Florentino Idoate, S.J., "La contemplación para alcanzar amor en un mundo secularizado" (The Contemplation to Attain [Divine] Love in a Secularized World), 2, in "Reunión-Ejercicios," 145.

207. Ibid., 1.

208. Florentino Idoate, S.J., "Discurso del rector de la Universidad Centroamericana

Throughout the afternoon and evening the Jesuits worked to produce the outlines of an apostolic plan to concretize their own conversion, first in a general assembly, then in small task forces, and finally in a plenary session called for 8 p.m. They gathered after evening Mass for a final session in order to approve "The Final Document of the San Salvador Meeting," which recommended three "presuppositions"[209] for a yet-to-be-written apostolic plan: (1) the province's communal commitment to the "redemption and liberation" of Central America as part of the Third World; (2) a strengthening of the spirit of community, mutual respect, and simplicity of lifestyle in the province; and (3) a deepening of the spirit of the willingness to put oneself and the works of the province at the service of the poor, as expressed in the retreat. A three-month "Work Plan"[210] was then approved with the express purpose of moving the process forward.

## Only a Beginning

Fr. Hernández-Pico suggests that, officially, it was first here at the 1969 retreat that "the Jesuits committed themselves to . . . attend to the cries that were coming from the unjustly impoverished and oppressed majorities of Central America, putting aside disordered affections for established works and lifestyles [in order to promote] . . . efficacious action on behalf of the poor."[211] With this monumental shift in horizons the process of renewal accelerated quickly, including "the rapid naming of a new master of novices (Fr. Juan Ramón Moreno) and the creation of a new work, that of the Delegate for Formation, for which Fr. Azcue nominated Fr. Ignacio Ellacuría."[212] Both nominees would be assassinated nineteen years later at the UCA. Within three months the province leadership[213] embraced many of the recommendations from the retreat, including the idea that Jesuit formation be geographically and spiritually relocated within the historical reality of Central America.[214]

The new provincial, Fr. Miguel F. Estrada, then called a second meeting of delegates selected to represent the various "works and nations"[215] of the province in September 1970, at the Santa Tecla Jesuit center in San Salvador dedicated specifically to the question of "apostolic programming." Not surprisingly, the first months of Fr. Estrada's tenure were largely focused on preparations for this critical gathering, including the completion of a "sociological survey"

---

José Simeón Cañas, Forentino Idoate, con motivo de la inauguración de la Universidad," *Planteamiento universitario 1989* (San Salvador: UCA, 1989), 135, 136.

209. "Documento final de la reunión de San Salvador," 4.

210. "Plan de trabajo" (Work Plan), 1, in "Reunión-Ejercicios," 182.

211. Hernández-Pico, *Historia reciente*, 8, 9.

212. Ibid., 9.

213. This meeting, formally called the Congregation of Procurators, had been previously scheduled as a mandated meeting of the leadership of the province.

214. Hernández-Pico, *Historia reciente*, 9, 10.

215. Ibid., 10.

of the Central American region (twelve volumes), which was presented at the meeting with "provisional conclusions."[216] Fr. Hernández-Pico reports that after much debate and discussion it was decided at this second meeting that "our apostolates should . . . foment attitudes of commitment to the social liberation our peoples, giving the latter the theological depth of being viewed as an integral part of the redemptive liberation of Jesus Christ."[217] And he concludes that the most important achievement of the gathering was the development of the outlines of the new apostolic plan called for at the December retreat.

> In this same meeting the Central American Jesuits determined an order of apostolic priorities. Their presupposition was the affirmation of the Rio Letter that "the social problem of Latin America" should have "absolute priority in our apostolic strategy" and, thus, . . . should translate into the allocation of "a part of our apostolic efforts toward the innumerable and believing mass of those who have been abandoned." The meeting named a series of apostolic activities (not concrete works) as priorities. (1) The formation of young Jesuits; (2) socio-philosophical-theological reflection on the Central American reality; (3) attention to, and, in some cases, formation of diocesan priests and . . . male and female religious; [and] (4) community organizing. They also mentioned two others without distinguishing an order: exercising a liberating influence in the area of education, and the promotion of communication media.[218]

Clearly, the preferential option for the poor and the struggle for liberation it implies had officially replaced developmentalism as a defining aspect of the horizon of the Jesuits of Central America.

The debate by no means ended there, however.[219] An opposition group from the UCA and the diocesan seminary, which had emerged during the retreat, charged that the dramatic Christmas and Holy Week movement of the province toward the option for the poor had been a kind of religious coup d'état. Fr. Beirne says, "They pictured Ellacuría as controlling the younger group that did his bidding."[220] The new provincial, Fr. Estrada, was compelled to write to Fr.

---

216. Ibid.

217. Ibid.

218. Ibid., 10, 11.

219. Ibid., 10-14.

220. Beirne, *Jesuit Education and Social Change*, 86. Fr. Beirne notes that the group included Fr. Achaerandio, and Antonio Perez (both from the UCA); Fr. José Ignacio Scheifler (a member of the first UCA Board replaced by Ellacuría) and Santiago Anitua (both from the San Salvador Seminary); and Fr. Jesus Rodriquez Jalon (from an unidentified university; he and Anitua did not attend the retreat). Note that the information in parentheses was not provided by Fr. Beirne, but was extrapolated by the author from the retreat document ("Lista de asistentes," 1-4, in "Reunión-Ejercicios," 8-11; and "Distribución de los padres y hermanos de la provincía segun su trabajo de acuerdo con el ultimo catalogo," 1-2, in "Reunión-Ejercicios," 14-15).

Arrupe in Rome in order to refute these charges, to explain the depth of the changes taking place, and to report on the work of the survey team.[221] Responding immediately, Fr. Arrupe "praised the work of the sociological survey team and told Estrada not to be surprised by opposition."[222] Thus encouraged, the thirty-six-year-old provincial pressed forward.

Four months later, after reviewing the results of the important September meeting at Santa Tecla, Fr. Arrupe would write, "The conclusions, presuppositions, and results are worthy of approval and are within the spirit of the Vatican Council, the 31st General Congregation and the documents of Medellín."[223] He would describe statements in the sociological and theological sections of the documents that reflected the shift to the horizon of liberation as "correct," noting "they conform to recent developments of the social apostolate since Medellín . . . and are consistent with the orientation of the Society of Jesus in Latin America."[224] But he would caution Fr. Estrada to heed the importance of apostolic unity, and to respect the difficult changes in mentality that such a shift of horizons would require.[225]

Thus, Fr. Arrupe's approval cemented the commitment of the 1970 Jesuit leadership in Central America to the process of conversion called for by Latin America's bishops at Medellín, and the Jesuit provincials at Rio. As I have suggested, what had occurred could be described as a shift of apostolic horizons. Like many others, the Jesuits realized that the horizon of development, and its "historicization"[226] in programs such as the Alliance for Progress, had proved inadequate to deal with the painful historical realities of Latin America. Indeed, even as Jesuit superiors working in the provincial offices near the UCA struggled with recalcitrant priests at the UCA and the archdiocese, events were acceler-

221. Letter from Miguel Francisco Estrada to Pedro Arrupe (San Salvador: Archives of the Society of Jesus of Central America, September 3, 1970). Cited in Beirne, *Jesuit Education and Social Change*, 86.

222. Beirne, *Jesuit Education and Social Change*, 86. Fr. Beirne is summarizing the contents of the September 3, 1970 letter from Fr. Arrupe to Fr. Estrada.

223. Letter from Fr. Pedro Arrupe to Fr. Miguel F. Estrada (San Salvador: Archives of the Society of Jesus of Central America, February 25, 1971). Cited in Beirne, *Jesuit Education and Social Change*, 86.

224. Ibid.

225. Ibid., 86-87.

226. This concept of the "historicization" is developed by Ignacio Ellacuría in numerous places. See Ignacio Ellacuría, "The Historicization of the Concept of Property," in John Hassett and Hugh Lacey, eds., *Towards a Society That Serves Its People* (Washington, DC: Georgetown University Press, 1991), 105-37 [translated from *ECA* 31, nos. 335-336 (1976): 425-50]; Ellacuría, "The University, Human Rights, and the Poor Majority," in Hassett and Lacey, eds., *Towards a Society*, 208-20 [translated from "Universidad, derechos humanos y mayorías populares," *ECA* no. 406 (August 1982): 791-816]; Ellacuría, "The Kingdom of God and Unemployment in the Third World," in Jacques Pohier and Dietmar Meith, eds., *Unemployment and the Right to Work* (New York: Seabury Press, 1982), [translated from "El reino de Dios y el paro en el tercer mundo," *Concilium* 180 (Madrid: Ediciones Cristiandad, 1982): 588-96.

ating across town. Salvador Cayetano Carpio was recruiting students from the National University for an "armed revolutionary struggle"[227] under the new banner of the FPL (the Popular Forces of Liberation), the first of the FMLN's eventual five political-military organizations. And in March 1970 the country's land barons, their supporters, and the Salvadoran military party rudely slammed the door in the face of a growing chorus of proposals for agrarian reform.

Fr. Arrupe's support for the results of the Santa Tecla meeting and the new direction of the province completed the first stage of the conversion of the Central American Jesuits from developmentalism to a historical commitment to Medellín's preferential option for the poor and the struggle for justice and liberation it implies. It was a big step forward. But as the gathered members of the province had realistically concluded in December, "It is only a beginning."[228] The first fervor of this epoch-changing conversion was about to meet the historical realities of the UCA and El Salvador.

---

227. "Morales Erlich y Dada Hirezi candidatos a junta" [Morales Erlich and Dada Hirezi candidates for junta], *Prensa Gráfica* (January 7, 1980). Cited in Montgomery, *Revolution in El Salvador,* 103.

228. "Documento final de la reunión de El Salvador," 4.

# 2

# *Taking Responsibility for the Historical Reality of El Salvador (1969-1979)*

## FROM THE OPTION FOR THE POOR
## TO THE UCA COUP

The University of Central America (UCA) felt the shock waves of the Jesuit province retreat almost immediately as 1970 began. But it would take an entire decade for the university community and its leadership to articulate a new horizon for its work. Jon Sobrino describes the 1970s as the decade during which the UCA developed the *theoria* of its self-understanding as a Christian university. He distinguishes this decade from the 1980s, which he says were "more focused on the *praxis* of the University."[1] Sobrino notes that lay faculty played a key role in this process of self-definition: "people like Román Mayorga [who] was much more influential in the University than [many] Jesuits."[2]

Román Mayorga, who joined the university in 1971 and served as president from December 1974 to October 1979, argues for the historical importance of several documents written during the decade that "officially defined the very model of what kind of university the UCA was trying to be." He suggests, "These documents had, at least during the years of the 1970s, the greatest importance in the UCA's understanding and creation of itself; they demanded a . . . prolonged reflection, a . . . consensual approval, and a . . . global effort to carry them out."[3]

He goes on to argue, however, that "not only the documents, but the process of elaborating them, adopting them, and carrying them out was important in the history of the UCA, inasmuch as they contributed to shaping the institution which actually came to exist, as well as a very developed model for that institution."[4] Fr. Juan Hernández-Pico likewise believes that it is important to pay attention to the collaborative nature of this process.

---

1. Interview with Jon Sobrino, S.J., by Robert Lassalle-Klein, April 19, 1994, 3.
2. Ibid., 2.
3. Letter from Román Mayorga Quirós to Charles J. Beirne, S.J., January 21, 1994 (typescript), 11 (used with permission of Román Mayorga Quirós).
4. Ibid.

Historically it's important to say that there was a process of conversion among persons on the teaching faculty and the administration of the UCA. It was not only a process of conversion among the Jesuits, but among a group of lay persons who had a lot of influence here at the UCA. And this group, Jesuits and lay persons together, developed a common vision. Here I am speaking from the analogy of the conversion of the Province. And it was this group that developed the vision.[5]

Fr. Charles Beirne offers an evocative description of what these years were like in his historical study.

The development of drafts of [these documents] are examples of this collaboration which took place not only in formal sessions on campus but also at social events in the homes of lay colleagues.[6] Jesuits and lay colleagues celebrated birthdays and anniversaries together; they went to the beach for holidays, and they became close friends. Luis Achaerandio, the rector, contributed significantly to encouraging this community atmosphere. Although major decisions continued to be the sole responsibility of the Board of Directors, these decisions tended to represent a consensus from the university community rather than just dictates from above. This spirit not only produced creative ways of being a university, it laid the groundwork for a solid community that would face adversity in the coming years.[7]

This is not to say, however, that there were not conflicts and tensions regarding the emerging direction of the university.

The Jesuit community managed ongoing internal tensions between the "gradualists" and the "liberationists" for the better part of the decade. This manifested itself in separate living arrangements for the two groups, and constant disagreements on the Board of Directors regarding "timing, topics, and emphases" in implementing the university's new direction, about which there was nevertheless general agreement.[8] On the one hand, Ellacuría's combination of intellectual brilliance and "charismatic genius"[9] helped push the UCA toward the emerging commitment of the Central American Jesuits to the option for the poor articulated by the Latin American bishops at Medellín. On the other

---

5. Interview with Juan Hernández-Pico, S.J., by Robert Lassalle-Klein, July 1, 1994.

6. Interview with Román Mayorga Quirós by Charles J. Beirne, S.J., March 21, 1994. Cited in Charles Beirne, *Jesuit Education and Social Change in El Salvador* (New York: Garland Publishing, 1996), 114.

7. Beirne, *Jesuit Education and Social Change*, 114.

8. See ibid., 92-93.

9. This is the characterization used by Juan Hernández-Pico to explain Ellacuría's extraordinary role in the transformation of both the UCA and the Central American Province. Interview with Fr. Juan Hernández-Pico, S.J., by Robert Lassalle-Klein, San Salvador, July 7, 1994, 8.

hand, Mayorga, who says he moved to the UCA "at the beginning of 1971,"[10] was more the consensus builder. Hernández-Pico notes that Mayorga "was the practical mediator between two lines of thought [that of Ignacio Ellacuría and Luis Achaerandio] among the Jesuits on the Board of Directors, part arbitrator and mediator."[11] Thus, what Hernández-Pico calls Mayorga's "intellectual and moral prestige"[12] allowed him to play a critical role in the planning processes that translated the university's emerging vision into institutional form culminating with the documents in question.

Fr. Cardenal asserts that "very strong lay–Jesuit tensions" began to emerge toward the end of the decade between the university's Jesuit leadership and "those who wanted more power in the UCA in order to turn it into the university of the Christian-Democratic Party, just as the National University had become the home of the left."[13] He says, "Ellacuría strongly opposed this vision of the lay Christian Democrats at the UCA," and that Mayorga and others "eventually left to form part of the government" in the reformist 1979 coup.[14] Nonetheless, Sobrino, Mayorga, Hernández-Pico, and Beirne all agree that the UCA experienced a period of dynamic collaboration among lay and Jesuit faculty and staff during the 1970s, which eroded after 1979. All emphasize the importance of the documents produced by that collaboration, both in the formation of a new vision for the UCA during the 1970s and for the process of confronting the

---

10. Román Mayorga, "Recuerdo de diez Quijotes" (unpublished manuscript, Montevideo and Washington, DC, March 1991), 10; published as *Recuerdo de diez Quijotes* (San Salvador: Ministerio de Relaciones Exteriores, 2010).

11. Ibid.

12. Ibid.

13. Rodolfo Cardenal, S.J., August 18, 2009, correspondence with author, transcript in personal files.

14. Jon Sobrino has suggested, "Without a group of lay people, this type of project is impossible. I'm convinced of it." But, as regards the centralization of decision making in the Jesuit Board of Directors which took place during the 1980s (and the consequently decreased role of lay faculty and staff in key decisions) he argues: "Why was the leadership in the hands of Jesuits? Under the circumstances of persecution and a university that wants to confront structurally, the Jesuits were able to do it best. That's because they were Jesuits. In 1980, when things got tough, many of the lay people left. The 'total commitment' was different. Some lay people resented that, sometimes with good reasons. [But r]emember, in 1979 30% of the [lay] faculty went to the government. These things don't happen in universities [in the United States]. We see them down there. [For instance, w]hen lay faculty come to the United States to study, they leave the university when they come back. I think that it is an illusion to think you can find a group of lay people totally committed to the university." Thus, while recognizing the problematic aspects of this centralization of power for collaboration between lay and Jesuit faculty and staff, he argues, "without the Board of Directors the university would have collapsed. But we still need to address the need for the participation of others, and to develop along more democratic lines." (All quotes from interview with Jon Sobrino by Robert Lassalle-Klein, April 19, 1994.) Román Mayorga Quirós, on the other hand, seems to feel that the university could have survived while still preserving more of the previous participation of lay faculty in decision making (letter from Román Mayorga Quirós to Charles J. Beirne, January 21, 1994).

national reality of El Salvador as a university community. And they agree that an important aspect of the decline of this collaborative spirit was the aforementioned exodus of many outstanding lay faculty to the government as part of the short-lived 1979 reformist coup, which the Jesuit provincial, Fr. César Jerez, S.J., told superiors in Rome was being called the "UCA Coup."[15]

In this chapter I will summarize and attempt to establish the context for the development and historicization of the vision captured in these 1970s documents, which the university placed at the heart of its collection of official writings defining its mission and identity, published shortly before the assassinations in 1989.[16]

## Toward a University That Serves Its People:
### The Presidency of Fr. Luis Achaerandio (1969-1974) and the Speech to the Inter-American Bank

It is no accident of history that in late 1970 it was Ignacio Ellacuría, S.J., with assistance from Román Mayorga, who wrote the address of university treasurer, Fr. Gondra,[17] outlining a new vision of the UCA for representatives of the Inter-American Development Bank (BID) gathered in Washington, DC. The speech was delivered to celebrate the October 27, 1970, signing of the BID loan financing early development the university's material foundation.[18] Its writers would lead the UCA as successive presidents from December 1974 until Mayorga's departure to lead the government in October 1979, and Ellacuría's assassination on November 16, 1989.

Mayorga recalls that the plan to obtain the loan was hatched in 1969: "I was working at the National Council for Economic Planning and coordination (CONAPLAN) preparing educational development projects for the Ministry of

---

15. Letter from Fr. César Jerez, S.J., to Fr. Pedro Arrupe, S.J., Archives of the Society of Jesus, Central American Province, San Salvador, El Salvador, no. 42, October 23, 1979. Cited in Beirne, *Jesuit Education and Social Change*, 145 n. 72.

16. The following are included under the title "Official documents": 1. "Discurso de la Universidad Centroamericana José Simeón Cañas en la firma del contrato con el BID," in *Planteamiento universitario 1989* (San Salvador: UCA, 1989), 9-14 (delivered as an address in 1970 by Rev. José Maria Gondra, S.J., written by Ignacio Ellacuría and Román Mayorga Quirós); 2. "Consideraciones justificativas y aclaratorias del escalafón de la Universidad," in *Planteamiento*, 15-36 (published by the Board of Directors in January 1974 after university-wide consultation); 3. "Las funciones fundamentales de la universidad y su operativización," in *Planteamiento*, 37-121 (published by the Board of Directors in May 1979 after university-wide consultation; final draft written by Sobrino and one other person); 4. Ignacio Ellacuría, "20 años de servicio del pueblo Salvadoreño," in *Planteamiento*, 125-29 (written and delivered by Ignacio Ellacuría at the UCA on September 15, 1985).

17. In 1969 Fr. Florentino Idoate, S.J., was president of the UCA; Fr. José Maria Gondra, S.J., was treasurer; and Fr. Joaquín López y López, S.J. (later assassinated) was general secretary. All were well connected with El Salvador's wealthy families through long years at the Externado San José, the Jesuit high school in San Salvador.

18. "Discurso de la Universidad Centroamericana José Simeón Cañas en la firma del contrato con el BID," 9-14.

Education" when "Fr. Gondra and Fr. Luis Achaerandio, S.J., asked me . . . if I would help them plan the University's development."[19] Mayorga remembers that he worked "for many months in a CONAPLAN office" with Fr. Achaerandio and Fr. Luis de Sebastián, S.J., and the architect Juan José Rodriguez. Together, he says, "we prepared the first plan for the development of the UCA, which provided the material foundation for the University and permitted them to create the structure of an institution capable of becoming what it is today."

Fr. Beirne, who has closely examined the documentation leading up to and supporting the loan request, notes that at some point during this process the Jesuit leadership of the university concluded that a loan would be necessary, but could not find favorable interest rates or long-term financing in Central America.[20] So academic vice-president Luis de Sebastian, S.J., and Mayorga developed a proposal for the Inter-American Development Bank in Washington, DC. University treasurer, Fr. Gondra, "thought in terms of a few hundred thousand dollars, but Román Mayorga recommended a goal of two million"![21] Mayorga says the proposal "had the clear intention" of financing the construction of "the infrastructure or basic platform of the University."[22] Beirne says it provided "for nine buildings, the basics of a library, laboratory equipment, more full-time personnel, graduate studies for faculty, and technical assistance."[23] Happily, Mayorga was able to convince CONAPLAN to declare the project "a high national priority," and the "Central Reserve Bank of El Salvador indicated its willingness to make it fully guaranteed."[24]

Inside the university, however, not everyone was content with the proposal. Ellacuría, who had never worked with Mayorga, wrote an internal memo attacking its characterization of the UCA as "triumphal, confusing desire with reality . . . in a disgraceful lack of self-criticism."[25] Mayorga himself later conceded that the proposal was "inspired by a certain *developmentalism* without any explicit reference to the problems of class divisions and domination."[26] But Mayorga felt that "the nature of the document did not lend itself to larger ideological concerns," and feared that mentioning such realities would scare off the bankers. For his part, Ellacuría saw the loan's approval as an opportunity to "go public" with a new vision of the university.

---

19. Román Mayorga, "Recuerdo de diez Quijotes" (March 1991), 5-6.

20. Beirne, *Jesuit Education and Social Change*, 95-96.

21. Ibid.

22. Román Mayorga Quirós, *La Universidad para el cambio social* (San Salvador: UCA Editores, 1976), 32.

23. Beirne, *Jesuit Education and Social Change*, 96. Here Beirne follows Román Mayorga Quirós, *La Universidad para el cambio social*, 31.

24. Mayorga Quirós, *La Universidad para el cambio social*, 31.

25. Ignacio Ellacuría, "Algunas notas sobre el resumen del survey de la Universidad J.S. Canas," April 10-11, 1970, Survey Vol. VII, UJSC, 22, Archives of the Central American Province of the Society of Jesus. Cited in Teresa Whitfield, *Paying the Price: Ignacio Ellacuría and the Murdered Jesuits of El Salvador* (Philadelphia: Temple University Press, 1994), 47 n. 20.

26. Mayorga Quirós, *La Universidad para el cambio social*, 31.

Mayorga recalls, "The first time I spoke with Ignacio Ellacuría, or *Ellacu* as we who were his friends knew him, was around the middle of 1970 when BID approved the loan to finance the UCA's first development plan."[27] The Board of Directors had designated Ellacuría to prepare the speech and asked Mayorga to provide "suggestions" on what the document should contain. Mayorga says, "I offered some ideas about the possibility . . . of creating a new kind of university in Central America, a university that would put its whole self at the service of social change simply as a university, that is to say, by means of the specific functions of this type of institution." Delighted, Ellacuría "told me these ideas coincided with those he had been elaborating from a theological angle" for the speech. Subsequently, "he showed me a draft, and we revised it together."[28]

Mayorga later accompanied Fr. Gondra to Washington for the signing speech, which he says was so well received that "they later offered Fr. Gondra a job at BID"! Mayorga recalls, "When I told this story to *Ellacu* . . . he laughed out loud and baptized the first of our collaborations as 'our speech given by Gondra.' It would be the beginning of a friendship that lasted to the end of his life."[29] A few days before the assassinations Ellacuría sent his old friend a copy of the recently published 1989 collection of the UCA's defining documents, which Mayorga fondly notes, "began with 'our speech given by Gondra.'"[30] The gift reached Mayorga after the assassinations with the poignant dedication, "For Román, still so present in this book and in the University."[31]

### "A Critical and Creative Conscience" for the Salvadoran People

Though Gondra's speech mentions neither Vatican II (1962-1965) nor Medellín (1968), the Council's insistence that the church "carries the responsibility of reading the signs of the times . . . in light of the gospel" (*Gaudium et spes* §4) is clearly in the background. Following Medellín's 1968 "option for the poor," the address is built on the premise that the UCA has a responsibility to respond to the social, political, and cultural forces oppressing El Salvador's suffering people. Thus, Medellín's interpretation of the Council's mandate forms one leg of what Ellacuría called the "theological angle"[32] driving the speech's claim that the UCA's "principal problem, now that our launch is assured by the loan from the Inter-American Development Bank, is to work out our particular university identity within the specific *historical reality* that we are living today in Central America."[33]

---

27. Román Mayorga, "Recuerdo de diez Quijotes," 10.

28. Ibid.

29. Ibid.

30. Ibid. See "Discurso de la Universidad Centroamericana José Simeón Cañas en la firma del contrato con el BID," 9-14.

31. "Discurso de la Universidad Centroamericana José Simeón Cañas en la firma del contrato con el BID," 12.

32. Ibid., 10.

33. Ibid., 9. My emphasis.

The other more formally theological dimension of this angle is Ellacuría's oft-repeated Ignatian conviction, implicitly assumed here, that "there are not two histories, a history of God and a human history; a sacred and a profane history. Rather, there is a single *historical reality* in which both God and human beings take part, so that God's participation does not occur without some form of human participation, and human participation does not occur without God's presence in some form."[34] These premises converge in the document's assertion that the UCA's mission is to respond as a university to the *historical reality of Central America*. And this assertion is informed by Ellacuría's conviction that *historical reality* is not only the arena in which the university must fulfill its various functions in secular society, but also the *locus theologicus* for its encounter with God.

These assumptions (explicit and implicit) lead Ellacuría and Mayorga to write, "For this reason we ask ourselves here today before this authentic Latin American forum, what would be the best university service we could render to the people with whom we live?"[35] This query, which drives the rest of the speech, merges the aforementioned concerns with the characteristic emphasis of Ignatian spirituality on discerning God's will and doing the *magis* (sometimes understood as the "greater" good) in carrying it out. The writers presume that if the Jesuit apostolic ideal is to be realized at the UCA, it must be enacted in institutional activities that *most effectively* promote the values of the Kingdom of God within the particular "historical reality" of the people the university hopes to serve. Thus, the document suggests that the UCA will start from an analysis of the historical reality of *what is* in order to discover *what should be done*. It will move from the national reality of El Salvador to the specifics of how its ethics should be lived out in that reality, rather than vice versa. This effectively moves the speech beyond Vatican II's generalized mandate "of reading the signs of the times in light of the gospel" toward a commitment to take positions on the specific historical realities of Central America and El Salvador guided by the discernments of church leaders at Medellín, Vatican II, and Rio. The UCA would soon discover that there is a big difference between teaching students the abstract principles of Catholic Social Teaching and taking public positions on the defining public of the day!

The speech then defines "How the University of Central America José Simeón Cañas understands its mission as a university,"[36] asserting that the UCA does not understand its mission "as a utopian search for timeless truth" but rather as a form of "service to the people that gave it being." Accordingly, if the university's functions are to be carried out in a "strictly historical" manner they must be concretized in response to "the historical situation of the peo-

---

34. Ignacio Ellacuría, "Historicidad de la salvación cristiana," *Escritos teológicos*, II (San Salvador: UCA Editores, 2000), 539; reprinted from *Revista latinoamericana de teología* 1 (1984): 5-45. My emphasis.

35. "Discurso de la Universidad Centroamericana José Simeón Cañas en la firma del contrato con el BID," 9.

36. Ibid.

ple it should serve." With this in mind, the speech then proceeds to examine the historical meaning of what the authors define as the university's three key functions: the commitment to promote human *development* outlined in UCA's founding documents, and its dual obligations to pursue *truth* and *liberty*, traditional obligations of the Latin American university.[37] Ellacuría and Mayorga outline strategies for *historicizing* each of these functions at the UCA, which Ellacuría describes as "demonstrating the impact of certain concepts within a particular context."[38]

Beginning with *development*, the document asserts, "When our University began its foundational labors in 1965 it thought that its service should be focused on the concept of development." However, they note that the university soon discovered that "the work of development, which struggles for the urgent advancement of the neediest, carries within itself the dynamic that leads to its own subordination."[39] As evidence the document asserts that "BID itself" has discovered that the work of development is best understood as "a means for human and social transformation" that points beyond itself toward "a higher ideal which, while incorporating development, goes beyond it." For both BID and the UCA, then, development turns out to be the means to a higher end, the "unavoidable precondition for a life that is humane, personal, and free for our peoples." While not the final goal, development is the necessary condition for attaining that goal.

Ellacuría and Mayorga then turn to the concept of *integral development*, which we have seen was promoted in church documents after 1967, using it to define how development should be historicized in the work of the UCA.

> Before subordinating the concept of development as the ultimate objective of the University, we must insist that it is *integral development* that the University must pursue, as stated in the memorable document [of Pope Paul VI], "development cannot be reduced to mere economic growth. In order to be authentic it must be *integral*, that is, it

---

37. Ibid., 10.

38. There are two distinct but related meanings of *historicization* found in Ellacuría's work. In addition to the meaning stated above, Ellacuría uses the term in his *Philosophy of Historical Reality* to refer to the incorporative and transformative power that human praxis exerts over the historical and natural dimensions of reality. For my description, see Robert Lassalle-Klein, "Ignacio Ellacuría's Debt to Xavier Zubiri: Critical Principles for a Latin American Philosophy and Theology of Liberation," in Kevin Burke and Robert Lassalle-Klein, eds., *Love That Produces Hope: The Thought of Ignacio Ellacuría* (Collegeville, MN: Liturgical Press, 2006), 109. For the original sources, see Ignacio Ellacuría, *Filosofía de la realidad histórica* (San Salvador: UCA Editores, 1990), 169; and Ignacio Ellacuría, "La historización del concepto de propiedad como principio de desideologización," *ECA* nos. 335-336 (1976): 425-50, at 427-28; translated as "The Historicization of the Concept of Property," in John J. Hassett and Hugh Lacey, *Towards a Society That Serves Its People: The Intellectual Contribution of El Salvador's Murdered Jesuits* (foreword Leo J. O'Donovan; Washington, DC: Georgetown University Press, 1991), 105-37, at 109.

39. "BID," 10.

must promote the development of all people and of the entire person" (*Populorum progressio* §14).[40]

The authors then provide three reasons why "this approach requires a profound renovation of the traditional structures of the University in order to impact the full development of all."

First, the commitment to integral development implies that "the mission of the University is to serve everybody and not just a group of privileged students"[41] who become professionals. The authors recognize that while some students use their education for selfish purposes that undermine "the just promotion and distribution of the national wealth," others faithfully "comply with this sacred obligation of service." They insist, however, that the modest contributions of the latter group should not lead the university to "appease its conscience by thinking it is impacting the entire nation through the professionals formed there," or by imagining that it has thereby "integrally fulfilled its mission of service."

Second, the writers argue that "the University should put itself at the service of all," and that it should do this by "directing its attention, its efforts, and its functioning as a university to the study of structures . . . that influence the lives of each citizen for good or for ill."[42] They say the university "should analyze [these structures] critically, it should contribute in a university manner to the denunciation and destruction of those that are unjust, and it should create new models which can be implemented by society and the state." And they conclude, "This is the irreplaceable work of the University in its service to the country as a whole and to each of its citizens," comprising a "critical and creative task" that the university fulfills for the nation.

Third, the authors argue that the university has a duty "to conscienticize" the Salvadoran people, "not with moralizing preaching, but with conclusive studies."[43] The idea is that the UCA "should strive to awaken in everyone an acute awareness of the human rights of every Central American," both at home and before the "international community." They assert, "Only in this way" will the university be able "to promote integral development without repeating the errors that have historically plagued developmentalism."

Next, having addressed the university's commitment to promote *human development*, the speech moves to the role of *truth* in the mission of the UCA. The document argues that "the University should be a kind of laboratory for the truth," reflecting the UCA's effort "to define itself by means of the search for truth, a social truth" that helps the nation to understand and to bring about "the realization of what is owed to each."[44] Thus, "the University understands its principal mission as that of being a *critical and creative conscience* for

---

40. Ibid., my emphasis.
41. Ibid., 11.
42. Ibid.
43. Ibid.
44. Ibid., 12.

the Salvadoran reality within the Central American context."[45] This powerful articulation of the UCA's new vision for itself would appear again and again in subsequent statements of the UCA's mission. Aware of the possibility of misinterpretation, however, Ellacuría and Mayorga immediately add, "We do not intend to be activists, but we do demand for ourselves the autonomy of thought and communication that will permit access to every source of truth, will allow us to communicate it, and will tolerate that sublime form of action which is thinking that brings about liberty with justice."

Finally, having argued that development will be historicized through the promotion of *integral development*, and that truth will be historicized through the university's role as a *critical and creative conscience* for the country, Ellacuría and Mayorga conclude that *liberty* can be fully historicized at the UCA only through university-style efforts to promote *liberation and freedom* for the Central American people. The text says, "Liberty must be initially understood in the current situation of our peoples as *liberation*" from "what is oppressive," or in the words of Pope Paul VI, "as liberating humanity from slavery, and enabling it to become its own agent responsible for its own material, moral, and spiritual development" (*Populorum progressio* §34).[46] The document insists, however, that "in order to know what kind of development to promote and for whom, or to know how development should be subordinated to liberation and freedom, what is needed is a new vision of the university, and a new kind of courage in carrying out the university task."

The talk then ends where it began, with Fr. Gondra thanking the no-doubt surprised bank officials for financing the UCA's intention to create a new kind of university.

> The fact is that this contract with the Inter-American Development Bank offers us the possibility for a *new liberty* to search for and communicate the *truth*, and the opportunity to work without compromise for the *true development* of our people. This is something that deserves our deepest thanks and the gratitude of the country to whose service this University has publicly committed itself.[47]

In the end, the address functioned as a kind of public announcement by the university's next two presidents, one lay and the other a Jesuit priest, that the UCA was embracing the *preferential option for the poor* outlined by the Latin American bishops at Medellín. We should note, however, that the UCA's understanding of its role in historicizing the university's commitments to development, truth, and liberty was, at this point, largely mediated through the agency of the country's elites. It would not be until the end of Archbishop Oscar Romero's three-year leadership of the archdiocese, and the failure of both the "UCA

---

45. Ibid., 12, my emphasis.
46. Ibid.
47. Ibid., 14, my emphasis.

Coup" and the FMLN's "final offensive," that Ellacuría and the UCA would find the practical means to focus the resources of the university on the agency of the poor and their emerging role in Salvadoran civil society.

### The Central American Jesuits Incorporate the Option for the Poor into Their Apostolic Planning

For their part, the Central American Jesuits continued to press ahead with the task of incorporating the newly adopted horizon of the Medellín bishops into their apostolic planning. Here too Ellacuría played a significant, if controversial role. Fr. Arrupe had described Ellacuría as "a little radicalized with some explosive ideas"[48] and approved the latter's appointment by Fr. Miguel Estrada as head of Jesuit formation only *ad experimentum*. Fr. Estrada, the first native-born provincial of Central America, was himself appointed in April 1970, just after the 1969 retreat, despite the fact that at thirty-six he was clearly identified with the new generation of "liberationists" considered by Luis Achaerandio and others to be under the influence of Ellacuría.[49]

As expected, changes followed quickly. College and philosophy studies for Jesuit seminarians were returned almost immediately from abroad to the province. Small communities were opened, some in close proximity to the poor. One small community moved to a rural town, Aguilares, a little over twenty miles from the capitol where in September 1972, Fr. Rutilio Grande and his team began a new form of "rural evangelization"[50] that would lead to his assassination in 1977. In 1974 Ellacuría founded the Center for Theological Reflection, where Jesuit seminarians, for the first time, could study theology in the country. Hernández-Pico notes that "All this was possible because . . . [Fr. Azcue] named Ignacio Ellacuría as delegate for formation."[51]

Of course it was Miguel Estrada who approved these innovations, marshaled crucial support both within the province and from Rome, and, from his first day in office, "exerted himself in order to make the options and conclusions of the meeting of 1970 a reality in the Province."[52] In addition to the items mentioned above, Fr. Hernández-Pico says Estrada's term saw "the birth and development of small communities capable of a great sense of community and simplicity"; "the foundation of the Centers for Research and Social Action (CIAS) in the Province"; and "support . . . for the most progressive vision at the UCA in San Salvador and the *Externado*," the Jesuit high school in San Salvador.

---

48. Segundo Azcue to Pedro Arrupe, December 21, 1969, cited in Rodolfo Cardenal, S.J., "La Provincia de Centro América," 92, Archives of the Central American Province of the Society of Jesus. Also cited in Whitfield, *Paying the Price*, 45.

49. Beirne, *Jesuit Education and Social Change*, 84-85.

50. Hernández-Pico, *Historia reciente*, 12.

51. Hernández-Pico interview by Lassalle-Klein, 4.

52. Hernández-Pico, *Historia reciente*, 11. Here Hernández-Pico refers to the second Province Congregation of 1970 during September at Santa Tecla in which the Jesuit leadership officially committed itself to the new horizon or "category of liberation" (ibid., 10).

Hernández-Pico asserts that Estrada's decision to return Jesuit seminary formation from abroad to Central America "began to reverse the shortage of vocations." He admires Estrada's "courageous" confrontation with the Nicaraguan dictator, Anastasio Somoza, regarding the latter's attempts to interfere with the Jesuit-sponsored UCA of Managua. And he praises Estrada's role in fostering an emerging "coherence" between the option for the poor of the 1969 retreat and the reality of the "apostolic and community" works of the Society of Jesus in Central America.[53]

In fact, from 1969 to 1974 the Society of Jesus waged a largely internal struggle to apply its new option for the poor to the mundane reality of its work in Central America. At the UCA Luis Achaerandio and Ignacio Ellacuría were the respective spokespersons for the competing "gradualist" versus "liberationist" Jesuit positions.[54] Fr. Beirne notes that Achaerandio had been elected president of the UCA on August 19, 1969, just four months before the December retreat and about a year after both Medellín and the important Jesuit meeting at Rio. Fr. Beirne asserts that "opposition to the [sociological] survey," which tried to document the existence of oppressive social structures in Central America, "had come mainly from Achaerandio" and a group of others who "pictured Ellacuría as controlling the younger group."[55] Hernández-Pico says this same group opposed the province's official adoption of the horizon of "liberation" at Santa Tecla.

Not surprisingly, Ellacuría recalls "being in a constant struggle and in the minority on votes"[56] during the first eight years following his 1967 election to the Board of Directors. Beirne describes how Jesuit living arrangements at the university reflected this split. "UCA I" was home to the gradualists (Achaerandio, Gondra, Ibisate, Sáinz, López y López, and Esnaola), while "UCA II" housed the "liberationists" (Ellacuría, de Sebastián, Montes, Cortina, Sobrino, Martín-Baró, Arroyo, Mariscal, and, subsequently, Rodolfo Cardenal). But Beirne also notes that "the gradualist and liberationist factions worked together, at times sparring, at times uniting their forces, especially when bombs began to explode after 1976, and after the assassination of Fr. Rutilio Grande, . . . [when] the Board had tilted toward Ellacuría's positions, thanks to a 3-2 majority (Ellacuría, Mayorga, and de Sebastián)."[57]

During the earlier period, however, Beirne says,

> Both groups reached general agreement on goals statements such as Gondra's 1970 speech at the IDB loan signing, the operational manual of the UCA, and even Ellacuría's 1975 article in *Estudios centroamericanos* (*ECA*) that explained the basic characteristics of the university.

---

53. Ibid., 12.

54. This terminology is that of Fr. Beirne, *Jesuit Education and Social Change*, 84.

55. Ibid., 88.

56. Letter from Juan Hernández-Pico, S.J., to Charles J. Beirne, S.J., July 1993. Cited in Beirne, *Jesuit Education and Social Change*, 92.

57. Beirne, *Jesuit Education and Social Change*, 92-93.

On issue after issue, however, they disagreed as to timing, topics, and emphases. And yet, an integrated university model came out of the dynamic tension between the two sectors.[58]

This was no doubt due, in part, to the leadership provided by Achaerandio during his presidency. Mayorga, who joined the Board as its first non-Jesuit member in 1970, offers a balanced view of Achaerandio's leadership. He insists,

> It is neither fair, nor remotely realistic, to pin labels on him like "reactionary" by some, and "radical" by others. There is one aspect, at least, in which one would have to be more explicit: he was a visionary in the contracting of lay persons and was generous in the integration of their contributions. Many of the lay persons that I mentioned before came to the UCA during his presidency. In my opinion, no other Jesuit saw with such clarity the importance of the university community, nor facilitated as much as he its growth and integration.[59]

Thus, despite their disagreements over the proper horizon for the work of the university, the UCA's Jesuit leadership managed to work with one another and their lay collaborators to develop the vision for a new kind of post-Vatican II university inspired by Medellín's preferential option for the poor. Their achievement seems all the more remarkable when one considers that it occurred as the social, political, economic, and military elites of El Salvador degenerated into polarized and irreconcilable camps.

### Strategic Planning to Implement the UCA's New Vision

The UCA's gradual incorporation of the horizon of the option for the poor, and the struggle for liberation and justice it implies, into its key documents during the 1970s consistently subordinated these concepts to the more general and encompassing horizon of "historical reality."[60] The BID speech, which initiated the UCA's official commitment to this process, begins with the premise that "the principal problem [of the UCA] . . . is to find our own university identity in the concrete historical reality which we are living today in Central America."[61] It then argues in a derivative manner for the adoption of liberation as the proper horizon for the work of the Central American university because it constitutes the proper response to "the present situation of our peoples."[62] Likewise, the key 1979 document that culminates this process, and still occupied the preeminent

---

58. Ibid., 93.

59. Letter from Román Mayorga Quirós to Charles J. Beirne, S.J., Washington, DC, January 21, 1994, 14. Used with permission of Fr. Beirne.

60. When the intent is to refer to the historical reality of El Salvador, the term "national reality" is used.

61. "BID," 9.

62. Ibid., 12.

position in the university's own handbook in 1989, affirms, "The UCA seeks to be an institutional university response to the historical reality of the country. . . . It does this in a university manner and . . . with a Christian inspiration."[63]

This subordination of the option for the poor and liberation to the more encompassing notion that they represent the proper Christian response to the demands of historical reality reflects a general tendency in Latin American ecclesial and theological thought. At the UCA, however, it was Ignacio Ellacuría who emphasized this relationship and constantly sought to ground its adoption by the UCA in a philosophical foundation. In 1972 Ellacuría published an article in *ECA* that used the work of the Spanish philosopher Xavier Zubiri to propose the following model for human intelligence:

> We have, accordingly, a theoretical intelligence, a practical intelligence, and an historical intelligence. The three are not only legitimate as aspects of intelligence, but they are, moreover, mutually implicated: theoretical knowledge demands a practice and both shapes and is shaped by a situation; practical knowledge is a situated knowledge and both implies and produces a theoretical knowledge; historical knowledge is at the same time both theory and action. [But] the supreme form of intelligence would be that which would fulfill to the highest degree all three dimensions of intelligence.

Ellacuría argues thus because he believes that not only intelligence but reality itself is formally historical. Thus intelligence is ultimately a response to, and must therefore have reference to, historical reality. Accordingly, he concludes that the university is most theoretically astute when it is engaged in "a form of effective thinking"[64] about the present historical reality in which it is situated.

Ellacuría's 1973 book, *Freedom Made Flesh*,[65] situates this action-oriented understanding of thinking, which he believes should take place at the university, in an explicitly religious and Christian context. Building on the work of Karl Rahner, Ellacuría suggests, "If people work within the world for the new future of history, and if they live on the basis of Christian promise and hope, then they are working for the definitive appearance of God as the absolute future of man (Rahner)." He goes on to suggest, however, that "we must affirm God, not only as the Absolute of individual experience, but also as the Absolute of historical experience itself."[66]

Ellacuría's point is that not only human understanding and political libera-

---

63. "Las funciones fundamentales de la universidad y su operativización," in *Planteamiento*, 47.

64. Ellacuría, "Filosofía y política," in *Veinte años de historia en El Salvador (1969-1989)*, vol. I (San Salvador: UCA Editores, 1991), 53.

65. Ignacio Ellacuría, *Freedom Made Flesh* (Maryknoll, NY: Orbis Books, 1976). Originally published as *Teología política* (San Salvador: Ediciones del Secretariado Social Interdiocesano, 1973).

66. Ellacuría, *Freedom Made Flesh*, 108.

tion, but the very act of contemporary Christian belief in the liberating character of God's salvific communication and self-revelation, must be situated within the general horizon of historical reality. He asserts,[67] "Christians . . . must insist that the presence of God in natural and historical reality is not the presence of a demiurge who miraculously rewards or punishes the religious behavior of individuals and nations." He says this implies "on the theoretical level they must seek a line of action that will transform the world and human society," while on the practical level "they must implement it in their praxis." As a result, Christian action for justice "will serve as the essential sign, without which man's transcendent salvation cannot be rendered present." For this reason, then, "Christians must insist that history is the locale of God's revelation, and that this revelation is meant to show us here and now that God is revealing himself in history."[68]

The suggestive English title of this work, *Freedom Made Flesh*, highlights Ellacuría's conviction that God's freedom was incarnated in the historical life lived by Jesus of Nazareth. It also highlights what he sees as the free choice facing the church and individual Christians whether or not to embrace or reject Medellín's "decisive turning towards the poor" as an essential aspect of "the mission of the Church in Latin America."[69] Typically, the reasoning he offers has less to do with internal church concerns and the teaching authority of its bishops than with the demands of the historical reality of Latin America, when interpreted in light of the gospel. Ellacuría writes,

> In Latin America "the poor" are not a fringe group; they are the majority. In a real sense they define what Latin America is: poor in health, poor in education, poor in living standard, poor in having a say in their own destiny. [Thus, both] by virtue of the universal vocation of the gospel, and by virtue of the historical summons specific to the region in which the Latin American church lives, it must be the Church of [and for] the poor.[70]

We must not miss the implication here that the poor are still "other" for Ellacuría's implied reader. Thus, the challenge to the church that believes it is called by God to make a preferential option for the poor is to overcome its distance from the poor through solidarity and compassion grounded in real relationships.

It is not surprising, then, that the documents of the early 1970s through which the UCA began to redefine its mission as a Christian university should characterize the UCA's embrace of the option for the poor, and the struggle for liberation and justice it implies, as the reasonable and informed response in light of the gospel to the demands of "historical reality." Neither is it surprising that these documents should demonstrate a certain preoccupation with the institutional forms designed to translate that horizon into thinking about "effec-

---

67. His understanding of this term would now be described as post-modern.
68. Ellacuría, *Freedom Made Flesh*, 18.
69. Ibid., 146.
70. Ibid.

tive history"[71] designed to change the national reality of El Salvador through the leadership of the country's elites.

Mayorga's 1976 history of the UCA describes 1970-1974 in terms that reflect this preoccupation. He characterizes 1970 as the "year of the ideological crisis"[72] when the university officially embraced the "thesis . . . 'of liberation'"[73] in the BID speech. He says the university's plan was to bring the horizon of liberation to the country's elites by means of policy proposals and professionals formed through dialogue and solidarity with the poor.

> The form in which the university was to contribute to this liberation, was by means of the study of reality, the scientific denunciation of oppressive structures, the search for effectively liberating solutions, and the preparation of professionals capable of implementing those solutions; [all done] in dialogue and solidarity with oppressed people.[74]

Recognizing the difference between these ideals and the actual accomplishments of the UCA, however, Mayorga immediately insists that in 1970 there remained a great "distance between this thesis and the reality of the University."[75]

The year 1971 followed as a "year of expansion"[76] for both the UCA's physical plant and its new self-understanding. Mayorga offers an important sketch of a process created to help the UCA faculty and staff deepen their commitment to the new horizon, and to implement it in the actual work of the university.

> In 1971 a seminar was held which included the participation of students, professors and directors, that is to say, with the representation of all spheres [of the university community], in which the commitment of the university to work for liberation was reaffirmed. This caused the orientation that was supposed to be guiding the university to penetrate, at least intellectually, into larger sectors than had participated in the initial discussion. . . . In fact, it constituted the first public examination of conscience, open to all spheres and profoundly critical, that the UCA dared to have with a degree of self-confidence.[77]

On the practical side, the university press published *An Analysis of a National Experience,* which documented government repression during the 1971 National Association of Salvadoran Educators (ANDES) teachers' strike. The piece was so "effective" that it led President Fidel Sánchez Hernández to eliminate the

---

71. Hans-Georg Gadamer, *Truth and Method,* trans. Joel Weinsheimer and Donald G. Marshall (2nd ed. rev.; New York: Crossroad, 1960, 1975, 1991), 302.

72. Ibid.

73. Mayorga Quirós, *La Universidad para el cambio social,* 37. See also pp. 37-40.

74. Ibid., 37.

75. Ibid., 38.

76. Ibid., 40. See also pp. 40-44.

77. Ibid.

UCA's annual subsidy from the 1972 national budget, which was approved by the National Legislative Assembly (more on this later).[78]

Mayorga characterizes 1972 as the "year of the organic structuring of the university to the order of its goals."[79] He recalls, "At the beginning of 1972 a project for the organization of the university was prepared which had been in the works since the preplanning for the renewed ideological orientation."[80] The process produced the "Organizational Handbook of the University,"[81] which envisioned a three-pronged structure through which the university would transform its commitment to the option for the poor, and the struggle for liberation and justice it implies, into an historically effective horizon for the national reality of El Salvador. This document outlined a detailed structure for the "coordinated realization of . . . appropriate university-style activities (Teaching, Research, and Social Outreach)."[82]

The year 1973 then followed as the "year of the institutionalization of research and of social outreach."[83] An institute for research was created with Dr. Guillermo Ungo as its first director, and a Center for Social Outreach was established as well. A steady stream of studies bringing the university's commitment to the option for the poor to bear on the national reality began to flow from the UCA. These studies embodied the UCA's growing efforts to focus the university's research and social outreach on the historical reality of El Salvador, historicizing its self-proclaimed mandate to "create new models so that society and the state can implement them."[84]

The year 1974 proved to be a "year of consolidation"[85] dedicated to correcting "imperfections," "deficiencies," and "lacunae" in the newly operative model of the university. Mayorga cites two major initiatives in this regard. First, in January the Board of Directors and the superior council of the university approved an important document intended to create an infrastructure to retain and recruit lay collaborators for the UCA's new mission in the decade ahead. This document ("Justifying and Clarifying Considerations for the Salary Scale of the University"[86]) appears in the university's own handbook, and is cited by Mayorga, both in his history and personal correspondence, as one of the key documents of the 1970s.[87]

---

78. Ibid., 41. Rodolfo Cardenal confirms this scenario in private correspondence with author, August 18, 2009.

79. Mayorga Quirós, *La Universidad para el cambio social*, 44.

80. Ibid., 46.

81. Mayorga Quirós includes important sections of this manual in his history. See *La Universidad para el cambio social*, 212-24.

82. "Manual de Organización de la Universidad," from *La Universidad para el cambio social*, 213.

83. Mayorga Quirós, *La Universidad para el cambio social*, 49. See also pp. 49-59.

84. "BID," 11.

85. Mayorga Quirós, *La Universidad para el cambio social*, 59. See also pp. 59-64.

86. "Consideraciones justificativas y aclaratorias del escalafon de la Universidad," in *Planteamiento*, 15-36.

87. Mayorga Quirós, *La Universidad para el cambio social*, 59-62. Also letter from Román Mayorga Quirós to Charles J. Beirne, S.J., January 21, 1994.

With these developments the UCA issued a bold call to reform the university's internal structures.

> On numerous occasions the UCA's "being the critical and creative conscience of the national reality" has manifested itself in severe criticisms against the injustice of social structures that deny human beings access to the authentic fullness of life. The university has constantly exerted itself to point out paths for a process which, because of the present characteristics of the life of the Central American people, should be initially understood as a process of radical social transformation which seeks to liberate the people from diverse forms of structural oppression.
>
> [But] only with difficulty could the university present itself as authentic in its statements, if it did not focus its critical lens on its own realities, and did not try to eliminate, to the greatest degree possible, whatever traces of injustice or oppression that could be found in its own structures.[88]

The document argues that the current salary scale at the UCA had become unjust because: (1) it was unresponsive to the "visible elevation in the cost of living during the year of 1973"; (2) it was "disordered," "intuitive," and "lends itself to interpretations of personal favoritism"; and (3) it promoted "a frankly competitive" atmosphere among faculty and staff at the UCA."[89] It then establishes a new salary scale based on eleven criteria. Mayorga's history says that this new system broke "the schemas of hierarchy and exploitation which . . . [were] usual in the Salvadoran economy."[90] And he proudly notes that the highest salary possible was only 3.5 times the upper limit for the lowest category of manual labor.

Other major initiatives cited by Mayorga include the creation of a sliding scale for tuition based on a student's ability to pay,[91] the permanent establishment of the Center for Theological Reflection, and the addition of new majors in political science and sociology. Thus, it seems that by the end of 1974 the university community and its leadership felt justified in their belief that the UCA was ready to expand and to test the validity of its commitment to the option for the poor through an examination of the impact of the UCA's teaching, research, and social outreach on the broader historical reality of El Salvador.

---

88. "Consideraciones justificativas," 15.

89. Ibid., 16.

90. Mayorga Quirós, *La Universidad para el cambio social*, 60.

91. "Resolución de la Junta de Directores y el Consejo Superior Universitario sobre cuotas diferenciadas de pagos estudiantiles y sus anexos," in Román Mayorga Quirós, *La Universidad para el cambio social*, 63-64.

## Historicizing the Vision:
### Risky Engagements with El Salvador's Elites

It is important to understand the changes underway at the UCA as the beginning of a university-style attempt to support increasing calls for needed social change in the country, and to avoid the violent confrontation taking shape among El Salvador's increasingly polarized political, ecclesial, economic, and military elites. A brief look at the developments taking place in the national reality of the country help to explain the urgency driving the aforementioned changes at the UCA.

### Taking Positions on Political Debates: Agrarian Reform, Revolution, and the Status Quo

Any list of key events from this period must include the National Agrarian Reform Congress convened in January 1970, only weeks after the Jesuit retreat. President Fidel Sánchez (1967-1972) had proposed a mild program of agrarian reform in August 1969, and in what Román Mayorga calls a "small *coup d'état*,"[92] a coalition of reformist members of the official party (the PCN [National Conciliation Party]), the Christian Democratic Party (PDC), and certain members of the government called the Congress for January 1970. The unexpected opening soon emerged as the defining moment of 1970 for Salvadoran secular and church leaders interested in pursuing agrarian reform through democratic means. Its controversial conclusion would be that it is "not only a right of the State but a duty" to carry out "massive expropriation [of underutilized land holdings] for the sake of the common good."[93]

The Catholic Church was among the many governmental, nongovernmental, business, and labor groups invited to participate in the Congress. Archbishop Luis Chávez y González sent a delegation of priests and laity, which created a "strong commotion"[94] according to Archbishop Rivera Damas by vigorously supporting calls for agrarian reform. However, much of the wealthy and landowning private sector united in polar opposition to the proposals before the Congress and exited *en masse* during the first session. Rodolfo Cardenal recalls, "The private sector expected the UCA to leave the room with them. But not only did they not leave, but they supported the project of agrarian reform."[95] Mayorga adds, "The brilliant and independent interventions of the UCA representatives at the Congress attracted considerable attention and provided an important landmark in the development of the institution."[96]

---

92. Mayorga Quirós, *La Universidad para el cambio social*, 35.

93. "Resoluciones y recomendaciones del Primer Congreso Nacional de Reforma Agraria," *Economía salvadoreña* 28 (1969): 109.

94. Tommie Sue Montgomery, *Revolution in El Salvador: From Civil Strife to Civil Peace* (Boulder, CO: Westview Press, 1995), 82.

95. Cardenal, correspondence with author, August 18, 2009.

96. Mayorga Quirós, *La Universidad para el cambio social*, 35.

Unfortunately, the dangers of moving from broad statements about Catholic Social Teaching to politically controversial positions on the defining issues of the day soon became apparent. Hours after speaking strongly in favor of agrarian reform, the archbishop's spokesperson, Fr. José Inocencio Alas, was "beaten, drugged, and left naked on the edge of a cliff in the mountains south of San Salvador."[97] Fr. Cardenal says the fact that the university's representatives did not walk out with its donors "was interpreted by members of the private sector as *a betrayal* by the UCA. The university, which they had regarded as a defender of their interests, had abandoned them." Cardenal emphasizes that this sense of betrayal "strongly influences the perception of the UCA in the private sector even today."[98]

Chastened, the government party manipulated the national elections that followed two months later, effectively removing agrarian reform from the presidential and legislative agendas until the mid-1970s. But as the decade began the Agrarian Congress had clearly placed land reform and the rights of peasant farm workers to organize at the top of the agenda of those pressing for economic and political reform through democratic means.

Another sector of Salvadoran society, however, had already abandoned reform in favor of armed revolution as the only way to bring about significant economic, political, and military change.[99] The first of what would become the five political-military organizations constituting the National Liberation Party (FMLN) was founded in 1970 by Salvador Cayetano Carpio.[100] Carpio had become secretary-general of the Communist Party of El Salvador (PCS) during the 1960s, a party that, in its own words, had "renounced the armed struggle"[101] after the disastrous *matanza* of 1932. Carpio would later recall,

> After a long process of ideological struggle within the traditional organizations [or political parties] it became evident that they . . . denied the possibility and necessity of the Salvadoran people undertaking the process of revolutionary armed struggle. [However,] by the end of 1969 it was very clear that El Salvador, its people, needed an overall strat-

---

97. Montgomery, *Revolution in El Salvador,* 82.

98. Cardenal, correspondence with author, August 18, 2009.

99. For a fuller account of the details of the founding of the various revolutionary political-military organizations in El Salvador during the 1970s, see Montgomery's account, on which the information in the next two paragraphs is based. See Montgomery, "The Revolutionaries," in *Revolution in El Salvador,* 101-26.

100. Salvador Cayentano Carpio (his *nom de guerre* was "Marcial") committed suicide on April 12, 1983, in Managua, Nicaragua, after being implicated in the assassination of another top leader of the FPL, Mélida Anaya (known as "Ana María"). For an interesting and provocative analysis of this event, see José Antonio Morales Carbonell, "El suicidio de Marcial ¿Un asunto concluido?," *ECA* 49, no. 549 (July 1994): 653-89.

101. "Declaración del CC del PCS en ocasión del 50 aniversario del levantamiento armado de 1932" [Declaration of the Central Committee of the Salvadorean Communist Party on the 50th anniversary of the 1932 armed uprising], El Salvador, January 1982. Cited in Montgomery, *Revolution in El Salvador,* 103.

egy in which all methods of struggle could be used and combined in dialectical fashion.[102]

Thus, Carpio resigned from the Communist Party of El Salvador, went underground, and founded the Popular Forces of Liberation (FPL) in 1970.

This sector of Salvadoran society would become increasingly important as the decade progressed. In 1972 the Revolutionary Army of the People (ERP) also emerged from the Communist Party (PCS) with a different, younger, and more diverse constituency. And in 1975 the Armed Forces of the National Resistance (FARN) was formed by a group that left the ERP when a hard-line faction assassinated Roque Dalton, El Salvador's most important living poet (then a member of the ERP), ostensibly because of his insistence on the need to emphasize political as well as military revolutionary activities. The following year, on January 26, 1976, the Revolutionary Party of Central American Workers (PRTC) was founded comprising union workers, individuals who had left the group that founded the ERP in 1972, and others. And finally, in 1979 the PCS itself decided that the time for armed struggle had come. Thus, the PCS formed the Armed Forces of Liberation (FAL), which grew out of militias created after the February 28, 1977, massacre in the Plaza Libertad that preceded the assassination of Fr. Rutilio Grande, S.J., by only two weeks.[103]

Each of these groups had a political arm, including mass-based organizations for political mobilization and education. But it was the steadily worsening standard of living and the increasingly brutal military, paramilitary, and right-wing suppression of civil society that fueled the steady growth of these political-military organizations during the 1970s. Ultimately, the interaction of all these factors with the failure the 1979 "Young Officers" or "UCA" coup (and its plans for agrarian, political, economic, and military reform), would create the conditions for the outbreak of true civil war in 1980.

A third sector, or social grouping, that would play a significant role in the coming decade was the coalition between the El Salvador's oligarchy (mostly large land-holders) and the military. Military candidates stole both national legislative and presidential elections during the 1970s, defrauding their rival civilian candidates of victories won at the polls. The fact that members of the oligarchy not only allowed this to happen but actually promoted the military consolidation of political power must be partially explained by the shared interest of these two groups in both the institutionalized system of corruption and the military repression of civil society in the name of anti-communist ideology.

According to retired Lieutenant Colonel Mariano Castro Moran, corruption was endemic in public life. Moran,[104] a graduate of El Salvador's military academy, participated in the successful 1944 rebellion against Hernández Martinez,

---

102. Mario Menendez, "Salvador Cayentano Carpio: Top Leader of the Farabundo Martí FPL," *Prensa Latina*, February 1980. Cited in Montgomery, *Revolution in El Salvador,* 103.

103. Montgomery, *Revolution in El Salvador,* 105.

104. This biographical information is from Montgomery, *Revolution in El Salvador,* 280 n. 44, 280.

and was a member of the Civilian-Military Directorate, which ruled after the U.S.-supported, anti-communist countercoup of January 25, 1961. In 1984 he wrote in *ECA*,

> It is a notorious and public fact that corruption has come to pervade all levels of public administration. The continuation in government of the regime's functionaries is not only because of political ambition but because they try to continue enriching themselves. . . . It is the survival imperative of a mafia encrusted with power.[105]

In this article Moran describes the 1970s construction of El Salvador's international airport and the freeway connecting it to San Salvador, along with several other incidents, as examples of the magnitude of the country's institutional corruption.

Montgomery summarizes a graphic description of how military officers gradually became part of this system of corruption in a 1980 interview with Cuban-born Peter Dumas, part-owner and general manager of the San Salvador Sheraton during the 1960s and 1970s.

> Peter Dumas, of the San Salvador Sheraton Hotel, asserted . . . that the private sector was "more corrupt" than the army. He explained that as long as officers were in the barracks there was no opportunity for them to become corrupt. When they assumed positions in state-owned companies such as ANTEL (the telecommunications company), however, opportunities for corruption abounded. Dumas described how the system might work for him: an officer would be invited to dinner at the hotel, to return and bring his family, and to use hotel facilities (gratis, of course) for a birthday party or similar event; there would follow an invitation to spend the weekend at the manager's beach house. Later the officer would be offered the opportunity to buy 10 percent of a business with guarantees that if he needed a loan one would be available at attractive interest rates, courtesy of a bank owned by members of the oligarchy. This, Dumas concluded, was only one example of how a "very elastic system" of corruption worked.[106]

In this way the economic and political self-interests of important military leaders became personally and institutionally intertwined with that of the wealthy land-owners who were virulently opposed to agrarian and political reform.

In 1972, however, the army-dominated government of President Fidel Sánchez Hernández (1967-1972) seriously alienated the majority of El Salvador's

---

105. Mariano Castro Moran, "Función política del ejercito Salvadoreño en el presente siglo" [Political function of the Salvadoran Army in the present century] (San Salvador: UCA Editores, 1984), 242. Cited in Montgomery, *Revolution in El Salvador,* 65.

106. Montgomery, *Revolution in El Salvador,* 65. Material cited from interview by Tommie Sue Montgomery with Peter Dumas, January 1980.

wealthy land-owning families with his modest attempts to develop a public consensus for a "democratic program of agrarian reform."[107] The 1970 National Agrarian Reform Congress had unified the oligarchy in polar opposition to all discussion of the topic. And Sánchez's tolerance for political opposition made possible the electoral defeat of his hand-picked successor, presidential chief of staff Colonel Arturo Armando Molina. Molina's victorious opponent was the former mayor of San Salvador, José Napoleon Duarte, whose platform included the promise of real agrarian reform. Predictably, however, the PCN-controlled Central Elections Council, which had already disqualified on technicalities the most likely winners among the opposition candidates for the National Assembly, fraudulently declared Colonel Molina the winner of the February 20, 1972, presidential election. As a result, on March 25, 1972, reformist army officers, led by Colonel Benjamin Mejia, instigated yet another coup.

The coup was soon defeated by the Air Force and security forces, and Molina was inaugurated. But the legitimacy of the new presidency had been weakened by the coup, by the blatant electoral fraud, and by the military's sullied reputation as an institution not committed to democracy. Now alienated from the reformers, the new president turned toward the oligarchy and the right wing for political support, unleashing the ideology of anti-communism against the National (public) University, an important voice for agrarian reform since at least the 1940s. Molina charged that the university was communist controlled, and at his request the National Assembly annulled the university's autonomy. Military troops occupied its campuses, arrested faculty, staff, and students, and closed the university until September 1973, when it reopened under government control. A July 1972 *ECA* editorial said the takeover "calls into question the value of any university and its freedom to realize its university mission."[108] But the intervention was popular among the increasingly reactionary land barons who saw both democratic and revolutionary strategies for agrarian and political reform as two sides of the same socialist coin.[109]

This narrow alliance between the military and the oligarchy proved to be politically unstable, however, and disruptive of bilateral relations with the United States.[110] Thus, in 1976, the U.S. Agency for International Develop-

---

107. Casa Presidencial press release, *Prensa Grafica*, August 15, 1969. Cited in Montgomery, *Revolution in El Salvador,* 61.

108. Unsigned editorial, *ECA* (July 1972): 438. Rodolfo Cardenal notes that all editorials in *ECA* are unsigned "because it is considered the official voice of the University, and its direction is closely associated with the Vice-president for Social Outreach." Rodolfo Cardenal, S.J., August 18, 2009, private collection.

109. Stephen Webre, *José Napoleón Duarte and the Christian Democratic Party in Salvadoran Politics 1960-1977* (Baton Rouge: Louisiana State University Press, 1979), 185; Mario Flores Macal, "Historia de la Universidad El Salvador" [History of the University of El Salvador], *Anuario de Estudios centroamericanos* 2 (1976): 13-35; cited in Montgomery, *Revolution in El Salvador,* 66.

110. The information in this paragraph is from Tom Barry and Deb Preusch, *The Central America Fact Book* (New York: Grove Press, 1986), 216-19.

ment (AID) persuaded Molina to implement a mild program of agrarian reform involving only 4 percent of the national's land. The program was to be jointly implemented by the military and two U.S. AID-supported projects: the Agrarian Transformation Institute (ISTA) and the Salvadoran Communal Union (UCS).

In response, the oligarchy waged a fierce and ultimately successful campaign of extreme anti-communist rhetoric and violence against the program. And a year later the hard-line minister of defense, General Carlos Humberto Romero, replaced Colonel Molina in yet another fraudulent election. This was followed by an unprecedented wave of persecution against the church, the Jesuits, and the UCA as part of a larger violent repression of Salvadoran civil society by government and clandestine right-wing groups.

## An Emerging Role in National Events

*ECA* played an increasingly important role in giving the UCA a voice in public affairs during this period. In early 1969 the Central American Jesuits passed control of the journal to the university. Rodolfo Cardenal describes Ellacuría's role in bringing *ECA* to the UCA, and the significance of its first issue.

> The need to efficaciously project the university into society motivated . . . [Ellacuría] to search for an organ to publish the truth uncovered by research at the UCA and to denounce injustices. Therefore he arranged that the UCA should assume the direction of the magazine *ECA*. The first issue of this new era of *ECA* was . . . dedicated to analyzing the causes and consequences of the war with Honduras. In this edition of the magazine the true causes of the conflict were unmasked by demonstrating that the root of the problem was in the unjust [system of] land tenancy. . . . [And] from this edition forward, *ECA* has been the principal and most constant organ for the publication of the critical thought of the university, and the most important professor's chair occupied by Fr. Ellacuría.[111]

The October 1970 BID speech written by Ellacuría and Mayorga further clarified the university's commitment to the option for the poor and the struggle for liberation and justice it implies. The plan was to engage the country's elites in developing policy proposals for change, and to produce professionals formed through "dialogue and solidarity with the oppressed."[112] *ECA*, together with a series of individual studies published by the university, would become one of the primary vehicles for implementing this during the last half of the decade.

---

111. Rudolfo Cardenal, "Ser jesuita hoy en El Salvador," *ECA* 44, nos. 493-494 (November-December 1989): 1017.

112. Mayorga Quirós, *La Universidad para el cambio social*, 37.

## ECA and the War with Honduras

On July 14, 1969, the Armed Forces of El Salvador invaded Honduras.[113] In response, Ellacuría's lead editorial in the UCA's new flagship journal boldly asserts, "The university would be failing in one of its most grave responsibilities, that of being an intellectual conscience for the nation, if it did not confront this crisis, offering an intellectual diagnosis."[114] He explains that the issue will therefore be dedicated to an in-depth examination of the war from a variety of perspectives, including a chronology of the events themselves; analyses of the effects of the war; its impact on the economy (the war had disastrous effects, eating up one-fifth of the budget[115]); the role of the Organization of American States in the conflict; legal issues; and a comparative statistical analysis of possible outcomes.[116]

William LeoGrande provides a historical perspective on the conflict, explaining that before 1969 Honduras played an important role easing long-simmering tensions in El Salvador over land tenure patterns: "With over 600 people per square mile, El Salvador's population density was the highest in Latin America. Over a quarter of rural families (26.1%) were completely landless, and another 60% owned too little land to support a family."[117] Fortunately, though El Salvador had no open land to develop, "Illegal emigration to less populous Honduras acted as a safety valve for the potentially explosive situation in the countryside." Montgomery adds that by the end of the 1960s this population had grown to "at least 300,000 Salvadoran settlers," many of whom were "second generation immigrants" and "successful small farmers."[118] A crisis emerged in April 1969 when Honduras, "using a new agrarian reform law, notified Salvadoran farmers that they had thirty days to leave their land." Two months later, the country "reversed its open-border immigration policy and closed its border." In response, El Salvador tried to close its own border to the returning immigrants, filed a complaint with the inter-American Commission on Human Rights, and invaded Honduras.

Though Salvadoran forces destroyed the Honduran Air Force on the ground

---

113. Recall that Ellacuría and Mayorga Quirós would suggest that the university "must understand its principal mission as that of being the critical and creative conscience of the Salvadoran reality within the Central American context" ("BID," 12).

114. *ECA* 24 (1969): 389.

115. Webre, *Duarte*, 93, 97. Cited in Montgomery, *Revolution in El Salvador*, 61.

116. The 1969 war with Honduras was referred to as the "Soccer War" because nationalistic sentiments stirred during the World Cup soccer competition between the two countries provided political cover for the El Salvadoran military to start a five-day war in July with Honduras over its decision to expel up to 300,000 Salvadoran peasants farming there, some for multiple generations. See William M. LeoGrande, *Our Own Backyard: The United States in Central America, 1977-1992* (Chapel Hill: University of North Carolina Press, 1998), 34; Montgomery, *Revolution in El Salvador*, 59-60; Hugh Byrne, *El Salvador's Civil War: A Study of Revolution* (Boulder, CO: Lynne Rienner, 1996), 20.

117. LeoGrande, *Our Own Backyard*, 34.

118. Montgomery, *Revolution in El Salvador*, 60.

and advanced far into the country, a cease-fire brought about by U.S. pressure on the Salvadoran government brought the war to an end after five days. While the war had been popular, it ate up one-fifth of the annual budget, and tens of thousands of landless Salvadoran peasants returned home. Byrne notes that the number of landless peasants in El Salvador more than doubled during this period from 19.8 percent in 1961 to 41.1 percent in 1971.[119] This had the effect of both intensifying ongoing tensions over land distribution and accelerating parallel problems with income distribution. Accordingly, from 1970 to 1980 the income of the poorest fifth of the population dropped from 3.7 percent to 2 percent of national income, and the richest fifth went from 50.8 percent to 66 percent of the national total.[120]

Ellacuría's treatment of the 1969 war with Honduras in *ECA* is unremarkable in that it provides an ethical justification for the position of the Salvadoran government in the conflict. What is notable, however, is his characterization of the desperate socio-economic and political predicament of El Salvadoran peasants as a "limit-situation."[121] He cites Karl Jaspers, "who used this term to refer to those situations in which one cannot live without struggle and suffering . . . , situations which place our whole existence in question and flood it with light."[122] This leads him to make two key points: "first: the presence of a limit situation itself is a condemnation of an unjust structure that demands radical change; [and] second, when a person or a people enter a limit-situation, decisions are always ambiguous and therefore those who make and implement these decisions must refuse to be swept up by the passions aroused by the impact of that situation."[123]

Ellacuría concludes with a good deal of prescience that if the present situation of El Salvador continues unchanged in which "fundamental human rights are being obscured due to legal and political arrangements," the result will be a contradiction or "antinomy between justice and [the] law."[124] Lest we miss the point, Ellacuría says that he is talking about "situations such as that of resistance to totalitarian regimes, revolution against unjust structures, revolutionary violence. . . . " Clearly, this is a man who hopes to avoid violence by alerting leaders in the government and civil society to the storm he sees gathering on the horizon, and who is aware months before the December 1969 retreat of the dangers of embracing Medellín's preferential option for the poor.

---

119. Byrne, *El Salvador's Civil War,* 20.

120. Ibid. Byrne (*El Salvador's Civil War*) cites Carlos M. Vilas, *Between Earthquakes and Volcanoes: Market, State, and the Revolutions in Central America,* trans. Ted Kuster (New York: Monthly Review Press, 1995), 68.

121. Ignacio Ellacuría, S.J., "Fundamental Human Rights and the Legal and Political Restrictions Place on Them," in Hassett and Lacey, *Towards a Society That Serves Its People,* esp. 96-99 (translated from "Los derechos humanos fundamentales y su limitación legal y política," *ECA* 24, nos. 254-55 [1969]: 435-49).

122. Ibid., 96-97.

123. Ibid., 99.

124. Ibid.

## Land Reform

The style that would characterize the UCA's adoption of the option for the poor and integral development as the horizon for its work in the 1970s was further developed in two issues of *ECA* on the subject of land reform. The second release (January-February, 1970) of the new *ECA* under the UCA's direction took up the subject, and Ellacuría's lead editorial offers nine principles that he argues should guide reform. The editorial tries to provide a rational basis for further dialogue with its analysis that any comprehensive proposal for Salvadoran land reform should provide both for a more "just land distribution," and "an increase in productivity,"[125] two aspects of land reform considered mutually exclusive by some participants in the reform congress.

1. On the one hand, he argues that the land ownership system should not be an obstacle to socio-economic and human development.
2. It should take into account the common good when promoting its own interests,
3. It should not accumulate benefits through unjust wages.
4. On the other hand, he says that profitable use should be made of the land, which will ensure stable employment.
5. The government should contribute to economic and human development by providing basic and vocational education, and promoting community development and organization.
6. Production and work should be adapted to promote both economic efficiency, and high employment.
7. Land productivity should be improved through fertilization, infrastructure and appropriate crop cultivation.
8. Adequate credit resources should be established to promote private agronomic development.
9. [The country should] improve national and international marketing and quality control techniques, provide economic incentives to promote development, and enhance the availability of technical information.[126]

In 1973 *ECA* again returned to the issue.[127] This time, however, all the articles emphasized the need for political change in order to pressure the wealthy to address their historically unjust monopoly of El Salvador's land and economy. Mayorga says this special edition of *ECA* was intended to serve as a "point of departure"[128] both for a series of seminars that the UCA would offer to governmental- and private-sector bureaucrats during the month of April, and for high-level conversations with government officials regarding "possible technical collaboration" by UCA scholars and administrators in developing a national

---

125. Ibid.
126. *ECA* 25, nos. 256-257 (January-February 1970): 3.
127. *ECA* 28, nos. 287-298 (July-August 1973).
128. Mayorga Quirós, *La Universidad para el cambio social*, 53.

plan for agrarian reform. Mayorga's history notes with some tact, however, that following "the well-known events in September of that year in Chile" (the U.S.-sponsored assassination and coup that overthrew the agrarian-reform-minded government of Salvador Allende), the government officials who had attended the seminars "unexpectedly resigned their positions, the conversations between the UCA and the government were terminated, and the theme of agrarian reform seemed to fall into official neglect once again."[129] The UCA was learning just how hard it would be to achieve even minor changes in government policy regarding land reform in El Salvador through the agency of sympathetic and conscientious elites.

## Two Important Books on the National Reality

In 1971, UCA faculty produced a controversial interdisciplinary study of the ANDES teachers' strike (*An Analysis of a National Experience*) applying the university's newly adopted principles "to a concrete case involving the study of the [national] reality, and the denunciation of oppressive structures."[130] Mayorga recalls, "The case was red hot at the moment," and the study proved to be explosive.

> This low-bred research project . . . caused the withdrawal of the 1972 national subsidy which the executive branch had already presented to the legislature. The subsidy disappeared "as if by magic," through instructions from the executive branch just before the appropriation was to have been voted. High government officials claimed later that urgent public needs had come up at the last minute, and made necessary a pull back of the UCA subsidy.[131]

Ellacuría's contribution to the volume summarized the chronology of events and offered an ethical analysis.[132] The Salvadoran National Legislature had passed a basic "Salary Law for the National Teaching Profession," but ANDES protested vigorously on three fundamental points: (1) the law exemplified a "totalitarian" encroachment upon the legitimate prerogatives of non-governmental bodies in educational institutions (the teachers union demanded an appeals board for administrative decisions;[133] (2) the basic salary scale was unjust;[134] and (3) the Assembly was both manipulating the legislative process and excluding the legitimate participation of important non-governmental offi-

---

129. Ibid., 53-54.

130. Ibid., 41.

131. Ibid.

132. Ignacio Ellacuría, "Estudio ético-político del proceso conflictivo ANDES-ministerio," in *Análisis de una experiencia nacional* (San Salvador: UCA Editores, 1971), 123-54. Reproduced in Ignacio Ellacuría, *Veinte años de historia en El Salvador (1969-1989): Escritos políticos* (San Salvador: UCA Editores, 1991), 523-56.

133. Ibid., 525.

134. Ibid., 528.

cials.[135] Ellacuría notes that ANDES warned it "was going to strike" if their proposal for a "raise in salaries and a mixed appeals board was not approved." But "the legislative assembly and the executive branch were not intimidated . . . and did not change the disputed points [in the law]."[136] As a result the teachers went on strike for three months.[137]

Though the volume criticizes both the Ministry of Education and the teachers' union, it raised the curtain on a host of issues particularly troubling to the government: the right to unionize and strike (farm worker unions were still banned), the control of the press by the right, the urgent need for profound educational reform, and the effect on the educational system of the fundamentally unjust distribution of economic resources in the country, among others. Hernández-Pico's informal history cites the effort as early "proof of the capacity of a university institution to become a critical conscience for the national reality."[138] Known simply as "the yellow book," Whitfield says the study was "badly printed" and "largely unread."[139] But it was clearly an important moment for the UCA in beginning to apply its new horizon to the historical realities of El Salvador, and to discover the limits of its strategy for concretizing its option for the poor through the agency of the country's elites.

The project also led Ellacuría to establish a critical principle regarding the nature of civil society that would shape his thinking in social ethics to the end of his life. After praising ANDES for assuming its role as "a political force," he warns that "there is a . . . sense of politicization that is directed to the change of the government in order to put oneself in its place," much like "a political party." While conceding, "This can be legitimate and necessary," he states that it is not the proper "meaning of a guild group like the teachers' [union]."[140]

Juan Hernández-Pico has argued that this development must be considered "important because it shows that Ellacuría consistently wanted a strong civic [or civil] society capable of being a social force over against political forces such as the state and political parties."[141] According to Beirne, Hernández-Pico argues that the insight gained in this exchange would "lead him to urge the emergence in the 1980s of a 'third (social) force' with an important role alongside the Salvadoran government and the FMLN insurgency." Later, we shall see the absolutely critical role this idea played in Ellacuría's discovery of practical strategies for linking the teaching, research, and social outreach of the university to the country's poor majorities as the agents of their own destiny.

Emphasizing the point a few months later, the August-September edition of

---

135. Ibid., 529.

136. Ibid., 531.

137. The teachers were on strike from June 7 until September 1, 1971, which falls during the Salvadoran academic year.

138. Hernández-Pico, *Historia reciente*, 12.

139. Whitfield, *Paying the Price*, 51.

140. Ellacuría, "Estudio ético-político," 534

141. Beirne, *Jesuit Education and Social Change*, 103. Beirne cites a letter from Juan Hernández-Pico, S.J., to Charles J. Beirne, S.J., July 1993.

*ECA* supported the union's demand to raise teachers' salaries. But Ellacuría's lead editorial again cautioned, "ANDES should deepen its consciousness of the need to serve the country. It should avoid certain characteristics of a movement closed in upon itself; . . . [and] it should avoid the temptation to turn itself into a political party."[142] As structures in civil society began to emerge and promote mass mobilization in El Salvador in the 1970s and 1980s, challenging a society dominated by land-holding families and the military, the implications of this line of thought became increasingly apparent.

Two years later, in June 1973, the UCA published *El Salvador: The Political Year of 1971-1972*,[143] demonstrating that the military related PCN had stolen the 1972 elections for the Molina government. Mayorga Quirós (who was one of the authors) believes that the yellow book "marked a culminating point in a gradual process in the relations between the institution and the state from a more or less presupposed collaborationism . . . to an exercise, in this case, of the critical university function."[144] He also states that the decision to actually publish the study provoked "an internal crisis [at the UCA] . . . only matched, in its conflictive character, by the ideological crisis of 1970, and perhaps even more intense."

When Ellacuría told the UCA Board he was recruiting CIAS scholars César Jerez and Juan Hernández-Pico for a joint research project on the elections, Román Mayorga cautioned that the UCA publish the work with the following prologue: "(a) This is a scientific piece of historical investigation of ideas and falls within the mission of the university; [and] (b) it is the sole responsibility of its authors and it does not commit the rest of university personnel for or against its content."[145] But Whitfield nonetheless observes, "The study . . . became the focus of extreme tension among the Jesuits. Lines were drawn between those who saw in the publication of the book a test case of whether the university was able to live up to its rhetoric and those more conservative Jesuits, still in a majority on the Board of Directors, and including the [president] . . . Luis Achaerandio, who feared the political and financial consequences that publication would bring with it."[146]

Such fears were confirmed when the book's assertion that the election had been stolen played a role in the Jesuits being dismissed after fifty-seven years as directors of the country's diocesan seminary. In September 1972 Archbishop Chávez and the secretary of the bishops' conference, Bishop Oscar Romero (who spearheaded the move), came to inform the Jesuit provincial, Fr. Estrada, that the Jesuits' tenure as directors of the diocesan seminary (which dated to 1915), was about to end. The final letter of dismissal, written by Bishop Romero

---

142. *ECA* 26, nos. 274-275 (August-September 1971): 481.

143. Juan Hernández-Pico, César Jerez, Ignacio Ellacuría, Emilio Baltodano, and Román Mayorga Quirós, *El Salvador: Año político, 1971-72* (San Salvador: UCA Editores, 1973).

144. Mayorga Quirós, *La Universidad para el cambio social*, 51-52.

145. "Minutes of the Board of Directors of the UCA" (San Salvador: Archives of the University of Central America, November 9, 1972).

146. Whitfield, *Paying the Price*, 51.

at Estrada's request, stated that the service of the Jesuits was no longer needed because the local diocesan church had attained sufficient "maturity" to take control of the operation itself. Whitfield argues, however, that the real issue was resistance by conservative bishops to the implementation of Vatican II and Medellín at the seminary, and to the contractual "autonomy" of the Jesuits to carry out the Council's directives.[147] Cardenal details a series of skirmishes that led to Rutilio Grande's nomination as seminary rector being vetoed in 1970.[148] The final blow came two years later when a number of seminarians who had seen the study refused an invitation to sing and serve at a solemn Mass to be attended by the recently inaugurated president, Colonel Molina, whose government, the seminarians said, "had been rejected by the people."[149]

The dispute even spread to Guatemala, where some Jesuits from the Rafael Landivar University sent an anonymous letter to the UCA protesting the decision made for security reasons to publish the work in their country.[150] Despite the difficulties, however, the volume was published, and Rodolfo Cardenal reports that copies were smuggled into the country hidden in a truck belonging to the uncle of Fr. César Jerez.[151] In the end, the book was important beyond Jesuit circles because it exposed the national elections as a charade whose real purpose was to provide political legitimation for military rule and the suppression of political dissent in the service of El Salvador's wealthy elites.

### Slander and Political Repression

Not surprisingly, relations with the Molina government quickly deteriorated, resulting in outright hostility toward other Jesuit-sponsored efforts to implement the new orientation. Hernández-Pico recalls that when administrators tried to implement Medellín's option for the poor at their high school across town (the *Externado San José*), "the government of Colonel Molina [began] . . . accusing various Jesuits of violating the Constitution."[152]

The problem began on April 27, 1973, with a letter from the high school parents' association to the school's president, with copies to Fr. Estrada and Fr. Arrupe in Rome, complaining that field trips designed to expose their sons to the national realities of El Salvador "should be realized with a Christian

---

147. Ibid., 48-49.

148. Rodolfo Cardenal, *Historia de una esperanza: Vida de Rutilio Grande* (San Salvador: UCA Editores, 1985, 2002), 114-39, 155-86.

149. "Apuntes ante la salida de la Compañía de Jesús del Seminario Central de San José de la Montaña de San Salvador" (San Salvador: Archives of the Central American Province of the Society of Jesus), 20. Cited in Whitfield, *Paying the Price*, 50.

150. Rodolfo Cardenal, "La Provincia de Centro América en sus diez ultimos años, 1969-79" (unpublished manuscript, San Salvador: Archives of the Central American Province of the Society of Jesus), 144. Cited in Whitfield, *Paying the Price,* 52.

151. Rodolfo Cardenal, S.J., correspondence with author, August 18, 2009. Whitfield says the books were transported by car. Whitfield, *Paying the Price,* 52.

152. Hernández-Pico, *Historia reciente*, 14.

spirit and not oriented by the doctrine of class struggle."[153] The upset parents reported that their newly enlightened children now "repeatedly accuse their families of living like bourgeoisie, as if the effort to maintain an economic well-being was a crime." The conflict escalated with an editorial written by Bishop Oscar Romero for the May 27, 1973, edition of *Orientación*, the newspaper of the San Salvador archdiocese. Whitfield's account is succinct:

> The editorial was a direct attack on a "certain school"[154] whose Marx-ist teachers had perverted the principles of Medellín with "pamphlets and literature of known red origin." Rapidly reprinted throughout the press as the authentic opinion of the Salvadoran church, it touched off an unprecedented campaign against the Jesuits as "Communists in sheep's clothing"[155] and "a threat to peace and social order." On June 11 the prosecutor general himself weighed in to charge the *Externado* with "teaching classes of Marxist orientation." Jesuits, staff, and parents of the *Externado* were called upon to testify, hour after hour and day after day, as the scandal absorbed the nation.[156]

During May, June, and July 1973 the local newspapers and radio stations were filled with attacks and half-truths. The crisis peaked on June 11, 1973, when Molina's attorney general formally charged the school with "teaching classes of Marxist orientation."[157] Archbishop Chávez finally intervened and appointed a commission to investigate the accusations, which fully exonerated the Jesuits and others teaching at the *Externado San José*. At the same time Ellacuría gathered a group of UCA Jesuits who combined forces with some of their counterparts at the *Externado* to publish a six-part series in the local media entitled, "The *Externado* Thinks Like This."[158] The series refuted the charges of Marxist ideological indoctrination and un-Christian anti-family atti-tudes and provided a rational framework for the entire enterprise of educational reform in the spirit of Medellín.

Juan Hernández-Pico says the piece played an important role in deflating the accusations. However, he believes that it was "the strong and courageous position of Archbishop Chávez and Father Estrada that succeeded in paralyz-ing" the attempt to bring authorities at the *Externado* to trial for violating the Constitution.[159] Rodolfo Cardenal agrees, recalling that the elderly archbishop

---

153. "Asociación de Padres de Familia del 'Externado San José' to Rev. Padre Francisco Javier Colino, S.J. (San Salvador: Archives of the Central American Province of the Society of Jesus, April 27, 1973).

154. *Orientación* (May 27, 1973).

155. *Diario Latino* (June 8 and 26, 1973).

156. This entire paragraph from Whitfield, *Paying the Price*, 54.

157. Ibid., 54.

158. Hernández-Pico provides this detail on the collaborative nature of the project. See Hernández-Pico, *Historia reciente*, 14.

159. Hernández-Pico, *Historia reciente*, 14. Also, letter from Juan Hernández-Pico, S.J., to Charles J. Beirne, S.J., July 1993. Cited in Beirne, *Jesuit Education and Social Change*, 107.

"negotiated, persuaded, and convinced" President Molina to relent, and the Jesuits agreed "to quietly withdraw the sociology professors at the end of the course."[160]

The affair finally abated when a poll revealed the *Externado* parents themselves overwhelmingly supported the work of the Jesuits at the school. But the message was clear: there would be serious consequences if the UCA and the Society of Jesus continued its efforts in the spirit of Medellín to make the suffering of El Salvador's impoverished majorities an issue for the next generation of the nation's civil and governmental elites.

### Consolidating the New Idea of the University: The Presidency of Dr. Román Mayorga (1975-1979)

The years 1974 and 1975 were important ones at the UCA in that they completed the shift to the option for the poor as the official horizon of the university. Luis Achaerandio finished his term on the Board and departed in December 1974 for Rome to attend the Thirty-Second General Congregation of the Jesuits, a worldwide meeting of the order to determine its agenda for the years ahead. Hernández-Pico makes the remarkable assertion (widely confirmed by other scholars) that the meeting "elevated as the [apostolic] vision of the universal Society" the difficult decisions of 1969-1970.[161] Ironically, the departure of Achaerandio, who had resisted those decisions, created the opening for a similar shift on the Board of the UCA. Román Mayorga was named university president (the only lay person ever so named). The following year, Fr. Luis de Sebastian, a Jesuit economist from Spain living in the "UCA II" community and committed to the "liberation thesis," was appointed university vice-president, assuming Achaerandio's place on the Board. This shifted the balance to a three to two majority, with Ellacuría, Mayorga, and de Sebastián favoring a more assertive emphasis of the UCA's commitment to the option for the poor through explicit support for social, political, and economic change.

### *Mayorga's Presidency Completes the Shift*

This shift did not come about without pain, however. In April 1974 the province had its own congregation in preparation for the worldwide December meeting. Rodolfo Cardenal describes it as "the longest and most conflictive in the history of the province . . . a forum in which were aired resentments, suspicions, aggressions and calumnies."[162] Hernández-Pico recalls,

> With its hard confrontations, it left behind a vapor trail of intense emotion and pain. This outcome was, on the one hand, a living reflection

---

160. Rodolfo Cardenal, S.J., correspondence with author, August 18, 2009.

161. Hernández-Pico, *Historia reciente*, 16.

162. Cardenal, "La Provincia de Centro América," 151. Cited in Whitfield, *Paying the Price*, 58.

of an apostolic body which was being overrun for the first time by the challenge of [Central America's] social conflicts and by the suffering of the great majorities of the poor. On the other hand, it offered a precise X-ray of the lack of maturity with which we confronted each other with our positions.[163]

On the positive side, the delegates were able to agree by sizable majorities on six "postulates" to guide the province in putting the decisions of 1970 into practice: (1) taking positions in favor of the poor in public disputes; (2) practicing the Jesuit vow of poverty as a means of solidarity; (3) allowing more participation by younger members in the province congregations; (4) a commitment to agrarian reform at the farm owned by the province; (5) embracing the role of high schools and universities in the work for justice and solidarity; and (6) ending the province's juridical dependence on Spain and elevation to the status of an independent province within the Jesuits.

However, two men who had led the province through the initial years of its commitment to the option for the poor suffered stunning defeats. Hernández-Pico notes with bitter irony (in light of the petition for independence from Spain) that "the first Provincial born in Central America was not elected to [attend] the Thirty-Second General Congregation"[164] in Rome. In a humbling turn of events the more conservative Luis Achaerandio defeated the provincial, Fr. Estrada, by a single vote on a secret ballot.[165] Fr. Arrupe and his consulters in Rome were deeply concerned at the depth of the divisions described in the documents and represented by the decision not to concelebrate the congregation's final Mass.

Further, in the aftermath of the divisive meeting, Ellacuría was removed as delegate for formation and prohibited, for the time being, from holding any other position in the province government. Fr. Hernández-Pico, who was installed in Ellacuría's place, believes (as did Ellacuría himself) that "Fr. Arrupe . . . [was] under pressure from Fr. Paolo Dezza" to remove Ellacuría as formation superior "because [Dezza] did not have confidence in Ellacuría's orientation."[166] Known as a traditionalist, Fr. Dezza was Fr. Arrupe's general assistant for education and influential at the Vatican as the former confessor of Pope Paul VI and John Paul I. Cardenal believes that the plan was to reduce Ellacuría's influence over

---

163. Hernández-Pico, *Historia reciente*, 15.

164. Ibid., 14-15. A province with full status in the Society of Jesus would automatically send its provincial, together with one elected delegate. Since Central America was still formally a vice-province of Spain, they were allowed only one elected candidate. Hernández-Pico implies that it was to be expected that the Jesuits would elect their provincial to represent them in Rome.

165. This bit of information was provided by Whitfield, *Paying the Price*, 58.

166. Interview with Fr. Juan Hernández-Pico, S.J., by Robert Lassalle-Klein, July 1, 1994, 4. Whitfield reports the detail about Ellacuría's belief citing *Notícias SJ* (San Salvador: Archives of the Central American Province of the Society of Jesus, December 1989), 8; and interview of Hernández-Pico by Teresa Whitfield, June 15, 1991.

Fr. Estrada, since Rome believed his "government was polarized by his [Ella-curía's] very presence."[167]

The irony of these moves, however, is that they set the stage for the elevation of Román Mayorga and Ignacio Ellacuría as successive presidents of the UCA, and the realization of their vision for the university articulated in the 1970 BID speech. As we saw earlier, when Luis Achaerandio left for Rome he gave up the presidency of the UCA and his position on the Board. Mayorga, who fully embraced the commitment of the UCA to the preferential option for the poor, but was seen as a mediator, emerged as the choice of all factions for the presidency of the UCA. Educated at Massachusetts Institute of Technology (MIT), gracious, and well prepared to deal with El Salvador's technological problems, Mayorga and his family, as Fr. Beirne notes, "had been close friends of the *gradualists*."[168] And, though Mayorga was a young age (33), as Hernández-Pico recalls,

> Román had a lot of prestige. He was a good scientist, a good economist, and had worked in government agencies, specifically in the ministry of planning. He had left this work to come to the university for less salary. So he also had moral prestige. And he was a good writer. He used to write in *ECA*, and he wrote a book about the mission of the university.[169]

Hernández-Pico emphasizes Mayorga's "great capacity to arbitrate,"[170] concluding, that is one "reason . . . [Mayorga's presidency] is very important. Because he was the practical arbitrator between two lines of thought among the Jesuits on the Board of Directors, part arbitrator and mediator."

But Fr. Achaerandio's departure and the shift of the Board toward the option for the poor also made it possible for Ellacuría to be elected president in 1979. Hernández-Pico believes that after Ellacuría's removal from Jesuit government "there was a change in his interest, of emphasis. It's not that his project was itself different, but that perhaps the means, or the platform . . . changes [from] formation and his influence on young Jesuits [to] . . . the university itself. But this is not an instantaneous change . . . I would say it lasts five years until 1979 when they named him . . . [president] of the university."[171] Rodolfo Cardenal disagrees somewhat, stating, "In my opinion the UCA was always first, and his work on formation revolved around the UCA. However, he obviously had more time for the UCA when he no longer had responsibility for the Jesuit students."[172]

---

167. Cardenal, "La Provincia de Centro América," 227. Cited in Whitfield, *Paying the Price*, 59.

168. Beirne, *Jesuit Education and Social Change*, 119.

169. Interview with Fr. Juan Hernández-Pico, S.J., by Robert Lassalle-Klein, July 1, 1994, 8.

170. Ibid.

171. Ibid. Rodolfo Cardenal concurs with this opinion. See Cardenal, "Ser Jesuita hoy en El Salvador," 1016.

172. Rodolfo Cardenal, S.J., correspondence with author, August 18, 2009.

What is not in dispute, however, is that the shift in the Board made possible by Fr. Achaerandio's departure created the opportunity to move toward the kind of university Ellacuría had envisioned since 1969.

### Clarifying and Institutionalizing the New Idea of the University

The immediate result of these changes was heightened focus by Román Mayorga and Ignacio Ellacuría on the task of defining what Jon Sobrino calls the *theoria* of the university's self-understanding. The next five years (1974-1979) would be especially productive in this regard, culminating in the synthetic statement of 1979. In what follows I will look briefly at some of the contributions of the UCA's next two presidents to this process.

Juan Hernández-Pico says that in 1974, "four months after ceasing to be delegate for formation, Ellacuría founded the Center for Theological Reflection"[173] (CRT). This center, which Mayorga describes as an initiative of the Society of Jesus,[174] was a milestone in Ellacuría's efforts to shift the physical and spiritual focus of Jesuit formation to Central America. Hernández-Pico, Ellacuría's successor as director of formation, writes,

> Formation . . . began . . . to be done in Central America. . . . [The novitiate was established at Santa Tecla in San Salvador, and] undergraduates and those studying philosophy studied at the UCA. . . . [As a result] the Jesuit students did their undergraduate and philosophy studies together. . . . Then in 1974 the Center for Theological Reflection was founded [by Ellacuría] which [brought some of the] masters of theology students of the Jesuits [to the UCA as well]. All this was possible because [Fr. Azcue] named Ignacio Ellacuría as delegate for formation.[175]

But the CRT was driven by a larger vision than the training of young Jesuits. Its goal was the dynamic renewal of priests, religious, and lay workers throughout the archdiocese and all of Central America in light of the changes in the Latin American church since Medellín. The center's impact on the Salvadoran church can be seen in a "very confidential" 1975 memo written for the Pontifical Commission on Latin America by the conservative bishop Oscar Romero. The document names the Jesuits as the most important of "Three Factors in the Priests' Political Movement in El Salvador,"[176] and it singles out Ellacuría's three pet projects as having been particularly influential: the work of the CRT; the book, *El Salvador: The Political Year 1971-72*;[177] and *ECA*.

---

173. Ibid., 6.

174. Mayorga Quirós, *La Universidad para el cambio social*, 64.

175. Hernández-Pico, S.J., interview with Robert Lassalle-Klein, July 1, 1994, 8.

176. James R. Brockman, *Romero: A Life* (Maryknoll, NY: Orbis Books, 1989), 56. Cited in Whitfield, *Paying the Price,* 102-3.

177. Hernández-Pico, Jerez, Ellacuría, Baltodano, and Mayorga Quirós, *El Salvador: Año Político, 1971-72*.

The year after Jon Sobrino's permanent return to the UCA in 1974 from doctoral studies in Frankfurt, he recalls, "Ellacuría said very clearly to me . . . , now
you take over the theology program, and I will do something else."[178] Sobrino
received his first death threat in 1975 (announced without his name on Salvadoran television) for his work at the CRT and the UCA.[179] The following year
Ellacuría assumed formal directorship of his beloved *ECA*. Mayorga offers an
evocative recollection of the energy the Basque Jesuit brought to this task:

> Ellacuría was the director of *ECA* from 1976, and you had to see him
> in the [editorial] sessions preparing for the magazine. He was a fund
> of ideas and unfurled with abandon his virtues of boundless creativity,
> and commitment to intellectual production. He would propose themes,
> write editorials, prepare his own articles, solicit collaborative projects,
> invent new sections, comment on manuscripts, and stimulate all of us
> to produce more and better work.[180]

Cardenal states simply, "Under his direction, *ECA* became the most authori-
tative magazine on the reality of the country."[181] And he suggests that it was
first through Ellacuría's work on President Molina's "agrarian transformation of
1976, [that] his figure began to acquire a public dimension. From that moment
on, Fr. Ellacuría was always present in the great crises of the country with his
sharp and critical analyses."[182] Indeed, it seems that Bishop Romero had been
correct in that it was primarily through the CRT, his books, and the pages of
*ECA* that Ellacuría began to assume the mantle as the preeminent *public intellectual* of the Salvadoran church.[183] As we shall see later, however, the Jesuit
would study at the feet of his former adversary, Oscar Romero, when the latter
became archbishop of San Salvador from 1977 to 1980.

Mayorga, on the other hand, focused his varied talents in administration,
analysis, and consensus building on the creation of a comprehensive process
of long-range "planning . . . for the second decade of the university," focused
on "how to use its institutional influence for the liberating transformation of
society."[184] The new president was especially concerned that the university
"should not enclose itself . . . in a narrow world in which everybody convinces
themselves and satisfies themselves in the belief that they are doing a lot for the

---

178. Interview with Jon Sobrino by Robert Lassalle-Klein, July 1, 1994, 8.

179. This detail is from Martha Doggett's chronology of death threats and attacks against
the Jesuits in El Salvador. See Martha Doggett, *Death Foretold: The Jesuit Murders in El
Salvador* (Washington, DC: Georgetown University Press, Lawyers Committee for Human
Rights, 1993), 301.

180. Román Mayorga, "Recuerdo de diez Quijotes," 11.

181. Cardenal, "Ser Jesuita hoy," 1018.

182. Ibid., 1019.

183. Cardenal adds that Ellacuría also taught a widely attended course on theology for lay
people during the second semester of the year offered in the evening at the Externado San
José, and repeated on Saturday mornings at the UCA.

184. Mayorga Quirós, *La Universidad para el cambio social*, 65.

country, while the miserable living conditions of the immense majority of the population, whom the UCA says it wants to serve, do not change in any way at all."[185] Thus, the university staff began a UCA-wide effort that produced three volumes[186] with specific goals and objectives for the university and its departments in the areas of research, teaching, and social outreach.

Noting the shortage of qualified persons and facilities for research, the plan outlines a strategy to increase the full-time faculty by 100 percent, while augmenting the student body by only 34 percent from 1976 to 1981. It lays initial plans to build science, library, and computer facilities as essential university infrastructures needed to promote research. And the document asserts that teaching at the UCA should be designed

> to prepare professionals who want to and who can contribute to a process of social change which better satisfies the needs of the vast majority of the population and liberates them from the conditions of injustice and oppression in which they currently find themselves. This means in the long and the short run the production of goods and services, and profound structural changes in the distribution of wealth, income and social organization.[187]

The plan explicitly asserts that "no prescribed sequence . . . timetable or . . . model of society" is being taught at the UCA. But it opts for a curricular plan balancing introductory courses in the social scientific study of "the social realities of Central America" and open registration courses offered by the university's three faculties (science/engineering, business/economics, and human sciences), with courses emphasizing specialization and electives for advanced training.

Finally, the plan outlines specific areas of university activity that are to be dedicated to social outreach. These include publication, public statements, broadcasts, editorials, and student social service (700,000 hours for the period of 1976 to 1981). However, it cautions that UCA's social outreach is to be understood as the responsibility and cumulative impact of the entire university on the national reality of El Salvador. Other important elements include a proposed "Center for Political and Social Documentation" (which would become one of the few sources of reliable data on El Salvador during the 1980s), a student loan fund, efforts to develop the long-term commitment of faculty and staff to the goals and values of the UCA's vision, and a proposal to develop a new faculty-staff salary scale.

---

185. Ibid., 66.

186. Universidad Centroamericana Simeón Cañas," *Plan Quinquenal, 1977-81*, vols. I-III (San Salvador: UCA Editores, 1976). The following description of this document is based on the summaries provided by Román Mayorga Quirós and Fr. Beirne. See Mayorga Quirós, "1975: Año de evaluación y planificación," *La Universidad para el cambio social*, 65-67; and Beirne, "Planning for 1976-1981," in *Jesuit Education and Social Change*, 120-26.

187. *Plan Quinquenal, 1977-81*, I, 158. Cited in Beirne, *Jesuit Education and Social Change*, 121.

The plan established a permanent office for planning and implementation, which embodied Mayorga's leadership style: collaborative, gracious, and given to developing consensus. Fr. Hernández-Pico notes, however, that the collaborative spirit of this period declined at the end of the decade when many key lay faculty and administrators left the university to join the reformist coup. This was followed a little over a year later by the beginning of the civil war.

> In 1979 many left. The war came, and some lay persons stayed. But, more than anything, the university began to function more vertically, centered on the Jesuits, and with less collaboration. It would be important, however, not to confuse these characteristics of centralization and clericalization with the process of conversion [which took place at the UCA during the 1970s].[188]

Jon Sobrino also recognizes that the influence of lay faculty and staff was unfortunately diminished by the "centralization" of decision making in Jesuit circles during the early 1980s, but tends to see the change as a product of the national environment of assassination and repression on day-to-day life at the UCA. He insists on the one hand that "without a group of lay people, this type of project is impossible. I'm convinced of it."[189] On the other hand, he agrees that a temporary centralization of decision making in the Jesuit Board of Directors took place during the 1980s, which he sees as a result of understandable decisions made by lay and Jesuit leaders under the threat of death.

> Why was the leadership in the hands of Jesuits? Under the circumstances of persecution and a university that wants to confront social structures, the Jesuits were able to do it best. That's because they were Jesuits. In 1980, when things got tough, many of the lay people left. The commitment was different. Some lay people resented that, sometimes with good reasons. [But] remember, in 1979 30 percent of the [lay] faculty went to the government. These things don't happen in [most] universities. But we see them down here. [For instance,] when lay faculty come to the United States to study, they often leave the university when they return to El Salvador. I think that it is an illusion to think you can find a group of lay people totally committed to the university.[190]

Thus, while acknowledging the negative impact on lay-Jesuit collaboration produced by this centralization of power, Sobrino argues that "without the Board of Directors the university would have collapsed." He does insist, however, that "we still must address the need for the participation of others, and to develop along more democratic lines."

---

188. Interview with Juan Hernández-Pico, S.J., by Robert Lassalle-Klein, July 1, 1994.

189. All quotes in the paragraph from interview with Jon Sobrino by Robert Lassalle-Klein, April 19, 1994.

190. Ibid.

As noted earlier, while similarly acknowledging the key role of lay leadership in the UCA model, Rodolfo Cardenal emphasizes the cumulative impact on the UCA of political ambitions nurtured by certain lay faculty and staff, and external attacks against the university.

> It would be impossible to run the UCA without lay people. . . . But this centralization was a response to the situation of the country and the UCA. Perhaps it was caused in large part by the failed attempt of certain lay faculty and staff to take control of the direction of the UCA in order to make it a tool of the Christian Democrats. But it was largely due to the political crisis, which made it necessary to make quick and strong decisions confronting attacks against the UCA, including its economic viability.[191]

For his part, Román Mayorga complained while still president in 1978 of "a pattern of excessive concentration of power in the Board of Directors,"[192] which was populated mainly by Jesuits. Thus, it is not surprising that he believes that the university could have survived both the exodus to the government and external attacks while still preserving more of the vigorous participation by lay faculty in decision making during the 1980s.[193] In 1982, Ellacuría himself would bemoan the "bureaucracy and verticalism" that afflicted the UCA under his leadership, "so that the UCA could appear at times to be governed from a higher center which is inaccessible and considerably unknown."[194]

Looking back, we can say that Mayorga and Ellacuría complemented each other in many ways from 1975 to 1979. The combination of Ellacuría's "charismatic genius" and Mayorga's "great capacity to arbitrate" fostered a creative synergy that allowed the UCA to forge a dynamic vision, and the real beginnings of "a different kind of university."[195]

### Blueprints from Mayorga and Ellacuría

Mayorga and Ellacuría were well prepared to make good use of the institutional resources mentioned above in the hard work of formulating and developing a consensus around the new vision for the work of the university. In this section I will briefly review two key statements of that vision articulated in documents

---

191. Rodolfo Cardenal, S.J., correspondence with author, August 18, 2009.

192. Cited in Beirne, *Education and Social Change*, 125.

193. Letter from Román Mayorga Quirós to Charles J. Beirne, January 21, 1994.

194. This is a quote from the meeting of the UCA's Board of Directors in which Ellacuría was elected to his second term as president. See "Minutes of the Board of Directors" (San Salvador: Archives of the University of Central America José Simeón Cañas, October 25, 1982).

195. Ignacio Ellacuría, "Diez años después: es posible una universidad distinta?" *ECA* nos. 324-325 (1975): 605-28 (translated by Phillip Berryman as "Is a Different Kind of University Possible?" in Hassett and Lacey, eds., *Towards a Society That Serves Its People*, 177-207).

written during 1975, the first year of Mayorga's presidency and the new majority for the option for the poor and liberation on the UCA Board.

During that year Mayorga somehow found time to revise the draft of the manuscript he had written earlier "in order to clarify for myself the . . . 'Project of the University.'"[196] He published it in 1976 as a "proposal, invitation, and challenge to the entire university community of the UCA." The intention was to stimulate conversation on what the UCA might become in its second decade (1975-1985).

In the first chapter Mayorga proposes "four general characteristics which . . . should typify the UCA in the next ten years." He envisions a university that (1) is truly committed to serving the Salvadoran people "ninety percent of which finds itself oppressed"[197]; (2) is open to "all sectors and in permanent contact with their needs and painful realities";[198] (3) serves as "a critical and creative conscience" for the nation;[199] and (4) operates with a "functional," "disciplinary," and "communal" integration in its research, teaching, and social outreach.[200] The second chapter summarizes the history of UCA's first decade (1965-1975). Chapter 3 offers a wealth of data documenting the terrible social and cultural polarities defining Salvadoran society: developed–underdeveloped, elitism–marginality, domination–dependence. Chapters 4 through 6 offer critical evaluations of the state of research, teaching, and social outreach at the UCA. And the final chapter outlines a series of challenges that Mayorga believes the UCA must confront in the decade ahead.

The book represents a remarkably clear statement by a young president of his vision for the UCA. What is more impressive, however, is the continuity it shows with statements developed later in the 1970s and 1980s. Mayorga demonstrates a profound appreciation for the work of the university's founders, as well as the importance of the recent commitment after 1969 to a preferential option for the poor and the struggle for liberation and justice it implies. He is also able to offer a realistic summary of obstacles that the university must overcome in order to continue moving forward, offering a convincing argument for the university-wide process of "evaluation and planning"[201] which followed shortly. Thus, the book was an important step in the self-understanding of the UCA and its appreciation for the need to plan the future. But just as its strength embodies Mayorga's ability to communicate the horizon of the option for the poor to a broad and very diverse university community, so it is also derivative of the work of Ellacuría and others in reformulating the horizon of Medellín as the context for the work of a Christian university in the Third World.

The shift in Ellacuría's focus toward the UCA and his growing profile as a public theologian can be seen in a series of programmatic articles published in

196. Mayorga Quirós, *La Universidad para el cambio social*, 5.
197. Ibid., 10.
198. Ibid.,13.
199. Ibid., 15.
200. Ibid., 17-19.
201. Ibid., 65-67; also 199-212.

1975, following his removal from Jesuit government the year before. The year began with two short overviews of "The Political Mission of the University"[202] and "The Philosophical Anthropology of Xavier Zubiri,"[203] the subject of Ellacuría's doctoral dissertation and his intellectual mentor. This was followed by perhaps his most important and original programmatic article on theological method, "Toward a Philosophical Foundation for Latin American Theological Method."[204] It is not unfair to say that one must grasp the basic concepts first stated programmatically in this article, and developed in his other writings, if one is to understand the overarching rationality that informs his entire intellectual project, including the work of the UCA itself.

The article begins with four principles from the work of the influential philosophical theologian Emerich Coreth and derived from the philosophical hermeneutics of Martin Heidegger, Hans-Georg Gadamer, and Wilhelm von Humbolt, which Ellacuría argues were currently held by many European theologians: (1) understanding has a circular structure that compromises the independence of its claims; (2) understanding is basically the comprehension and description of the structures of human meaning; (3) the "world" and the things that we take for granted as our "horizon" are human structures created for the communication and maintenance of meaning; and (4) all knowledge, including theological knowledge, is basically a search for meaning.[205] Ellacuría argues somewhat surprisingly that these assertions reflect a set of philosophical presuppositions that "must be overcome" in order to "do justice . . . to the reality of human knowing and . . . Latin American theological thought."

His alternative is embodied in what he describes as three "fundamental principles for a proper conceptualization of . . . human intellection" as it operates in a truly "Latin-American theological method."[206] First, human intelligence is first and foremost a sensory and biological adaptation. He quotes Zubiri's dictum that "a species of idiots is not biologically viable," and he argues that intelligence never loses this practical character, even in its most abstract expressions. Second, "the formal structure of intelligence . . . is not to understand and grasp meaning, but to apprehend reality and to confront itself with that reality." Here, Ellacuría first develops his three famous dimensions of "confronting oneself with real things as real": (1) grasping what is at stake in reality; (2) assuming responsibility for reality; and (3) taking charge of, or transforming reality,[207] to

---

202. Ignacio Ellacuría, "Misión política de la Universidad," *ABRA* 8 (El Salvador, 1975), 2-7.

203. Ignacio Ellacuría, "La antropología filosofica de Xavier Zubiri," in *História universal de la medicina*, VIII (ed. Pedro Lain Entralgo; Barcelona, 1975), 109-12.

204. Ignacio Ellacuría, "Hacia una fundamentación del método teológico latino-americano." *ECA* 30, nos. 322-323 (August-September 1975): 409-25.

205. Ibid., 418.

206. Ibid., and 418-21.

207. Ibid., 419-20. The Spanish reads: "el hacerse cargo de la realidad," "el cargar con la realidad," and "el encargarse de la realidad." My translation follows that of Jon Sobrino; see Jon Sobrino, "Jesus of Galilee from the Salvadoran Context: Compassion, Hope, and

which Jon Sobrino says, "I would add that we must 'allow ourselves to be carried along by reality.'"[208] And third, "Human intelligence is not only always histori-cal, but this historicity belongs to the essential structure of intelligence."[209]

Ellacuría's fourth article of 1975 embodies perhaps the most important pro-grammatic statement of his vision for the UCA, and serves well to demonstrate the "cash value" of the aforementioned ideas. He outlines his program for "a different kind of university, one that as a university and in a university manner, responds to its mission in history, one that demonstrates its political effective-ness in a university manner by . . . [helping] impart shape to a new society and to a new form of state power."[210] The key point is that the Christian university must define itself through the arduous task of interacting with, and taking positions on, the historical reality in which it lives. He then argues that this can only be done by getting to know, taking responsibility for (in harmony with its values), and contributing to the transformation of the national reality within which the university is situated, (in this case) El Salvador.

Ellacuría's final major article of 1975 is a contribution to a theological "trib-ute to Karl Rahner," whom Sobrino describes as Ellacuría's most important theological mentor. The piece is a programmatic treatment of Ellacuría's vision for theology in a series (127) of "Theses Regarding the Possibility, Necessity and Meaning of a Latin American Theology."[211] One can hear unmistakable echoes

---

Following the Light of the Cross," *Theological Studies* 70, no. 2 (2009): 449-50; also Jon Sobrino, interview by Robert Lassalle-Klein, November 4, 2009, Santa Clara University; personal papers. A more literal translation might read: "realizing about reality"; "picking up (or carrying) reality"; and "taking care of (or taking charge of) reality." However, the Spanish, which involves a play on words, cannot really be translated literally. Ellacuría says they connote (respectively): "a being in the reality of things—and not only being before the idea of things or the meaning of things . . . ," "the fundamentally ethical character of intelligence," and "the praxical character of intelligence." Jon Sobrino characterizes the three in terms of the *noetic, ethical, and praxical* dimensions of intelligence. See Jon Sobrino, "Ignacio Ellacuría, the Human Being and the Christian: 'Taking the Crucified People Down from the Cross,'" in Kevin Burke and Robert Lassalle-Klein, eds., *Love That Produces Hope: The Thought of Ignacio Ellacuría* (Collegeville, MN: Michael Glazier/Liturgical Press, 2006), 18-19.

208. Jon Sobrino, *La fe en Jesucristo, ensayo desde las víctimas* (San Salvador: UCA Editores, 1999), 102; also Jon Sobrino, "La teología y el 'principio liberación,'" *Revista latinoamericana de teología* 35 (1995): 138. I believe that the former is mistranslated as "let ourselves be burdened with reality," in Jon Sobrino, *Christ the Liberator: A View from the Victims* (Maryknoll, NY: Orbis Books, 2001), 52. Perhaps the meaning is clearer when Sobrino speaks of "corresponding to and being carried by the *more* of reality," in Jon Sobrino, *Liberación con espíritu: apuntes para una nueva espiritualidad* (San Salvador: UCA Editores, 1985, 1994), 29, which is adequately translated as "willingness to be swept along by the *more* of reality," in *Spirituality of Liberation: Toward Political Holiness* (Maryknoll, NY: Orbis Books, 1988), 19.

209. Ibid.

210. Ignacio Ellacuría, "Is a Different Kind of University Possible?" in Hassett and Lacey, eds., *Towards a Society That Serves Its People*, 179.

211. Ignacio Ellacuría, "Tesis sobre la posibilidad, necesidad y sentido de una teología Latinoamericana," in A. Vargas Machua, ed., *Teología y mundo contemporáneo: homenaje a Karl Rahner* (Madrid: Ediciones Cristiandad, 1975), 325-50.

of the philosophical horizon outlined above in his claim that "What . . .Latin America has achieved as its fundamental interpretation of what constitutes reality . . . is the importance of the historical dimension, of history, as a realization of humanity and as the realization and revelation of the absolute."[212] Students of theology will not miss Rahner's influence in the way Ellacuría correlates the urgent questions of secular history with the embodiment of God's self-offer in the life and death of Jesus, and the witness of his disciples.

> We [in Latin America] are historically in a situation of faith . . . at the same time that we are in a historical situation and preoccupied with its transformation. From this necessary situationality, and with the determinate horizon of a faith which asks itself about its secular dimension, it is inevitable that one's questions regarding the historical situation and the Christian message would be mutually conditioned and evaluated.[213]

But he parts company with his German mentor in his self-conscious commitment to the historical specificity of the Latin American context. And this makes all the difference! For it is precisely this context that allows Ellacuría to argue: "One can recognize a clear interaction between Latin-American theological thinking and pastoral praxis, which is what has put it into motion." It is the experience of the Latin American church that leads him to conclude, "What is fundamentally accepted is the intention to present the serious needs of the oppressed majorities in terms of Christian liberation."[214] And it is precisely this historical specificity that leads Ellacuría to assert Latin American Christians will make their contribution to the universal church. For, "In the reconversion of the [Latin American] church to the world of the oppressed, one sees a profound principle of renovation for the [universal] church of its mode of evangelization and its mode of doing theology."

In the end, 1975 proved to be a very productive year for the UCA's efforts to more clearly define its horizon. Both Ellacuría and Mayorga produced important proposals that outlined a path toward the more fully elaborated vision of the UCA that emerged at the end of the decade. And Ellacuría was able to formulate a programmatic challenge to philosophers, theologians, university educators, and others to *grasp what is at stake* in, to *take responsibility for*, and to *take charge of doing something* to support and promote the ongoing irruption of the poor as agents of their own future in El Salvador and Latin America.

### The Synthetic Statement of 1979

Three years later, in April and May of 1978, the Board of Directors initiated a series of meetings with each of the academic departments of the university

---

212. Ibid., 339.
213. Ibid., 348.
214. Ibid., 336.

designed to produce a synthetic statement of the UCA's self-understanding as a university. The document they produced recalls that the land reform proposals offered by the government of General Humberto Romero, as well as the UCA's application for a second loan from the Inter-American Development Bank, "seemed to have put the UCA into a new stage."[215] A team of twenty persons was formed, which conducted a five-month consultation involving all sectors of the university community. Jon Sobrino was asked to synthesize the results into a final document, which the Board adopted with some revisions in May 1979.

The final document is the mature statement of a university with nine years' experience living with the new horizon of the preferential option for the poor and the struggle for liberation and justice it implies marked out by the Latin American bishops at Medellín. Looking back to the UCA's emerging role on the political scene during the early 1970s in the view of its final authors, the statement asserts that it "presupposes six or seven years of *doing things* at the UCA."[216]

The first section is dedicated to "The Proper Identity of the UCA."[217] Its charter statement maintains:

> The UCA seeks to be an institutional university response to the historical reality of the country, considered from an ethical perspective as an unjust and irrational reality which should be transformed. This is rooted . . . in a purpose: that of contributing to social change in the county. It does this in a university manner and . . . with a Christian inspiration.[218]

It is interesting that by this point the rhetoric of option for the poor and the struggle for liberation and justice has been almost completely subordinated to the more general and encompassing horizon of formulating a Christian value-based response to the demands of "historical reality." As we have seen, this reflects both the intellectual influence of Ignacio Ellacuría's work on the philosophical foundations for Latin American liberation thought, as well as a general tendency within that body of thought itself.

The document then elaborates three elements as constitutive of the UCA's identity: (1) the UCA should be working "for social change"; (2) it should be doing so "in a university manner"; and (3) its efforts should be guided by and grounded in the "Christian inspiration" of Jesus and the gospels. There is no need to review the first two, by now familiar, characteristics. But the third merits further comment. The section dedicated to this topic argues that UCA's Christian inspiration draws the university's attention to three Christian values. First, while Christian faith sees human history and achievement as the medium of God's self-revelation, it also takes sin seriously as a historical reality, and it

---

215. "Las funciones fundamentales de la universidad y su operativización," in *Planteamiento*, 43.

216. Interview with Jon Sobrino by Robert Lassalle-Klein, April 19, 1994, 1.

217. "Las funciones fundamentales," 47-54.

218. Ibid., 47.

is critical of any effort to absolutize history or its achievements. Second, Christian faith struggles against the historical effects of sin as they are embodied in oppressive structures, and it sees this struggle as a practical dimension of Jesus' call to love of neighbor. And third, Latin American Christian faith works for the salvation of the whole person and all of humanity through its compassionate solidarity with the part of humanity that suffers most (the poor majority). Accordingly the document concludes:

> The most explicit testimony of the Christian inspiration of the UCA will be putting itself really at the service of the people in such a way that in this service it allows itself to be oriented by the oppressed people themselves. This will make the university see and denounce what there is of sin in our reality; it will impel it to create models that historically correspond better to the Reign of God; and it will make it develop typically Christian attitudes, such as operational hope, the passion for justice, the generous self-giving to other, the rejection of violent means, etc.[219]

The second section outlines how the UCA should "operationalize" its "fundamental functions" of teaching, research, and social outreach guided by the "charism" of the three basic characteristics noted above and "the actual circumstances of our actual historical experience."[220] The document cautions, however, that the UCA does not elevate any of its three basic functions as the most important of the university's tasks. Rather,

> The UCA realizes its mission by means of three functions [together]: social outreach, research, and teaching. . . . These functions, related among themselves, form a structure. Although teaching is the material base that conditions the other two, it is social outreach that should give meaning to research and teaching. And it is research that should illuminate what outreach and teaching should be.[221]

What must be understood here is that the subordination of teaching to the synergistic interaction of all three variables (teaching, research, and social outreach) flows essentially from the notion that the university exists to serve the Salvadoran people as a whole, not just the privileged students who study there.[222] This point is made clearly in the section on the UCA's identity, which insists,

---

219. Ibid., 53.
220. Ibid., 54.
221. Ibid., 55.
222. Here it is important to address Ellacuría's oft-quoted remark that students were a "necessary evil" for the work of the UCA. Jon Sobrino claims that this "was a cynical comment. It was not part of [Ellacuría's understanding] of the model." Rodolfo Cardenal says that Ellacuría used to say that, "by definition, the University has students, it forms them as professionals, and it grants titles," which "consumes most of its human and financial

The UCA exists [primarily] neither for itself, nor for its members. Its center is not located within itself, within its students, within its professors, or within its authorities. [The university] exists for the Salvadoran people, and this should be the center and the ultimate orientation of its activity. More specifically still, [its center should be] the majority of the population which suffers inhuman conditions, and which suffers them by virtue of certain structures which should be transformed. This means the work of the UCA is decidedly oriented by social outreach.

Thus, the work of the university is to be subordinated to the Christian and human vocation *to grasp what is at stake in, to assume responsibility for,* and *to take charge of doing something about* the historical reality in which it lives. In this context, it is worth noting that the historical reality of El Salvador and the Third World has sensitized this community of scholars to the dangers of unnecessarily reducing the work of the university to what it can accomplish through the tiny minority of the world's population privileged to study there.

The third and final section of the document then concludes with a series of specific recommendations intended to "operationalize" the "goal" stated in Part One and the "functions" outlined in Part Two.[223] This section amounts to a rather specific outline or plan for the UCA's development over the next several years. The document concludes with three tasks that would prove to be prophetic in the breach. The first recommendation is that "there should be a better and more active participation of all its personnel in the diverse functions and activities of the UCA."[224] Unfortunately, the aforementioned "verticalization" of the UCA's decision-making, together with the devastating loss of 30 percent of its faculty to the government only three months after the approval of this document, would result in what Fr. Beirne argues by 1989 had become "a glaring problem: over dependence on a few key people rather than sustained development of a multi-layered cadre of lay and Jesuit colleagues to implement the model."[225] Both Fr. Beirne and Román Mayorga believe this situation would cripple the UCA's efforts to recover after the assassination of its top Jesuit lead-

---

resources." But, he says, "Ellacuría is clear: professionals as such are not agents of change, since they seek to enter the established order, to find a well-paying job, and to support a family, etc., their objectives are very different from an agent of change." Sobrino makes a similar point, interpreting Ellacuría's point ironically: "In fact, he used to say that it would be fantastic if 10% left the UCA committed [to the option for the poor], and 50% were less right wing; he used to say that such an outcome would [strongly] affect the collective consciousness [of the country]." Thus, Cardenal concludes, "For Ellacuría, change does not come from the student side of the work, but from the institution of the university as a whole which has the task of transforming the national reality."

223. "Operativación de la finalidad y funciones de la UCA," in *Planteamiento*, 95-121.

224. Ibid., 117.

225. Beirne, *Jesuit Education and Social Change*, 235. Fr. Beirne's conclusion on this point is consistent with the analysis of Román Mayorga Quirós (see Juan Mayorga, letter from Román Mayorga Quirós to Charles J. Beirne, S.J., Washington, DC, January 21, 1994. Used with permission of Román Mayorga Quirós.)

ership in 1989, and potentially confuse future commentators trying to understand its role in the model.

Jon Sobrino suggests, however, "The problem in 1989 . . . was not participation, but a lack of creativity at all levels, Jesuits and lay faculty."[226] Rodolfo Cardenal says, "I'm inclined to agree with Jon. After the assassinations the UCA went through an 'institutional' depression that lasted for five or six years."[227] Reflecting on his own experience of these years, Cardenal observes, "It was complicated to accept the change of direction at the top; the new times and challenges, etc.; the nostalgia for the past, in particular for the people and the models broken by the historical process. This is what caused the depression." Whichever the case, what is clear is that the UCA was unprepared to deal with the loss of its top leadership.

The synthetic statement of 1979 also emphasizes the need for an "articulation of the Christian inspiration of the UCA."[228] During the 1980s the university would admirably fulfill its claim that "the principal articulation of the Christian inspiration of the UCA consists in . . . making Christian values efficaciously seen in its [work]." However, there would be a concerted, and ultimately largely successful, propaganda campaign waged by enemies of the UCA to convince military and government officials that the work of the university was only marginally and perversely linked to Christianity. For example, in a confidential 1987 report for the Conference of American Armies, Ignacio Ellacuría and eight other theologians are described as "aligned with Marxist ideology." The report concludes that "because of their attitudes and means of operation they have marginalized themselves from serious theological discussion."[229] The U.N. Truth Commission would later note that one of the authors of this slanderous report, Colonel Juan Orlando Zepeda, El Salvador's vice-minister of defense, helped to plan the assassination of Fr. Ellacuría and his companions. This kind of slander fostered an attitude in military circles toward Ellacuría and the UCA in which a former student of Fr. Segundo Montes (José Ricardo Espinoza) could become one of the assassins, though, as we saw, Espinoza would weep through the gunshots.[230]

---

226. Jon Sobrino, Note to Robert Lassalle-Klein, July 24, 1995, Santa Clara, CA: University of Santa Clara.

227. On this point, see Beirne, *Jesuit Education and Social Change*, 235-39; Mayorga Quirós, letter from Román Mayorga Quirós to Charles J. Beirne, S.J., January 21, 1994.

228. "Operativización de la finalidad y funciones de la UCA," in *Planteamiento*, 119.

229. Doggett, *Death Foretold*, 307. Referencing the source document for this quote, Doggett notes, "Ignacio Ellacuría and eight other theologians are named in a document attacking liberation theology prepared for a meeting of the Conference of American Armies, which includes the armed forces of 15 nations in the Americas, including El Salvador and the United States. . . . The theologians are mentioned in a chapter entitled, 'Strategy of the International Communist Movement in Latin America through Different Means of Action.' Colonel Juan Orland Zepeda, El Salvador's vice-minister of defense, is part of the working group responsible for the document."

230. Espinoza provides this detail in his extrajudicial declaration. See "El Caso de la masacre de la UCA: Sentencia interlocutona para detención provisional," *ECA* nos. 393-

Finally the 1979 document sensibly concludes by recommending the importance of good public relations and communications in order to "avoid risks, problems and dangers," which it describes as "unnecessary and repairable." A decade later, Archbishop Rivera Damas would say in his Sunday homily of November 19, 1989, the day the Jesuits and the two women were buried,

> There is no doubt that such an abominable action had been decided beforehand and the groundwork was laid by an irresponsible campaign of accusations and slanders—above all in some print media—against several of the distinguished academics of the UCA who now are dead. These accusations and slanders poisoned minds and ultimately put weapons in the hands of the assassins.[231]

### The Church in Defense of Civil Society

The brutal repression of Salvadoran civil society by agents of the state forms the backdrop for the efforts of the UCA Jesuits and their colleagues to follow the examples of Fr. Rutilio Grande and Archbishop Romero to accompany and empower the poor in their efforts to bring about reform through mass mobilization. Virtually all such advocates of reform faced brutal repression under the military presidencies of Colonel Julio Rivera (1961-1967), General Fidel Sánchez (1967-1972), Colonel Arturo Armando Molina (1972-1977), and Colonel Carlos Humberto Romero (1978-1979), administrations committed to protecting and consolidating the political monopoly by the Salvadoran army.[232] Like others before them, elections in this period continued to be marred by fraud and military control.

The scenario changed somewhat in 1972, however, when Christian Democrat José Napoleon Duarte and social democrat Guillermo Ungo joined together under the banner of the National Opposition Union (UNO) to win a somewhat more "open" election over the "official candidate," Colonel Arturo Armando Molina. As we have seen, however, they were soon deprived of their victory by yet another case of blatant fraud by the military. The Legislative Assembly elections that followed on March 12, 1972, were similarly manipulated, which, in turn, led to the unsuccessful coup of March 25, 1972. The 1974 mayoral and Assembly elections were defaced by still more military manipulation. And, going from bad to worse, the UNO coalition boycotted the 1976 elections, with the result that there was no official opposition for the first time in fourteen years.

---

394 (November-December 1989): 1155-68. Also see the final report of the Jesuit Lawyers Committee: Doggett, *Death Foretold*, 115 and 64-71.

    231. *Proceso*, §409, November 29, 1989, 4. Cited in Doggett, *Death Foretold*, 34.

    232. Here I follow the argument of Edelberto Torres Rivas, "Crisis and Conflict, 1930 to the Present," in Leslie Bethell, ed., *Central America since Independence* (Cambridge: Cambridge University Press, 1991), esp. 101.

## *Military Control of the State and the Defeat of Land Reform*

In this context, the fate of Molina's 1976 plan for agrarian reform illustrates how the declining credibility of the electoral process impacted the work of the UCA and accelerated the rise of political repression at the end of the decade. Not long after the 1976 mayoral and Assembly elections, Colonel Molina and the National Assembly formulated a modest plan for agrarian "transformation" in an effort to restore some credibility to the government. (Molina explained, "We don't use the term agrarian reform because that is communist terminology."[233]) The official decree announced the government's intention to nationalize 61,000 hectares (150,731 acres) of cow pastures and cotton fields in Usulután and San Miguel. It used a 1974 law allowing expropriation of fallow and underutilized land in order to place the property under the Salvadoran Institute of Agrarian Transformation (ISTA), created in 1975. The land was to be distributed to 12,000 campesino families.

The UCA lent its credibility to the project following a June phone call from Atilio Vieytez, a former UCA faculty member working as minister of planning in Molina's government, asking the UCA's support. Rodolfo Cardenal asserts that "President Molina himself made a personal promise to the Jesuit team from the UCA to not step back" from the proposal.[234] The vote went to the university superior counsel and Guillermo Ungo recalls that UCA faculty from the opposition party "didn't think that there existed the real conditions for agrarian reform, but Ellacuría thought that was because of a dogmatic and sectarian position we held as the opposition."[235] The proponents argued that the UCA had been a vigorous advocate of agrarian reform since the Agrarian Reform Congress of 1970, so the Jesuits and Mayorga concluded that the "rational and Christian" position was to support Molina's plan as "an indispensable first step." A July statement expressed the university's real "hope" for the agrarian scheme.[236]

A special issue of *ECA* on agrarian reform to be edited by Fr. Ignacio Martín-Baró was planned for September. But before the special issue could be released, Molina gave in to the furious protests of the large land holders and supported changes in the legislation (introduced October 20, 1976), which insured its failure. Ellacuría's scathing editorial, *"A sus ordenes, mi Capital!"* ("At your orders, my Capital!") reminded Molina of his vow, "I only promise what I am sure of accomplishing."[237] The editorial denounced Molina's capitulation to El Salvador's wealthy land barons with bitter irony: "The government has given in to

---

233. Cited in Robert Armstrong and Janet S. Ruben, *El Salvador: el rostro de la revolución* (San Salvador: UCA Editores, 1983, 1993; translated from *El Salvador: The Face of Revolution* [Boston: South End Press, 1982]), 83. Also cited in Whitfield, *Paying the Price*, 67.

234. Rodolfo Cardenal, S.J., August 18, 2009, private collection.

235. Interview with Guillermo Ungo by Teresa Whitfield, December 15, 1990. Cited in Whitfield, *Paying the Price*, 68.

236. "Pronunciamiento del consejo superior de la Universidad Centroamericana José Simeón Canas," *ECA* nos. 335-336 (September-October 1976): 419.

237. Ignacio Ellacuría, "A sus órdenes, mi Capital!" *ECA* no. 337 (November 1976): 641.

the pressure of national capitalism . . . ; the government has given in, the government has submitted, the government has obeyed. After so much hot-air of foresight, strength, and decision, the government has ended up saying: At your orders, my Capital!"

Sadly, Molina's decision also signaled a turn away from the politics of compromise toward political repression as the language for political debate. Two small bombs exploded later that month (September 1976) at the UCA. On the night of December 2-3, 1976, an explosion blew a large hole in the UCA's central administration building, and the White Warriors Union claimed responsibility. Six months later, on June 20, 1977 (three months after the assassination of Rutilio Grande), the same group threatened to assassinate any Jesuit who did not leave the country within thirty days. In response, Fr. Pedro Arrupe, S.J., worldwide superior general of the Jesuits, replied after consulting with his men, "They may end up as martyrs, but my priests are not going to leave [El Salvador], because they are committed to its people."[238]

Not surprisingly, as the space for economic, political, and military reform grew smaller at the end of the decade in the face of the government's increasingly brutal repression of civil society, armed opposition groups and their political supporters began to gain strength. Tens of thousands of people mobilized for rallies and public protests against the government's policies and increasingly egregious abuses of human rights. Then, on February 20, 1977, Molina's hand-picked successor, General Carlos Humberto Romero, won the presidency in yet another fraudulent election, and the government slammed the door on reform with an escalating campaign of political repression and murder. Forces on all sides of the political spectrum could see that the country was sliding rapidly toward civil war.

### Fr. Rutilio Grande, S.J.: The Seed That Falls into the Ground

As we have already said, developments at the UCA must be situated in the larger context of the option for the poor by the Latin American Catholic Church at Medellín in 1968 and by the Central American Jesuits in 1969-1970. The immense creativity and generosity of Catholic and other religious leaders in supporting and promoting the renewal of Salvadoran civil society during the late 1970s, and the brutal persecution they suffered for these efforts, are too rich and complex to summarize here.[239] We can do no more than briefly describe

---

238. Penny Lernoux, *Cry of the People* (New York: Doubleday, 1980), 77 n. 61.

239. For a small sample, see Phillip Berryman, *The Religious Roots of Rebellion: Christians in Central American Revolutions* (Maryknoll, NY: Orbis Books, 1984); Phillip Berryman, *Stubborn Hope: Religion, Politics and Revolution in Central America* (Maryknoll, NY: Orbis Books, 1994); Donna Whitson Brett and Edward T. Brett, *Murdered in El Salvador: The Stories of Eleven U.S. Missionaries* (Maryknoll, NY: Orbis Books, 1988); Kevin F. Burke, *The Ground beneath the Cross: The Theology of Ignacio Ellacuría* (Washington, DC: Georgetown University Press, 2000); Ann Butwell et al., eds., *The Globalization of Hope: Central America, Mexico and the Caribbean in the New Millennium*, I (Washington, DC: EPICA, 1998);

the examples of Fr. Rutilio Grande, S.J., and Archbishop Oscar Romero, their struggles with the politics of repression, and the impact of their efforts on the emerging self-understanding of the UCA at the end of the decade.

As we saw, the Jesuits were dismissed as directors of El Salvador's diocesan seminary in a meeting of Archbishop Chávez and Bishop Oscar Romero with the Jesuit provincial, Fr. Miguel Estrada, in September 1972. This followed a series of skirmishes with conservative bishops by Fr. Grande and other Jesuits over their efforts to implement Vatican II and Medellín at the seminary, resulting in the rejection of Rutilio's nomination as seminary rector in 1970.[240] Shortly thereafter, Fr. Grande gained approval for a leave of absence from the seminary in order to study at the Latin American Pastoral Institute in Quito, Peru, during 1971-1972.[241] As noted earlier, the final decision to terminate the Jesuits' more-than-fifty-year tenure at the seminary came when the students refused to sing and serve at a solemn Mass attended by the newly inaugurated president, Colonel Arturo Molina, after his fraudulent 1972 election was exposed by a team of Jesuits at the UCA. Upon Fr. Grande's return, and in light of the fact that the Jesuits were no longer needed at the seminary, Archbishop Chávez named him pastor of the parish church in Aguilares on September 22, 1972. The parish was to be the site of a new Jesuit ministry among rural farm workers, the poorest residents of this "Third World" country. Fr. Grande had traded the comfortable confines of the diocesan seminary for a dangerous new rural ministry among El Salvador's increasingly restive farm workers.

The rural ministry of Fr. Grande and his team among El Salvador's impoverished campesinos at Aguilares (about seventy miles north of San Salvador) symbolized the promise and the price of the church's vision for El Salvador in the late 1970s. This undoubtedly crossed the minds of some among the crowd of forty Jesuits, almost two thousand campesinos, and many friends gathered at

---

Ann Butwell et al., eds., *We Make the Road by Walking: Central America, Mexico and the Caribbean in the New Millennium*, II (Washington, DC: EPICA, 1998); Rodolfo Cardenal, *Historia de una esperanza: Vida de Rutilio Grande* (San Salvador: UCA Editores, 1985); Ricardo Falla, *The Story of a Great Love* (Washington, DC: EPICA, 1998); Pablo Galdámez, *Faith of a People: The Life of a Basic Christian Community in El Salvador, 1970-1980* (Maryknoll, NY: Orbis Books, 1986); María López Vigil, *Don Lito of El Salvador* (Maryknoll, NY: Orbis Books, 1990); María López Vigil, *Death and Life in Morazán: A Priest's Testimony from a War Zone in El Salvador* (Washington, DC: EPICA, 1989); Thomas R. Melville, *Through a Glass Darkly: The U.S. Holocaust in Central America* (Xlibris Corp., 2005); Jack Nelson-Pallmeyer, *War against the Poor: Low-Intensity Conflict and Christian Faith* (Maryknoll, NY: Orbis Books, 1989); Judith M. Noone, M.M., *The Same Fate as the Poor* (2nd ed.; Maryknoll, NY: Orbis Books, 1994); Anna L. Peterson. *Martyrdom and the Politics of Religion: Progressive Catholicism in El Salvador's Civil War* (Binghamton, NY: SUNY Press, 1997); UCA José Simeón Cañas, *Rutilio Grande: Mártir de la evangelización rural en El Salvador* (San Salvador: UCA Editores, 1978); Daniel Santiago, *The Harvest of Justice: The Church of El Salvador Ten Years after Romero* (New York: Paulist, 1993); Whitfield, *Paying the Price*.

240. Cardenal, *Historia de una esperanza*, 130-33.
241. Ibid., 133-39, esp. 136.

the parish on December 5, 1976, to see Bishop Arturo Rivera Damas[242] ordain two Jesuit seminarians, Carlos Cabarrús and Luis Pellecer, to the priesthood, and a classmate, Jorge Sarsanedas, to the deaconate.[243] This seemed to be the first harvest of an earlier planting.

The short history of Fr. Grande's life by the Central American Jesuits[244] reports that the city of Aguilares had "10,000 inhabitants; El Paisnal, 2,000 inhabitants, and the rest of the population of the parish—around 18,000— . . . dispersed in 170 square kilometers around the town."[245] The economy of the area was dominated by thirty-five great *latifundial* estates, where the local population worked as seasonal day laborers for about three dollars a day[246] (in 1975 a Salvadoran family of six needed to earn $704 per year to provide for life's basic necessities).[247] By June of 1974, two years later, Grande and his team had trained 326 lay catechists who gave pre-baptismal instruction (37) and instruction in the faith (38), ran a youth group with 96 participants (18), animated twelve music groups (12), and trained a team to facilitate the development of new communities (58), seventeen of whom went on to work in other communities.[248] That same year, Ellacuría, still head of Jesuit formation, sent a group of young Jesuits studying at the CRT and the UCA to live in Aguilares with the understanding that their collaboration in the ministry would enrich their studies.

But this seemingly simple initiative was soon complicated by what Cardenal describes as "a series of problems and needs that motivated the agricultural laborers to take another step in their consciousness and political activity," based on their "need not only to come together, but to organize themselves."[249] The

---

242. Juan Hernández-Pico reports that Bishop Rivera Damas did the ordination (*Historia reciente*, 20). Whitfield names Archbishop Chávez (Whitfield, *Paying the Price*, 100), although she does not cite her source.

243. Within a year, Cabarrús would be thanking Archbishop Romero for personally saving his friend, Panamanian Jesuit priest Fr. Jorge Sarsanedas, who had been kidnapped on May 1, 1977, on his way back from saying Mass, and detained incommunicado by the infamous National Guard. Cabarrús would later use the experiences in Aguilares for his doctoral thesis: *Génesis de una revolución: Análisis del surgimiento y desarrollo de la organización campesina en El Salvador* (Mexico City: Ediciones de la Casa Chata, 1983). Regarding this incident, see Hernández-Pico, *Historia reciente*, 24-25; and Whitfield, *Paying the Price*, 64-65 and 106-7. On June 9, 1981, Fr. Luis Pellecer, S.J., was kidnapped in Guatemala, held for several months by the armed forces, tortured, and brainwashed. On September 30, 1981, he appeared on national television in a propaganda spectacle organized by the armed forces, denouncing the role of the Jesuits in Guatemala. See Hernández-Pico, *Historia reciente*, 59-61.

244. The book was written by Fr. Rodolfo Cardenal but not published under his name. This is clear in the "Introduction" to Cardenal, *Historia de una esperanza*, 13-20, esp. 13.

245. *Rutilio Grande: Mártir de la evangelización rural,* 64. The information in this paragraph is from pp. 64-66.

246. This latter detail is from Whitfield, *Paying the Price*, 62.

247. Manuel Sevilla, "Visión global sobre la concentración económica en El Salvador," *Boletín de ciencias económicos y sociales* (May-June 1984): 179, 188-89. Cited in Montgomery, *Revolution in El Salvador,* 70.

248. *Rutilio Grande: Mártir de la evangelización rural,* 75.

249. Ibid., 433.

rapidly expanding but still illegal Christian Federation of Salvadoran Farm Workers, FECCAS (temporary farm workers were legally prohibited from unionizing), was becoming increasingly active in the area, benefitting from the training and mobilization of agricultural workers by the church. Founded in 1969 to revive the failed Union of Catholic Workers,[250] Cardenal explains that FECCAS "actively supported the Christian Democratic Party," and had a presence in some campesino communities in 1974.[251] In this environment, at the end of the year a local activist, Apolinario Serrano (or Polín as he was affectionately known), invited three of the Jesuit students to a meeting "in El Líbano, where the first FECCAS group was formed" in the area, followed shortly by foundation of another group in Los Gramales attended by one of the students.[252] A few weeks later in December 1974 the seminarians living in Aguilares "offered to collaborate with FECCAS,"[253] helping to organize a seminar attended by some two hundred campesinos. For this reason, Cardenal concludes that in Aguilares, "FECCAS was born at the breast of the Church, which provided economic and social support." He adds, however, that "soon, after just a few months, FECCAS claimed its autonomy."[254]

The implications of this autonomy would soon become apparent to both the seminarians and the older Jesuits as the organizational goals of FECCAS to acquire and use the power of the state fundamentally diverged from the work of the parish in its pastoral accompaniment of the campesino community. Whitfield reports that in 1975 three of the young Jesuits, "two Guatemalans, Alberto Enriquez and Fernando Ascoli, and the Nicaraguan Antonio Cardenal, realized they shared a conviction that the Christian commitment awakened in the people of Aguilares would need to move toward armed revolution if the injustice of their lives was to be redressed."[255] Rutilio and his team in Aguilares raised serious objections to this line of thought, however, and at the UCA Ellacuría insisted that the leadership role being played by the seminarians was a dangerous mistake compromising both the autonomy of FECCAS and the integrity of the church's work in Aguilares.[256] Confirming the fears of the older Jesuits, in 1975 the three seminarians would be present in the cathedral when the BPR (the Popular Revolutionary Block) was founded, and would soon leave the Jesuits to join the revolutionary fronts.

Juan Hernández-Pico asserts that the decision of the Jesuit seminarians to pursue a revolutionary commitment was deemed as "incompatible with the vocation of the Society of Jesus."[257] Thus, their choice to leave the seminary formed a dramatic contrast to the ordination in Aguilares of three of their

---

250. Ibid., 434.

251. Ibid., 434-35.

252. Ibid., 436.

253. Ibid.

254. Ibid., 457.

255. Whitfield, *Paying the Price*, 64.

256. Ibid., 65.

257. Hernández-Pico, *Historia reciente*, 20.

former Jesuit colleagues on December 5, 1976. Hernández-Pico says that Ella-curía, who had strongly opposed the role of the departed seminarians in the popular movement, was "destroyed" by the leaving of the Nicaraguan, Antonio Cardenal.[258] Nonetheless, he recalls that when Fr. Gondra complained at the 1978 Province Congregation that "all we are doing with our formation is losing the young," Ellacuría rose to respond, saying, "We may have lost them for the Society, but they are not a loss for the people of El Salvador." The Jesuits, who had been reduced to silence, burst into applause.[259] However, they would soon find themselves tarred with the same brush as their former colleagues.

This brings us back to the events of December 5, 1976, in which the crowd gathered for the Jesuit ordinations would be linked to an unrelated confronta-tion just a few kilometers down the road. About 250 farm workers (some of whom were members of the newly formed chapter of FECCAS) had gone to the home of Francisco Orellana to protest their forcible dislocation from land where some had lived for over fifty years. When the leaders asked to speak with the landowner, however, he fired his gun "in panic," accidentally killing his brother Eduardo Orellana.[260] Hernández-Pico notes that the now departed Jesuit semi-narians involved in the foundation of FECCAS "had been living for two years in the parish of Aguilares assigned to Rutilio [Grande]." He says that, in the minds of some, this created an "irrational" association of the FECCAS tragedy "to the huge crowd [gathered] at Aguilares with the result that the ordination of the first young Jesuits formed at the Center for Theological Reflection in San Salvador was punctuated by the . . . unleashing of a hate campaign against the church and the Jesuits. One of its lowlights would be the assassination of Rutilio Grande."[261]

The campaign began ominously on December 7, 1976, with articles in *El Diario de Hoy*, El Salvador's second largest newspaper, published by Napoleon Viera Altamirano, vilifying the crowd as "hoards of assassins organized by Third-World priests." We should note that a 1981 cable from the U.S. Embassy later identified Altamirano as a "principal figure" during this period of self-imposed exile in Miami of financing the creation of "rightist death squads" in El Salvador "trying to destroy the moderate reformist government by terrorizing its officials as well as businessmen who cooperate with its reform program."[262] *La Prensa Gráfica* described the Spanish Jesuits as "Marxist leaders protected by official tolerance, bloodying our soil!"[263] And President Molina, whose fraudulent 1972

258. Interview of Juan Hernández-Pico by Teresa Whitfield, June 15, 1991. Cited in Whitfield, *Paying the Price*, 66. The meaning of this word is clearly metaphorical, suggesting "devastated" as another possible translation.

259. Ibid.

260. *Rutilio Grande: Mártir de la evangelización rural*, 92.

261. Hernández-Pico, *Historia reciente*, 20.

262. This cable was released under the freedom of information act. "Millionaires' Murder, Inc.," secret cable from Mark Dion, U.S. Embassy, San Salvador, to Secretary of State, January 5, 1981. Cited in Montgomery, *Revolution in El Salvador*, 132-33.

263. Cited in Whitfield, *Paying the Price*, 100.

election had been exposed by the UCA, went on television to denounce liberation theology as the "number one" enemy of El Salvador.[264] Rodolfo Cardenal says that "Archbishop Chávez publicly defended his priests and the mission of the Church,"[265] but the media campaign continued unabated for months.

Sadly, on March 12, 1977, the explosive anti-Jesuit rhetoric of organizations such as the "Committee for the Defense of the Fatherland" sowed its inevitable harvest when Fr. Rutilio Grande, S.J., was ambushed and taken from his jeep, with an old man and a fifteen-year-old boy, by armed members of the national police and executed.[266] One month earlier, on February 13, Rutilio had said in his homily to a large crowd gathered to protest the government's expulsion of the pastor of the neighboring parish in Apopa (Colombian priest, Fr. Mario Bernal): "It is dangerous to be a Christian in our environment, . . . practically . . . illegal . . . because the world that surrounds us is radically rooted in an established disorder, before which the simple proclamation of the gospel . . . is subversive."[267]

### Archbishop Oscar Romero: Prophetic Defender of Civil Society and the Poor

The church's ministry in Aguilares would never fully recover from the assassination of Fr. Grande and the repression that followed. Yet in a real way the government's brutal repression of this experiment in rural evangelization, which had involved such a rich collaboration with the UCA, would open up new and unimagined possibilities. Fr. Miguel Estrada recalls his thoughts as he sought to avoid the recently appointed Archbishop Romero[268] when the latter arrived at the Aguilares church the night of Fr. Grande's funeral: "These are the consequences of your calumnies. You said we were Marxists and now they are killing us"![269]

It was midnight by the time the archbishop finished concelebrating the funeral Mass with the Jesuit provincial, Fr. Jerez, and some others.[270] But he

---

264. Interview with Jon Sobrino by Teresa Whitfield, March 7, 1991. Cited in Whitfield, *Paying the Price*, 100.

265. *Rutilio Grande: Mártir de la evangelización rural*, 92.

266. Doggett reports, "a medical examination indicated that shots were fired from both sides of the road and that 9 mm. bullets were fired from a Mauser, the type of weapon then used [only] by the police. The three surviving children were interviewed, and identified one of the gunmen as Benito Estrada. An arrest warrant was issued for Estrada, a 35-year-old resident of El Paisnal . . . [and] customs agent (policía de aduana). . . . He was never apprehended . . . and the murder remains unsolved. See Doggett, *Death Foretold*, 24.

267. *Rutilio Grande*, 108. Also Hernández-Pico, *Historia reciente*, 23.

268. On February 22, 1977, Romero had been appointed archbishop of San Salvador.

269. Interview with Fr. Miguel Estada by Teresa Whitfield, February 6, 1991. Cited in Whitfield, *Paying the Price*, 104.

270. The information in this paragraph is from the recollection by Jon Sobrino of the events. See Jon Sobrino, *Archbishop Romero: Memories and Reflections* (Maryknoll, NY: Orbis Books, 1990), 6-8 (translated from *Monseñor Romero* [San Salvador: UCA Editores, 1990]).

asked the priests and sisters (some campesinos as well) to stay and help him formulate the church's response. Someone mentioned that the informal autopsy revealed the victims had been killed by weapons used only the government. Jon Sobrino recalls, "Agitated, perturbed . . . he must have been afraid. . . . The hour had come in which he would have to face up to the powerful—the oligarchy and the government." Sobrino adds, however,

> I shall never forget how totally sincere he was in asking for our help— how his words came from the heart. An archbishop was actually asking us to help him—persons whom a few weeks before he had regarded as suspect, as Marxist! I felt a great tenderness for this humble bishop who was asking, practically begging us, to help him bear the burden that . . . had [been] imposed on him, a far heavier burden than his shoulders, or anyone else's, could ever have borne alone.[271]

Years later, three months before his death in 1980, the archbishop himself would recall how his relationship with his brother priests evolved after Rutilio's death.

> I asked them to help me carry on with the responsibility; there was much enthusiasm from the clergy to help me and I felt that I would not be alone . . . but that I could count on all of them. That union with the clergy vanquished all our fears. They had the idea that I was con- servative, that I would maintain relations with the government, with the rich, and that I would ignore the people's problems, the repression, the poverty. . . . Some of them feared I would stop everything and asked what I was thinking of doing. My response was that they should continue and that we should try to understand each other well, and to . . . [promote] the Church's work as Vatican II and Medellín had asked us to do.[272]

Yet something further remained, for up to this point Romero had still not publically confronted the government on its brutal repression of Salvadoran civil society. Archbishop Romero himself clarifies what changed.

> Father Grande's death and the death of other priests after his impelled me to take an energetic attitude before the government. I remem- ber that because of Father Grande's death I made a statement that I would not attend any official acts until this situation [of who had killed Grande] was clarified. I was very strongly criticized, especially by diplomats. A rupture was produced, not by me with the government but the government itself because of its attitude.[273]

271. Ibid., 6-7.
272. Interview of Archbishop Oscar Romero with Tommie Sue Montgomery, December 14, 1979. Cited in Montgomery, *Revolution in El Salvador,* 95.
273. Ibid.

Fr. Hernández-Pico's poetic description is evocative of the dramatic transformation seemingly brought about by Fr. Grande's death: "Monseñor Romero kept vigil at the body of Fr. Grande on that night of blood [so] generously shed, and awakened to his prophetic vocation."[274] The people would call it "Rutilio's miracle." But perhaps it is more accurate to say that Archbishop Romero made a decision to finally confront the government on its brutal suppression of Salvadoran civil society, which was provoked by the suffering the Salvadoran church, including its priests, for its preferential option for the poor. The archbishop himself concludes the preceding statement by declaring that, in the end, "I support all of the priests in the [poor] communities," through whose work "we have managed to combine well the pastoral mission of the church, preference for the poor, to be clearly on the side of the repressed, and from there to clamor for the liberation of the people."[275]

There are some disagreements among Archbishop Romero's friends and followers on the nature of the change that took place. Bishop Gregory Rosa Chávez, a close associate of Archbishop Romero who worked with the archbishop in communications[276] and interviewed him weekly on the diocesan radio station, YSAX,[277] argues that Archbishop Romero didn't have a conversion, but rather experienced a gradual evolution toward a decision to take a public position on the abuse of human rights. In support of this theory Bishop Rosa Chávez cites a documentary done by a Swiss journalist who spent a week with the archbishop during the final phase of his life. Rosa Chávez says the journalist asked, "Have you been converted, Monseñor Romero?" and he says that Romero responded, "I wouldn't say *converted*. Rather, it's been a gradual evolution that led to a decision to respond to the situation in the country as a pastor."[278]

If this is correct, then what role did the assassination of Rutilio Grande play in this process? Bishop Rosa Chávez says, "There are two theories about the conversion of Monseñor Romero, the Jesuits' and ours. The Jesuits say that he was converted thanks to Rutilio. But we say that he was already in a process of conversion."[279] Laying out the dilemma, Rosa Chávez explains, "Before being named archbishop he was bishop in a poor rural area where he met many campesinos, while always questioning, 'What is God asking of me?' On the other hand, he was very close friends with Rutilio Grande, and Fr. Grande's death affected him deeply. They were very similar as pastors."

Monsignor Ricardo Urioste, vicar general of the diocese of San Salvador under Romero, similarly asserts, "I don't think the killing of Rutilio Grande

274. Hernández-Pico, *Historia reciente*, 24.

275. Interview of Archbishop Oscar Romero with Tommie Sue Montgomery, December 14, 1989. Cited in Montgomery, *Revolution in El Salvador*, 95.

276. Interview of Bishop Gregorio Rosa Chávez by Robert Lassalle-Klein, San Salvador, November 12, 2009.

277. Brockman, *Romero*, 116.

278. Interview of Bishop Gregorio Rosa Chávez by Robert Lassalle-Klein, San Salvador, November 12, 2009.

279. Ibid.

provoked the conversion of Monseñor Romero."[280] As evidence of Romero's prior concern for the poor, Urioste cites an incident in 1976 when Romero, as bishop of the diocese of Santiago de Maria, "opened his bishop's house to the poor." James Brockman's biography of Oscar Romero recounts the details of this incident, noting that the bishop criticized the "selfishness" of the coffee growers for denying a "just wage" to the harvesters, forcing them to spend cold nights sleeping in the public square of Santiago de María during the harvest. In response, Romero opened the cathedral rectory, the diocesan offices, and a hall for clergy meetings in the bishop's residence so that "hundreds of workers thus had at least a roof over their heads at night and shelter from the cold."[281] Brockman asserts, however, that while Romero "did what he could to alleviate the hardships of the harvesters," on the other hand, he offered "no solution for the injustice beyond wishing that the landowners were not so selfish and fraudulent." Brockman asserts that public interventions of this sort would have to wait until "after he became archbishop" and the death of Rutilio Grande, when, like the campesinos of Aguilares, "he would come to recognize that the oppressed must organize in order to pressure for their rights, and he would vigorously defend the rights of their organizations."[282]

Granting the validity of these differing perspectives, I would argue that Sobrino, Bishop Rosa Chávez, and Monsignor Urioste are all partially correct in that their claims address different pieces of the puzzle of the transformation or "conversion" of Archbishop Romero. Clearly, Romero's embrace of Medellín's call to a preferential option for the poor may be properly described in his own words cited by Bishop Rosa Chávez as "a gradual evolution that led to a decision to respond to the situation in the country as a pastor."[283] On the other hand, the archbishop himself distinguishes the "gradual evolution" of his option for the poor from his later "decision to respond to the situation in the country as a pastor." Here the archbishop differentiates his own early evolution toward a preferential option for the poor from his later decision to publically denounce the situation in the country. Using the language of conversion developed by Donald Gelpi, S.J.,[284] I would argue that we can distinguish Romero's *personal conversion*, characterized by his gradual decision to assume personal responsibility for the suffering of the poor, from the archbishop's *socio-political conversion* following the assassination of Rutilio Grande and other priests. For it was only after the death of Rutilio Grande that Romero began to take full responsibility as archbishop for the systematic and ongoing violations of human rights by the

---

280. Speech and interview of Monsignor Ricardo Urioste by Robert Lassalle-Klein, Santa Clara University, April 28, 2010.

281. Brockman, *Romero*, 56.

282. Ibid., 55

283. Interview of Bishop Gregorio Rosa Chávez by Robert Lassalle-Klein, San Salvador, November 12, 2009.

284. Donald Gelpi, S.J., *The Gracing of Human Experience: Rethinking the Relationship between Nature and Grace* (Collegeville, MN: Liturgical Press/Michael Glazier, 2001), 292-93 and 297-301.

government and others through public denouncements of this ongoing pattern that defined the "situation in the country" through the end of his life.

The story of the founding of the Mothers of the Disappeared told by Alicia García and her companions gives eloquent testimony to this change in Archbishop Romero produced by what I am calling his *political conversion*. Alicia's daughter, Patricia, recalls, "Our committee was born through the desperate efforts of mothers searching for their children after the National Guard ambushed the student march from the National University to the Plaza Libertad in San Salvador on July 30, 1975."[285] Rodolfo Cardenal writes that more than two thousand students had taken to the streets that morning to protest government and private contributions of thirty million dollars to host the upcoming "Miss Universe" contest, as well as the National Guard's brutal repression of an earlier protest by university students in Santa Ana.[286] Cardenal says the soldiers surrounded the crowd, cut off all escape routes, and opened fire on the unarmed students "leaving at least 37 dead and several dozen 'missing.'"

Alicia García, who observed the massacre from the Maternity Hospital where she worked, was forced to enter the chaotic scene of dead and dying victims in order to pick up blood for a transfusion from the blood bank down the street. She was horrified to witness a government steam roller crush the bodies, and her daughter describes what happened three days later.

> On August 3rd my mother joined the other women looking for missing relatives when she realized her brother must have been arrested or "disappeared" along with the other students. She went to various prisons until she found him with four young people in custody at San Francisco Gotera, along with 159 others imprisoned there. They discovered that his anus had been seriously injured through torture. When the women left to buy medicine at the pharmacy, however, they were not allowed to reenter the prison. Fortunately they saw a priest and begged him to bring the medicine to the boys. An hour later the priest emerged and said he had attended to all four, including the most seriously injured. That evening they went back to Santiago de María with the priest because it was too far to travel to San Salvador, and he insisted that they stay the night. In the morning they discovered he was Bishop Romero.[287]

Bishop Romero's response to the plight of the women and their children fits the pattern of the earlier story, demonstrating real compassion and concern for their suffering. Stories like this provide evidence for the claim of Bishop Rosa

285. Testimony of Patricia García and interview by Robert Lassalle-Klein, San Salvador, January 5, 2011.

286. Rodolfo Cardenal, *Manual de historia de Centroamérica* (San Salvador: UCA Editores, 1996), 397.

287. Testimony of Patricia García and interview by Robert Lassalle-Klein, San Salvador, January 5, 2011.

Chávez and Monsignor Urioste that Romero's heart was open to the suffering of his people before he became archbishop, and that he had made a personal option for the poor. But it is equally true that, like the earlier example of the harvesters, there is no record that Bishop Romero publically denounced the government's role in either the student massacre of July 30, 1975, or the illegal imprisonment and torture of innocent civilians that followed. Things would change after the death of Rutilio Grande.

Patricia García recalls, "Two years later after he was named archbishop we were excited, so we went to see him." She recalls, however, that the women encountered a different man when they saw him again eight months after the death of Rutilio Grande. She says, "He invited us to the seminary on Dec. 24, 1977, and suggested that we form the committee. Our name was *The Committee of Mothers of Persons Who Were Captured, Disappeared or in Prison.* My mother Alicia asked if we could use his name. But he said, 'Not unless something happens to me.' He loved to call us *the mothers.*"[288]

This testimony points to the change that had occurred in Archbishop Romero who, by December 1977, was now ready to stand publically with those being tortured and abused, and to publically denounce those who carried out these acts. This impression is confirmed by a story about Archbishop Romero told to Pope John Paul II by *the Mothers* a couple of years after Romero's death. Patricia García recalls,

> The Mothers were invited to Europe in 1982 to talk about our work. When we were in Rome we asked to see the Pope. He was busy, so Mother Alicia went on the radio and said she was sad the Pope couldn't find time to meet with the Mothers of the Disappeared. The next day a message came that the Pope would meet with us for forty-five minutes. We spent two hours with him. He wanted to know what role Monseñor Romero had played with us. My mother said, "Saint Romero was the one who gave us the idea to form this committee. He was with the common people of El Salvador, and he accompanied us in recovering our lost and tortured husbands, wives, sons, and daughters." She also told the Pope that when Monseñor Romero returned to El Salvador after his visit to Rome as archbishop he was very sad. When the Pope asked why he was so sad, Mother Alicia told him, "It was because you didn't understand him. None of the poor were spreading terror. We were just trying to protect ourselves and asking for human rights."[289]

---

288. Ibid.

289. Ibid. The account appears to refer to the May, 7, 1979, meeting between Archbishop Romero and Pope John Paul II. Romero's personal diary entry for that day states, "I left, pleased by the meeting, but worried to see how much the negative reports of my pastoral work had influenced him." See Oscar Romero, *A Shepherd's Diary,* trans. Irene B. Hodgson (Cincinnati, OH: St. Anthony Messenger Press, 1993), 215.

Patricia concludes, "The Pope asked her all about the country, and it was after that meeting that he came to visit El Salvador."

While many things could be said about this recollection, both the Mothers and the Pope seem to recognize that Archbishop Romero had made "a decision to respond to the situation in the country as a pastor."[290] This decision to take public responsibility for the situation of the country is what I am calling a political conversion. Aside from the archbishop's own words, his actions after this point demonstrate a new willingness to publically criticize the government. Perhaps more than anything else this is what begins to distinguish the ministry of Archbishop Romero after the assassination of Rutilio Grande from that of the compassionate bishop of San Francisco Gotera who remained silent about horrific outcome of the July 30, 1975, student massacre.

### The Root of Romero's Prophecy: Civil Society and the Body of Christ

In the space that remains I will briefly evoke the broad significance for the country's suffering people and the UCA Jesuits of the three-year ministry of Archbishop Romero as the church's response to the brutal repression of Salvadoran civil society. The future of that ministry was captured in the response of the archbishop to the violent military repression that followed the assassination of Rutilio Grande.[291] On May 11, 1977 (two months after the killings), Fr. Alfonso Navarro became the first diocesan priest to die when he was murdered at the rectory of his parish, La Resurrección, in Miramonte, a middle-class neighborhood in San Salvador.[292] On May 13 local newspapers published a statement from the notorious right-wing death squad, the *White Warriors Union*, claiming responsibility for the murders.[293] Then on May 19, the army launched a full-scale military siege of Aguilares, appropriately entitled "Operation Rutilio." Soldiers depopulated the town and broke into the church, shooting an old sacristan frantically ringing the bells, and spraying the altar with bullets. The parish's three remaining Jesuits were whisked into a waiting car and deported from the country. A state of emergency was declared, and about fifty people, including a number of campesino leaders, were assassinated.[294]

---

290. Interview of Bishop Gregorio Rosa Chávez by Robert Lassalle-Klein, San Salvador, November 12, 2009.

291. Much of the information in this paragraph is from Sobrino, *Archbishop Romero*, 25-31.

292. Jon Sobrino and Rodolfo Cardenal believe it was "La Parroquia de la Resurrección." Jon Sobrino, correspondence with author, July 24, 1995, and Rodolfo Cardenal, S.J., correspondence with author, August 18, 2009. The detail on the neighborhood is from Berryman, *The Religious Roots of Rebellion*, 126.

293. Inter-American Commission on Human Rights, Organization of American States, "Report on the Situation of Human Rights in El Salvador," Chapter II, Case 2336, 9.3., OEA/Ser.L/V.II.46 doc 23 rev. 1 (November 17, 1978), http://www.cidh.org/countryrep/el salvador78eng/chap.2.htm.

294. Doggett, *Death Foretold*, 303.

A month later, on June 19, 1977, the archbishop drove from San Salvador to Aguilares, despite an official ban on entering the area, in order to celebrate Mass with the terrorized community and to install a new pastor (Fr. Jon Cortina, S.J.) with his team. A number of local clergy and church workers, who had been living in a state of siege, accompanied him. In his homily Romero publicly thanked the Jesuits for the work of Fr. Grande and his team, and he thanked the sisters who courageously took the parish after the priests had gone. The campesinos, who had been terrorized with impunity for weeks by paramilitary and army forces, flocked to hear the words of consolation preached by the archbishop. He told them, "We suffer with those who have suffered so much. . . . We suffer with the lost—those who have had to run away and do not know what is happening to their families . . . [and] we are with those who are being tortured."[295]

Jon Sobrino, who was there, offers a remarkable description of what happened next.[296] Mass ended with a procession of the Blessed Sacrament out of the church, Archbishop Romero in the rear and the crowd in front. The crowd flowed out into the square in front of the church in order "to make reparation for the soldiers' desecration of [both] the sacramental Body of Christ, and the living Body of Christ, the murdered campesino." Armed troops were stationed across the square by the town hall looking "sullen, arrogant, and unfriendly." As the procession approached the soldiers the crowd stopped, uneasy, and afraid. Sobrino writes,

> We had no idea what might happen. . . . [So] we all instinctively turned around and looked at Monseñor Romero, who was bringing up the rear, holding the monstrance. *"Adelante"* (Forward!), said Monseñor Romero. And we went right ahead. The procession ended without incident. From that moment forward Monseñor Romero was the symbolic leader of El Salvador. He made no such claim. He had sought no such thing. But this is the way it was. From then on Monseñor Romero led us, marching at our head. He had been transformed into the central reference point for the church and for the country. Nothing of any importance occurred in our country over the next three years without our all turning to Monseñor Romero for guidance and direction, for leadership.[297]

Sobrino concludes, "This miracle does not happen every day. But it happened here. The campesinos of Aguilares came into Monseñor Romero's heart and stayed there forever."

By 1978 the archbishop's 8:00 a.m. Sunday morning homily had become the most popular radio program in the country. Thousands of campesinos who could neither read nor write, along with their more educated urban counter-

---

295. Ibid., 27.
296. Ibid., 27-28.
297. Ibid., 28.

parts, would tune in to the archbishop's sermon. It was always followed by church announcements, the events of the week in El Salvador, and a reading of the names of persons who had been killed, assaulted, tortured, or kidnapped (no matter who the perpetrator).[298] In addition, Romero broadcasted weekly interviews and commentaries on important events via the archdiocesan radio station, YSAX, also allowing the UCA a daily slot.

Ellacuría, de Sebastian, Sobrino, and other Central American Jesuits and UCA faculty became important resources for the archbishop in developing his homilies, commentaries, and interview materials. The Jesuits played an especially important role in helping the archbishop develop his annual Pastoral Letters. Jon Sobrino wrote the basic text of second letter, "The Church, the Body of Christ in History."[299] For the third and fourth letters the archbishop provided guidelines to diverse teams who developed several drafts and had numerous meetings both at the archdiocese and the UCA. But according to numerous close observers it would be grossly inaccurate to accept the distorted portrayal offered by the reactionary Bishop Romeo Tovar Astorga that "the Third World clergy manipulated Monseñor Romero and of course that meant the Jesuits."[300] Rather, the vast majority of observers agree with the opinion of Hector Dada, a lay economics professor at the UCA and an advisor for the archbishop: "He gathered up the opinions of half the world and so, yes, often he did say things that one of the Jesuits might have written for him. But at other times he'd say the opposite of what I or any Jesuit had advised him."[301]

### The UCA Coup: Voice of Reform

In some ways Archbishop Romero's increasingly urgent pleas on behalf of his persecuted people represented the rapidly deteriorating situation of Salvadoran civil society in the face of brutal government repression. In 1977, despite the conviction of U.S. Ambassador Frank Devine that "President [Carlos Humberto] Romero recognized that human rights had become a serious issue,"[302] the fraudulently elected regime governed with rigid conservatism over a toxic brew of spiraling mass demonstrations, strikes, military repression, murder of government critics by right-wing death squads, and left-wing kidnappings. The stolen elections were immediately followed on February 28, 1977, by the massacre in

---

298. Interview with Luis de Sebastian by Tommie Sue Montgomery, Fall 1979. Cited in Montgomery, *Revolution in El Salvador,* 96.

299. See Archbishop Oscar Romero, *Voice of the Voiceless: The Four Pastoral Letters and Other Statements* (Maryknoll, NY: Orbis Books, 1985) (translated from *La voz de los sin voz: La palabra viva de Monseñor Oscar Arnulfo Romero* [San Salvador: UCA Editores, 1980]).

300. Interview of Bishop Tovar Astorga by Teresa Whitfield, Zacoteluca, April 12, 1991. Cited in Whitfield, *Paying the Price,* 112.

301. Interview of Hector Dada by Teresa Whitfield, January 9, 1991. Cited in Whitfield, *Paying the Price,* 115.

302. Montgomery, *Revolution in El Salvador,* 73.

the Plaza Libertad; the assassination of Rutilio Grande on March 12; the April kidnapping by the FPL (the Popular Forces of Liberation) of Mauricio Borgonovo, minister of external relations; the assassination of Fr. Alfonso Navarro at the rectory of his parish on May 11; the army siege of Aguilares on May 19; the June 20, 1977, threat by the White Warriors Union to assassinate any Jesuit who did not leave the country within thirty days; and the December 24, 1977, founding of the Mothers of the Disappeared at the invitation of Archbishop Romero in response to the sickening wave of government and right-wing kidnappings, torture, and murder.[303]

Following a long-standing pattern of reformist coups and reactionary countercoups,[304] this bloody spectacle, combined with the government's inability to deal with the worsening economic situation of the country, fomented increasing dissatisfaction among a group of young officers frustrated with General Romero's apparent inability to gain even the smallest political concessions from the military and the oligarchy. In March and April 1979 Lieutenant Colonel René Guerra y Guerra and his brother Rodrigo, a businessman, tried unsuccessfully to find military support to force the new president's resignation. On May 2 the National Police opened fire on several hundred demonstrators, killing twenty-two unarmed citizens supporting the BPR, which had occupied the cathedral to protest the imprisonment of five of their leaders. Then on July 17, 1979, the military was startled to see Anastasio Somoza's hated National Guard landing on Salvadoran beaches in full flight from a revolution with broad popular support from Nicaraguan civil society, which it had brutally repressed. Recognizing that the building crisis could lead to a similar outcome in El Salvador, a group of "young officers" led by Colonel Alfredo Arnoldo Majano and Lieutenant Colonel René Guerra y Guerra began to meet during the summer of 1979 discussing plans for a reformist coup.[305]

On October 12, 1979, the officers approached Román Mayorga, president of the UCA, with a request that he join the planned junta. Ellacuría's advice was stark: "It's possible you'll be burned by this, or worse, but in the circumstances I don't think you have a choice. It is the only way, if there is one, to avoid bloodshed while at the same time searching for a positive change for the country."[306] Mayorga responded to the officer's request with a conditional "yes" based on three demands: (1) he must be allowed to select the new government's proclamation from the three possibilities he had been shown; (2) there must be a purge of military officers who had been engaged in corruption and serious human rights abuses; and (3) the most important political opposition (the

303. Armstrong and Ruben, *El Salvador*, 93; Byrne, *El Salvador's Civil War*, 44-48; LeoGrande, *Our Own Backyard*, 37-40.

304. Montgomery, *Revolution in El Salvador*, 37-39.

305. Rodolfo Cardenal, *Manual de historia de Centroamérica* (San Salvador: UCA Editores, 1996), 406-7; Montgomery, *Revolution in El Salvador*, 74; Armstrong and Rubin, *El Salvador*, 112.

306. Román Mayorga, "Recuerdo de diez Quijotes," 11; Whitfield, *Paying the Price*, 125.

Popular Forum) must be represented on the junta.[307] In the end the junta consisted of five members: Mayorga, president of the UCA; Colonel Adolfo Arnoldo Majano, representing the younger officers; Colonel Jaime Abdul Gutiérrez, who replaced Guerra y Guerra and represented the most conservative military wing; Dr. Guillermo Ungo, director of research at the UCA and the candidate selected to represent the Popular Forum; and Mario Andino, representing the private sector.

On October 15, 1979, the coup dispatched General Romero into exile in Guatemala and published its platform, "Proclamation of the Armed Forces of El Salvador."[308] Full of idealism, the document stated that the junta had assumed power in order "to create the conditions so that all Salvadoran can have peace and live with human dignity."[309] It promised "to carry out authentically free elections"; "to lay the foundations" for "economic, social and political" change; and "to guarantee the rule of human rights." It proposed to initiate the reconstruction of Salvadoran civil society by "permitting the constitution of political parties of all ideologies," granting "the right to organize in all sectors of the work force," conducting timely elections, and offering "amnesty to all exiles and political prisoners." It also promised "the dissolution of ORDEN,"[310] the despised security organization, and the reorganization of its much-feared parent, the military-intelligence organization ANSESAL.[311] And finally, the proclamation announced plans to promote an "equitable distribution of the national wealth" through programs promoting agrarian reform, price controls, increased domestic production, and guarantees for "the right to housing, food, education, and health of every inhabitant.[312]

In many ways the platform represented the last best hope for real economic, political, and military reform, which the UCA had been promoting throughout the 1970s. Indeed, so many officials of the new government came from the university that it was commonly referred to as the "UCA Coup." The *Diario de Occidente* displayed the headline, "People say the Jesuits have taken power in our country."[313] And the Jesuit provincial, Fr. Jerez, wrote to Fr. Arrupe in Rome predicting, "If this new attempt fails we will not escape the hatred and the criticism of the extreme Right and the extreme Left, . . . being like a sandwich. We will try to maintain our independence. But being realistic we cannot

---

307. Interview of Román Mayorga Quirós by Teresa Whitfield, May 1, 1991. Cited in Whitfield, *Paying the Price*, 125.

308. "'Proclama de la Fuerza Armada de El Salvador,' October 15, 1979," in *ECA* 34, nos. 372-373 (October-November 1979): 1167; also in Rafael Menjívar Ochoa, *Tiempos de Locura: El Salvador 1979-1981*, Appendix 2 (San Salvador: Flasco, 2006), 266-68.

309. "Proclama," in Ochoa, *Tiempos de Locura,* 267.

310. Ibid.

311. Byrne, *El Salvador's Civil War*, 54; and James Dunkerley, *The Long War: Dictatorship and Revolution in El Salvador* (London: Junction Books, 1982), 143.

312. Byrne, *El Salvador's Civil War,* 54. Also Cardenal, *Manual de historia de Centroamérica*, 408.

313. Diario de Occidente, October 27, 1979. Cited in Whitfield, *Paying the Price,* 127.

escape the image of being participants."[314] More than anything, the coup was an attempt to avoid civil war by responding to the demands of Salvadoran civil society for political, economic, and military reform.

The new government made serious efforts to carry out the promised reforms. The junta won the fatal enmity of Major Roberto D'Aubuisson and other military personnel identified with political murder and repression by keeping its promise to move against the abuses of the security agencies, ORDEN and ANSESAL. On October 16, 1979, a general amnesty was declared for all political prisoners and Salvadorans living in exile. In November the junta dissolved ORDEN and created a special commission that identified political detainees and recommended the prosecution of officials involved in torture and illegal detention. And on December 7, decree §43 was issued retroactive to October 15, banning the transfer of properties of more than 247 acres (100 hectares) in preparation for the agrarian reform program (designed with U.S. planners) that followed.[315] "The Basic Law for Agrarian Reform," designed with U.S. planners,[316] was promulgated by the second junta on March 5, 1980.[317]

William LeoGrande explains that Phase One of the proposed program of land reform "expropriated large estates in excess of 1,250 acres and transferred ownership to the resident workers . . . constituting about 14.7% of the nation's arable land, and about 30,000 families" as beneficiaries.[318] He continues, "Phase Two called for expropriating estates between 250 and 1,250 acres . . . comprising about 12% of the arable land, and approximately 50,000 families as beneficiaries." And he concludes, "The affected farms produced 35% of El Salvador's coffee, 40% of its cotton, and 20% of its sugar."[319] Another report done for the Pentagon provides a certain amount of perspective, stating, "Phase II . . . was the most important part of the program affecting the largest number of properties, the most productive acreage, and the agricultural base of the coffee oligarchy." In fact, "Phase III, sometimes called the land-to-the-tiller program, involved no further land redistribution, but allowed renters and sharecroppers to purchase title for the land that they had been working [and] . . . scheduled

---

314. Letter from Fr. César Jerez, S.J., to Fr. Pedro Arrupe, S.J. (San Salvador: Archives of the Central American Province of the Society of Jesus, October 23, 1979). Cited in Beirne, *Jesuit Education and Social Change*, 145.

315. Segundo Montes, *El Agro Salvadoreño (1973-1980)* (San Salvador: UCA Editores, 1986), 240.

316. Benjamin C. Schwarz, *American Counterinsurgency Doctrine and El Salvador: The Frustrations of Reform and the Illusions of Nation Building* (Santa Monica, CA: National Defense Research Institute, 1991), 45.

317. "Ley Básica de la Reforma Agraria," *ECA* (December 1979): 1114-5. Cited in Schwarz, *American Counterinsurgency Doctrine and El Salvador,* 45.

318. LeoGrande, *Our Own Backyard,* 166-67.

319. Ibid., 167. LeoGrande cites the testimony by Roy Prosterman in the U.S. House of Representatives, *Presidential Certification on El Salvador, Vol. II*, 146; John D. Strasma, *Agrarian Reform in El Salvador* (Checchi and Co, USAID, 1983), 168-75; and Nina M. Serafino, *The Post-Election Situation of Agrarian Reform in El Salvador* (Washington, DC: Congressional Research Service, 1982).

almost half the country's farmland for redistribution to one-half to two-thirds of poor rural households.[320]

Unfortunately, the reformist plans captured in the proclamation and the early decrees issued by the *Young Officers' Coup* or *UCA Coup* were never implemented as the military proponents of political repression asserted control over the reins of government. The new regime had tremendous ideas grounded in the values of Catholic Social Teaching, and talented administrators trained in the best social science of the day, but as Mayorga would later admit, "We were forgetting the little detail of military power, and the impossibility that human qualities alone can triumph."[321]

320. Schwarz, *American Counterinsurgency Doctrine and El Salvador*, 45.

321. Mayorga Quirós interview by Whitfield, May 1, 1991. Cited in Whitfield, *Paying the Price*, 127.

# 3

# *Transforming the Historical Reality of El Salvador (1979-1989)*

## FROM THE AGENCY OF THE ELITE TO THE HEART OF THE PEOPLE

The armed conflict that wracked El Salvador from 1980 to the signing of the Peace Accords in January 1992 began and ended in a struggle over civil society: over what expression civil society would be allowed to take, over its influence in public debate, over who would control it, and how. The Right fought to protect its own economic power . . . first of all on the ground of civil society, attempting by all means available to subordinate, or subdue, the forces unleashed . . . by church groups, unions, and the Left in the 1960s.[1]

### Battle for the Soul of Civil Society: State-Sponsored Violence versus the Voice of Prophecy

The trailhead of the path trod by those who murdered Ignacio Ellacuría and his companions was blazed many years before. The U.N. Truth Commission asserts that the assassinations of Archbishop Romero and the University of Central America (UCA) Jesuits, which bracketed the 1980s, were the outcome of long-standing patterns of violence by agents of the state and their collaborators against their critics and opponents in civil society. Reflecting this truth, both right-wing apologists for military repression and National Liberation Party (FMLN) rebels traced their roots to the 1932 slaughter of Salvadoran indigenous and peasant farm workers led by General Hernández Martínez, known simply as "la Matanza" (the Massacre). The massacre was considered by many on the right to have been an unfortunate but necessary means of social control, an attitude emblemized by the infamous 1980s death squad, the General Maximiliano Hernández Martínez Anti-Communist Brigade.[2] On the

---

1. Michael W. Foley, "Laying the Groundwork: The Struggle for Civil Society in El Salvador," *Journal of Interamerican Studies and World Affairs* 38, no. 1 (Spring 1996): 67-104.

2. Cynthia J. Arnson, "Window on the Past: A De-classified History of the Death Squads

other hand, the rebel FMLN took its name from the executed leader of the unsuccessful revolt.

In its analysis of the March 24, 1980, assassination of Archbishop Romero, the U.N. Truth Commission states,

> Violence has formed part of the exercise of official authority [in El Salvador] . . . throughout the country's history, in a pattern of conduct within the Government and power elites of using violence as a means to control civilian society. The roots of this situation run deep. In the past 150 years, a number of uprisings by peasants and indigenous groups have been violently suppressed by the State and by civilian groups armed by landowners.
>
> A kind of complicity developed between businessmen and landowners, who entered into a close relationship with the army and intelligence and security forces. The aim was to ferret out alleged subversives among the civilian population in order to defend the country against the threat of an alleged foreign conspiracy. When controlling internal subversion became a priority for defending the State, repression increased.[3]

The report goes on to outline three "stages" in evolution of state-sponsored violence against Salvadoran civil society in the twentieth century

The first period began with the formation of the National Guard, which was "created and organized in 1910," and "cooperated actively with large landowners . . . to crack down brutally on the peasant leaders and other rural groups that threatened their interests."[4] The report states that "local National Guard commanders . . . hired out guardsmen to protect landowner's materials interests," which spawned a "practice of using the services of 'paramilitary personnel,' chosen and armed by the army or the large landowners . . . [as] a kind of 'intelligence network' against 'subversives' or [as] a 'local instrument of terror.'" The defining moment of this stage came in the aforementioned 1932 bloodbath carried out by "National Guard members, the army and paramilitary groups, with the collaboration of local landowners . . . [against] peasants in the western part of the country in order to put down a rural insurrection."[5]

The insurrection planned for January 22, 1932, was sparked by a right-wing military coup seven weeks earlier, on December 2, 1931, in which General Martínez overthrew the mildly reformist government of President Arturo

---

in El Salvador," in Bruce B. Campbell, Arthur David Brenner, eds., *Death Squads in Global Perspective: Murder with Deniability* (New York: Palgrave Macmillan, 2002), 86.

3. United Nations, *Report of the Commission on the Truth for El Salvador, From Madness to Hope: The 12-Year War in El Salvador,* March 15, 1993, 132-33.

4. Ibid.

5. Ibid. I will say more on this later. See Thomas P. Anderson, *Matanza: El Salvador's Communist Revolt of 1932* (Lincoln: University of Nebraska Press, 1971), 136.

Araujo after the latter proposed modest reforms to assist peasant farmers suffering from the collapse of the coffee market in the Great Depression of 1929.[6] Municipal and legislative elections followed on January 5 and 10, 1932, in which campesino winners were denied official recognition.[7] In frustration, farm workers in the west of the country began organizing for a January 22 revolt, and the communist party, led by Augustín Farabundo Martí, agreed to mobilize urban forces in support.

Unfortunately for its supporters, the rebellion was subverted by lack of coordination between the rural campesinos and their urban counterparts when Farabundo Martí was captured four days before the planned uprising.[8] General Martínez quickly and brutally repressed the insurrection, and unleashed an extended reign of terror against indigenous campesinos that scholars say eventually took somewhere between ten thousand and thirty thousand lives.[9] Anderson asserts that less than 10 percent of those killed actually participated in the revolt, with the rest being massacred by General Martínez in a general assault against indigenous campesinos and their demands for labor and political reform.[10] Farm worker unions were outlawed, political organizations were prohibited, and a situation of extreme inequality was frozen in place through military control.

Following the 1932 "Matanza," military governments would rule El Salvador for the next fifty years, until 1982, when the United States demanded elections and a civilian government. The United Nations observes that "from virtually the beginning of the century, a Salvadorian State security force, through a

---

6. Edward T. Brett, *"La Matanza* 1932 Peasant Revolt," in Immanuel Ness, ed., *International Encyclopedia of Revolution and Protest* (Malden, MA: Wiley Blackwell Publishing, 2009), Blackwell Reference online: http://www.blackwellreference.com/public/book?id=g 9781405184649_yr2010_9781405184649; accessed February 4, 2011. U.S. attaché for Central American military affairs, Major A. R. Harris, described the economic situation following his visit shortly after the 1932 Martínez coup: "Roughly 90 percent of the wealth of the country is held by about one half of 1 percent of the population. Thirty or forty families own nearly everything in the country. They live in almost regal splendor . . . , send their children to Europe or the United States to be educated, and spend money lavishly . . . [while] the rest of the population has practically nothing." On the political side, leftist Salvadoran intellectual Jorge Arias Gómez writes, "December 2, 1931, marks an era in the political life of the nation [in] which . . . the oligarchy ceased to govern directly . . . [and] withdrew from the political game in order to leave it to military tyranny." See Arias Gómez, "Augustín Farabundo Martí," *La Universidad* 96, no. 4 (July-August 1971): 181-240. Cited in Tommie Sue Montgomery, *Revolution in El Salvador: From Civil Strife to Civil Peace* (Boulder, CO: Westview Press, 1995), 37.

7. Rodolfo Cardenal, *Manual de historia de Centroamérica* (San Salvador: UCA Editores, 1996), 383.

8. Montgomery, *Revolution in El Salvador,* 36-37.

9. Anderson uses the figure of 10,000, while UCA historian Rodolfo Cardenal, S.J., says, "The most reliable calculations indicate that some 30 thousand campesinos were shot." Anderson, *Matanza,* 136; and Cardenal, *Manual de historia de Centroamérica,* 384.

10. Anderson, *Matanza,* 129, 136.

misperception of its true function, was directed against the bulk of the civilian population."[11]

The military dictatorships that followed the 1932 massacre kept the government in the hands of a small group of military and civilian elites with a very narrow base of support that "kept itself in power . . . by using 'selective violence.'" Tommie Sue Montgomery explains that the inherent instability of this arrangement produced the following cycle of coups and countercoups from December 1931 through January 1980: (1) a military coup by reactionary officers followed by consolidation of power through violent repression of dissent from civil society; (2) reaction against the repression by the general public and a progressive military faction culminating in a progressive military counter coup, and the promulgation of reforms; and (3) the reemergence of the most repressive military faction culminating in yet another coup and the use of violence to reconsolidate its power over the military and the state.[12]

The second major period in the evolution of Salvadoran state-sponsored violence against its critics runs from 1967 to 1979.[13] During this period "General José Alberto Medrano, who headed the National Guard, organized the paramilitary group known as ORDEN . . . to identify and eliminate alleged communists among the rural population[, and founded] the national intelligence agency, ANSESAL." The United Nations says, "These institutions helped consolidate an era of military hegemony in El Salvador, sowing terror selectively among alleged subversives identified by the intelligence services. In this way, the army's domination over civilian society was consolidated through repression in order to keep society under control."

The third major period in the evolution of state-sponsored violence against Salvadoran civil society began with the October 15, 1979, reformist coup, which the United Nations says "altered the political landscape in El Salvador," and "ushered in a new period of intense violence."[14] The star of this drama would be ex-major Roberto D'Aubuisson.

### D'Aubuisson's Vision of "National Salvation"

The new government installed by the October 15, 1979, coup won the enmity of right-wing landowners and their traditional agents of repression and social control with its plans for moderate land reform and decrees suppressing the dreaded security agency ORDEN and ANSESAL. As we saw earlier, Phase One of the junta's program for land reform, largely developed by U.S. planners, proposed to expropriate 14.7 percent of El Salvador's arable land concentrated in undeveloped estates of over 1,250 acres, transferring it to about

---

11. Ibid.

12. Montgomery, *Revolution in El Salvador*, 37-38.

13. Ibid., 133.

14. United Nations, *Report of the Commission on the Truth for El Salvador*, 134 and 133.

30,000 campesino families working the land.[15] Phase Two planned to move 12 percent of the arable land from estates between 250 and 1,250 acres to about 50,000 farmworker families. This posed a more serious threat to the interests of large landowners since "35% of El Salvador's coffee, 40% of its cotton, and 20% of its sugar"[16] were grown there. Phase Three, the "land-to-tiller" program, "scheduled almost half the country's farmland for redistribution to one-half to two-thirds of poor rural households,"[17] providing assistance to renters and sharecroppers hoping to purchase properties under eighteen acres.

The anger of the land barons and military forces opposed to the elimination of ORDEN and ANSESAL crystalized in a toxic brew of furious and ultimately successful opposition to the junta, unleashing a wave of terror against anyone advocating reform. On the one hand, "Members of the army, the Treasury Police, the National Guard and the National Police formed '[death] squads' to do away with their enemies." On the other, "Private and semi-official groups . . . set up their own squads or linked up with existing structures within the armed forces,"[18] producing a virulent variety of terrorist organizations "supported or tolerated by State institutions [which] . . . operated in coordination with the armed forces[,] and acted as a support structure for their activities."[19] In the face of the junta's inability to control the military, the United Nations states that "various circles in the armed forces and the private sector vied for control of the repressive apparatus." As a result, "Hundreds and even thousands of people perceived as supporters or active members of a growing guerrilla movement . . . were murdered."

The principal authors of this mayhem, according to U.N. Truth Commission, belonged to "a core of military officers who sought to pre-empt the groups that had staged the coup and also any reform movement."[20] The report highlights the leadership of ex-Major Roberto D'Aubuisson in this group, whose previous access to government intelligence and willingness to use "illegal force" against political opponents "catapulted" him in the view of right-wing leaders "to undisputed national political leadership of the only faction capable 'of preventing a left-wing takeover.'"[21]

---

15. William M. LeoGrande, *Our Own Backyard: The United States in Central America, 1977-1992* (Chapel Hill: University of North Carolina Press, 1998), 166-67.

16. Ibid., 167.

17. Benjamin C. Schwarz, *American Counterinsurgency Doctrine and El Salvador: The Frustrations of Reform and the Illusions of Nation Building* (Santa Monica, CA: National Defense Research Institute, 1991), 45. Also see Hugh Byrne, *El Salvador's Civil War: A Study of Revolution* (Boulder, CO: Lynne Rienner, 1996), 52.

18. United Nations, *Report of the Commission on the Truth for El Salvador*, 133.

19. Ibid., 134. The report adds, "The Salvadorian armed forces also maintained within the Joint Staff under Department 5, Civilian Affairs, a secret, clandestine intelligence unit . . . [for] the 'elimination' of individuals." See ibid., 136.

20. Ibid., 134.

21. Ibid., 135, and 239 n. 422, citing "General Framework for the Organization of the Anti-Marxist Struggle in El Salvador," document confiscated at the San Luis estate of Roberto D'Aubuisson on May 7, 1980, order of May 12, 1980, placing the detainees at the disposal of the military examining judge, exhibit no. 4.

D'Aubuisson was a protégé of General Medrano and "third in command of ANSESAL" until 1979, when he resigned from the army after the reformist junta decided to eliminate the agency.[22] The ex-military officer took "part of the agency's archives" with him, utilizing them to create a right-wing political-military structure with its own death squads, which he used to assassinate supporters of the reformist junta.

In the fall, following the October 15, 1979, reformist coup, the ex-major met in Guatemala with Mario Sandoval Alarcon, founder of the fascist National-ist Liberation Movement. Alarcon advised D'Aubuisson and his associates on the politics of political murder and put him in contact with weapons smugglers and wealthy reactionary Salvadoran exiles in Miami.[23] The Miami connection, described in a 1981 memo from the U.S. embassy in El Salvador entitled "Millionaires' Murder, Inc.," provided millions of dollars to finance the wave of repression that descended on El Salvador.[24] The cable asserts that six Salvadoran millionaires "have directed and financed right-wing death squads [in El Salvador] for nearly a year, that they are trying to destroy the moderate reformist government by terrorizing its officials as well as the businessmen who cooperate with its reform program[, and] that a wave of recent kidnappings is very likely their work." The cable observes that "many Salvadoran and some official Americans have been aware that rightist death squads are financed and directed by a group . . . in Miami, that the publisher of the *Diario de hoy* N [Enrique] Viera Altamirano is a principal figure," and that "they organize, fund and direct death squads through their agent Roberto D'Aubuisson."[25]

The 1993 U.N. Truth Commission pointedly notes that the U.S. government under the Reagan administration "tolerated, and apparently paid little official heed to the activities of [these] Salvadoran exiles living in Miami . . . between 1979 and 1983 . . . [who] directly financed and indirectly helped run certain

---

22. Ibid., 134; Montgomery, *Revolution in El Salvador,* 76.

23. Craig Pyes, "D'Aubuisson's Fledgling Party Finds a Mentor in Guatemala," *Albuquerque Journal,* December 18, 1983; Craig Pyes, "Right Built Itself in Mirror Image of Left for Civil War," *Albuquerque Journal,* December 18, 1983; Craig Pyes, "A Chilling Plan Maps a Terror Road to Rule," *Albuquerque Journal,* December 19, 1983; Christopher Dickey, *With the Contras* (New York: Simon & Schuster, 1985), 87. Cited in Montgomery, *Revolution in El Salvador,* 132.

24. This cable was released under the freedom of information act. "Millionaires' Murder, Inc.," secret cable from Mark Dion, U.S. Embassy, San Salvador to Secretary of State, January 5, 1981.

25. "Millionaires' Murder, Inc." Cited in Montgomery, *Revolution in El Salvador,* 133. Note that I have eliminated Montgomery's mistaken interpolation of the name *Napoleon* into the text for the letter N and substituted the name *Enrique*. Napoleon is clearly incorrect since Napoleon Viera Altamirano died August 8, 1977. Further, Ambassador Robert White testified on February 6, 1984, before the House Foreign Affairs subcommittee on Latin America that the group of six included "Enrique Viera Altamirano, publisher of the conservative newspaper *Diária de hoy*"; see Associated Press, "White Says White House 'Created' Salvadoran Rightest Leader," *Sarasota Herald-Tribune,* Tuesday, February 7, 1984, 5-A.

death squads."[26] The rationale was provided by D'Aubuisson who insisted that the junta had been "infiltrated by Marxist officers," which he predicted would "be fatal for the independence and freedom of the Salvadorian fatherland if the anti-communists in the population failed to act."[27] And the campaign of murder and intimidation was financed by "wealthy civilians who feared that their interests would be [negatively] affected by the reform program announced by the Government Junta, . . . [and] were convinced that the country faced a serious threat of Marxist insurrection which they had to overcome."[28]

As horrific as the activities of the death squads were, however, the armed forces were worse. The United Nations states,

> The Commission on the Truth registered more than 22,000 complaints of serious acts of violence that occurred in El Salvador between January 1980 and July 1991. . . . Those giving testimony attributed almost 85% of cases to agents of the State, paramilitary groups allied to them, and the death squads. . . . Armed forces personnel were accused in almost 60% of complaints, members of security forces in approximately 25%, members of military escorts and civil defense units in approximately 20%, members of death squads in more than 10% of cases. The complaints registered accused [the] FMLN in approximately 5% of cases.[29]

The report goes on to state that "this violence originated in a . . . mind-set that viewed political opponents as subversives and enemies. Anyone who expressed views that differed from the Government ran the risk of being eliminated as if they were armed enemies on the field of battle . . . [through] extrajudicial executions, enforced disappearances and murders of political opponents."[30]

In this context, then, it is important to understand that the 1979 coup was closely associated with the UCA. When Román Mayorga resigned as UCA president on October 15, 1979 (on the advice of Archbishop Oscar Romero[31]), he and Guillermo Ungo left to join the five-person junta, taking over a dozen faculty members with them.[32] Ignacio Ellacuría soon replaced Mayorga as president.

Once in power, the 1979 junta was unable to implement its program while trying unsuccessfully to restrain the increasing military repression until the

---

26. United Nations, *Report of the Commission on the Truth for El Salvador*, 137.

27. Ibid., 134, and 239 n. 421.

28. Ibid., 134.

29. Ibid., 43.

30. Ibid.

31. Archbishop Romero states in his personal diary that Román Mayorga Quirós "asked my opinion of his becoming part of the civilian-military junta," to which he responded that Mayorga Quirós "was the appropriate person" before providing his personal blessing. See Archbishop Oscar Romero, *A Shepherd's Diary* (Cincinnati, OH: St. Anthony Messenger Press, 1993), 355.

32. Charles J. Beirne, S.J., *Jesuit Education and Social Change in El Salvador* (New York: Garland Publishing, 1996), 149.

civilians finally resigned en masse a little over two months later.[33] Tommie Sue Montgomery offers a brief account, confirmed by Fr. Cardenal,[34] of how the most reactionary elements gained control of the military and sabotaged the goals of the coup.

> Despite the months of planning and the socioeconomic commitments of the *golpistas*, their objectives were derailed in the days before and immediately after the coup occurred; [Colonel Jaime Abdul] Gutiérrez and his cohorts thwarted them. First Gutiérrez arranged [the young reformer] René Guerra's removal as one of the two military members of the Junta by calling a meeting of the Young Military (as the conspirators came to be known) to which Guerra and his followers were not invited. Gutiérrez argued that as a lieutenant colonel, Guerra was too junior in rank for such an important position; Gutiérrez was elected in his stead. Second, hours after General Romero departed the country, Gutiérrez, without consultation with or authorization from his colleagues, called Colonel José Guillermo García in San Vicente and offered him the post of minister of defense. Third, García invited Colonel Nicolás Carranza, who was on the CIA payroll at $90,000 a year [and founder of both ORDEN and ANSESAL], to be vice-minister of defense. In short, before the coup was twenty-four hours old, the most reactionary remnants of the officer corps had reasserted control over the armed forces.[35]

During its ten short weeks of life the reformist junta careened from one crisis to the next. Death squads controlled by Roberto D'Aubuisson and sectors of the armed forces carried out brutal attacks on civilians. The National Guard and the Treasury Police moved with increasing savagery against demonstrations, strikes, and occupations of embassies and government buildings. And on December 26, 1979, the civilian members of the government were informed that attempts by the junta to control the armed forces would be rejected.

Guillermo Ungo remembers that on December 26 the new vice-minister of defense, Colonel Vides Casanova, declared, "Colonel García gives the orders, not the Junta."[36] Vides Casanova would soon rise to be commander of El Salvador's National Guard, serving from 1979 to 1983 during the most horrific period of human rights abuses, including the December 2, 1980, rape and murder of four U.S. church women about which the U.N. Truth Commission found that he

---

33. Mario Andino, the private sector representative, resigned on January 4, 1980. Montgomery, *Revolution in El Salvador*, 78-79; and LeoGrande, *Our Own Backyard*, 42-43.

34. Cardenal, *Manual de historia de Centroamérica*, 409.

35. Montgomery, *Revolution in El Salvador*, 75-76.

36. Interview with Guillermo Ungo by Teresa Whitfield, December 15, 1990. Cited in Teresa Whitfield, *Paying the Price: Ignacio Ellacuría and the Murdered Jesuits of El Salvador* (Philadelphia: Temple University Press, 1994), 132.

had substantial information and that he covered up.[37] Following this declaration of refusal to accept civilian rule, Mayorga and Ungo resigned with the entire civilian cabinet on January 3, 1980 (except Mario Andino, who resigned a day later), at a meeting at the seminary arranged by Archbishop Romero to mediate the dispute.[38] The officers then formed a second junta with civilian allies, and the government took a sharp turn to the right, perpetrating previously unthinkable actions of political terror against every sector of civil society associated with the opposition.[39]

As predicted by Fr. Jerez, Ellacuría and the UCA Jesuits now topped the lists of D'Aubuisson's death squads and military elements that wanted the first junta to fail. It became common wisdom in the right-wing media that the 1979 reformist coup had been planned at the UCA, and that "the leadership of the FMLN," which declared war a year later, had "been indoctrinated in these centers of Jesuit instruction."[40]

This attitude persisted and was promoted in the media by the radical right during the 1980s. In 1988 D'Aubuisson stated, "With [Ellacuría's] declarations it can be confirmed what has always been said: that the real ringleaders of [the] subversive movements . . . are not in the mountains, but near the UCA."[41] And in 1989, the year of the Jesuit assassinations, a slanderous book entitled *Marxist Infiltration in the Church* charged that the mobilization of Salvadoran civil society from 1977 to 1989 in favor of social, economic, and political reform was "the direct responsibility of a group of foreign conspirators ensconced in [the UCA]. These Jesuits—above all Ellacuría and Sobrino—have been the real brains who have remained hidden behind all the subversive movements that have been stirred up by the clergy in our country."[42]

---

37. United Nations, *Report of the Commission on the Truth for El Salvador,* 62. Trained in counterinsurgency at the School of the Americas in the United States, Vides Cassanova was appointed minister of defense in 1984 and held the post until 1988, when he immigrated to the United States, where he lives today.

38. See also Dario Moreno, *U.S. Policy in Central America: The Endless Debate* (Miami: Florida International University Press, 1990), 71-81, esp. 71-74; and Byrne, *El Salvador's Civil War,* 53-69.

39. Elements of the preceding account taken from the following sources: LeoGrande, *Our Own Backyard,* 40-43; Robert Armstrong and Janet S. Ruben, *El Salvador: el rostro de la revolución* (San Salvador: UCA Editores, 1983, 1993), 112-29; Montgomery, *Revolution in El Salvador,* 73-79; Whitfield, *Paying the Price,* 120-28; Berryman, *Stubborn Hope,* 63-64; Thomas M. Leonard, *Central America and United States Policies, 1820s-1980s: A Guide to Issues and References* (Claremont, CA: Regina Books, 1985), 37; Byrne, *El Salvador's Civil War,* 53-69.

40. *Diario de hoy,* June 13, 1988. Cited in Martha Doggett, *Death Foretold: The Jesuit Murders in El Salvador* (Washington, DC: Georgetown University Press, Lawyers Committee for Human Rights, 1993), 29.

41. Quote from Roberto D'Aubuisson, *Diario de hoy,* September 17, 1989. Cited in Dogget, *Death Foretold,* 29.

42. A. Jerez Magaña, *La infiltración Marxista en la iglesia* (San Salvador: Editorial Dignidad, Institutio de Relaciones Internacionales, 1989), 23. Cited in Doggett, *Death Foretold,* 22.

Here, then, lies the trailhead of the path traveled by the killers to the Jesuit assassinations ten years later. The same logic appears in the words of Colonel Benavides ordering Lt. Espinoza, the former Jesuit student, to carry out the murders: "Alright men, we're playing for all the cards, it's either them or us, seeing as they are the intellectuals who have been directing the guerrillas for a long time."[43] There was no room for civilian non-combatants in this world, and neither the church nor the university could expect the space to pursue truth on its own terms.

In the minds of the right the UCA Jesuits had joined other leaders in Salvadoran civil society as military targets. Thus, on December 27, 1979, three bombs exploded outside the UCA computer center. On February 16, 1980, the Jesuit residence of Fr. Ellacuría was fired upon with machine-guns, leaving one hundred bullet holes. On February 18, a bomb destroyed part of the UCA library. On March 22, the National Police entered the UCA campus at 1:15 p.m., shooting their weapons and killing a math student, Manuel Orantes Guillén. And two days later, on March 24, Archbishop Oscar Romero, while saying Mass, was assassinated at "the order" of Roberto D'Aubuisson by "members of his security service, acting as a 'death squad.'"[44]

The United Nations offers the following account:

> Former Major Robert D'Aubuisson, former Captain Alvaro Saravia and Fernando Sagrera were present on March 24, 1980, at the home of Alejandro Caceres in San Salvador. Captain Eduardo Avila arrived and told them that Archbishop Romero would be celebrating a mass that day. Captain Avila said that this would be a good opportunity to assassinate the Archbishop. D'Aubuisson ordered that this be done and put Saravia in charge of the operation.[45]

Captain Avila then left to pick up the sniper and rendezvoused with the others in the parking lot of the Camino Real Hotel, where the gunman got into a red, four-door Volkswagen driven by Amado Antonio Garay, Saravia's driver. At least two vehicles drove across town to the chapel, waiting as the sniper got out and shot the archbishop through the heart in front of the stunned Mass-goers as he preached his homily. D'Aubuisson later paid 1,000 *colones* to Walter Antonio "Musa" Alvarez, who, in turn, paid the gunman. In September 1981, Alvarez himself was kidnapped and murdered.

Five weeks later, on May 7, 1980, a startling break in the case occurred. Twelve active and retired military personnel with an equal number of civilians were arrested at a wealthy estate in Santa Tecla. The group, led by D'Aubuisson, was formally accused of plotting a coup against the reformist government that

---

43. Extrajudicial confession of Gonzalo Guevara Cerritos, January 13, 1990, as reprinted in *ECA* nos. 493-494 (November-December 1989): 1161. My translation. Also cited in Doggett, *Death Foretold*, 22.

44. United Nations, *Report of the Commission on the Truth for El Salvador*, 127.

45. Ibid.

included many former members of the UCA faculty and staff. The arresting officers found three explosive documents in the course of the raid: a list of accusations against Oscar Romero; a diary belonging to former Captain Alvaro Rafael Saravia, which was filled with the details of the planning and logistics of the murder; and a strategic plan for a campaign of assassination of repression entitled "General Framework for the Organization of the Anti-Marxist Struggle in El Salvador."

The U.N. Truth Commission asserts, "Their goal was to seize power in El Salvador, and their political plan provided for 'direct action' . . . [and] 'activities of combat networks,' including 'attacks on selected individuals.'"[46] Despite this evidence, however, D'Aubuisson and the others were immediately released. Only Saravia was ever charged (seven years later on November 24, 1987!), but the Supreme Court invalidated the evidence. It would be thirteen years before a governmental body (the U.N. Truth Commission) exposed the truth of what happened, chastising the Supreme Court of El Salvador for having "ensured . . . impunity for those who planned the assassination."[47]

It is no accident, then, that the assassination of Archbishop Romero coincided with the rise of Roberto D'Aubuisson on the Salvadoran scene. Indeed, Romero's assassination symbolized the apparent triumph of D'Aubuisson's "doctrine of national salvation" over the visions of other elite groups, including the church's 1970s vision from Medellín of social reform through the renewal and mobilization of civil society. The U.N. Truth Commission explains that the assassination played an important role in the ex-major's rise to prominence on the extreme right.

> After the assassination of Monsignor Romero, which, in very close circles, D'Aubuisson took credit for having planned . . . , his prestige and influence grew among the groups that wielded economic power, gaining him further support and resources. The San Luis estate incident and his temporary stay in Guatemala did not interrupt his political plans, since it was in Guatemala that he was able to establish contact with internationally linked anti-communist networks and organizations and individual anti-communists such as Mario Sandoval Alarcon, Luis Mendizábal and Ricardo Lao.[48]

As noted above, the UCA Jesuits, and especially Ignacio Ellacuría, soon joined the reformist leaders of Salvadoran civil society at the top of D'Aubuisson's list.

Accordingly, on June 29, 1980, three months after Romero's assassination, and six weeks after D'Aubuisson's brief arrest, the Salvadoran Anticommunist Army detonated two bombs at the UCA, destroying the printing press and a student center. On October 24, two powerful bombs exploded at the residence of Fr. Ella-

---

46. Ibid., 129 (§399).
47. Ibid., 131 (§415).
48. Ibid., 135 (§424).

curía, where ten Jesuits were sleeping. On October 27, the residence was bombed again, becoming uninhabitable. And on November 26, Ellacuría sought refuge in the Spanish embassy, fleeing the next day for a seventeen-month exile after a tip from Captain Francisco Mena Sandoval, one of the plotters of the reformist Young Officers Coup, warning that the Jesuit would be assassinated that night.[49] Thus, the decade began with the same sterile logic of state-sponsored violence against political opponents in civil society with which it would end.

### Revolution or Death! Civil War in Defense of the People

After the Junta collapsed, events in El Salvador accelerated rapidly toward war. On January 22, 1980, guards and snipers fired from the roof of the National Palace, killing between twenty and fifty-two civilians gathered in the national square for the largest demonstration in Salvadoran history.[50] On February 8, 1980, the second junta said it would recognize the Constitution of 1962 only "where it was compatible" with the rulers' "line of government."[51] In mid-month Roberto D'Aubuisson publicly accused Mario Zamora Rivas, leader of the Christian Democratic Party and attorney general of El Salvador, of being a communist and a member of "a revolutionary group, the FPL." The U.N. Truth Commission states that a few days later, on February 23, 1980, six "members of a state security force" in ski masks entered Mr. Zamora's home through the roof carrying weapons with silencers, and executed him in the bathroom." The Commission adds that the Military High Command worked "to conceal the identity of the perpetrators . . . with the result that the necessary investigation was never made."[52]

On March 6, 1980, a national state of emergency was declared suspending significant legal rights and protections. Though it had to be renewed every thirty days, the emergency would continue (with one brief interlude) for seven years! And in March 1980, most of the remaining civilians resigned from the government. The collapse of this "second" junta put the military completely in control of the government and foreclosed participation from the center and the left. Then, at the behest of U.S. advisors, on March 9, 1980, University of Notre Dame graduate José Napoleon Duarte agreed to represent the Christian Democrats on the junta, ostensibly because "the objective" of Zamora's murder had been "to force us out of the government, [and] we were determined not to let them succeed."[53] This provided the Salvadoran military and the U.S. govern-

---

49. Doggett, *Death Foretold*, 304; also Beirne, *Jesuit Education and Social Change*, 165.

50. "Central America 1980: Nicaragua, El Salvador, Guatemala," 18; *Amnesty International Annual Report*, 1980, 134. Cited in Americas Watch, *El Salvador's Decade of Terror: Human Rights since the Assassination of Archbishop Romero* (New Haven: Yale University Press, 1991), 8.

51. Decree 144, Article 1. Cited in America's Watch, *Decade of Terror*, 8.

52. United Nations, *Report of the Commission on the Truth for El Salvador*, 140, 141.

53. José Napoleon Duarte, *My Story* (New York: G.P. Putnam's Sons, 1986), 113-15; cited in Montgomery, *Revolution in El Salvador*, 136.

ment with political cover for Washington's increasing financial and logistical support. The new government lasted two years, until March 28, 1982, when Roberto D'Aubuisson was elected president of the National Assembly after the United States brokered a deal to keep him from being appointed provisional president by the military-related party, ARENA, which had formed a coalition of parties to achieve plurality with him as their candidate.

In April 1980, Guillermo Ungo, Duarte's running mate in the infamous 1972 election, which the UCA showed had been stolen by Colonel Molina, led to the unification of many former government officials, civilian political groups, nonaligned trade unions, and professional organizations in the formation of the Democratic Front (FD). The group negotiated a common platform with the Revolutionary Coordinator of the Masses and formed the Democratic Revolutionary Front (FDR). The FDR then began to function as the political branch of the armed revolutionary opposition. Finally on October 10, 1980, the various revolutionary organizations united to form the FMLN.[54]

The political space for reform and opposition had almost completely collapsed. Following the resignation of the first junta, *ECA* published a statement from the university superior counsel recognizing the sad state of affairs.

> The important thing is to notice that a group of capable and honest people, after placing all their dreams and their talents at the service of profound reforms, became witnesses to the impossibility of accomplishing this goal in a society in which opponents of change hold sway, and when the process is headed by armed forces whose institutional, historical and psycho-social characteristics have rendered them incapable of defending the real interests of the popular masses.[55]

Ellacuría's editorial in the March 1980 edition of *ECA* provisionally endorsed the FDR's political platform. Noting certain "grave difficulties," it concluded, "After examining as a totality all objective and subjective conditions, those favorable and unfavorable, and in the light of the experience of the centrist solution of these past six months, it is not unreasonable to affirm that the FDR, from the political point of view, offers better prospects as a new national project which might lift the country from its current desperate situation."[56] The September 1980 editorial conceded the inevitability of civil war and appealed to both sides to act in a humane manner.[57]

Finally on January 10, 1981, the FMLN launched its long-expected "final offensive." It came almost exactly a year after the January 3, 1980, resignations of Mayorga and Ungo, and the failure of the "UCA coup." The FDR had prepared for the offensive by calling two general strikes the year before. The first on June 24-25, 1980, virtually shut down the country for forty-eight hours. The

---

54. Montgomery, *Revolution in El Salvador,* 110, 101-26.
55. *ECA* 35 (January-February 1980): 5-18.
56. *ECA* 35 (March 1980): 172.
57. *ECA* 35 (September 1980): 793-98.

second strike was called on August 13-15, 1980, in order to mobilize and test the organizational structure for a general insurrection.[58] Three levels were examined: guerrilla units oriented to armed combat; civilian militias composed of peasants and workers for civilian self-defense, vigilance, and military engineering; and neighborhood committees with responsibility for supplies, logistical support, and grassroots political education.[59] Preparations for the offensive had begun three months before when the FMLN was officially formed on October 10, 1980.

At 6:30 p.m. on January 10, 1981, guerrilla units took control of several radio stations in San Salvador and broadcast the call of Salvador Cayetano Carpio for a general insurrection, which the FMLN General Command was convinced would follow.

> The hour to initiate the decisive military and insurrectional battles for the taking of power by the people and for the constitution of the democratic revolutionary government has arrived. We call on all the people to rise up as one person, with all the means of combat, under the orders of their immediate leaders on all war fronts and throughout the national territory. The definitive triumph is in the hands of this heroic people. . . . Revolution or death. We will triumph! [*Revolución o muerte. Venceremos!*][60]

During the first forty-eight hours, the FMLN commandeered the military base at San Francisco Gotera in Morazán, where Captain Mena Sandoval, who helped plan the 1979 reformist coup and warned Ellacuría of his impending assassination, with another officer led eighty soldiers from the Second Brigade at Santa Ana to join the revolt. Mark Danner explains that Mena Sandoval proved to be an important asset in a series of battles in the following weeks with the elite Atlactl Battalion, perpetrators of the 1989 UCA murders, because he "had the foresight to steal an Army radio when he came over to the guerrillas." Mena Sandoval's "knowledge of the enemy's codes" allowed the rebels "to keep one crucial step ahead of their opponents," and to inflict casualties while avoiding capture and losses.[61]

But while some like Mena Sandoval and his colleagues interpreted the demand of Archbishop Romero a year earlier to "stop the repression!" as a call to join the rebels, the promised "general insurrection" did not occur. The Salvadoran armed forces retained control of the capital and many other areas

---

58. Adolfo Gilly, "Experiencias y conquistas de una huelga limite," *Uno más Uno*, August 21, 1980. Cited in Montgomery, *Revolution in El Salvador,* 112.

59. See "En los Cerros de San Pedro el FMLN construye el poder popular," *Venceremos* 1, no. 2 (January 1982): 8. Also Montgomery, *Revolution in El Salvador,* 111-13.

60. Press release, *SALPRESS*, Mexico City, January 12, 1981. Cited in Montgomery, *Revolution in El Salvador,* 112.

61. Mark Danner, "The Truth of El Mozote," *The New Yorker*, December 6, 1993, http://www.markdanner.com/articles/print/127; accessed August 16, 2011.

while the FMLN retreated to its home bases in the north and the east of the country.[62] As a result, it soon became clear that the government would not fall anytime soon, and that the FMLN had no unified plan and insufficient coordination for waging a sustained war. Thus, judged as a "final" effort, the offensive failed to achieve its objective of a Nicaraguan-style overthrow of a repressive regime. Instead, the government and the FMLN seemed destined for a long and bloody civil war.

Captain Mena Sandoval, however, and his colleagues provide a dramatic contrast to the Atlacatl Battalion, who Danner reveals "had been trained, in large part by . . . Mena Sandoval" at the San Francisco Gotera Commando Center not long before the offensive. Sadly, eight months after the aforementioned exchange, the U.N. Truth Commission reported that the Atlacatl Battalion committed one of the worst human rights atrocities of the decade in the village of El Mozote, Morazán.[63] The report offered the following facts: "On December 10, 1981, in the village of El Mozote . . . Morazan, . . . the Atlacatl Battalion detained, without resistance, all the men, women and children who were in the place. The following day, December 11, . . . they were deliberately and systematically executed . . . over 200. The figure is higher . . . [with] unidentified victims."[64]

The report continues:

> During the morning, they [the troops] proceeded to interrogate, torture and execute the men in various locations. Around noon, they began taking out the women in groups, separating them from their children and machine-gunning them. Finally they killed the children. A group of children who had been locked in the convent were machine-gunned through the windows. After exterminating the entire population, the soldiers set fire to the buildings.[65]

The massacre was planned as part of a larger operation involving other military units entitled "Operation Rescate,"[66] which perpetrated over a period of days similar slaughters of women and children in the surrounding villages of La Joya, La Rancheria, Los Toriles, Jocote Amarillo, and Cerro Pando. The United Nations states that the Armed Forces High Command of El Salvador then "repeatedly denied the massacre occurred" while its own chief of staff, who "was aware that the massacre had occurred, . . . failed to undertake any investigation."[67]

---

62. These details from Montgomery, *Revolution in El Salvador,* 112, 113.

63. United Nations, *Report of the Commission on the Truth for El Salvador,* 114-21, esp. 114.

64. Ibid., 114.

65. Ibid., 115.

66. Ibid.

67. Ibid., 121.

Thus, with all other avenues seemingly closed, the words of Archbishop Romero to the journalist José Calderón Salazar two weeks before the prelate's assassination epitomized the flickering hopes of those committed to the church's vision of reform through the mobilization and renewal of Salvadoran civil society.

> I have often been threatened with death. [But] I must tell you, as a Christian, I do not believe in death without resurrection. If I am killed, I shall arise in the Salvadoran people. I say so without boasting, with the greatest humility.
>
> As a shepherd, I am obliged by divine mandate to give my life for those I love—for all Salvadorans, even for those who may be going to kill me. If the threats are carried out, from this moment I offer my blood to God for the redemption and for the resurrection of El Salvador.
>
> Martyrdom is a grace of God that I do not believe I deserve. But if God accepts the sacrifice of my life, let my blood be a seed of freedom and the sign that hope will soon be reality. Let my death, if it is accepted by God, be for my people's liberation and as a witness of hope in the future.
>
> You may say, if they succeed in killing me, that I pardon and bless those who do it. Would, indeed, that they might be convinced that they will waste their time. A bishop will die, but God's church, which is the people, will never perish.[68]

Sadly, what some see as the fulfillment of Romero's prophecy that he would rise in the Salvadoran people would be preceded by another decade of murder and grievous persecution against Salvadoran civil society.

### Hypocrisy and Failure:
### U.S. "Nation Building" in El Salvador

Four days after launching its general offensive, the FDR–FMLN announced the formation of a Political-Diplomatic Commission, implementing its plan to be recognized by the government as a "representative political force"[69] for peace negotiations. At this point the conflict was still essentially a local matter, and at least some of the combatants recognized the futility of an extended war. But the United States had a different view.

---

68. James R. Brockman, *Romero, A Life* (Maryknoll, NY: Orbis Books, 1989, 2005), 247-48.

69. This was the term used in the Mexican-French proposal for peace negotiations immediately after the offensive. See Ignacio Ellacuría, "La declaración conjunta mexicano-francesa sobre El Salvador," *ECA* 36, no. 395 (April-May 1981): 845-66. Reprinted in Ignacio Ellacuría, *Veinte años de historia en El Salvador (1969-1989): Escritos políticos* (San Salvador: UCA Editores, 1991), 1235-69.

In 1977 a State Department official testified to Congress that the United States had "no strategic interests" in El Salvador.[70] However, the July 19, 1979, triumph of the Sandinistas in the Nicaraguan revolution led the United States to view developments in El Salvador through a Cold War lens. Thus, four days after the beginning of the FMLN offensive the Carter administration reinstated military aid, increasing it again on January 17 with a pledge to "support the Salvadoran Government in its struggle against left-wing terrorism supported covertly . . . by Cuba and other Communist nations."[71] In 1982 the new Reagan administration targeted the FMLN insurgency as the most important Cold War conflict since Vietnam, announcing the United States would "draw the line" in El Salvador against "communist aggression"[72] with an ambitious counterinsurgency campaign. Thus, the explicit goal of successive Republican administrations during the 1980s became the military defeat of the FMLN.

A 1991 report prepared by the Rand Corporation for the Pentagon ["Pentagon Report"] explains that the Reagan administration saw the Salvadoran civil war as the "ideal testing ground"[73] for post-Vietnam "low-intensity conflict doctrine."[74] The official U.S. Army/Air Force statement on counterinsurgency stated that low-intensity conflict comprised "the full range of measures taken by a nation to promote its growth and to protect itself from subversion, lawlessness, and insurgency. The strategy focuses on building viable political, economic, military and social institutions that respond to the needs of society."[75] The report notes with some cynicism that the strategy was known as "nation building."

The seriousness of U.S. involvement in this "experiment" is reflected in the financial commitment it entailed. The Pentagon report states,

> The conflict there has been the most expensive American effort to save an ally from an insurgency since Vietnam. El Salvador has absorbed at

---

70. U.S. Congress, House of Representatives, Committee on International Relations, Subcommittee on International Organizations, the Recent Presidential Elections in El Salvador: Implications for U.S. Policy. Hearings, March 9 and 17, 1977, 95th Congress, 1st Session (Washington, DC: Government Printing Office, 1977), 15. Cited in America's Watch, *El Salvador's Decade of Terror,* 177.

71. U.S. Department of State, Press Statement, January 17, 1981, 1, cited in Cynthia Arnson, *Crossroads: Congress, the President, and Central America: 1976-1993* (University Park, PA: Pennsylvania State University Press, 1993), 51.

72. William LeoGrande, "A Splendid Little War: Drawing the Line in El Salvador," *International Security* 6, no. 1 (Summer 1981): 27; Lou Cannon, *President Reagan: The Role of a Lifetime* (New York: Simon & Schuster, 1991), 344.

73. Lewis Tambs and Lt. Com. Frank Aker, "Shattering the Vietnam Syndrome: A Scenario for Success in El Salvador," unpublished manuscript, 11. Cited in Michael Klare and Peter Kornbluh, eds., *Low Intensity Warfare: Counterinsurgency, Proinsurgency and Antiterrorism in the Eighties* (New York: Random House, 1988), 112.

74. Schwarz, *American Counterinsurgency Doctrine and El Salvador,* 1.

75. Headquarters, Department of the Army, Department of the Air Force, *Military Operation in Low Intensity Conflict,* FM 100-20/AFM 2-X4, Final Draft, June 24, 1988 (1988), 2.14-2.15. Cited in Schwarz, *American Counterinsurgency Doctrine and El Salvador,* 7.

least $4.5 billion, over $1 billion of which is in military aid. When combined with over $850 million in unsubsidized credits and an estimated CIA investment of over $500 million, the total expenditure approaches $6 billion. Only five countries receive more American aid each year than El Salvador, a nation of 5.3 million people.[76]

But every war needs a public rationale, and this one found its classic statement in the January 10, 1984, report of the National Bipartisan Commission on Central America chaired by Henry Kissinger, former secretary of state under Richard Nixon.[77] The Pentagon study says the Kissinger Commission committed itself to a thorough application of counterinsurgency doctrine in El Salvador, marking the first time "a comprehensive strategy for meeting the threat of instability and insurgency in the Third World had been given the status of national policy."[78]

Designed as a lofty apologetic for the application of U.S counterinsurgency policy in El Salvador, the Kissinger Commission stated that increases in military aid would

> be made contingent upon the Salvadoran government's demonstrated progress toward free elections; freedom of association; the establishment of the rule of law and an effective judicial system; and the termination of the so-called death squads, as well as vigorous action against those guilty of crimes and the prosecution to the extent possible of past offenders.[79]

The Pentagon report asserts, however, that Kissinger and his co-authors rendered these claims meaningless with an endnote, "which declared, in effect, that since the survival of the Salvadoran regime was crucial to American security, the United States could not allow human rights abuse to stand in the way of its support of El Salvador."[80] This line of reasoning would insure U.S. support for a decade of murder and sorrow in El Salvador, driven by the underlying demands of U.S. Cold War electoral politics.

The U.N. Truth Commission outlines the real-life implications of this approach, offering the infamous El Mozote massacre carried out by the U.S. trained Atlacatl Battalion as an example of its impact on U.S. counterinsurgency

76. Schwarz, *American Counterinsurgency Doctrine and El Salvador*, 2.

77. National Bipartisan Commission on Central America, *Report of the National Bipartisan Commission on Central America* (January 10, 1984). Cited in Schwarz, *American Counterinsurgency Doctrine and El Salvador*, 10-11.

78. Schwarz, *American Counterinsurgency Doctrine and El Salvador*, 11. The quotation is a citation from Christopher M. Helman, "Protracted Insurgent Warfare: Development of an Appropriate U.S. Doctrine," in Richard H. Schultz, et al. (eds.), *Guerrilla Warfare and Counterinsurgency: U.S.-Soviet Policy in the Third World* (Lexington, MA: Lexington Books, 1989), 127.

79. National Bipartisan Commission, *Report*, 102.

80. Schwarz, *American Counterinsurgency Doctrine and El Salvador*, 12. For the statement in question see National Bipartisan Commission, *Report*, 130.

policy in El Salvador. The United Nations explains that the Atlacatl Battalion was a Rapid Deployment Infantry Battalion (BIRI) "specially trained for counter-insurgency warfare." In fact, "It was the first unit of its kind in the armed forces and had [just] completed its training, under the supervision of United States military advisers, at the beginning of that year, 1981."[81] The United Nations warns, however, that the massacre should not be misunderstood as a wartime aberration or divergence quickly corrected by U.S. trainers, but rather as indicative of a pattern of serious human rights violations by a U.S. trained battalion that spanned the decade, including 1989 murders of UCA martyrs.

The Pentagon report is even more insistent on this point.

> The very battalion whose members murdered the Jesuits had been created, trained, and equipped by the United States; it was, indeed, the first Salvadoran battalion designed to serve as a model of a clean efficient weapon in the fight against the FMLN.[82] The Atlacatl Battalion has had a particularly ferocious history, massacring [over 200] peasants in El Mozote in 1981, killing dozens of villagers from Tenancingo and Copapayo in 1983, and slaughtering 68 in the hamlet of Los Llanitos and 50 at the Gualsinga River in 1984.[83]

Indeed, the Atlacatl Battalion would interrupt a 1989 training session with U.S. advisors in order to carry out the UCA assassinations, but we will say more about that later. Thus, the Pentagon report insists that the activities of the battalion must be understood as an element of U.S. counterinsurgency policy in El Salvador. This is particularly disturbing in light of the U.N. report that in the convent where the soldiers locked the children, "143 bodies were identified, including 131 children under the age of 12 [whose] . . . average age . . . was . . . six." The United Nations adds that they were all murdered with "United States-

---

81. National Bipartisan Commission, *Report,* 116.

82. FMLN is an acronym for the Farabundo Martí National Liberation Front. It was officially formed on October 10, 1980, when several of the most important political-military organizations working to overthrow the government of El Salvador united under its banner (the following five organizations would eventually constitute the FMLN). In 1970 the first of what would become the five political-military organizations constituting the FMLN was founded when Salvador Cayentano Carpio resigned from the Communist Party of El Salvador (PCS), went underground, and founded the Popular Forces of Liberation (FPL). In 1972 the Revolutionary Army of the People (ERP) also emerged from the Communist Party with a different, younger, and more diverse constituency. In 1975 the Armed Forces of the National Resistance (FARN) was formed by a group that left the ERP when a hard-line faction assassinated Roque Dalton, El Salvador's most important living poet (then a member of the ERP), ostensibly because of his insistence on the need to emphasize political as well as military revolutionary activities. The following year, on January 26, 1976, the Revolutionary Party of Central American Workers (PRTC) was founded during a congress of union workers, individuals who had left the group that founded the ERP in 1972, and others. Finally, in 1979, the PCS itself formed the Armed Forces of Liberation (FAL).

83. Schwarz, *American Counterinsurgency Doctrine and El Salvador,* 35-36.

manufactured M-16 rifles," firing ammunition "manufactured for the United States Government at Lake City, Missouri."[84]

In what follows I will briefly summarize the Pentagon report's evaluation of the three defining aspects of U.S. counterinsurgency doctrine in El Salvador: (1) military reform; (2) land reform, and (3) political reform.

## The Failure of Military Reform

The analysis begins with an illuminating post-mortem of the failure of Salvadoran military reform in light of the supposed twin pillars of U.S. counterinsurgency policy: military effectiveness (or "tactical performance") and human rights.[85]

It notes that the 1981 "Report of the El Salvador Military Strategy Assistance Team," written a decade earlier, concluded that the Salvadoran armed forces would require a thorough restructuring in order to carry out U.S. policy on counterinsurgency war. The list of undesirable characteristics included a disengaged officer corps; a "nine-to-five, five-day-a week" force mired in a "garrison [bound] mentality"; forced service by conscripts (as young as fourteen) with little will to fight; excessive reliance on long-distance firepower and helicopters rather than on ground troops for holding territory; and a highly motivated enemy. In light of this shortcoming, U.S. advisors proposed the creation of "hunter-killer" squads, "imaginative psychological warfare," and the resurrection of "civil defense units."[86]

In the following decade, however, U.S. advisors found Salvadoran military forces "stubbornly resistant to change" for a variety of reasons. First, the "tanda" system, in which each graduating class from the military academy moved up together through the ranks proved to be a major obstacle. U.S. advisors quickly discovered that the Salvadoran military "operated not through a clear chain of command but through a complex system of consensus within and between tandas." Described as "a sort of West Point Protective Association gone berserk"[87] in another influential 1988 Pentagon study known as the *Colonels Report*, class members shielded one another from prosecution and punishment during the 1980s for even the most egregious of human rights violations. A 1990 report by the Congressional Arms Control and Foreign Policy Caucus noted the pervasive influence of this system:

---

84. United Nations, *Report of the Commission on the Truth for El Salvador,* 117 (§354), 118 (§357), 119 (§366).

85. Schwarz, *American Counterinsurgency Doctrine and El Salvador;* see especially "The Effort to Transform El Salvador: Military Reform," 17-43.

86. Ibid., 17-18.

87. A.J. Bacevich, James D. Hallums, Richard H. White, and Thomas F. Young, *American Military Policy in Small Wars: The Case of El Salvador* (Washington, DC: Pergamum, Brassey's International Defense Publishers, 1988), 26. Cited in Americas Watch, *El Salvador's Decade of Terror,* 21.

> Of the 15 primary commanders [of the Salvadoran armed forces], 12 are members of the Tandona . . . [of] 1966. . . . This unprecedented concentration of power permits the Tandona to protect its members from removal for corruption, abuses or incompetence. The Tandona at times shows more loyalty to its members than to the rule of law or even to the president.[88]

The same report found that fourteen of the fifteen highest-ranking army officers in May 1990 had commanded troops who committed atrocities at some point during their careers.[89]

Second, the Pentagon report finds the 1980s' Salvadoran military rife with "self-serving interests and . . . institutional barriers" to advancement for those who did not enter through the military academy. Citing a "tradition that views the structure of the armed forces as comprising only a commissioned officer elite and peasant conscripts who serve it,"[90] it says this attitude was reinforced by institutional corruption in which officers embezzled the salaries of non-existent conscripts.

> Every year 20,000 pay slots for soldiers are divided among the Salvadoran Army's regional commanders. Since the Salvadoran armed forces have no central roster and hence no way to detect fraud, most commanders fill a portion of these slots with nonexistent soldiers, collecting the "ghost soldier" salaries themselves. Brigades generally have at least one 50-man "ghost" company that brings the brigade commander $60,000 annually. The salary of a re-enlistee is nearly double that of a conscript. Imaginary re-enlistees are therefore quite profitable to an individual commander, and many actively discourage genuine re-enlistment because it would cut into their ghost soldier profits.[91]

Compounding the problem, a portion of every soldier's salary was matched by the Salvadoran government and paid into the armed forces' social security fund. At $150 million, this fund constituted the largest source of liquid capital in the country in 1991, allowing the military to maintain their own commercial bank and investment portfolio. However, though all contribute to the fund, "the only members of the armed forces eligible to receive these benefits are officers and a very small number of re-enlistees."[92]

Third, the Pentagon study cites "corrupt and ubiquitous practices [such] as commanders selling goods at inflated prices to their men, siphoning funds from

---

88. Arms Control and Foreign Policy Caucus, "Barrier to Reform: A Profile of El Salvador's Military Leaders," May 21, 1990, 2. Cited in Americas Watch, *El Salvador's Decade of Terror*, 21.

89. Ibid.

90. Schwarz, *American Counterinsurgency Doctrine and El Salvador*, "The Effort to Transform El Salvador," 19. He is citing Bracevich et al., *American Military Policy*, 27-28

91. Ibid.

92. Ibid., 20.

food and clothing budgets, and leasing their troops as guards and laborers to landowners and businessmen."[93] The report notes, "Many officers have detailed knowledge of each others' questionable financial activities and can use this information to blackmail those officers who might otherwise . . . bring human rights abusers to justice."[94]

Fourth, the report draws the devastating conclusion that "the Salvadoran military does not wish to win the war because in so doing it would lose the American aid that has enriched it for the past decade."[95] It notes that when the United States began pouring more than a million dollars a day into El Salvador and quintupled[96] the size of the army between 1980 and 1987, the opportunities for self-enrichment multiplied. To appreciate the institutional momentum toward insularity and corruption created by U.S. intervention, consider the incredible reach into civilian society attained during the 1980s by military owned financial institutions (all ending in "FA") including: the Armed Forces Mutual Savings Bank (CAMFA), a press and propaganda office (COPREFA), a chain of drugstores (CEFAFA), a supermarket and department story (COOPFA), an electronics center (CITFA), a mortuary (FUDEFA), and a rehabilitation and job placement center for disabled veterans (CERPROFA).[97] Accordingly, the report concludes that outdated structures, corruption, brutal human rights practices, and incredible wealth generated by U.S. aid helped to create (1) a closed, insular, apparently unreformable culture; and (2) an institutional self-interest on the part of the Salvadoran military leadership in the indefinite continuation of a brutal civil war.

## Cynicism and Deceit

The Pentagon report predictably states that U.S counterinsurgency policy promoted respect for human rights as a sine qua non for gaining popular support and government legitimacy. However, it notes that U.S. counterinsurgency expert Colonel John Waghelstein characteristically subordinated such U.S. values to strategic concerns when he argued, "the only territory you want to hold is the six inches between the ears of the campesino."[98] And the report frankly concedes that efforts to promote human rights were frustrated throughout the decade by "the military's killing and brutalizing of civilians."[99]

The real-life meaning of this statement, and the absurdity of trying to win "hearts and minds" through brutal repression, is well illustrated by the story

93. Ibid.

94. Ibid., 21.

95. Ibid.

96. Montgomery, *Revolution in El Salvador*, 199.

97. The information in this sentence is from Montgomery, *Revolution in El Salvador*, 199-200.

98. Speech by Colonel John Waghelstein, "LIC in the Post-Vietnam Period" (American Enterprise Institute: January 17, 1985). Cited in Schwarz, *American Counterinsurgency Doctrine and El Salvador*, 22.

99. Schwarz, *American Counterinsurgency Doctrine and El Salvador*, 24.

of Rosa Marina Zavala and her family, rural peasants from the village of Santa Marta, El Salvador.[100] About 5:00 in the afternoon March 17, 1981, the deafening sound of exploding bombs and bullets filled the streets as Marina (age 24), her future husband, José Antonio (age 28), and thousands of terrorized men, women and children grabbed whatever they could and fled.

The situation in the countryside was desperate. The U.N. Commission provides the historical context: "During the years 1980, 1981 and 1982 [the U.S. backed Salvadoran government carried out] . . . mass executions . . . in which members of the armed forces, in the course of anti-guerilla operations, executed peasants—men, women and children who had offered no resistance—simply because they considered them to be guerrilla collaborators."[101] An adaptation of U.S. counterinsurgency tactics from the Vietnam War, it was part of "a deliberate strategy of eliminating or terrifying the peasant population in [order] . . . to deprive the guerrilla forces of . . . supplies and information and of the possibility of hiding. . . ."[102]

The Pentagon report explains that rural pressures for land reform had reached critical mass by the beginning of 1980, driven by the fact that "over 70% of the land was owned by only 1% of the population, while over 40% of the rural population owned no land at all and worked as sharecroppers on absentee owners' land or as laborers on large estates."[103] Norberto, a peasant farm worker, remembers, "We would go to the coffee plantations, . . . to the cotton plantations and . . . the sugar cane fields," but "the wages were unfair . . . and our children were naked."[104] Eventually, he recalls, "the people got organized and said, 'Now we are going to protest,' . . . but they answered us with death, and a great repression."

By 1981 peasants like Marina and her family knew exactly what this meant. Thus, she recalls, "The Salvadoran army invaded Santa Marta, so we fled with most of the village on foot." Their plan was to sneak with thousands of terrified neighbors through the deadly cordon encircling and bombarding the town, and to flee north with whatever they could carry in hopes of crossing the Lempa River and finding refuge in Honduras. Normally a two-and-a-half-hour walk, Marina says that it took hours and hours because of "pregnant women with

---

100. This account and all quotes unless otherwise noted are from José Antonio Zavala and Rosa Marina Zavala, interview by author, June 24, 2010, Pittsburg, CA, transcript, files of author; and José Antonio Zavala and Rosa Marina Zavala, interview by Marybeth, 1990, Oakland Catholic Worker, transcript, files of author. U.S. federal immigration judge Bernard J. Hornbach of the Ninth Circuit Court of Appeals granted political asylum to José Antonio Zavala and seven other family members on January 31, 1990, based on an expanded version this account and supporting documentation.

101. United Nations, *Report of the Commission on the Truth for El Salvador*, 126.

102. Ibid.

103. Schwarz, *American Counterinsurgency Doctrine and El Salvador*, 44.

104. "Norberto, Mesa Grande," in Renato Camarda, *Forced to Move: Salvadorean Refugees in Honduras* (foreword Ronald V. Dellums; San Francisco: Solidarity Publications, 1985), 8.

swollen stomachs, small children, old people, and people who were injured or sick on stretchers." To avoid being heard, mothers squeezed crying children so tightly to their chests that some were asphyxiated. Thousands of peasants joined the march from other villages similarly under attack so that, "When we reached the Lempa River we were about 11,000 people."

José Antonio describes what happened next. "We got to the river at about 11:00 that night. Most of the people did not know how to swim, so we looked for tires, boards, or whatever could serve as a raft." Since he knew "a little bit" how to swim, José Antonio grabbed a branch and began swimming back and forth, ferrying frantic riders across the river. "By 3:00 in the morning I couldn't take it anymore," he recalls, but thousands more continued their desperate attempts to cross.

> A rope had been stretched across the river so that the people could grab it and try to make it over. Many people entered the river carrying children on their shoulders, using their hands to hold the few things they had brought. This worked fine until they got to the middle where it was too deep to stand and the weight made them drown, including the children. Sometimes we were able to save one or two who could swim a bit, but many disappeared. At about 6:00 in the morning when the Salvadoran and Honduran armies woke up they came to the high ground on either side of the river and began throwing grenades and firing machine guns at the people crossing in the water. A terrible cry filled the air. The bullets fell on the water like rain.[105]

Everyone ran for cover, dragging bloody and dying relatives under rocks and whatever cover they could find. José Antonio has a vivid memory of when the firing started, "I carried Marina's little brother, Adán, on my last trip across the river. When we reached the middle a mortar fell on the river bank we had just left, and we saw a mother and her child blown to pieces. Adán panicked and tried to break free, but I wouldn't let go until we got to the other shore and were able to hide in the underbrush." Rosario, a young eighteen-year-old mother, was not so lucky,

> It was a massacre. . . . They shot my baby in my arms and wanted me to fall into the river and be swept away in the current just like those five hundred who were swept away at the Sumpul River massacre. I carried my baby through the long hike to Los Hernández [two miles away]. All the while I was thinking, "I can't bear this." The women had to forcibly take her out of my arms that night and I watched them bury her just as she was, wrapped in a cloth.[106]

---

105. Ibid. For photographs of the crossing, an asphyxiated child with her grieving father, the flight to the refugee camps, and other firsthand accounts of the massacre, see Camarda, *Forced to Move*, esp. 18-21.

106. Yvonne Dilling, "Suffering Together at Valle Nuevo," Center for Christian

Remembering their near escape, José Antonio concluded, "Maybe God helped me." Marina reflected, "I prayed to the Virgin, I believed she would save us. They were firing bullets that just missed our heads. It was a miracle. We should have died that day. I felt that the Virgin was protecting me with a covering. I could feel the bullets flying on either side of my head."

Marina and José Antonio survived and were eventually forced to move to the Mesa Grande United Nations refugee camp, where they lived as refugees in very poor conditions for most of seven years. They were married there by Archbishop Rivera Damas of El Salvador, who succeeded Archbishop Romero after his assassination by Roberto D'Aubuisson, intent on silencing his protests against the repression. Marina and José Antonio had four children in the camp, Oscar, Elmer, Elsi, and Wil, and finally returned to their village in El Salvador in December 1987 with thousands of other refugees over protests from the military. But the U.S.-backed war was raging, and campesinos living in areas controlled by the rebels were still considered enemy collaborators. Marina recalls, "The army was killing many of the people who had returned from Honduras. And the civilian paramilitary groups would kill people, cut off the head, and bring it to military where they would receive extra points. They did this to Danielito Rivera, the husband of my cousin, Carmela Zavala."

Knowing they were certainly next, José Antonio and his cousin Chepe, a church worker who had been captured and tortured, found a *coyote* and immigrated illegally to the United States. Both were captured by the border patrol on January 31, 1987, and signed claims for political asylum, which were eventually granted nine years later. The moment of decision arrived for Marina and the children in mid-1988. "The area commander came to my mother's house and told her he was going to kill all of us. He said we had come from Honduras and that we were all guerrillas." Marina immediately wrote to José Antonio who recalls, "I was really concerned when I heard what had happened, and realized that the only way I would ever see Marina and the children alive was if they fled to the U.S." They arrived with the help of human rights workers in December 1988.

In 1989, a former high-ranking State Department official commented with some cynicism that the Salvadoran armed forces have "always found it a lot easier to kill labor leaders than guerrillas."[107] This assessment was sadly reflective of the 1983 evaluation offered by U.S. Army Major Victor Rosello of the Salvadoran military's "National Plan" to win hearts and minds:

> Any gains made by the National Plan are quickly offset by government linked or sponsored repression. Even if one were to assume that the government officials are not involved in unlawful detentions, arrests,

Ethics at Baylor University (Copyright © 2005), http://www.baylor.edu/christianethics/SufferingarticleDilling.pdf.

107. Interview with unnamed former high-ranking State Department official by Benjamin C. Schwarz, November 1989. Cited in Schwarz, *American Counterinsurgency Doctrine and El Salvador*, 25.

> tortures, or murders, the success of counterinsurgency is threatened
> by the fact that the government . . . cannot guarantee public safety. . . .
> It is ludicrous to sponsor a counterinsurgency program under these
> conditions.[108]

Indeed, in light of the record, it is difficult to avoid the conclusion that the supposed emphasis of U.S. counterinsurgency doctrine in El Salvador amounted to a secondary concern (at best), or simply propaganda.

As we saw, the 1984 the Kissinger Commission report recommended military aid be "conditioned" on the "establishment of a rule of law and an effective judicial system."[109] Accordingly, shortly after his inauguration in 1984 President José Napoleon Duarte formed a U.S.-financed team to investigate the 1980 murder of Archbishop Romero; the 1981 "Sheraton Murders" of two U.S. labor advisors and the head of El Salvador's agrarian land reform program; two peasant massacres; and the 1980 killing of a U.S. journalist. The report notes, however, that the commission was disbanded fifteen months later "without having achieved any of its objectives."[110] In 1985 another commission was formed that added several other cases of political violence to the previous commission's mandate. The Pentagon report notes, however, "Despite $15 million in American aid for this body . . . six years later none of the cases with which they have been concerned has been adequately resolved, and the commission has forgone investigations of human rights abuses, focusing instead on common crimes."[111]

The report then offers a stunning list of judicial failures to effectively prosecute outrageous military crimes:[112] (1) a kidnap-for-profit ring cracked by the F.B.I. during 1986 in which death squads posed as leftist rebels while abducting the nation's wealthiest businessmen; (2) the 1987 political amnesty law that liberated two enlisted men convicted for the Sheraton murders, and effectively pardoned "tens of thousands of human rights violations";[113] (3) the September 1988 massacre of peasants living in the village of San Sebastian; (4) the 1988 ruling by the Salvadoran Supreme Court that dismissed testimony considered "convincing" by U.S. diplomats implicating ex-Major Roberto D'Aubuisson of the murder of Archbishop Romero; and (5) the November 16, 1989, murder of the UCA Jesuits and the two women by the Atlacatl Battalion.[114] After review-

---

108. Major Victor Rosello, "An Assessment of the National Campaign Plan for El Salvador: Planning for Success or Failure?" DTIC AD-A139932 (unpublished M.A. thesis, University of Chicago, March 1984), 49. Cited in Schwarz, *American Counterinsurgency Doctrine and El Salvador*, 25.

109. National Bipartisan Commission, *Report*, 104.

110. Schwarz, *American Counterinsurgency Doctrine and El Salvador*, 26.

111. Ibid., 26-27.

112. Ibid., 27.

113. The United Nations Truth Commission charges that the UCA assassinations were ordered by the chief of staff of the El Salvadoran Military High Command in collusion with other members of the high command. United Nations, *Report of the Commission on the Truth for El Salvador*, 53.

114. Schwarz, *American Counterinsurgency Doctrine and El Salvador*, 25-35.

ing this atrocious list, the report arrives at the following unavoidable and certainly understated conclusion:

> Attempts to investigate and punish human rights abuses have been blocked by the armed forces, death squads linked to those forces, and a rightist-dominated court system and legislature. Such obstacles . . . are certainly counterproductive to an effort to win hearts and minds. The conviction of only two officers, in a situation in which up to 40,000 political murders have been attributed to the armed forces and death squads operating with or by them, constitutes a violation of the state's obligation to investigate, prosecute, and punish crimes, particularly those committed by its agents.[115]

One wonders, then, why U.S. funding for this barbarity continued. The report notes (with some irony) that "forgetting that between 1965 and 1977 the United States had trained the majority of the Salvadoran officer corps and that it was precisely these officers who carried out the worst bloodletting in Central American history," the 1984 Kissinger Commission had nonetheless portrayed the brutality of the Salvadoran armed forces as a "technical problem of inadequate training."[116] The 1991 Pentagon report rejects this thinking, however, as naive at best, citing the example of the Atlacatl Battalion, which bracketed its bloody decade with the El Mozote massacre and the Jesuit assassinations.[117]

As evidence, the report cites still other aspects of Salvadoran military activity that the United States tolerated throughout the decade, including the tendency to temporarily reduce human rights violations for a short period so as to maintain U.S. aid while avoiding real reform,[118] the ongoing role of the death squads in the Salvadoran military,[119] and the conviction of Salvadoran military leaders that the issue of human rights was at best ancillary to the real goal of U.S. policy in El Salvador: the military defeat of the FMLN. Indeed, Alfredo Cristiani, Salvadoran president at the time of the Jesuit assassinations, criticized the United States for bogging down the war effort with its "human rights psychosis."[120]

---

115. Ibid., 34-35.

116. Ibid., 35.

117. Ibid., 35-36.

118. Ibid., 35-37.

119. Ibid., 41-43. See U.S. Congress, Permanent Select Committee on Intelligence, *U.S. Intelligence Performance on Central America: Achievements and Selected Instances of Concern*, Staff Report of the Subcommittee on Oversight and Evaluation, 97th Congress, 2nd Session, September 22, 1982. According to this report, a U.S. Embassy study found that "both on and off duty members of the security forces are participants" in the death squads and that it was "unofficially confirmed by right-wing spokesman Robert D'Aubuisson that security force members used the guise of the death squad when a potentially embarrassing or odious task needed to be performed." Cited in Schwarz, *American Counterinsurgency Doctrine and El Salvador*, 41.

120. Brook Larmer, "The Politics of Polarization," *Christian Science Monitor*, October 24, 1988. Cited in Schwarz, *American Counterinsurgency Doctrine and El Salvador*, 39.

The culminating effect of such trangressions was to undermine support for the war in the United States. Indeed, the United States was directly implicated in these violations by virtue of its massive commitment to military funding, and by the presence of its advisors at many levels of the conflict.[121] U.S. personnel had direct and indirect knowledge of, and roles in covering up, the brutal and systematic violations of human rights at El Mozote and elsewhere, all paid for by U.S. dollars and carried out, as noted above, with M-16 cartridges made in Lake City, Missouri.

## The Failure of Land Reform

The second pillar of U.S. counterinsurgency strategy in El Salvador was the land redistribution program announced by the 1979 junta. Partially implemented by succeeding governments in the 1980s, it was designed by U.S. experts, financed by U.S. aid, and mainly implemented by U.S. organizers and technicians. The Pentagon report recognizes the inherent logic in the FMLN cause, arguing that El Salvador's "highly concentrated pattern of ownership caused a gross maldistribution of wealth . . . and hence appalling poverty for the majority of the population and gross political inequality."[122] As noted earlier, the U.S. supported plan was designed to change this intolerable situation in three phases.[123]

The report argues that the story of the failure of this promising land reform program "reflects the political history of El Salvador since the program's inception." While the reformist junta of October 1979 helped develop the program with a "progressive vision of reforming the agrarian structure of the country," by the middle of the following year "military hardliners and the traditional agrarian oligarchy supplanted most of the reformers." The result was that "land reform thus fell under the control of those who had historically opposed it."[124]

Reviewing what was achieved, the report notes that Phase I was implemented in 1980 after the collapse of the reformist junta. It expropriated 14.7 percent of the country's arable land, though 69 percent had been deemed suitable only for cattle grazing, while only 9 percent included coffee growing areas. In response,

---

121. On May 29, 1983, the *Philadelphia Inquirer* presented the front-page headline: "How U.S. Advisers Run the War in El Salvador." While it was difficult to prove at the time, journalist Rod Norland explained that "American officers have moved quietly into the top levels of the Salvadoran military and are . . . actually making critical decisions about the conduct of the war. . . . [They serve] as strategists, tacticians and planners." (See Rod Norland, "How U.S. Advisers Run the War in El Salvador," *Philadelphia Inquirer*, May 29, 1983. Cited in Montgomery, *Revolution in El Salvador,* 166.) Montgomery notes that by the late 1980s, every brigade and battalion in the country was accompanied by U.S. military advisors. Indeed, during the November 1989 offensive, U.S. journalists reported overhearing a U.S. military advisor giving combat intelligence to Salvadoran troops on the ground. (See Frank Smyth, "Caught with Their Pants Down," *Village Voice*, December 2, 1989, 17.)

122. Schwarz, *American Counterinsurgency Doctrine and El Salvador,* 45.

123. Ibid.

124. Ibid., 46-47.

however, the armed forces declared a state of siege (which lasted from March 1980 until January 1987!) and expropriated recently distributed estates, allowing the landowners to "intimidate peasants into abandoning the cooperatives or not applying for title to them in the first place." The net results were disastrous for the program's supposed beneficiaries:

> The number of peasants killed by security forces in 1980 was highest in those areas affected by Phase I; over 500 peasant leaders, dozens of land reform officials, and hundreds of peasant union and cooperative members were assassinated. The military also rampantly demanded extortion payments from the newly formed cooperatives; these efforts were so effective that by 1982, 78 cooperatives had been abandoned or had reverted to their former owners. Intense intimidation of cooperatives by the military and civil defense forces, often directed by the oligarchy, continued until 1983, by which time thousands of cooperative workers had been killed.[125]

D'Aubuisson was elected head of the Constituent Assembly in March 1982, and "Phase II, the centerpiece of the program, was gutted by ARENA in 1983."[126] Two mechanisms were inserted into the constitution and the legislation itself, allowing large landowners to circumvent the reform. The report notes glumly that "No Phase II land has been redistributed."

Finally, Phase III, the land-to-the-tiller program allowed 52,000 families to buy about 24,000 acres. However, an audit by the General Accounting Office found that by 1984 one-third of the applicants "were not working the land because they had been threatened, evicted, or had disappeared."[127] The redistributed land contained "the country's poorest and most exhausted soils, and were mostly located in areas where the fighting was the worst. The report concludes, "Many of those who did benefit received too little land to feed their families, or land only marginally suitable for farming."[128]

The report's overall evaluation of Salvadoran land reform efforts during the 1980s concludes on a sobering note: "Instead of regarding land reform as a means to defeat the insurgency, the right has attacked the program with tenacious hostility, first seeking to prevent it and then succeeding in eviscerating it. . . . And despite a decade of reform, 80% of farm land still belongs to its original owners."[129] As a result, "In the 11 years since the program began, wealth has become more concentrated in El Salvador, and the disparity between rich and poor has grown."

---

125. Ibid., 45-46.

126. Ibid., 47.

127. Quotation from "Salvadoran Land Program Is Criticized," *New York Times*, February 15, 1984. Cited by Schwarz, *American Counterinsurgency Doctrine and El Salvador*, 47.

128. Schwarz, *American Counterinsurgency Doctrine and El Salvador*, 47, 48.

129. Ibid., 48.

## The Failure of Political Reform

The third leg of U.S. counterinsurgency in El Salvador was political reform. The report outlines the fate of three "civil-military pacification programs" developed and "imposed" by the United States on a reluctant Salvadoran government and its military. It explains, "The ultimate goal of these programs is to erase the population's perception of the military as an oppressive force and to promote a more benign image of the central government."[130] The first program was the 1983 National Campaign Plan. It proceeded in three phases attempting, first, to clear the FMLN from the economically vital southern half of El Salvador. The second phase called for massive funding by the U.S. Agency for International Development (AID) to be funneled to the Salvadoran National Commission for Restoration of Areas (CONARA) and focused on "reconstructing damaged housing and infrastructure, implementing the land reform program, and providing basic services such as water and electricity. The third phase attempted to establish local civil defense units.[131] The report notes that the plan failed to clear the FMLN from the area, that "the notoriously corrupt CONARA swallowed American aid," and that "the peasants perceived civil defense units to be ugly symbols of uncontrolled repression."[132]

The second civic-action program of the mid-1980s, United for Reconstruction (UPR), followed the pattern of the first and suffered the same fate. The third, Municipalities in Action (MEA), provided funds directly to mayors with the idea that local communities could then decide how to spend them. However, while one study characterized MEA as "the most effective counterinsurgency strategy"[133] of the decade, its very success was premised on circumventing the Salvadoran government and its military. The report concludes with a sober and realistic assessment of the mistaken premises underlying the entire effort:

> Civic action . . . assumes that the rural populace is either ignorant of political issues or that its loyalty can . . . be purchased. Failure to recognize the real issues at the root of the insurgency . . . [has meant that] civil action in El Salvador has thus far failed to uproot either poverty or mistrust. . . . The means employed by civic action will not—cannot—accomplish the goals desired. Those goals will be reached only when El Salvador transforms itself from an unjust, corrupt, brutal, and divisive society. . . .[134]

The Pentagon report finally attributes U.S. efforts to stimulate political reform in El Salvador to the misguided "pretense" that "America . . . can create

---

130. Ibid., 50.

131. Ibid., 51.

132. Ibid., 52.

133. Research Triangle Institute, CONARA Impact Evaluation, September 20, 1988, 11. Cited in Schwarz, *American Counterinsurgency Doctrine and El Salvador.*

134. Schwarz, *American Counterinsurgency Doctrine and El Salvador,* 55-56.

democracy abroad."[135] The report notes that by October 1988, reporter Brook Larmer captured the almost total collapse of the counterinsurgency rational when she wrote, "Nearly everyone here, from conservative Army colonels to leftist political leaders, openly criticizes the U.S. 'project,' questioning whether it can produce genuine change or end the war."[136] Still, the war and U.S. funding would continue through 1991.

The report appropriately cites the realism of a U.S. diplomat who states, "We say we are here to fortify democracy. Well, hell, we could be doing that forever,"[137] and highlights the "ludicrous positions" created by this "democracy" rationale. For instance, the United States spent between $6 and $8 million organizing the 1982 elections. Yet when it became clear that "ARENA and the other radical right-wing parties that controlled the Assembly would elect . . . D'Aubuisson as president," the U.S. pre-empted the process and forced the democratically elected Assembly to select a candidate more to its liking.[138]

Similarly, the United States spent $10.4 million in the 1984 presidential elections: "AID paid organizers to encourage workers and peasants to vote for Duarte over D'Aubuisson, and the CIA channeled funds to the Christian Democrats to prevent what was considered to be a likely D'Aubuisson victory."[139] Yet the United States later found its ally manipulating and damaging the credibility of El Salvador's key democratic institutions, the legislature and the judiciary, precisely in order to defeat the U.S. program of military, agrarian, social, and political reform. The report asserts that the United States was well aware of these actions on the part of the Salvadoran government. Yet it continued to fund its activities, all the while promising the public at home that it could reshape the Salvadoran government and military in the United States' own image.

After more than a decade of this, the Pentagon report finally had the sanity to ask the following question:

> If a regime is incapable of governing—controlling its own territory, imposing order among its population, winning support when it has been given reasonable assistance sufficient to compensate for help given to its internal enemies—it then becomes necessary to question whether that regime will survive and whether it deserves to survive.[140]

The same question had provoked the reformist 1979 coup and the slide toward civil war a decade before. One wonders what took the U.S. policy makers so long

135. Ibid., 71.

136. Brook Larmer, "The Shifting Battlefront," *Christian Science Monitor*, October 20, 1988. Cited in Schwarz, *American Counterinsurgency Doctrine and El Salvador*, 71.

137. James LeMoyne, "The Guns of El Salvador," *New York Times Magazine*, February 5, 1989, 55. Cited in Schwarz, *American Counterinsurgency Doctrine and El Salvador*, 73.

138. Schwarz, *American Counterinsurgency Doctrine and El Salvador*, 72.

139. Ibid., 72.

140. Ibid., 73.

to ask it? Were they unaware of the struggles of the 1970s, blinded to the reality of El Salvador by anti-communist ideology, or cynically ready to sacrifice El Salvador on the altar of Cold War politics?

### *In the Name of God, Stop the Repression!*
### *The UCA Follows Archbishop Romero*

For those committed to reform and social change, the brutal repression of Salvadoran civil society, the failure of the reformist 1979 Young Officers Coup, the assassination and apparent eclipse of Archbishop Romero by Roberto D'Aubuisson, and the disappointment of the FMLN's hopes for a general insurrection closed the door for the foreseeable future on the major projects of the 1970s. The only realistic alternatives seemed capitulation or war.

In this section I will briefly explain how this situation and the events that followed drew the UCA away from a focus on El Salvador's elites toward a university praxis emphasizing the role of Salvadoran civil society in creating a peace process and achieving a negotiated solution to the war. We will examine how the UCA Jesuits and their companions learned from the example of Archbishop Romero to operationalize their option for the poor in a university-style engagement with El Salvador's disenfranchised, and mostly poor, majorities. From Archbishop Romero they would learn to trust the common people, and to promote the emergence of a functioning civil society capable of developing its own alternatives to the projects of various competing elites: the military, the FMLN and the left, the land barons and their allies on the right, those in charge of the state, and their patrons in the United States. As we shall see, this important new development would become the vehicle for what some regard as the ultimate realization of Archbishop Romero's prophecy.

### U.S. Cold War Politics Extend the War

The failure of the FMLN's "final offensive" created a new historical moment: the possibility of serious negotiations between the right, which controlled the government, and the left, represented by the FMLN. In a February 1981 cable to Washington, U.S. Ambassador Robert White described "both sides fighting to a draw."[141] The FMLN began to promote a negotiated settlement to the conflict, and a variety of voices, including acting Archbishop Rivera Damas, urged the beginning of negotiations. Ignacio Ellacuría and the UCA Board decided to press for a "mediated negotiation,"[142] a position they held through the end of the war. Román Mayorga, who had gone into exile in January 1981, called for negotiations in *ECA* saying prophetically, "Neither of the two sides in the conflict has sufficient strength to achieve a total victory over the other, even though each

---

141. U.S. Embassy/State Department cable, February 18, 1981, no. 1363, "NSA's El Salvador: The Making of U.S. Policy." Cited in Arnson, *Crossroads*, 145.

142. Minutes of the Board of Directors of the University of Central America, José Simeón Cañas (San Salvador: Archives of the University of Central America, March 11-12, 1981).

will be able to inflict significant damage for an indefinite period of time. This could become extraordinarily long and costly in suffering, human lives, and the economic future of El Salvador."[143] U.S. Ambassador Robert White promoted "a political solution."[144] And on August 28, 1981, Mexico and France offered a proposal for negotiations based on recognizing the FDR-FMLN coalition as a "representative political force."[145]

The incoming Reagan administration, however, was determined to internationalize the essentially local Salvadoran conflict using it to symbolically "draw the line"[146] against international communism. Thus White was immediately removed as ambassador by the new administration. And on February 23, 1981, an administration White Paper was released entitled, "Communist Interference in El Salvador," which argued, "the insurgency in El Salvador has [become] . . . another case of indirect armed aggression against a small third world country by communist powers acting through Cuba."[147]

For its part, the leadership of the church in El Salvador was convinced that Washington's Cold War ideology was getting the better of historical reality. Acting Archbishop Arturo Rivera Damas wrote to Vice-President Bush on April 6, 1981, arguing that the new administration was misreading the Salvadoran situation. He writes,

> The Administration does not understand the composition and nature of the Junta. Specifically, I think you underestimate the power and resistance of the right-wing military to true political change, including the kind of political dialogue which I am sure is the only road to peace in our country. . . . The United States must clearly indicate it is in favor of a political solution through negotiations or [they] will not occur.[148]

But the archbishop's appeal fell on deaf ears. The administration had already faced this question and accepted the downsides of a military approach. Indeed,

---

143. *ECA* 36, no. 395 (April-May 1981): 367-82.

144. Testimony of Hon. Robert E. White, U.S. Congress, House Committee on Foreign Affairs, Subcommittee on Inter-American Affairs, *U.S. Policy toward El Salvador*, March 11, 1981 (Washington, DC: U.S. Government Printing Office, 1981), 133. Cited in Arnson, *Crossroads*, 146.

145. Ignacio Ellacuría, "La declaración conjunta mexicano-francesa sobre El Salvador," *ECA* 36, no. 395 (April-May 1981): 845-66. Reprinted in Ignacio Ellacuría, *Veinte años de historia en El Salvador (1969-1989): Escritos políticos* (San Salvador: UCA Editores, 1991), 1235-69.

146. These words were used by Reagan's first secretary of state, Alexander Haig, in a briefing for the congressional leadership on the State Department's White Paper "Communist Interference in El Salvador." See LeoGrande, "A Splendid Little War," 27. He also used this phrase in briefing the National Security Council. See Cannon, *President Reagan*, 344.

147. Department of State, Bureau of Public Affairs, "Communist Interference in El Salvador," Special Report No. 80, February 23, 1981. Cited in Arnson, *Crossroads*, 56.

148. Letter of apostolic administrator of San Salvador, Arturo Rivera Damas, to Vice-President George Bush, April 6, 1981. Cited in Montgomery, *Revolution in El Salvador*, 147.

on February 25, 1981, two days after the aforementioned White Paper, former Ambassador White had starkly posed the following question to U.S. policy makers on the first day of congressional hearings regarding Reagan policy in El Salvador.

> The security forces in El Salvador have been responsible for the deaths of thousands and thousands of young people, and they have executed them on the mere suspicion that they are leftists or sympathize with leftists. The real issue is how do you supply military assistance to a force that is going to use that military assistance to assassinate, to kill, in a totally uncontrolled way? Do you want to associate the United States with the type of killing that has been going on down there in El Salvador?[149]

Unfortunately, the Reagan administration's unapologetic acceptance of such liabilities as part of the cynical calculus of Cold War politics would find an ambivalent but reliable collaborator in Congress, establishing a pattern that would continue for the next decade.

## Ellacuría Shifts to Negotiations and Civil Society

As we saw, the failure of the reformist 1979 coup led the UCA not only to accept the "inevitability" of the offensive, but to place some hope in it (albeit with much ambivalence) as a possible solution. The *ECA* editorial of December 1979 formulated the dilemma as follows:

> In the face of the utter failure of the most generous, technically qualified and motivated effort seen in recent years, we are confronted brokenheartedly with the question: is it that even a profound reformism is not possible in El Salvador? The least we can say is that it has not been possible with this approach, with these men, and with this political project. And that is not because they were not competent. Rather, it is that maybe the reformist model is no longer viable in our country, and that in order to change something it is necessary to carry out a true revolution.[150]

A month and a half after the failure of the FMLN's "final offensive," however, Ellacuría came out in favor of "A Process of [Political] Mediation for El Salvador,"[151] a position that he held for the rest of his life. The Jesuit's think-

---

149. Testimony of Robert White, U.S. Congress, House Committee on Appropriations, Subcommittee on Foreign Operations, Foreign Assistance and Related Programs Appropriations for 1982, Hearings, Part 1, 97th Congress, 1st Session (Washington, DC: U.S. Government Printing Office, 1981), 3, 17. Cited in Arnson, *Crossroads*, 58-59.

150. *ECA* 34, no. 374 (December 1979): 1038.

151. "Ignacio Ellacuría, "Un proceso de mediación para El Salvador," *ECA* 36, nos. 387-388 (March 1981): 3-16.

ing was shaped not only by the military reality that neither side had sufficient strength to win, but he also questioned whether the government or the FMLN truly represented the majority of the Salvadoran people.

In August of 1981,[152] Ellacuría expanded his argument in favor of negotiations, invoking a principle that Juan Hernandez Pico believes emerged from Ellacuría's involvement in the 1971 ANDES strike: the need for "a strong civic society capable of being a social force over against political forces such as the state and political parties."[153] In this article Ellacuría introduced the concept of *third forces* whose interests were directly represented by neither the government nor the FMLN. This idea would lead Ellacuría and the university to devise ways during the 1980s of interacting more directly with the vast array of grassroots groups through which disenfranchised, poor, and unrepresented Salvadorans had begun to act as agents of their own destiny. As an FMLN comandante would explain looking back a decade later,

> The contribution of Ellacuría was that he understood that this country is sadly polarized, and that the positions of the two sides, the two poles, have radicalized. But between one camp and the other there are an enormous number of people who are not expressing themselves politically, people who want to see a solution to the problems of the country without being connected either to the FMLN or the government. Ellacuría insisted on the need for these forces to express themselves and play a real role in society.[154]

The failure of the FMLN offensive and the prospect of a long and bloody civil war pushed Ellacuría and the UCA to identify this reality as an important force in favor of negotiations and a foundation for a political future.

## Archbishop Romero Teaches UCA to Trust the Common People

Reflection on the life and ministry of Archbishop Romero among the country's poor majorities played a crucial role in drawing the UCA's attention from El Salvador's elites to its common people. In 1985 the UCA presented a posthumous doctorate to Archbishop Romero, and Ellacuría insisted that, while the UCA offered consultation during the archbishop's tenure, "no one doubted who was the teacher and who was the assistant, who was the pastor setting the direction and who was the implementer, who was the prophet revealing the mystery and who was the follower, who was the one who encouraged and who was the one

---

152. Ignacio Ellacuría, "La responsabilidad de las 'terceras fuerzas,'" editorial, *ECA* no. 394 (August 1981): 750.

153. Letter from Juan Hernández-Pico, S.J., to Charles J. Beirne, S.J., July 1993. Cited in Beirne, *Jesuit Education and Social Change*, 103.

154. Interview with Gerson Martinez by Teresa Whitfield, March 18, 1991. Cited in Whitfield, *Paying the Price*, 294.

encouraged, who was the voice and who was the echo."[155] But what was it the UCA learned from Romero? Ellacuría explained that the award represented "a commitment to do in our university way what he did in his pastoral way."[156] And Jon Sobrino has suggested that the UCA learned how to fulfill its mission as a university by watching what it meant to run an institution like the archdiocese from the perspective of a preferential option for the poor.[157]

In a liturgy celebrated at the UCA eight months after the March 24, 1980, assassination, Ellacuría offered four points summarizing what the UCA had learned from its self-proclaimed mentor.[158] First, Ellacuría says that the UCA believed the archbishop offered a new model of how "to historicize the power of the Gospel"[159] in the Salvadoran context. Second, just as Oscar Romero had learned from Rutilio Grande how to historicize the gospel in the present moment, so the UCA was committed to learn from both of them what it meant to be "dedicated . . . to evangelizing the poor" in a way that "led the poor to historicize their own salvation" and to give "historical flesh to the eternally new word of God."[160]

Third, Ellacuría says the archbishop taught the university that its initial conversion to God's preferential option for the poor should be historicized by letting the crucified people become "the guiding light" of its apostolic ministry. As a result Romero "changed his location, he changed his situation, and what had been an opaque, amorphous and ineffective word became a torrent of life to which the people drew near in order to quench their thirst."[161] Fourth, the archbishop taught the university to look to the common Salvadoran people themselves in order to find the salvation preached by their mentor. Thus, while universities are by nature institutions for the elite, Archbishop Romero showed the UCA that the purpose of the university was to empower the "poor majorities of El Salvador" to become active participants in shaping their future.[162]

Though the university had been living with the option for the poor for over a decade, these words would suggest that it was just learning how to make it into an effective "historical force." While the frustration and failures of the strategic visions nurtured by the UCA, the church, and the left during the 1970s seemed to block the way forward, their apparent failure drew the UCA's attention away from the agency of El Salvador's political, economic, ecclesial, and university

---

155. Ignacio Ellacuría, "La UCA ante el doctorado concedido a Monseñor Romero," *Escritos teológicos*, III (San Salvador: UCA Editores, 2002), 104; reprinted from *ECA* no. 437 (1985): 168.

156. Ibid., 102.

157. Interview of Jon Sobrino by Robert Lassalle-Klein, May 8, 1994, 4.

158. Ignacio Ellacuría, "Monseñor Romero, un enviado de Dios para salvar a su pueblo," *Escritos teológicos*, III, 93-100; reprinted from *Sal Terrae* 811 (1980): 825-32 and *ECA* 19 (1990): 5-10.

159. Ellacuría, "Monseñor Romero," 94.

160. Ibid., 96.

161. Ibid., 98.

162. Ibid., 100.

elites toward the renewal of Salvadoran civil society taking place through the emerging agency of the country's dispossessed majorities. And it soon became clear to Ellacuría that the vast majority of Salvadorans wanted political, economic, social reform, *and* an end to the war.

## Gradual Emergence of a New Kind of Christian University

At the end of the 1970s, therefore, the UCA's emerging model of the university was influenced by watching Archbishop Oscar Romero run the archdiocese grounded in a commitment to Medellín's preferential option for the poor.[163] Drawing on the 1985 speech in which Ellacuría presented an honorary doctorate to the deceased archbishop, the UCA found in Archbishop Oscar Romero (1) a model of how to historicize the force of the gospel, (2) through a liberating evangelization of the poor, (3) which the vast majority of Salvadorans experienced as consistent with the gospel, (4) with such force that many were disposed to live their Christian vocation by imitating his example.

In this section, therefore, I will briefly outline how the UCA tried to implement what it learned from the archbishop through a variety of initiatives designed to enact the mission articulated in the 1979 document summarized above.[164] The reader will recall that the document asserted the UCA should be "for social change," "in a university manner," driven by "Christian inspiration."[165] In what follows, then, I will first examine how the UCA tried to historicize this mission through the creation of innovative practical programs for social outreach. Second, I will examine how and why the UCA began actively promoting a military-political solution to the war after the failure of the FMLN's "final offensive" in 1981. And third, I will examine some of the ecclesial politics generated by the UCA's way of implementing its understanding of the role of a Christian university in society. These elements will then prepare us to examine the gradual realization by Ellacuría and the UCA that a military-political solution depended on the continued emergence of El Salvador's socially marginated majorities as the primary agents for a solution to the conflict.

### Practical Vehicles for a University-Style Preferential Option for the Poor

As noted earlier, on December 2, 1975, the UCA Board approved the foundation of the Center for Political and Social Documentation[166] in order to provide basic research data for teaching, research, and social outreach (the university's three basic functions). This realized one aspect of the long-range "planning for

---

163. Interview of Jon Sobrino by Robert Lassalle-Klein, May 8, 1994, 4.

164. "Las funciones fundamentales de la universidad y su operativización," in *Planteamiento*, 37-121. For more information on this point, see section of this chapter entitled "The Synthetic Statement of 1979."

165. See "Las funciones fundamentales," 47.

166. The Spanish title was Centro de Documentación y Apoyo a la Investigación (CIDAI).

. . . the second decade of the University" initiated in 1975 by the UCA's new president, Román Mayorga, after the "liberation thesis" gained the support of a majority of the Board. Recall that Mayorga had initiated the planning process in order to help the UCA "consider the question of how to use its institutional influence for the liberating transformation of society."[167] Thus it was felt that the university would need a center to better understand the "national reality" it so hoped to transform.

After Ellacuría became president, in May of 1980 the Center for Political and Social Documentation became the Center for Information, Documentation, and Research Support (CIDAI), under the direction of Ricardo Stein. In the 1980s CIDAI and its weekly publication, *Proceso,* would become the most important source of independent documentation and analysis of current events in El Salvador. While Ellacuría was in exile from November 1980 to April 1982 he supported an increased role for CIDAI in helping the Board to analyze and adapt to rapidly evolving events.

Accordingly, on March 11-12, 1981, the Board considered input from Ellacuría on this and other questions conveyed through former provincial Miguel Estrada, S.J., before developing its plan for the first semester of 1981 (March-July). Following a schema presented at the March 9, 1981, meeting by recently appointed acting vice-president, Ignacio Martín-Baró,[168] the Board discussed how CIDAI might be integrated into "the directing and thinking nucleus of the UCA"[169] in order to provide the university's "analysis and reflection with the maximum academic quality." Confirming this direction, Ellacuría's subsequent April 1981 letter to the Board explicitly emphasized the importance of CIDAI in "clarifying and grounding [the] analysis" guiding the university's social outreach "from which all its activities receive their overall orientation."[170]

The key point here is that the Board realized the need for sophisticated yet practical tools through which to document and analyze the rapidly evolving national reality of El Salvador. Thus, while the pages of *ECA* had provided insightful analysis since 1969, the 1980s witnessed a quantum leap in the UCA's practical ability to document and analyze unfolding events. Indeed, by mid-decade the UCA was publishing seven scholarly journals analyzing economics, social psychology, sociology, theology, national issues, and the documentation of key events. In 1985 Segundo Montes would found the Human Rights Institute of the UCA (IDHUCA), and in July 1986 Ignacio Martín-Baró led the creation of the University Institute for Public Opinion (IUDOP). Together these centers

---

167. Mayorga Quirós, *La Universidad para el cambio social*, 65.

168. Ignacio Martín-Baró, "La UCA en El Primer Ciclo Académico de 1981," Minutes of the Meeting of the Board of Directors of the University of Central America, March 9, 1981 (San Salvador: Archives of the University of Central America), appendix.

169. Minutes of the meeting of the Board of Directors of the University of Central America, March 11-12, 1981 (San Salvador: Archives of the University of Central America), 2.

170. Letter from Rev. Ignacio Ellacuría to the Board of the University of Central America, José Simeón Cañas (San Salvador: Archives of the University of Central America, April 27, 1981), 1, 2.

would make the excruciating reality of El Salvador's suffering majorities available to the nation itself and interested parties abroad. The importance of this achievement cannot be overemphasized in light of the brutal suppression of El Salvador's independent media by the government and the military, and the consistent attempt by the U.S. mission to downplay the grotesque human rights violations of its ally. Two examples must suffice.

First, starting in 1985 Segundo Montes began to publish annual studies (1985, 1986, 1987, 1988, 1989)[171] that brought international attention to the startling reality that the war had made refugees of between 20 and 25 percent of the population of El Salvador. These played an important part in exposing the insensitivity of U.S. administrations during the 1980s to the human rights violations suffered by refugees seeking political asylum in the United States and helped to refute the logic of the repression. Montes's 1987 study presented data that led to the incredible conclusion (unrefuted as far as I know) that Salvadoran refugees living abroad (primarily in the United States) represented the largest source of foreign capital in the country.[172] One important political implication of this discovery was that it directly contradicted claims that either the flourishing wealth of the oligarchy or U.S. economic aid was the most important factor for the economic survival of El Salvador.

Second, under the leadership of Ignacio Martín-Baró, IUDOP offered the average Salvadoran a "social mirror" providing an objective basis from which to conclude that their own dangerous opinions against the war were, in fact, shared by many, if not most other citizens.[173] IUDOP pointed out that, for instance, in May 1988 over 40 percent of the population supported a negotiated solution to the war, even though one could be executed for voicing this opinion publicly!

Martín-Baró compared the empowering effect of such information to the homilies of Archbishop Romero, which, as we saw, documented the reality of the nation on his weekly broadcasts. He argued that "public opinion polls can be a way of returning their voice to the oppressed peoples, an instrument that, as it reflects the popular experience with truth and meaning, opens the consciousness to a sense of a new truth to be constructed in history."[174] To this end IUDOP conducted twenty-three such surveys under Martín-Baró from July

---

171. Segundo Montes, *El Salvador 1985: Desplazados y refugiados* (San Salvador: IDHUCA, 1985); *El Salvador 1986: En busca de soluciones para los desplazados* (San Salvador: IDHUCA, 1986); *El Salvador 1987: Salvadoreños refugiados en los Estados Unidos* (San Salvador: IDHUCA, 1987); co-author with J. J. Garcia, *Salvadoran Migration to the United States: An Exploratory Study* (Washington, DC: Center for Immigration Policy and Refugee Assistance, Georgetown University Press, 1988); *Refugiados y repatriados, El Salvador y Honduras* (San Salvador: IDHUCA, 1989).

172. Montes, *El Salvador 1987*, 103-21, esp. 120-21.

173. Ignacio Martín-Baró, "La encuesta de opinión pública como instrumento desideoloizador," *Revista de psicología de El Salvador* 35 (January-March 1990), 11. Cited in Whitfield, *Paying the Price*, 253.

174. Martín-Baró, "La encuesta de opinión pública," 21. Cited in Whitfield, *Paying the Price*, 253.

1986 to September 1989. These studies not only reflected the national reality but helped to shape it by articulating and reinforcing the opinions of El Salvador's underrepresented majorities as an important social force.

Ready access to such material also put Martín-Baró in a position to make extremely important and internationally recognized scholarly contributions to the study of the psychological reality of the country. In a 1988 article published in the UCA's journal of social psychology Martín-Baró asserted that the military, with the help of U.S. advisors, had shifted the focus of its efforts from the *"dirty war* of the early eighties" to a "psychological war," which was having serious effects on the mental health of the nation. He explained the logic of this shift in terms of the Salvadoran military's appropriation of the U.S. counterinsurgency project suggesting, "The primary goal of the North American project is the elimination of the revolutionary movement; the restoration of democracy in the country is only secondary, or derivative."[175] Referring to the first half of the decade, he notes, "That is why, when the time was propitious, the project set out to get rid of all insurgent groups, rapidly and brutally, combining military action with a massive campaign of repression against the civilian population." However, "When this campaign failed, the project entered into a new phase that sought to achieve the same objective through democratic forms that would justify the project itself." He also revealed the roots of this shift in the exigencies of U.S. politics: "Essentially, the North American project for El Salvador had to find a form of dirty war that would allow it to realize its goals but spare it from having to pay the political costs. And the answer was thought to have been found in psychological warfare."

The article then goes on to explain that the dirty war and the psychological war shared three important objectives: (1) a dismantling of the grassroots mass organizations; (2) an elimination of many of the most significant opposition figures; and (3) a weakening of the support bases of the revolutionary movement in virtually all sectors of the overall population.[176] Both employed violence, polarization, and the institutionalized lie. But the psychological war was able to use terrorist repression more selectively, thereby reducing it to levels acceptable in the United States and emphasized psychological tactics geared to producing psychic trauma, insecurity, inhibition, flight, and moral discrediting of politicizing themes.

In another 1988 article published in the same UCA journal, "Political Violence and the War as Causes of Psychosocial Trauma in El Salvador," Martín-Baró goes on to document how this campaign produced a national epidemic of "psychosocial trauma, which is to say, the traumatic crystallization of dehumanized social relations in persons and groups. The social polarization tends to be somatized, the institutionalized lying precipitates grave identity problems, and

175. Ignacio Martín-Baró, in *Towards a Society That Serves Its People*, 307; reprinted from "From Dirty War to Psychological War: The Case of El Salvador," in A. Aron, ed., *Flight, Exile, and Return: Mental Health and the Refugee* (San Francisco: CHRICA, 1988).

176. Ibid., 308-9.

the violence occasions a militarization of the very mind."[177] He then concludes, "These realities make it urgent to undertake a psychosocial project of depolarizing, deideologizing and demilitarizing the country." His strategy would include a negotiated end to the conflict.

One other innovation worth mentioning is Ellacuría's 1984 creation of a "Chair for the National Reality." As we have seen, U.S. advisors tried to moderate the all-out government-sponsored war on civil society that had characterized the early 1980s. As a result, a small space opened for unions, grassroots organizations, and political parties to operate, and the UCA found itself in a good position to create a forum for the public exchange of ideas, something sorely lacking at the time. As a result, Ellacuría's *Cátedra de la Realidad Nacional* quickly became the most important national forum for virtually every major policy proposal regarding the future of the country. The forum also energized the other dimensions of the UCA's program of social outreach. For instance, the 1987 November-December *ECA* was totally dedicated to a *Cátedra* on the Esquipulas II peace proposal, which included labor groups, Archbishop Rivera Damas, and virtually the entire political leadership of the country except ARENA.

### From the 1970s Visions of the Elites to the Majority's Wish for Negotiations and Peace

Two documents written in 1981 capture the essence of the "negotiated solution" to the conflict promoted by Ellacuría and the UCA Board after the failure of the FMLN's "final offensive" in 1981. In this section I will briefly summarize these documents as examples of the aforementioned shift away from the agency of elites toward the concerns of everyday Salvadoran civil society in the UCA's efforts to "historicize" the gospel at the beginning of the decade.

As mentioned above, though Ellacuría would remain in exile from November 27, 1980, to April 1982, he continued to play an active role in decision making through regular contact with the Board and other elements of the university leadership. Following this pattern the Board traveled to San Jose, Costa Rica, on March 28, 29, 1981, to meet with their leader while considering a global and strategic reevaluation of the many "functions of the UCA" in light of the current "situation of El Salvador." In the minutes Ellacuría is listed as president while the acting president, Axel Solderberg, appears merely as vice-president.[178]

After the meeting Ellacuría developed a proposal outlining an important new direction for the university's social outreach. This document, which appears as

---

177. Ignacio Martín-Baró, "La violencia política y la guerra como causas del trauma psicosocial in El Salvador," *Revista de psicología de El Salvador* 28 (April-June 1988): 123.

178. Ignacio Ellacuría, "La proyección social de la UCA hoy." Appendix to Minutes of the Board of Directors of the University of Central America (San Salvador: Archives of the University of Central America, José Simeón Cañas, April 27, 1981). Cited in Beirne, *Jesuit Education and Social Change*, 174. All citations from Board meetings in this section are taken from Beirne, *Jesuit Education and Social Change*, 169-206.

the first order of new business in the Board minutes for April 27, 1981, argues that "the social outreach of the UCA should now ground itself in the perspective of a political solution and . . . a process of mediation"[179] for the civil war. It insists this strategic commitment must be carried out in a thoroughly "university manner"[180] through the activities of the president; the editorial, production, and distribution work of the university's overall communications center; its press (UCA Editores) and journals (administration, engineering, economics, etc.); the Center for Information, Documentation, and Research Support (CIDAI) and *ECA*; and the Social Service Center, which placed students for their community service hours. It also envisions a vigorous agenda of public events such as "round tables, conferences, congresses, etc.," ongoing contacts with leading "politicians, economists, religious, military figures, etc.," and the addition of a university radio station and weekly newspaper, all designed to stimulate the "national collective consciousness" of Salvadoran civil society through reflection on current events.[181]

The document manifests a new sensitivity to the need to be in dialogue with a broad range of non-elite social groups, including professional organizations, owners of small- and middle-sized businesses, other universities, labor unions, political and military personnel, the FMLN-FDR, and student organizations. To this end it proposes the creation of a new social outreach council. On May 15, 1981, the Board approved the document and appointed Jon Sobrino the interim coordinator for the new council. Later, on September 6, 1982, the Board established a vice-president for social outreach, and Ellacuría himself was named to the position (in addition to his role as president).

In June 1981, Ellacuría wrote to the acting president, Axel Solderberg, stating his views on the current situation and advocating an activist role for the UCA in promoting a negotiated solution to the conflict.

> I see the UCA as . . . doing useful things . . . to advance the process that leads to a solution to end the hell in which the majority of the people in this country lives, a situation aggravated by war, repression, insecurity and the most profound economic crisis. . . .
>
> It seems to me that in the short run of the next months there will be no solution. The Left is not going to defeat the Government, nor will the Government achieve a victory over the Left. As a result, social and economic disaster is going to continue and worsen. [But] will this worsening bring about a new situation that will require a negotiated political solution? . . . [No,] because the United States and the military believe, or want to believe, that they can accomplish a definitive military victory relatively soon. . . . All the other groups, including the

---

179. Ellacuría, "La proyección social de la UCA hoy," 3.
180. Ibid., 5.
181. Ibid., 1-3.

Christian Democrats, both inside and outside the country, are pushing for a negotiated agreement despite the difficulty in achieving it..[182]

But what sort of negotiated solution does Ellacuría envision?

Two weeks after his letter to the UCA Board, on May 11, 1981, Ellacuría outlined a framework for a "political-military solution" that would define the university's position for the next several years.[183] After explaining his approach, Ellacuría summarizes his view of the current state of affairs in El Salvador. He states that after the failure of Colonel Molina's 1976 agrarian reform, the country moved steadily toward an intolerable "limit situation" involving military repression of civil society.[184] He notes that every electoral victory by the opposition has been "stubbornly annulled" since 1972,[185] and that both parties to the current conflict have committed themselves to a "military" solution,[186] despite the fact that neither side was capable of achieving victory.[187] Thus, with virtually every other international government except the United States pressuring for a political settlement,[188] and both sides at least talking about a political settlement, he affirms a building consensus that the Salvadoran situation cannot tolerate the prolongation of a civil war.[189]

Ellacuría then proposes three principles for a negotiated solution: (1) a purely military solution cannot resolve the current situation; (2) a purely political solution is not a realistic possibility; and (3) a combined political-military solution is the most likely path to resolution. He argues that the latter, in order to be effective, must "give birth to and guarantee a political project and a structure that responds to the objective needs of the national reality, to the just demands of the organized community, and to the present correlation between [political and military] forces inside and outside the country."[190] With these principles in hand both Ellacuría and the UCA would dedicate much of its social outreach for the rest of decade to promoting a negotiated solution to the war.

### Structural and Ecclesial Implications of the UCA's New Way of Being a University

A closer examination of the aforementioned Board meeting of March 11-12, 1981, serves to illustrate the role of social analysis in shaping the UCA's inter-

---

182. Letter from Ignacio Ellacuría to Axel Soderberg, June 1981. Cited in Beirne, *Jesuit Education and Social Change*, 178.

183. Ignacio Ellacuría, "Solución política o solución militar para El Salvador?" *ECA* nos. 390-391 (May 1981): 295-324; reprinted in *Veinte años de historia*, 951-95. The article is dated May 11, 1981.

184. Ellacuría, *Veinte años de historia*, 957.

185. Ibid., 960.

186. Ibid., 962.

187. Ibid., 964.

188. Ibid., 966.

189. Ibid., 966-72.

190. Ibid., 980-95.

pretation of its new way of being a university. As suggested earlier, the work of the Board that day was dedicated to "planning for university activities for the first semester of 1981 (March to July)" following the outline suggested by Martín-Baró.[191]

Fr. Beirne's study of the UCA uses this document to "help us see the major issues to which the Board and the UCA would dedicate time during this crucial year."[192] The document emphasizes that, despite the worsening situation in the country, "the University . . . cannot renounce" the UCA's "explicit option . . . for the total liberation of the Salvadoran . . . people," its "Christian inspiration," or its plans "to conserve and . . . increase the academic quality of its services . . . , especially in teaching."[193] It then outlines a series of strategies designed "to collaborate in a university fashion with the current national process" through the university's teaching, research, and social outreach.[194]

Examples include linking the university's proposal for a negotiated settlement to the war to the work of CIDAI, *ECA*, *Proceso*, UCA Editores (the university press), and communications with political and church groups. The minutes emphasize the practical importance of teaching for maintaining the student population and the "prestige linked to the university's "scientific and Christian seriousness."[195] There was a call for practical measures to support the faculty and staff and to promote the work of teaching," including "revitalizing the University High Council."[196] The Board asserted that research analyzing the current national reality comprised a critical "contribution by the UCA to the current situation."[197] Overall, the document demonstrates a preoccupation with maintaining and finding practical avenues to advance the university's mission in the circumstances of brutal repression and war.

The October 11, 1982, meeting was largely taken up with responding to explosive "accusations against the UCA"[198] by a Salvadoran bishop closely aligned with the military. On October 7, 1982, the right-wing newspaper, *El Diario de Hoy*, had quoted charges by Bishop Pedro Aparicio of San Vicente, E.S., that whole sections of the UCA faculty exhibited "Marxist tendencies" and that "all of its teaching programs include Marxist points."[199] Additionally,

---

191. Minutes of the meeting of the Board of Directors of the University of Central America, March 11-12, 1981 (San Salvador: Archives of the University of Central America), 1; cited in Beirne, *Jesuit Education and Social Change*, 171-74. All citations from Board meetings in this section are taken from Beirne, *Jesuit Education and Social Change*, 169-206.

192. Beirne, *Jesuit Education and Social Change*, 171.

193. Ibid.

194. Minutes of the meeting of the Board of Directors of the University of Central America, March 11-12, 1981, 1-4.

195. Ibid., 3.

196. Ibid.

197. Ibid., 2.

198. Letter from Ignacio Ellacuría to the Board of Directors, October 8, 1982. Minutes of the meeting of the Board of Directors of the University of Central America, October 11, 1982 (San Salvador: Archives of the University of Central America).

199. Letter from the Board of Directors to the Episcopal Conference of El Salvador,

the bishop insinuated that Román Mayorga and Guillermo Ungo, leaders of the reformist 1979 coup who "had come out of the UCA," were Marxists, and made the politically explosive charge that "FECCAS and other campesino organizations were born at . . . [the] university." Axel Soderberg and Fr. Miguel Estrada, S.J., were sent to meet with Bishop Aparicio and reported at the October 25, 1982, meeting that the bishop claimed he was misquoted and promised a public statement "discounting the accusations."[200] These kinds of events formed a significant part of the background to the technical discussion about the legal status of the university.

A few months later the Board meeting of February 21, 1983, was preoccupied with concerns in Rome over tensions with elements of the Salvadoran hierarchy. On February 13, 1983, Fr. Paolo Dezza, S.J. (then one of two special papal delegates governing the Society of Jesus), wrote to Ellacuría urging greater cooperation with the Salvadoran bishops. The background for this letter was complaints from the most politically conservative Salvadoran bishops about the work of the UCA. It seems that the papal nuncio for El Salvador had sent an eighteen-page document to the Vatican alleging that "the UCA had deviated from its foundational purpose in the positions it was taking, but especially in its independence from the hierarchy."[201] On April 28, 1982, the nuncio asked the Sacred Congregation for Catholic Education and the Jesuit curia "to remove from the UCA some rather radical Jesuits." Then in August 1982 the Congregation delivered to Fr. Dezza letters from the papal nuncio and the episcopal conference announcing "the intention of the bishops to establish [their own] Catholic university 'in light of the impossibility of arriving at an understanding with the Fathers of the University.'"[202]

Ellacuría was sent to Rome to meet with Fr. Dezza and his advisors on December 19, 1982. He reported to the Board on February 21, 1983, that,

> Fr. Dezza's position is that the UCA should be oriented as a Catholic university as much in what it teaches and does, as in its indirect dependence on the Jesuit hierarchy. Consequently he maintains that even though we do not depend directly on the bishops of El Salvador, but rather directly on the pope through the Jesuit chain of command, we should seek to achieve dialogue and good relations with them, but should avoid inopportune intrusions [on their part].[203]

---

October 12, 1982. Minutes of the meeting of the Board of Directors of the University of Central America, October 11, 1982 (San Salvador: Archives of the University of Central America).

200. Minutes of the meeting of the Board of Directors of the University of Central America, October 25, 1982 (San Salvador: Archives of the University of Central America), 1.

201. Minutes of the meeting of the Board of Directors of the University of Central America, February 21, 1983 (San Salvador: Archives of the University of Central America), 1.

202. Ibid.

203. Ibid.

Dezza's solution was to stop "publicly emphasizing" the UCA's legal autonomy, and to begin "a dialogue" with the bishops. He strongly encouraged this approach, while refusing the path of granting either juridical or practical control over the university to the bishops.

Significant differences in approach and tensions also existed among the Jesuit universities of the larger region. On February 27, 1984, the Board heard a report from Ignacio Martín-Baró on his role as proxy for Ellacuría at a meeting held in Mexico city of the Jesuit university presidents from Mexico and Central America. When he mentions the centrality of the option for the poor in orienting the research, social outreach, and teaching of the UCA, he says the approach "either was [genuinely] not understood or they didn't want to understand it." He notes with disappointment that "the publication program of the [Salvadoran] UCA hardly brought any surprise or admiration," adding "the same thing occurred regarding the social outreach programs . . . [of] the UCA in Nicaragua." Overall, the UCA's academic vice-president felt "the discussion was generally made up of positions that were overly spiritualistic . . . and a boiling down to the general affirmation of the importance of the 'university apostolate' of the Society of Jesus."[204]

Fr. Charles Beirne has studied the correspondence between Jesuit superiors in Rome and El Salvador from the founding of the university through the death of the martyrs in 1989. While these documents and many of the particulars of this correspondence cannot be made public (due to its confidential nature and the fact that many of the principals are still alive),[205] some of Fr. Beirne's observations and conclusions may be introduced into our discussion.[206] He tells us that during 1984 Jesuit superiors in Rome continued to express concern about the need to overcome polarizing attitudes attributed to certain Jesuits in the unintellectual apostolates.[207] Fr. Peter Hans Kolvenbach, S.J., elected head of the Society of Jesus on September 13, 1983, was quite concerned about Jesuit tensions with the bishops of Nicaragua over the close relationship between the Jesuit university in Managua and the Sandinista government. Regarding the San Salvador UCA, however, recently named provincial of Central America, Fr. Valentin Menendez, S.J., continued to emphasize in his correspondence with Rome the crucial role being played in the country by the university through its educational work, especially with its publications and their influence on policy debates raging in the country. Likewise, Fr. Menendez continued to interpret

---

204. Memorandum from Ignacio Martín-Baró to Ignacio Ellacuría, February 20, 1984. Minutes of the meeting of the Board of Directors of the University of Central America, February 27, 1984 (San Salvador: Archives of the University of Central America).

205. The Jesuit curial staff of the Central American Province of the Society of Jesus has asked that this material remain confidential until such time they give permission for its use.

206. Charles J. Beirne, S.J., "Murder in the University: Jesuit Education and Social Change in El Salvador" (unpublished manuscript, May 2, 1994), 183-92. Used with permission of author.

207. Ibid., 183.

and defend the UCA's crucial contribution to promoting dialogue to end the civil war.[208]

Fr. Beirne shows that these same themes surfaced repeatedly in this correspondence throughout the 1980s. A series of Jesuit provincials were called upon to explain and interpret the work of the UCA to superiors in Rome who had received notably mixed reports from critics on the scene, or from Jesuit observers from outside. UCA Jesuits themselves were asked to make a series of institutional adjustments and to deal with shortcomings in carrying out the work of the university. These were undertaken, but, in general, the work continued with strong support from the Society of Jesus in Rome.

Fr. Beirne's unpublished review of these documents shows that, right up until weeks before the assassinations, provincial correspondence between El Salvador and Rome reflects concerns with issues of overwork, the need to attend to a union of hearts and minds within the Jesuit order, and what is seen as a certain overemphasis on the university's autonomy from ecclesiastical superiors. The overall tone, however, amounts to a solid endorsement for the UCA's real, influential, and positive presence in almost every serious effort to develop solutions for the most serious problems of the country.[209] With its emphasis on the role of the gospel in the UCA's efforts, this correspondence reflects the province's affirmation that the UCA was finding its own way to "historicize" in the 1980s what it learned from Archbishop Romero the decade before.

## Role of the UCA in the Life, Death, and Resurrection of Salvadoran Civil Society

It is important to understand that the UCA's commitment to negotiations between the FMLN and the government was an extremely dangerous position when Ellacuría and the UCA assumed it in 1981. In 1983 the ARENA party, through what the CIA describes as its clandestine "paramilitary organization,"[210] made a direct threat on the lives of all who would dare to advocate dialogue: "Dialogue is treason to the fatherland, and so we warn all the parties, political and military forces interested in negotiating the future of the country, that the eyes and the guns of the true patriots of El Salvador are on them."[211] Within days a bomb exploded at the UCA II residence, and fliers were found claiming responsibility for the group who had issued the warning: the Secret Anti-Communist Army (ESA). This was the situation until 1984 when U.S. counterinsurgency helped promote the election of José Napoleon Duarte.

---

208. Ibid.

209. Ibid., 191.

210. CIA/State Department, "Briefing Paper on Right-Wing Terrorism in El Salvador," October 27, 1993. U.S. document declassified on November 1993, Washington, DC. Cited in Whitfield, *Paying the Price*, 292.

211. "Comunicado del ESA, atribuyéndose las acciones terroristas del 6 de septiembre de 1983," *ECA* no. 419 (October 1983): 903. Cited in Whitfield, *Paying the Price*, 292.

The reader will recall that Duarte's election was strongly endorsed by the Reagan administration, with the CIA providing covert financial and logistic support. Duarte had won the presidential elections of 1972, which the military had stolen (as documented by the UCA), and had graduated from the iconic U.S. Catholic university, Notre Dame. The 1984 election campaign, which featured nasty exchanges between Duarte and Roberto D'Aubuisson, cemented Duarte's standing in the United States as the candidate of reform. However, Duarte had run on a platform promoting peace negotiations that created a problem for his patrons in the Reagan administration who were committed to continuing the war and achieving a military victory over the FMLN. Accordingly, Duarte was asked to sign a joint communiqué in Washington the week before he assumed the presidency. The agreement stated that increased U.S. aid was needed both to achieve peace and to pursue the successful prosecution of the war.[212] The United States would oppose serious negotiations for the remainder of the decade, but the new president of El Salvador had another idea.

### 1984: La Palma and Ayagualo

Duarte surprised all sides by announcing in his October 8, 1984, speech to the General Assembly of the United Nations that he was inviting the FDR-FMLN to peace talks in La Palma, Chalatenango. The FDR-FMLN had made a peace proposal five months before in May 1984, but few expected Duarte to reciprocate. The meeting was arranged for October 15, 1984, and came off because of remarkable cooperation between the two sides with assistance from the Catholic Church, the International Red Cross, and several Latin American governments. A nationwide cease-fire was arranged, and Salvadorans came out to line much of the one-hundred-kilometer road from San Salvador to La Palma. They waved white paper doves at the passing cars carrying the government and FMLN leadership to the meeting chanting, "We want peace!"[213] Ellacuría was later told that his *ECA* editorial, "The Military and Social Peace,"[214] was read aloud to Defense Minister Vides Casanova during the ride to La Palma, and actually played a constructive role in the talks.[215] Archbishop Rivera Damas presided at the meeting, and both sides agreed to meet again in a month.

The next meeting took place on November 30, 1984, at Ayagualo, a town outside of San Salvador. Between the two meetings both sides had come under intense pressure not to yield on key points from important constituencies who did not favor a peace process. The FMLN presented a "Comprehensive Pro-

---

212. "Comunicado conjunto del Presidente de los Estados Unidos y el Presidente Electo de El Salvador," May 21, 1984, *ECA* no. 428 (June 1984): 466.

213. These details provided by Montgomery, who was present. See *Revolution in El Salvador*, 188.

214. Ignacio Ellacuría, "Los militares y la paz social" (unsigned editorial) *ECA* nos. 429-430 (July-August 1984): 475-90.

215. This incident is mentioned in Whitfield, *Paying the Price*, 293. Author cites Ignacio Ellacuría, *Notebooks*, no. 9, October 12, 1984.

posal for a Negotiated Political Solution and Peace," which many observers interpreted as "hard line," and was rejected on national television that night by Duarte as a threat to the peace process.[216] The country waited to see what the outcome would be. On December 28, 1984, Ellacuría wrote a long article summarizing, critiquing, and pointing out the possibilities inherent in the two positions. He was quite critical of the pressure on both sides to rigidly maintain their positions and continue the war.

> For the extreme right and for large sectors of the Armed Forces, the total ruin of the dialogue would be seen as a total success; for the United States, a relative failure of the dialogue would be seen as a mild success; while, on the other hand, the success of the dialogue would be a partial success for Duarte, and the total success of the dialogue would be an important success for the FMLN-FDR. Not to look at it in this way is an error for the left, which could return to a position in favor of making the situation harder because it does not understand the present moment, just as it did not in 1976 with the agrarian transformation, in 1979 with the October coup, and in 1980 with the moderate positions of Colonel Majano.[217]

The article concludes by declaring prophetically, "If the opportunity for dialogue is lost, then once again the fervent hope of most Salvadorans will be squandered and destroyed. And the responsibility will belong to those who have frustrated it, or simply not given it the support they should have done."[218] It was the last meeting the two sides would have for three years.

### 1987: Paths to a Solution: Ellacuría's Proposal

The next real breakthrough did not come until August 7, 1987, in Esquipulas, Guatemala, when Costa Rican President Oscar Arias led the Central American presidents to agree on a regional framework for a comprehensive Central American peace. The *Arias Plan* envisioned processes of national reconciliation in each country, amnesty, dialogue between belligerents, cease-fires, and the opening of democratic processes leading to broad representation through free elections. Unfortunately, the regional peace process collapsed in El Salvador under the weight of political assassination, government intransigence, and resistance from Washington (still intent on a counterinsurgency victory). But a historic paradigm shift had begun. The UCA's national opinion poll showed over

---

216. The UCA provided a summary of the events at La Palma and Ayagualo in *Proceso* nos. 161 and 162 (October 15, October 22, 1984). The comments on the FMLN proposal are from Montgomery, *Revolution in El Salvador*, 188-89.

217. Tomas R. Campos (pseudonym for Ignacio Ellacuría), "Las primeras vicisitudes del diálogo entre el gobierno y el FMLN-FDR," in *Veinte años*, 1326; reprinted from *ECA* no. 434 (1984): 885-903. The text notes that the article was written on December 28, 1984.

218. Ibid.

80 percent of Salvadorans favored dialogue and an immediate resolution of the war.[219] Equally important, a host of non-governmental groups that were revitalizing the country's civil society after its brutal repression during the early 1980s (e.g., unions, teachers, human rights groups, political parties, church leaders, the press, village and neighborhood organizations, professional associations, etc.), were becoming articulate spokespersons for this unrepresented national majority and its demand for peace.

In 1987, Ignacio Ellacuría was one of the first to perceive the changes underway and to appreciate their significance. That year he published "Paths to a Solution for the Present Crisis of the Country,"[220] in the UCA's flagship journal, *ECA*. His thesis was that the collective existence of such groups constituted a new *third force* capable of being a key actor in moving the country from its stalemate toward a solution. For Ellacuría and for El Salvador this new development represented the practical means to move from a habitual emphasis on the agency of the government and the FMLN elites to a focus on the type of institutions through which the much talked about *popular majorities* themselves could initiate significant action at the national level.

In the article's first section Ellacuría proposes the creation of a process of national reflection, which Archbishop Rivera Damas and the UCA would soon turn into a series of events called the *National Debate*. Some consider the creation of this national conversation on the future of the country to be the most important political development of 1988 and the beginning of the process that would lead from the start of serious negotiations through the FMLN offensive and the UCA assassinations to peace. In section four Ellacuría asserts that the emergence of a *third force* in Salvadoran politics has the potential to "become an important element both for defending the just interests of the lower-class majority, and for creating a political solution for the conflict and its causes."[221] Ellacuría stresses that this third force is not a political organization but a social one, and he links it to an emerging theme in Catholic Social Teaching, namely, social organization and civil society as an important means through which individuals' interests can be defended against oppressive state power.[222]

Ellacuría's notion of the third force also fits into a larger discussion among Latin American theorists regarding civil society and its role in the continent's transition to democratic forms of government and social organization after decades of military rule. In an excellent summary of the international conversation on *Civil Society and Political Theory*[223] from around the time of Ellacuría's death, Jean Cohen and Andrew Arato suggest the following:

---

219. Ignacio Martín-Baró, *La opinion pública salvadoreña (1987-1988)* (San Salvador: UCA Editores, 1989), 90. Cited in Whitfield, *Paying the Price*, 315.

220. Ignacio Ellacuría, "Caminos de solución para la actual crisis del país," in Ellacuría, *Veinte años*, II, 1151-69; reprinted from *ECA* no. 462 (April 1987): 301-12.

221. Ibid., 1162.

222. Ibid.

223. Jean L. Cohen and Andrew Arato, *Civil Society and Political Theory* (Cambridge, MA: MIT Press, 1992).

The main concern of Latin American theorists and their collaborators has been the transition from a new type of military-bureaucratic
authoritarian rule: First, involving a period of *liberalization* (defined
as the restoration and/or extension of individual and group rights);
and second, a stage of *democratization* (understood in terms of the
establishment of a citizenship principle based on at least a procedural
minimum of participation). But these transitions are seen as strongly
dependent on the *resurrection of civil society*. Here, civil society
stands for a network of groups and associations between (in some versions, including) families and face-to-face groups on one side and outright state organizations on the other, mediating between individual
and state, private and public.[224]

This approach is reflected in Ellacuría's argument. He explicitly mentions
labor (including two of El Salvador's most important union movements, the
National Union of Salvadoran Workers (UNTS), and the National Union of
Workers and Campesinos (UNOC); large identifiable segments of El Salvador's
unrepresented majorities (the unemployed, refugees, marginated communities living in shanty towns); and those organizations doing social development
work: churches, educators, private business (such as the National Association for
Private enterprise [ANEP]), and professionals.[225]

Ellacuría is also clearly trying to develop institutional alternatives to the military-bureaucratic organizations of the state and those vying for control of the
government such as the FMLN as means to enhance the agency of the country's
dispossessed majorities. Avoiding the dispute over control of the state, the goals
of such organizations will focus on structural justice, a negotiated solution to
the war, and the mobilization of independent social groups. Ellacuría then proposes a program for the political mobilization and coordination of Salvadoran
civil society, arguing, "To flee from this [needed] effort, claiming that it might
be subject to political manipulation, is to ignore the fundamental distinction
between the social and the political, and it is to abdicate a fundamental obligation for each and every social power: putting their specific weight and capacity
for pressure at the service of the lower-class majorities and toward the solution
of the national conflict."[226] He adds that Salvadoran civil society should use
means that are non-violent and focused on conscientization, mobilization, organization, pressure, and negotiation.

In November 1987 Ellacuría piqued the interest of the man who would play
the key role in operationalizing this proposal: San Salvador's Catholic Archbishop Arturo Rivera Damas.

---

224. Ibid., 48. My emphasis.
225. Ellacuría, "Caminos de solución," 1163.
226. Ibid., 1167.

### 1988: El Salvador's National Debate[227]

Many saw 1988 as a critical year for El Salvador. The Reagan presidency was coming to an end with elections in the United States. Legislative elections were scheduled for March in El Salvador in which the right-wing ARENA party would soundly defeat the incumbent Christian Democrats. Despite numerous election irregularities and marginal participation from the left, the results were widely read as a stinging rejection by the Salvadoran people of the fruits of eight years of Christian Democratic rule and U.S. counterinsurgency. The following year ARENA would also wrest the presidency from the Christian Democrats, whose political program had become synonymous with their patrons in Washington, DC. At the same time important changes underway in the Soviet Union under Mikhail Gorbachev had brought *perestroika* to the fore in relations with the West. Thus, as the international rationale for U.S. counterinsurgency evaporated, and El Salvador's electorate chose the only viable national party offering an alternative to eight years of U.S.-sponsored Christian Democratic rule, the FMLN nurtured hopes for a *year of decision*.

Ellacuría, however, understood from the UCA's national opinion poll that the population was in no mood to continue the war and had tired of the negative prospects for peace. He therefore found little more than a promise for business as usual in the aforementioned events. In an article published early in the year he wrote:

> 1988 does not offer important new events from which one can hope for substantive change; rather, it presents a series of characteristics which make it a year of indefinition, a year of transition to who knows what, a year lost for great solutions. This presents us with the question of what to do during a year whose potential and possibilities are from the beginning so negative, the question of how to extract from the negative some positive dynamics in favor of a truly liberating process.[228]

By now the archdiocese and the UCA had begun their own planning for a different kind of initiative (based on Ellacuría's April proposal in *ECA*) designed to coordinate and multiply the impact of El Salvador's emerging *third forces*. In late November 1987 Archbishop Rivera Damas and Ellacuría agreed that the UCA and the archdiocese should both work to establish a national forum for a political discussion on the future of the country.[229] At an early December meeting of many of the country's leaders at the UCA the archbishop presented his official public proposal for "a public debate of all the viable forces of the

---

227. This section basically follows the narrative of Whitfield, *Paying the Price,* 317-20.

228. Ignacio Ellacuría, "1988, un año de transición para El Salvador," in Ellacuría, *Veinte años,* I, 453-66; reprinted from *ECA* nos. 471-482 (1988): 5-20.

229. Ignacio Ellacuría, *Notebooks,* no. 189, November 20, 1987; cited in Whitfield, *Paying the Price,* 317-18.

country,"[230] recommending the UCA as a partner for the planning process. Due to ecclesiastical politics, however the archbishop felt it necessary to exclude Ellacuría from the planning team, and the latter's influence on the process was not publicly acknowledged. But the initiative did come to fruition with the help of the UCA where Ellacuría was president.

On July 20, 1988, invitations went out to 102 organizations. The process was designed to elicit a number of points on which broad consensus existed in the country. The cover letter expressed the hope that these points of consensus would "help the government, the armed forces and the political parties, on the one hand, and the FDR-FMLN, on the other, to bring the conflict to an end through dialogue and negotiation."[231]

In the following months the conference and ensuing events seriously altered the country's political landscape. El Salvador's third forces were able to make themselves heard on the national scene as never before. In his editorial for the August-September 1988 issue of *ECA* dedicated to the National Debate, Ellacuría wrote:

> The national debate has been one of the important events of 1988 in El Salvador. During more than two months—July and August—it became the newest and most dynamic factor in the socio-political process. It drew attention and obligated practically all the significant forces of the country to take a position before its conclusions. The government, the Armed Forces, the political parties, private business, the church, the FMLN, and of course, the active participants in the national debate spoke about it. The communication media gave it a lot of space, to the point of making it into one of the principal themes of discussion.[232]

On the other hand, Ellacuría was well aware of the limitations of what had been achieved. Many groups, for example, had refused the invitation to participate. Nevertheless, there was a majority consensus on no less than 147 statements, and unanimity on several key points such as absolute priority of the need to direct economic resources away from the war toward the basic needs of the population, and the criterion that "the solution must be Central American and not a U.S. *intervention*."[233]

Most importantly, however, the process mobilized the opinion of the people themselves and articulated the outline of a broad national consensus. Even Alfredo Cristiani, the presidential candidate of the right-wing ARENA party, which had long supported the brutal suppression of Salvadoran civil society,

---

230. "Cátedra Universitaria de Realidad Nacional: Propuestas de solución después de Esquipulas II," *ECA* 42, nos. 469-70 (November-December 1987): 863.

231. "Carta de invitación del Señor Arzobispo de San Salvador," in *Debate Nacional 1988*, San Salvador, 1988, as cited by Whitfield, *Paying the Price*, 318.

232. Editorial: "El significado del debate nacional," *ECA* 43, nos. 478-479 (August-September 1988): 713.

233. Ibid., 741.

stated he agreed with 85 percent of the conclusions. He also committed his government, if elected, to a "permanent dialogue" with the FMLN.[234] The initiative had swung from the government and the FMLN to El Salvador's civil society, or what Ellacuría called its third force. The National Debate, by giving expression to the overwhelming desire for peace, had focused and increased the momentum for negotiations to a point that demanded a response from both the FMLN and the government.

### 1989: Collapse of Negotiations, War, Assassination, and Resurrection

Cynthia Arnson's excellent study of U.S. policy on Central America describes the situation as 1989 began.

> The far-right ARENA party won control of El Salvador's National Assembly in March 1988, putting former Major Roberto D'Aubuisson, suspected mastermind of the assassination of Archbishop Romero, in a key position of power. President Duarte, himself suffering from incurable liver cancer, seemed to personify the multiple ills of his administration. Economic austerity measures had taken a devastating toll on the party's urban base, eroding popular support for the regime. Violent abuses by the army and death squads were resuming an upward spiral, prompting Duarte to decry the "extremist death squads that seem to be coming back to life." The Christian Democrats themselves were badly divided over who should succeed Duarte as candidate in the 1989 presidential elections.[235]

Then on January 23, 1989, just as the election season swung into full gear, the FMLN surprised everyone with a proposal to postpone the upcoming presidential elections for six to eight months (September 15, 1989) to implement a series of guarantees for a free and fair election, and to abide by the results.[236] The Duarte government rejected the proposal, but the administration of George H. W. Bush (1978-1982) encouraged a reconsideration. Three weeks later, on February 20-21, 1989, the FMLN met in Mexico with thirteen political parties and proposed to renounce the armed struggle and incorporate into the political process. After a brief period of hope, however, negotiations collapsed. The military party, ARENA, was confident of victory in the upcoming elections, which it eventually won with 54 percent of the vote on March 19, 1988. And in the months between the elections of March 1989 and Cristiani's inauguration in June the far right escalated its campaign of violence and murder against reform-

---

234. "Los candidatos y la paz," *Carta a las iglesias*, October 1-15, 1988. Cited in Whitfield, *Paying the Price*, 320.

235. Ibid.

236. Montgomery, *Revolution in El Salvador*, 213-14.

ist officials while the FMLN, which had been planning an offensive since 1987, began a series of assassinations against government officials.

Ellacuría and the UCA, however, remained powerful voices in favor of negotiations both in El Salvador and the North, which made them threats to the economic and political interests on the far right and to the military leadership. Why? As noted earlier, the Pentagon Report states that right-wing landowners remained virulently opposed to land reform.[237] Military leaders were largely corrupt, enjoyed impunity for violations of human rights, and did "not wish to win the war because in so doing it would lose the American aid that has enriched it for the past decade"[238] The government depended on U.S. aid for survival and shared a commitment to defeat the FMLN, but there was little confidence and often outright opposition among the civilian-military elites to aspects of U.S. counterinsurgency promoting reforms directed at disenfranchised peasants.

In this atmosphere the extreme right saw an opportunity to carry out its long-held desire to assassinate Ignacio Ellacuría as part of its most recent campaign of terror intended to paralyze civil society and halt the increasing momentum toward peace. Accordingly, on March 3, 1989, the Crusade for Peace and Work denounced the "tiny group of satanic brains led by Ellacuría and a pack of communist hounds" ruining the country.[239] On March 14, a grenade exploded at the university's emergency electric power plant. On March 18, a paid advertisement denounced the "deceptive Jesuits Ignacio Ellacuría, Segundo Montes, and others, who with their doctrines, are poisoning many young minds." On April 16 the Armed Forces High Command published an ad charging Segundo Montes with defending the FMLN's use of land mines, and placing him with "groups and individuals who insist on defending the terrorism of the FMLN-FDR and its front groups." On April 19, the rebels bombed the residence of the new vice-president, Francisco Merino, and Attorney General Roberto Garcia Alvarado was murdered by a bomb on the roof of his jeep. The following day Colonel Juan Orlando Zepeda said the UCA is a "refuge for terrorist leaders, from where they plan the strategy of attack against Salvadorans." And on April 28, three bombs exploded at the UCA printing press.

The threat of negotiations and peace nevertheless continued to build. When the new president, the businessman Alfredo Cristiani, took office on June 1, 1989, he revealed a surprising five-point plan for talks with the FMLN that did not make surrender a precondition. Talks began September 13-15, 1989, in Mexico, and continued October 15-17 in San Jose, Costa Rica. Both sides agreed to a third meeting November 20 and 21, 1989, in Caracas, Venezuela. The September talks in Mexico produced a rebel proposal for a cease-fire to begin by November 15, 1989, with peace by January 31, 1990. At the October

---

237. Schwarz, *American Counterinsurgency Doctrine and El Salvador,* 46-50.

238. Ibid., 21.

239. Unless otherwise cited, the attacks mentioned in this paragraph are from the Jesuit Lawyers Committee chronology, "Attacks on El Salvador's Jesuits." See Doggett, *Death Foretold,* 308.

talks in San Jose, Costa Rica, the government demanded an immediate cease-fire, and Cristiani said he could not guarantee safety for the combatants. Both sides nonetheless agreed to create a special commission for carrying out accords related to life, liberty, and freedom of assembly and organization as well as electoral and judicial reform. There was also a general agreement to address the economy and reduce the size of the armed forces.

During the next few weeks, however, military events and pressure for war from the right and the left closed the space for political negotiation, while congressional support for continued U.S. military aid solidified. On October 17 (the last day of the talks) the daughter of Colonel Edgardo Casanova Vejar was brutally assassinated outside her home. Two days later bombs exploded in the homes of political opposition leader Ruben Zamora and his sister-in-law. Cristiani called FMLN demands to restructure the Supreme Court and the armed forces "absurd,"[240] and the rhetoric on both sides rapidly escalated. Then on October 31, 1989, bombs exploded in the offices of both the Committee of Mothers of the Detained, Disappeared, and Assassinated (COMADRES) and the National Trade Union Federation of Salvadoran Workers (FENASTRAS). Ten union leaders were killed and thirty-five people wounded. Whitfield observes, "Watching in horror as Febe Elizabeth Velazquez, one of the most important of all the leaders of the popular movement, ran out of the wreckage, the back of her head quite visibly blown right off, a sickening fear descended on the country."[241]

Ten days earlier Ellacuría had departed on a three-week trip to Europe to raise money, receive a prize given to the UCA by the Comin Foundation in Barcelona, witness the inauguration of the Xavier Zubiri Foundation in Madrid (Ellacuría's intellectual mentor), and participate in a meeting of university presidents. Shortly after the bombing, Colonel Juan Antonio Martinez Varela called Ellacuría in Spain with a message worriedly imploring him to serve on a commission to investigate the FENASTRAS bombing. On November 9, 1989 (his fifty-ninth birthday), Ellacuría sent the following response from Salamanca to the letter awaiting him there from Cristiani's minister of the presidency, Colonel Juan Antonio Martinez Varela: "I am stunned by this act of terrorism. I am ready to work for the promotion of human rights, I am convinced that President Cristiani rejects these types of actions and that he has proposed this commission with good will. I would like to support any reasonable effort that may help negotiation advance in the most effective way possible."[242] Little did he know that his immediate return would rob him of that opportunity.

---

240. "Crónica del mes-octubre," *ECA* no. 492 (October 1989): 865. Cited in Whitfield, *Paying the Price*, 342.

241. Whitfield, *Paying the Price*, 343.

242. Quotation by Whitfield, *Paying the Price*, 345, of a letter from Ignacio Ellacuría to Colonel Juan Antonio Martínez Varela, November 9, 1989 (photocopy). Whitfield notes that Ellacuría asked to postpone his decision until November 13, 1989, when he was returning to the country.

Major Erik Warren Buckland, senior U.S. military advisor to Salvadoran Psychological Operations, later testified to the FBI that a week or two earlier (late October or early November 1989[243]) his Salvadoran counterpart, Colonel Carlos Armando Avilés Buitrago (chief of psychological operations for the Salvadoran Joint Command), had revealed that a group of high-ranking Salvadoran military officers was planning to assassinate Fr. Ellacuría and other UCA Jesuits. According to the major, Avilés recruited Buckland to accompany him on a mission from Colonel René Ponce, chief of staff and second ranking officer of the Salvadoran Military High Command, in order "to solve a problem with Colonel Benavides."[244] When they arrived, Buckland was told to wait outside, but Avilés later reported that Benavides said Ellacuría "was a problem," and that "they wanted to handle it in the old way by killing some of the priests."[245] Major Buckland did nothing to prevent the planned murders, however. He later testified that he thought if "Chief of Staff Ponce had assigned a senior Colonel (Avilés) to address the problem," then it meant the assassinations "would not happen."[246] The major would soon realize he had been manipulated.

On November 11, 1989, two days after Ellacuría's response to Cristiani's invitation, the streets of the capital were lit with gun battles and military flares as the FMLN launched its nationwide offensive. Guerrillas assumed entrenched positions in poor neighborhoods around the city. Clashes occurred at the National University, at the Cuscatlan Stadium, and at military housing across from the UCA. Later the Air Force bombed and strafed working-class neighborhoods and shanty towns where the guerrillas were ensconced. The Military High Command found itself considering "the possibility that they could lose power, or that San Salvador could become a divided capital, much like Beirut."[247]

As we saw earlier, the U.N. Truth Commission reports that on the fifth day of the offensive, November 15, 1989, Colonel René Emilio Ponce, chief of staff of the armed forces, called "a meeting of General Staff with military heads and commanders" at the military academy at 6:30 p.m.[248] At that meeting Colonel Ponce "authorized the elimination" of civilian opposition leaders, and the bombing of civilian neighborhoods. One of the attendees reports that the session broke up around 10:00 p.m.[249] The United Nations asserts, "the officers

---

243. Doggett, *Death Foretold*, 225.

244. Sworn statement by Eric Warren Buckland, January 11, 1990, handwritten addendum, Washington, DC, p. 10 (on file at Lawyers Committee for Human Rights). Cited in Doggett, *Death Foretold*, 225.

245. Sworn statement by Eric Warren Buckland, January 11, 1990, handwritten addendum. Cited in Doggett, *Death Foretold*, 225.

246. Doggett, *Death Foretold*, 226.

247. Ibid., 38.

248. United Nations, *Report of the Commission on the Truth for El Salvador*, 50.

249. Written statement of General Humberto Larios, Fourth Criminal Court, August 29, 1990; INTERJUST, Sistema Informativo de la Corte Suprema de Justícia, September 4, 1990. Cited in Doggett, *Death Foretold*, 57.

stayed in the room talking in groups,"[250] and that "Colonel Ponce called over Colonel Guillermo Alfredo Benavides [director of the Military Academy] and, in front of the four other officers, ordered him to eliminate Father Ellacuría and to leave no witnesses . . . [and] to use the unit from the [U.S.-trained] Atlacatl Battalion."

Confirming this scenario, one month after the murders, on December 20, 1989, Major Buckland said that he learned from Avilés that Colonel Benavides had indeed ordered an Atlacatl commando unit to assassinate Ellacuría and his companions, and that an active cover up was underway. The major would come under intense pressure from the U.S. Embassy, the FBI, and his own military superiors, to back away from his story.[251] And in fact, a week after his January 12, 1990, testimony, Buckland would recant the portion admitting prior knowledge of the plot to assassinate Ellacuría and the other Jesuits. *Newsweek* later reported, "'The [George H. W. Bush] administration didn't want that story to come out,' sources said, because it 'wasn't productive to the conduct of the war.'"[252] Buckland continued to insist, however, that Avilés said Benavides had ordered the assassinations, information the major had already shared with his sister, Carol Buckland, a CNN reporter, first by telephone and later in a letter dated December 25, 1989. This testimony would play an important role in breaking through the wall of lies supporting the cover-up and protecting those who had ordered and committed the murders.

Accordingly, at approximately 1 a.m. on November 16, 1989, three hundred Salvadoran soldiers operating under the cover of darkness, including at least one hundred members of the elite U.S.-trained Atlacatl Battalion, surrounded the campus of the Jesuit-run UCA in San Salvador.[253] Having reconnoitered the virtually empty campus around 6:30 p.m., a force of fifty soldiers entered the university through the pedestrians' gate and gathered in the nearby university parking lot. After about thirty minutes they began shooting up nearby cars and set off at least one grenade, simulating a guerrilla attack. Leaving some of the group in the parking lot, others quietly formed a deadly inner ring, several scampering to the rooftops of neighboring houses and buildings, as they tightened the noose around the newly inhabited Jesuit community residence attached to the Archbishop Oscar Romero Center for Theological Reflection. Sleeping unawares inside was their quarry, Fr. Ellacuría, with five other Jesuit priests, and (unbeknownst to the soldiers) the housekeeper, her daughter, and a woman inhabiting a small dwelling at the rear entrance to the Jesuit community. Once in position, the smaller "select" group entrusted with the killings began banging on doors seeking entry to the building at multiple points.

---

250. United Nations, *Report of the Commission on the Truth for El Salvador,* 50.

251. Doggett, *Death Foretold,* 143-45, 166-68, 221-36.

252. Ibid., 228.

253. Unless otherwise noted, this account is based on extrajudicial testimonies by some of the participants; see United Nations, *Report of the Commission on the Truth for El Salvador,* and other primary sources summarized in Doggett, *Death Foretold,* 64-71, 281-83.

Twenty-six-year-old Private Oscar Amaya Grimaldi ("Pilijay"), designated the "key man" and entrusted with the battalion's only AK-47 for the murders, recalls that Fr. Ellacuría came to the balcony in his bathrobe and said, "Wait. I am coming to open the door. But don't keep making so much noise."[254] At that moment another group entered the lower floor of the attached Romero Center, destroying computers, books, and whatever else they found. After about ten minutes of banging Fr. Segundo Montes finally opened the first set of doors and was taken to the front lawn where Fr. Amando López, Fr. Ignacio Martín-Baró, Fr. Juan Moreno, and Ellacuría were being held. Martín-Baró left with one of the soldiers to open the side gate of the residence near the Chapel of Christ the Liberator. On the way they passed by the guest bedroom, where the angry voice of Fr. Martín-Baró heard by witnesses suggests that Sub-sergeant Tomás Zarpate Castillo was already holding the cook, Elba Ramos, and her daughter Celina at rifle point. Once inside the compound, Amaya and Sub-sergeant Antonio Ramiro Avalos (nicknamed "Satan") ordered the priests to lie down on the back lawn, where a neighbor testified they began a kind of "rhythmic whispering, like a psalmody of a group in prayer."[255] At that moment, as we saw earlier, Lieutenant José Ricardo Espinoza, a graduate of the Jesuit high school across town when Fr. Segundo Montes was there, gave Avalos the order to "proceed." This was relayed to Private Amaya, someone yelled "Now!" and the shooting began. Espinoza testified in his extrajudicial confession, as noted earlier, that he retreated from the Jesuit residence with tears in his eyes.[256]

"Pilijay" murdered Ellacuría, Montes, and Martín-Baró with the AK-47. "Satan" opened fire on Juan Ramón Moreno and Amando López. Tomás Zarpate repeatedly shot Elba and Celina until they ceased moaning, the mother's arms wrapped protectively around her daughter. At that moment Fr. López y López emerged from the door of the residence. Seeing the corpses he fled back into the house where he was executed by Colonel Pérez Vásquez. A blood-soaked copy of Jürgen Moltmann's book *The Crucified God* was found by his body. The entire operation took about one hour.

Thus, while negotiations for peace had offered a hopeful counterpoint to the drums of war, the voice of Salvadoran civil society had once again been brutally silenced by repression and murder. And Ellacuría's hope that the "profound and wide-ranging" national conversation generated by the National Debate might lead to a negotiated solution lay in ruins.

Indeed, the early morning executions at the new Jesuit residence on November 16, 1989, seemed to symbolize the eclipse of dialogue and negotiation by the purveyors of state-sponsored violence against civil society and the voices of reform. Most of the top Jesuit leadership of the UCA was dead, with their friend, Elba, and her daughter Celina, who had sought refuge with the Jesuit

---

254. Doggett, *Death Foretold*, 67.

255. These are the words of Martha Doggett describing the account of a neighbor; Doggett, *Death Foretold*, 68.

256. Doggett, *Death Foretold*, 115 and 332.

community that night. Some of the bodies of El Salvador's leading intellectuals had their brains dislodged by a soldier's boot. One assailant took the time to symbolically reenact the assassination of Archbishop Oscar Romero by carefully shooting through the heart the dead prelate's picture hanging in the office. The ruin emblemized the utter defeat of the UCA's hopes to historicize the gospel by supporting the efforts of the country's marginated third forces to construct a politics of negotiation and reconciliation for El Salvador.

### Conclusion

The story of the UCA martyrs does not conclude with their deaths, however. For international outrage occasioned by the murders, combined with military realties exposed by the surprising offensive, sowed seeds of doubt that would blossom in the months and years ahead. Three weeks after the assassinations, on December 8, 1989, the *Christian Science Monitor* reported that "the rebel offensive, now entering its fourth week, has shaken the political and military realities of El Salvador so profoundly that . . . [it] may be slowly convincing some of the country's elite that concessions have to be made."[257] Military actors in El Salvador and the United States finally admitted that neither party was strong enough to defeat the other. A secret CIA National Intelligence Estimate written in February 1989 had asserted, "We believe that the government is likely to grind down the insurgency as a military force over the next three to five years."[258] Yet on February 8, 1990, shortly after the offensive, General Maxwell R. Thurman, head of the U.S. Southern Command, told the Senate Armed Service Committee when asked if the Salvadoran government could defeat the rebels, "I think they will not be able to do that."[259] For their part the rebels believed, according to one leader, "The offensive laid down the parameters of what we could achieve by military means and what we couldn't. We believed we had made an impressive show of force but it was not something we could do every six months."[260] Meanwhile, a January 29, 1990, article in the *San Francisco Examiner* suggested, "Intense reaction to the Jesuit murders and the FMLN offensive has raised profound doubts about the success of U.S. policy there in general, assuring, at the very least, the first major debate in five years over Washington's future role in El Salvador."[261]

---

257. Chris Norton, "After Salvador's Rebel Offensive," *Christian Science Monitor,* December 8, 1989, 4.

258. U.S. Declassified Documents I, CIA, "El Salvador: Government and Insurgent Prospects," February 1989, iii-iv. Cited in Byrne, *El Salvador's Civil War,* 170.

259. Michael R. Gordon, "U.S. General Says Salvador Cannot Defeat the Guerrillas," *New York Times,* February 9, 1990, 9. Cited in Byrne, *El Salvador's Civil War,* 172.

260. Facundo Guardado interview by Hugh Byrne, February 19, 1993, in Byrne, *El Salvador's Civil War,* 173.

261. Phil Bronstein, "No Cuts Likely in U.S. Aid to Salvador," *San Francisco Examiner,* January 28, 1990, A14. Cited in Byrne, *El Salvador's Civil War,* 172.

One by one over the next two years all the major power brokers and political actors (the U.S. government, the Salvadoran Military High Command, the FMLN, the Salvadoran oligarchy, and the government itself) would be forced to admit that their own strategic visions for the country had not fully succeeded, and absent massive ongoing U.S. aid, had no future without the approval of the country's vast majorities. The FMLN had demonstrated that a military victory by the government was impossible. The government had demonstrated it could survive but not win, even with U.S. support. And the country's poor majorities were now mobilized and insisting on peace and the creation of the minimal institutional structures necessary to guarantee an end to the brutal repression of civil society. El Salvador's third forces had created a formidable non-aligned political force undermining the claims of the various power brokers. And El Salvador's increasingly independent and influential civil society was now an important player in promoting a viable politics of national reconciliation. Ironically, the strategic vision diligently promoted by Ellacuría, the UCA, and so many others was given new life through the impact on the peace process of the deaths of the martyrs.

Thus, by the end of 1990 it was clear that the Jesuit murders in combination with the successful offensive had done serious damage to the case of the Salvadoran government for continued Washington aid (especially after the fall of the Berlin Wall in November 1989). Cristiani journeyed to Washington in February 1990 to contain the damage, but he encountered a distinct change in congressional attitudes. Days after the president's visit Senator Christopher Dodd introduced a bill to cut U.S. aid to El Salvador by 50 percent unless the FMLN blocked progress in the negotiations and threatened the viability of the government. This proposal would become a framework for congressional attempts to limit aid in the months ahead.

In late April 1990 the House Foreign Affairs Committee took up Dodd's proposal. On April 30, 1990, the Moakley task force said the investigation of the Jesuit case was at a "virtual standstill" and revealed aspects of Major Buckland's allegations (which the administration had suppressed). On May 22, 1990, the House adopted the Moakley-Murtha amendment, which contained a version of the Dodd formula to cut military aid by half. In the debate Congressman Moakley protested, "Enough is enough. They killed six priests in cold blood. I stood on the ground where my friends were blown away by men to whom the sanctity of human life bears no meaning—and men who will probably never be brought to justice."[262] A Republican substitute to cut military aid by 25 percent failed 175 to 243, and the Moakley-Murtha version passed 250 to 163 with thirty-one Republicans in favor and only twenty-eight Democrats opposed.[263]

Though the effect was largely symbolic, it was clear that the Jesuit murders had seriously wounded the now-fragile remains of the bipartisan compromise first articulated by the Kissinger Commission in favor of the Salvadoran coun-

---

262. *Congressional Record*, May 22, 1990, H 2712. Cited in Arnson, *Crossroads*, 255.
263. Arnson, *Crossroads*, 254-55.

terinsurgency effort. Without the artificially constructed pipeline of U.S. dollars supporting the war, the Salvadoran government, like the FMLN, soon realized it would have to start paying attention to the results of the IUDOP polls and the demand of the country's third forces that their voices (particularly their insistence that the war must end) play a role in shaping the future of El Salvador.

Responding to these forces, in 1991 the United Nations and its secretary-general, Javier Pérez de Cuéllar of Peru, assumed a crucial if somewhat frantic role in tortuous peace negotiations that concluded at the United Nations in New York twenty-eight minutes after the end of 1991 and the expiration of his term. Peace accords ending the decade-long war were signed in Mexico City on January 16, 1992, and the final documents contained significant provisions for military, political, economic, and social reform. In the end, the very existence of the treaty demonstrated the inadequacies of the strategic visions for El Salvador that the country's elites had attempted to impose on the Salvadoran people and civil society during the 1980s.

The hope of U.S. policy makers for a military victory over the FMLN had proved unachievable due to its cost and lack of support from the common people, though the United States did succeed in preventing a rebel victory. The far right's ideology of national salvation through state-sponsored violence against civil society, embraced by the military and the Salvadoran government, had wrought a terrifying decade of murder and economic ruin. The edifying visions of the reformist 1979 coup had been defeated by the military arm of the state. The rebels' dream that vast numbers of Salvadorans would rise up in a general insurrection had proved to be unrealistic (despite several important military offensives). And the murders of Archbishop Romero, the Jesuits, and so many others had demonstrated the impotency of the gospel against the power of the state. Ironically, however, the triumph of state-sponsored violence against Salvadoran civil society simultaneously revealed and refined the courageous resiliency, independence, and importance of the country's third forces, including their defender and prophet, Archbishop Romero, simultaneously providing legitimacy to the cause of the rebels and reinforcing the cause of peace.

In the end, it seems that Ellacuría was correct in 1987 when he argued that El Salvador's emergent civil society embodied the mobilization of the country's poor majorities, giving expression to their demands for peace and a credible promise of reform (so often expressed in IUDOP's polls). And he was prescient in his assertion that the UCA could best historicize the church's option for the poor in the Salvadoran context through solidarity with the country's third forces and their demands for reform. Indeed, the demands of civil society for peace and reform provided the outline for the final agreement articulated in the peace accords for the future of El Salvador.[264]

---

264. Though peace and some significant reforms would come to El Salvador as a result of the accords, the country's fundamental social and economic problems (e.g., landlessness, economic development, various forms of poverty as indicated by extremely low social indicators, political extremism, and human rights violations, etc.) remain to be addressed.

So what, then, is to be learned from the U.S. involvement in this disturbing story? The Pentagon report concludes that during the 1980s the Salvadoran government, the right-wing landowners and their allies, and the Salvadoran military knew that they "had America trapped,"[265] and had concluded the United States was prepared to make a kind of "pact with the devil" in order to insure that "El Salvador not fall to the FMLN." Sadly, in light of the insistence on torture as a legitimate weapon in the war against terror by former vice-president Chaney and other former U.S. officials,[266] the Pentagon report seems prescient in pointing to the potential threat to basic and enduring American values posed by the practical aspects of U.S. counterinsurgency and anti-terrorist policy. The Pentagon report asserts that, by making victory for an inept and corrupt ally the cornerstone of its counterinsurgency objectives in El Salvador, the United States helped to defeat its own efforts to promote development and human rights. The report concludes, "In attempting to reconcile these objectives, . . . we pursued a policy by means unsettling to ourselves, for ends humiliating to the Salvadorans, and at a cost disproportionate to any conventional conception of the national interest."[267]

For those interested in the future of the Catholic university, it must be said that the commitment of Ignacio Ellacuría and the UCA to the option for the poor led them to confront violent, powerful, and dehumanizing forces with a reasoned and compassionate plea for negotiations and peace. In the end, the sanity and humanity of this approach proved a serious threat to ongoing U.S. support for an immoral ally in a brutal and unnecessary civil war. Twenty-five years after their deaths, the UCA martyrs remind us of the risks to individuals and institutions whose lives and work embody a commitment to the dignity of every person, especially the marginated, through effective opposition to the sometime follies of U.S.-financed wars on foreign soil.

What cannot be denied, however, is that the emphasis that the UCA Jesuits placed on supporting the mobilization and the hopes of Salvadoran civil society, with the country's poor majorities as important actors, played a significant role in helping to establish a historically effective tradition for the agency of the dispossessed in a viable national politics of reconciliation for El Salvador. The

---

Likewise, the UCA faces serious problems in the years ahead (see Beirne, "Murder in the University," pp. 220-42. However, the author believes that the birth of a growing Salvadoran civil society representative of the interests of the country's poor majorities (whose role Ellacuría prophetically enunciated in 1987) is one of the nation's most important assets for facing the daunting challenges ahead. One can only hope that its autonomy and significance will be respected by the government, the opposition, the extreme right, and foreign governments such as the United States who have interests in the region. No doubt the voice of the UCA will continue to be heard on this subject.

265. Schwarz, *American Counterinsurgency Doctrine and El Salvador*, 82.

266. Former Vice-President Dick Cheney, "Keeping America Safe" (remarks made at the American Enterprise Institute for Public Policy Research), May 21, 2009; http://www.aei.org/speech/100050, accessed March 2, 2014.

267. Schwarz, *American Counterinsurgency Doctrine and El Salvador*, 84.

question remains, however, what does this history offer to the current generation of Salvadorans that grows increasingly disenchanted with glaring inequities of El Salvador's politics of peace? And what does it say to those of us whose hearts sink at the prospect of sustaining a spirituality of Christian solidarity in the context of the *realpolitik* of U.S. foreign policy and national interest in an ambiguous world of deals and compromises?

I believe an answer to this question is to be found in the real life stories of the martyrs and their colleagues and the many ways they historicized their option for the poor. These Jesuits and their colleagues were drawn to appreciate the political significance of the mobilization and institutionalization of El Salvador's third forces through a spirituality disposed to recognize the mediation of grace through the agency of the poor. Ellacuría and his friends spoke evocatively of solidarity with *the crucified people* of our world. More importantly, however, they historicized this spirituality by dedicating themselves to supporting the faint patterns of hope and progress emerging among the confusing details of El Salvador's historical reality during the 1980s.

Twenty-five years after their deaths we can honestly say that the hard work, the political analysis, and the sense of public accountability and responsibility demanded to create a functioning civil society and a viable politics of national reconciliation grounded in the agency and aspirations of the country's poor majorities of El Salvador has only just begun. But while the road to a better future has yet to be constructed, the path is clearly marked for millions of Salvadorans by the examples of Archbishop Oscar Romero and the UCA martyrs. For their journeys serve as living signs of faith that the risen Jesus lives in the country's poor and marginated majorities, hope for a future grounded in the values of the Reign of God, and love for the resilient and courageous people of El Salvador.

In Part II, we will explore the spiritual, philosophical, historical, and theological roots of this conviction and the vision of the Christian university that emerged from it.

# Part II

# *Doing Theology with the Crucified People and Those Who Love Them*

## IGNACIO ELLACURÍA'S FUNDAMENTAL THEOLOGY

Ellacuría . . . had the gift to let reality talk.

Ellacuria did what he did not only because he had an idea, but because he was moved by reality. . . . If we go back, however, . . . and ask what helped him to conceptualize this reality, it was Zubiri and Rahner.

Jon Sobrino[1]

### Introduction

Ignacio Ellacuría's transformative journey with the people of El Salvador, his colleagues, and Archbishop Oscar Romero finds voice in an extraordinary collection of writings that spans fourteen volumes and a variety of themes spanning theology, philosophy, political analysis, science, the nature of the university, literature, and more. In the following chapters I will explore how the historical reality of El Salvador led Ellacuría to develop fresh and at times paradigm-changing interpretations of his sources, which he uses to respond to the historical reality of El Salvador's people and to formulate the outline of a remarkable new contextualized approach to fundamental theology for Latin America.

In Part I I told the University of Central America's (UCA's) story of blood and ink, which Ellacuría described as trying "to do in our university way what [Archbishop Romero] did in his pastoral way"[2] while leading the archdiocese of San Salvador guided by the discernment that God was calling the church to a preferential option for the poor. Each of the three chapters above spoke of

---

1. First quote: Interview with Jon Sobrino by Robert Lassalle-Klein, San Salvador, April 19, 1994, 1. Second quote: Interview with Jon Sobrino by Robert Lassalle-Klein, Santa Clara, CA, March 17, 1994, 1.

2. Ignacio Ellacuría, "La UCA ante el doctorado concedido a Monseñor Romero," *Escritos teológicos*, III (San Salvador: UCA Editores, 2002), 104.

writers, books, teaching and learning, service projects, faith and politics, public forums, policy analyses, and collaborations with leading actors as part of some aspect of the UCA's attempts to understand and communicate the truth about U.S.-funded state-sponsored violence against Salvadoran civil society. It was also the story of the UCA's efforts to fulfill its mission as a Christian university to take El Salvador's crucified people down from the cross by analyzing and supporting their struggles to bring about liberation and justice and to create a society where dignity, love, compassion, and sanity might prevail.

In Part II I will summarize the transformations produced by Ignacio Ellacuría in the spiritual, philosophical, ecclesiological, and theological sources he uses in order to develop a contextual fundamental theology for Latin America. Ellacuría and his colleagues were changed by the process narrated above and experienced what he and Jon Sobrino describe as a mystical encounter with the risen Jesus mediated through their love and solidarity with El Salvador's suffering people. Ellacuría's fundamental theology and Sobrino's Christology bear the marks of this transformative experience, which is not surprising in light of Sobrino's assertion that "we have done nothing more than—starting from Jesus—elevate the reality we are living to the level of a theological concept."[3]

First, then, I will analyze the central role of the *Spiritual Exercises* of St. Ignatius and Ignatian spirituality in Ellacuría's life and thought. I will do this by (1) documenting their relationship to his philosophy of historical reality, (2) analyzing their role in the December 1969 option for the poor of the Central American Jesuits and Ellacuría's personal sense of being called to take the crucified people of El Salvador down from the cross, and (3) exploring Ellacuría's conviction that Rutilio Grande, Archbishop Romero, and their followers became living signs of the Christ of the 1969 San Salvador retreat and the action of the Word of God in history.

Second, I will summarize Ellacuría's appropriation of Xavier Zubiri's critique of what he calls a persistent strain of reductionist idealism in Western philosophy and his concepts of sentient intelligence and the primacy of the formal dimension of reality. I will identify five areas in which Ellacuría's confrontation with the historical reality of Latin America moved his thinking beyond that of his philosophical mentor. And I will suggest what Ellacuría's philosophy contributes to his work on behalf of El Salvador's poor majorities.

Third, I will suggest that, more than anyone else, Archbishop Romero shaped Ellacuría's historical encounter with God in the crucified people of El Salvador and the worldly mysticism that forms the core of his mature writings and work. I do this by arguing that Archbishop Romero showed Ellacuría how to be the prophetic voice of the church to Salvadoran society; by teaching him to love, to trust, and to find Christ in the common people of El Salvador; and by inspiring Ellacuría and others to follow his example by bringing God close to the suffer-

---

3. Jon Sobrino, *Jesucristo liberador: Lectura histórica-teológica de Jesús de Nazaret* (San Salvador: UCA, 1991), 30, my translation; see Jon Sobrino, *Jesus the Liberator: A Historical-Theological View* (Maryknoll, NY: Orbis Books, 1993), 8.

ing poor and by leavening their struggle for liberation with the message of Jesus in a salvific way for the historical process of El Salvador.

Fourth, I will examine Karl Rahner's contributions to the *fundamenta* developed by Ignacio Ellacuría to interpret the human face of God revealed by Archbishop Romero in the suffering people of El Salvador. I will first explain Ellacuría's insistence that *historical reality* is the proper object of a truly Latin American theology and that human beings apprehend an absolute (or *theologal*) dimension of reality, showing how it builds on key insights from Rahner's metaphysics of being as well as Zubiri's post-Newtonian realism. Second, I will show how Ellacuría's use of Zubiri's *model of sentient intelligence to conceptualize the role of human knowing in Latin American theological method* mimics aspects of the theory of knowing (the role of the hylomorphic theory and the agent intellect) behind Rahner's transcendental Thomism. Third, I will examine Ellacuría's notion that *historical reality has been transformed by grace,* showing how it draws upon and historicizes aspects of Rahner's concept of the supernatural existential. And fourth, I will examine Ellacuría's *theology of sign* and its application to the crucified people, showing how it echoes the trinitarian pattern of Rahner's "theology of symbol."

Finally, this summary of how Ellacuría's fundamental theology builds upon and produces changes in his sources will put us in position to do the work of Part III. There I will show how Jon Sobrino's Latin American Christology uses the theological *fundamenta* outlined here to make sense of the life, death, and resurrection of Archbishop Romero and examine Ellacuría's claim that the crucified people are the defining sign of the times and a privileged *locus theologicus* for God's historical self-offer today.

# 4

# *The Spiritual Exercises of St. Ignatius*

## LATIN AMERICA'S RETREAT MASTER,
## MIGUEL ELIZONDO, S.J.

The life and thought of Ignacio Ellacuría cannot be understood apart from the journey from Portugalete to San Salvador to which he was called by his master of novices, Fr. Miguel Elizondo, S.J., in 1948, after just one year in the Jesuits. Ellacuría and his six companions would be prepared for the great challenges and transformations ahead by the action-oriented mysticism of the *Spiritual Exercises* of St. Ignatius passed on to them by Elizondo, and fortified by companions with a deeply shared sense of call to the mission of the Society of Jesus in Latin America. Ellacuría's adult life is best understood as his response to this characteristically Jesuit sense of call and a passionate desire to collaborate with God's work in the world, concretized after Vatican II in a profound commitment to the efforts of the Jesuits to discern and respond to the signs of the times in Central America. As we have seen, his journey would become a sign of the "yes" of the Salvadoran church to God's preferential option for the poor.

We begin, then, by asking how the life of Ignacio Ellacuría became so intertwined with the defining classic of Ignatian spirituality, and how its methods and insights shaped his life and thought?

Ignacio Ellacuría was born November 9, 1930, in Portugalete,[1] the heart of the Basque country on the northern (Atlantic) coast of Spain. The fourth of six children and five sons, in 1940 he was sent to southern Navarro, 143 miles from home, for studies at the Jesuit high school in Tudela, Spain.[2] Here, young Ignacio began the study of Latin, Greek, and the classics of Western literature,

---

1. Rudolfo Cardenal, "Ser jesuita hoy en El Salvador," *ECA* nos. 493-494 (1989): 1013-21, esp. 1013, henceforth cited as Cardenal "Ser jesuita hoy." For revised and expanded versions of this article, see Rudolfo Cardenal, "Ignacio Ellacuría (1930-1989)," http://www.uca.edu.sv/ martires /new/ella/fella.htm (San Salvador, September 1999), henceforth cited as Cardenal, "Ignacio Ellacuría." See also Rodolfo Cardenal, S.J., "De Portugalete a San Salvador: de la mano de cinco maestros," in J. Sobrino and R. Alvarado, eds., *Ignacio Ellacuría, "Aquella libertad esclarecida"* (San Salvador: UCA Editores, 1999); Teresa Whitfield, *Paying the Price: Ignacio Ellacuría and the Murdered Jesuits of El Salvador* (Philadelphia: Temple University Press, 1994), 15-17.

2. Cardenal, "Ser jesuita hoy en El Salvador," 1013.

his knowledge of which would impress later mentors in the humanities[3] and philosophy.[4] He also nurtured what became a lifelong passion for soccer.[5]

Reserved and intense, Ellacuría was not invited to a meeting of promising recruits by the spiritual father of the senior class at Tudela.[6] Still, he graduated at age sixteen and became the fourth of five brothers to enter the seminary in the Jesuit novitiate at Loyola on September 14, 1947, the ancestral home of Ignatius Loyola, founder of the Jesuits. There he made the famous thirty-day silent retreat known as the *Spiritual Exercises* of St. Ignatius under the direction of Fr. Miguel Elizondo, S.J., then master of novices. The first of his great teachers, Elizondo would mentor Ellacuría in a vigorous and thoroughly updated version of Ignatian spirituality.

After only one year in the novitiate, Ellacuría was invited to "volunteer" with five other novices to accompany Fr. Elizondo on an exciting new mission to open the doors of the first-ever novitiate for the Society of Jesus in Central America. Thirty-five years later Ellacuría would recall with some humor that his affirmative response to Elizondo's offer reflected, more than anything else, the fact that "back then we had a very simple understanding of obedience."[7] Ellacuría recalled, "It wasn't a sacrifice or heroism,"[8] adding, "I have never regretted having begun an American life." His choice of words, however, betrays the ongoing influence of Spain in Ellacuría's perspective thirty-five years after his formative journey from Portugalete to San Salvador. U.S. readers will notice that Ellacuría uses the adjective "American" to describe his move to Central America, while Central Americans will wonder why he eschews the more typical "Latin" or "Central" American modifiers. From either perspective, like the Castilian accent he retained throughout his life, Ellacuría's sense that he was living an "American life" reveals a distinctively Spanish worldview.

This small detail echoes the reality that Ellacuría lived his entire adult life at the crossroads of Spain and Central America. Viewed correctly, this aspect of his intellectual and personal biography makes the transformations he experienced all the more remarkable and interesting. It is no secret that friends and foes alike identified Ellacuría with the sometimes overbearing influence of Spanish Jesuits on the Society of Jesus in Central America.[9] Five of the six mur-

---

3. Whitfield, *Paying the Price,* 25.

4. Cardenal, "Ignacio Ellacuría," 4.

5. Ibid., 6; and Cardenal, "Ser jesuita hoy," 1017.

6. José Ellacuría, in a talk at the UCA, San Salvador, November 15, 1990. Cited in Whitfield, *Paying the Price,* 16; and in Cardenal, "Ignacio Ellacuría," 1.

7. Cardenal, "De Portugalete," 43.

8. Ignacio Ellacuría, "El volcán jesuita: entrevista con el Padre Ellacuría, Rector de la Universidad Centroamericana," *ABC*, Madrid, March 28, 1982; cited in Whitfield, *Paying the Price,* 17; and in Cardenal, "De Portugalete," 44.

9. November 13, 1989, three days before the assassinations, *La Prensa Gráfica* stated, "it is of the utmost urgency that the Jesuits are thrown out of the country," and falsely charges "the Spanish Jesuit priest Ignacio Ellacuría "with making the University a guerrilla arms depot." See Doggett, *Death Foretold,* 309.

dered priests, all of whom played important roles at the university, were Spanish. Yet, within two years of the assassinations, many younger Jesuits (though loyal to the ideals of the martyrs) called openly for reduced Spanish influence in key Jesuit positions in order to promote the "Central-Americanization" of the province.[10] It is likewise significant that, by the end of his second year as president of the University of Central America (UCA) and seven years after becoming a Salvadoran citizen, Ellacuría had spent only thirteen of his fifty-two years in the country!

These details help us to appreciate that Ignacio Ellacuría is best understood as a bridge figure. He was among the most brilliant of a generation of mid-twentieth-century Spanish Jesuits sent to serve the Catholic Church of Latin America. But he is loved and remembered mainly for having embraced, and been transformed by, a lifetime of sharing the suffering, hopes, and aspirations of the "crucified people" of El Salvador.

Faced with the puzzle of preparing his charges to face the unforeseen challenges and transformations that would emerge after World War II, Elizondo sought to instill both personal freedom and the deep spirituality of St. Ignatius Loyola in his novices. As noted in Chapter 1, he challenged them to interiorize the spirituality of the *Spiritual Exercises* by studying the founding history and documents of the Society of Jesus and by learning to use their own judgment in adapting to Central America. This seemed better to Elizondo than depending on Spanish convention regarding "what one can consider essential in the vocation of the Society."[11]

Elizondo is revered for his work as the spiritual director of the final stage of Jesuit formation for Latin America through three decades (1968-1995) after Vatican II. Looking back on the challenge of forming mainly Spanish novices to serve in the Americas, Elizondo recalls being guided by Ignatius's motto, *Ad majorem Dei gloriam* (for the greater glory of God). He says, "I felt totally free of my past, of my antecedents as a Jesuit and as a novice master, although I was a 'novice' in that myself."[12] As noted earlier, Fr. César Jerez, S.J., the native-born and much-loved provincial of Central America during its first persecutions and martyrdoms, said shortly before his death that Elizondo "taught us not to be afraid."[13]

### A Daring Challenge

This would prove to be a valuable quality. For as we saw, on December 24-31, 1969, Elizondo and his former protégé, Ellacuría, led the Jesuits of Central

---

10. This issue is mentioned as the central challenge facing the province in the brief history by Juan Hernández-Pico; see Juan Hernández-Pico, S.J., *Historia reciente de la Provincia de Centroamérica (1976-1986)* (San Salvador: Ediciones Cardoner, 1991), 3. See also "Interview of Jesuits in Formation," by Robert Lassalle-Klein (San Salvador, July 1994).

11. Interview with Fr. Miguel Elizondo (1990); cited in Whitfield, *Paying the Price*, 22; see also 21-24.

12. Whitfield, *Paying the Price*, 21.

13. Interview with César Jerez (1991); cited in Whitfield, *Paying the Price*, 24.

America through the *Spiritual Exercises* as they sought to discern "the call" of the Society of Jesus in Central America after Medellín (1968) and Vatican II (1962-1965).[14] Not surprisingly, Elizondo's efforts would be directed toward fostering a profound appreciation in his colleagues, based on the latest research, of the founding traditions of Jesuit spirituality. Two talks given by the former novice master and provincial at the beginning of the retreat capture his understanding of the essence of Ignatian spirituality and its relationship to the present historical moment.[15] They revolve around four points that would define the spirituality of an entire generation of Latin American Jesuits and can be found at the heart of Ellacuría's life and work.

First, in responding to the call of Vatican II, Medellín, and the Latin American Jesuit provincials to renew their sense of mission and identity, Elizondo asserts, "If we have to renew ourselves, we won't begin by renewing *things*, nor will we begin by renewing ourselves as persons; rather we will begin by renewing our spirituality . . . [our experience] of the God who has communicated himself to us" in the *Spiritual Exercises*.[16] But where is this God to be found?

Elizondo's second point is that Ignatius believes that God is to be found, with the help of the *Exercises*, through "a dialogical encounter of the whole province . . . with the Christ of today, with his church of today, and with the Christ located here, in this province."[17] His point is that the renewal of the Central American Jesuits should begin and end with the living Christ of today encountered by the bishops at Medellín, the Jesuit provincials at Rio, and the retreatants gathered in El Salvador. This assertion had the effect of transforming the training for radical freedom rooted in the *Spiritual Exercises*, which Elizondo had tried to instill in his many charges from 1949 forward, into a prophetic call to discern and cooperate with how God was acting in the present historical moment. As

---

14. "Presentación," 1, in "Reunión-Ejercicios de la viceprovincia Jesuitica de Centroamérica, Diciembre 1969," 2, in *Reflexión teológico-espiritual de la Compañía de Jesús en Centroamérica,* II (San Salvador: Archives of the Society of Jesus, Central American Province, Survey S.J. de Centroamérica, December 1969), 1, henceforth cited as "Reunión-Ejercicios." Juan Hernández-Pico asserts that this discussion, and a corresponding proposal developed at the Province Congregation of 1970, contributed seminal ideas to what eventually became the famous "Decree Two: The Jesuits Today," of the worldwide 32nd General Congregation of the Society of Jesus, December 2, 1974 to March 7, 1975; see Juan Hernández-Pico, *Historia reciente,* 9-10.

15. Elizondo delivered the following talks: "The Theological and Spiritual Meaning of a Communal Meeting of the Vice-Province"; "The First Week as the Indispensable Beginning of Conversion"; "The Ignatian Vision of the Following of Christ"; "Prayer in the Society of Jesus." See "El sentido teológico y espiritual de una reunión comunitaria de la viceprovincia," "La primera semana como comienzo indispensable de conversión," "La visión ignaciana del seguimiento de Cristo," and "La oración en la Compañía de Jesús," in "Reunión-Ejercicios," 31, 37-45, 46-57, 76-83, 88-95.

16. Elizondo, "Sentido teológico," 1, in "Reunión-Ejercicios."

17. Ibid., 5.

he later recalled, "I wanted to prepare in them the openness that is necessary for what the future will bring, without ever knowing what the future may be."[18]

Third, as noted earlier, Elizondo asserts, "The Ignatian vocational experience consists in a Trinitarian experience, an experience of [cooperating with] the Trinity present and operative in this world, . . . realizing its plan for the salvation of the whole world."[19] He insists that the essential Ignatian insight is that the Trinity acts "not only by means of the presence and operation of God, but through the insertion of humanity in history." This is so because "Christ, the human *par excellence*, enters into that history of salvation bringing with him all persons chosen to actively cooperate with the work of the Trinity in realizing the salvific plan of God. "[20]

And fourth, Elizondo argues that the notion that we are called to be integral collaborators with God's action in the world reflects the spiritual experience of St. Ignatius himself.[21] He says, "When St. Ignatius feels that this is the call, that the one calling him . . . is . . . the God of salvation, he emerges from his solitude and . . . engages the world." Accordingly, "The definitive God of Ignatius is going to be the God of this world," and "the world is [going to be] the location for the encounter with God." As a result, for Ignatius and his followers, "Action becomes a totally different category," and "love will not be principally affective or contemplative, but a love which is realized in works, which translates into service, which is realized in this cooperation with God." In the end, therefore, "action will be for St. Ignatius the response to this Trinitarian God, and the sign of the active presence of the Trinity in Ignatius and the life of his Society."[22] In Elizondo's view this is the root of the Jesuit mystical tradition of "contemplation in action" in which apostolic service is the proper response to God's invitation to collaborate with the work of the Trinity in saving the world.

Building on this mystical understanding of the Ignatian vocation from Elizondo, Ellacuría would electrify the gathered priests, brothers, and seminarians in the days that followed with a bold new Jesuit apostolic vision emerging from the preferential option for the poor of the Latin American bishops.[23] By the fifth

---

18. Interview with Miguel Elizondo by Teresa Whitfield, December 31, 1990. Cited in Whitfield, *Paying the Price*, 24.

19. Elizondo, "La primera semana como comienzo indispensable de conversión," 3, in "Reunión-Ejercicios" (Día 25:3), 48.

20. Ibid.

21. In November 1537 Ignatius had a vision confirming this Trinitarian service-oriented mysticism at a chapel in the village of La Storta outside Rome in which the Father says to Ignatius, "I wish you to be our servant," and instructs the Son, "I wish you to take him as your servant" (Joseph N. Tylenda, S.J., *A Pilgrim's Journey: The Autobiography of Ignatius of Loyola* [San Francisco: Ignatius Press, 2001], 177-78).

22. Elizondo, "The Theological and Spiritual Meaning of a Communal Meeting of the Vice-Province," in "Reunión-Ejercicios."

23. Ellacuría delivered the following talks: "The Goal and the Meaning of the Meeting"; "Our Collective Situation Seen from the Perspective of the First Week"; "The Problem of Translating the Spirit of the *Exercises* to the Vice-Province"; "The Third World as the Optimal Place for the Christian Life of the *Exercises*." See "Finalidad y sentido de la reunión," "Nuestra

day of the 1969 retreat many of the gathered Jesuits had become restless and fearful in the face of the epoch-defining challenges that lay ahead. Then, as we saw earlier, in a bold and classically Ignatian move, on December 29 Ellacuría turned the church's dangerous and looming confrontation with the hopeless historical reality of Latin America's innumerable "poor majorities" into the ultimate apostolic challenge. Ellacuría argues that the *Spiritual Exercises* are leading the Jesuits to serve, and to willingly share the fate of the crucified Christ of the Latin American poor. He warns that Medellín's call to a preferential option for the poor is bringing the Society of Jesus face to face with the sometimes terrifying forces shaping the historical reality of Central America. But he also reminds them that the *Spiritual Exercises* of St. Ignatius are built around a deeper call to love and service rooted in Jesus Christ, who he insists will give them the strength to handle the dangers of a life for others.

Ellacuría states his belief that the province's willingness to accept suffering for love is leading them toward a mystical encounter with the Christ of the *Exercises*, and that the option for the poor they are about to assume will mediate an encounter with the Christ of the retreat. Turning conventional wisdom on its ear, he argues that the Third World is "the optimal place for the Christian to live the *Exercises*."[24] He says that the upside-down logic of the *Exercises* is leading the Jesuits of Central America to the unexpected conclusion that "Christ is in the poor," and that, "It is not us who have to save the poor, but the poor who are going to save us."[25] Indeed, he says that it is by choosing to serve the poor that the Jesuits of Central America will truly come to know that the power of Christian love and friendship are greater than the terrible powers of this world. How prescient that insight would prove to be!

Ellacuría asserts that the atmosphere of generosity, prayer, and openness to God's will generated by *Exercises* is the appropriate place to confront the historical reality of what he will later call the "crucified people" as both the defining "sign of the times" and a "sign of contradiction." He says that people in the First World turn away from the suffering produced by their domination of the world's resources because its reality "would either drive them crazy or convert them from a whole pattern of being and acting."[26] He argues, however, that the spirit of Medellín and Rio is leading Third World Jesuits to discover that solidarity with the poor "offers the real possibility of making the experience of the *Exercises* visible and effective in the secular world"[27] through sharing in the

---

situación colectiva vista desde la perspectiva de la primera semana," "El problema del traslado del espíritu de los Ejercicios a la Vice," "El tercer mundo como lugar óptimo de la vivencia cristiana de los Ejercicios" in "Reunión-Ejercicios," 31, 32-36, 58-71, 99-115, 124-38.

24. "Ellacuría, "El tercer mundo como lugar óptimo de la vivencia Cristiana de los Ejercicios" [The Third World as the Optimal Place for the Christian to Live the *Exercises*] (Dia 29:1), 1-12, "Reunión-Ejercicios," 127-38.

25. Ibid., 4.

26. Ignacio Ellacuría, "El reino de Dios y el paro en el tercer mundo," *Concilium* 180 (1982), 593.

27. Ellacuría, "El tercer mundo como lugar óptimo," 6.

historical "schema of death and resurrection"[28] that Jesus lived. And he asserts this is because the Christ of the *Spiritual Exercises* in San Salvador is embodied in the country's suffering poor.

This background, then, helps us appreciate the meaning of the following assertion by Fr. Juan Hernández-Pico regarding the role of the *Spiritual Exercises* in Ellacuría's life and ministry.

> What Ignacio Ellacuría did in his apostolic life as a mature Jesuit, although he did not formulate it programmatically in these words, was to first lead the Central American Province [of the Society of Jesus] to enter into the spirit of the *Spiritual Exercises*, . . . and later the University of Central America "José Simeón Cañas" (the UCA). Then finally, building on this, he tried to bring the national reality of El Salvador through the same experience. . . .[29]

While one may disagree with Ellacuría's reading of the *Exercises* in light of the option for the poor, or his interpretation of what he calls the "preeminent" sign of the times, what cannot be doubted is that he believed that love and solidarity with the struggles of the "crucified people" of Central America to survive and thrive in the midst of poverty and repression were the path to which the Jesuits of Central America were being called by Medellín. Thus, he boldly states that their "yes" to the discernment of Medellín at the 1969 Christmas retreat would eventually transform them into living signs of the *Exercises* and the ongoing presence of Jesus Christ in their midst. And Ellacuría would dedicate the last twenty years of his life (1969-1989) to variations on the claim that it was by embracing Medellín's option for the poor[30] that the church would fulfill its destiny to become a "sacramental" and "mediating sign"[31] of the ongoing

---

28. Ibid., 10.

29. See Juan Hernández-Pico, S.J., "Ellacuría, Ignaciano," in Jon Sobrino and Rolando Alvarado, eds., *Ignacio Ellacuría, "Aquella libertad esclarecida"* (San Salvador: UCA Editores, 1999), 305, translation mine.

30. Ignacio Ellacuría, "Aporte de la teología de la liberación a las religiones Abráhamicas en la superación del individualismo y del positivismo." *Revista latinoamericana de teología* 10 (1987): 9, 15.

31. Ignacio Ellacuría, *Teología política* (San Salvador: Ediciones del Secretariado Social Interdiocesano, 1973), 47-48; and Ellacuría, "Fe y justicia," in Ellacuría, Arnaldo Zenteno, and Alberto Arroyo, eds., *Fe, justicia y opción por los oprimidos*, I (Bilbao, Spain: Editorial Española, Desclee de Brouwer, 1980), 23. Ellacuría makes analogous claims regarding "Latin American theology," the "Christian University" and its graduates, Archbishop Oscar Romero, Latin American philosophy, the "Abrahamic religions," those who "seek truth," advocates of human rights, etc. See Ignacio Ellacuría, "Hacia una fundamentación del método teológico latinoamericano," *Escritos teológicos*, I (San Salvador: UCA Editores, 2000), 187-218; Ignacio Ellacuría, "Tesis sobre la posibilidad, necesidad y sentido de una teología Latinoamericana," in A. Vargas Machua, ed., *Teología y mundo contemporáneo: homenaje a Karl Rahner* (Madrid: Ediciones Cristiandad, 1975), 325-50; Ignacio Ellacuría, "Diez años despúes; ¿es posible una universidad distinta?" *ECA* 30, nos. 324-325 (October-November 1975): 605-28; Ignacio Ellacuría, "La inspiración cristiana de la UCA en la docencia," *Planteamiento universitario*

presence of Jesus Christ to the "crucified peoples"[32] of a broken world. Indeed, Ellacuría himself would finally be caught up in the personal implications of his famous claim that the principal sign of the times "by whose light all the others should be discerned and interpreted . . . is . . . the crucified people."[33] Thus, Jon Sobrino, his closest friend and Jesuit companion, asserts that Ellacuría came to believe that "the foundation of his life, his vocation as a Jesuit, and deeper still, as a human being," was "to take the crucified people down from the cross."[34]

## Theologian of the *Spiritual Exercises* of St. Ignatius

Given this background, it is not surprising that two of Ellacuría's most influential ideas, his philosophy of historical reality and his theology of sign, are best understood in the context of the *Spiritual Exercises* of St. Ignatius. J. Matthew Ashley, in an important study of Ellacuría's writings on the Ignatian theme of contemplation in action and posthumously discovered notes for a course on the *Spiritual Exercises*,[35] maintains,

> The briefest look at his biography makes it clear that Ignacio Ellacuría was a man passionately committed to Ignatian spirituality, who sought to put it at the service of the Church in Latin America. The thesis of this essay is that he did this in large measure by seeking philosophical

*1989* (San Salvador, El Salvador: Universidad Centroamericana José Simeón Cañas, 1989), 195-200; Ignacio Ellacuría, "Monseñor Romero, un enviado de Dios para salvar a su pueblo," *Sal Terrae* 811 (1980): 825-32; Ignacio Ellacuría, "Función liberadora de la filosofía," *ECA* 40, no. 435 (1985): 45-64; Ignacio Ellacuría, "Aporte de la teología de la liberación a las religiones Abráhamica," 3-27; Ignacio Ellacuría, "Voluntad de fundamentalidad y voluntad de verdad: conocimiento-fe y su configuración histórica," *Revista latinoamericana de teología* 8 (1986): 113-32; Ignacio Ellacuría, "Human Rights in a Divided Society," in Alfred Hennelly and John Langan, eds., *Human Rights in the Americas: The Struggle for Consensus* (Washington, DC: Georgetown University Press, 1982), 52-65.

32. Ellacuría, "El pueblo crucificado, ensayo de soteriología histórica," *Escritos teológicos*, II (San Salvador: UCA Editores, 2000), 137-70; reprinted from I. Ellacuría et al., *Cruz y resurrección: anuncio de una iglesia nueva* (Mexico City: CTR, 1978), 49-82.

33. Ignacio Ellacuría, "Discernir *el signo* de los tiempos," *Escritos teológicos*, II (San Salvador: UCA Editores, 2000), 133-35; reprinted from *Vida nueva* 1258-59 (1980-1981): 35-36; and *Diakonía* 17 (1981): 58, 59; translated as "The Crucified People," in *Mysterium Liberationis* (Maryknoll, NY: Orbis Books, 1993), 580-604.

34. Jon Sobrino, "Ignacio Ellacuría, el hombre y el cristiano, 'Bajar de la cruz al pueblo crucificado'" (San Salvador: Centro Monseñor Romero, 2001), translated as "Ignacio Ellacuría, The Human Being and the Christian: 'Taking the Crucified People Down from the Cross,'" in Kevin Burke and Robert Lassalle-Klein, eds., *Love That Produces Hope: The Thought of Ignacio Ellacuría* (Collegeville, MN: Liturgical Press, 2006), 5.

35. Ignacio Ellacuría, "Lectura latinoamericana de los Ejercicios Espirituales de San Ignacio," *Revista Latinoamericana de teología* 23 (1991): 111-47; from unpublished notes, "Curso de Ejercicios," San Salvador, University of Central America: Archives of Ignacio Ellacuría, 1974; Ignacio Ellacuría, "Fe y justicia," *Christus* (August 1977): 26-33; and *Christus* (October 1977): 32-34.

and theological language and arguments to articulate the encounter with Christ that is structured by Ignatius Loyola's *Spiritual Exercises*.[36]

Ashley goes on to assert, "While he had the particular dilemma of the Latin American church in mind, his contribution has much to say for the rest of the church as well." Indeed, he argues that Ellacuría "deserves a place among those Jesuit theologians, such as Karl Rahner, Henri de Lubac, and Pierre Teilhard de Chardin, who have sought to elaborate the conceptual presuppositions and implications of Ignatian spirituality for late modernity."[37]

In what follows I will argue that Ellacuría's *philosophy of historical reality* and *theology of sign* both shaped and were shaped by his interpretation of the *Spiritual Exercises* and the challenge of Medellín at the 1969 retreat recounted above. Before proceeding, however, a brief word on the meaning of these concepts is warranted.

The core insight of Ellacuría's magnum opus, *Philosophy of Historical Reality*,[38] which is further elaborated in later theological works,[39] is that *historical reality* is the proper object of a contextualized Latin American approach to philosophy and theology. Ellacuría derives this concept from the philosophy of science of his mentor, Xavier Zubiri (1898-1983), the brilliant Spanish philosopher and student of Edmund Husserl (1859-1938) and Martin Heidegger (1889-1976). Zubiri says that the proper object of philosophy is the cosmos, understood in the classical sense "as an ordered and harmonious system,"[40] which he interprets as "a single complex and differentiated physical unity"[41] comprising interactive and progressively more complex systems of matter, biological life, sentient life, and human history (which includes both personal and social dimensions). Historical reality is the "last stage of reality" in which the material, biological,

---

36. J. Matthew Ashley, "Contemplation in the Action of Justice: Ignacio Ellacuría and Ignatian Spirituality," in Kevin Burke and Robert Lassalle-Klein, eds., *Love That Produces Hope: The Thought of Ignacio Ellacuría* (Collegeville, MN: Liturgical Press/Michael Glazier, 2006), 144.

37. Ibid.

38. Ignacio Ellacuría, *Filosofía de la realidad histórica* (San Salvador: UCA, 1990), 42. For book-length studies and collections on the philosophical roots of Ellacuría's theology, see Kevin Burke, S.J., *The Ground beneath the Cross: The Theology of Ignacio Ellacuría* (Washington, DC: Georgetown University Press, 2000); Michael E. Lee, *Bearing the Weight of Salvation: The Soteriology of Ignacio Ellacuría* (New York: Crossroad, 2009); and Burke and Lassalle-Klein, eds., *Love That Produces Hope*; Héctor Samour, *Voluntad de liberación: La filosofía de Ignacio Ellacuría* (Granada: Comares, 2003); José Sols Lucia, *La teología histórica de Ignacio Ellacuría* (Madrid: Trotta, 1999); and Jon Sobrino and Rolando Alvarado, eds., *Ignacio Ellacuría, "Aquella libertad esclarecida"* (Santander: Sal Terrae, 1999).

39. Ellacuría, "Hacia una fundamentación," 207-9; Ignacio Ellacuría, "Tesis sobre la posibilidad, necesidad y sentido de una teología latinoamericana," in A. Vargas Machua, ed., *Teología y mundo contemporáneo: homenaje a Karl Rahner* (Madrid: Ediciones Cristiandad, 1975), 325-50, esp. 339; Ignacio Ellacuría, "Función liberadora de la filosofía," *ECA* 40, no. 435 (1985): 45-64, esp. 63.

40. "Cosmos," in *Oxford English Dictionary* (online edition, 2nd ed.).

41. Ellacuría, *Filosofía de la realidad histórica*, 31.

sentient, personal, and social dimensions of reality are all made present in human history, and "where all of reality is assumed into the social realm of freedom."[42]

Ellacuría diverges from his mentor, however, by making *historical reality* (rather than the cosmos) the proper object of philosophy and theology, and he develops the concept of *historicization* (a more limited term in Zubiri) to describe the process of how historical reality comes to be. The term has two primary meanings in Ellacuría's work. The first, more general meaning refers to the incorporative and transformative power that human praxis exerts over the historical and natural dimensions of reality.[43] Here, "the historicization of nature consists . . . in the fact that humanity makes history from nature and with nature."[44] And in a second, more narrow meaning, Ellacuría says, "Demonstrating the impact of certain concepts within a particular context is [also] . . . understood here as their historicization."[45] Here historicization refers to a procedure for testing and validating truth claims associated with a concept. This is derived from the idea that if the truth of a historicized concept lies in its "becoming reality," then it follows that the concept's "truth can be measured in [its] results."[46]

These ideas, then, lead Ellacuría to reinterpret and historicize Rahner's famous notion of the supernatural existential historical reality transformed by grace and to historicize Rahner's theology of symbol as a theology of sign (more on these in the section on Ellacuría as an interpreter of Rahner in Chapter 7). Taken together these ideas provide theological foundations for Ellacuría's emphasis on the call of Vatican II to read the signs of the times and interpret them in light of the gospel[47] and for his assertion that the "mission of the Church" is to be "a sign, and only a sign, of the God who has revealed himself in history, . . . of Jesus, the Lord, the Revealer of the Father."[48]

Turning to the role of Ellacuría's philosophy of historical reality in his interpretation of Ignatian spirituality, Ashley asserts that Ellacuría uses "the philosophical term *historicization* to identify and deploy what he took to be

---

42. Ibid., 43.

43. Ibid., 169

44. Ibid.

45. Ignacio Ellacuría, "La historización del concepto de propiedad como principio de desideologización," *ECA* 31, nos. 335-336 (1976): 425-50; translated as "The Historicization of the Concept of Property," in John Hassett and Hugh Lacey, eds., *Towards a Society That Serves Its People* (Washington, DC: Georgetown University Press, 1991), 109.

46. Ellacuría, "La historización del concepto de propiedad," 428.

47. Karl Rahner, "Theology of the Symbol," *Theological Investigations*, IV (Baltimore: Helicon, 1966), 221-52, at 224, 225, 234. Ellacuría's theology of *sign* is most fully articulated in *Freedom Made Flesh* (Maryknoll, NY: Orbis Books, 1976). Laurence A. Egan, M.M., in the book's foreword (vii-ix, at viii), describes Ellacuría as a "former student of Karl Rahner" who "has tried to combine the insights of Rahner with those of the Theology of Liberation—a synthesis . . . imbued with the reality of Central America."

48. Ellacuría, *Teología política*, 48; *Freedom Made Flesh* 89.

the central dynamism of the *Spiritual Exercises*."[49] As we saw above, the term *historicization* has two meanings in Ellacuría's work, and I would argue that a brief inspection of his notes for the course on the *Exercises* reveals how he capitalizes on both. First, he asserts that the *Exercises* "participate in the more general form of historicization that implies the active listening to the word of God," and "make[s] what is historical the essential dimension of the structure of the Christian encounter with God."[50] Second, however, Ellacuría says that the *Exercises* "also historicize the word of God"[51] in the narrower sense as well. Here, they "turn their attention to historical, personal, and circumstantial signs so that they can [help retreatants to] discover" how the word of God is, *or is not*, acting "concretely" in a particular historical reality. This distinction reflects Ellacuría's high regard for the *Exercises* as a critical tool for discerning whether a given sign of the times (e.g., the crucified people) is a reflection of grace or the anti-kingdom.

Ashley's article does not mention this distinction, but both meanings of historicization appear in his work. On the one hand, he describes Ellacuría's treatment of the meditations of the Second Week of the *Exercises* and the Ignatian theme of contemplation in action as examples of what I have called Ellacuría's "more general" understanding of historicization. Ellacuría sees the focus of the retreat on the life of Jesus and the invitation of Ignatius to an "election" regarding a "life-determining" decision[52] as examples of how "the *Exercises* interweave one's own individual history with the broader world-history . . . , and . . . the history of God's salvific work in the world with its definitive manifestation in Jesus' history."[53] Ashley argues, "The goal, as Ellacuría stresses, is not simply knowledge of God and God's will, but a decision to incarnate that will in one's life,"[54] which he says Ellacuría sees as an example of historicization (in its more general sense, I would add).

On the other hand, however, Ashley highlights Ellacuría's assertion that the historical character of the various signs of God's activity in the world also creates the need for something like Ignatian discernment. Ellacuría himself argues that when one confronts historical signs, "an endeavor of discrimination and discernment is required since the sign is not univocal, but rather requires interpretation."[55] And he asserts (citing Rahner) that this is precisely why the *Exercises* constitute "a method to find a will of God that cannot be deduced from universal principles."[56] Ashley correctly cites this argument as an example of the principle of historicization, though I would add that it exemplifies the

49. Ashley, "Contemplation in the Action of Justice," 145.

50. Ellacuría, "Lectura," 115.

51. Ibid., 113.

52. Ashley, "Contemplation in the Action of Justice," 147.

53. Ibid., 147-48.

54. Ibid., 148.

55. Ellacuría, "Lectura," 114.

56. Ibid. He cites Karl Rahner, "Die Logik der existentiellen Erkenntnis bei Ignatius von Loyola," in *Das Dynamische in der Kirche* (Freiburg: Herder Verlag, 1958), 74-148.

second, narrower, more critical meaning of the term. He says this is why Ella-curía sees the *Exercises* as the perfect vehicle for those seeking to answer "the challenge that the Latin American Church had set itself at Medellín: to read the signs of the times in the light of the gospel in its own specific reality, and to respond adequately to them."[57]

When we place this emphasis on the dynamics of historicization operating in the *Exercises* in the context of Ellacuría's theology of sign, we begin to under-stand why he sees historicization as a sign for God. Indeed, as Ashley notes, Ellacuría believes that the *Exercises* are ordered to help one's life become a living sign of the action of the word of God in history.

Ashley explains that Ellacuría sees the goal of the *Exercises* as "effecting a historical continuation—Ellacuría named it a *progressive historicization*—"[58] of the historical mission of Jesus "governed by 'the spirit of Christ who animates those who follow him,'"[59] rather than reflecting a naive ahistorical attempt to simply recapitulate the historical details of the life of Jesus. He insists that "what is involved is a contemplation of God in things, that gives way to *con-templation in action* with things."[60] And he says that, for Ellacuría, the "crucial point" is that "the God becoming present, the person making God present, and the person becoming present to a God who is at work—are strictly correlative and simultaneous."[61] Thus, "We find God in all things by laboring in the midst of all things."

This provides a theological framework for the point made earlier by Fr. Hernández-Pico, for as Ashley asserts, Ellacuría "was convinced that the *Exer-cises* could do this not only for individuals, but corporately, if only the adequate philosophical and theological structures could be formulated to unleash their power."[62] Ellacuría himself states the point in positive terms: "The fact that St. Ignatius himself saw that it was possible to give the spirit of the *Exercises* a body in the Society of Jesus is proof of the capacity for historicization that they possess."[63] Ashley asserts that Ellacuría believes that the mistaken priority assigned to *theoria* over *praxis* in Greek thought and Western spirituality made it almost "impossible to fully unleash the power of . . . contemplation in action, both generally speaking, and in its specifically Ignatian form."[64] He argues,

---

57. Ashley, "Contemplation in the Action of Justice," 146.

58. Ibid., 148.

59. Ibid., citing Ellacuría, "Lectura," 127.

60. Ibid., 146.

61. Ibid., 155.

62. Ibid., 148. On Ellacuría's novitiate and the important role Elizondo gave to the *Exercises* for inculturating his charges, see Whitfield, *Paying the Price*, 15-24. On the 1969 corporate retreat, see Juan Hernández-Pico, "Ellacuría, Ignaciano," 305-26; Robert Lassalle-Klein, "The Jesuit Martyrs of the University of Central America: An American Christian University and the Historical Reality of the Reign of God" (Ph.D. diss., Graduate Theological Union, 1995), 51-56; and Charles Beirne, S.J., *Jesuit Education and Social Change in El Salvador* (New York: Garland, 1996), 84-87.

63. Ellacuría, "Lectura," 114.

64. Ashley, "Contemplation in the Action of Justice," 156.

therefore, "It is not too much to say that *the* objective of Ellacuría's 'philosophy of historical reality' was to overcome this bias, so pervasive to the philosophical tradition." Viewed in this way, Ellacuría's philosophy of historical reality must be interpreted in light of its practical application by Ellacuría himself in helping to actualize his understanding of the intention of Ignatius that the lives of his men gathered for the 1969 retreat should become living signs of the action of the word of God in history.

These reflections, then, draw our attention to the central role of the *Spiritual Exercises* of St. Ignatius and the Ignatian spirituality they embody in Ellacuría's life and thought. In what follows, I will argue, after tracing their roots, that the various philosophical, political, and theological themes and concepts running through Ignacio Ellacuría's life and thought were shaped by an overarching sense of vocation and call. And I will suggest Ellacuría's understanding of his vocation to follow Christ was historicized through his discernment that he was being called as a Jesuit, a Christian, a university president, and a human being into active collaboration with God's loving design to strengthen the faith, hope, and love of the crucified people of El Salvador by taking them down from the cross, and by supporting and enabling their struggles for freedom and life. Ignacio Ellacuría and his colleagues committed themselves to this path in December 1969, and over the next twenty years it transformed them into living signs of the Christ of the San Salvador retreat and the action of the Word of God in history.

# 5

# *Ellacuría's Philosophy of Historical Reality*

## Xavier Zubiri's Sentient Intelligence and Neuroscience

In this chapter I will examine the philosophical roots of what I call Ignacio Ellacuría's Christian historical realism. My purpose is to explore what Ellacuría's philosophy of historical reality contributes to his relationship (and that of the University of Central America [UCA]) with what he called El Salvador's poor majorities. Ignacio Ellacuría's philosophy of historical reality is built on the groundbreaking work of Xavier Zubiri, considered by some to be the greatest Spanish philosopher of the last half of the twentieth century. Zubiri's powerful philosophical work on the nature of human intelligence integrates cutting-edge insights from the natural sciences, including Einstein's theory of relativity, systems theory, and perceptual psychology; the epoch defining phenomenology of Husserl and existentialism of Heidegger; post-modern thought; and the great traditions of classical and medieval philosophy while remarkably anticipating recent breakthroughs in cognitive neuroscience.

Ellacuría's philosophy of historical reality, which assures his place among Latin America's most important twentieth-century philosophers, builds on Zubiri's work. More importantly for our purposes, Ellacuría utilizes Zubiri's groundbreaking categories to conceptualize the encounter with the Christ encountered in the epoch-defining discernment of the Central American Jesuits to embrace Medellín's preferential option for the poor at the 1969 *Spiritual Exercises* retreat. In this section I will briefly summarize how Ellacuría builds on and reinterprets aspects of the work of Xavier Zubiri in formulating the Christian (or theological) historical realism that allows him to make sense of the profound implications of the 1969 retreat while revolutionizing Catholic fundamental theology in ways that have yet to be fully appreciated and understood outside Latin America.

## Mentor and Student

Ellacuría was ordained a priest on July 26, 1961, during his final year studying with Karl Rahner at Innsbruck. Six weeks later while visiting his family in
Bilbao, Spain, he decided to seek out the famous Spanish philosopher Xavier
Zubiri at his home. Ellacuría had written several unanswered letters to the philosopher and in a letter to his provincial says he went there to tell Zubiri "that
I wanted to do a doctoral dissertation with him and about him." The surprise
visitors were met by the Basque philosopher's sister-in-law who said that Zubiri
was at Mass, and "didn't usually receive visitors." She added, however, that
Zubiri had a standing exception for priests, and when Zubiri returned Ellacuría
recalls that he greeted them "with great simplicity and spontaneity." Seeing "the
moment was ripe," the young man made his request, which "sat well" with the
philosopher, and even "flattered" him. Ellacuría says that Zubiri then inquired,
"What would I claim?" recalling, "I quickly replied that I saw in him a model
of the intersection between the classical and the modern, between the essential
and the existential." Zubiri liked this answer, for "he smiled and said that this
had actually been the goal of his work. Then he promised to put himself entirely
at my disposal for whatever I needed."[1]

Cardenal says that "Zubiri was so impressed with his new disciple that he
immediately wrote to his wife to say he had met 'a brilliant young Jesuit' who
even knew Greek, the language in which he was weakest."[2] During the Franco
regime Zubiri had severed all direct ties with the university and determined
"never to direct another thesis."[3] Nonetheless, he steadfastly supported Ellacuría through "problems with the academic authorities . . . who rejected the
idea of writing a dissertation about a living philosopher." Ellacuría eventually
found a faculty member willing to direct but not interfere with the writing
of the dissertation. He presented the outline to Zubiri in October 1963 and
defended *La principalidad de la esencia en Xavier Zubiri* at the University of
Complutense in Madrid in 1965. Near the end of this process Ellacuría made
the *Spiritual Exercises* of St. Ignatius in Ireland and took final vows in the Society of Jesus on February 2, 1965.

It is interesting that both teacher and student shared a predilection for
theology and an interest in Rahner. In their first conversation Zubiri spoke at
great length about theology and his desire to spend two years with Rahner at
Innsbruck and two more studying scripture in Jerusalem.[4] Zubiri dedicated the

---

1. Ignacio Ellacuría, "Entrevista con Zubiri (San Sebastián, 8 de septiembre de 1961)," in
*Escritos filosóficos*, II (San Salvador: UCA Editores, 1999), 26.

2. Rudolfo Cardenal, "Ignacio Ellacuría (1930-1989)," http://www.uca.edu.sv/martires /
new/ella/fella.htm (San Salvador, September 1999), 6; henceforth cited as Cardenal, "Ignacio
Ellacuría."

3. Rodolfo Cardenal, S.J., "De Portugalete a San Salvador: de la mano de cinco maestros,"
in J. Sobrino and R. Alvarado, eds., *Ignacio Ellacuría, 'Aquella libertad esclarecida'* (San
Salvador: UCA Editores, 1999), 53.

4. Ellacuría, "Entrevista con Zubiri," II, 20.

introduction of an unpublished monograph on God to Rahner, and it appears as the conclusion to his final book, *El hombre y Dios.*[5] Cardenal adds that Zubiri once confessed that theology "satisfied him more than philosophy."[6] For his part Ellacuría completed the courses for a doctorate in theology at the University of Comillas in Madrid in 1965.

After two more years with Zubiri, however, it was determined that Ellacuría would be sent to the UCA in San Salvador, which had opened its doors a year earlier. On January 29, 1967, while this decision was being considered, Zubiri wrote to Ellacuría that their collaboration was "unsurpassed and irreplaceable. Nobody understands me like you, and only you have my full trust."[7] Later that year Zubiri wrote personally to Fr. Pedro Arrupe, S.J., superior general of the Jesuit order, requesting that Ellacuría be missioned to work with him full time in Spain. Arrupe was "very impressed" by the letter and approved the request, but superiors in San Salvador did not agree. As a compromise it was decided that Ellacuría would return to work with Zubiri in Madrid for three or four months each year during vacations and summer.

Ellacuría wrote in 1968, summarizing the current state of their collaboration, that "all the materials are ready for you to begin publishing, and for me to do the dissertation in theology."[8] But Ellacuría never wrote the dissertation, and Zubiri died September 21, 1983, still editing the manuscript on the philosophy of God. Ellacuría finished editing the manuscript, did an introduction, and published *El hombre y Dios* posthumously in 1984. As Zubiri's closest collaborator and intellectual heir, he was named first director of the Xavier Zubiri Foundation in Madrid and promoted distribution and understanding of Zubiri's writings around the world. Not surprisingly, many Latin American Jesuits from this period have studied Zubiri's work.

More than anyone else Xavier Zubiri shaped the philosophical categories informing the sweeping Christian historical realism formulated by Ignacio Ellacuría. But Ellacuría's posthumously published magnum opus, *Philosophy of Historical Reality*, moves definitively beyond the work of his mentor by making "historical reality"[9] the proper object of his work in philosophy and theology.[10] Ellacuría explicitly accepts the systemic hypothesis of Zubiri's philosophy of science that "all worldly reality constitutes a single complex and differentiated

---

5. Ignacio Ellacuría, "Presentación," in Xavier Zubiri, *El hombre y Dios* (Madrid: Alianza Editorial, 1984), ix. Ellacuría explains that it was his editorial decision to append this introduction as the conclusion to Zubiri's posthumously published *El hombre y Dios*.

6. Cardenal, "De Portugalete," 55.

7. Ignacio Ellacuría, "Carta de I. Ellacuría a X. Zubiri (29 de enero de 1967)," *Escritos filosóficos*, II, 59.

8. Ignacio Ellacuría, "Carta de I. Ellacuría a X. Zubiri (15 de agosto de 1968)," *Escritos filosóficos*, II, 65.

9. Ignacio Ellacuría, *Filosofía de la realidad histórica* (San Salvador: UCA Editores, 1990), 42.

10. Ellacuría substitutes "historical reality" for Zubiri's more abstract "unity of intramundane reality"; see ibid., 30, 25.

physical unity."[11] And he builds carefully on Zubiri's philosophical integration of the theory of evolution, analyzing matter, biological life, sentient life, and human history (in its personal and social dimensions) as different systems comprising the more comprehensive reality of the cosmos.

However Ellacuría shifts the emphasis from Zubiri's more abstract focus on the unity of the material cosmos to his own concentration on "historical reality" as the object of philosophy and theology. He justifies this move with the argument that "historical reality is where reality is 'more,' . . . both 'more its own,' and 'more open.'"[12] It is here that reality becomes decisively human in his view. And he believes that contemporary philosophy and theology have the duty to explore the limits and possibilities this freedom entails. Indeed, it is on this point (which is derived from Zubiri) that Ellacuría will focus his most creative efforts.

This important theoretical change explains in part how Ellacuría moves beyond Zubiri and his other mentors (including Rahner) by grounding his philosophical and theological work in the specific historical reality of Latin America. It is this move that allows him to treat the preferential option for the poor made by the church in Latin America as a "concrete universal"[13] (in Rahner's sense of the term) of significance for the whole church. It also grounds his prophetic cry that the "crucified people" constitute the "principle . . . sign of the times" and must orient the "universal historical mission" of the church in the world today.[14] This image can be understood as a metaphor for the universal significance of Medellín's discernment that God was calling the Latin American church to a preferential option for the poor embraced by the Central American Jesuits at the 1969 retreat.

## Zubiri's Critique of the Evasion of Reality in the West

Ignacio Ellacuría lamented what he saw as the disastrous inability of Latin American philosophy, theology, and political rhetoric to address the "brute reality"[15] of the continent's suffering people. For this purpose he recommended the thought of Xavier Zubiri, in which he found "an adequate manner to face up to reality and come to terms with it," and which he says, "without claiming to do so, is very helpful in . . . exposing and breaking down the idealist and

---

11. Ellacuría, *Filosofía de la realidad histórica,* 31.

12. Ibid.

13. Karl Rahner, *Spirit in the World* (New York: Continuum, 1968, 1994), 124; and Karl Rahner, "The Orientation towards Universality in the Particular and Successful History of Revelation," in *Foundations of Christian Faith* (New York: Crossroad, 1978), 161. See Ignacio Ellacuría, *Freedom Made Flesh* (Maryknoll, NY: Orbis Books, 1976). 145, 146.

14. Ellacuría, "Discernir *el signo* de los tiempos," *Escritos teológicos,* II (San Salvador: UCA Editores, 2000), 134, 135.

15. Ignacio Ellacuría, "Zubiri, cuatro años después," *Escritos filosóficos,* III (San Salvador: UCA Editores, 2001), 402.

ideological monstrosities" served up by politicians, academics, religious leaders, and the press.[16]

In 1988, the year before his assassination, Ellacuría treated Zubiri's critique of what he called idealist reductionism and the question of reality in an article entitled "Zubiri's Solution to Idealist Reductionism."[17] Given both the nature and the timing of the article, it constitutes perhaps the closest thing we have to an explicit synthetic statement of how Zubiri's broad-reaching thought and massive philosophical corpus shaped Ellacuría's own thought on these subjects. I will use this article in tandem with a number of other sources to show how Ellacuría builds on Zubiri's groundbreaking proposals that anticipate breakthroughs in twenty-first-century cognitive neuroscience in creating an approach for contextual theologies around the globe seeking alternatives to the (sometimes) reductionist idealism and empiricism of the West.

Ellacuría adopts Zubiri's notion that these positions reflect and perpetuate the fact that a good deal of "modern philosophy is laboring under the affliction of idealism."[18] And he builds on Zubiri's neurologically cogent and post-modern[19] approach grounded in a powerful critique of idealism, which he argues (in some of its forms) has afflicted the history of Western philosophy. Zubiri asserts,

> Sensing, it is said, is one thing; intellection is another. This perspective on the problem of intelligence contains, at bottom, an affirmation: intellection is posterior to sensing, and this posteriority is an opposition/dichotomy. This has been an initial thesis of philosophy since Parmenides, which has quietly loomed, with a thousand variants, over all of European philosophy.[20]

Zubiri's rejection of this thesis, which is central to his entire project, anticipates what some consider a key claim of twenty-first-century cognitive neuroscience that human perception and thought is a neurological event at every stage of the process so that sensing and intellection must be considered an integral unity. Ellacuría explains that Zubiri believes the unfortunate dichotomization of sensing from intellection[21] has produced two "distortions" in Western philosophy, which he calls (1) the "logification of intelligence" and (2) the "entification of reality." Ellacuría argues these distortions must be overcome in order to construct

---

16. Ignacio Ellacuría, "La superación del reduccionismo idealista en Zubiri," *Escritos filosóficos*, III, 403; reprinted from *ECA* no. 477 (1988): 633-50.

17. Ibid., 403-30.

18. Ibid.

19. Diego Gracia situates Zubiri in a "postmodern philosophical horizon." Diego Gracia, *Voluntad de verdad: Para leer a Zubiri* (Barcelona: Editorial Labor, 1986).

20. Xavier Zubiri, *Inteligencia sentiente: Inteligencia y realidad* (Madrid: Alianza Editorial, 1980), 11-12.

21. Zubiri's aforementioned distinction between sensing (apprehending something by means of an impression) and "pure sensing" (the mere stimulation of the senses) is critical here. He asserts that the opposition should not be between "intellection and sensing," but between "pure sensing and intellection" (Zubiri, *Inteligencia sentiente*, 80).

a truly contextualized "Latin American" philosophy and theology[22] capable of explaining the faith of Archbishop Romero and his followers. In the following subsections I will describe each of these distortions, occasionally highlighting where Zubiri's insights anticipate recent insights from cognitive neuroscience.

### The "Logification of Intelligence"

Ellacuría begins by explaining Zubiri's assertion that Greek philosophy made a wrong turn in its understanding of perception, the mind, and the brain. He says that Zubiri traces the roots of idealist reductionism in Western philosophy to the "progressive subsuming" of other aspects of intellection into what the mind, acting as "logos," affirms, proposes, or predicates about its objects.[23] Zubiri calls this the "logification of intelligence."[24] And both agree that this reductionist narrowing of intelligence impoverishes our appreciation of non-conceptual aspects and sources of knowing. Most especially it reduces sense-based forms of knowledge to the status of mere sense data.

Zubiri uses the famous puzzle of how the brain turns electromagnetic waves hitting the retina into the perception of color in order to make his point. He asserts, "The color is not produced by the wave (as critical realism holds)." Instead, he says, "the visual perception of color *is* the electromagnetic wave *in* the perception."[25] He says this is so because, "Within the ambit of perception (and only there), the [perceptual] qualities and the [electromagnetic] waves are . . . one and the same thing, not two, as they would have been if the waves had been caused by the qualities. Sensible qualities are realities, within the ambit of perception, . . . of something beyond them in the cosmos."[26] As a result, "We will ask ourselves . . . how the waves, as realities existing outside the perception, cause the quality apprehended in the perception (e.g., the color green) to appear." Writing in the 1970s he says, "this is a problem for science" and at the heart of "the scandal" of the as-yet-unsolved puzzle of the nature of human perception.

Zubiri's point, which has now been explored in great detail by twenty-first-century neuropsychology, is that we *see* much more (or sometimes less) than is present on the retina. Just as in a gestalt or in the case of materials that obstruct or distort the passage of light on its way to the retina, the mind adds or eliminates aspects of what it concludes is lacking or extraneous in its perception of the object. A prominent neuropsychologist who describes the mind as "an emergent property of the brain" wonders, "How far down in the perceptual stream does this constructive activity occur?" He responds, "It does not affect what reaches the retina, obviously (except that attention and goals direct where

---

22. Ignacio Ellacuría, "Zubiri en El Salvador," *ECA* nos. 361-362 (1978): 949-50, esp. 950.
23. Ellacuría, "La superación del reduccionismo idealista," 407.
24. Zubiri, *Inteligencia sentiente*, 86.
25. Ibid., 186.
26. Ibid., 187.

the retina looks)." But "does it affect what reaches the thalamus? Probably not." However, while "I don't know whether it affects what reaches the amygdala, . . . it certainly biases the strength of response there," and "past that point what reaches the cortex is probably selected and even modified by biasing systems." Thus, "At the level of visual cortex the information is already selected/biased by a task set and by an emotional set (survival value)." And "by the time it reaches consciousness, when you see the object, the information has been heavily biased or edited. So if you see the object, you really see it—but you only see the object if your bias systems allow it."[27]

This reflection demonstrates that while the activity of the mind when "you see the object" may be distinguished from that of the brain (the thalamus, the amygdala, and the visual cortex), it makes no sense to treat the mind as dichotomous from or posterior to the sensing activity of the brain (understood as part of the central nervous system), or as anything less than part of a profoundly integrated system. Yet these are exactly the errors that Ellacuría and Zubiri assert afflict Western thought in the form of reductionist idealism (which would tend to dichotomize the mind from the brain) and empiricism (which would tend to reduce the mind to the brain). Ellacuría explains that both distortions are rooted in what Zubiri calls the *logification of intelligence*, which he traces through the history of Western philosophy. In what follows, however, I will focus our discussion on Ellacuría's description of the logification of intelligence in twentieth-century phenomenology due to its massive influence on contemporary philosophy and theology.

Before proceeding, however, we must ask what counts as truth in human perception and whether science and the humanities have similar answers. Edmund Husserl (1859-1938), considered by many as the founder of modern phenomenology, developed one of the most influential twentieth-century philosophical responses to this question. Zubiri says Husserl felt that philosophy had become "a mixture of positivism, historicism and [crude] pragmatism founded in the last instance in the science of psychology."[28] He believed Western thought was being distorted by reductionist empiricism and its tendency to equate truth with factual propositions validated by logic or empirical data.[29] But Husserl rejected the casual subordination of cultural phenomena such as beauty, valuing, judging, knowing, etc., to the causality of the physical world, which he found in his contemporaries. And as an alternative, Zubiri says, "Husserl created phenomenology," beginning with "a severe critique" of crass empiricism and turning "away from the psychological to the things themselves."[30]

---

27. Joel Nigg, Director, Division of Psychology, Professor of Psychiatry, Pediatrics, and Behavioral Neuroscience, Oregon Health and Science University, Portland, OR. Personal correspondence with author, August 17, 2012.

28. Xavier Zubiri, "Dos etapas," *Revista de Occidente* 4, no. 32 (1984): 47. Cited in Gracia, *Voluntad de verdad*, 33.

29. D. W. Hamlyn, "Empiricism," *Encyclopedia of Philosophy* (New York: Macmillan Publishing, 1967), 504.

30. Gracia, *Voluntad de verdad*, 33.

Husserl thus abandoned the naive "natural attitude" of everyday life and ordinary science regarding observation and sense data and began to ask how objects "constitute themselves" in consciousness.[31] The reader will note this approach fits well with our discussion of the intersection between cognitive neuroscience and Zubiri's philosophical critique of the logification of intelligence.[32] Not surprisingly then, Zubiri asserts that "Phenomenology was the key movement that opened an appropriate ground for philosophizing as such," overcoming both the reductionist empiricism of naive approaches to science, while avoiding the idealist trap that reduced sense-based forms of knowledge to the status of *mere* sense data for consideration by a faculty of judgment.[33]

Phenomenology would play an important role in a variety of twentieth-century approaches, including the philosophies of being, language, existentialism, hermeneutics, pragmatism, semiotics, symbolic logic, science, mind, consciousness, and more. And Ellacuría and Zubiri would incorporate contributions gained through each. But while Zubiri would build on Husserl's phenomenology, he also exposed and rejected the version of reductionist idealism that he found there.

Diego Gracia highlights the breakthrough importance of Zubiri's critique of Husserl in the development of Zubiri's thought. Gracia explains that early in his career Zubiri "clearly identifies himself with [Husserl]"[34] in his efforts to create an alternative to classical realism and modern transcendental idealism through "the discovery of a philosophically viable route for the phenomenological method."[35] If this is accurate (and I believe it is), the philosophies of both Zubiri and Ellacuría should be seen as attempts to "correct" *from within* what they saw as two important errors in the phenomenological tradition.[36] On the other hand, I would also argue that Zubiri and Ellacuría go beyond phenomenology when they assert that the phenomenological description of the object must be limited to the status of a methodological first step in the philosophical process. Thus, while philosophy will involve phenomenology, they will argue that it must be more than that.

*First, then, I would agree with Gracia's assertion that Zubiri attempts to "correct" phenomenology by hypothesizing that the primogenital location of intellection is actually sensation itself rather than Husserl's "pure consciousness," or Heidegger's better formulated "understanding of Dasein."*[37]

---

31. Christian Beyer, "Edmund Husserl," *Stanford Encyclopedia of Philosophy* (2011), online at http://plato.stanford.edu/entries/husserl; accessed September 3, 2012.

32. Zubiri also wrote his licentiate thesis on Husserl. Xavier Zubiri, "Le problème de la objectivité d'Après Ed. Husserl: I, La logique pure" (Louvain, 1921). Cited in Gracia, *Voluntad de verdad*, 35.

33. Gracia, *Voluntad de verdad*, 33.

34. Ibid., 89.

35. Diego Gracia, "Zubiri, Xavier," in R. Latourelle and R. Fisichella, eds., *Dictionary of Fundamental Theology* (New York, Crossroad, 1995), 1165-69, esp.1165.

36. Gracia, *Voluntad de verdad*, 89, 90.

37. Xavier Zubiri, *Sobre el hombre* (Madrid: Alianza Editorial, 1986), 439-40. Cited in Gracia, *Voluntad de verdad*, 68.

Four implications of this move are of particular significance for Ellacuría and Zubiri. First, it allows Zubiri to make the argument that intelligence and sensation are unified in what he will call "sensing" or "sentient intelligence."[38] Second, phenomenological philosophy will be compelled to confront the stubborn sense of being something "in its own" right (*en propio*) or something "of its own" (*de suyo*), which characterizes the way the objects of sense are manifested by sensible apprehension.[39] Third, Zubiri will call this the phenomenological *reality* of the thing, defining reality by the way that things actualize themselves when they are apprehended as being something "of their own" (*de suyo*).[40] And, fourth, Ellacuría and others will insist that Zubiri's position is nothing like a naïve realism since "reality" does not refer directly to things as they exist in the world "outside" apprehension and independent of it.

*Second, I would argue that Zubiri makes another key "correction" to Husserl's approach by carefully limiting the scope of Husserl's insistence that phenomenology must bracket or withhold judgment on the question about the reality or existence of the thing.* He does this by reframing Husserl's distinction between *noesis* (the "act" of consciousness in grasping the phenomenal object) and *noema* (the referent of *noesis*, or the thing as it is grasped or "intended" by consciousness). Zubiri switches this to a distinction between the *formal reality* (or *reity*) of the thing as it imposes itself in the sensible apprehension and the *reality* of the thing as it exists outside of sensible apprehension (*reality*).[41] And he insists that *noesis* comprises the "primordial apprehension" of the thing as being something "of its own" (its formal reality) which is "re-actualized" before the distancing and predicating judgments[42] of the logos.[43] This leads him to insist that since the formal reality of the thing (its *reity*) is a physical actualization of the thing in the apprehension, therefore it is proper for the deepening, measuring, and searching thought of reason to develop provisional models, hypotheses, and postulates about the *reality* of the thing as it exists outside the perception.

---

38. Recall that for Zubiri and Ellacuría the primordial act of intellection is sensation, which Zubiri says "consists in apprehending something by means of an impression," Zubiri, *Inteligencia sentiente*, 79.

39. I find this aspect of autonomy akin to what C. S. Peirce means by "secondness."

40. Zubiri writes, "Given the completely distinct character that the term 'reality' can have in vulgar and even in philosophical language, that of knowing reality outside of any apprehension, the term 'reidad' can serve in order to avoid confusion. [However,] I will employ the two terms indiscriminately: 'reidad' will mean here simply 'reality,' simply being 'of itself'; see Zubiri, *Inteligencia sentiente*, 57.

41. Diego Gracia argues, "it is important to keep in mind that the word 'reality' has two meanings in Zubiri: 'reality as formality' (or reality *qua* given in apprehension) and 'reality as fundamentality' (or reality as the actualization in a sensible apprehension of the thing beyond apprehension)" ("Zubiri, Xavier," *Dictionary*, 1166).

42. Zubiri actually argues that intellection engages in three types of judgments when it assumes the posture of the logos: affirmative, propositional, and predicative. See Xavier Zubiri, *Inteligencia y logos* (Madrid: Alianza Editorial, Sociedad de Estudios y Publicaciones, 1982), 152, 155-56, 161.

43. Zubiri, *Inteligencia sentiente*, 4, 64-67; Zubiri, *Inteligencia y logos*, 52.

In this way Zubiri limits Husserl's bracketing of the question of the reality of the thing (or *epoche*) to the status of a methodological first step in the philosophical process. Zubiri's unification of the formal reality of the thing (its *reity*) with its reality as it exists outside of sensible apprehension (its *reality*) ends up limiting the role of the *epoche* to establishing the formal reality of the thing (*reity*) as it is first manifested in the primordial apprehension of the reality of the object. As a result, Zubiri explicitly rules out ontological or metaphysical claims based on the *epoche*[44] while simultaneously asserting that once the question of reality has been raised, philosophy and science have the obligation to pursue it. This leads him to conclude that philosophy will have to be more than simply phenomenology, which is the substance of his second "correction" of Husserl's understanding of the phenomenological approach to philosophy.

### The "Entification of Reality"

This brings us, then, to a second set of "distortions" that Zubiri says lie at the root of idealist reductionism in the Western philosophical tradition: *the reduction of reality to a form or a subcategory of being*. Using the Spanish word *ente*[45] for *being*-as-a-thing or *entity*, Zubiri and Ellacuría call this the "entification of reality."[46] The substance of this critique can be captured in three points.

*First, Ellacuría argues that for Zubiri the entification of reality means that the being-of-an-entity* (ente) *and the larger category of being itself* (ser) *have improperly displaced reality in philosophy.* Zubiri puts the point concisely.

> Classical philosophy has addressed the problem of being from the perspective of what I have called conceiving intelligence. Intellection is "understanding"; and understanding is intellection that something "is" [*es*]. This was a primary thesis for Parmenides. . . . [Later] grounded in Parmenides, both Plato and Aristotle continued to subsume the act of intellection to the work of the logos. This was what . . . I have called a *logification of the intelligence*. But it is something else as well, for it is assumed that what has been intellected is "being" [*ser*]. And this implies that reality is just a form of being, though certainly its fundamental form . . . : it is *esse reale* (real existence). In other words,

---

44. Zubiri criticizes Heidegger for this, first praising what he calls Heidegger's "theory of ontological knowledge," then rejecting what he calls Heidegger's notion that the *comprehension of being* constitutes a *mode of being*. See Xavier Zubiri, *Sobre la esencia* (Madrid: Gráficas Cóndor, Sociedad de Estudios y Publicaciones, 1962, 1980), 441-42.

45. I have chosen to translate this word as the "being-of-an-entity" because, even though *ente* is the ablative form of the Latin word *ens* [real being], *entis,* the Spanish word *ente* is closer in meaning to what medieval philosophers meant by *esse,* or *esse real* [real existence]; (see Zubiri, *Inteligencia sentiente,* 226).

46. Ellacuría, "La superación del reduccionismo," 409-18. Zubiri's position on this point shares important elements with Martin Heidegger's criticisms of the Western philosophical tradition in *Being and Time.*

... reality has the character of an entity. This is what I call an *entification of reality*. And in this way, the logification of intellection, and the entification of reality, intrinsically converge. The "is" of intellection consists in an affirmation, and the "is" that is conceived by intellection has the character of an entity. This convergence (between the act and the object of intellection) has largely framed the path of European philosophy.[47]

*Second, Ellacuría says that Zubiri is arguing that the entification of reality reverses the proper priority of reality over meaning in thinking and knowing.* He explains that Zubiri's philosophical "search for truth" requires a "method through which the most reality, qualitatively and quantitatively understood, might be actualized in the intelligence."[48] And this demands a serious critique of the tendency to reduce reality to a thing, or to the meaning we assign it in conceptualization and thinking. Ellacuría notes that Zubiri's approach also has both theoretical and ethical value in that "dedicating one's life to the search for truth" in this way also makes one "more honest, . . . more free and . . . more useful."[49] Zubiri "is, of course, including . . . intellection in all its complexity in reality."[50] I shall return to this point in a moment.

*Third, Ellacuría says that the priority Zubiri assigns to reality in the search for the true and the good "actualizes the transformative capacities of . . . philosophy" in three respects:*[51] (1) it arms the person "with adequate tools"[52] to verify or critique truth claims; (2) it contributes to a sufficiently complex way of thinking about the biological and human dimensions of reality and the need to develop their contributions to "each and every person";[53] and (3) Zubiri's "contribution . . . makes it possible . . . with added effort, but without distortions, to better . . . realize" philosophy's transformative promise.[54] This focus on praxis epitomizes Ellacuría's approach to Zubiri's work.

These assertions, then, capture the essence of Ellacuría's appropriation of Zubiri's critical rereading of the phenomenological tradition. Ellacuría says that he learned from Zubiri that "the return [of phenomenology] to things is not enough . . . if that turn presupposes reducing them to their being, or to their meaning."[55] He insists instead on the need "to return to the *reality* of things because, anchored in that reality, restrained by it and driven by it, one can reach

---

47. Zubiri, *Inteligencia sentiente*, 224-25.
48. Ellacuría, "La superación del reduccionismo idealista," 417.
49. Ibid., 418.
50. Ibid.
51. Ibid.
52. Ibid.
53. Ibid.
54. Ibid.
55. Ibid., 639.

both being and meaning, *as the being and meaning of reality.*[56] The implications of this claim can be seen in the story of Archbishop Romero, whose early resistance to Medellín's preferential option for the poor was shaped by what priestly colleagues call "a very odd view of the documents" driven by "prejudices" against what he called "charlatans using them as a pretext to justify outlandish ideas"[57] and "fanatical propaganda"[58] for "an anti-Christian revolution."[59] As we will see in the next chapter, however, Romero says that it was as bishop of Santiago de María, where he "ran into suffering," which opened him to the reality revealed there, that he began to change.[60]

### Free to Get Real:
### Sentient Intelligence and the Primacy of Reality

What alternative, then, do Ellacuría and Zubiri provide to what they see as the reductionist idealism of the West and its role in the evasion of reality? In this section I will first examine Zubiri's model of *sentient intelligence*, briefly suggesting how it anticipates key insights from twenty-first-century cognitive neuroscience while providing a viable alternative to the *logification* of intelligence.[61] Second, I will examine what they call "the primacy of reality" as an alternative to the *entification* of reality.[62] And third, I examine some aspects of the role of sentient intelligence and the primacy of reality in Ellacuría's scientifically informed Christian historical realism.

Before proceeding, however, it must be said from the outset that sentient intelligence and the primacy of reality function as reciprocal concepts for Zubiri and Ellacuría. Thus, Zubiri insists "that an instrinsic priority of knowing over reality, or of reality over knowing is impossible." He says this is because "knowing and reality are in their very root strictly and rigorously related. There is no priority of one over the other."[63] In a moment we will examine the radical implications of this claim for Rutilio Grande, Oscar Romero, and Ignacio Ellacuría.

---

56. Ibid.

57. Oscar Romero, Editorial, *Orientación* 1234 (September 24, 1971): 3. Cited in Zacarías Diez and Juan Macho, "En Santiago de María me topé con la miseria," *Dos años de la vida de Monseñor Romero (1975-1976), Años de cambio?* (San Salvador: Imprenta Criterio, del arzobispado de San Salvador, 1995), 117.

58. Oscar Romero, Editorial, *Orientación* 2030 (August 12, 1973), 3. Cited in *Dos años de la vida de Monseñor Romero*, 118.

59. Oscar Romero, Editorial, *Orientación* 2036 (September 23, 1973), 3. Cited in *Dos años de la vida de Monseñor Romero*.

60. Diez and Macho, "En Santiago de María me topé con la miseria."

61. Ellacuría, "La superación del reduccionismo idealista," 419.

62. Ibid., 426.

63. Zubiri, *Inteligencia sentiente*, 10.

### Sentient Intelligence: Integrating the Mind and the Brain

So why use the word *intellection* to define *intelligence,* and what is the meaning of *sentient intelligence?* Zubiri and Ellacuría use the term *intellection* to emphasize that intelligence must be understood as an action (that of apprehending and knowing) rather than as a faculty or a thing. This forms the basis for the further claim that intellection is comprised of the sensible and intellectual apprehension of whatever we encounter as real. Thus, sensible and intellectual apprehension cannot be understood as separate moments in a sequence, but must rather be seen as aspects of a single action or process. Stated analogously, we could say that what we mean by the mind and the brain must be defined in the context of their role in the process of human perception and decision making. For Ellacuría this implies that the intellectual activity of the university exists to serve society, that every course should treat the national reality, and that the active participation of the country's poor majorities in civil society was El Salvador's best hope for creating a truly rational and humane future.

Ellacuría says that *sentient intelligence* is captured in Zubiri's notion "that *intellection* formally consists in apprehending the real as real, and that sensing is apprehending the real as an impression."[64] And he makes two assertions in support of this important thesis, which I suggest anticipate the more recent claims from cognitive neuroscience.

*First, Ellacuría says that Zubiri correctly insists that "the structural unity of intellection and sensing"*[65] *form two dimensions of a single act of sentient intelligence.* Zubiri writes,

> It is not only that human sensing and intellection are not in opposition. Rather, their intrinsic and formal unity constitutes a single and distinct act of apprehension. As sentient, the act is an impression. As an intellection, the act is an apprehension of reality. In this way, the distinct and unified act of sentient intellection is an impression of reality. Intellection is a way of sensing. And, in human persons, sensing is a mode of intellection.[66]

Ellacuría asserts that Zubiri's point is "much more radical" than the usual idea that intelligence apprehends reality by thinking about data given by the senses.[67] He says Zubiri argues instead that the "distinct and indivisible act of intellection" is not only an apprehension of reality (the intellective moment) but also an impression of reality (the sensible moment).[68] The intellection of

---

64. Ellacuría, "La superación del reduccionismo idealista," 420, citing Zubiri, *Inteligencia sentiente,* 12.

65. Ibid.

66. Zubiri, *Inteligencia sentiente,* 13.

67. Ellacuría, "La superación del reduccionismo idealista," 421.

68. Ibid., 422.

the object is not simply the product of affirmative, propositional, or predicative judgments about a collection of sense data. Rather, "reality is already actualized in sensing itself, in the sensible actualization itself." Juan Bañón explains: "Intellecting, then, is not judging. Judging is nothing but a single mode, and not the most elemental or primary one, which the human person has of confronting themselves with things as realities. This depends on a [more] elemental act, which is the primordial apprehension of reality."[69]

Ellacuría is quick to point out that Zubiri's critique of idealism also entails a rejection of reductionist empiricism. Indeed, he insists that Zubiri is not at all interested in reducing the various other aspects of intellection "in one way or another to sensing."[70] Zubiri's claim is that "intellective sensing does not simply yield contents that can be subsequently gathered and interrelated, etc." Rather, "the formal dimension of reality manifests itself in these contents themselves," which is "something neither the sensualists nor the idealists understood."

Ellacuría uses the distinction between stimulus-response and true human intellection to make his point, arguing that "an impression of reality implies a state of really being affected by a cause, and not simply by a stimulus." Thus, "the thing affecting me manifests itself with the variability of reality, and not only as an objective sign." And "that which is apprehended imposes itself on me with its own force, not the force of a stimulus, but with the force of a reality." The idea is that "the sentient character of intellection is not only a source of contents, and a motor for the subsequent deployment/unfolding of intellection itself." Rather, sensing turns out to be the impression of the formal dimension of a reality itself, so that "reality will have as many ways of presenting itself as there are different ways of sensing."

*Second, the act of intellection (which consists in the sentient apprehension of the real as real) has three moments or aspects.* Ellacuría summarizes his agreement with Zubiri's argument in three points.

*One, intellection begins with what Zubiri calls the sentient or primordial apprehension of a thing as being something "in and of itself"* (en y por sí mismo) *or simply "in itself"* (en propio).[71] Ellacuría says that reality "makes itself present in the impression of reality," which is why Zubiri calls it "a primary apprehension of the real," and the "formal" aspect of how we apprehend reality." Zubiri says, "This installation in . . . reality is physical and real, because the transcendentality of the impression of reality is physical and real." He treats this apprehension as the actualization of a relationship that "is physical and real, because the transcendentality of the impression of reality is physical and real." The first volume of Zubiri's magisterial trilogy on intelligence, *Sentient Intelligence: Intelligence and Reality* (1980), is dedicated to the analysis of this moment.[72]

---

69. Juan Bañón, Metafísica y noología en Zubiri (Salamanca: Publicaciones Universidad Pontificia de Salamanca, 1999), 24.

70. Ellacuría, "La superación del reduccionismo idealista," 422.

71. Ibid., 423.

72. Zubiri, *Inteligencia sentiente*.

*Two, intellection then moves to a "second moment" to determine "what is real with respect to other real things" that have been apprehended.*[73] *Here,* Zubiri says that intellection can be described as an act of the logos, where objects are categorized and named. It is noteworthy that Zubiri insists that this action occurs "within" the apprehension. It involves a move, however, from what he calls "primordial apprehension" to a "dual apprehension."[74] The idea is that intellection "reactualizes"[75] the moment of "primary apprehension of the thing," and relates it to the sensible apprehension of "other real things" through affirmative, propositional, and predicative judgments[76] (e.g., "this thing is a tree"). With this development, intellection has moved into the mode of the logos. Zubiri's critique of the "logification of intelligence" is intended to prevent the reduction of the entire process of intellection to this moment. The second volume of Zubiri's trilogy, *Intelligence and Logos* (1982), is a study of this moment of judgment, locating it within the larger process of intellection.

*And three, intellection finally takes us beyond "what can be apprehended directly, immediately, and as a single unit" by forcing us to see what we apprehend as "a worldly reality" vis-à-vis other "already apprehended realities."*[77] *Here, intellection has the character of an act of reason.* Ellacuría explains that the first two moments of intellection are actions that take place within the field of apprehension. In the third moment, however, intellection becomes reason, which Zubiri says "is simply the march from reality as a field [of apprehension] to a reality as a world." Ellacuría says that though reason "is a transcendental march toward the world," the act of reason nonetheless remains "grounded in the sentient character of intelligence." Thus, in its final stage, intellection operates as reason, developing provisional models, hypotheses, and postulates about the reality of things as they exist outside of sensible apprehension (the *noema*). Zubiri dedicates the third volume of his trilogy, *Intelligence and Reason*, to the role of sentient reason in intellection.[78]

Zubiri returns to the example of the perception of color to illustrate his concept of sentient intelligence, which allows us to show again how his work anticipates key aspects of current research in cognitive neuroscience. Zubiri writes, "Moving toward the real that exists outside the perception is something inexorably necessary, an intrinsic moment in perception of sensible qualities. Every quality is perceived not only in and of itself as such and such a quality, but also as a *pointing toward*. The reality of the qualities that are *only* in the perception is exactly what constitutes their radical insufficiency as moments of the real. They are real, but they are really insufficient. In their insufficiency, however,

73. Ellacuría, "La superación del reduccionismo idealista," 424.

74. Zubiri, *Inteligencia y logos*, 55, 56.

75. Ibid., 52.

76. Ibid., 109-10.

77. Ellacuría, "La superación del reduccionismo idealista," 424-25.

78. Xavier Zubiri, *Inteligencia y razon* (Madrid: Alianza Editorial, Sociedad de Estudios y Publicaciones, 1983).

these qualities . . . are . . . *pointing toward* the real that is outside the perception. Indeed, this is what gives rise to science."[79]

Alva Noe makes a similar point in explaining why the neuroscience of visual perception requires a unity-in-distinction between the mind and the brain, though his position is not without controversy. "We experience the visual world as sharply focused and uniformly detailed even though the eye, by dint of its nonuniform resolving power, cannot create such a representation, at least not without the brain's help. Again, we don't experience the retinal image; we don't experience *any* image, in that sense. We experience *the world*, and we do so not by depicting it internally but by securing access [to the world]. . . . Seeing is a kind of coupling with the environment, one that requires attention, energy, and, most of the time, movement."[80] Here Noe is arguing (in agreement with Zubiri) that the operation of the brain in visual perception is demonstrably shaped by the practical goal of the conscious creature to see and interact with a real object (a tree, dog, cat, etc.), rather than the idealist notion that we interact with pictures or representations, which we then examine.

Ellacuría concludes by stressing the importance of the structural unity of intellection and sensing and the formal character of sentient intelligence. He argues that reductionist empiricism and closed materialism are unable to account for the facts of perception or (by extension) the mind/brain distinction mentioned above. He says these insights have far-reaching implications for disputes about method and what counts as knowledge in academic disciplines and about what is truly human in politics.[81] Demonstrating his point, Ada María Isasi-Diaz uses Ellacuría's notion of sentient intelligence to argue that the everyday reality of marginated and oppressed Latinas (their *realidad cotidiana*) must be taken seriously as an intellectual source for theology and the social sciences.[82]

### Post-Newtonian Realism: The Formal Nature of Our Apprehension of Reality and Its Primacy

Ellacuría and Zubiri criticize the tendency to reduce reality to a form or subcategory of being in Western philosophy, which Ellacuría links to the crippling inability of Latin American academic and political writers to adequately address the "brute reality" of the continent. The underlying philosophical problem in their view is that *being* cannot be said to formally exist (in the phenomenological sense described earlier), and Western idealism makes a substance out of an event better described as an "*act* of being." This position flows from Zubiri's studies

---

79. Zubiri, *Inteligencia sentiente*, 184.

80. Alva Noe, *Out of Our Heads: Why You Are Not Your Brain, and Other Lessons from the Biology of Consciousness* (New York: Hill & Wang, 2009), 144-45.

81. Ellacuría, "La superación del reduccionismo idealista," 426.

82. Ada María Isasi-Diaz and Eduardo Mendieta, eds., *Decolonizing Epistemologies: Latina/o Theology and Philosophy* (New York: Fordham University Press, 2012), 48-49, 95, 98-101, 105; Ada María Isasi-Díaz, *La Lucha Continues: Mujerista Theology* (Maryknoll, NY: Orbis Books, 2004), 93.

of pre-war breakthroughs in physics and other sciences, which convinced him that "space, time, consciousness, and being" have been improperly turned into substances.[83] He says, "It has been thought that things are in time and space, that they are apprehended in the acts of consciousness, and that their ontic character is a moment of being." But emerging studies of the brain in human perception and relativity theory suggest that "space, time, consciousness, being, are not four receptacles for things . . ." and "real things are not *in* space or time, as Kant thought (following Newton), but rather real things are spatial and temporal." Thus, "Intellection is not an act of consciousness, as Husserl thought," and "there is not [a thing called] consciousness; there are only conscious acts." In fact, it appears that "neither consciousness, nor *the* unconscious, nor *the* subconscious exist; there are only conscious, unconscious and subconscious acts."[45]

But how are we to conceive of reality in a post-Newtonian world if being, space, time, and consciousness cannot be said to exist? Ellacuría argues that Zubiri's *formal concept of reality* and his insistence on the philosophical *primacy of formal reality* provide a scientifically informed notion of reality while addressing the problem of the "entification of reality" in the West. Ellacuría summarizes the conclusions he draws from Zubiri's position in three key assertions.

*First, Ellacuría answers the question, "What is reality?" by asserting that, for Zubiri, intellection consists in the actualization of the real as formally real.*[84] He makes three key points in this regard. (1) Zubiri argues that "it is in the act of intellection and only in the act of intellection, formally considered, where the real manifests itself as real." (2) Reality is first actualized for intelligence as the sensible apprehension of a formal reality. And a formal reality is whatever is sensibly apprehended as being something "in itself" (*en propio*), as something "of its own" (*de suyo*), or "as something that already is what it is before its presentation, as a *prius*, more in a metaphysical than a temporal sense."[85] (3) The "formality of reality opens us . . . to the arena of real things as real."[86] Here Ellacuría emphasizes that, for Zubiri, "even if reality is a formality, real things are not a formality, but rather simply real things."[87] Ellacuría makes this distinction more empirical when he asserts that the "reality of the real thing has to be measured—for there are degrees of reality—in terms of the degree to which it is 'of itself.'" The idea is that as the ecology of material, biological, sentient, and human systems evolve epigenetically one from the other each becomes progressively more self-directed "until in human persons their physical '*of its ownness*' becomes '*their own*' physicality." Thus, it is precisely the human person's awareness of their own formal reality (as being something "of its own") that finally "permits them to be reduplicatively self-possessed"[88] as an acting subject.

---

83. Xavier Zubiri, *Naturaleza, historia y Dios* (Madrid: Alianza Editorial, Fundación Xavier Zubiri, 1987, 2004), 15.

84. Ellacuría, "La superación del reduccionismo idealista," 426.

85. Ibid., 427.

86. Ibid., 428.

87. Ibid.

88. Ibid., 429.

*Second, Ellacuría says Zubiri insists on the philosophical primacy of "formal reality" for philosophical approaches informed by contemporary physics while emphasizing the importance of his argument that reality has a "transcendental function."*[89] Ellacuría explains that Zubiri is arguing for the primacy of reality "in the dual sense that reality is both the end and the origin [of] . . . everything else," and that "being, existence, meaning, etc., sprout within and from reality." He explains that, for Zubiri, the sensible apprehension of the formal reality of a thing (the quality of being something "of its own") has a transcendental function that opens the subject "to more and more reality."

Ellacuría describes this as a function "through which, by being installed in real things and without abandoning or annihilating them, we physically extend and expand ourselves by means of our modest intellective sensibility toward the real as real, toward a reality which is always open." He insists that it is precisely here "where any type of reality can make itself present in one way or another, including the absolutely absolute reality that we call God."[90] He says its formal reality places a claim upon the subject that cannot be ignored (he calls this the "transcendental function" of formal reality). And he suggests this claim is at the heart of Zubiri's argument for the primacy of reality as well as its status as a truly "positive" alternative to the entification of reality.

*Third, Ellacuría follows Zubiri in insisting that we are not only open to reality and located in reality, but we are bound to reality.*[91] The point is not just that reality forcefully makes itself present, or simply that reality imposes on us its formal character as being something "of its own" (*de suyo*). Rather, reality places certain claims on us that cannot be ignored. The idea is that "intellective sensing not only opens us to both reality and being," it also "drives us irresistibly to endlessly explore every type of reality and every form of being" that we encounter. Zubiri calls this our "bondedness" (or *religación*) to reality.[92]

Zubiri then asserts that the "bondedness" of the subject to reality means that when a reality is actualized *as real* for us (the subject), it creates a corresponding demand for the self-actualization of our own reality (the reality of the subject).[93] We are therefore confronted with a decision about whether and how to live by the truth of the formal reality actualized by their own sentient intelligence. Ellacuría's point is that through the day-by-day actualization of the real as real by sentient intelligence "a life is being constructed in which the force, the richness, and the power of the real intersect and intertwine with the problematic

---

89. Ibid. Diego Gracia correctly notes that "the word 'reality' has two meanings in Zubiri: 'reality as formality' (reality *qua* given in apprehension), and 'reality as fundamentality' (reality *qua* the actualization in a sensible apprehension of the thing beyond apprehension)"; see Gracia, "Zubiri, Xavier," *Dictionary*, 1166.

90. Ellacuría, "La superación del reduccionismo idealista," 429-430.

91. Ibid., 430.

92. Zubiri, *El hombre y Dios*, 92-94, 139-40.

93. Ibid., 248.

presented by reality itself."[94] Thus, as a result of our fundamental and unavoidable relationship with the "power of the real," we are faced by a steady diet of choices regarding whether and how to appropriate ourselves in relation to the realities we encounter.

Ellacuría concludes that it is "only by grasping and being grasped by more reality" that the human person can "become not just more intelligent, but, finally more real, and more human."[95] And he says this "giving in to reality in a will-to-truth, in a will-to-live, and in a will-to-being is a splendid way to overcome reductionist idealism." In the next chapter we will see how he uses it to explain the transformative impact on Archbishop Romero of his encounter with the historical reality of Rutilio Grande's priestly ministry with the peasants of Aguilares.[96]

### Ellacuría's Christian (or Theological) Historical Realism: Innovations

Having summarized Ellacuría's appropriation of Zubiri's concepts of sentient intelligence and the primacy of the formal dimension of reality the question remains, what transformations were produced by Ellacuría's encounter with the crucified people of El Salvador? In this section I will briefly suggest five areas in which Ellacuría's confrontation with the historical reality of Latin America moved his thinking beyond that of his philosophical mentor.

*First, Ellacuría diverges from Zubiri by explicitly grounding virtually all aspects of his work as a Christian philosopher and theologian in the historical reality of Latin America.* While it may seem obvious, I believe the Latin American contextualization of Ellacuría's thought is the most important source of its striking originality. One can find its roots in his talks for the 1969 retreat when he argues passionately for the historical reality of "The Third World as the Optimal Place for the Christian to Live the Exercises."[97] Though he correctly warns that the ideas expressed in the documents of Medellín will lead to persecution and death, it is here that the Central American Jesuits nonetheless first embrace God's preferential option for the poor.

In an important aside, Ellacuría describes his interpretation of Medellín's epoch-changing challenge as a "small" effort to go beyond the work of his teacher, Karl Rahner, by attempting to focus on Latin America's "worldly reality

---

94. Ellacuría, "La superación del reduccionismo idealista," 427.

95. Ibid., 430.

96. Ignacio Ellacuría, "Monseñor Romero, un enviado de Dios para salvar a su pueblo," *Escritos teológicos,* III (San Salvador: UCA Editores, 2002), 93-100.

97. Ignacio Ellacuría, "El tercer mundo como lugar óptimo de la vivencia Cristiana de los Ejercicios" (Dia 29:1), 1-12, in "Reunión-Ejercicios de la viceprovincia Jesuitica de Centroamérica, Diciembre 1969," 127-38, in *Reflexión teológico-espiritual de la Compañía de Jesus en Centroamerica, II* (San Salvador: Archives of the Society of Jesus, Central American Province, Survey S.J. de Centroamérica, December 1969).

and to conceive of it in theological terms."[98] Virtually all of Ellacuría's subsequent work follows the same pattern. And it can be argued that Ellacuría's entire philosophical and theological output is a response to the historical reality of Latin America, which he argues is defined by the continent's "poor majorities."[99]

*Second, Ellacuría identifies "historical reality"*[100] *as the proper object of philosophy and theology, and he argues that the process of facing up to real things as real has three dimensions.*[101] On the one hand, he explicitly accepts what he calls Zubiri's "strictly intramundane [or world-centered] metaphysics,"[102] building carefully on Zubiri's cosmology, analyzing matter, biological life, sentient life, and human history (in its personal and social dimensions) as different types of boundary maintaining systems, which build epigenetically upon the lower levels, integrating them into the more complex comprehensive reality of the cosmos.

On the other hand, however, Ellacuría makes an important change when he asserts that "historical reality" is the proper object of philosophy and theology. He agrees with Zubiri that historical reality comes to be through the appropriation and transformation of the historical (i.e., tradition-centered) and natural

---

98. Ibid., 2.

99. Ignacio Ellacuría, "Función liberadora de la filosofía," *ECA* 40, no. 435 (1985): 46. See also "Historización del bien común y de los derechos humanos en una sociedad dividida," in E. Tamez and S. Trinidad, eds., *Capitalismo: violencia y anti-vida*, II (San José, 1978), 81-94; *Freedom Made Flesh* (Maryknoll, NY: Orbis Books, 1976), 7-11, 127-63; "Hacia una fundamentación del método teológico latinoamericano," *Escritos teológicos*, I (San Salvador: UCA Editores, 2000), 187-218; "Tesis sobre la posibilidad, necesidad y sentido de una teología latinoamericana," in A. Vargas Machuca, ed., *Teología y mundo contemporáneo: homenaje a Karl Rahner en su 70 cumpleaños* (Madrid: Ediciones Cristiandad, 1975), 325-50; "La historización del concepto de propiedad como principio de desideologización," *ECA* nos. 335-336 (1976): 425-50; "Fe y justicia," in I. Ellacuría et al., *Fe, justicia y opción por los oprimidos* (Bilbao: Editorial Desclée de Brouwer, 1980), 9-78; "El pueblo crucificado, ensayo de soteriología histórica," *Escritos teológicos*, II, 137-70; "Monseñor Romero, un enviado de Dios para salvar a su pueblo," *Sal Terrae: Revista de teología pastoral* 811 (1980): 825-32; "Discernir *el signo* de los tiempos," *Diakonia* 17 (January/April 1981): 57-59; "Universidad, derechos humanos y mayorías populares," *ECA* no. 406 (August 1982): 791-816; "El reino de Dios y el paro en el tercer mundo," *Concilium* 180 (Madrid: Ediciones Cristiandad, 1982), 588-96; "Historicidad de la salvación cristiana," *Revista latinoamericana de teología* 1 (1984): 5-45 ["The Historicity of Christian Salvation," in I. Ellacuría and J. Sobrino, eds., *Mysterium Liberationis: Fundamental Concepts of Liberation Theology* (Maryknoll, NY: Orbis Books, 1993), 251-89]; "Aporte de la teología de la liberación a las religiones Abráhamicas en la superación del individualismo y del positivismo," *Revista latinoamericana de teología* 10 (1987): 3-27; "La teología de la liberación frente al cambio socio-histórico de América Latina," *Revista latinoamericana de teología* 12 (1987): 241-64; "Utopia y profetismo desde America Latina: un ensayo concreto de soteriología histórica," *Revista latinoamericana de teología* 6 (1989): 141-84.

100. Ignacio Ellacuría, *Filosofía de la realidad histórica* (San Salvador: UCA Editores, 1990), 42.

101. Ellacuría, "Hacia una fundamentación," 208.

102. Ellacuría, *Filosofía de la realidad histórica*, 26.

(i.e., the material, biological, and sentient) dimensions of reality[103] and that the process of human self-definition, or *historicization*, is driven by the fact that when something "is already given as a reality . . . I am forced to "become aware of it" or "to realize about it [*hacerse cargo de ella*] as a reality."[104] But he moves beyond Zubiri when he argues that the process of "facing up to real things as real has a triple dimension,"[105] which he asserts involves not only (1) "becoming aware of," "realizing about," or "grasping what is at stake in reality" (*hacerse cargo de la realidad*), but also (2) an ethical demand "to pick up" or "assume responsibility for reality" (*cargar con la realidad*), and (3) a praxis-related demand to change or "to take charge of reality" (*encargarse de la realidad*).[106] I will say more about this in a moment. But for now what is important is to understand that, for Ellacuría, every aspect of the process of human self-definition (or *historicization*) will have to pass through these three steps.

*Third, Ellacuría develops Zubiri's principle of historicization into a contextualized truth test for the claims of theology and philosophy.* Zubiri accepts Nietzsche's criticism of what he sees as the artificial split between intelligence and sensibility, arguing that it is largely responsible for the various forms of reductionist idealism. And building on Zubiri's model of sentient intelligence Ellacuría argues that the exclusion of sensibility from intellection has serious political implications by denigrating the knowledge of common people as an intellectual source and creating a dichotomy with the "true" conceptual knowledge of elites. At the same time, he shifts the focus of his work to historical intelligence from Zubiri's emphasis on sentient intelligence, in part, by using historicization as the method *par excellence* for the verification of truth claims.

As noted earlier, there are two primary uses of the term "historicization" in Ellacuría's work. First, in the *Philosophy of Historical Reality,* Ellacuría uses the term to refer to the incorporative and transformative power that human praxis exerts over the historical and natural dimensions of reality.[107] And second, in a 1976 article, Ellacuría suggests that "demonstrating the impact of certain concepts within a particular context is also . . . understood here as their historicization."[108] It is this secondary sense of the term that predominates in the great majority of Ellacuría's occasional pieces.

---

103. For the two primary meanings of "historicization," see Ellacuría, *Filosofía de la realidad histórica* 169; and "La historización del concepto de propiedad como principio de desideologización," *ECA* nos. 335-336 (1976): 425-50, at 427-28.

104. This is Ellacuría describing Zubiri in "La historicidad del hombre in Xavier Zubiri," 526. See Zubiri, *Sobre la esencia,* 447.

105. Ellacuría, "Hacia una fundamentación," 208.

106. Ibid. My translation of Ellacuría's three famously difficult phrases generally follow those of Jon Sobrino, in Jon Sobrino, "Jesus of Galilee from the Salvadoran Context: Compassion, Hope, and Following the Light of the Cross," in "The Galilean Jesus," *Theological Studies* 70, no. 2 (2009): 449 (special issue; ed. Robert Lassalle-Klein).

107. Ellacuría, *Filosofía de la realidad histórica,* 169.

108. Ignacio Ellacuría, "The Historicization of the Concept of Property," in John Hassett and Hugh Lacey, eds., *Towards a Society That Serves Its People* (Washington, DC: Georgetown

This brilliant development of historicization as a method for verifying truth claims provides methodological criteria concretizing three key themes in his work. *First, historicization operationalizes Ellacuría's Christian (or theological) historical realism.* Ethical concepts, for instance, are said to be historicized "when they refer to historical realities."[109] Ellacuría says this is the opposite of being abstract, in the negative sense. *Second, historicizing concepts subjects them to validity tests, which means that they must be constructed to be verifiable in order to be considered valid.* Using a classic notion of counterfactual proof, Ellacuría argues that if a "hypothesis cannot be nullified by data, it is not . . . [historicized]."[110] Indeed, he suggests, in that case "one is falling into sheer idealism, no matter how much the realist or materialist one might claim to be."[111] And *third, historicization becomes a procedure for testing truth claims.* Ellacuría holds that the truth of a historicized concept is actualized in its "becoming reality." Thus, its "truth can be measured . . . in its results,"[112] though nowhere does Ellacuría say that truth is identical with those results. This means that it will be necessary to continually revise the content of a given concept in light of its historical effects in order to maintain the "essential meaning" of that concept. The meaning of a concept is determined, at least in part, by the practical effects or impact of that concept on historical reality.[113]

*Fourth, Ellacuría historicizes his key theological concepts.* Ellacuría's historicization of *transcendence* provides an excellent example. He argues that a "historicized" treatment of the concept of transcendence will reject "pernicious philosophical influences," which identify transcendence with "separateness" and teach that "historical transcendence is separate from history."[114] He says such approaches operate under the mistaken assumption that "the transcendent must be outside or beyond what is immediately apprehended as real." For them, the transcendent is always "other, different . . . separated . . . in time, . . . space, or . . . essence"[115] from the historical object.

Ellacuría argues instead that revelation and history should be treated as correlative realities.

> I will assume that there are not two histories, a history of God and one of humanity; a sacred and a profane history. Rather there is a single

University Press, 1991), 109 (trans. from "La historización del concepto de propiedad como principio de desideologización," *ECA* 31, nos. 335-336 (1976): 425-50.

109. Ibid., 427.

110. Ibid.

111. Ibid.

112. Ibid., 428.

113. I have argued elsewhere that Ellacuría's use of historicization as a truth test exhibits important parallels with the "pragmatic maxim" of C. S. Peirce, founder of philosophical pragmatism. See Robert Lassalle-Klein, "The Body of Christ: The Claim of the Crucified People on North American Theology and Ethics," *Journal of Hispanic-Latino Theology* 5, no. 4 (May 1998): 68-74.

114. Ellacuría," Historicity of Christian Salvation," 254.

115. Ibid.

historical reality in which both God and human beings intervene, so that God's intervention does not occur without some form of human participation, and human intervention does not occur without God's presence in some form.[116]

He portrays transcendence, therefore, as "something that transcends in and not as something that transcends away from [history]; as something that physically impels to more, but not by taking out of; as something that pushes forward, but at the same time retains."

Thus, "God can be separated from history, but history cannot be separated from God. Sin does not make God disappear, but rather crucifies God."[117] Ellacuría therefore asserts that, no matter how much one might deny the idea of God, the saving presence of God continues to permeate historical reality. Thus, a truly theological understanding of salvation history will hold that "when one reaches God historically . . . one does not abandon the human, . . . [and] real history, but rather deepens one's roots, making what was already there more present and more effective."

This leads Ellacuría to ask to ask what efforts by the Latin American church to promote liberation socio-political and personal oppression and from sin have to do the Kingdom of God preached by Jesus?[118] His answer is to frame this as "the problem of Christians who, compelled by their faith, and as an objective realization of that faith, seek to make human action correspond as much as possible to God's will [or the Kingdom of God]." Thus, embracing what biblical scholars call the "eschatological reserve" of Jesus in regards to the Reign of God, Ellacuría says that Latin American theology is obliged to analyze ways that the Kingdom of God is *already* being realized in history, while at the same time analyzing how it is *not yet* fully realized in these efforts as a result of sin. For our purposes this could be described as a theological version of the problem faced by the Central American Jesuits at the 1969 retreat.

Ellacuría insists, on the one hand, that active opposition to historicizing the values of the Reign of God has real implications, including persecution and death, for God's prophets and his people. On the other hand the solidarity of Jesus and the martyrs—who accept crucifixion as the price for love and solidarity—function as historical signs of transcendence and hope in the resurrection as the final validation that Christ is present in their neighbor. In this way Ellacuría rejects cosmic dualisms as the final explanation for the inhumanity of sin, asserting "It may be possible to divide history into a history of sin and grace; but the division presupposes the real unity of history."

What this means is that we bear responsibility for our actions. And, more positively, *we have a crucial role to play in historicizing the Kingdom of God.* Thus, Ellacuría's profound Christian historical realism and his commitment to

---

116. Ibid.
117. Ibid., 255.
118. Ibid., 253.

the unifying role of grace in history lead him to assert that it is historical reality itself (which includes the reality of the Kingdom as well as the anti-Kingdom) that places a radical claim on the Christian disciple to take the crucified people down from the cross.

*Fifth, Ellacuría transforms Zubiri's epistemological principle that intellection involves the reciprocal actualization of reality and the subject into an ethical challenge with deeply religious implications.* Diego Gracia argues that "in Ellacuría, Zubiri's thesis that the human person must *realize about reality* is transformed into an ethical imperative."[119] Ellacuría appears to confirm this interpretation when he asserts in a 1979 paper, "Biological Foundation for Ethics,"[120] that the human person "formally constitutes himself as a moral reality" precisely "by having to open himself to reality, to what things are 'of their own,' . . . [and] by having to confront himself and things as real."[121]

In an earlier article Ellacuría reveals that Zubiri's notion that we must *confront ourselves with* (*enfrentarse con*) or "realize about reality" (*hacerse cargo de la realidad*)[122] is an "explicit allusion" to Heidegger's claim that humans experience a sense of having been "thrown" into existence (as Dasein).[123] Ellacuría explains that Zubiri has modified Heidegger's idea, arguing instead that human beings experience a certain coercion to give themselves over "to the thrownness of the real thing as real." The basic principle is that when something "is already given as a reality, I not only have to allow it to be [*dejar que sea*], but I am forced to face up to it [*hacerse cargo de ella*] as a reality,"[124] and "when I confront a determinate thing, I am not only being in the thing, but I am being-together with reality." As a result, he insists, it is only "in this being-together [that] the human person is able to reappropriate him- or herself as a reality."

As we saw above, Ellacuría moves beyond Zubiri when he argues that the process of apprehending "real things as real has a triple dimension,"[125] and when he asserts that the actualization (or *historicization*) of the human subject will have to pass through the same steps. What, then, is the meaning of these steps in his own life?

First, Ellacuría says that *becoming aware of, realizing about,* or *grasping what is at stake in reality* "assumes being in the reality of things—and not merely being before the idea of things or their meaning."[126] Jon Sobrino calls this the *noetic* moment of facing up to reality, noting the Ellacuría's idea is that sentient intelligence must be "incarnated in reality."[127] Gustavo Gutiérrez eloquently articulates

119. "Diego Gracia," Central America Province News, 1993; quoted in letter from Dean Brackley, S.J., to Charles Beirne, S.J., September 2, 1993.

120. Ignacio Ellacuría, "Fundamentación biológica de la ética," *ECA* 368 (1979): 419-28.

121. Ibid., 422.

122. Ellacuría, "Hacia una fundamentación," 207.

123. Ellacuría, "La historicidad del hombre in Xavier Zubiri," 526.

124. Ibid.

125. Ellacuría, "Hacia una fundamentación," 208.

126. Ibid.

127. Jon Sobrino, "Ignacio Ellacuría, el hombre y el cristiano, 'Bajar de la cruz al pueblo

the personal impact of Ellacuría's "confrontation" with the historical reality of the poor. He says Ellacuría's encounter with the oppressed people of El Salvador provided a fundamental frame of reference that came to define his life, his encounter with God, and death. Gutiérrez writes,

> The life Ignacio chose makes us understand the scope of the death he encountered. Like Jesus, Ignacio could say, "No one takes my life; I give it freely" (Jn 10:18). He gave it, in fact, out of love for the God of the Bible, and for the people he made his own. The people compelled him to learn about the scandal of their poverty and their unending suffering. Thus he came to understand the central role that justice has in the gospel message, and that without it there is no authentic peace.[128]

Gutiérrez's words capture beautifully and precisely what Ellacuría means when he writes that realizing about reality "implies being among the reality of things through their material and active mediations."[129] Here the meaning of truth, justice, and love emerge as "noetic" aspects of Ellacuría's encounter with the historical reality of El Salvador's poor majorities.

Second, Ellacuría says that *picking up* or *assuming responsibility for reality (cargar con la realidad)* "expresses the fundamentally ethical nature of intelligence."[130] He asserts that "intelligence was not given to humanity so that it might evade its real obligations, but rather so that it might pick up and carry what things really are, and what they really demand."[131] Sobrino interprets this to mean that "intelligence is interrogated by reality and must respond to its demand."[132]

In moving words, undoubtedly drawn from his own experience, Gutiérrez speculates about the inner conflicts Ellacuría must have faced in accepting the sense of responsibility implied in a real relationship with the poor.

> His choice made him see that he couldn't follow in Jesus' footsteps without walking with the people in their aspiration to dignity, life, and liberation. Yet in the face of this difficult challenge, he did not take refuge—and this is another of the traits that give him his special place—in something he had at hand. It was something that could have hidden the fear of solidarity and its demands from others, and even

---

crucificado'" (San Salvador: Centro Monseñor Romero, 2001), translated as "Ignacio Ellacuría, The Human Being and the Christian: 'Taking the Crucified People Down from the Cross,'" in Kevin Burke and Robert Lassalle-Klein, eds., *Love That Produces Hope: The Thought of Ignacio Ellacuría* (Collegeville, MN: Liturgical Press, 2006), 19.

128. Gustavo Gutiérrez, "No One Takes My Life from Me; I Give It Freely" (trans. James Nickoloff), in Burke and Lassalle-Klein, *Love That Produces Hope*, 69.

129. Ellacuría, "Hacia una fundamentación," 208.

130. Ibid.

131. Ibid.

132. Sobrino, "Ignacio Ellacuría, the Human Being and the Christian," 19.

from himself, namely, an intellectual life flowing quietly along in the purely academic world. This kind of life, although it might occasionally reflect what was happening to the marginalized, would in fact be far from them and their afflictions. Chances to excel in the university world were not lacking, this we know. He possessed a solid formation in philosophy and theology, and he was well known as the favorite student of a great teacher, Xavier Zubiri. The academy's doors stood open to him.[133]

In fact, as we saw earlier, Zubiri petitioned the superior general of the Jesuits to release Ellacuría from the University of Central America (UCA) and to assign him to Spain so they could collaborate.[134] But it was decided that Ellacuría would return to El Salvador with permission to collaborate with Zubiri in Spain during summer and vacations,[135] allowing Ellacuría to stay rooted in the reality of El Salvador and its suffering people. Sobrino describes Ellacuría's path as one of "fidelity to the real,"[136] a way of accepting responsibility for the reality of the poor and a decision "to be faithful to that reality regardless of where it might lead."[137]

Third, Ellacuría says that *changing* or *taking charge of reality* "points to the praxis-oriented nature of intelligence."[138] He argues that "intelligence only actualizes its nature, including its character of knowing reality and comprehending its meaning, when it undertakes really doing things." And he continues, "Precisely because of the priority that reality has over meaning, there is no real change of meaning without a real change in reality; to try to change the first without trying to change the second is to distort intelligence and its primary function." For Sobrino, however, Ellacuría's third dimension of facing up to things as real implies both "taking charge of reality" and "'allowing oneself to be carried by reality' (the dimension of a graced experience)."[139] Gutiérrez says that Ellacuría did this by using his education, guided by the gospel, to serve the people of El Salvador.

We cannot know . . . how many tensions and perplexities, vacillations and inconsistencies, bad moods, and painful impasses he experienced along the path he chose to follow. But naturally his could be neither

---

133. Gutiérrez, "No One Takes My Life," 69.

134. Letter from Ignacio Ellacuría to Xavier Zubiri, April 30, 1968. Cited in Teresa Whitfield, *Paying the Price: Ignacio Ellacuría and the Murdered Jesuits of El Salvador* (Philadelphia: Temple University Press, 1994), 42.

135. Letter from Paolo Dezza to Segundo Azcue, April 23, 1968. Cited in Whitfield, *Paying the Price*, 42.

136. Jon Sobrino, S.J., *Spirituality of Liberation* (Maryknoll, NY: Orbis Books, 1988), 14, 17 (trans. Robert R. Barr from *Liberación con espíritu* [San Salvador: UCA Editores, 1985]).

137. Ibid., 17.

138. Ellacuría, "Hacia una fundamentación," 208.

139. Jon Sobrino, "Jesus of Galilee from the Salvadoran Context," 449–50.

a tranquil nor a triumphal journey. It never is. What is certain is that he put his intelligence, his analytical acumen, and all his intellectual talent to work doing the discernment necessary to find the correct path amid the jumble of events taking place in El Salvador and Latin America. Not only did he not forget his philosophical formation. He used it as a source of criteria for acting in a changing situation full of surprises. Thus he gave his academic formation its due, and . . . made clear the role that it can play in the daily life of individuals, no matter how conflictual. . . . One of my old professors . . . said, "There is nothing more practical than a good theory." Ignacio lived out this kind of theorizing with passion.[140]

In Part III we will see that Jon Sobrino goes one step further when he asserts that Ellacuría became the prophetic voice of the church in El Salvador after the murder of Archbishop Romero. In Part I we saw that this decision led to his death, which played a role in the collapse of U.S. military aid to El Salvador and the end of the war. In the chapters that follow I will suggest that Ellacuría's own life illustrates the meaning of these concepts by showing what it meant for him to become aware of, to take responsibility for, and to help change the historical reality of the suffering people of El Salvador.

What tools, then, does Ellacuría leave to help us come to terms with the practical, ethical, and religious implications of Zubiri's insight that human knowledge involves the reciprocal actualization of both the subject and its object? First, he articulates a powerful theoretical foundation for historicizing the noetic, the ethical, and the praxical dimensions of intelligence. Second, he offers a historical model for what each contributes to the humanizing journey of a theologian, a professor, and a university president who encountered the Christ of the San Salvador retreat in the crucified people of El Salvador.[141] And third, he stands humbly before the example of Archbishop Romero whose remarkable journey demonstrates the transformative power of the crucified people. We turn now to Ellacuría's relationship with Archbishop Oscar Romero.

---

140. Gutiérrez, "No One Takes My Life," 70.

141. Ignacio Ellacuría, "La teología como el momento ideologics de la praxis ecclesial," *Escritos teológicos,* I (San Salvador: UCA Editores, 2000), 163-85.

# 6

# *Gloria Dei, Vivens Pauper*

## Archbishop Oscar Romero[1]

Given the depth and complexity of Ignacio Ellacuría's writings in theology and philosophy, it is not surprising that there is disagreement about their starting point and unifying themes. Some rightly emphasize the profound influence on Ellacuría's thought of the *Spiritual Exercises* of St. Ignatius,[2] others, the philosophical historical realism of Xavier Zubiri,[3] while still others, the groundbreaking theology of Karl Rahner, S.J., which influenced Vatican II and Medellín.[4] Some properly highlight Ellacuría's explicit commitment to developing "critical and creative"[5] principles for a Latin American philosophy of liberation[6] or a theology of liberation grounded in a Christian understanding of salvation in history.[7] But Jon Sobrino, Ellacuría's closest friend and collaborator, looks elsewhere.

---

1. *Gloria Dei, vivens pauper* (the glory of God is the poor person who lives) is the adaptation by Archbishop Romero of the famous statement of St. Irenaeus, *Gloria Dei, vivens homo* (the glory of God is the human person alive). See Archbishop Oscar Romero, "Una experiencia eclesial en El Salvador, Centro América," in *La voz de los sin voz: La palabra viva de Monseñor Oscar Arnulfo Romero* (San Salvador: UCA Editores, 1980, 1996), 193.

2. J. Matthew Ashley, "Contemplation in the Action of Justice: Ignacio Ellacuría and Ignatian Spirituality," in Kevin Burke and Robert Lassalle-Klein, eds., *Love That Produces Hope: The Thought of Ignacio Ellacuría* (Collegeville, MN: Liturgical Press, 2006), 144-65.

3. Diego Gracia, "Filosofía práctica," in José A. Gimbernat and Carlos Gómez, eds., *La pasión por la libertad* (Navarra, Spain: Editorial Verbo Divino, 1994), 329-52.

4. Martin Maier, "Karl Rahner: The Teacher of Ignacio Ellacuría," in Kevin Burke and Robert Lassalle-Klein, eds., *Love That Produces Hope: The Thought of Ignacio Ellacuría* (Collegeville, MN: Liturgical Press, 2006), 128-43

5. Ignacio Ellacuría, "Función liberadora de la filosofía," *ECA* 40, no. 435 (1985): 47; henceforth "Función liberadora."

6. Ellacuría, "Función liberadora," 46. See Héctor Samour, *Voluntad de liberación: la filosofía de Ignacio Ellacuría* (Granada, Spain: Editorial Comares, 2003), 3; Antonio González, "Assessing the Philosophical Achievement of Ignacio Ellacuría," in *Love That Produces Hope*, 73-87; also in *La pasión por la libertad*, 307-27; José Mora Galiana, *Ignacio Ellacuría, filósofo de la liberación* (Madrid: Editorial Nueva Utopia, 2004).

7. Ignacio Ellacuría, "Hacia una fundamentación del método teológico latinoamericano," *Escritos teológicos*, I (San Salvador: UCA Editores, 2000). See Juan José Tamayo Acosta, "A la paz por la justicia: praxis de liberación," in José A. Gimbernat and Carlos Gómez, *La pasión*

For Sobrino, it is Ellacuría's historical encounter with the Mystery of God revealed in the crucified people of El Salvador that forms the core of the latter's writings and work. And he believes it is Ellacuría's relationship with Archbishop Romero, especially the latter's love and reverence for the Salvadoran people as the human face of God, that ultimately shaped Ellacuría's mature life and thought. In Sobrino's 2009 "Letter to Ellacuría," entitled "Archbishop Romero and You," Sobrino asserts,

> Romero became someone very special for you, different from what Rahner or Zubiri had been. He got inside you, touching your deepest fibers. I had that feeling from the beginning. And it always stuck with me when you said in your homily at the funeral mass we had in the UCA [University of Central America]: "With Monseñor Romero God visited El Salvador."[8]

Here and elsewhere Sobrino insists, which many commentators miss, that Ellacuría's relationship with God and his people, and hence a fundamental aspect of Ellacuría's identity, was changed by knowing Archbishop Romero. Sobrino explains, "People know that both of you were eloquent prophets and martyrs." But he says, "I like to remember another important similarity, which is how you began. Each of you was given a Christian and Salvadoran torch, and without any kind of discernment made the fundamental choice to keep it burning. Monseñor Romero received it from Rutilio Grande the night they killed him. And when Monseñor Romero died, you picked it up."[9] Sobrino says his point "is to remember and emphasize that in El Salvador there was a grand tradition" that he says was "passed from hand to hand" of "dedication and love for the poor, confrontation with oppressors, steadiness in conflict, and the hope and the dream [of the Kingdom of God]" grounded in "the Jesus of the gospel and the mystery of his God." He insists, therefore, "We must not squander that legacy, and need to make it available to the young."

In this section, then, I will first argue that Oscar Romero's encounter with the suffering of his people and the vilification and murder of his clergy for defending them were the driving forces behind his decision to accept Medellín's

---

*por la libertad* (Navarra, Spain: Editorial Verbo Divino, 1994) 127-51; José Sols Lucia, *La teología histórica de Ignacio Ellacuría* (Madrid: Editorial Trotta, 1999); Kevin Burke, *The Ground beneath the Cross: The Theology of Ignacio Ellacuría* (Washington, DC: Georgetown University Press, 2000); Michael E. Lee, *Bearing the Weight of Salvation* (New York: Herder & Herder/Crossroad, 2009).

8. Jon Sobrino, "Monseñor Romero y tú," Carta a Ellacuría 2009, http://www.foroellacuria. org/otra_mirada.htm, 4; accessed July 27, 2013. Also cited in Jon Sobrino, "Ignacio Ellacuría, el hombre y el cristiano, 'Bajar de la cruz al pueblo crucificado'" (San Salvador: Centro Monseñor Romero, 2001), translated as "Ignacio Ellacuría, The Human Being and the Christian: 'Taking the Crucified People Down from the Cross,'" in Kevin Burke and Robert Lassalle-Klein, eds., *Love That Produces Hope: The Thought of Ignacio Ellacuría* (Collegeville, MN: Liturgical Press, 2006), 43.

9. Ibid., 1.

discernment that God was calling the Latin American church to support and defend the poor. And second, I will suggest that it was Archbishop Romero more than anyone else who, like Jesus, taught Ignacio Ellacuría not only to defend but to know and love the common people of El Salvador.

### "In Santiago de María I Ran into Suffering" (1970-1977)[10]

The story of Archbishop Romero and his gradually deepening concern for the poor provides dramatic confirmation for Ellacuría's thesis regarding the disclosive and transformative power of the encounter with reality. Following the December 1969 retreat led by Ignacio Ellacuría and Miguel Elizondo the Central American Jesuits began reorganizing their works around Medellín's call to a preferential option for the poor, which they understood to entail active support for the rights of campesinos and civilian movements promoting social, economic, and political reform and the end of military rule. But Oscar Romero's actions and statements while auxiliary bishop of San Salvador from 1970 to 1974 betray a deep suspicion and even hostility toward calls inspired by Medellín for the church to collaborate with and support movements for social change. By the late 1970s, however, Archbishop Romero would emerge as the prophetic voice of the Salvadoran church denouncing state-sponsored violence against campesinos and civil society and demanding in the name of God that the state should "stop the repression!" Romero's journey from often strident critic of Medellín's proponents to defender of the poor would challenge, fascinate, and inspire Ignacio Ellacuría to his core.

In this section I will argue (in agreement with Romero's colleagues and coworkers while bishop of Santiago de María) that his encounter during those years with the terrible suffering of rural farm workers opened his heart and mind to Medellín's preferential option for the poor. And I will suggest that it was the vilification and later murder (in San Salvador) of Romero's clergy for supporting and defending their suffering farm workers that was the driving force behind the archbishop's decision to take a more assertive and public posture against government repression.

### *Auxiliary Bishop of San Salvador (1970-1974)*

The reader will recall that by 1970 Ellacuría and the UCA had begun to historicize their commitment to the option for the poor by reframing the university's "principal mission as that of being the critical and creative conscience"[11] of El Salvador and by dedicating the pages of *ECA* to land reform and criticism of the

---

10. Oscar Romero, cited in Zacarías Diez and Juan Macho, "En Santiago de María me topé con la miseria," *Dos años de la vida de Monseñor Romero (1975-1976), Años de cambio?* (San Salvador: Imprenta Criterio, del arzobispado de San Salvador, 1995),

11. José María Gondra, S.J., "Discurso de la Universidad Centroamericana José Simeón Cañas en la firma del contrato con el BID," *Planteamiento universitario 1989*, 12.

July 1969 war with Honduras. The following year the university lost government funding for its role in exposing military violence during the 1971 ANDES teachers' strike. In 1972 Rutilio Grande began the new rural ministry in Aguilares; in 1973 the UCA exposed the fraudulent national elections of the previous year; and in 1974 Ellacuría founded the Center for Theological Reflection at the UCA, where Jesuit seminarians could finally study in Central America, and local religious could learn theological approaches grounded in the spirit of Medellín and Vatican II. Ellacuría also published *Teología política* (1973) and numerous articles during this period outlining philosophical and theological foundations for a Latin American philosophy and theology of liberation grounded in the work of Medellín, Karl Rahner, Xavier Zubiri, and the *Spiritual Exercises* of St. Ignatius.

Interestingly enough, Oscar Romero emerged at almost the same moment as a countervailing voice among the Salvadoran bishops to the calls of people like Ellacuría for more church involvement in social questions. Ordained a priest in Rome on April 4, 1942, Oscar Romero served as secretary for the Episcopal Conference of El Salvador from 1967 to 1974 and was ordained auxiliary bishop of San Salvador on June 21, 1970. Bishop Romero held very different views from Ellacuría at this time regarding the proper role of the church in society. While there is no detailed study of Romero's thinking on this issue (several important studies of his life exist[12]), I would suggest that before becoming archbishop, he held what one author calls a traditionalist "quasi-corporatist" view of the role of the church in society, found alongside the preferential option for the poor that begins to appear in the documents of Medellín.[13] Here the church's role is that of a unifying social institution promoting what Medellín calls "socialization understood as a sociocultural process of personalization and communal growth" so that "all of the sectors of society, . . . [especially] the social-economic sphere, should, because of justice and brotherhood, transcend antagonisms in order to become agents of national and continental development."[14]

Bishop Romero's commitment to this view of the church as unifier and social glue, along with other more personal factors, rendered him deeply suspicious of theological and pastoral approaches pushing the church toward prophetic denunciations of state-sponsored violence against reformist groups mobilizing civil society in support of social change. Romero's public statements and writings during this period as editor of the diocesan newspaper, *Orientación*,

---

12. A small sample would include James Brockman, *Romero, A Life* (Maryknoll, NY: Orbis Books, 1989); Jesús Delgado, *Oscar A. Romero, Biografía* (San Salvador: UCA Editores, 1986); Zacarías Diez and Juan Macho, "En Santiago de María me topé con la miseria"; Martin Maier, *Monseñor Romero, Maestro de espiritualidad* (San Salvador: UCA Editores, 2001); Jon Sobrino, *Archbishop Romero: Memories and Reflections* (Maryknoll, NY: Orbis Books, 1990); María López Vigil, *Oscar Romero: Memories in Mosaic* (Washington, DC: Ecumenical Program on Central America and the Caribbean, 2000); Scott Wright, *Oscar Romero and the Communion of the Saints: A Biography* (Maryknoll, NY: Orbis Books, 2010).

13. William T. Cavanaugh, "The Ecclesiologies of Medellín and the Lessons of the Base Communities," *Cross Currents* (Spring 1994): 72.

14. Second General Conference of Latin American Bishops, "Document on Justice," 13.

consistently characterize more activist views of the church as politically naive distortions of Catholic teaching unduly influenced by communist approaches dangerously politicizing the role of the church in Salvadoran society. As a result, during his years as auxiliary bishop, Romero engaged in a series of confrontations with Jesuits, diocesan priests, religious, and small Christian communities who understood Medellín's option for the poor as a mandate to promote the conscientization and mobilization of campesinos and others promoting human rights and the end of military rule.

One lay friend from this period says the new bishop "began to oppose"[15] the more activist posture of the church toward society inspired by Medellín, while a diocesan priest describes him as an emerging "ideological warrior" who nonetheless "played fair."[16] Juan Hernández Pico recalls an early encounter with Romero shortly after the latter's appointment as auxiliary bishop of San Salvador. The story captures the new bishop's way of using the pages of _Orientación_ in his self-appointed role as the guardian of orthodoxy who believed the church must preserve its neutrality in the area of politics. Hernández Pico remembers that Archbishop Chávez had asked him and another Jesuit, Néstor Jaén, to offer a retreat on the _Spiritual Exercises_ of St. Ignatius for the priests of San Salvador. He says, "All the priests attended and they ran the whole gamut of the different political tendencies" in the diocese. Naturally enough one evening the clergy got into "a big heated argument on faith and politics and the role of the priest in all of it."[17]

> Suddenly we saw a priest in black robes enter. He moved in all quiet and stealthy-like, and he just stayed there in the back, hidden, without saying anything.
>
> "Who's that?" I whispered to Néstor.
>
> "That's the new auxiliary bishop, Oscar Romero."
>
> When we finished the debate, Néstor said to me: "I wonder how Romero's going to react after hearing everything we said."
>
> He was right to wonder. Two weeks later an article signed by Romero appeared in _Orientación_ saying that two Jesuits—and it gave our names—had led spiritual exercises that didn't have anything spiritual about them, that they were pure sociology and practically Marxist sociology at that! . . .

Hernández Pico recalls, "I got mad and wrote a fiery letter attacking him. I said that it was precisely those kinds of accusations that were endangering people's lives, and that Medellín had called for us to make changes in the Church," adding, "Let's see if he's fair enough to publish that in _Orientación_! I bet he won't!" Much to Pico's surprise, however, he says, "I was wrong. He published it. In

---

15. Interview with Ana María Godoy, in María López Vigil, _Oscar Romero: Memories in Mosaic_, 40.

16. Interview with Rutilio Sánchez, in López Vigil, _Oscar Romero_, 43.

17. Interview with Juan Hernández Pico, in López Vigil, _Oscar Romero_, 44-45.

its entirety." Pico notes, however, that the new bishop had "gotten in the last word! . . . Though he would allow my views to be voiced, he stood by his judgment, and claimed that he would prove that we were Marxists. Nobody could beat him at being stubborn"!

These were dangerous accusations, and Romero's very public attacks against clergy critical of the government helped to marginalize their voices and served to legitimate repressive actions against those calling for change. The reader will recall that the Central Elections Council controlled by the ruling right-wing party fraudulently declared Colonel Arturo Armando Molina winner of the February 20, 1972, presidential election over José Napoleon Duarte and Guillermo Ungo, whose winning platform had included the promise of real agrarian reform.[18] When the stolen election was exposed by a UCA investigation many diocesan seminarians refused to sing at the inaugural liturgy, charging that its location in the cathedral along with the presence of the papal nuncio provided wrongful legitimation for a fraudulent government. Romero saw the protest as a dangerous foray by the church into politics, and Hernández Pico says he "made the problem his personal issue. The pope and his nuncio had been attacked, and the hierarchy of the church had been insulted. How could it be worse?"[19]

As a result Romero "started to actively support the expulsion of the Jesuits from the seminary" saying, "we were the ones that were putting ideas into the seminarians' heads and we had to go," adding ominously, "If they're not removed, we reserve the right to take other measures." This was a threat (at least in part) to bring the matter to the attention of Vatican officials, which Romero later did on this and other issues. In the end the Jesuits were removed after fifty years of service and "Monseñor Romero took charge of the seminary." Pico says, "He was satisfied. Orthodoxy had triumphed."[20] Years later Archbishop Romero would apologize to Fr. Amando López (part of the seminary faculty) for his role in pushing the Jesuits out of the seminary.[21] For the time being, however, he was content!

Romero considered good relations with the government to be a top priority throughout this period. Colonel Molina assumed office on July 1, 1972, and just over two weeks later, on July 19, Molina ordered troops to invade the campus of the National University with tanks and helicopters, arresting eight hundred people and closing its doors for a year. In his public statement the new president justified the invasion with the assertion that the university had "fallen into the hands of the communist party of El Salvador and . . . opportunists."[22] Shortly

18. Rodolfo Cardenal, *Manual de historia de Centroamérica* (San Salvador: UCA Editores, 1996), 396.

19. Interview with Juan Hernández Pico, in López Vigil, *Oscar Romero*, 51.

20. Ibid., 52.

21. Interview of James R. Brockman, S.J., with Amando Lopez, S.J.; cited in Brockman, *Romero*, 51.

22. "Mensaje del Señor Presidente de la República Coronel Arturo Armando Molina," cited in *La investigación y la docencia en la educación universitaria de El Salvador* (San Salvador: Proyecto UCA/PRENDE-OEA, 1990), 144; and Teresa Whitfield, *Paying the Price:*

thereafter, according to a contemporary priest from the archdiocese, "The Bishops' Conference published a paid ad in the newspapers, written and signed by Monseñor Romero as secretary, defending the occupation of the university with a rationalization taken straight from the government's statement: that the university was a hotbed of subversion, and that it was necessary to take measures against it."[23]

Looking back, the Central American Jesuit provincial, Francisco Estrada, recalls, "He looked for reasons to be in conflict with us."[24] What is certain is that Romero considered the conviction of the Central American Jesuits, expressed in their teaching and writings, that the preferential option for the poor implied public opposition to state-sponsored violence against the poor and civil society to be a dangerous perversion linking the teachings of Medellín to Marxism.

The vehemence of Romero's commitment to this position and the danger it posed for the objects of his ire is clearly demonstrated by the 1973 crisis at the prestigious Jesuit high school in San Salvador, the *Externado San José*, provoked by Romero's criticism of field trips to poor neighborhoods and the use of class analysis to interpret their meaning. Fr. Estrada recalls,

> He hurled virulent accusations at us, first in *Orientación*, . . . and then in *El Diario Latino, La Prensa Gráfica* and *El Diario de Hoy* . . . that our Marxist teachings pitted children against their parents, [and that] . . . we were using "pamphlets of communist origin" in our religion classes. Outrageous accusations! He put together a whole campaign against us. . . . It was a national campaign all provoked by that man.[25]

Fortunately, the aged Archbishop Chávez intervened forcefully in the newspapers and with the government on behalf of the Jesuits, conducting his own investigation that found the charges baseless and persuading President Molina to drop charges of teaching classes of Marxist orientation. Fr. Estrada, whose ecclesial authority was equivalent to that of a bishop, recalls his attempt to discuss the affair with Bishop Romero.

> "Look," I told him rather angrily, "You're accusing us of very serious things and I want you to tell me what you're basing these accusations on. Because the authority that I recognize—the only authority I recognize—is [that of your superior] Archbishop Chávez, and he knows exactly what's being taught in our school. We've never taken a single step without his approval. . . ."

Estrada says that Bishop Romero "didn't even look at me," and recalls thinking that "even though he waged heated battles, he was really a timid man." So the

---

*Ignacio Ellacuría and the Murdered Jesuits of El Salvador* (Philadelphia: Temple University Press, 1994), 50.

23. Interview with Pedro Declerc/Noemí Ortiz in López Vigil, *Oscar Romero*, 47.
24. Interview with Francisco Estrada, in López Vigil, *Oscar Romero*, 52.
25. Ibid.

Jesuit provincial again demanded, "I want to know what you are basing these accusations on!" Romero, however, "kept his eyes downcast, and responded simply: 'I have reliable sources of information.'" Frustrated, Estrada insisted, "What reliable sources could you possibly have? In the case of the school, the only sources are me, the provincial of the Society of Jesus, and the archbishop of San Salvador, of whom you are simply an auxiliary! What other source could you possibly have to be causing such an uproar? Tell me!"

Estrada continues, "He didn't look up," but just repeated, "I have reliable sources of information" without changing "his words or his tone." "But I've already told you who the only reliable sources are! What are these sources of yours?" Estrada demanded. "I have reliable sources," Romero simply repeated. Summarizing the exchange Estrada recalls, "That man drove me totally crazy. He didn't give me single argument or a single reason. He didn't dialogue. He didn't ask me questions. He didn't want to know."[26]

In the end the charges were dropped due in large part to the intervention of Archbishop Chávez, who contradicted the May 27, 1973, accusations made in *Orientación* by Oscar Romero, his auxiliary bishop. Public opinion turned in favor of the Jesuits after a survey revealed that an overwhelming majority of parents supported their work at the school, and Ellacuría published a six-part series in the local media written by Jesuits from the UCA and the high school entitled "The *Externado* Thinks Like This."[27]

About this time Romero suffered another important setback in his efforts to restrain what he saw as the excesses wrought by over-zealous supporters of Medellín. When the Jesuits were ousted at the end of 1972 as directors of the diocesan seminary the bishops designated Oscar Romero as rector of the new diocesan-led administrative team and faculty with Monsignor Freddy Delgado as vice-rector.[28] The remaining theology and philosophy students were either dismissed or sent elsewhere, and the seminary began afresh in February 1973. But numbers were low, and Monsignor Delgado was having problems with the seminarians, so Romero orchestrated a graceful exit by arranging for him to become adjunct secretary of the bishops' conference.[29] Problems escalated, however, when Bishop Aparicio withdrew his students, and by midyear the seminary was deemed financially unsustainable and closed. Thus, after more than half a century of successful operation under Jesuit direction the national seminary had collapsed in less than a year under Romero's leadership.

As the conflicts continued, Romero's fellow auxiliary bishop, Arturo Rivera Damas, reports that his colleague's spirits began to fall. Rivera Damas recalls a 1974 meeting of the Salvadoran Episcopal Conference when Romero attempted to resign both as director of *Orientación* and as editor of a proposed pastoral

---

26. Ibid., 52-53.
27. Hernández-Pico provides this detail on the collaborative nature of the project. See Juan Hernández-Pico, S.J., *Historia reciente de la Provincia de Centroamérica (1976-1986)* (San Salvador: Ediciones Cardoner, 1991), 14.
28. Brockman, *Romero*, 51.
29. Ibid., 52.

letter on the family. His intention was to reclaim a position he had earlier abdicated as delegate to the October 1974 synod of bishops in Rome. Bishop Rivera Damas, who had been selected to go in Romero's place, recalls, "He had reservations about me, I was considered too liberal." He says Romero "did it because he did not agree that I, who was so progressive in his opinion, should represent El Salvador at the synod; he didn't trust me."[30] But Rivera Damas refused to step aside on canonical grounds and his view prevailed with the support of Rome. Looking back he says, "I believe Monseñor Romero was going through an emotional depression, he seemed quite exhausted."[31]

### Bishop of Santiago de María (1975-1976)

The tide soon shifted, however. For during the synod in Rome on October 15, 1974, Romero was named bishop of Santiago de María in Usulutan, seat of a rural diocese about seventy-one miles slightly southeast of San Salvador.[32] Romero's final editorial in *Orientación* one week later on October 21, 1973, offers insight into his state of mind. On the one hand, Romero laments what he sees as "the possible loss of faith . . . among notable individuals from the church itself," which he associates with "hysterical and histrionic postures of demagogic revolutionism" that "foster disorder and do not offer . . . solutions."[33] On the other hand, however, he asserts that, as editor, he has always "respected the authorities" and emphasized "evangelization" over "human promotion," while rejecting the accusation that he may have "neglected" the latter. And there is no mistaking Romero's disdain for those (like the Jesuits) who believed that Medellín was calling to the church to confront the state on injustices against the poor and to collaborate with movements in civil society promoting social change. Comparing himself to his opponents, he writes,

> What we do regret, more with an understanding silence of tolerance and patience than with an attitude of polemical resentment, is the explicitly worldly, violent and uncontrolled conduct of those who have tried to make use of religion to destroy the spiritual basis of religion. . . . For our part, we have preferred to adhere to that which is certain, to cling with fear and trembling to the Rock of Peter, to seek assurance in the shade of the church's teachings, and to put our ears to the lips of the pope instead of leaping like reckless and foolhardy acrobats to the speculations of impudent thinkers of social movements of dubious origin. . . .[34]

---

30. Diez and Macho, "En Santiago de María me topé con la miseria," 46, 47.
31. Ibid., 47.
32. Brockman, *Romero*, 52.
33. Diez and Macho, "En Santiago de María me topé con la miseria," 48-49.
34. Ibid., 48; and López Vigil, *Oscar Romero*, 59.

Brockman notes that Romero explicitly frames his episcopal appointment as vindication from Rome of his views on the proper role of the church in society expressed in *Orientación* when he writes,

> This trust of the pope in its editor must also be interpreted as the most solemn backing of the church's magisterium for the ideology that has inspired the paper's pages under this editorship. This silent approval from so high a source constitutes the best reward and satisfaction for all of us who work together for this ideal, at the same time that it determines the route to follow.[35]

Given his criticisms of Medellín and its proponents, it is notable that Romero identifies the teaching magisterium of the church with Rome while failing to even mention Medellín as an authentic expression of that charism.

Several of Romero's contemporaries see his confrontation as bishop in Santiago de María with the "misery" of his people as the key to his conversion to the option for the poor.[36] Unfortunately for the Central American Jesuits and others, Romero nonetheless remained an "ideological warrior" who looked to Rome for support of his commitment to contain what he saw as dangerous threats posed by overzealous supporters of Medellín to the church's neutrality before the Salvadoran government. In this connection Romero was named consultant to the Pontifical Commission on Latin America on May 18, 1975, and stayed on in Rome after the meeting to attend a November 5, 1975, talk by Bishop Alfonso López Trujillo, secretary-general of the Conference of Latin American Bishops. Following the presentation on "Priests' Political Movements in Latin America: Present Situation, Dangers, and Proposal for Remedies,"[37] Romero spoke against what he saw as the improper politicization of the clergy in El Salvador. The next day he submitted a "very confidential" memo to the commission outlining "Three Factors in the Priests' Political Movement in El Salvador."[38]

The memo begins by highlighting the decisive influence of "the Jesuits"[39] in politicizing the church in El Salvador. Romero complains about Ellacuría's *Teología política* as the subject of criticisms submitted to the Congregation for the Doctrine of the Faith in Rome despite having been published with a *nihil obstat* from the Salvadoran curia and the Interdiocesan Social Secretariat. Following this backhanded swipe at the diocesan curia, the new bishop cites a government memo characterizing UCA classes offered by a certain lay professor as "antigovernment political rallies." He attacks the university for its Jesuit-inspired commitment to "liberating education," for its publication of a "new Christology" (by Jon Sobrino), for a weekly feature on "new Christians" in the local

---

35. Brockman, *Romero*, 52-52. I was unable to find this quote in the source cited by Brockman.

36. Diez and Macho, "En Santiago de María me topé con la miseria," 58-141.

37. Brockman, *Romero*, 56.

38. Diez and Macho, "En Santiago de María me topé con la miseria," 49-53.

39. Ibid., 50.

newspaper (*El Mundo*), and for teaching theology courses to lay students and Jesuit seminarians without official episcopal oversight.

Looking past Archbishop Chávez to Rome, the memo revives the discredited accusation of "Marxist indoctrination" levied against the Jesuit high school (the *Externado San José*) by "various parents" without mentioning Romero's role in provoking "the scandal" or noting the refutation of the charges by Archbishop Chávez.[40] He denounces "the politicization" of the national seminary under Jesuit leadership, citing as evidence the rector's (Amando López, S.J.) defense of the students' refusal to sing at the 1972 installation of "the president whose election they considered fraudulent" as a legitimate form of "conscientious objection." He attacks Rutilio Grande's team in Aguilares for its role in accelerating "promotion" (or community organizing), and he worries about the Jesuits' politicizing "influence on religious communities and Catholic colleagues."

The rest of the memo exemplifies how Romero had come to see himself as allied with authorities in Rome against dangerous elements in the local church. In section two he denounces "social-political problems" generated by the "Interdiocesan Social Secretariat" and the "Justice and Peace Commission" under the leadership of Fr. Juan Ramón Vega. He describes a chaotic and divided curia in which this rogue appointee of Archbishop Chávez is free to produce "negative and scathing criticism against capitalists and the government" through a diocesan bulletin edited and produced by his "paid" assistant, Fr. Fabián Amaya, and distributed by politicized priests and opposition leaders "with the economic support of *Misereor* [the anti-poverty agency of the German bishops] and the moral support of Bishop Rivera [y Damas]." Romero complains, "The Episcopal Conference has asked the Archbishop several times that it be suspended, the government has complained on multiple occasions about its critical tendencies, and many people are resentful." And he concludes with the incriminating observation, "There are several Central American bishops who cannot explain how this priest can represent the Peace and Justice Commission if he does not have the confidence of the bishops and he cannot achieve a healthy collaboration with the government. . . ."[41]

In section three Romero attacks "groups of priests, religious orders, and *committed Christians* from all the dioceses [of the region . . . working] in perfect intercommunication."[42] Echoing the government he says, "They spread their ideas in the peasant development centers [operated by the church], which have already been identified by the government as 'centers of subversion.'" Yet he sounds isolated when he states that the diocesan radio station (YSAX), retreat centers, and small Christian communities have become home to priests, religious, and lay leaders who "know and practice 'Marxist analysis.'" He accuses them of planning "the occupation of the cathedral" following the July 30, 1975, massacre of university students by the government, and says "they go behind

---

40. Ibid., 51.
41. Ibid., 52.
42. Ibid.

the backs of the bishops to whom they run when there is trouble." He also criticizes their belief "that the church cannot be apolitical because all of its actions have political repercussions" (his interpretation of an idea from *Teología política*) at the same time that he admits the church faces both "a repressive military government that wants to remain in power and to destroy all opposition," and "a cruel social differentiation in·which a few have everything and the majority live in misery."[43]

After positioning himself with the anti-Medellín faction of the Salvadoran bishops in a divided and politicized church, the letter concludes by insisting that the bishops nonetheless defend their priests, reaffirming his corporatist view of the role of the church in society.

> The bishops defend their priests in all conflicts. They try to be timely in their declarations in order to head off *pronouncements* from these groups. In dialog with the central government, they warn it about false information. Their greatest pastoral concern is the spiritualizing of the clergy in order to give witness of the true hope and transcendence of Christianity, while simultaneously seeking the most effective pastoral policy for uniting the social classes and . . . for maintaining good relations and healthy collaboration with the government.[44]

In a few short years Romero would shift the priority he assigned to good relations with the government in favor of a more prophetic stance, using the pulpit to defend his priests and his people against state-sponsored violence. Looking back it is fascinating to observe that the criticisms and suspicions found in Romero's 1975 letter to the pontifical commission and his final editorial in *Orientación* reappear as slanderous and deadly accusations in the 1989 pamphlet by Monsignor Freddy Delgado entitled, "The Popular Church Was Born in El Salvador."[45]

Published the year before the Jesuit assassinations and eight years after Romero's murder, the reader will recall that Monsignor Delgado was Romero's vice-rector in the failed 1972-1973 seminary project before being moved at his suggestion to adjunct secretary of the bishops' conference (Romero was the secretary). Delgado claims, "The principal strategy of the Communist Party in order to make El Salvador a *Socialist Republic of Workers and Campesinos* and a satellite of the Soviet Union has been the instrumentalization of the Catholic Church in the communist revolution. . . ."[46] And he asserts, "The targets in El Salvador are clear: to politicize the clergy, to divide the Episcopal Conference internally and externally between *progressives and reactionaries,*

---

43. Ibid., 53.

44. Ibid.

45. Monsignor Freddy Delgado, "La iglesia popular nació en El Salvador, memorias de 1972 a 1982" (San Salvador: privately produced, 1989).

46. Ibid., 1.

and once divided, to make the *progressives* docile and efficacious instruments of the revolution."

Monsignor Delgado then claims to have discovered an international Jesuit-led conspiracy to create "grassroots" groups of priests that would give birth to a Salvadoran "church that is born in the people, by the people and for the people,"[47] and to elect Oscar Romero "as successor to Archbishop Luis Chávez y González."[48] He argues that even though "until then, Bishop Romero had always spoken against the pastoral approach of Medellín,"[49] he was chosen by the Jesuits and their allies because his "psychological weakness [and] . . . personal insecurity," made him "manageable."[50] He charges that "from February 24 to 28, 1977, Monseñor Romero was closeted with a group of priests in the Seminary" who performed "a psychoanalysis" on the vulnerable prelate while "analyzing the national situation through a Marxist framework."[51] Once under their control, he says the Jesuits and their allies made moves "to fully instrumentalize the church . . . [as] a means for power . . . in the cause of the communist revolution."[52]

Not surprisingly, Monsignor Delgado was well known for his extremist positions, and the Jesuits received reassurances from both Archbishop Rivera Damas and the papal nuncio, Monsignor de Nittis, that they had written to Rome to refute the charges. But the ultra-rightist daily, the *Diario de Hoy*, published by D'Aubuisson's financial supporter, Enrique Viera Altamirano, wrote that Delgado's book confirmed that "all those groups at the service of international communism were planned and organized in the installations of the UCA with the active participation of its Jesuit leaders, beginning with the sadly infamous Ignacio Ellacuría, the most nefarious individual ever to set foot on Salvadoran soil."[53] From the perspective of history, then, it does not seem unfair to say that Oscar Romero, the "ideological warrior" of *Orientación* and Santiago de María, planted some of the seeds of distortion that later justified both his own murder and that of the UCA martyrs.

On the other hand, Romero's charges must be seen against the background of his encounter while bishop of Santiago de María (1975-1977) with the suffering of his people and the efforts of his clergy to defend them. The reader will recall that in 1976 Romero opened the cathedral rectory, diocesan offices, and a hall in the bishop's residence to hundreds of temporary farm workers gathered for the harvest so they might have a roof over their heads and shelter from the cold.[54] And in 1975 Romero traveled from prison to prison with Alicia Garcia

---

47. Ibid., 1-2.

48. Ibid., 28.

49. Ibid., 29.

50. Ibid., 27.

51. Ibid., 29.

52. Ibid., 28.

53. *Diario de Hoy*, January 25, 1989; cited in Whitfield, *Paying the Price*, 327.

54. Diez and Macho, "En Santiago de María me topé con la miseria," 146-49; Brockman, *Romero*, 55-56.

(founder of the Mothers of the Disappeared) and other frantic mothers and sisters searching for relatives following the National Guard ambush and massacre during the July 30, 1975, student march from the National University to the Plaza Libertad in San Salvador. When the group finally found their relatives at San Francisco Gotera almost one hundred miles to the east, Romero brought medicine to Alicia's brother, who had been brutally tortured, and offered overnight hospitality to the women at the parish. In neither case, however, did Romero do more than lament the "selfishness" of the growers or in any way publically rebuke the role of the government in the massacre. Indeed, in his memo to the Pontifical Commission on Latin America written four months later Romero rebukes priests involved in occupying the cathedral one block from the site of the massacre.[55] He also denounces the criticisms "against capitalists and the government" published in the diocesan newspaper by the Interdiocesan Social Secretariat and the Justice and Peace Commission.[56]

Two incidents, however, capture Romero's brewing ambivalence about the authorities and his growing empathy for the suffering of rural farm workers and the clergy who supported them. On June 21, 1975, members of the National Guard entered the village of Tres Calles at 1:00 a.m., ransacking the houses of five campesinos while looking for weapons and murdering the unarmed men in front of their families. Passionist fathers Zacarias Diez and Juan Macho recall that they and other local priests told Romero, "We must do something, Bishop,"[57] proposing several forms of public response. "But Monseñor was on another wavelength and didn't think like us," they recall. Instead, Romero wrote an anguished personal letter to his friend, President Colonel Arturo Armando Molina, and a summary of the events for the Salvadoran bishops. Looking back the priests say, "It is true; he did something: it was an energetic protest and a strong denouncement." On the other hand, however, "it was not public, it was private, since he still believed that denunciations from authority to authority were more effective."

Despite such limitations, however, the pain and outrage in Romero's letter are palpable: "Mr. President, . . . it rent my soul to hear the bitter tears of widowed mothers and orphaned children who, with inconsolable sobs, told their story . . . of cruel abuse and mourned having been left as orphans."[58] At the same time Romero's letter to the bishops betrays an emerging element of self-doubt when he writes, "I didn't think any public pronouncement was necessary."[59] He justifies this conclusion by explaining his conviction that direct intervention with the authorities would be "more effective," by noting that the church was "not directly involved," and by citing a lack of certainty about the "true motives" of the killers and the "conduct" of the victims. On the other hand, however, he

---

55. Ibid., 52.
56. Ibid., 51.
57. Ibid., 61.
58. Ibid., 62.
59. Ibid., 67.

writes, "My beloved brother bishops, I implore you to evaluate these actions [I have taken] and to suggest what else might be done pastorally and perhaps collegially" to respond to these events. Here we see Romero struggling to adapt his convictions about the role of the church in society to the realities of Santiago de María. For the first time, Romero finds himself issuing "protests and ringing charges against the 'security forces' . . . on behalf of the poor and their right to dignity and life."[60]

A second incident involved one of the church's peasant training centers, which Romero characterizes "as *centers of subversion*"[61] in his November 1975 memo. Earlier that year the papal nuncio had expressed suspicions about the center in Los Naranjos, and Romero was considering whether to close or reorient the project when one of its priests joined the occupation of the San Salvador cathedral following the July 30, 1975, student massacre.[62] Then, on August 16, the center director, Fr. Juan Macho, was refused entry at the airport into El Salvador and forced to return to Madrid after being told by migration, "Look, you have a lot of problems in Jiquilisco [your parish]. . . . The order is that you cannot get off the plane."[63] Romero again wrote to Molina, this time defending Fr. Macho's "priestly actions . . . [as] the director of the Los Naranjos Center for Campesino Development."[64] The letter was successful, and Fr. Macho was allowed to return, but the center was temporarily closed and an interim director installed.[65]

Romero then left for the October 20-22, 1975, meeting of the Pontifical Commission in Rome, and Brockman reports that shortly after his return in early December he invited Bishop Marco René Revelo, head of the catechetical commission and auxiliary bishop of Santa Ana, to meet with him and the priests of Los Naranjos. The priests saw Romero as consumed by "prejudices"[66] that the center was manipulating the teachings of Medellín and preoccupied with "charlatans who use them as a pretext"[67] to promote political agendas. Not surprisingly, Revelo and Romero concluded that certain classes had "manipulated" the documents of Medellín and distorted Catholic Social Teaching in a way that confused the politicized catechists.[68]

On the other hand, however, the dialogue with the Passionists produced an agreement in which the work would continue, but courses taught by center staff would be shifted to parishes where the campesinos lived so that Romero and the local priests could oversee the process.[69] The government, the nuncio, and

---

60. Ibid., 64.

61. Ibid., 52.

62. Brockman, *Romero*, 59.

63. Diez and Macho, "En Santiago de María me topé con la miseria," 72.

64. Ibid., 74.

65. Brockman, *Romero*, 59.

66. Diez and Macho, "En Santiago de María me topé con la miseria," 117.

67. Ibid., citing Romero's editorial from *Orientación* 1234 (September 25, 1971): 3.

68. Jesús Delgado, *Oscar A. Romero, Biografía* (San Salvador, UCA Editores, 1986), 65.

69. Brockman, *Romero*, 60; the agreement appears in Diez and Macho, "En Santiago de María me topé con la miseria," 129-34.

the priests from the center were all satisfied, and Fr. Macho became both director of the center and vicar for the diocese where he began working closely with
Romero. The net result was, "From that day forward Romero became more
focused on better understanding Medellín." A breakthrough had been achieved
in the view of the Passionists as "an outcome of the Los Naranjos affair, to that
point that it can be said that the experience finally opened his mind to Medellín, since until then it had been closed by suspicions and doubts to the teaching
of such an important document."[70]

That same month, Pope Paul VI published *Evangelii nuntiandi* (December
8, 1975), linking evangelization in the modern world to powerful denunciations
of poverty and oppression like those found in the documents of Medellín. All of
these factors, then, led Romero to reconsider the previously unquestioned priority he had assigned to maintaining good relations between the church and the
government in the face of state-sponsored violence against his people. At the
end of the day, therefore, it was Oscar Romero's encounter as bishop of Santiago
de María with the suffering of his people and the vilification of his clergy for
educating and defending them that played a decisive role in opening his mind
and heart to Medellín's discernment that God was calling the Latin American
church to support and defend the poor.

### Monseñor Romero: Sent by God
### to Save His People (1977-1980)

Ellacuría's relationship with God and the Salvadoran people, not to mention his
own vocation, was deeply impacted by knowing Archbishop Romero. Sobrino
recalls that while Romero used to say, "With this people it is easy to be a good
shepherd," Ellacuría responded, "Monseñor was a grace for the people. We
were the ones to be grateful."[71] But what exactly was the nature of this grace
and its impact on Ellacuría? Sobrino writes,

> I think that Monseñor was a grace for Ellacuría in a very special way.
> I often thought that Ellacuría may have considered himself more or
> less a colleague of Zubiri in philosophy and colleague of Rahner in
> theology. . . . But he never considered himself a colleague of Monseñor
> Romero. And the reason is because he always saw Monseñor as some-
> one who was ahead of him, as in the way Monseñor Romero placed
> himself before the mystery of the ultimate, [his] faith in God. As I have
> written, . . . I think his [Ellacuría's] faith was carried . . . by the faith
> of Monseñor Romero. In other words, he found in Monseñor someone

---

70. Delgado, *Oscar A. Romero*, 66; Diez and Macho, "En Santiago de María me topé con
la miseria," 120.

71. Jon Sobrino, "El padre Ellacuría sobre Monseñor Romero, ayudas para poner a
producir en las iglesias la herencia de Jesús," *Revista latinoamericana de teología* 65 (2005):
136.

who had the power, without imposing, "to draw you" toward him in faith. That is the grace.[72]

But in what sense did Ellacuría believe that Romero had gone ahead of him in faith? Eight months after Romero's assassination Ellacuría published an article entitled, "Archbishop Romero, sent by God to save his people."[73] Here Ellacuría reflects on what I have called the political dimension of Romero's conversion to Medellín's option for the poor (his *political conversion*), which Romero himself asserts began when "Father Grande's death and the death of other priests after his impelled me to take an energetic attitude before the government."[74] Romero says, "I remember that because of Father Grande's death I made a statement that I would not attend any official acts until this situation [of who had killed Grande] was clarified." As a result, "A rupture was produced, not by me with the government but [by] the government itself because of its attitude."

But what was the nature of the process unfolding in Archbishop Romero? Ellacuría believes that the murder of Rutilio Grande confronted the new archbishop with a reality that produced changes in his attitude toward Medellín's option for the poor. He outlines three stages or developments in Romero's three-year ministry as archbishop (1977-1980). These parallel Ellacuría's threefold process discussed earlier of "facing up to real things as real."[75]

Here Ellacuría argues that facing up to the reality of Fr. Grande's death confronted Romero with three imperatives: (1) a demand to "become aware of," "realize about," or "grasp what is at stake" in the reality of Fr. Grande's priestly ministry with the peasant farm workers of Aguilares and why it led to his death (*hacerse cargo de la realidad*); (2) an ethical demand "to pick up" or assume public responsibility as part of his mission as archbishop to accompany and defend the terrorized peasants of Aguilares and El Salvador whom Fr. Grande left behind (*cargar con la realidad*); and (3) a praxis-related demand as archbishop "to take charge of" the reality of those peasants before the church and Salvadoran society (*encargarse de la realidad*), thereby creating a salvific historical trajectory for those disposed to follow his example. Ellacuría's reflections provide a window into his perceptions of how Oscar Romero, who as auxiliary bishop had tried to suppress the early response to Medellín, eventually "went ahead" of Ellacuría and his colleagues by historicizing its discernment that God was calling the Latin American church to a preferential option for the poor.

In this section I will briefly describe Ellacuría's insights, using them as clues as to how Romero's three-year ministry as archbishop of San Salvador helped

---

72. Ibid., 136-37.

73. Ignacio Ellacuría, "Monseñor Romero, un enviado de Dios para salvar a su pueblo," *Escritos teológicos,* III (San Salvador: UCA Editores, 2002), 93-100; reprinted from *Sal Terrae* 811 (1980): 825-32; and *ECA* 19 (1990): 5-10.

74. Interview of Archbishop Oscar Romero with Tommie Sue Montgomery, December 14, 1979; cited in Tommie Sue Montgomery, *Revolution in El Salvador: From Civil Strife to Civil Peace* (Boulder, CO: Westview Press, 1995), 95.

75. Ellacuría, "Hacia una fundamentación," 208.

to transform Ellacuría's relationship with God, his theology, and his relationship with the people of El Salvador as UCA president and a prophetic successor to Romero. Ellacuría begins by noting that before becoming archbishop, "Monseñor Romero . . . was considered an opponent of . . . Medellín. Interested mainly in orthodoxy, he was wary of . . . the theology of liberation and . . . attacked those who denounced the country's structural injustice as infected with Marxism."[76] And he insists that "it was not his appointment as Archbishop of San Salvador that changed Monseñor Romero," stating that "he was chosen so that the preferential option for the poor emerging in the diocese might be contained and subordinated within more traditional channels."[77] Rather, things changed when "the assassination of Fr. Grande, the first of the priest martyrs he was called to bury, shook his conscience [so that] the veils hiding the truth were torn away." As a result, though some saw Fr. Grande's assassination as simply "a political event," Archbishop Romero was able to see "something new . . . and this transformed him."

But what exactly did he see? Ellacuría says that Rutilio's death presented Archbishop Romero with a demand to "come to terms with"[78] or to *see* the reality of Fr. Grande's life and ministry. He was therefore confronted with "the illuminating light of a priest who had dedicated himself to evangelizing the poor, [and] who through that evangelization had led the poor to historicize their own salvation, giving historical flesh to the eternally new word of God."[79] Thus, the authenticity of Fr. Grande's priestly ministry and his love for the rural peasants of Aguilares,

> revealed to him what it meant to be apostle in El Salvador today; it meant being a prophet and a martyr. And so the career of a prophet and martyr began, not because he had chosen it, but rather because God filled him with historical voices of the suffering of his chosen people and with the voice of blood of the first to die as a martyr in El Salvador today, so that all might have life and so that the whole church might regain its by now barely perceptible prophetic pulse.[80]

On the one hand, then, Ellacuría realized long before Oscar Romero that Medellín's preferential option for the poor implied solidarity with the struggles of Latin America's poor majorities for liberation from poverty, military rule, and state-sponsored violence. On the other, however, it was Archbishop Romero who pioneered a path as the church's prophetic voice to Salvadoran society.

Jon Sobrino writes, "Each of you was given a Christian and Salvadoran torch, and . . . made the fundamental choice to keep it burning."[81] The call to

---

76. Ellacuría, "Monseñor Romero, un enviado de Dios para salvar a su pueblo," 95.
77. Ibid.
78. Ellacuría, "Hacia una fundamentación," 208.
79. Ellacuría, "Monseñor Romero, un enviado de Dios para salvar a su pueblo," 96.
80. Ibid.
81. Sobrino, "Monseñor Romero y tú," 1.

prophecy came to Oscar Romero through the murder of Rutilio Grande and the military suppression of his rural ministry (1972-1977), eventually suffusing his three-year ministry as archbishop of San Salvador (1977-1980). Then, just when it seemed that Roberto D'Aubuisson's ideology of "national salvation" had extinguished Romero's flame, it somehow passed to Ellacuría, illuminating his ten-year ministry as president of a Christian university committed to the preferential option for the poor. In this way Archbishop Romero went ahead of Ignacio Ellacuría, showing him what it meant to be the prophetic voice of the church to Salvadoran society.

Ellacuría's second point is that Archbishop Romero's emerging role as the voice of prophecy to the Salvadoran state was only the beginning of a deeper transformation. He argues, "Through this initial conversion, which was nothing but the start of something that could have ended there, Monseñor Romero . . . [was] beginning a profound conversion of his mission." Ellacuría asserts, "It is this mission, and his fidelity to it, that finally transforms him . . . into a fundamental factor in the history of salvation of El Salvador."

But what changed in the mission of Archbishop Romero? Ellacuría asserts that after Fr. Grande's murder and the campaign of military terror against his flock ("Operation Rutilio") Romero's mission acquires a "new meaning" that "sanctifies him more and more."[82] He says it is true that Romero "had 'also' been concerned about the poor and oppressed" while bishop of Santiago de María, but after Rutilio's martyrdom the suffering peasants of El Salvador "became the guiding light of his pastoral ministry." Why? Ellacuría says that Rutilio's assassination moved the "preferential option for the oppressed" from a "theoretical" consideration about Medellín to a question for Romero about "faithfulness to the gospel" and Rutilio's ability "to see the historical Jesus in this oppressed people." He says this change led Archbishop Romero down a path that he followed "to its ultimate consequences when he recognized in this people without a voice the voice of God himself, when he saw in the crucified people the God of salvation, [and] when he understood their struggles for liberation as the path toward a new earth and a new heaven."

Sobrino asserts that Ellacuría came to believe that his vocation as a human being, a Christian, and a Jesuit was to take the crucified people down from the cross. However, it was Archbishop Romero who first traveled at great risk to celebrate Mass with traumatized and isolated peasants of Aguilares three months after the assassination of Rutilio Grande. And it was Romero who first told them, "You are the image of the pierced savior . . . who represent Christ nailed to the cross and pierced by a lance"; and you are "the image of all those towns who, like Aguilares, will be broken and defiled."[83] Thus, it was Ellacuría who followed Romero when eight months later in a February 1978 essay written

---

82. Ellacuría, "Monseñor Romero, un enviado de Dios para salvar a su pueblo," 97.

83. Oscar Romero, "Homilía en Aguilares [June 19, 1977]," *La voz de los sin voz: La palabra viva de Monseñor Oscar Arnulfo Romero* (San Salvador: UCA Editores, 1980), I, 207-12, at 208.

before the meeting of the Latin American bishops at Puebla[84] he spoke of "the crucified people" as that "vast portion of humankind that is literally and actually crucified by natural . . . historical, and personal oppressions,"[85] and three years later in 1981 when he described the crucified people as the "principal" sign of the times "by whose light the others should be discerned and interpreted."[86]

Here, then, is the second area in which Romero "went ahead" of Ellacuría, shaping his faith and transforming his future. Ellacuría told his fellow Jesuits in 1969 that "Christ is in the poor" and that the Third World is "the optimal place for the Christian to live the *Exercises*."[87] But eight years later, Archbishop Romero developed personal relationships with the common people of El Salvador that went far beyond what Ellacuría had achieved to that point. Romero came to know and love the poor of El Salvador in a personal way, seeing Christ in them, risking his life to defend them, and pioneering the idea of the crucified people that would later come to define Ellacuría's theology and sense of call.

The significance for the terrorized peasants of Aguilares of Romero's interpretation of their plight as "the image of . . . Christ nailed to the cross"[88] and the theological power of Ellacuría's corresponding notion of *the crucified people* is evident. But the question remains, did anything change in the real world? This brings us to the third and most crucial claim of Ellacuría's article that "one can and should say that with him there began to be realized, in a surprisingly efficacious manner, the salvation of the historical process that is being realized in El Salvador."[89]

Ellacuría's point provides an interesting twist on Marx's 1845 criticism of the German philosopher Ludwig Feuerbach: "The philosophers have only interpreted the world . . . ; the point, however, is to change it."[90] Cutting in what would appear to be the opposite direction, Ellacuría asserts that Archbishop Romero "never tired of repeating that political processes, however pure and idealistic, are not enough to bring humanity's liberation."[91] Tying this position to St. Augustine's claim that "in order to be human one must be *more* than human," Ellacuría asserts that for Archbishop Romero "history that . . . tries to be only human, quickly ceases to be so." He explains this is why Romero "never stopped calling [us] to transcendence" in homilies about "the word of God, [and]

---

84. This detail is from Sobrino, "El padre Ellacuría sobre Monseñor Romero," 120.

85. Ignacio Ellacuría, "El pueblo crucificado, ensayo de soteriología histórica," *Escritos teológicos*, II (San Salvador: UCA Editores, 2000), 138.

86. Ellacuría, "Discernir *el signo* de los tiempos," *Escritos teológicos*, II, 134.

87. "El tercer mundo como lugar óptimo de la vivencia Cristiana de los Ejercicios" (Dia 29:1), 1-12, in "Reunión-Ejercicios de la viceprovincia Jesuitica de Centroamérica, Diciembre 1969," 127-38, in *Reflexión teológico-espiritual de la Compañía de Jesús en Centroamerica*, II (San Salvador: Archives of the Society of Jesus, Central American Province, Survey S.J. de Centroamérica, December 1969).

88. Romero, "Homilía en Aguilares," 208.

89. Ellacuría, "Monseñor Romero, un enviado de Dios para salvar a su pueblo," 100.

90. Karl Marx, *Theses on Feuerbach*, in *Collected Works of Karl Marx and Frederick Engels* (New York: International Publishers, 1988), V, 8.

91. Ellacuría, "Monseñor Romero, un enviado de Dios para salvar a su pueblo," 98-99.

the action of God in breaking through human limits." Like St. Augustine, then, Archbishop Romero spoke of "a transcendence that was never presented as the abandonment of what is human, as the escape from what is human, but rather as its improvement and perfection."

This claim finds validation, I would suggest, in the method and the content of Romero's preaching. Seven months after the death of Rutilio Grande, Archbishop Romero explained that his homilies were intended to offer (1) a "word of consolation to those who suffer"; (2) "a word denouncing crime . . . [and] violence"; (3) "a word of support for the just demands of our people"; (4) "a word of hope"; and (5) a word "in these hours of tragedy, blood, [and] pain to sow a vision of hope for something more, not as an opiate of the people as communism says, . . . but rather as a push to be more just in this world."[92] For Archbishop Romero, then, there was no history other than the real history of El Salvador within which to sow the word of Good News about Jesus Christ. Accordingly, on August 6, 1977, just two months after the homily to the terrified peasants of Aguilares, he states,

> we have to save ourselves within our own history, but a history that is thoroughly penetrated by the light of salvation, of Christian hope. The entire history of El Salvador, its politics, its economy, and everything that constitutes the lived reality of Salvadorans must be illuminated by faith. There is no need for a divorce. [Rather, the history of salvation] . . . has to be the history of the country, penetrated by God's plan, in order to live it with faith and hope as a history that leads us to salvation in Christ.[93]

Accordingly, Archbishop Romero insisted that there cannot be two histories, as some theologians have taught. Rather, salvation history must be salvation in the history of El Salvador, and the history of El Salvador must be a part of salvation history.

But what hope does such an argument offer to a crucified people? Ellacuría says, "This is why he was always searching for an authentic *salvation* of the historical process" while simultaneously respecting its autonomy from the question of salvation.[94] Ellacuría says Romero's respect for the autonomy of history from the question of salvation protected him from dehistoricizing "the real historical process with its particular worldly qualities." Instead, "What he did was to assume the burden of its sin" and to point the Salvadoran people toward the "best opportunities for transcendence." He did this by "fighting against any absolutization of what is finite and human, above all . . . power and wealth, but also . . . dogmatism . . . and . . . sectarianism," and by defending "justice, love,

---

92. Monseñor Oscar Romero, "Los signos de los tiempos" (Homily of October 30, 1977), *Homilías Monseñor Óscar A. Romero,* I (San Salvador: UCA Editores, 2005), 422-24.

93. Oscar Romero, "La Iglesia, cuerpo de Cristo en la historia" (Homily of August 6, 1977), *Homilías Monseñor Óscar A. Romero,* I (San Salvador: UCA Editores, 2005), 231.

94. Ellacuría, "Monseñor Romero, un enviado de Dios para salvar a su pueblo," 98-99.

solidarity, and liberty" in the name of "Jesus as the model for faith and Christian transcendence."[95]

In response, Ellacuría says, "The people opened themselves to Christian transcendence." Day by day, "The word, the life, [and] the example of Monseñor Romero made the Christian message credible to ever larger sectors of the Salvadoran people [as] . . . he opened up to an ever increasing and more pure kind of hope." Ellacuría says "he saw more light than darkness, more life than violence" in El Salvador's tortured political process, and he spoke "in favor of the oppressed" while avoiding "identification *with*" any particular political party or solution.[96] As a result, the Salvadoran people "received from Monseñor Romero a new strength to hope, to struggle in hope, [and] to offer their lives in heroic sacrifices full of meaning" so that "their struggles for liberation acquired through him a transcendent meaning. . . ."

Sobrino says that Ellacuría thought the Salvadoran people learned from "Monseñor Romero . . . how to be the people of God."[97] And he believed this "may be the unique contribution of Monseñor Romero as *archbishop*: introducing Christian leaven into these historical struggles for justice and liberation." Thus, while "historical struggles and Christianity are not easy to combine," Sobrino says "that [is the] miracle Ellacuría saw realized in the ministry of Monseñor Romero."

Ellacuría argues, then, that Archbishop Romero "became an exceptional example of how the power of the gospel can become a transformative historical force."[98] And he concludes, "This is why he continues living after his death." Ellacuría's point is that it is not sufficient that "there are many who remember him," or that "he removed the blindfold that kept them from recognizing the truth of the gospel" in the birth of a new society. Rather, Archbishop Romero lives on "because there are many who are disposed to follow his steps, knowing that Monseñor Romero was an exemplary follower of Jesus of Nazareth in the last three years of his public life." As we have already seen, Ellacuría himself was one such person.

Here, then, is Ellacuría's interpretation of the fulfillment of Romero's prophecy, spoken two weeks before his 1980 death to José Calderón Salazar from the Mexican newspaper *Excelsior*:

> I must tell you, as a Christian, I do not believe in death without resurrection. If I am killed, I shall arise in the Salvadoran people. . . . Let my blood be a seed of freedom and the sign that hope will soon be reality. Let my death, if it is accepted by God, be for my people's liberation and as a witness of hope in the future. . . . A bishop will die, but God's church, which is the people, will never perish.[99]

---

95. Ibid., 99.

96. Ibid., 100.

97. Sobrino, "El padre Ellacuría sobre Monseñor Romero," 122.

98. Ellacuría, "Monseñor Romero, un enviado de Dios para salvar a su pueblo," 100.

99. Words of Oscar Romero to José Calderón Salazar, published in *Orientación* (April 13): 1980; cited in Brockman, *Romero*, 248.

Romero's prophecy is a prayer that his thirst for love and justice rooted in faith would be passed from hand to hand among those "disposed to follow his steps as a faithful follower of Jesus."

Romero words spoken just moments before his death appear to confirm this interpretation. His final homily draws a parallel between the death of Jesus and the sacrifice of Salvadoran martyrs whose struggle for justice is grounded in "the love of Christ and service of others."[100] He asserts that "every effort to make society better, especially when society is so immersed in injustice and sin, is an effort that God blesses, that God wants, and that God demands." He says, "I beg all of you, beloved brothers and sisters, that we look at these [deaths] . . . with this [kind of] hope, with this spirit of devotion and of sacrifice, and do what we can."[101] He then concludes with a remarkable and self-implicating appeal to the dangerous memory of Jesus Christ: "May this immolated body and this flesh sacrificed for humanity fire us to also give our bodies and blood over to suffering and pain, like Christ: not for itself, but rather in order to bring . . . justice and peace to our people."

Here, then, is the third way in which Oscar Romero "went ahead" of Ignacio Ellacuría and others by helping shape the people of El Salvador into a people of God. Ellacuría embraced Medellín's challenge to the Latin American church long before Romero. But following the example of Rutilio Grande, Archbishop Romero forged ahead of Ellacuría and his colleagues, keeping company with the peasants of Aguilares, bringing God close to the suffering poor, and leavening their struggle for liberation with the message of Jesus in a way that mediated salvation to the historical process of El Salvador.

And how did all of this influence the work of Ellacuría and his colleagues at the UCA? Ellacuría's reflections eight months after the death of Archbishop Romero are helpful here as well.[102] First, the UCA learned from Oscar Romero how "to historicize the power of the gospel"[103] for El Salvador by running the university, like the archdiocese, from the perspective of a preferential option for the poor.[104] Five years later, on the occasion of an honorary doctorate granted to Archbishop Romero by the UCA, Ellacuría explained that the award represented "a commitment to do in our university way what he did in his pastoral way."[105] Thus, Romero "was the teacher" and the UCA "was the assistant"; Romero "was the voice and . . . [the UCA] was the echo."[106]

---

100. Monseñor Oscar Romero, "La última homilía de Monseñor" (Homily of March 24, 1980), *Homilías Monseñor Óscar A. Romero* (San Salvador: UCA Editores, 2009), VI, 455.

101. Ibid., 457.

102. Ellacuría, "Monseñor Romero, un enviado de Dios para salvar a su pueblo," 93-100.

103. Ibid., 94.

104. Interview of Jon Sobrino by Robert Lassalle-Klein, May 8, 1994, 4.

105. Ignacio Ellacuría, "La UCA ante el doctorado concedido a Monseñor Romero," *Escritos teológicos*, III (San Salvador: UCA Editores, 2002), 102; reprinted from *ECA* no. 437 (1985): 168.

106. Ibid., 104.

Second, Oscar Romero empowered "the poor to historicize their own salvation" and to give "historical flesh to the eternally new word of God."[107] This had the effect, given the strategic failures of the 1970s visions of the church, the center, and the left for El Salvador, of drawing the UCA's attention away from its earlier almost exclusive focus on the agency of El Salvador's elites. As a result, during the 1980s, the UCA became increasingly involved in the renewal of Salvadoran civil society taking place through the increasing participation of the country's dispossessed majorities in shaping their own future.

Third, Archbishop Romero showed the UCA that by embracing the sufferings and hopes of El Salvador's poor majorities "what had been an opaque, amorphous and ineffective word became a torrent of life to which the people drew near in order to quench their thirst."[108] And following Romero's death the prophetic torch passed to Ellacuría and the UCA, who worked tirelessly for a negotiated end to the war and social-political-economic reforms as the foundation for peace with justice.

And fourth, Archbishop Romero showed the UCA how "the power of the gospel could become a transformative historical force,"[109] making God's preferential option for the poor real for El Salvador. Following Romero's example, in 1982 Ellacuría told the graduates of Santa Clara University that "a university of Christian inspiration is one that focuses all its university activity . . . within the illuminating horizon of . . . a Christian preferential option for the poor."[110] He says the role of the university is to "intellectually incarnate itself among the poor in order to be science . . . [and] intellectual support for those who . . . possess truth and reason, . . . but who do not have the academic arguments to justify and legitimate them." And his counsel to those moved by the example of Archbishop Romero and the UCA is as follows:

> Just place some of your potential as a university and your whole human heart . . . before the reality of a crucified world, and ask yourselves the three questions Ignatius of Loyola put to himself as he stood before the . . . representative of all those who are crucified: What have I done for this world? What am I doing for it now? And above all, what should I do? . . . The answer lays both in your personal and academic responsibility. . . .[111]

For Ignacio Ellacuría, the answer to this question was embodied in the life, death, and resurrection of Archbishop Romero. Romero was the teacher and Ellacuría the student because "with Monseñor Romero God visited El

---

107. Ibid., 96.

108. Ibid., 98.

109. Ibid., 100.

110. Ignacio Ellacuría, "Discurso de graduación en la Universidad de Santa Clara," *Escritos universitarios* (San Salvador: UCA Editores, 1999), 226.

111. Ibid., 228.

Salvador."[112] Archbishop Romero more than anyone else, like Jesus, taught Ignacio Ellacuría to love the common people of El Salvador, to trust them, to see Christ in them, and to discover his vocation to take this crucified people down from the cross. And Romero's faith helped transform Ellacuría, like so many others, into a living sign of God's love and promise of resurrection to the Salvadoran people. Jon Sobrino writes,

> In Monsignor Romero, in his compassion for the suffering, his denunciations in their defense, his uncompromising love, you witnessed the God who is "Father" of the poor. In his conversion, his venture into the unknown and uncontrollable, in his moving forward without institutional church support, in his standing firm wherever the road might lead, you witnessed the Father who continues to be "God." And perhaps in Monseñor Romero you also saw that, in spite of everything, commitment is more real than nihilism, joy is more real than sadness, and hope is more real than absurdity.[113]

---

112. Sobrino, "El padre Ellacuría sobre Monseñor Romero," 126.
113. Sobrino, "Monseñor Romero y tú," 6.

# 7

# *Mysterium Salutis*

## KARL RAHNER

In this chapter I will summarize Karl Rahner's contribution to the *fundamenta* developed by by Ignacio Ellacuría to describe the face of God revealed by Archbishop Romero in the crucified people of El Salvador. Ellacuría was deeply moved by Karl Rahner, S.J., both as a theologian and as a Christian. In an open letter to Ellacuría dated a year after the assassinations Jon Sobrino recalls, "I remember one day in 1969 you told me . . . your great teacher Karl Rahner bore his doubts with great elegance, which made you say that faith was not something obvious for you either, but rather a victory."[1] In this chapter I will suggest that if Jon Sobrino is correct that Ellacuría's faith was "carried by the faith of Monseñor Romero,"[2] then it was Rahner who supplied many of the fundamental theological categories that Ellacuría used to interpret the human face of God revealed by Oscar Romero in the suffering people of El Salvador.

In the last chapter I argued that Ellacuría's conviction that "facing up to real things as real has a three-fold dimension" is reflected in his assertion that Archbishop Romero's three-year ministry moved through three stages: (1) grasping what was at stake in Fr. Grande's priestly ministry with El Salvador's oppressed farm workers; (2) assuming public responsibility as archbishop to accompany and defend El Salvador's terrorized peasants as central to his mission; and (3) introducing a salvific trajectory into El Salvador's historical process by inspiring many others to follow his example as "an exemplary" disciple of Jesus." I then used those stages to explore how Archbishop Romero "went ahead" of Ellacuría, reshaping his experience of God, his theology, and his relationship with the people of El Salvador.

I asserted first that Archbishop Romero showed Ellacuría what it meant to be the prophetic voice of the church to Salvadoran society. Second, Romero

---

1. Jon Sobrino, "Ignacio Ellacuría, el hombre y el cristiano, 'Bajar de la cruz al pueblo crucificado'" (San Salvador: Centro Monseñor Romero, 2001), translated as "Ignacio Ellacuría, The Human Being and the Christian: 'Taking the Crucified People Down from the Cross,'" in Kevin Burke and Robert Lassalle-Klein, eds., *Love That Produces Hope: The Thought of Ignacio Ellacuría* (Collegeville, MN: Liturgical Press, 2006), 79.

2. Jon Sobrino, "El padre Ellacuría sobre Monseñor Romero, Ayudas para poner a producir en las iglesias la herencia de Jesús," *Revista latinoamericana de teología* 65 (2005): 137.

taught Ellacuría to love the common people of El Salvador, to trust them, to see Christ in them, and to discover his vocation to take this crucified people down from the cross. And third, Romero inspired Ellacuría and many others to follow his example, bringing God close to the suffering poor and leavening their struggle for liberation with the message of Jesus in a way that mediated salvation to the historical process of El Salvador. In all of this I suggested that Archbishop Romero fostered Ellacuría's historical encounter with the Holy Mystery of God animating the crucified people of El Salvador, thereby historicizing a worldly mysticism that forms the core of his mature writings and work.

In Chapters 8 and 9, I will argue that the theologies of Ignacio Ellacuría and Jon Sobrino are unified by a shared conviction that the principal analogue (*analogatum princeps*) of the life, death, and resurrection of Jesus of Nazareth is to be found today among the "crucified peoples" of the globe and those who take them down from the cross. In this chapter I will show how Ellacuría uses concepts from Zubiri and the other sources to build upon and extend elements of Rahner's fundamental theology in making the argument above. I will also briefly examine the contribution of these developments to Ellacuría's argument that the love of Oscar Romero (and his followers) for the crucified people functions sacramentally as an efficacious sign and means of grace, drawing his followers into a historical relationship with the risen Jesus and the work of the Trinity in the world. Ignacio Ellacuría brought this interpretation of Rahner's ideas to Archbishop Romero and died like him, in part, for the pastoral praxis they informed. This chapter tries to capture the spirit of gratitude that Ellacuría always maintained toward Rahner as a great theological teacher and mentor whose ideas helped him to interpret the saving Mystery of God embodied in the three-year ministry of Archbishop Romero and unfolding at the heart of the historical reality of El Salvador.

### Studies with the Great Theologian of the Council

Ellacuría left San Salvador in 1958 after undergraduate studies in Ecuador to study for a master's in theology with the Jesuit faculty at Innsbruck, Austria, from 1958 to 1962. Given the ambivalence that Ellacuría manifests about this period of his Jesuit formation, it is interesting that Aurelio Pólit, S.J., president of the Universidad Católica of Ecuador, renowned authority on Sophocles and Virgil, and Ellacuría's first great undergraduate teacher in the humanities, cautions the recently arrived student,

> I think it is a tremendous advantage that you will be in a position to profit from all the German contributions to science and criticism. But I would consider it a disaster if you so subordinate yourself to its influence that you lose your freedom of spirit, and the clear-headed trust in your own judgment and the aesthetic perspective that we Latinos bring.[3]

---

3. Letter from Aurelio Pólit to Ignacio Ellacuría, 1958. Quoted in Rudolfo Cardenal,

Cardenal reports that Austria seemed "cold and gloomy" to Ellacuría, who "missed the spirit of the Central American [Jesuit] community in Ecuador" and his friends who were "spread all over Europe."[4] In a play on national stereotypes, certain students called Ellacuría "the Sun King"[5] for his aloof and ironic brilliance and the Spanish-speaking enclave that formed around him. The group made no secret of "its discontent with . . . the antiquated restrictions on the daily life of the theologian and the surprisingly poor quality of instruction."[6]

On the other hand, with one German and two Austrians they demonstrated a holy enthusiasm for soccer, forming a Jesuit team that won the Austrian national university championship much to the horror of their superiors at Innsbruck and Rome. He maintained a lifelong devotion to the sport, organizing weekend matches at the University of Central America (UCA) and combing the sports section for news of his favorite teams. Ellacuría later recalled with good humor "how he had to defend the theologate soccer team to the Jesuit superiors."[7] Their reaction, however, was not so positive. Despite having excelled in classes, won a national championship, and been a leader among the Latin Americans, the local superior's final evaluation complains, "Though he is exceedingly talented, his character is potentially difficult, his . . . critical attitude is constant, he is not open to others, and he separates himself from the community with a small group in which he exercises a strong influence."[8]

It is worth noting that Ellacuría's frustration with the "preconciliar structures" at Innsbruck between 1958 and 1962 was hardly unique among students of that period. Cardenal recalls, "He used to say that the only thing that made the [Innsbruck] theologate worthwhile was the opportunity to study with Rahner."[9] Ellacuría took various courses during these years with Fr. Karl Rahner, S.J. In October of 1961 Rahner was appointed private advisor to Cardinal Franz König of Vienna for the upcoming Second Vatican Council. He soon emerged as among the "most powerful"[10] theological *periti* of Vatican II. Martin Maier, S.J., suggests, "one can imagine that Rahner frequently shared his thoughts about the preparations for . . . [the Council] with his class," which included "the young Ellacuría."[11]

---

"Ignacio Ellacuría (1930-1989)," http://www.uca.edu.sv/martires /new/ella/fella.htm (San Salvador, September 1999), 5.

4. Cardenal, "Ignacio Ellacuría," 5.

5. Victor Codina, "Ignacio Ellacuría, teólogo y mártir," *Revista latinoamericana de teología* 21 (September-December 1990): 263; cited in Cardenal, "Ignacio Ellacuría, 28.

6. Rodolfo Cardenal, "Ser jesuita hoy en El Salvador," *ECA* nos. 493-494 (November-December 1989): 1015.

7. Ibid.

8. Cardenal, "Ignacio Ellacuría," 6.

9. Cardenal, "Ser jesuita hoy," 1015. Cardenal adds, however, that Ellacuría was also impressed by Hugo Rahner and Andres Jurgmann.

10. See Herbert Vorgrimler, *Understanding Karl Rahner: An Introduction to His Life and Thought* (New York: Crossroad, 1986), 99 (trans. by John Bowden from *Karl Rahner verstehen: Eine Einfuhrung in sein Leben und Denken* (Freiburg: Verlag Herder, 1985).

11. Martin Maier, "Karl Rahner, the Teacher of Ignacio Ellacuría," in Kevin Burke and

Ellacuría clearly saw his own work as a development of Rahner's. His earliest and most significant theological statements are explicitly framed as interpretations of what he learned from this great theologian of the Council. As we have seen, he presents the key talk of the 1969 retreat discussed above as a "small attempt" to apply Rahner's categories to the "reality [of the Third World] and to conceive of it in theological terms."[12] Also the English foreword to Ellacuría's first book (1973) describes the author (with his approval, one supposes) as a "former student of Karl Rahner," whose book represents "a synthesis" that "has tried to combine the insights of Rahner with those of the Theology of Liberation."[13]

I have argued elsewhere that Ellacuría should be regarded as Rahner's most important Latin American interpreter.[14] In this section I will examine four important assertions supporting this claim, each of which builds on Rahner's insights while attempting to historicize them for a Latin American context. First, Ellacuría argues that *historical reality is the proper object of a truly Latin American theology* and that *human beings apprehend an absolute (or theologal) dimension of reality.* The first part of this claim combines key insights from Rahner's metaphysics of being with what I described earlier as Zubiri's post-Newtonian realism and his assertion of the primacy of reality over being. The second part reformulates Rahner's assertion that all human beings experience a non-objective preapprehension of Absolute Being in terms of Ellacuría's philosophy of historical reality. Second, Ellacuría uses Zubiri's *model of sentient intelligence to conceptualize the role of human knowing in Latin American theological method,* an approach that he argues is more adequate than previous accounts. Ellacuría's account mimics important aspects of the role of the hylomorphic theory and the agent intellect in Rahner's transcendental Thomism

---

Robert Lassalle-Klein, eds., *Love That Produces Hope: The Thought of Ignacio Ellacuría* (Collegeville, MN: Liturgical Press, 2006), 2.

12. Ignacio Ellacuría, "El tercer mundo como lugar óptimo de la vivencia Cristiana de los Ejercicios" (Dia 29:1), in "Reunión-Ejercicios de la viceprovincia Jesuitica de Centroamérica, Diciembre 1969," in *Reflexión teológico-espiritual de la Compañía de Jesus en Centroamerica, II* (San Salvador: Archives of the Society of Jesus, Central American Province, Survey S.J. de Centroamérica, December 1969), 2.

13. Laurence A. Egan, M.M., "Foreword," in Ignacio Ellacuría, *Freedom Made Flesh: The Mission of Christ and His Church* (Maryknoll, NY: Orbis Books, 1976), viii (trans. by John Drury from *Teología política* [San Salvador: Ediciónes del Secretaridado Sociál Interdiocesano, 1973]).

14. Robert Lassalle-Klein, "Ignacio Ellacuría's Rahnerian Fundamental Theology for a Global Church," *Philosophy and Theology* 25, no. 2 (2013): 275-99; Robert Lassalle-Klein, "Rethinking Rahner on Grace and Symbol: New Proposals from the Americas," in Paul Cowley, ed., *Rahner beyond Rahner: A Great Theologian Encounters the Pacific Rim* (Lanham, MD: Rowman & Littlefield, 2005), 87-99; and Robert Lassalle-Klein, "La historización de la filosofía de la religión de Rahner en Ellacuría y Zubiri," in Juan A. Nicolás and Héctor Samour, eds., *Historia, ética, y liberación: La actualidad de Zubiri* (Granada: Comares, 2007), 113-230; and Robert Lassalle-Klein, "Jesus of Galilee and the Crucified People: Contextual Christology of Jon Sobrino and Ignacio Ellacuría," in Robert Lassalle-Klein with Virgilio Elizondo and Gustavo Gutiérrez, eds., special issue, "The Galilean Jesus," *Theological Studies* 70, no. 2 (Spring 2009): 350.

while using what I would argue is a more scientifically viable account of human intellection and perception. Third, Ellacuría develops a theological anthropology rooted in the notion that *historical reality has been transformed by grace* that draws upon and historicizes aspects of Rahner's famous concept of the supernatural existential. And fourth, Ellacuría develops what he calls a *theology of sign* that mimics aspects of Rahner's "theology of symbol" while historicizing it to support the claim that the crucified people are the defining sign of the times.

In all of this it must be emphasized that there is no systematic treatment of Rahner in Ellacuría's work and, with one exception that I will examine later, very little explicit critique. Thus, the aforementioned suggestions should be seen mainly as my own reconstruction of continuities, developments, and differences that appear in what Ellacuría portrayed in the 1969 Jesuit retreat as his attempt to use Rahner's contributions to conceive of the historical reality of Latin America in theological terms.

### Historical Reality and Holy Mystery

Ellacuría uses the concept of historical reality and his insistence on its primacy in Latin American theological method (building on the work of Zubiri) to clarify and extend the implications of key theological concepts he inherits from Rahner. This is emblemized in a well-known article on the historical reality of Christian salvation in which Ellacuría says that Latin American theology must answer the questions, "What do human efforts toward historical and even sociopolitical liberation have to with the establishment of the Reign of God that Jesus preached?" and, "What do the proclamation of the Reign of God and its realization have to do with the historical liberation of the oppressed majorities?"[15]

Of course these are issues that Rahner never explicitly addressed. But Ellacuría says they raise questions about the nature of "Christian historical transcendence" in regard to the relationship between "so-called profane history and salvation history" and "the specifically Christian contribution" to historical transcendence.[16] He summarizes Rahner's response to these questions in a short article from 1962,[17] which Ellacuría says contains principles that remain "fundamental" throughout Rahner's thought despite coming from a time when he was less interested in religion as a political force. He says Rahner insists that "the history of salvation occurs in and is interwoven with the history of the world," while simultaneously asserting that "salvation history is different from

---

15. Ignacio Ellacuría, "Historicidad de la salvación cristiana," *Escritos teológicos*, II (San Salvador: UCA Editores, 2000), 539.

16. Ibid., 569; Ignacio Ellacuría, "The Historicity of Christian Salvation," in Michael Lee, ed., *Ignacio Ellacuría: Essays on History, Liberation, and Salvation* (Maryknoll, NY: Orbis Books, 2013), 144.

17. Karl Rahner, "History of the World and Salvation-History," *Theological Investigations* V (London: Darton, Longman & Todd, 1966), 97-114 ("Weltgeschichte und Heilgeschichte," *Schriften zur Theologie* V [Einsiedeln: Benziger, 1962], 115-35).

profane history," and "in the final analysis, profane history is the condition for the possibility of the history of Christ, which is also the history of God."[18] As a result, salvation history clarifies human history "by demythologizing it" and by exposing it as "existentially powerless" without Christ.

Students of Rahner will note that he is rejecting the rigid distinction drawn by neoscholastic theology between sacred and the profane history, which he undermines with the claims that a "Christian theology of history cannot but say that salvation-history takes place within the history of the world," and "salvation-history takes place right in the midst of ordinary history."[19] Ellacuría certainly agrees, but he extends and radicalizes the point by explicitly rejecting the admittedly analytical distinction between salvation history and profane (or human) history[20] found in Augustine's view of history as a contest between the city of God and the city of man. Ellacuría insists that it is crucial to use the language of just one history, "the great history of God," which he says (in harmony with Rahner) includes "what God has done with all of nature, what God does in human history, and what God wants to happen as a result from his ongoing self-giving, which can be imagined as passing from eternity to eternity."[21] He also explicitly rejects the distinction between "what is natural and what is supernatural in this one history of God"[22] (language that Rahner preserves but mitigates), arguing that human history, which he says "has a more profane appearance" and includes the history of sin, is also constitutive "of the great history of God with humanity."[23]

Here Ellacuría's insistence on the unity of human history, grounded in his philosophy of historical reality, simply clarifies and extends Rahner's claim that the distinction between salvation history and human history, like the distinction between what is supernatural and what is natural, is only analytical. Ellacuría insists that the fundamental tension in history is not between the history of God and the history of humanity (profane history) or "between nature and the supernatural" since they are both "part of the one history of God who, in creating humanity, has elevated us [in order] to participate personally in his own divine life." This allows him to emphasize, which he sees as crucial for Latin American theology, that the fundamental tension in the one and only history that exists (the great history of God with humanity), "is between grace and sin":

---

18. Ellacuría, "Historicidad de la salvación cristiana," 570.

19. Rahner, "History of the World and Salvation-History," 98, 99.

20. Gustavo Gutiérrez argues that in the aforementioned article Rahner rejects the "old dualities" of sacred vs. profane and supports, though in a somewhat "more ambiguous" manner than other authors, through his agreement with what Gutiérrez describes as the fundamental affirmation that "there is only one history—a *Christo-finalized* history." See Gustavo Gutiérrez, *A Theology of Liberation: History, Politics, and Salvation* (rev. ed., with new intro. Maryknoll, NY: Orbis Books, 1988), 86 n. 14.

21. Ellacuría, "Historicidad de la salvación cristiana," 570; "The Historicity of Christian Salvation," 146.

22. Ellacuría, "Historicidad de la salvación cristiana," 575.

23. Ibid., 571.

There are actions that kill (divine) life, and there are actions that give (divine) life. The former belong to the reign of sin, while the latter belong to the reign of grace. There are social and historical structures that objectify the power of sin and also serve as vehicles for that power against humanity, against human life; and there are social and historical structures that objectify grace and also serve as vehicles for that power in favor of human life. The former constitute structural sin and the latter constitute structural grace.[24]

So Ellacuría does not disagree with Rahner, but tries to clarify and further historicize the point that salvation history is better conceptualized as a form of transcendence that occurs within, rather than over against, Latin American history. He wants to focus on a kind of historical transcendence "that allows one to speak of an intrinsic unity without implying a strict identity" between human and salvation history. He does this in part by explicitly rejecting the neoscholastic language of two histories and insisting that a Latin American approach "will assume that there are not two histories, a history of God and a human history; a sacred and a profane history. Rather, there is a single *historical reality* in which both God and human beings take part, so that God's participation does not occur without some form of human participation, and human participation does not occur without God's presence in some form."[25]

Thus, Ellacuría argues that there is only one historical reality and that human beings apprehend an absolute (or *theologal*) dimension of that historical reality, which plays a key role in mediating our encounter with God. In the following two sections I will show how this position draws from and reconfigures elements of Rahner's metaphysics of being and hylomorphic theory of knowing.

### From Rahner's Metaphysics of Being to Historical Reality

In this section I will summarize Ellacuría's argument that *historical reality is the proper object of a truly Latin American theology* and that *human beings apprehend an absolute (or theologal) dimension of reality*. I will argue that the first assertion combines key insights from Rahner's metaphysics of being with Zubiri's formal concept of reality and his assertion of the primacy of reality over being. And I will argue that the second assertion uses Ellacuría's philosophy of historical reality to reformulate Rahner's argument that all human beings experience a non-objective preapprehension of Absolute Being.

We begin, then, with a brief summary of an important dimension of Rahner's metaphysics of being and Ellacuría's appreciative critique of one element of this approach (through Heidegger). Rahner describes the question of *being* as "the chief concern of metaphysics," asserting that it must be understood "if we

---

24. Ibid., 576.

25. Ibid., 541. See the excellent translation by Michael Lee, "The Historicity of Christian Salvation," 142.

are to grasp what is meant by *God*."[26] Rahner's analysis is built around a two-fold philosophical definition of being that distinguishes "common being" (which Ellacuría might call the *being-of-an-entity*) from Absolute, or Infinite, Being,[27] which functions as the horizon for our existence. Referring to what he calls "common being," Rahner writes, "We call 'a being,' or entity, any conceivable object of knowledge, anything that is not nothing."[28]

Moving next to what he calls "Absolute Being," Rahner asserts that "the individual object is encountered within a 'horizon' which is non-objectively and implicitly involved whenever the mind grasps individual objects."[29] He asserts this horizon "is the a priori condition of all particular knowledge," without which "we could neither compare things nor . . . form unqualified judgments." And he identifies the preapprehension of this horizon as a privileged moment in our experience of God, stating,

> The term of this *a priori* gasp (Transcendence) . . . [is what] we call Being, . . . *actus purus*, absolute Being, *simpliciter*, absolute mystery, God, . . . the fontal infinitude of Being *simpliciter*, to which as to incomprehensible mystery the transcendence of man is ordered in every act of knowledge—though he does not conceive of it for itself—and which is the source not only of the knowledge but of the reality of every being.[30]

Ellacuría and Zubiri have great appreciation for this distinction between "common being" and Absolute, or Infinite, Being (which cannot be an object of experience).[31] Rahner claims to find it in Thomas Aquinas, but commentators assert that his sensitivity to the issue has also been influenced by Heidegger's famous claim to have uncovered a fundamental "ontological difference"[32] between the "being of things (entities)" and "being itself." Thomas Sheehan argues that in *Spirit in the World* Rahner "uses Heidegger in order to extort an existential transcendental turn out of Aquinas, and uses Aquinas to extort an affirmation of God out of Heidegger."[33] Something like this can be seen in Rahner's use of the aforementioned distinction to support his transcendental claim that "metaphysical *objects*—existents which cannot be experienced—are accessible only insofar as the *object* of metaphysics, *common being* (which in

---

26. Karl Rahner and Herbert Vorgrimler, "Being," in *Theological Dictionary* (New York: Herder & Herder, 1965), 53-54.

27. Karl Rahner, *Spirit in the World*, trans. William Dych, S.J. (New York: Continuum Publishing, 1957, 1968, 1994), 388.

28. Rahner and Vorgrimler, "Being," 53.

29. Ibid.

30. Ibid., 54.

31. Rahner, *Spirit in the World*, 388-89.

32. Martin Heidegger, *Being and Time*, trans. John Macquarrie and Edward Robinson (New York: Harper & Row, 1962), 32.

33. Thomas Sheehan, *Karl Rahner: The Philosophical Foundations* (Athens, OH: Ohio University Press, 1987), 114.

itself is not an object, not a thing in itself), already presupposes them as its ground, without this ground itself being an object which could be investigated by itself."[34]

Zubiri highlights the importance of this twofold approach to being in Heidegger's work when he speaks appreciatively of the "unquestionable merit . . . of having posed the question of *being itself* apart from that of the *being of things*."[35] Using Heidegger's famous metaphor of being as the light that illuminates *Dasein* (the *there-being* of human beings), Zubiri explains,

> Heidegger will tell us that the presence of being in *Da-sein* is like light. In the true being of *Da-sein*, being is not present as a thing—that would make being into a thing [entity]—, but rather "being is the luminescence itself." Being is the luminescence of every entity and being is that which constitutes the very essence of man.[36]

Affirming this insight, Zubiri concludes, "If Heidegger had been content to assert the understanding of being . . . there would not have been the least objection . . . "[37] on his part. Unfortunately, he says, "Heidegger is looking for an Ontology,"[38] and mistakenly "regards the understanding of being as not just the act in which being is *manifested* to itself and from itself, but rather as a *mode of being* . . . of being [itself]." Thus, while he agrees with Heidegger that the understanding of being can be described as a function of the continually receding horizon of our being-in-the-world, he asserts that this does nothing to resolve the underlying problem that Heidegger has illegitimately changed what should be understood as an "act of being" into a substance. Going still further, Zubiri protests (as we saw above) that while there are *acts* of being, in point of fact, "real being does not exist."[39] Indeed, "only *being real* exists, or *realitas in essendo*, as I would say."

Like Rahner and Heidegger, then, Zubiri distinguishes the being-of-an-entity (what he calls *ente*) from being itself (or *ser*). He argues, however (as we saw earlier), that both the "being-of-an-entity (*ente*) and being (*ser*) have [improperly] displaced reality in philosophy."[40] Starting from the phenomenological perspective of Husserl's call to return "to the thing!" he says that our study of "what is" should properly begin with how things are actualized in our

---

34. Rahner, *Spirit in the World*, 388-89.

35. Xavier Zubiri, *Sobre la esencia* (Madrid: Gráficas Cóndor, Sociedad de Estudios y Publicaciones, 1962, 1980), 441.

36. Ibid.

37. Ibid., 442.

38. Ibid.

39. Xavier Zubiri, *Naturaleza, historia y Dios* (Madrid: Alianza Editorial, Fundación Xavier Zubiri, 1987, 2004), 16.

40. Xavier Zubiri, *Inteligencia sentiente: Inteligencia y realidad* (Madrid: Alianza Editorial, 1980), I, 637.

intelligence.[41] Echoing Husserl, Zubiri argues against Heidegger that in a truly phenomenological approach "what formally characterizes the human person is not the *understanding of being*, but rather the mode of our *apprehension of things*."[42] On the other hand, however, he argues against Husserl that the mode of our apprehension of things is defined by "sentient intelligence." Thus, the proper beginning point for a strictly intramundane (world-centered) philosophy grounded in science will be the formal "reality" that characterizes the way things are actualized by our sentient intelligence as apprehensions possessing the character of being something "in its own" right *(en propio)*, or as something "of its own" *(de suyo)*.

So how, then, does Ellacuría use these concepts, which we studied earlier, to advance the argument made by Rahner using the metaphysics of being and its role in our encounter with God? First, building on Zubiri's argument that the question of *reality* has been improperly subordinated to that of *being* in Western philosophy, Ellacuría shifts the focus from the *metaphysics of being* to an *intramundane metaphysics of the sentient intellection of reality*. He says this is necessary because "intellection . . . consists in the actualization of the real as formally real," and "real things only show themselves as real in the act of intellection."[43] Students of Rahner will observe that "Ellacuría is making the same move as Rahner" since "the major contribution of *Spirit in the World* is precisely its account for the claim that we have no access to being without sentient intellection of reality."[44] Is this correct?

On the one hand, it is absolutely correct that Rahner's argument for "the origin of sensibility as conversion to the phantasm" in *Spirit in the World* can be understood as simply another way of arriving at what Ellacuría and Zubiri call *"the structural unity of intellection and sensing,"*[45] which is the hallmark of sentient intelligence. So we may wonder if Ellacuría's sentient intelligence is simply another name for Rahner's *conversion to the phantasm*? On the other hand, however, as we saw in Chapter 5, Zubiri's account of sentient intellection requires no conversion to a phantasm in order to achieve what he describes as the *primordial apprehension of reality*, an approach that I also argued is more consonant with contemporary research on the role of the brain in human perception. As we saw, the intellection of reality seems to occur earlier in the perceptual stream of the brain and the central nervous system than what occurs in the visual cortex. It directs where the retina looks, filtering visual messages through the thalamus according to their behavioral relevance, and biasing the strength of the reaction at the amygdala so that what reaches the visual cortex (producing a phantasm) has

---

41. Zubiri, *Sobre la esencia*, 451.

42. Ibid.

43. Ignacio Ellacuría, "La superación del reduccionismo idealista en Zubiri," in *Escritos filosóficos* (San Salvador: UCA Editores, 2001), 426. Also see Zubiri, *Inteligencia sentiente*, 648.

44. Peter Fritz, personal correspondence with Robert Lassalle-Klein (August 17, 2013), transcript in personal files of the author.

45. Ellacuría, "Reduccionismo," 420; Zubiri, *Inteligencia sentiente*, 644.

already been selected and modified by what can only be described as the activity of the mind. Thus, while I would agree that Zubiri's notion of sentient intelligence functions in Ellacuría's theology in ways that are quite parallel to Rahner's conversion to the phantasm in *Spirit in the World*, it must be said that there are important differences as well, not the least of which is their commensurability with scientific accounts of perception.

Second, Ellacuría argues that the self-transcending character of *historical reality*[46] is the proper object of theology and philosophy.[47] While this again parallels Rahner's interest in the luminescence of being found in the sensible world, Ellacuría builds on Zubiri's more mundane (and scientifically oriented) analysis using systems theory to describe the natural cosmos as an integrated unity of four major types of self-transcending systems (material, biological, sentient, and historical reality), each comprising complex boundary-maintaining systems that build epigenetically upon the lower levels that are integrated into a larger systemic whole. Ellacuría then asserts that historical (or human) reality constitutes the most self-possessing (*de suyo* or "of its own") and/or "last stage of reality." This is where the other levels of reality are all made present, and "where we are given not only the highest forms of reality, but also the field of the maximum possibilities of the real."[48] He says this is so, in part, because the human person's awareness of their own historical reality (as being something "of their own") "permits them to be reduplicatively self-possessed,"[49] which is why he insists that historical reality is the proper object of Latin American theology and philosophy. While there is nothing about this approach that contradicts Rahner, the terms of the argument are different.

Third, Ellacuría asserts that not only are we part of reality and apprehend reality through sentient intellection, but we are also bound to reality. He says, "We are open to reality, and we are installed there, but we are also bound to reality. Reality does not just make itself present as . . . the force of reality that imposes itself primarily on the intelligence, but rather as the force that also makes itself present as a power that dominates us."[50] Accordingly, "Intellective sensing not only opens us to both reality and being," it also "drives us irresistibly to endlessly explore every type of reality and every form of being"[51] that we encounter. He explains this is so because the fundamental and unavoidable relationship of sentient intelligence to the "power of the real" presents the self with ongoing choices regarding whether and how to appropriate itself in relation to the realities it encounters.[52] Thus, Ellacuría concludes, "it is by submerg-

---

46. Ignacio Ellacuría, *Filosofía de la realidad histórica* (San Salvador: UCA Editores, 1990), 42.

47. Ellacuría substitutes "historical reality" for Zubiri's more abstract "unity of intramundane reality"; see ibid., 30, 25.

48. Ibid., 43.

49. Ibid.

50. Ellacuría, "Reduccionismo," 430.

51. Zubiri, *Inteligencia sentiente*, 649.

52. Ibid., 648.

ing oneself in reality and taking up all its dynamisms, as modest as they might appear, that the human person will capture and be captured by more reality, and thus become not only more intelligent, but finally, more real, and more human."[53]

Fourth, Ellacuría uses his philosophy of historical reality to reframe and extend Rahner's argument for the preapprehension of Absolute Being as a privileged moment in our historical encounter with God. He argues instead that sentient intelligence apprehends an absolute or "theologal" dimension of *reality*, and that our *historical reality* is inevitably defined by our response to this *theologal* reality, which mediates our encounter with God.[54]

Ellacuría argues that the self-determination of the subject is an integral aspect of the apprehension and intellection of what he calls the *theologal* or absolute dimension of reality in an important 1986 article entitled "A Will-to-Fundamentality and a Will-to-Truth: Knowledge-Faith and Their Historical Configuration."[55] He asserts that intellection is at least partially a response to the absolute or *theologal* dimension of reality, which forces a subject to freely and habitually choose how to actualize oneself in response to that reality.[56] He asserts that faith (which he calls commitment) builds on knowledge (or intellection) as a series of decisions to live by one's intellections of the absolute or *theologal* dimension of reality.[57] Thus *faith* is the decision to live by one's intellections of the absolute dimension of reality, and he asserts that decisions not to live by those intellections tend to cause one to confuse concepts with reality, and to objectify oneself and others.

Here Ellacuría foregrounds what Rahner treats only briefly at the end of *Spirit in the World*[58] where he suggests that the process of conversion to the phantasm involves not just sensation and intellection but also implies a self-determination or decision by the subject about who he or she will be in the world.[59] Rahner writes,

> God shines forth only in the limitless breadth of the pre-apprehension, in the desire for being as such by which every act of man is borne, and which is at work not only in his ultimate knowledge and in his ultimate decisions, but also in the fact that the free spirit becomes, and must

---

53. Ellacuría, "Reduccionismo," 430.

54. Ignacio Ellacuría, "Voluntad de fundamentalidad y voluntad de verdad: conocimiento-fe y su configuración histórica," *Revista latinoamericana de teología* 8 (1986): 113-32. Zubiri and Ellacuría distinguish the theologal or absolute dimension of reality from the theological dimension of reality, which explicitly thematizes its relationship to God.

55. Ibid., 113.

56. Ibid., 121.

57. Xavier Zubiri, *El hombre y Dios* (Madrid: Alianza Editorial, Sociedad de Estudios y Publicaciones, 1984, 1985), 234

58. Rahner, "The Possibility of Metaphysics on the Basis of the Imagination" in *Spirit in the World* (New York: Continuum, 1968, 1994), 387-408.

59. This important aspect of Rahner's conversion to the phantasm was pointed out to me by Peter Fritz. Personal correspondence with Robert Lassalle-Klein (August 17, 2012).

become, sensibility in order to be spirit, and thus exposes itself to the whole destiny of this earth. Thus man encounters himself when he finds himself in the world and when he asks about God.[60]

Ellacuría's move from the metaphysics of being to a metaphysics of reality, however, leads him to reframe what he learns from Rahner's argument about *the preapprehension of Absolute Being* as a privileged medium for our encounter with God. He argues instead that we apprehend the reality of God indirectly through the experience of what Zubiri calls *the absolute power of the real* as the foundation or ground of our personal being.[61] Zubiri says, "The immediate presence of the enigma of reality in our bondedness to the power of the real is a directional presence of the reality of *something*," which our intelligence concludes is God.[62] The key is that "God is only directionally present in the real," and "the human person does not know anything more than that the one who is directionally present is God." The question for theology, then, "is not so much whether there is a God, but whether something of what is there is really God."[63]

Ellacuría says this means on the one hand that, whether we know it or not, the experience of the absolute power of the real that we have been discussing is an experience of God.[64] More exactly, there is a way in which our experience of bondedness to the absolute power of the real both is and is not a primary apprehension of God. Following Rahner's conviction that God cannot be an object if human freedom is to be preserved, Ellacuría writes,

> What is not a primary apprehension . . . is that what we are apprehending when we apprehend the power of the real as a foundation of our personal being, and when we apprehend our personal being as grounded in the power of the real, is that this foundation is God, and is divine and divinizing. Nor do we know the personal characteristics of this God whom we apprehend as the foundation of our own self-development.[65]

On the other hand, however, he says that these experiences form what we might call an *analogous primary apprehension of the reality of God*. To make his point, Ellacuría uses Zubiri's reading of a famous text in which St. Thomas discusses the connaturality of knowledge of God: "Knowing God in a certain confused and general way is something that is naturally infused. . . . But this is not knowing *simplicitur* that God exists; in the same manner that knowing that somebody is coming, is not knowing Pedro, even though it is Pedro who

---

60. Rahner, *Spirit in the World*, 406.
61. Ellacuría, "Voluntad de fundamentalidad," 116.
62. Ibid., citing Zubiri, *El hombre y Dios*, 230.
63. Zubiri, *El hombre y Dios*, 230.
64. Ellacuría, "Voluntad de fundamentalidad," 116.
65. Ibid.

is coming."[66] Ellacuría says the point is that "the human person immediately apprehends that someone is coming, [and] that we have apprehended something very important. What we do not know, for the moment, is what to call it, even though some of its fundamental characteristics are already given to us in a certain manner."[67]

In the end, therefore, despite the analogous character of our primordial apprehension of the power of the real as the ground of human subjectivity, both Ellacuría and Zubiri insist that this is an experience of God. For students of Rahner it is not difficult to see that Ellacuría has reframed Rahner's argument that human beings have a non-objective preapprehension of Absolute Being,[68] clarifying and extending his claim that the conversion to the phantasm of human spirit-in-the-world exposes it "to the whole destiny of this earth."[69] I would argue, therefore, that Ellacuría builds upon, extends, and implicitly critiques certain aspects of Rahner's argument when he uses Zubiri's framework to argue that each person apprehends an absolute (or "theologal") dimension of reality, which serves as a key medium for our encounter with God. It is this absolute or *theologal* dimension of reality that will allow Ellacuría to assert in all seriousness that "with Monseñor Romero God visited El Salvador."[70]

### From Rahner's Hylomorphic Knowing to Sentient Intelligence

The second major area in which Ellacuría simultaneously builds upon insights from Rahner while attempting to historicize them for a Latin American context can be found in his assertion that *sentient intelligence provides the most adequate model for conceptualizing the role of human knowing in Latin American theological method.* Ellacuría's argument for sentient intelligence follows important aspects of Rahner's account of the role of the hylomorphic theory and the agent intellect in his theory of knowing (a defining aspect of his transcendental Thomism). But Rahner's moves are resituated in a framework that I would suggest offers a clearer and more scientifically viable account of certain key aspects of human intellection and perception. I will offer four points in this section explaining and defending this thesis.

First, Rahner develops an interpretation of the hylomorphic theory of Thomas and Aristotle that supports his treatment of being. He defines hylomorphism as

> the doctrine of Aristotle, supplemented by the Scholastics, that every physical being is essentially constituted of matter (Gr. ὕλη) and form (Gr. μορφή), which combine to make a single entity. It is based on the notion that physical being has a substantial essence, constituted by

---

66. Ellacuría, "Voluntad de fundamentalidad," 116.
67. Ibid.," 116.
68. Rahner and Vorgrimler, "Being," 54.
69. Rahner, *Spirit in the World,* 406.
70. Sobrino, "El padre Ellacuría sobre Monseñor Romero," 126.

"prime matter" (*materia prima*, potency, mutability) and "form" (act), a (variable) substantial principle of configuration which is produced by an external efficient cause, is the basis of specific difference, and makes matter what it was in potency to be. The structure of the resultant palpable "second matter" is thus always hylomorphic.[71]

Stephen Fields explains that Rahner's approach rejects the traditional notion that form relates to matter as efficient causality, working externally from the outside to produce an effect that is not intrinsic to matter. For Rahner, this view diminishes the dynamically unified character of being, tending to reduce being to "an entity," the first aspect of his aforementioned twofold definition of being.

Rahner argues instead that form gives "itself away"[72] when it is emanated in matter. Rahner believes that form and matter are ontologically congenial, constituting a unity-in-difference in which matter incarnates form. The problem, however, is that the emanation of form in matter does not bring about the perfection of that form. Rahner argues, therefore, that form is perfected only when it returns to itself through its material emanation, following the cycle of Being's emanation and return that defines the cosmology of Thomas Aquinas.

As we saw above, Rahner insists that *being* is "the chief concern of metaphysics" and must be grasped "if we are to grasp what is meant by *God*."[73] So it is not surprising that Rahner's hylomorphism serves his treatment of being. Building on Aquinas he says that being emanates its material medium precisely so that being can become realized by returning to itself by being known. In this view matter exists to serve as a medium for being so that being can return to itself by being known (by the soul). Here being is grasped in its material medium by the intellect, which is possible only because the medium of matter incarnates and expresses being's formal intelligibility.

Second, Rahner uses this hylomorphic approach to being to develop his theory of being as symbol (or *realsymbol*). Building on his position that both the substance and the intelligibility of form are incarnated in its material medium, Rahner insists on the need for a theological and a philosophical account of how being is symbolized or expressed in its material medium. For this purpose he develops what he calls "an ontology of symbol."[74] He says "the basic principle" of this ontology of symbol will be that "all beings are by their nature symbolic, because they necessarily *express* themselves in order to attain their own nature."[75] He postulates, "Our task will be to look for the highest and most primordial manner in which one reality can represent another—considering

---

71. Rahner and Vorgrimler, "Hylomorphism," in *Theological Dictionary*, 217.

72. Karl Rahner, "The Theology of Symbol," trans. Kevin Smyth, *Theological Investigations*, IV (Baltimore, MD: Helicon Press, 1966), 231; Stephen M. Fields, S.J., *Being as Symbol: On the Origins and Development of Karl Rahner's Metaphysics* (Washington, DC: Georgetown University Press, 2000), 7.

73. Rahner and Vorgrimler, "Being," 53.

74. Rahner, "The Theology of Symbol," 222.

75. Ibid., 224.

the matter primarily from the formal ontological point of view."[76] He says he will "call this supreme and primal representation, in which one reality renders another present (primarily *for itself* and only secondarily for others), a symbol [or *realsymbol*]: the representation which allows the other *to be there*." Thus he concludes by asserting that the "symbol strictly speaking (symbolic reality) is the self-realization of a being in the other, which is constitutive of its essence."[77]

Rahner then distinguishes being as *symbol* (or *realsymbol*), which instrinsically represents what it signifies, from similar "concepts which point linguistically and objectively in the same direction: *eidos* [εἶδος], *morphe* [μορφή] sign, figure, expression, image, aspect, appearance, etc."[78] He says this is crucial for theology because,

> In a real theology of the symbol, based on the fundamental truths of Christianity, a symbol is not something separate from the symbolized (or different, but really or mentally united with the symbolized by a mere process of addition), which indicates the object but does not contain it. On the contrary, the symbol *is* the reality, constituted by the things symbolized as an inner moment of moment itself, which reveals and proclaims the thing symbolized and is itself full of the thing symbolized, being its concrete form of existence.[79]

Rahner thus marries hylomorphism with his ontology of symbol in order to explain how being is symbolized in its material medium. This allows him to assert that the soul and the body are a metaphysical unity, and to elude the dichotomies of sensation vs. knowing and body vs. soul that Ellacuría and Zubiri believe plague Western philosophy.

Rahner argues both that the body must not be understood as independent from or "prior to the reality of the soul,"[80] and that the soul must not be understood as ontologically pre-existing the body or as the body's efficient cause,[81] either of which would undermine the innate unity-in-distinction of the body and soul. Instead, he argues, "The body is the symbol [or *realsymbol*] of the soul, in as much as it is formed as the self-realization of the soul, though it is not adequately this, and the soul renders itself present and makes its *appearance* in the body which is distinct from it."[82] Fields observes that, for Rahner, "Although the body constitutes the matter, or substrate, in which the soul dynamically expresses itself, it is the soul that, emanated in the body, informs it, thus making the person a *spirit-in-the-world*."[83]

---

76. Ibid., 225.
77. Ibid., 234
78. Ibid., 224.
79. Ibid., 251.
80. Ibid., 246, 247.
81. Fields, *Being as Symbol*, 8.
82. Rahner, "The Theology of the Symbol," 221-52, esp. 247.
83. Fields, *Being as Symbol*, 8; Rahner, *Spirit in the World*, 406-7.

Third, Rahner develops a famously original interpretation of the role of the agent intellect in uniting the mind and its object as a key element of his episte-mology. Rahner's theory of knowledge builds on his interpretation of the agent intellect, the faculty of human knowing in the philosophies of Aristotle and Thomas. Rahner states, "The agent intellect is introduced again and again in Thomas as the *a priori* condition, inherent in thought itself, of the possibility of something [becoming] actually intelligible."[84] He explains that Thomas uses this idea to resolve the underlying problem that "sensibility does not reach any-thing actually intelligible."[85] We will return to this idea in a moment since the model for *sentient intelligence* adopted by Ellacuría and Zubiri, which I have suggested is consonant with recent neuroscientific research on the role of the brain in human perception, eliminates this problem.[86]

Thomas believes, however, that "human universal knowing needs a faculty," so he turns to Aristotle's idea of "the *agent intellect*, which makes the species [the form] received from sensible things intelligible."[87] Rahner cites Thomas's succinct statement of the problem.

> Aristotle maintained that they (the forms existing universally in them-selves) subsist only in sensible things (hence always in an already real-ized concretion). Therefore he considered it necessary to posit some power which would make what was potentially intelligible actually intelligible by *abstracting* the species [or *forms*] of things from mat-ter and from individuating conditions. This power is called the *agent intellect*.[88]

Fields explains that, using this model, Rahner argues that objects become intel-ligible to knowing subjects by means of their sensuous intuition and ontological assimilation from the data of the form that gives substance to the object.[89] He says the data is intuited and consolidated by the imagination, which mediates it from the lower sensuous level to the higher level of the soul. The imagination synthesizes and integrates the input, creating a perceptual unity (percept) or "phantasm,"[90] which is an ontologically accurate representation of "the object whose form it contains."[91] Summarizing the results, Fields says, "The *agent intel-*

---

84. Rahner, *Spirit in the World*, 136.

85. Ibid., 137.

86. See Chapter 5.

87. Rahner, *Spirit in the World*, 137, citing Thomas Aquinas, *Summa contra Gentiles* II, 96.

88. Ibid., citing Thomas Aquinas, *De spiritualibus creaturis* a.9; *Summa Theologiae* I, a. q. 54, a.4; q. 79, a.3; *De Anima* a.4; *De spiritualibus creaturis*. a.10; *De Anima* lect. 10, n. 731; *Summa contra Gentiles* II, 59; II, 77.

89. This section follows Fields, *Being as Symbol*, 9-13, interspersed with my own interpretations of citations from Rahner's work.

90. Fields, *Being and Symbol*, 9.

91. Ibid., 10.

*lect*, a power properly of the soul, *abstracts the form from the phantasm that contains* it, thus making it known to the intellect as a concept or a universal."[92]

Granting the accuracy of this summary, we must note that Rahner repeatedly insists that the abstraction by which the form is "*liberated* from the matter in which and by which it is individuated"[93] in the phantasm, "cannot be thought of in a naive interpretation . . . as a production in the intellect of an intellectual *double* of what is sensibly given in intuition, [or] as an *image (Bild)* which the intellect looks at as sensibility looks at its objects."[94] He argues instead that "being can never be *liberated (abgelost)* in the abstractive concept . . . but can only be re-realized (*nachvollzogen*) in that synthesis of the universal and the singular, of form and subject, of possibility and actuality which is . . . the affirmative synthesis of the judgment."[95]

But how, then, does the agent intellect abstract the form from the phantasm if not by creating some sort of condensed image or representation of it? Rahner responds that the universal must be known in the phantasm itself, and that the agent intellect achieves this through what he calls (following Thomas) a *conversion to the phantasm* by means of which the intellect makes a judgment about the universal nature of the sensible form found in the phantasm. In response, then, to the question, "What does conversion to the phantasm mean?"[96] Rahner replies, "The term says that the intelligible universal, the intelligible species [or *form*] in the strict sense, is known only in and at the sensibly known, and so in a turning to it." Using the image of light in a different but complementary sense to what we saw earlier from Heidegger, Rahner says, "The conversion to the phantasm is nothing other than the illumination of the phantasm by the light of the agent intellect, through which illumination the abstraction is already accomplished."[97]

This image works for Rahner, as it does for Heidegger and Aquinas, because (as we saw earlier) being cannot be an object of thought. Thus, Rahner says its presence is more like light, providing the illumination that serves as the condition for the possibility of seeing the object, to which it yields the stage. This brings us to the role of Aquinas's notion of *excessus* in Rahner's theory of the agent intellect. Rahner writes, "If, according to Thomas, the ground of metaphysics is disclosed only by the fact that it shows itself to be a condition of the possibility of . . . the conversion to the phantasm, then *excessus*, negation and comparison must be the ground of metaphysics in such a way that they are the condition of the possibility for the knowledge of world by that mode of thought which is essentially dependent on sense intuition."[98]

Fields explains that Rahner follows Scholastic tradition in affirming that,

---

92. Ibid.
93. Rahner, *Spirit in the World*, 138.
94. Ibid., 140-41.
95. Ibid., 201-2.
96. Ibid., 265.
97. Ibid., 264.
98. Ibid., 395.

when the agent intellect abstracts the form from the phantasm through its judgment about the sensible form, "the agent intellect knows the universal as distinct from other modes of Being."[99] But he asserts that Rahner "parts company with this tradition in his analysis of the inner structure of abstraction, *excessus*."[100] He says that, for Rahner, "the universal is grasped when the intellect perceives it as an intelligible form that transcends the sensuous particularity of the phantasm that embodies and limits it. Seeing the contrast between the universal and the particular in the phantasm, the intellect negates that particular, thus determining the universal by *excessus*." He explains, however, that "this negation requires as its condition of possibility a further negation" because "in order to recognize the universal precisely as an essence . . . it is [necessarily] perceived as limited against the intellect's implicit awareness of the Infinite and Absolute."

Explaining this second negation, Fields writes,

> The origin of this second excessus lies in the immanent dynamism of intelligence, capable of affirming, not merely the finite mode of Being as a universal in a particular, but the unlimited existence of the one ground of Being. This capacity, the "preapprehension of absolute being" (*Vorgriff*), grasps the Being of beings, not as a determinable object, but as the original unity and totality of reality, the "horizon" against which all objects can be known. As being's horizon, the Absolute is the intellect's final cause immanent in it, not intuitively as an implicit concept, but as any cause is necessarily immanent in its effect.[101]

Fields says that Rahner follows the Scholastic tradition with the claim "that knowledge of the universal is never separable from the material data that embody it."[102] But he asserts that Rahner diverges from the tradition with his insistence that the abstraction of the form from the phantasm and the conversion to the phantasm are not two separate acts but rather two moments of a single act of abstraction and judgment based on the intellect's ability to contrast the sensuous form with its preapprehension of Absolute Being.[103]

Without going any further into the weeds of Transcendental Thomism this discussion is important for us because it draws our attention to the role in Rahner's thought of the "preapprehension of absolute being" and the "conversion to the phantasm" in overcoming the assertion by Aquinas that "sensibility does not reach anything actually intelligible."[104] It demonstrates that Rahner recognizes the problematic nature of the gulf in Thomas's theory of knowing between sensation and intellection, and between the phantasm and the agent intellect, and

---

99. Ibid., 187.

100. Fields, *Being as Symbol*, 10.

101. Ibid., 10-11.

102. Ibid., 11.

103. Ibid., 10.

104. Ibid., 137.

tries to resolve it. His solution is a creative integration of hylomorphism with ontology, emphasizing the role of the agent intellect.

Fourth, though he never asserts as much, Ellacuría's notion of sentient intelligence mimics and reframes aspects of the role of the agent intellect and the conversion to the phantasm in solving the aforementioned problem in Rahner's thought. Rahner's solution demonstrates an awareness of the dichotomy between sense data and thought that Ellacuría says (with Zubiri) runs through much of Western philosophy. However, as I argued above, Rahner's conversion to the phantasm, which occurs in the act of abstraction, stops well short of the neuroscientific implications of Zubiri's claim that "the structural unity of intellection and sensing"[105] is rooted in the *primordial apprehension* of the reality of the object at the beginning of perception and intellection.

Thomas's claim that "sensibility does not reach anything actually intelligible"[106] contradicts Ellacuría's assertion that the intellection of reality is not simply the product of affirmative, propositional, or predicative judgments about sense data, but that "reality is already actualized in sensing itself, in the sensible actualization itself."[107] And Rahner's reliance on the agent intellect and the conversion to the phantasm to solve this problem, though fundamental, refer to an event that occurs later in the process of perception and intellection and that therefore cannot be described as primordial. As a result, I would suggest that Ellacuría uses Zubiri's analysis of the role of sentient intelligence in knowing in order to clarify and extend key aspects of Rahner's ingenious integration of *hylomorphism* with the *agent intellect*, modeling an approach that fits well with contemporary studies of perception in cognitive neuroscience. This allows Ellacuría to agree with Rahner that the soul and the body form a metaphysical unity while historicizing aspects of his notion that the human person is a spirit-in-the-world. Ellacuría wants to emphasize that the human person is a historical reality, a sentient intelligence-in-the-world able to apprehend the absolute dimension of reality revealed in the everyday, and to take a stance on his or her encounters with God's action-in-the-world mediated through the history of El Salvador.

Though his terms differ in some respects from those of Thomas and his students, Ellacuría agrees with Rahner that the "metaphysics of knowledge is Christian when it summons the human person back to the here and now of their finite world, because the Eternal has also entered into their world so that the human person might find Him, and in Him might find themselves anew."[108] This is the conviction that drives Ellacuría's 1969 insistence that the Christ of the San Salvador retreat should guide the renewal of the Central American Jesuits after Medellín and Vatican II.[109] This Christ revealed himself eight years later

105. Ellacuría, "Reduccionismo," 644.

106. Rahner, *Spirit in the World*, 137

107. Ibid.

108. Ibid., 408.

109. Ellacuría, "El problema del traslado del Espíritu de los Ejercicios a la vice" (Dia 28:1), 1-12, in "Reunión-Ejercicios de la viceprovincia Jesuitica de Centroamérica, Diciembre 1969," 104-15, in *Reflexión teológico-espiritual de la Compañía de Jesús en Centroamerica*,

to Oscar Romero through the crucified people he so loved and who defined his ministry as archbishop before passing the prophetic torch to Ellacuría who thereby discovered his own call as a human being and a Christian to take this crucified people down from the cross.

### The Crucified People: Scandal and Sign of Salvation

I have argued thus far, then, that Ellacuría uses his concepts of *historical reality* and *sentient intelligence* to clarify, reframe, and extend aspects of Rahner's metaphysics of Being and his hylomorphic theory of knowing. I have also addressed the role of these concepts in Ellacuría's assertion that human beings apprehend an absolute (or *theologal*) dimension of reality that is a privileged locus for our encounter with God. Thus *historical reality* and *sentient intelligence* can now be seen as *philosophical-theological fundamenta* for what I have described as Ellacuría's Christian (or theological) historical realism. One author wonders whether, based on these arguments, "perhaps Ellacuría shows people what Rahner meant all along, though in language more accessible and less beholden to the overwrought distinctions of 1930s neo-Thomism."[110]

The question that preoccupies us in this section, however, is the role of these concepts in Ellacuría's specifically *theological fundamenta* for Latin American theologies and the contribution to this discussion of what he learns from Rahner. In the following two sections, therefore, I will address the influence of Rahner's concept of the *supernatural existential* and his *theology of symbol* on the defining theological elements of what I have called Ellacuría's Christian historical realism.

### *From Rahner's Supernatural Existential to Historical Reality Transformed by Grace*

In this section I will argue that Ellacuría develops a theological anthropology grounded in the affirmation that *historical reality has been transformed by grace*, which I will suggest clarifies and attempts to further historicize[111] (beyond what Rahner has already done) aspects of what some consider Rahner's best-known theological concept, the *supernatural existential*. Drawing on his philosophy of historical reality Ellacuría argues, "History is, in effect, a tran-

---

*II* (San Salvador: Archives of the Society of Jesus, Central American Province, Survey S.J. de Centroamérica, December 1969).

110. Peter Fritz, personal correspondence with Robert Lassalle-Klein (August 17, 2012).

111. I am indebted here to the early work of Martin Maier, S.J., who presents Ellacuría as an important interpreter of Karl Rahner, especially through the latter's efforts to "historicize" Rahner's supernatural existential, and Maier's assertion that Ellacuría seeks to develop "a theology of the signs of the times." See Martin Maier, "Theologie des gekreuzigten Volkes: Der Entwurf einer Theologie der Befreiung von Ignacio Ellacuría und Jon Sobrino" (doctoral dissertation, University of Innsbruck, 1992); and Maier, "Karl Rahner: The Teacher of Ignacio Ellacuría," 128-43.

scendental openness because it encompasses in itself both the opening of reality and the doubly unified opening of the intelligence and the will, of the apprehension and choice." Then, citing Rahner, he asserts, "This openness, which for each person is the elevated transcendental openness of a *supernatural existential* (Rahner), is, in history as a whole, the elevated transcendental openness of a gratuitous historicity."[112] Ellacuría believes this move toward an explicitly historical account of grace will allow him to provide theologies seeking God's word in the signs of the times with a fully elaborated account of the personal and social dimensions of the hearer of the Word grounded in scripture, tradition, and contemporary science.

Ellacuría accepts Rahner's notion that the human existential has been elevated and transformed by God's self-offer (or grace) into a supernatural existential, or a spirit-in-the-world who is a "hearer of the Word."[113] However he clarifies and historicizes Rahner's point based on philosophical grounds and Judeo-Christian biblical narratives of "salvation history" when he asserts that, thanks to God's historical self-communication, "*history* is in itself [*de suyo*] transcendentally open, and in that transcendentality God is already present, at least in an inchoate way."[114] Thus, Ellacuría implies that Rahner's supernatural existential is better understood in terms of the one historical reality that has been elevated and empowered by grace.

As we saw earlier, Ellacuría clarifies and historicizes Rahner's attempt to overcome the dichotomy between salvation history and human history by rejecting the neoscholastic terms of the argument (which Rahner does not) and by insisting that fundamental tension in history is not between the history of God and the history of humanity, or between nature and the supernatural, but is rather between the action of grace and sin in human history (the great history of God). Students of Rahner will correctly insist that this is precisely his point. But I would argue, as noted above, that Ellacuría's category of historical reality clarifies and allows Ellacuría to further historicize the point. How did Ellacuría arrive at this position and what are its implications for his theology?

First, it is important to understand that Ellacuría's position emerges in response to the well-documented influence of Martin Heidegger's existential philosophy (and his concept of *Dasein*) on Rahner's "supernatural existential." Regarding Heidegger's influence on his student, Rahner himself states, "Although I had many good professors in the classroom, there is only *one* whom I can revere as my *teacher*, and he is Martin Heidegger," adding that "Catholic

---

112. Ignacio Ellacuría, "Historia de la salvación," *Escritos teológicos,* I (San Salvador: UCA Editores, 2000), 604; reprinted from *Revista latinoamericana de teología* 28 (1993): 8. Posthumous, from an unpublished manuscript dated 1987.

113. Rahner says that the human situation or existential is defined by the fact that we are always confronted by God's self-offer (or grace) and have an unrestricted openness toward that self-offer, which he calls our "obediential potency for listening to an eventual word of God . . . should such a word be spoken. . . ." See Karl Rahner, *Hearer of the Word: Laying the Foundation for a Philosophy of Religion* (New York: Continuum, 1941, 1994), 16.

114. Ellacuría, "Historia de la salvación," 604.

theology . . . can no longer be thought of without Martin Heidegger."[115] Given
the centrality in Rahner's work of the notion of God as the Absolute Mystery
that forms the horizon of our everyday experience, the following words leave
little doubt that Heidegger's influence was profound.

> Surely he has taught us *one thing*: that everywhere and in everything
> we can and must seek out that *unutterable mystery* which *disposes*
> over us, even though we can hardly name it with words. And this we
> must do even if, in his own work and in a way that would be strange
> for a theologian, Heidegger himself abstains from *speech* about this
> mystery, speech which the theologian must *utter*.[116]

Thomas Sheehan draws our attention to an article written by Rahner the
year after the 1939 publication of *Spirit in the World* suggesting how Rahner
understands and utilizes "The Concept of Existential Philosophy in Heidegger."[117]
Zeroing in on Heidegger's signature concept Rahner asserts, "*Dasein* designates
in Heidegger . . . the human being himself, . . . characterized by the fact that . . .
he can ask the question about being, that his is *the connatural transcendence
which orients him toward all being*."[118] While the accuracy of Rahner's interpretation of Heidegger may be contested, what is important for our purposes is that
it demonstrates his tendency to extend Heidegger's claim that *Dasein* must take
a stance on its own being into the claim that human beings must take a stance
on what Rahner sees (through Thomas Aquinas) as their transcendental orientation toward absolute or infinite being. As Sheehan and others have observed,
this conclusion seems to read Martin Heidegger through the eyes of Aquinas![119]

Sheehan suggests that Rahner's interpretation of *Dasein*, then, lays the foundation for what he would later call the "supernatural existential." And indeed,
ten years later Rahner explicitly argues that God's grace has "supernaturally"
elevated the human existential (or *Dasein*), planting the seed of a relentless self-
transcending orientation toward all being, which ultimately leads toward union
with God.[120]

Second, as we have seen, Ellacuría is influenced by Zubiri's appreciative critique of Heidegger. As noted earlier, when Ellacuría arrived in Madrid after
four years in theology with Rahner at Innsbruck (1958-1962), Zubiri had just
finished his most important work, *Sobre la esencia* (1962), and was entering his

115. Karl Rahner, "On Martin Heidegger," in Thomas Sheehan, *Karl Rahner: The Philosophical Foundations* (Athens, OH: Ohio University Press, 1987), xi.

116. Rahner, "On Martin Heidegger," xi-xii.

117. Karl Rahner, "Introduction au concept de philosophie existentiale chez Heidegger," *Recherches de sciences religieuses* 30 (1940): 152-71.

118. Rahner, "The Concept of Existential Philosophy in Heidegger," 131; cited in Sheehan, *Karl Rahner*, 119.

119. Sheehan, *Karl Rahner*, 114.

120. Karl Rahner, "Concerning the Relationship between Nature and Grace," *Theological Investigations*, I (New York: Crossroad, 1961), 297-317.

most productive and creative period. The book presents Zubiri's *formal* definition of reality, which builds on elements of Heidegger's ontology of being and
his concept of *Dasein*, while making substantive changes to reflect progress in
relativity theory, evolutionary biology, and perceptual psychology. The Chilean
philosopher Jorge Eduardo Rivera, who studied with both Heidegger and
Zubiri, argues, "All, or almost all, of what Heidegger says about 'being' or about
'being itself' is captured by Zubiri in the word, 'reality.'"[121] Zubiri insists, however, that his formal approach to the question of "reality" avoids what he calls
Heidegger's substantivation of "being."

During these years in Madrid Zubiri also provided Ellacuría with the concept
of *historical reality*, which more specifically integrates and subordinates what
Heidegger means by *Dasein* within its horizon. The full story of the impact of
Heidegger's concept of *Dasein* on Zubiri's notion of *historical reality* cannot be
elaborated here. Briefly, however, Zubiri's formal concept of reality (or *reity*[122])
attempts to ground aspects of Heidegger's ontology of being in important breakthroughs in science consonant with Heidegger's philosophical claim that being
must not be understood as an existent *thing*. To this end he constructs what
he calls a "strictly intramundane [or world-centered] metaphysics,"[123] which
explains how *Dasein* emerges from the development of matter, biological life,
sentient life, and historical reality as different types of systems comprising the
larger unity of "the cosmos." He asserts that "the final aspect of the dynamism
[of reality] . . . is . . . history," which is "the constitution of a new kind of world,"[124]
and he argues that "reality becomes a world" through its "historical dynamism."
Analogously to *Dasein*, then, historical reality is that reality that must take a
stance on its personal and collective history-in-the-world, and all, or almost all,
of what Heidegger says about *Dasein* is captured by Ellacuría in the concept of
historical reality.

Ellacuría takes this concept somewhat beyond Zubiri, however, with the
assertion that "historical reality" is the proper object of philosophy and theology and by more fully elaborating how historical reality comes to be.[125] And
building on Zubiri's subordination of Heidegger's notion of being (and *Dasein*)
to reality, Ellacuría reinterprets Rahner's *supernatural existential* as a defining
aspect of historical reality, which has been elevated and transformed by God's
historical self-communication (or grace). Thus, while Heidegger always understood *Dasein* as a being-historical structure that cannot be divorced from the
wider horizon of being, the shift from *Dasein* to historical reality clarifies and
emphasizes the notion that changes in the object are inherently public, simultaneously personal and social, and therefore to a certain degree verifiable.

121. Jorge Eduardo Rivera, *Heidegger y Zubiri* (Santiago de Chile: Editorial Universitaria,
S.A & Ediciones Universidad Católica de Chile, 2001), 11.

122. Zubiri, *Inteligencia sentiente*, 57.

123. Zubiri, *Sobre la esencia*, 201, 210.

124. Xavier Zubiri, *La estructura dinámica de la realidad* (Madrid: Alianza Editorial,
1989), 325.

125. Ellacuría, *Filosofía de la realidad histórica*, 42.

This theological interpretation of historical reality allows Ellacuría to move toward a more fully contextualized theological reflection on both the substance and the criteria for discerning God's historical self-communication (or grace) mediated through Medellín's discernment of God's call to a preferential option for the poor. And it provides a powerful theological argument for Miguel Elizondo's insistence during the 1969 Jesuit retreat that the *Spiritual Exercises* were built on the conviction of Ignatius that the Trinity acts "not only by means of the presence and operation of God, but through the insertion of humanity in history."[126] Ellacuría then follows Rahner's trinitarian reading of Thomas's doctrine of emanation and return (*exitus–reditus*) to assert that "creation can be seen as the grafting *ad extra* of the trinitarian life itself."[127] Ellacuría insists this implies that all of reality participates in the divine life and that historical reality (in its personal and social dimensions), which we should note eventually produces the person of Jesus, must be seen as the means for "the *return* of all creation to its original source."[128]

As a result, Ellacuría insists, "Christianity must take very seriously the meaning of the Word made flesh in history. God has revealed himself in history, not directly, but in the sign that is human history. There is no access to God except by means of the sign of history."[129] He says this implies that "action on history, the salvation of social humanity in history, is the true path by which God will ultimately deify humankind. Therefore, it is not just that the *history of salvation* brings with it a *salvation in history*; it is also that the salvation of humankind in history is the only way the history of salvation can reach its conclusion."

Seen in this way, the option for the poor of the 1969 Jesuit retreat opens the path to a new kind of practical mysticism, an encounter with the historical reality of the risen Jesus mediated through the "crucified people" of El Salvador. And the personal transformation of Archbishop Romero brought about by his loving embrace of the terrorized peasants of Aguilares can be seen as validating Ellacuría's soteriological claim from the retreat: "It is not us who must save the poor, rather it is the poor who are going to save us."[130] This affirmation lies at the heart of Ellacuría's claim that Medellín's call to a preferential option for the poor is an invitation to accept God's saving self-communication mediated through the sign of the suffering people of El Salvador.

### From Rahner's Theology of Symbol to a Theology of Sign

This section explores the fourth and final *fundamenta* of Ellacuría's Christian historical realism that I would assert builds on elements from Rahner's fundamental theology. In what follows I will make four points in support of the claim

---

126. Miguel Elizondo, "La Primera Semana como comienzo indispensable de conversión," 3, in "Reunión-Ejercicios," Día 25:3, 48.

127. Ellacuría, "The Historicity of Christian Salvation," 276-77.

128. Ibid.

129. Ellacuría, *Teología política*, 9-10.

130. Ellacuría, "El tercer mundo como lugar óptimo," 4, in "Reunión-Ejercicios," 130.

that Ellacuría's *theology of sign* mimics key theological assertions from Rahner's *theology of symbol* while shifting its philosophical underpinnings and attempting to historicize its meaning for a Latin American context.

First, as discussed above, Rahner's theology of symbol weds his version of the hylomorphic theory with a twofold definition of being (distinguishing *common* and *absolute* being) in creating his theory of *being as symbol* (or *realsymbol*). Rahner's argument begins from the "basic principle" that "all beings are by their nature symbolic, because they necessarily 'express' themselves in order to attain their own nature."[131] Being emanates its form, which "gives itself away" to matter,[132] thereby forming a hylomorphic unity-in-difference of form and matter. Rahner describes the unity of form and matter that results from being's self-expression in its material medium as its *realsymbol*. This allows him to assert that the body is the *realsymbol* of the soul, that Jesus is the *realsymbol* of the Word (John 1:1-18), and that the Logos is the *realsymbol* of the Father. As we saw above, Thomas's doctrine of emanation and return influences Rahner's account of the conversion to the phantasm wherein the agent intellect abstracts the form from the phantasm of sensation, reuniting it with itself by making it known to the intellect.

Rahner's famous article on the theology of symbol limits the scope of his reflection to symbols that embody "the highest and most primordial manner in which one reality can represent another . . . from the ontological point of view." He admits that virtually "anything could be the symbol of anything else," and he concedes that "secondary cases of symbolism do of course exist." But as noted above he rules out forms of representation "which point linguistically and objectively in the same direction: *eidos* [εἶδος], *morphe* [μορφή], sign, figure, expression, image, aspect, appearance, etc." This approach reflects the justified preoccupation he shares with Heidegger of the need to correct the tendency in Western philosophy to reduce the always-receding horizon of "real being" (which Rahner associates with the Mystery of God) to the status of a thing, one more entity among the many that human beings encounter in their everyday world. This concern is reflected in Rahner's stated belief that a wider consideration of symbols "would make it impossible to distinguish really genuine symbols ('symbolic realities') from merely arbitrary 'signs', 'signals' and codes' ('symbolic representations')."[133]

Rahner's intention is to claim that the "fundamental truths of Christianity" are symbolic in nature, such as "the Logos is the image, likeness, reflection, representation, and presence—filled with all the fullness of the Godhead"[134]; "the body is the symbol of the soul, in as much as it is formed as the self-realization of the soul";[135] and "God's salvific action on man . . . takes place in such a way that

---

131. Karl Rahner, "The Theology of the Symbol," *Theological Investigations*, IV (Baltimore, MD: Helicon Press, 1966), 224, 225.

132. Ibid., 231.

133. Ellacuría, "Theology of the Symbol," 225.

134. Rahner, "The Theology of the Symbol," 237.

135. Ibid., 247.

God himself is . . . given to man and grasped by him in the symbol."[136] These are foundational claims that were controversial at the time, and the radically inclusive nature of the category of symbol for ways of talking about images or representations of God remains so. They work together with the various elements of Rahner's "ontology of symbol" to explain how humanity, understood as spirit-in-the world, can become a living symbol of the ever-receding horizon of the Mystery of God. For Rahner, of course, Jesus exemplifies this relationship as the symbol incarnate of the Logos.

Second, Rahner uses his theology of symbol to argue that natural and historical dimensions of reality unfold according to the pattern of the life of the Trinity. Rahner and Karl Barth are renowned in twentieth-century theology for their recovery of the ancient doctrine of the economic Trinity. Rahner formulates this doctrine as follows: "The Trinity in the history of salvation and revelation [the *economic* Trinity] *is* the *immanent* Trinity, because in God's self-communication to his creation through grace and incarnation God really gives himself, and really appears as he is in himself."[137] Thus, Rahner insists that all of our knowledge about God is based on how God has acted in creation and human history (the economic Trinity).[138]

Summarizing Rahner's view of how God exists in God's self (the *immanent* Trinity[139]) Fields writes,

> Unified by emanation and return, Father and Son constitute *the Being* in whom the Son, the Father's Word, perfectly expresses the Father. The Father possesses himself . . . in a relational opposition to the Son. Although the Son is other than the Father, he . . . is thus the Father's medium, emanated by the Father as his perfect image, co-equal in Being with him, yet the other through whom the Father returns to himself.[140]

Thus, Fields says that for Rahner, "In the Incarnation, the man Jesus becomes the Word's self-emanated other. As the human image of the Word, Jesus reflects the Word to the world, which he leads through himself to the Father, the source of the World. The incarnation is thus structured by the emanation and return that defines the Trinity's immanent relations."[141]

Rahner's own words are somewhat clearer when he asserts, "This means that the Logos is the *symbol* of the Father, . . . the *inward* symbol . . . where what is symbolized expresses itself and possesses itself." Yet "because God must express

---

136. Ibid., 245.

137. Karl Rahner, *Foundations of Christian Faith: An Introduction to the Idea of Christianity* (New York: Crossroad, 1978) 136.

138. Ibid.

139. See the definition of the "immanent" and the "economic" Trinity in Rahner and Vorgrimler, *Theological Dictionary*, 471.

140. Fields, *Being as Symbol*, 8.

141. Ibid., 8-9.

himself inwardly . . . he can also express himself *outwardly*," so that "the finite, created utterance *ad extra* is a continuation of the immanent constitution of 'image and likeness' [which] . . . takes place in fact *through* the Logos (John 1:3)."[142] This affirmation, then, amounts to the claim that creation is a dimension of the external expression (and thus a symbol) of the inner life of the Trinity. Rahner is careful to conclude by affirming "revelation as the starting-point" of his theology of symbol, which is clarified by philosophy but "is not capable of proof by purely philosophical arguments."[143]

Third, while Ellacuría's *theology of sign* borrows theological assertions from Rahner's *theology of symbol*, it offers different underpinnings from his philosophy of historical reality while attempting to historicize its claims in a Latin American context.[144] Accordingly, Ellacuría's theology of sign does not ask how Being returns to itself by knowing its self-emanated form in its material medium. Rather, he asks how the self-transcending power of the personal and social dimensions of historical reality (dynamics that can be observed and measured by the natural and human sciences) can function as a sign for God. Similarly, Ellacuría claims that "God revealed himself in history, not directly, but in a sign: . . . the humanity of Jesus,"[145] which readers will recognize as a version of Rahner's famous assertion from his theology of symbol that "the incarnate word is the absolute symbol of God in the world."[146] Thus, Ellacuría wants to historicize Rahner's reference to the "incarnate word" as a reference to the historical reality of Jesus, and he shifts the emphasis from symbol to *sign* in order to develop a theology of the signs of the times for Latin America.[147]

Accordingly, Ellacuría's theology of sign works hard to historicize its terms. (1) Reflecting his focus on historical reality as the proper object of philosophy and theology,[148] Ellacuría asserts that the "sign, by its very nature, should be something visible and verifiable."[149] (2) Utilizing conventional terms found in the semiotics of C.S. Peirce and others,[150] he says "the sign should, by its nature, refer to something that is both in relation to the sign, but which is not

---

142. Rahner, "The Theology of the Symbol," 236-37.

143. Ibid.; see note on 229-30.

144. Ellacuría's theology of *sign* is most fully articulated in *Freedom Made Flesh*.

145. Ellacuría, *Teología política*, 9; *Freedom Made Flesh*, 18.

146. Rahner, "The Theology of the Symbol," 237. The argument of this section is developed more fully in Robert Lassalle-Klein, "Rethinking Rahner on Grace and Symbol," 93-96.

147. Martin Maier contends that Ellacuría develops a theology of the signs of the times in response to the Council's mandate in *Gaudium et spes* to read the signs of the times and interpret them in light of the gospel. See Maier, "Karl Rahner: The Teacher of Ignacio Ellacuría," 135-37.

148. Ellacuría, *Filosofía de la realidad histórica*, 42.

149. Ignacio Ellacuría, "Iglesia y realidad histórica" *Escritos teológicos*, II (San Salvador: UCA Editores, 2000), 505; reprinted from *ECA* no. 331 (1976): 213-20.

150. For Peirce, see *Collected Papers of Charles Sanders Peirce*, vol. II, *Elements of Logic*, ed. Charles Hartshorne and Paul Weiss (Cambridge, MA: Harvard University Press, 1932), 2.22, 2.299, 2.247.

the sign itself," and "the sign does not have to resemble what it signifies" since "its effectiveness lies in transmitting the message." (3) Following Rahner's use of symbol to address the problem of nature and grace, Ellacuría asserts that "the sign is nothing but an active mediation between two extremes" or two distinct orders of reality "whose connection cannot be immediate." Then historicizing this claim, Ellacuría argues that in order to be "a sign . . . of the God who has revealed himself in history,"[151] the Salvadoran church must operationalize its preferential option for the poor through prophetic denunciations of state-sponsored violence against peasants and civil society.

Ellacuría's point is that it is only by taking real historical actions with real risks that the church will become a living sign of the Word of God as it was discerned by the Latin American bishops at Medellín. In 1973 he writes,

> God and humanity do not become one unless it occurs through a historical process that is salvation history; and the presence of God among humanity gains visibility and efficacy through a salvation history that is, in some way, a salvation of history. Thus, if the Church is capable of historically constituting itself in its historical activity as a historical sign of the presence of the reign of God among humanity, its apparent dualism will be overcome: its theologal and its historical aspects, without being identified, will be seen united.[152]

Then in 1981 Ellacuría further historicizes Medellín's discernment with the startling claim that the "principal" sign of the times "by whose light the others should be discerned and interpreted" is "the historically crucified people."[153] And he insists that this metaphor for Medellín's option for the poor places a claim on the Latin American church and all followers of Jesus. This was the challenge faced by the Central American Jesuits at the 1969 retreat, and their "yes" is what he believes opens the door to a historical encounter with the God of the poor. For in Ellacuría's historicized theology of sign,

> The oppressed are already in themselves the sacrament of Christ, the historical body of Christ, the history of his crucified divinity. They are the place where one should focus one's contemplation, but not treating them simply as an object of contemplation, but as a reality that captivates and obligates one to partake of their historical journey and their personal problems. They require an immersion in what they are and what they do.[154]

151. Ellacuría, *Teología política*, 48; *Freedom Made Flesh*, 89.

152. Ibid.

153. Ellacuría, "Discernir *el signo* de los tiempos," *Escritos teológicos*, II (San Salvador: UCA Editores, 2000), 134.

154. Ignacio Ellacuría, "Fe y justicia," *Escritos teológicos*, III (San Salvador: UCA Editores, 2002), 367.

As we will see in the next chapter Jon Sobrino and Ellacuría can be described as theological collaborators in a shared attempt to show how followers of Jesus are drawn into a mystical historical analogy between the life, death, and resurrection of Jesus Christ and the struggles of the crucified people to believe and to survive the "world of poverty . . . today."[155] The Greek Fathers describe this dynamic as *theōsis*, which Ellacuría and Sobrino apply to the option for the poor where the disciple is drawn into a transformative encounter with the divine mystery of the inner life of God. Building on the action-centered mysticism of the *Spiritual Exercises* of St. Ignatius, Rahner's recovery of the economic Trinity, and Augustine's contributions to Christian semiotics, the two Jesuits foster a theological interpretation of the crucified people as a sign of the salvation brought by Jesus.

Fourth and finally, I would argue that commentators have not sufficiently emphasized the significance of the fact that Ellacuría frames his entire theological project as a "theology of sign,"[156] his own development of Rahner's theology of symbol. In an unpublished letter Ellacuría insists that his work cannot be properly understood apart from the Rahnerian "theology of sign" that frames it.[157] Written a year after the 1973 publication of *Teología política* this letter successfully defends his book against criticisms expressed in writing by the office of the apostolic nuncio in San Salvador. Ellacuría argues that the unnamed reviewer "ignores and passes over what is essential in my work: salvation in history is a sign of the plenitude of a salvation that is meta-historical." Then, to remove any doubt, he adds the remarkable assertion,

> Not to have understood this theology of sign, which dominates the entire publication . . . presupposes a serious lack of depth in the interpretation and the evaluation of my work. Everything that is presented as salvation in history . . . is regarded as a sign of the history of salvation. It comes from that, and it moves toward that. My work tries to demonstrate the connection between the sign and what constitutes it as a sign.[158]

These words should draw the attention of interpreters to the many signs that framed the rest of Ellacuría's theological career and the unifying importance he assigns to this Rahnerian framework. In 1969, Ellacuría exhorts his fellow Central American Jesuits to embrace Medellín's call to serve the poor as Jesus did, saying, "The Province should be the efficacious sign of [the] Christ experi-

---

155. Jon Sobrino, *Christ the Liberator: A View from the Victims* (Maryknoll, NY: Orbis Books, 2001), 3-8, 4. See also Jon Sobrino, *Jesus the Liberator: A Historical-Theological View* (Maryknoll, NY: Orbis Books, 1993), 254-73.

156. Ellacuría, *Teología política*, 9-10, 44-69; *Freedom Made Flesh*, 15-18, 82-126.

157. Ignacio Ellacuría, "Respuesta crítica a 'Nota sobre la publicación *Teología política* del Reverendo Padre Ignacio Ellacuría, S.J.'" (San Salvador: Archivos Ignacio Ellacuría, April 24, 1974).

158. Ellacuría, "Repuesta crítica," 6-7.

enced in the [*Spiritual*] *Exercises* [of St. Ignatius]."[159] He asserts that Medellín is calling the church in Latin America to become a "sacramental" and "mediating sign"[160] of the ongoing presence of Jesus Christ to the "crucified peoples" of today.[161] And he famously argues that the principle sign of the times "by whose light all the others should be discerned and interpreted . . . is . . . the crucified people."[162] Jon Sobrino has said that this final asssertion placed such a powerful claim on Ellacuría that he came to believe "the foundation of his life, his vocation as a Jesuit, and deeper still, as a human being" was "to take the crucified people down from the cross."[163]

I have argued, then, that Ellacuría's *theology of sign* mimics aspects of Rahner's *theology of symbol* while reframing its underpinnings in terms of his philosophy of historical reality and historicizing its claims for a Latin American context. He will ask for historical signs to verify the truth claims associated with theologies of grace; he will build on conventional semiotic theory; and he will focus on the self-transcending power of historical reality and hope as a sign for God. But there is no denying the Rahnerian character of Ellacuría's theology of sign and its pervasive influence on his life and work. This is captured in the hope-filled historical realism of Ellacuría's Rahnerian claim that "salvation history tells us the fundamental sign of God is history itself, though not all history [especially the history of sin] in the same way."[164]

159. Ellacuría, "El problema del traslado del Espíritu de los Ejercicios a la vice-provincia," 6, in "Reunión-Ejercicios," 109.

160. Ellacuría, *Teología política*, 47-48; *Freedom Made Flesh*, 87-89; and Ignacio Ellacuría, "Fe y justicia," 317.

161. Ignacio Ellacuría, "El pueblo crucificado, ensayo de soteriología histórica," *Escritos teológicos,* II (San Salvador: UCA Editores, 2000), 137-70. Ellacuría makes analogous claims regarding "Latin American theology," the "Christian University" and its graduates, Archbishop Oscar Romero, Latin American philosophy, the "Abrahamic religions," those who "seek truth," advocates of human rights, etc. See Ignacio Ellacuría, "Hacia una fundamentación del método teológico latinoamericano," *Escritos teológicos,* I (San Salvador: UCA Editores, 2000), 187-218; "Tesis sobre la posibilidad, necesidad y sentido de una teología latinoamericana," in A. Vargas Machuca, ed., *Teología y mundo contemporáneo: homenaje a Karl Rahner en su 70 cumpleaños* (Madrid: Ediciones Cristiandad, 1975), 325-50; "Diez años después; es posible una universidad distinta?" *ECA* nos. 324-325 (1975): 605-628; "La inspiración Cristiana de la UCA en la docencia," *Planteamiento universitario 1989* (San Salvador: Universidad Centroamericana José Simeón Canas, February 1989): 195-200; "Monseñor Romero, un enviado de Dios para salvar a su pueblo," *Sal Terrae* 811 (1980): 825-32, and *ECA* 19 (1990): 5-10; "Función liberadora de la filosofía," *ECA* no. 435 (1985): 45-64; "Aporte de la teología de la liberación a las religiones Abráhamicas en la superación del individualismo y del positivismo," *Revista latinoamericana de teología* 10 (1987): 3-27; "Voluntad de fundamentalidad y voluntad de verdad," 113-32; "Human Rights in a Divided Society," in A. Hennelly and J. Langan, eds., *Human Rights in the Americas: The Struggle for Consensus* (Washington, DC: Georgetown University Press, 1982), 52-65.

162. Ellacuría, "Discernir *el signo* de los tiempos," 134.

163. Jon Sobrino, "Ignacio Ellacuría, el hombre y el cristiano," 240; "Ignacio Ellacuría, the Human Being and the Christian," 5.

164. Ignacio Ellacuría, *Teología política*, 47; *Freedom Made Flesh*, 88.

## Conclusion

In conclusion, then, I have examined Karl Rahner's contributions to both the *philosophical-theological* and the strictly *theological fundamenta* developed by Ignacio Ellacuría to interpret the human face of God revealed by Archbishop Romero in the suffering people of El Salvador. I argued first that Ellacuría insists that *historical reality* is the proper object of a truly Latin American theology and that human beings apprehend an absolute (or *theologal*) dimension of reality. I also examined how this claim builds on key insights from Rahner's metaphysics of being as well as Zubiri's post-Newtonian realism and his assertion of the primacy of reality over being. Second, I said that Ellacuría uses Zubiri's *model of sentient intelligence in order to conceptualize the role of human knowing in Latin American theological method*. Here I asserted that Ellacuría's account mimics aspects of the role of the hylomorphic theory and the agent intellect in Rahner's transcendental Thomism while using what I argued is a more scientifically accurate account of human intellection and perception. Third, I said that Ellacuría develops a theological anthropology rooted in the notion that *historical reality has been transformed by grace*, which draws upon and historicizes aspects of Rahner's concept of the supernatural existential. And fourth, I argued that Ellacuría develops a *theology of sign* that echoes the trinitarian pattern of Rahner's theology of symbol in support of the historicized claim that the crucified people are the defining sign of the times.

Finally, I suggested that Ellacuría's concepts of historical reality and sentient intelligence serve as *philosophical-theological fundamenta* and that his historicized theologies of grace and sign serve as *strictly theological fundamenta* for what I have called Ellacuría's Christian historical realism. Each of these points might have had its own chapter but this would have taken us astray. For my goal has been simply to offer a critical appraisal of their contributions to the claim of Jon Sobrino and Ignacio Ellacuría that Christian disciples are drawn into the paschal mystery of the life, death, and resurrection of Jesus when, like Oscar Romero, they are moved by compassion and solidarity to take the "crucified peoples" of the globe down from the cross. This is the subject of Part III.

# Part III

# *Bearing the Spirit to a Suffering World*

## THE CONTEXTUAL CHRISTOLOGY OF JON SOBRINO AND IGNACIO ELLACURÍA

### Introduction

How, then, do Ignacio Ellacuría and Jon Sobrino make sense from the perspective of faith in Jesus Christ of the suffering, death, and apparent defeat of the hopes and aspirations for liberation and life of so many Salvadorans and the people who loved them, including Archbishop Oscar Romero and his followers? The answer is to be found in the image of the crucified people and the notion that followers of Jesus are called to take them down from the cross, which emerged from Romero's homily to the terrorized peasants of Aguilares after the assassination of Rutilio Grande. In the following chapters I will show how the contextualized Christology of Jon Sobrino and Ignacio Ellacuría gives voice to the faith, hope, and love of the University of Central America (UCA) martyrs and what Sobrino calls the church of the poor. It is a theology that faces up to the common ruin that humanity continues to bring upon itself while at the same time showing how the life, death, and resurrection of Jesus open the way to a view of salvation history as a salvation-in-history.

In Part I, I explored the historical reality of the UCA martyrs, Archbishop Oscar Romero, and the Salvadoran people while tracing the birth of a new kind of Christian university. I argued that Ellacuría and his colleagues (both Jesuits and others) were among the first to appreciate the political significance of the mobilization in civil society of El Salvador's *third forces* thanks, in part, to a spirituality disposed to recognize God's grace and the face of Christ in the poor and their struggles for liberation from military rule and oppression. I examined how Ellacuría, Archbishop Romero, and their friends began to speak evocatively of *the crucified people* of El Salvador in their homilies and theological writings. And I showed how they historicized this spirituality by supporting the glimmers of hope and social reform emerging in El Salvador during the 1970s and 1980s and by denouncing state-sponsored repression intended to frustrate the call for reform.

In Part II, I explained how Ellacuría's encounter with God in the historical reality of El Salvador as embodied in Medellín's call for a preferential option for the poor led Ellacuría to reinterpret his sources in developing a Latin American fundamental theology able to make sense of the transformative experiences described above. These sources included (among others) the *Spiritual Exercises* of St. Ignatius; the philosophy of Xavier Zubiri; the fundamental theology of Karl Rahner; and, most importantly, the faith and spirituality of Archbishop Oscar Romero, emblemized in his love and support for El Salvador's suffering peasants. We saw that Ellacuría's critical and creative appropriation of these sources was epitomized in the notion, inspired by Archbishop Romero, that the mission of the Christian university and his own vocation as a human being, a Christian, and a Jesuit was to help take the crucified people of El Salvador down from the cross.

In Part III, I will explore key elements of the contextual Christology developed by Sobrino and Ellacuría in reflecting theologically on the ecclesial praxis of the Salvadoran church as a community of faith in solidarity with the poor. I have argued elsewhere that the fundamental theology of Ignacio Ellacuría and the allied Christology of Jon Sobrino form what may be the most fully developed contextual theology written since Vatican II.[1] This remarkable collaboration reflects epoch-shaping events in Latin America and the Catholic Church in El Salvador as well as long years of Jesuit friendship, shared ministry, persecution, and finally martyrdom. The Christology produced by these Jesuit "companions of Jesus"[2] is unified by its shared conviction that (1) the historical

---

1. This argument appears in Robert Lassalle-Klein, "Jesus of Galilee and the Crucified People: Contextual Christology of Jon Sobrino Ignacio Ellacuría," with Virgilio Elizondo and Gustavo Gutiérrez, eds., special issue, "The Galilean Jesus," *Theological Studies* 70, no. 2 (Spring 2009): 347-376, esp. 347. Note that the English titles of the Orbis Books editions of Jon Sobrino's two-volume Christology (which is the focus of much of this article) are mistranslated from the Spanish, casting them in the model of Edward Schillebeeckx's two volumes, *Jesus* and *Christ*, which obscures the focus of *both* volumes on Jesus Christ. *Jesucristo liberador: Lectura histórica-teológica de Jesús de Nazaret* (San Salvador: UCA, 1991) becomes *Jesus the Liberator: A Historical-Theological View* (Maryknoll, NY: Orbis Books, 1993); and *La fe en Jesucristo: Ensayo desde las víctimas* (San Salvador: UCA, 1999) becomes *Christ the Liberator: A View from the Victims* (Maryknoll, NY: Orbis Books, 2001). Where I translate directly from the Spanish rather than quote the English, the Spanish version is cited first, followed by the English. It should be noted that the voluminous writings of Ignacio Ellacuría and Jon Sobrino cover many topics other than fundamental theology and Christology in considerable depth.

2. Ignatius Loyola named the order he founded on August 15, 1534 (officially approved September 27, 1540, by Paul III), *La Compañia de Jesús*, and referred to its members as "companions of Jesus." The spirituality and the mystical theology of Ignatius embodied in the order's name find expression in the idea of Ellacuría and Sobrino that followers of Jesus are called not only to share the burden of his cross but also to take the crucified people down from the cross. This metaphor echoes the famous opening words of the 32nd General Congregation of the Society of Jesus (December 2, 1974, to March 7, 1975), partially inspired by a *postulatum* on justice submitted by the Central American Jesuits: "What is it to be a Jesuit? It is to know that one is a sinner, yet called to be a companion of Jesus as Ignatius was: Ignatius, who begged the Blessed Virgin to 'place him with her Son,' and who then saw

reality of Jesus, which brings joy and salvation, is the real sign of the Word made flesh; and (2) the *analogatum princeps* (primary analogue) of the life, death, and resurrection of Jesus of Nazareth is to be found today among the crucified peoples who are victims of poverty, inequality, structural injustice, and violence around the globe.

Sobrino summarizes the central themes associated with this claim in an evocative passage on Galilee written not long after the assassination of Ella-curía, his five Jesuit colleagues, and two lay coworkers on November 16, 1989.

> Galilee is the setting of Jesus' historical life, the place of the poor and the little ones. The poor of this world—the Galilee of today— are where we encounter the historical Jesus and where he is encoun- tered as liberator. And this Galilee is also where the risen Christ who appears to his disciples will show himself as he really is, as the Jesus we have to follow and keep present in history: the historical Jesus, the man from Nazareth, the person who was merciful and faithful to his death on the cross, the perennial sacrament in this world of a liberator God.[3]

This analogy embodies Sobrino's response to Vatican II's mandate "of read- ing the signs of the times and of interpreting them in light of the gospel"[4] in his two hope-filled volumes on the meaning of Jesus' ministry, resurrection, the sending of the Spirit, and his call to faith-filled discipleship. Methodologically, the analogy reflects forty years of living with the "preferential option for the poor" and the struggle for liberation it implies discerned by Latin American bishops shortly after Vatican II as God's will for the church, and places that discernment in a hermeneutical circle with the life, death, and resurrection of Jesus Christ.[5] Substantively, as noted earlier, the analogy reflects Sobrino's

---

the Father himself ask Jesus, carrying his Cross, to take this pilgrim into his company. What is it to be a companion of Jesus today? It is to engage, under the standard of the Cross, in the crucial struggle of our time: the struggle for faith and that struggle for justice which it includes" (Society of Jesus, "Jesuits Today" nos. 1 and 2, Decree 1, *Documents of the 31st and 32nd General Congregations of the Society of* Jesus (St. Louis: Institute of Jesuit Sources, 1977), 401.

3. Sobrino, *Jesus the Liberator,* 273.

4. *Gaudium et spes* §4, *Vatican Council II,* ed. Austin Flannery, O.P. (Northport, NY: Costello, 1975).

5. It is essential to evaluate the legitimacy and adequacy of Sobrino's methodological presuppositions in terms of the hermeneutical circle he seeks to create between the option for the poor of the contemporary church and the church's normative tradition regarding Jesus Christ. Sobrino asserts, "Latin American Christology . . . identifies its setting, in the sense of a real situation, as the poor of this world, and this situation is what must be present in and permeate any particular setting in which Christology is done" (Sobrino, *Christ the Liberator,* 28). Noted American Christologist William Loewe argues that Sobrino's Christology "admirably" represents the kind of theological reflection approved in *Libertatis conscientia,* claiming that, "while he insists on the church of the poor as the ecclesial setting of his theology, what is received in that setting as the foundation of his theology is the apostolic faith of the church" (William Loewe, "Interpreting the Notification: Christological Issues," in Stephen J.

claim that "I have done nothing more than—starting from Jesus—to elevate the reality we are living to the level of a theological concept, to theorize about a christological faith that we see as real faith."[6] And finally, as an icon of Christian discipleship, it reflects the influence on the Jesuits of El Salvador of Archbishop Romero as a model of Medellín's discernment and its confirmation in the 1969 Jesuit retreat that God was calling the Latin American church to a preferential option for the poor.

But what is the significance, if any, for 'Christians and non-Christians far removed from El Salvador of the analogy drawn by Sobrino and Ellacuría between the historical reality of Jesus Christ and the crucified peoples of today? Surely there are many crucified peoples around the planet, though most do not believe in Jesus Christ, and fewer still know much about El Salvador. In the following chapters I will discuss two elements of the approach to Jesus Christ developed by Sobrino and Ellacuría that I believe have the potential to both reshape Christian spirituality, theology, ethics, biblical studies, ecclesiology, and education, and to reposition Christian approaches to interreligious dialogue in the years ahead. First, Ignacio Ellacuría develops a profound Christian historical realism (and a corresponding theological historical realism) that is both intellectually rigorous and honest, and perfectly suited to preparing Christians to participate in the challenge of formulating a global ethic for a diverse and polarized world. And second, Sobrino integrates these concepts into a contextualized Latin American "saving history" Christology, which prepares Christians to enter intercultural and interreligious dialogue by starting "from below" with the historical reality of Jesus Christ.

In what follows, then, I will show how Ellacuría's Christian historical realism and Sobrino's "saving history" Christology are woven together in support of the claim that not only Christian disciples but all people are drawn into the paschal mystery of the life, death, and resurrection of Jesus when, like Oscar Romero, they are moved by compassion and solidarity to take the crucified peoples of the globe down from the cross.

---

Pope, ed., *Hope and Solidarity: Sobrino's Challenge to Christian Theology* [Maryknoll, NY: Orbis Books, 2008]), 143-52, at 146.

6. Sobrino, *Jesucristo liberador* 30, my translation. See Sobrino, *Jesus the Liberator*, 8.

# 8

# *Mysterium Liberationis*

## The Christian Historical Realism
## of Ignacio Ellacuría

What, then, are the key elements of Ignacio Ellacuría's Christian historical realism, and how do they frame Sobrino's christological understanding of the life, death, and resurrection of Jesus Christ and its significance for the crucified people of Latin America? In the last part I summarized the contributions of the *Spiritual Exercises* of St. Ignatius, Archbishop Romero, the philosophy of Xavier Zubiri, and the fundamental theology of Karl Rahner, S.J., as sources for Ellacuría's Latin American approach to theology. I said first that Ellacuría saw the 1969 option for the poor by the Central American Jesuits as historicizing the spirit of Medellín and the Christ of the San Salvador retreat in an apostolic plan that allowed them to collaborate with the ongoing work of the Trinity in the world.

Second, I suggested Archbishop Romero taught Ellacuría to love the common people of El Salvador, to trust them, to see Christ in them, and to discover his prophetic vocation to help take this crucified people down from the cross. Third, I asserted that Zubiri provided Ellacuría with a post-Newtonian concept of reality and a philosophical model for the emergence and operation of sentient intelligence that is consistent with recent neuroscientific research on the brain and human perception. And fourth, I examined the influence of Rahner and these other facts on four philosophical and theological *fundamenta* of Ellacuría's Latin American approach to theology. These were (1) historical reality as the primary object of theological reflection; (2) sentient intelligence as fundamental to an adequate theory of knowing; (3) a historicized theology of grace and sin; and (4) a theology of sign capable of interpreting the historicity of God's ongoing self-revelation and the signs of the times for Latin America. But what issue are these elements designed to address and how do they help to frame the contextual Christology of Jon Sobrino?

### Introduction: Liberation and the Historicity of Salvation

While the question of what drives Ellacuría's overall project is too complex to resolve here, it bears noting that the opening line of his first book, *Teología política* (1973), asserts, "One of the fundamental themes in contemporary theology, without which the other themes in theology gain neither their full precision nor meaning, is the historicity of salvation."[1] Similarly, the first line of his longest article on the subject, written a decade later (1984), again asserts, "The problem of the historicity of Christian salvation continues to be the most serious problem for the understanding and practice of the faith."[2] He proposes, therefore, "to rethink the classical problem of *the relationship between Christian salvation*, which would seem to be what formally defines the mission of the church and of Christians as Christians, *and historical liberation*, which would seem to be what formally defines the mission of states, social classes, citizens, and humans as human."[3] Here, then, is an overarching concern that we can safely say runs through Ellacuría's entire theological project and also plays a key role in shaping Sobrino's christological project.

This preoccupation with the historicity of salvation and liberation informs the title chosen by Ellacuría and Sobrino for their two-volume mini-summa, *Mysterium liberationis*, which summarizes the "fundamental concepts of liberation theology."[4] Jon Sobrino says the title was chosen as a twist on the important post-conciliar series *Mysterium salutis* (mystery of salvation). He recalls, "Ellacuría and I chose the title *Mysterium liberationis* because the contents and purpose of the project had to do with liberation" and in order to emphasize "liberation as a principal reality that theology must address."[5] Thus, they used the word *liberation* to interpret the Christian doctrine of *salvation*, thereby suggesting that salvation is being historicized by what Gustavo Gutiérrez calls the "irruption of the poor" and by the response of the Latin American church to Medellín's call to attend to "deafening cry [that] pours from the throats of millions of men and women asking their pastors for a liberation that reaches them from nowhere else."[6] Moreover, by combining *liberation* with *mystery* in the pattern of *mysterium salutis* the title points to the struggle of the poor for dignity and justice as a privileged medium for the human encounter with the Mystery of God. This foreshadows the argument of their work in Christology outlined below that the hopes and struggles of Latin America's poor majorities for liberation and life comprise a privileged *locus theologicus* and historical sign

---

1. Ignacio Ellacuría, *Teología política* (San Salvador: Ediciónes del Secretariado Sociál Interdiocesano, 1973), 1 (trans. by John Drury as *Freedom Made Flesh: The Mission of Christ and His Church* [Maryknoll, NY: Orbis Books, 1976]).

2. Ignacio Ellacuría, "Historicidad de la salvación cristiana," *Escritos teológicos*, I (San Salvador: UCA Editores, 2000), 535.

3. Ibid., my emphasis.

4. Ignacio Ellacuría and Jon Sobrino, *Mysterium liberationis, Conceptos fundamentales de la teología de la liberación*, vols. I and II (San Salvador: UCA Editores, 1990).

5. Jon Sobrino, personal correspondence with Robert Lassalle-Klein (September, 17, 2013), transcript in personal files of the author.

6. Second General Conference of Latin American Bishops, "Document on Poverty in the Church," section 2, in *The Church in the Present-Day Transformation of Latin America in the Light of the Council: II Conclusions* (Washington, DC: Division for Latin America–United States Catholic Conference, 1973).

of the salvation announced by Jesus Christ and the saving encounter with the Mystery of God in human history.

In the following section, then, I will briefly summarize four important claims regarding the historicity of Christian salvation that shape Ellacuría's treatment with Jon Sobrino of the crucified people as part of the saving mystery of Jesus Christ. First, Ellacuría asserts that history and salvation comprise two aspects of a larger unity that he describes as the great history of God. Second, he argues that salvation history is a salvation in history. Third, he argues that the historical reality of Jesus of Nazareth is the defining sign of the Word made flesh and must be the starting point for Latin American Christology. And fourth, he proposes what he calls a historical soteriology that draws an analogy between the saving historical reality of the crucified Jesus and the crucified people as victims of sin of the world and the bearers of its salvation.

### History and Salvation: Two Aspects of a Larger Whole

Ellacuría's treatment of the historicity of salvation is shaped by his critique of Western idealism and what he sees as distortions of Aristotle rooted in the metaphysics and epistemologies of Plato and Parmenides, summarized in Chapter 4.[7] Ellacuría asserts that this strain of Greek philosophy, which has been very influential in Christian theology, has produced "a continuing prejudice that salvation is ahistorical." As we saw earlier, this critique leads Ellacuría to not only criticize (following Rahner) the tendency of neoscholastic theology to overemphasize the distinction between salvation history and profane or human history, but to explicitly reject the terms of the argument. Instead, he insists (following Gustavo Gutiérrez) there can be only one history, "the great history of God,"[8] which he defines as "what God has done with all of nature, what God does in human history, and what God wants to happen as a result from his ongoing self-giving, which can be imagined as passing from eternity to eternity."

Emblematic of the theological dualisms undermining the unity of history in the West Ellacuría notes that "for centuries, due to a Greek philosophical mentality that is alien to the orientation of the Bible, the relationship of the supernatural to the natural has been a fundamental theme in theology."[9] He says, on the one hand, the *supernatural* was understood to encompass themes related to "the trinitarian God revealed by grace," while on the other, the natural was understood to comprise treatises on human persons "as they appeared to be" in themselves. Ellacuría insists this formulation "must be superseded," which he does by addressing the relationship of divinity and humanity in the context of the "more encompassing" horizon of history and transcendence.

---

7. Ellacuría, *Teología política*, 6; *Freedom Made Flesh*, 11.

8. Ellacuría, "Historicidad de la salvación cristiana," 570; "The Historicity of Christian Salvation," in Michael Lee, ed., *Ignacio Ellacuría: Essays on History, Liberation, and Salvation* (Maryknoll, NY: Orbis Books, 2013), 146.

9. Ellacuría, *Teología política*, 1; *Freedom Made Flesh*, 3.

### *Transcendence in History*

Ellacuría traces the Western lineage of a series of dichotomies (sacred vs. profane, salvation history vs. human history, natural vs. supernatural, etc.) to "pernicious philosophical influences" that equate transcendence with "separateness," and insist "historical transcendence is separate from history."[10] These philosophies are united, in his view, by their belief that "the transcendent must be outside or beyond what is immediately apprehended as real." For them, the transcendent is always "other, different, . . . separated . . . in time, . . . space, or . . . essence" from historical objects. The problem with this approach, however, is that it "tends to make humanity and God extrinsic to each other" with the result that "the problem of salvation history is launched down a dead-end street: two realities fundamentally extrinsic to each other, with each one closed in upon itself . . . so that they cannot coincide in one and the same salvation."[11]

Ellacuría insists, however, that "there is a radically different way of understanding transcendence, more in line with the way reality and God's action are presented in biblical thinking."[12] He says, "This is to see transcendence as something that transcends *in* and not as something that transcends *away from*; as something that physically impels to *more* but not by taking *out of*; something that pushes forward, but at the same time retains." The cash value of this approach for a theological understanding of salvation history is that "when one reaches God historically . . . one does not abandon the human, does not abandon real history, but rather deepens one's roots, making more present and effective what was already effectively present."

Drawing on this understanding of history and transcendence Ellacuría then makes the startling assertion, as noted earlier, that "God can be separated from history, but history cannot be separated from God. . . . Sin does not make God disappear, but rather crucifies God."[13] Thus, "It may be possible to divide history into a history of sin and another of grace, but that division presupposes the real unity of history, and the real and indissoluble unity of God and of the human being in history."[14] The idea here is that, from the perspective of Ellacuría's Christian historical realism, no matter how much one might deny the idea of God, in the end the saving presence of God continues to permeate historical reality.

On the one hand, then, the radical denial of the historical reality of God has real implications: the crucifixion of God and God's messengers by their opponents. On the other, however, it is precisely the solidarity of Jesus and the martyrs—who accept crucifixion as the price of love and solidarity and look toward

---

10. Ellacuría, "Historicidad de la salvación cristiana," 542; "The Historicity of Christian Salvation," 142.

11. Ellacuría, *Teología política*, 6; *Freedom Made Flesh*, 12.

12. Ellacuría, "Historicidad de la salvación cristiana," 542; "The Historicity of Christian Salvation," 142.

13. Ibid.

14. Ibid.

the resurrection in hope—that reveals them as historical signs of transcendence and hope. Thus, Ellacuría refuses cosmic dualisms as the final explanation for the inhumanity of sin, asserting instead that the fundamental historical conflict is not between history and transcendence or between nature and grace, but rather between sin and grace. His profound Christian historical realism is embodied in the notion that there is only one history, the great history of God. And though it is clouded by conflict between the saving acceptance of God's self offer (grace) and its rejection in sin, the great history of God and the world that emerges there comprise the one and only place wherein the self-transcending story of human sin and salvation can unfold. As a result, Ellacuría's approach to Christology will turn on the conviction that humanity bears responsibility for the crucified people of this world and that God's historical self-offer and the Reign of God are mediated to us through the invitation to take them down from the cross.

## Salvation History Is a Salvation in History

But how does this notion that history and salvation are part of the larger history of God shape Ellacuría's understanding of the historicity of salvation? In his longest and most sustained theological work Ellacuría responds that "salvation history is a salvation in history," which he says "is the theme of this entire book."[15] In this section, then, I will first summarize Ellacuría's careful analysis of the unity-in-distinction that he insists theology must recognize in the key concepts underlying this assertion (*salvation, salvation history*, and *salvation in history*), and I will explain the importance of these distinctions for what he calls *historical soteriology* when he claims that the crucified people are the bearers of salvation and an ongoing historical sign of God's self-offer in Jesus of Nazareth. Second, I will briefly summarize what these terms contribute to Ellacuría's argument that salvation history is a salvation in history.

### *Defining the Terms*

The influence of Karl Rahner and the post-conciliar break with neoscholastic theology can be seen in the care with which Ellacuría defines his terms and the emphasis he places on the unity-in-distinction of their meanings. This is the context for Sobrino's revelation (noted above) that the title of *Mysterium liberationis*, their collection on the mystery of liberation, was chosen as an explicit allusion to a famous post-conciliar series on the mystery of salvation. *Mysterium salutis* was an ambitious attempt by leading theologians after Vatican II to create a decisive break from pre-conciliar neoscholastic textbook theology through the publication between 1967 and 1976 of a multi-volume work reframing Catholic theology in terms of salvation history. Karl Rahner's contribution played a defining role in this project, and the claim of Ellacuría and Sobrino

---

15. Ellacuría, *Teología politica*, 8; *Freedom Made Flesh*, 15.

that liberation historicizes the mystery of salvation (captured in the title *Mysterium liberationis*) advances its core concern. Only three volumes of *Mysterium salutis* were published in English, but two of them, Rahner's treatise on the *Trinity* and *Mysterium paschale* by Hans Urs von Balthasar, came to be viewed as classics.[16] As we saw above, Ellacuría was a former student of Rahner, and his theological *fundamenta* are built upon and historicize Rahner's trinitarian theology of symbol and his theology of grace. The significance of Rahner's distinctions between salvation, salvation history, and soteriology for his treatments of the Trinity and grace is, therefore, relevant to our discussion.

Rahner argues that while *salvation* is "a basic concept of religion and theology," it is "not really a technical term of theology" since it signifies "a *subjective*, existential healing and fulfillment" that "is not yet given in this transient world by any objective redemption, [or] any grace of any Church, as constant human experience proves."[17] Rahner's point is that "salvation remains the essential object of hope," which, though it has a history, must never be thought of as having been fulfilled in this lifetime and, thereby, serves "to expose the common ruin in which the one human race is involved by man's own doing." He concludes, therefore, that "the concept of salvation should not be identified with grace but should retain that note of conclusiveness" that places it beyond history. Paradoxically, he says this "opens the way of salvation to humanity and the individual in Jesus Christ . . . and reveals history as saving history." Thus, Rahner insists, the meta-historical character of *salvation* demands that it must be related to, but not be conflated or confused with, the historical transcendence that characterizes *salvation history*. He says this distinction is necessary in order to preserve the historicity of grace, Christology, and the self-revelation of the trinitarian God in the economy of salvation.

Having established the unity-in-distinction between the meta-historical character of *salvation* and the historicity of *salvation history* in Jesus Christ, Rahner makes a similar distinction in regards to *soteriology*, which he defines as "the theology of redemption, the salvation (Gr. σωτηρία) of man."[18] On the one hand he asserts, "In the concrete economy of salvation, God himself in his literal self-communication is the salvation of man, with the result that all reality . . . can be considered from a soteriological point of view."[19] On the other hand he says, "But it is customary for *soteriology* to confine itself to examining Christ's redemptive death on the cross as the continuation of Christology: the death of the God-Man, suffered in loving obedience, in view of which God loves mankind as a whole and in which (because it is his own) he has accepted

---

16. Fred Sanders, *The Image of the Immanent Trinity: Rahner's Rule and the Theological Interpretation of Scripture* (New York: Peter Lang, 2005), 55-56.

17. Karl Rahner and Herbert Vorgrimler, "Salvation," in *Theological Dictionary* (New York: Herder & Herder, 1965), 419-20.

18. Karl Rahner and Herbert Vorgrimler, "Soteriology," in *Theological Dictionary* (New York: Herder & Herder, 1965), 441.

19. Ibid., 442.

and assumed the world."[20] Rahner's transcendental Christology integrates both perspectives by insisting on the one hand that creation is "the finite, created utterance *ad extra* . . . through the Logos (John 1:3)" of the trinitarian God,[21] and that "antecedently to justification by grace . . . man is already subject to the universal salvific will of God, he is already redeemed"[22] by God's universal self-offer to humanity. On the other hand, however, this meta-historical and universal character of God's salvific self-offer from eternity must be seen as part of God's definitive self-offer in the historical event of Jesus Christ. He insists, therefore, that

> within the framework of an essential Christology . . . we are trying to reflect upon the mystery . . . of "God becoming man," . . . the center out of which we Christians live, and which we believe. [For] it is only here that the mystery of the Trinity is accessible to us, and only here that the mystery of our participation in the divine nature is promised to us in a definitive and historically tangible way.[23]

For Rahner, then, soteriology focuses on the saving power for all peoples at all times of what he calls God's definitive self-offer in Jesus Christ. Thus,

> The mysteries of soteriology can . . . be reduced to the mystery of the Incarnation; all we have to do is to suppose . . . that the Word of God took on a nature from among the human race which, by the creative will of God, shared in solidarity one common history of salvation and disaster; and that this human nature of Christ was willed . . . as something to be actualized, and hence as freely accomplishing the human destiny of life and death. With these presuppositions . . . the whole doctrine of the redemption follows from the mystery of the Incarnation. We have thus listed a posteriori all the truths of faith which come in question as *mysteria stricte dicta* . . . : the Trinity, the Incarnation and the divinization of man in grace and glory.[24]

Rahner's approach to soteriology therefore remains christocentric (like all of his theology), which leads him to tie soteriology to theological reflection on God's self-offer from all eternity in Jesus Christ. To this end he introduces a distinction between what he calls the *objective* and the *subjective* dimensions of salvation so that soteriology is not simply conflated with the doctrine of grace. Soteriology

20. Ibid.

21. Karl Rahner, "The Theology of the Symbol," trans. Kevin Smyth, *Theological Investigations*, IV (Baltimore, MD: Helicon Press, 1966), 236-37.

22. Karl Rahner and Herbert Vorgrimler, "Existential, Supernatural," in *Theological Dictionary* (New York: Herder & Herder, 1965), 161.

23. Karl Rahner, *Foundations of Christian Faith* (New York: Seabury, Crossroad, 1978), 213.

24. Karl Rahner, "The Concept of Mystery in Catholic Theology," *Theological Investigations*, XXI (New York: Crossroad Publishing, 1991), 65.

therefore addresses how "*objective* redemption has made the religious situation of every individual, prior to any consent of his, something quite different from what it would be without Christ and his cross."[25] However, he asserts, "It is not soteriology but the doctrine of grace that deals with the subjective application of this *objective* redemption by the free acceptance of Christ's grace as God self-communication (*subjective redemption*)."[26] In either case, however, Christian fundamental theology insists on the meta-historical plenitude of *salvation* as the object of eschatological hope, which places the emphasis on the unity-in-distinction between eternity and history and the need for an adequate way of conceptualizing the historicity of salvation history, soteriology, and the doctrine of grace.

Ellacuría clearly follows Rahner in endorsing this view. This can be seen in his 1974 response to the official "note" from the office of the apostolic nuncio of El Salvador criticizing his first book, *Teología política*. The unknown author of the memo asserts that Ellacuría's notion that salvation history is also salvation-in-history "exaggerates this aspect of salvation in history" while shortchanging the "meta-historical" character of the "eternal truths" that comprise the object of faith.[27] Ellacuría responds, "The author says that I exaggerate the aspect of 'salvation in history' . . . but he does not show it. With this charge he ignores and passes over what is essential in my work: salvation in history is the *sign* of the plenitude of a salvation that is meta-historical."[28] Here, then, Ellacuría clearly distinguishes the meta-historical character of *salvation* from what he means by *salvation in history* while at the same time exploring their relationship.

Ellacuría insists, "Everything that is presented as salvation in history (which is not simply equivalent to salvation history) is regarded as a sign of the history of salvation, it comes from this and it moves toward it." In this way Ellacuría not only establishes the unity-in-distinction of *salvation* and *salvation in history*, but he does the same for *salvation history* and *salvation in history*. He then concludes, "Not to have understood this theology of sign, which dominates the entire publication (which, as I will say later, belongs to what must be understood today as fundamental theology) presupposes a serious lack of depth in the interpretation and the evaluation that follows. . . . My book tries to demonstrate the connection between the sign and what constitutes it as a sign." Thus, like his teacher Rahner, Ellacuría insists on the importance of relating, without conflating or confusing, the concepts of *salvation, salvation history*, and *salvation in history*. And he insists that these distinctions are crucial to his theology of sign (and hence his understanding of the Trinity and the history of salvation) as well as his notion that *salvation history* must also be *salvation in history*.

Four years later Ellacuría introduced the concept of *historical soteriology* as

---

25. Rahner, "Soteriology," 442.
26. Ibid.
27. Ignacio Ellacuría, "Respuesta crítica a 'Nota sobre la publicación *Teología política* del Reverendo Padre Ignacio Ellacuría, S.J.,'" *Revista latinoamericana de teología* 77 (2009): 206.
28. Ibid., 207.

the theological frame for his famous article on the crucified people, published eight months after Archbishop Romero's homily addressing the terrorized peasants of Aguilares as "the image of the pierced savior . . . who represent Christ nailed to the cross and pierced by a lance."[29] Locating what he calls *historical soteriology* in the context of the historicity of *salvation*, Ellacuría writes, "Historical soteriology is understood here above all as something that refers to salvation as it is presented in revelation. But the accent falls on its historical character."[30] He insists, therefore, that historical soteriology "must be a soteriology whose essential reference point is the saving work of Jesus, but it must likewise be a soteriology that historicizes this saving work and does so as the continuation and following of Jesus and his work." Thus, Ellacuría follows Rahner's understanding that soteriology is focused on the universal significance of God's self-offer in Jesus Christ and his "redemptive death on the cross."[31] But Ellacuría seeks to historicize this soteriology by asking, "How is the salvation of humankind achieved starting from Jesus? Who continues in history that essential function, that saving mission that the Father entrusted to the Son? . . . Which historically oppressed peoples serve as the continuation, *par excellence,* of the saving work of Jesus?"[32] Here, then, the inherent tension between the meta-historical dimension of salvation and the historicity of salvation drives Ellacuría to ask how the mystery of salvation is realized in the historical reality of the suffering and death of Jesus of Nazareth (the Christ) and how that is made real in history today? In Ellacuría's hands Rahner's christocentric approach becomes somewhat more Jesus-centric.

This approach clearly demonstrates the significance of Ellacuría's efforts to distinguish, without separating or conflating, the concepts of *salvation, salvation history, salvation in history,* and *historical soteriology.* Unfortunately, the otherwise excellent book by Michael Lee attempts to redefine soteriology in a way that obscures the importance of these distinctions and the need to tether *soteriology* (in Rahner's words) to the historical event of "Christ's redemptive death on the cross." Lee writes, "Traditionally, soteriology has focused specifically on the redemptive act wrought by Jesus Christ. However, this work suggests that soteriology refers to a broader *logos* about Christian salvation that deploys a whole constellation of ideas surrounding the divine–human relationship."[33] On the one hand, it is certainly true that for Ellacuría and Rahner the universal meta-historical character of God's self-offer to humanity and its realization in Jesus Christ includes a number of ideas about "the human–divine relationship."

---

29. Oscar Romero, "Homilía en Aguilares [June 19, 1977]," in *La voz de los sin voz: La palabra viva de Monseñor Oscar Arnulfo Romero* (San Salvador: UCA Editores, 1980), I, 208.

30. Ellacuría, "El pueblo crucificado, ensayo de soteriología histórica," *Escritos teológicos*, II, 138. See also Ignacio Ellacuría, "The Crucified People: An Essay in Historical Soteriology," in Michael Lee, ed., *Ignacio Ellacuría: Essays on History, Liberation, and Salvation* (Maryknoll, NY: Orbis Books, 2013), 196.

31. Rahner, "Soteriology," 442.

32. Ellacuría, "The Crucified People," 196.

33. Michael E. Lee, *Bearing the Weight of Salvation: The Soteriology of Ignacio Ellacuría* (New York: Herder & Herder/Crossroad, 2009), 158.

On the other hand, however, Lee's definition could be understood to nullify the point of Rahner's effort to distinguish soteriology from the doctrine of grace, and to weaken the insistence by both Ellacuría and Rahner that soteriology is essentially theological reflection on God's definitive self-offer in Jesus Christ. Lee's broader notion of soteriology then leads him to assert that "the distinguishing characteristic of Ellacuría's soteriology is the way he describes salvation as both historical and transcendent without conflating these characteristics." Again, in and of itself, this statement is true. However, the underlying preoccupation of Ellacuría's work with the problem of the *historicity of salvation* (his own statement) appears to have been displaced in Lee's approach by the question of *soteriology* using a definition of the term that does not match its general use in Ellacuría's work, which focused on the saving character of the historical reality of Jesus Christ.

Given the accuracy of the comments above regarding the meaning and significance of Ellacuría's efforts to distinguish (without separating or conflating) the meta-historical character of *salvation* from *soteriology*, which Ellacuría says is focused on the suffering and death of Jesus, I would argue for the need to highlight the Jesus-centric character of Ellacuría's approach to soteriology and its relationship to the underlying focus of Ellacuría's theological corpus on the *historicity of salvation*. This relationship fosters the historical *logos* that Ellacuría uses to reinterpret Christian salvation as a salvation-in-history. It also allows him to reconceptualize the nature of transcendence as a transcendence in history rather than as a transcendence away from history, which provides Ellacuría's treatment of the historicity of Christian salvation with its distinguishing characteristic. Thus, the underlying concern that informs Ellacuría's entire discussion is not so much an effort to develop a broader and more encompassing understanding of *soteriology* that includes the meta-historical dimensions of salvation but rather a concern with the *historicity of Christian salvation*, which Ellacuría calls "the most serious problem for understanding and practice of the faith."[34]

### Salvation in History

In this section I will briefly summarize the substance of Ellacuría's argument for the unity-in-distinction between "the plenitude of a salvation that is meta-historical"[35] and a salvation history that is also a *salvation in history*. He begins with the claim that if salvation is historical, then two things must be assumed: first, salvation "will differ according to the time and place in which it is realized"; and second, "it must be realized in the historical reality of humanity, in their entire specific reality."[36] This implies, however, that revelation is not fin-

34. Ellacuría, "Historicidad de la salvación cristiana," 535.

35. Ellacuría, "Respuesta crítica a 'Nota sobre la publicación *Teología política* del Reverendo Padre Ignacio Ellacuría, S.J.,'" 207.

36. Ellacuría, *Teología política*, 8; *Freedom Made Flesh*, 15.

ished and that the church and the followers of Jesus are obliged to pursue "an ongoing reading of revelation in the changing reality of human history."

Ellacuría asserts that the approach to historical transcendence implied in this statement compares favorably to the more primitive accounts arising from the reductionist materialism of Marx and the "escape into individualistic interiority" of Feuerbach.[37] In providing an alternative, however, he says Christians must communicate "that the presence of God in natural and historical reality is not the presence of a demiurge who rewards with miracles or punishes the religious behavior of individuals and their peoples."[38] Rather, Christian transcendence (like all other kinds of transcendence) must be understood as something that emerges in historical reality in response to its demands and possibilities. And action to transform the world and human society should be seen as the "essential sign" by which the salvation of humanity is made present, and Christians "should insist that history is the locale of God's revelation . . . that . . . God is revealing himself in history" and that salvation history is a salvation in history.

But how is the meta-historical character of salvation preserved in this schema? As we saw above, Ellacuría's theology of sign simultaneously preserves the plenitude of salvation while insisting that its historicity demands that it be a salvation in history. He historicizes the claim that the second person of the Trinity, the Word of God, became flesh in Jesus Christ by asserting that "God has revealed God's self in history, not directly, but in the sign that is human history."[39] He says this means "there is no access to God except through the sign of history," and he proposes that "the Christian assertion that there is no communication with God the Father except through the sign of the humanity of Jesus should be elevated to a transcendent and universal position." Indeed, he argues, "we should pick up again the assertion that Jesus has been constituted the Lord of history" and that "history is the interval between his first and second coming . . . where we must prepare the way of the Lord." Thus, he concludes, "action on history and the salvation of social humanity in history is the true path by which God will finally deify humankind. So it is not just that salvation history brings with it a salvation in history, but it is also that humanity's salvation in history is the only way salvation history can reach its culmination."[40]

Here, then, the mystery of salvation converges with the Mystery of God, which was the point all along in the view of Zubiri and Ellacuría. Zubiri writes,

> The power of the real . . . consists in that things are real *in* God. Thus, for Christianity, this "being real in God" consists in being like God. Real things are . . . God *ad extra*; and for Christianity, this *ad extra* is "being like God." This being like God admits of diverse modes and degrees, but they are always modes and degrees of a strict being like

37. Ellacuría, *Teología política*, 9; *Freedom Made Flesh*, 17.
38. Ellacuría, *Teología política*, 9; *Freedom Made Flesh*, 18.
39. Ibid.
40. Ellacuría, *Teología política*, 10; *Freedom Made Flesh*, 18.

God. . . . The human person is a formal projection of the divine reality itself, a finite manner of being God. [And] the finite moment of this becoming like God is what, in my view, constitutes that which we call "human nature." God is transcendent *in* the human person, being human as a deifying God. A transcendence of God *in* the human person is then, I repeat, being like God. . . . In my estimation, this is the essence of Christianity. Prior to being a religion of salvation (often repeated nowadays as if it were something evident), and precisely in order to be such, Christianity is a religion of becoming like God.[41]

Ellacuría seems to have this passage in mind when he writes, "As X. Zubiri so often pointed out . . . creation can be seen as the grafting *ad extra* of the trinitarian life itself, . . . an act of communication and self-giving by the divine life itself . . . [so that] each thing . . . is a limited way of being God." Echoing the Thomistic schema of *exitus–reditus* (emanation and return) that we saw in Rahner, Ellacuría argues, "God's . . . grafting *ad extra* of the divine life has gone through a long process toward . . . the human nature of Jesus and ultimately toward the *return* of all creation to its original source." Thus, "humanity as a formally open essence, and history in its essential openness, are the realities in which that grafting of the triune life are more and more present, although always in a limited way—open but limited, limited but open."[42]

Applying this Jesus-centric and trinitarian perspective (which we saw in the earlier discussion of soteriology) to the question of grace and sin, Ellacuría then argues that "from this perspective we see more clearly not only the unity of God's history, but the fundamental dimension in which to reflect on the problem of grace and sin. All created things are a limited way of being God, and the human being in particular is a small God because the human being is a relative absolute."[43] As a result, prior to being a religion of salvation, Ellacuría agrees with Zubiri and Rahner that Christianity turns out to be a religion of *theōsis* (deification, or coming into union with God). This is why the historicity of Christian salvation (and of *theōsis*) rather than soteriology emerges as what Ellacuría considers "the most serious problem for the understanding and practice of the faith."[44] This perspective shapes Ellacuría's Christian historical realism and his entire project. Thus, on the one hand, Ellacuría argues that the "yes" of the 1969 retreat to Medellín's call for a preferential option for the poor draws the Central American Jesuits into a deeper encounter with the Christ of the San Salvador retreat and a transformative participation in the saving life and work of the Trinity in the world. On the other hand, however, he insists that each person maintains the capacity to say "no" by converting "the self and its

---

41. Xavier Zubiri, *El hombre y Dios* (Madrid: Alianza Editorial, 1984), 380-81.

42. Ellacuría, "The Historicity of Christian Salvation," 276; "Historicidad de la salvación cristiana," 578.

43. Ellacuría, "The Historicity of Christian Salvation," 277; "Historicidad de la salvación cristiana," 579.

44. Ellacuría, "Historicidad de la salvación cristiana," 535.

freedom . . . into idols." He finds this approach in Archbishop Romero's fourth and final pastoral letter, "where he tries to expose the idolatries of our society . . . [including] the absolutization of wealth and private property, the absolutization of national security, and the absolutization of [popular] organizations."[45]

Here, then, we see the importance that Ellacuría places on the dynamics of *theōsis* (or "becoming like God") in addressing the historicity of salvation. For Ellacuría it is the dynamics of *theōsis* (or what Zubiri calls *deiformación*) that explains the human capacity to historicize transcendence by entering into a historical relationship with the divine. And it is *theōsis* that explains our capacity to create idols, making our own creations of wealth, property, national security, civic organizations, etc., into absolutes that, since they are not divine, negate God's self-offer mediated through the absolute (or *theologal*) dimensions of reality. This brings us, then, to Ellacuría's argument for the historical reality of Jesus of Nazareth as the historical sign and mediation of God's saving self-offer and the meta-historical plenitude of salvation.

### The Historical Reality of Jesus

Ellacuría's Jesus-centric approach to soteriology leads him to assert that "in order to determine how much and what kind of salvation there is in history we must center our reflection on Jesus, the culmination of salvation history."[46] Ellacuría insists, however, that if "theo-logical reflection on salvation in history demands a christ-ology," it must also be a "human logos" (or an anthropo-logos) in order to meet the standard of Christian belief about Jesus. So Ellacuría says we must ask "which *logos*" is capable of properly conceptualizing the historicity of Christian salvation in Jesus Christ?

He says scripture provides no definitive answer since "there are different Christologies in the New Testament" and "different readings of the same historical Jesus" depending on "the situation and the needs" of those seeking faith in Jesus.[47] For example, Paul's Christology "pays little attention to the flesh-and-blood Jesus . . . in order to jump too quickly to the Christ of faith," while Luke gives "more attention to the historical Jesus and his social and historical resonance." Thus, New Testament accounts of the details about Jesus and the *logos* they use to interpret those details will differ according to the time and place of the events and the needs of the audience.

In a similar way, Ellacuría asserts, "Today we need a new Christology" capable of explaining "how Jesus realizes his salvific mission to humanity in all its plenitude"[48] while at the same time giving "the flesh-and-blood Jesus and his history their full weight as revelation." Ellacuría says this new Christology will

---

45. Ellacuría, "The Historicity of Christian Salvation," 278; "Historicidad de la salvación cristiana," 580-81.

46. Ellacuría, *Teología política*, 11-12; *Freedom Made Flesh*, 23-24.

47. Ellacuría, *Teología política*, 11-12; *Freedom Made Flesh*, 25.

48. Ellacuría, *Teología política*, 13; *Freedom Made Flesh*, 26.

need "a historical-exegetical reading of what the life of Jesus really was" and "a historical *logos*, without which every other *logos* is just speculative and idealist." He says, "This historical *logos* will have to start from the fact, indisputable to the eye of faith, that the historical life of Jesus is the fullest revelation of the Christian God." But "it will have to operate methodologically as a *logos* of history that subsumes and goes beyond the *logos* of nature, which has frequently been confused with the *logos* of being and reality." Thus, he argues, "only a *logos* that takes into account *the historical reality of Jesus* can open the way for a full Christology and a Christology for the ever changing historical moment" because "only a historical *logos* can detect what there is of salvation in history in the history of salvation."[49]

Here, then, the full weight of Ellacuría's Christian historical realism and its underlying philosophy of historical reality are brought to bear on perhaps the central question for Christology: What is the nature of salvation in Jesus Christ? Ellacuría insists that a credible theological account of the salvific meaning for a Latin American audience of the life, death, and resurrection of Jesus Christ is impossible without a rigorous consideration of the *historical reality* of Jesus. But what exactly does Ellacuría mean by *the historical reality of Jesus*? It is certainly not what John P. Meier, a leading biblical scholar on the historical Jesus, calls *the real Jesus*, "the total reality of Jesus of Nazareth, that is, all that Jesus thought, said, did, and experienced during his lifetime, or even just during his public ministry."[50] Nor is it what Meier calls *the historical Jesus*, which he defines as "a scientific construct, a theoretical abstraction of modern scholars that coincides only partially with the real Jesus of Nazareth, the Jew who actually lived and worked in Palestine in the first century A.D." Indeed, it turns out that what Ellacuría means by the *historical reality of Jesus* is substantially different from what Meier calls the *real Jesus* and the *historical Jesus*.

In my discussion (in Chapter 4) of Ellacuría's concept of *historical reality* I said it could be understood as that (human) reality that must take a stance on its history-in-the-world. Thus, I would argue that what Ellacuría calls the historical reality of Jesus should be understood as the basic posture of Jesus on his history-in-the-world (my term), a stance that Ellacuría argues was publicly accessible to his followers and one that, not incidentally, also forms a subject of the Gospels. Understood in this way, the historical reality of Jesus is a different object from what Meier calls the *historical Jesus*,[51] which he identifies with positive claims made by scholars about the words, deeds, and larger narratives that can be credibly linked to Jesus (but not the defining commitments of Jesus mediated through them).

---

49. Ellacuría, *Teología política*, 13; *Freedom Made Flesh*, 27. My emphasis.

50. John Meier, *A Marginal Jew: Rethinking the Historical Jesus. Volume Two: Mentor, Message, and Miracles*, Anchor Bible Reference Library (New York: Doubleday, 1991), 4.

51. For a larger discussion on this point see Robert Lassalle-Klein, "Marina's Gospel and the Historical Reality of Jesus," in Robert Lassalle-Klein, ed. *Jesus of Galilee: Contextual Christology for the 21st Century* (Maryknoll, NY: Orbis Books, 2011), 99-118, esp. 107-11.

Likewise, the historical reality of Jesus is different from what Meier calls the *real Jesus*. The Gospels do not claim to know everything that Jesus said and did (Luke 1:4; John 20:30-31; 21:25; Mark 1:1; Matthew 13:51), and, I would submit, neither would most people claim to know the answer to that question about themselves! But the evangelists do in fact claim to know the defining elements of Jesus' stance on his history-in-the-world.[52] Indeed, the Gospels are in general agreement that the life and ministry of Jesus of Nazareth were defined (among other things) by his faithfulness as eschatological prophet to the history, scripture, traditions, and people of Israel even in the face of death; by his relationship as beloved Son sent by the Father; and by his sense of mission as having been sent to initiate the Reign of God as good news for the poor and for the rest of Israel as a light to the nations.

Ellacuría argues that this historical reality of Jesus of Nazareth should be understood as the defining sign of God's self-revelation, which has been confirmed by God's resurrection of Jesus. He assumes that we can "trust" (in the words of Pope Benedict XVI)[53] a critical reading of the Gospels, in concert with historical sources and the teaching of the Christian community, to provide faithful witness to the basic stance of Jesus on his history-in-the-world. In the next section we will see how, in his view, the historical reality of Jesus provides the ongoing standard for Christian discipleship and the church's mandate to read the signs of the times in the light of the gospel.

## Historical Soteriology and the Crucified People

This brings us then to Ellacuría's concept of *historical soteriology* and its role in his fundamental approach to Christology. Here Ellacuría draws an analogy between the historical reality of Jesus of Nazareth and the crucified people as victims of sin of the world, bearers of its salvation, and an ongoing historical sign of God's self-offer in Jesus Christ.

As noted above, this concept frames Ellacuría's reflections on the crucified people inspired by Romero's homily to the terrorized peasants of Aguilares. The article begins by asking, "What does the fact that the majority of humanity is oppressed mean for salvation history and in the history of salvation? . . . Can we consider them historically saved when they continue to bear the burden of the sins of the world? Can we consider them the savior of the world precisely because they bear the burden of the sin of the world? What relation do they have to the church as a sacrament of salvation?"[54]

Building on the understanding of *soteriology* discussed above, Ellacuría turns to Christ's redemptive death on the cross for answers. But in keeping with his conviction that "the problem of the historicity of Christian salvation

---

52. Ibid., 108, 111.

53. Pope Benedict XVI, *Jesus of Nazareth: From the Baptism in the Jordan to the Transfiguration* (New York: Doubleday, 2007), xxi-xxii.

54. Ellacuría, "El pueblo crucificado," 137. Ellacuría, "The Crucified People," 196.

continues to be of the most serious problem for . . . [Christian] faith,"[55] he insists that only a truly *historical soteriology* will do. Indeed, he asserts, while "many Christological and ecclesiological topics are wrapped up" in the questions above, "we could say that we find here the whole of Christology and ecclesiology in their character as historical soteriology."[56]

It is noteworthy that Ellacuría (or his editor Sobrino) adds four lines at this point to the original 1977 article when it was republished under a slightly different title in *Mysterium liberationis* the year after his death. This is important because the lines clearly follow, while historicizing, the narrower, more Jesus-centric understanding of soteriology outlined above. Thus, Ellacuría (or Sobrino) asks,

> How is the salvation of humankind achieved starting from Jesus? Who continues in history that essential function, that saving mission that the Father entrusted to the Son? The answer to these questions can give historical flesh to the people of God and thus avoid dehistoricizing this basic concept and also avoid spiritualizing or ideologizing it falsely. Historical soteriology provides an essential perspective in this regard.[57]

The key question, then, turns out to be how, and in what sense, the saving work of God in Jesus is continued in the crucified people? Ellacuría's definition of soteriology pushes him to suggest that not only is God's saving work in Jesus continued in the crucified people, but the very presence of Jesus is to be found there. Thus, Ellacuría insists that "historical soteriology . . . must be . . . a soteriology that has the saving work of Jesus as an essential point of reference; but it must also be a soteriology that historicizes that saving work, and historicizes it as a *continuation* and a following *of Jesus and his work*."[58]

Ellacuría's historical soteriology, therefore, is built upon a historical correlation that literally and figuratively "places the figure of Jesus together with that of oppressed humanity,"[59] a correlation that he says is required by Latin American theological method. Thus, "any historical situation must be seen in light of its corresponding key in revelation," and "revelation must be considered in light of the history to which it is addressed, although not every historical moment [e.g., sin] is equally valid for providing a proper focus."[60] This is the methodological core of what Ellacuría means by *historical soteriology*. As Michael Lee

---

55. Ellacuría, "Historicidad de la salvación cristiana," 535.

56. Ellacuría, "The Crucified People," 196.

57. Ibid. The reader should note that although Lee's translation follows the later slightly changed version of the article published in *Mysterium liberationis* under the title "El pueblo crucificado," he replaces this with the title of the original essay, "El pueblo crucificado, ensayo de soteriología histórica."

58. Ellacuría, "El pueblo crucificado, Ensayo de soteriología histórica," 138; Ellacuría, "The Crucified People," 196. My emphasis.

59. Ibid.

60. Ibid., 138-39.

explains, "Ellacuría correlates the Christian tradition's central salvific figure, Jesus, understood in light of the Suffering Servant of Isaiah, with the poor as the *crucified people*, who characterize the scandal of the present situation. Each figure illumines the other: the crucified people de-romanticize the passion of Jesus, while the passion of Jesus illumines the salvific importance of the crucified people today."[61]

Two questions immediately arise, however. First, what aspect exactly of the crucified people is being correlated with Jesus? On the one hand, Ellacuría justifiably says the mere fact "that there is a crucified people whose crucifixion is the product of actions in history . . . [is] not enough to prove that this crucified people is the continuation in history of the life and death of Jesus."[62] On the other hand, however, he insists that if the Gospel narratives of the suffering and death of Jesus are not flights of "expiatory masochism" then they must represent "the discovery of something real in history."[63] But what might that be, and to what does Ellacuría's historical soteriology intend to draw its correlation?

Ellacuría's response is that "Jesus' death makes it clear why really proclaiming salvation runs up against the resistance of the world and why the Reign of God struggles against the reign of sin . . . at the hands of those who make themselves gods, lording it over human kind." Indeed, Ellacuría says, "the reason could not be clearer: If the Reign of God and reign of sin are two opposed realities, and human beings of flesh and blood are the standard bearers of both, then those who wield the power of oppressive domination cannot but exercise it against those who have only the power of their word and their life, offered for the salvation of many."[64] So what, then, is the basis for the correlation Ellacuría wishes to draw between Jesus and the crucified people? Ellacuría says the parallel lies in the historical fact that their "resistance to oppressive powers and the[ir] struggle for historical liberation brought them persecution and death" in spite of the fact that their "resistance and struggle were . . . the historical product of a life lived in response to the word of God."[65]

Second, it is one thing to correlate the crucified people with Jesus, but quite another to insist they are the "continuation" of his historical presence! In what sense, then, can Ellacuría legitimately claim that the crucified people are the "continuation . . . of Jesus and his work"?[66] Here, as we saw earlier in Ellacuría's 1974 response to criticism of his work from the office of the apostolic nuncio of El Salvador, Ellacuría uses his theology of sign to argue that he

---

61. Lee, *Bearing the Weight of Salvation*, 89.

62. Ellacuría, "The Crucified People," 208.

63. Ibid., 203.

64. Ibid., 204.

65. Ellacuría, "El pueblo crucificado, Ensayo de soteriología histórica," 147; Ellacuría, "The Crucified People," 204.

66. Ellacuría, "The Crucified People," 196; "El pueblo crucificado, Ensayo de soteriología histórica," 138.

simply wants to examine how "salvation in history is the *sign* of the plenitude of a salvation that is meta-historical."[67] Thus, Ellacuría responds to the question about presence by asserting, "Our time is full of signs through which the historically saving God becomes present. The problem is in discerning . . . what God is saying through them and how we as humans must respond."[68] He then asserts, in perhaps his best-known text, "Among so many signs . . . , some striking and others barely perceptible, in every era there is a principal one in light of which all the others should be discerned and interpreted. That sign is always the historically crucified people, who combine with their abiding character the always distinctive historical form of their crucifixion." He adds the remarkable claim that "this crucified people is the historical continuation of the servant of Yahweh, whose human form is being taken away by the sin of the world, who are being stripped of everything by the powerful of this world, snatching away even their life, above all their life."[69] And he concludes by asserting that the crucified people place a serious claim on the church whose "universal historical mission should be calling humanity to turn with eyes of mercy—*Dives in misericordia*—toward this exploited and massacred humanity." Ellacuría's point is that, like Jesus and the suffering servant, the suffering innocence of the crucified people is a sign that invites and demands a compassionate response from followers of Jesus as an act of faith in the God of the Reign that he announced.

Here Ellacuría's Christian historical realism and his fundamental theology of sign frame his approach to Christology and the church. I argued earlier that Ellacuría's philosophy of historical reality leads him to historicize Rahner's theology of symbol as a theology of sign. I characterized his claim that "God revealed himself in history, not directly, but in a sign: . . . the humanity of Jesus,"[70] as a contextualized reinterpretation of Rahner's famous assertion that "the incarnate word is the absolute symbol of God in the world."[71] And I explained that Ellacuría shifts the emphasis from symbol to sign in part to cohere with the Council's mandate to read the signs of the times and interpret them in light of the gospel. Ellacuría's historical soteriology then further historicizes this theology of sign with the claim that the crucified people are the principal sign of the times, a historical sign of God's continuing self-offer in Jesus, and the object of the historical mission of the church. But he insists that the historical reality of "the crucified people has a twofold thrust" as both "victim of the sin of the world" and "bearer of the world's salvation."[72] Thus, the crucified people remain

67. Ellacuría, "The Crucified People," 207.

68. Ignacio Ellacuría, "Discernir *el signo* de los tiempos," *Escritos teológicos*, II (San Salvador: UCA Editores, 2000), 133.

69. Ibid., 134.

70. Ellacuría, *Teología política*, 9; *Freedom Made Flesh*, 18.

71. Karl Rahner, "Theology of the Symbol," *Theological Investigations*, IV (Baltimore, MD: Helicon Press, 1966), 237.

72. Ellacuría, "The Crucified People," 223.

a profoundly ambivalent sign of both sin and salvation, a sign that poses ongoing risks and challenges that each generation must face.

This can be seen in the story of Ignacio Ellacuría himself who, Sobrino says, defined "his life, and his vocation as a Jesuit and, deeper still, as a human being" in terms of "a specific service: *to take the crucified people down from the cross*."[73] Ellacuría insists this striking metaphor for Medellín's option for the poor places a claim on all human beings. Indeed, the entire christological project developed with Sobrino could be described as an attempt to show that followers of Jesus and those who act like him (whether disciples or not) are drawn into a mystical "analogy"[74] between the life, death, and resurrection of Jesus Christ, and solidarity with the struggles of the crucified people to believe and to survive the "world of poverty . . . today."[75] As noted above, this takes us into the realm of what the Greek Fathers called *theōsis* and what Zubiri calls *deiformación*.

Ellacuría and Sobrino argue that the one who follows the historical reality of Jesus (which Ellacuría also calls his praxis[76]) is drawn into a transformative participation with the work of the Trinity in the world and the divine mystery of the inner life of God. Ellacuría's reflections with Sobrino on the saving mystery of Jesus Christ are shaped by his deeply trinitarian theology of sign, the hallmark of his Christian historical realism, which (as we have seen) builds on the trinitarian mysticism of the *Spiritual Exercises* of St. Ignatius, Rahner's recovery of the economic Trinity in twentieth-century Catholic theology, Zubiri's realism and philosophy of God, and Romero's praxis of faith. Their approach is emblemized in Sobrino's claim that the disciple who responds to the grace-filled call to take the crucified people down from the cross becomes a living sign of the life, death, and resurrection of Jesus Christ, the sending of the Spirit, and the ongoing work of the Trinity in the world. I will say more about this intriguing and potentially controversial metaphor in the next chapter.

In this chapter, then, I have discussed the contribution of four claims regarding the historicity of salvation from Ellacuría's Christian historical realism to the contextual Christology he develops with Jon Sobrino. First, Ellacuría describes history and salvation as complementary aspects of the larger unity that he calls the great history of God. Second, he insists that salvation history must be experienced as a salvation in history if it is genuinely historical. Third, he argues that

---

73. Jon Sobrino, "Ignacio Ellacuría, el hombre y el cristiano, 'Bajar de la cruz al pueblo crucificado'" (San Salvador: Centro Monseñor Romero, 2001), translated as "Ignacio Ellacuría, the Human Being and the Christian: 'Taking the Crucified People Down From the Cross,'" in Kevin Burke and Robert Lassalle-Klein, eds., *Love That Produces Hope: The Thought of Ignacio Ellacuría* (Collegeville, MN: Liturgical Press, 2006), 1-67, at 5.

74. See Jon Sobrino, *Jesus the Liberator: A Historical-Theological View* (Maryknoll, NY: Orbis Books, 1993), 254-73; and Jon Sobrino, *Christ the Liberator: A View from the Victims* (Maryknoll, NY: Orbis Books, 2001), 3-8.

75. Sobrino, *Christ the Liberator,* 4.

76. Ignacio Ellacuría, *Filosofía de la realidad histórica* (San Salvador: UCA Editores, 1990), 599, 595.

the historical reality of Jesus of Nazareth is the defining sign of the Word made flesh and the starting point for a genuinely Latin American Christology guided by a historical *logos*. And fourth, this Christology is captured in a historical soteriology correlating the saving historical reality of Jesus with the crucified people as the victims of the sin of the world and bearers of its salvation.

# 9

# *Analogatum Princeps of the Historical Reality of Jesus*

## THE CRUCIFIED PEOPLE OF EL SALVADOR

### Introduction

If Ignacio Ellacuría is the leading figure in the conversion of the Central American Jesuits to Medellín's call to a preferential option for the poor, then Jon Sobrino has been its evangelist. Sobrino has traveled the world telling the stories of Archbishop Romero, Ignacio Ellacuría, the University of Central America (UCA) martyrs, the four religious women, and the crucified people of El Salvador in over two dozen books and hundreds of articles, short publications, interviews, presentations, courses, and seminars. These reflections are witness to a lifetime of bringing the hopes and aspirations for liberation of Latin America's impoverished majorities to bear on Christian spirituality, systematic theology (Jesus Christ, church, God, grace, the Holy Spirit), ethics, and a whole variety of historical events in what he calls "a fundamentally Jesus-centered and reality-centered theology."[1] Reflecting on his journey as a Central American Jesuit and a surviving companion of the UCA martyrs Sobrino writes, "God has come to meet me in a call that I used to name 'a vocation to religious life,' and which I now experience as a 'larger vocation' . . . of helping—together with others—to humanize this creation of God."[2]

In this chapter I will briefly summarize how Sobrino's two-volume Christology can be understood as a witness and response to the saving mystery of the crucified people of El Salvador and the church of Archbishop Romero. As he states in the introduction to Volume I, "in this book I have done nothing more than—starting from Jesus—elevate the reality we are living to the level of a theological concept, to theorize about a Christological faith that we see as real faith."[3] Sobrino's unique role as witness and interpreter of martyrdom and

---

1. In Valentí Gómez-Oliver and Josep M. Benítez, eds., *31 jesuítas se confiesan* (Barcelona: Ediciones Península, 2003), 491.

2. Ibid., 490, 491.

3. Jon Sobrino, *Jesus the Liberator: A Historical-Theological View* (Maryknoll, NY: Orbis Books, 1993), 30; and Jon Sobrino, *Christ the Liberator: A View from the Victims* (Maryknoll, NY: Orbis Books, 2001), 8.

hope is strikingly emblemized by the blood-stained pages of Jürgen Moltmann's *The Crucified God*—a subject of his 1975 dissertation[4] on Jürgen Moltmann— which fell from the bookshelf of his room into the blood of Juan Ramon Moreno on the morning of November 16, 1989. Sobrino's Christology opens a window to the meaning for both the UCA martyrs and Christians around the globe of the blood and ink so generously spilled in creating a post–Vatican II university guided by Medellín's call to take the crucified people down from the cross.

Sobrino's family fled persecution and war in Bilbao, Spain, before moving to Barcelona in 1937 where he was born the following year and lived until 1950. After studying with the Jesuits at the Colegio de Sarriá in Barcelona (1948-1950) and Nuestra Señora de Begoña in Bilbao (1950-1956) he entered the Jesuits on October 6, 1956. One year later, in October 1957, he and several classmates joined Fr. Miguel Elizondo at the new Jesuit novitiate at Santa Tecla in San Salvador, eight years after it began with Ellacuría and his classmates. Following vows, Sobrino began undergraduate studies in humanities from 1958 to 1960 with the Jesuit faculty in Havana, Cuba, moving on to St. Louis University between 1960 and 1963 where he completed undergraduate studies and obtained a licentiate in philosophy. He stayed on for a master's in structural engineering (1960-1965) and returned to San Salvador in 1965 to teach Latin, Greek, and literature at the diocesan seminary (San José de la Montaña) while teaching philosophy and mathematics at the UCA. One year later he was sent to Frankfurt, Germany, for theological studies the Hoch Schule Sankt Georgen and was ordained on July 6, 1969. He completed a licentiate in sacred theology in 1971 and returned permanently to El Salvador in 1974 before receiving the doctorate the following year for his dissertation, "A Comparison of the Christologies of W. Pannenberg and J. Moltmann."[5]

Theological studies pushed the young Jesuit to "demythologize" his faith, provoking what he calls a "painful" awakening from the "dogmatic slumber" of naive convictions and beliefs carried from his youth.[6] While "God and faith were no longer evident," he found solace in Ellacuría's 1969 self-implicating observation that "Karl Rahner carried his doubts about faith with elegance." Then, upon returning to El Salvador in 1974 Sobrino says, "I went through another awakening." This time, however, both the crisis and its impact on his faith were different. He recalls, "I had to wake up from the slumber of inhumanity and my Central American Jesuit companions helped me." We cannot review the details here, but the impact on Sobrino's faith of the option for the poor unfolding among his colleagues and the rising hopes for change among the common people of El Salvador shape the lifeworld out of which his Christology arises. What is important for our purposes, however, is Sobrino's surprising

---

4. Jon Sobrino, "Una comparación de las cristologías de W. Pannenberg y J. Moltmann" (Hoch Schule Sankt Georgen, Frankfurt, 1975).

5. Gómez-Oliver and Benítez, *31 jesuítas se confiesan*, 491; and Jon Sobrino, *Curriculum vitae*, personal files of Robert Lassalle-Klein.

6. Gómez-Oliver and Benítez, *31 jesuítas se confiesan*, 489.

observation that "in this waking up to the reality of the poor, God reappeared—in a new way." He recalls, "When I first came to El Salvador in 1957 I did not see things like this. However, when I returned for good in 1974 . . . the crucified people 'appeared to me,' *opthe*, . . . as it says in the appearances of the risen Jesus."[7] Sobrino insists, however, that beyond the simple fact of their irruption into his consciousness "the crucified people also appeared in another even more surprising way as good news, grace, and salvation, without which I would not have done anything." Here, then, is the true *locus theologicus* for Sobrino's mature encounter with God.

He says, "It is not that I now possess him, of course, or that the tragedy of this world no longer cries out for a theodicy [a theological explanation of how a good God can tolerate evil]. But . . . I woke up. So today I would not be true to myself if I did not mention, always with fear and trembling, God." Thus, he writes,

> In addressing the reality of this God I have written that he is the God of life, a defender of the poor and a denouncer of the oppressor, the God of the resurrection who gives hope to the victims and the crucified God who is like them, the *Deus semper maior* and the *Deus semper minor*, the God of the promise who is always before us and mysteriously draws us to him, the Father and Mother God, who welcomes us with forgiveness, compassion, and tenderness. With these words I can only stammer who this God is, God's essence, so to speak.[8]

Like Ellacuría, Sobrino says he has been shaped by Rahner's description of "God as Holy Mystery" and quotes Rahner's idea that "Catholic theology, despite its many dogmas and ethical norms, says only one thing: the mystery remains forever mystery."[9] Sobrino then historicizes this claim (like Ellacuría) quoting Porfirio Miranda, "The problem is not finding God, but encountering him where He said he would be'—which is the ongoing demand and invitation of Jesus in Matthew 25."

Sobrino occupies a unique role as both witness and interpreter to the unexpected grace that is the crucified people and those who love them. He writes, "I have been surrounded by an immense cloud of witnesses that 'have suffered the shedding of blood,' as it says in the Letter to the Hebrews [9:22], and it has fallen to me to live in the midst of it."[10] He says, "They are people still being martyred who resemble Jesus in the way they live, in their mission, in what they defend and denounce, and in the reasons for which they are persecuted and assassinated. Magnificent people, with limitations of course, who have made the gospel speak like nothing else, and who have made the depths of God and Jesus real with spontaneity and naturalness, without even a discernment: this is the greater love." Remarkably, Sobrino recalls that when he learned in Thailand

---

7. Ibid., 483-84.
8. Ibid., 489-50.
9. Ibid., 490.
10. Ibid., 484.

that the Salvadoran armed forces had assassinated his friends and companions he told the audience "spontaneously and with total conviction: 'I must give you bad news: they have assassinated my entire community. And I must tell you good news [as well]: I have lived with good men, men of compassion, truth, and love.'"[11]

This reaction provides the hermeneutical key to Sobrino's work: "gratitude and appreciation,"[12] tempered by a realistic awareness for the suffering caused by sin and idolatry. Sobrino says, "this book is written in the midst of crucifixion, but definitely in the hope of liberation" and that "liberation and crucifixion provide the basic tension for Christian faith and . . . christology on this continent."[13] He insists that "the situation of El Salvador does not render christology super-fluous, but makes it all the more necessary to put all one's intellect into elaborating a christology that will help the resurrection of the Salvadoran people." Thus, he says, "I have allowed myself to be welcomed by God and to try, in a modest way, to help God's creation become what his heart desires; to allow myself to be welcomed by the poor of this world and to help the human family grow. Needless to say Jesus has opened my eyes to all of this."[14]

In what follows, then, I will trace how Sobrino brings this spirit of gratitude and denunciation to his reflection on the saving Mystery of Jesus Christ. Summarizing his approach in a letter to a young Jesuit, Sobrino writes,

> My Christology fundamentally says that Jesus Christ is a good news, a *euaggelion*. This is the impression that I have, and I think it is important to make note of it because that is, in my opinion, what is most original in a Christology of mercy, the cross, and martyrdom. In other words, cross and martyrdom refer not only to "sin," but also to "grace." This seems to me the most important contribution from the "Salvadoran school" of theology (Ignacio Ellacuría, Monseñor Romero . . . ).[15]

As noted above, the contextual Christology developed by Sobrino and Ellacuría is unified by two fundamental claims: (1) the historical reality of Jesus, which brings joy and salvation, is the real sign of the Word made flesh; and (2) the *analogatum princeps* of God's self-offer in the life, death, and resurrection of Jesus is to be found today among the crucified peoples of the planet. In the following sections I will examine three important contributions that Sobrino's Christology makes to this argument. In the first section I will briefly summarize how he proposes to elaborate a Christology by starting from *the historical reality of Jesus*. Here Sobrino builds on Ellacuría's Jesus-centric and historical approach to soteriology outlined above. As part of this section I will

---

11. Ibid., 485.

12. Ibid., 494.

13. Sobrino, *Jesus the Liberator*, 1.

14. Gómez-Oliver and Benítez, *31 jesuítas se confiesan*, 494.

15. Jon Sobrino, S.J., personal letter to Hartono Budi, S.J., June 30, 1999, personal files of Robert Lassalle-Klein, 2.

examine Sobrino's assertions that a truly Latin American Christology must (1) take "into account the historical reality of Jesus";[16] (2) build on the insight that "the historical life of Jesus is the fullest revelation of the Christian God";[17] and (3) explain how the defining aspects of *the historical reality of Jesus* (e.g., the Reign of God as good news to the poor, his relationship with the Father, and his crucifixion) constitute a salvation in history.

In the second section I will examine Sobrino's claim that a Latin American christological faith views the "Easter experience"[18] as part of the historical reality of Jesus. Sobrino argues that the encounter with the risen Jesus places a demand on the person that changes them, referring them back to the historical reality of Jesus (the Gospels conclude that "God raised Jesus from the dead") and pushing them forward to live as Jesus lived (taking the crucified people down from the cross). Here Sobrino builds on Ellacuría's argument that the soteriological nature of the encounter with Jesus Christ, both before and after the resurrection, lies in its power to draw us to become more like Jesus, a transformative process that Sobrino and Ellacuría argue (along with Rahner and Zubiri) ultimately includes *theōsis* (or *deiformación*).

Finally, in the third section I will explore how Sobrino argues, building on Ellacuría's notion of historical soteriology, that God's saving self-offer in the historical reality of Jesus is continued in the crucified people and the invitation to take them down from the cross. Here the mystery of salvation embodied in Sobrino's historical soteriology (which asserts that the crucified people are the *analogatum princeps* of God's self-offer in Jesus Christ) converges with *theōsis* or *deiformación*. Sobrino's idea is that when we take the crucified people down from the cross we are drawn into the work of the Trinity in the world and the Mystery of God, echoing Zubiri's Rahnerian idea that "prior to being a religion of salvation . . . and precisely in order to be such, Christianity is a religion of becoming like God.[19]

## The Historical Reality of Jesus as Starting Point for Latin American "Saving History" Christology

I will begin by examining *the historical reality of Jesus* as the starting point for Sobrino's Latin American approach to Christology. Here Sobrino reframes Ellacuría's Jesus-centric and historicized approach to soteriology in terms of what Rahner calls "saving history Christology." The basic idea is that where historical soteriology asks how the historical reality of Jesus is continued today, the saving history approach asks how the historical reality of the disciples' encounter with

---

16. Ignacio Ellacuría, *Freedom Made Flesh: The Mission of Christ and His Church* (Maryknoll, NY: Orbis, 1976), 27; trans. John Drury from *Teología política* (San Salvador: Secretaridado Social Interdiocesano, 1973); cited in Sobrino, *Jesus the Liberator,* 46-47.

17. Ibid.; cited by Sobrino in *Jesus the Liberator,* 47.

18. Sobrino, *Christ the Liberator,* 226.

19. Xavier Zubiri, *El hombre y Dios* (Madrid: Alianza Editorial, 1984), 380-81.

the risen Christ, understood as "an act proper to God himself,"[20] occurs today. Next I will explore how Sobrino says the historical reality of Jesus is continued in the crucified people and how God acts through their hope against crucifixion to inspire and raise up followers of Jesus, who will take them down from the cross. First, however, I must briefly summarize Sobrino's argument in Volume I of his Christology that the historical reality of Jesus is a salvation-in-history. Sobrino states, "In this volume I set out the life of Jesus in relation to three central dimensions . . . : his service to the *Kingdom of God*, his relationship to *God-the-Father*, and his death on the cross . . . endeavor[ing] to stress the liberative, and so good-news, dimension of both Jesus' mission and his person."[21] Sobrino analyzes these dimensions, then, as defining aspects and liberating signs of God's self-offer and the salvation-in-history incarnated in the historical reality of Jesus.

Rahner outlines "two basic types of Christology,"[22] distinguishing what he calls *"saving history"* Christology, which interprets Jesus Christ "from below," as we see in the New Testament, from what he calls "the *metaphysical* type" of Christologies, which view Jesus "downwards from above,"[23] as represented by Chalcedon and the ecumenical councils of the early church. Rahner predicts this typology will be misunderstood, particularly his argument that Christology from below "understands, and must understand, this process of 'rising up' as an act proper to God himself." Recent criticisms of Sobrino's work confirm Rahner's prophecy.[24]

Rahner says that "the point of departure [for saving history Christology] . . .

---

20. Karl Rahner, "The Two Basic Types of Christology," *Theological Investigations*, vol. 13, trans. David Bourke (New York: Seabury, 1975), 213-23, 214.

21. Sobrino, *Jesus the Liberator*, 6.

22. Rahner, "The Two Basic Types," 213-23.

23. Ibid., 213-14.

24. Sobrino's assertion that the historical development of dogma about Jesus Christ reflects the historical character of the divine economy of salvation appears not to have been considered in the 2006 notification issued by the Congregation for the Doctrine of the Faith (CDF). The document clearly admits, on the one hand, that "Father Sobrino does not deny the divinity of Jesus when he proposes that it is found in the New Testament only 'in seed' and was formulated dogmatically only after many years of believing reflection." However, it criticizes a "reticence" that "fails to affirm Jesus' divinity with sufficient clarity," which, it asserts, "gives credence to the suspicion that the historical development of dogma . . . has arrived at the formulation of Jesus' divinity without a clear continuity with the New Testament" (CDF, "Notification on the Works of Father Jon Sobrino, S.J.," in Stephen J. Pope, ed., *Hope and Solidarity: Sobrino's Challenge to Christian Theology* (Maryknoll, NY: Orbis Books, 2008), 256. Reading Sobrino's work as an example of what Rahner calls "saving history" Christology, however, supports the interpretation that what the notification sees as "reticence" is instead a reflection of Sobrino's analytical focus on the church's "process of 'rising up'" from its first generation faith-filled response to the life, death, and resurrection of Jesus Christ to the fully elaborated fourth-century doctrinal claims of Chalcedon as an act inspired by the Holy Spirit and "proper to God himself." Referring to the criticism of the CDF, William Loewe correctly points out that "the Congregation does not insist that Sobrino *should* be read as saying this, nor does his text support such a reading. Rather the opposite is the case" (Loewe, "Interpreting the Notification" in *Hope and Solidarity*, 146, 150).

is the simple experience of the man Jesus, and of the Resurrection in which his fate was bought to its conclusion." He says,

> The eye of the believer in his experience of saving history alights first on the man Jesus of Nazareth, and on him in his *fully human reality*, in his death, in the absolute powerless[ness] and in the abidingly definitive state which his reality and his fate have been brought to by God, something which we call his Resurrection, his glorification, his sitting at the right hand of the Father.[25]

Sobrino ties his Christology to this "undertaking of Karl Rahner . . . to restore to Christ his true humanity," which "insisted on thinking of the humanity of Christ "sacramentally."[26] He therefore adopts the "basically chronological" pattern of christological reflection "found in the New Testament" where "Jesus' mission of service to the Kingdom" raises "the question about the person of Jesus," ultimately answered by the disciple's "confession of his unrepeatable and salvific reality."[27] Following Rahner's insistence on the unity of the historical Jesus and the Christ of faith he asserts, "As a result the *real* point of departure is always, somehow, the whole faith in Christ, but the *methodological* point of departure continues to be the historical Jesus. This is objectively, the best *mystagogy* for the Christ of faith."[28] And with Ellacuría he historicizes this claim by insisting that we come to know the risen Jesus mainly by picking up and carrying his message about the Reign of God[29] and by accepting the suffering that comes to those who do things to realize its values in society today.

But what, exactly, does Sobrino mean by the "historical reality" of Jesus? And what role does the historical reality of Jesus play in his saving history Christology? Sobrino asserts that the historical Jesus is both the way to Christ and the starting point for a truly contextual Christology. Thus, while Latin American Christology "presupposes . . . faith in the whole reality of Jesus Christ," it must also confront "the methodological problem" that remains: "Where does one start in giving an account of this whole?" Sobrino therefore asserts, "I have chosen as my starting point the *reality* of Jesus of Nazareth, his life, his mission and his fate, what is usually called the *historical Jesus*."[30]

---

25. Rahner, "Two Basic Types," 215, emphasis added.

26. Sobrino, *Jesus the Liberator,* 45.

27. Sobrino, *Jesucristo liberador,* 104; Sobrino, *Jesus the Liberator,* 55.

28. Ibid.

29. Like many theologians, Ellacuría and Sobrino, from Medellín on, place great emphasis on the Reign of God as a defining element of the message and ministry of Jesus. Ellacuría, however, characteristically links the fundamental theological significance of the Kingdom preached by Jesus to what he calls "the transcendental unity of the history of salvation," arguing that the Kingdom reveals that "there are not two histories but one single history in which the presence of the liberator God and the presence of the liberated and liberator human being are joined together" (Ignacio Ellacuría, "La teología de la liberación frente al cambio socio-histórico de América Latina," in *Escritos teológicos,* I [San Salvador: UCA Editores, 2000], 317).

30. Sobrino, *Jesus the Liberator,* 36-63, at 36.

Here it is worth noting that, while Sobrino generally refers to the "reality" of Jesus rather than Ellacuría's more precise "historical reality" of Jesus, the meaning and the approach are generally the same (with some exceptions owing to looser language on Sobrino's part). This conjunction of the terms *reality* and *historical Jesus* should alert us to Sobrino's affinity with the insistence by both Ellacuría and Rahner on the unity of history and transcendence in Jesus. This is clear in Sobrino's argument that "Jesus Christ is a whole that, to put it for now in a simplified way, consists of a historical element (Jesus) and a transcendental element (Christ), and the most characteristic feature of faith as such is the acceptance of the transcendental element: that this Jesus is more than Jesus, that he is *the* Christ."[31]

Sobrino's two-volume Christology then proceeds to examine "the meaning of the *historical dimension of Jesus* in Latin American Christology." Sobrino starts with what he calls "(1) the most *historical* aspect of Jesus: his practice with spirit,"[32] carried out in announcing the Reign of God as good news to the poor. He then moves "(2) from the practice of Jesus to the *person* of Jesus," as revealed in his willingness to accept death on the cross in order to fulfill his mission as Son of the Father to announce and initiate the Reign of God. And he concludes with an examination of the journey "(3) from the historical Jesus to the whole Christ,"[33] asserting that "the most adequate way of gaining access to the Christ of faith . . . [is] re-enacting . . . the practice of Jesus . . . [as] a declaration, albeit implicit, that he is the Christ."[34] Volume I, *Jesucristo liberador* (*Jesus Christ Liberator*), focuses on the New Testament and the movement from "the mission and faith of Jesus" to his crucifixion and death, while Volume II picks up the trail from the New Testament resurrection accounts to the development of Christology in the early church and the first ecumenical councils. In all this Sobrino makes it clear that the deposit of faith remains normative, and that he is reading the tradition from a Latin American ecclesial "setting"[35] defined by the option for the poor and the perspective of the victims of history.

In the following three subsections, I will summarize the core claims of Sobrino's two volumes on each of the aforementioned points while tracing the impact of Ellacuría's profound historical realism on his vision of a Latin American saving history Christology that starts "from below" with the historical reality of Jesus. Then, heeding Rahner's prescient warning, I will examine how Sobrino's

---

31. Ibid., 36-37.

32. Ibid., 50. Sobrino's notion of the "poor with spirit" goes back to an early essay by Ellacuría on the Beatitudes where he interprets the first beatitude of Matthew 5:3 as "Blessed are the poor *with* spirit" (Ignacio Ellacuría, "Las bienaventuranzas como carta fundamental de la Iglesia de los pobres," in Oscar Romero et al., eds., *Iglesia de los pobres y organizaciónes populares* (San Salvador, UCA, 1979), 105-18; reprinted in Ellacuría, *Escritos teológicos,* II, 417-37, see esp. 423.

33. Sobrino, *Jesucristo liberador,* 96, 100, 102; *Jesus the Liberator,* 50, 52, 54.

34. Sobrino, *Jesus the Liberator,* 55; *Jesucristo liberador,* 103.

35. Sobrino, *Jesus the Liberator,* 28.

saving history Christology interprets the "process of 'rising up'" from the historical reality of Jesus to the Christ of faith as "an act proper to God himself."[36]

## Historicizing the Reign of God: The Ministry of Jesus

Sobrino's examination of Jesus begins with a definition: "By 'historical Jesus' we mean the life of Jesus of Nazareth, his words and actions, his activity and his praxis, his attitudes and his spirit, his fate on the cross (and the resurrection)."[37] This inclusion of both the "spirit" and the resurrection of Jesus in what Sobrino calls the "historical" Jesus helps us see that his understanding of the historical reality of Jesus transcends the positivism of historical facts. Indeed, Sobrino argues that "the most historical aspect of Jesus is his practice, and . . . the spirit with which he engaged in it and . . . imbued it." But what exactly does Sobrino mean by Jesus' "practice with spirit," and the "spirit" of the practice of Jesus?

Sobrino says the "spirit" of Jesus' refers to his "honesty toward the real world, partiality for the *little ones*, deep-seated mercy, [and] faithfulness to the mystery of God."[38] But what is "historical," observable, or *real* about this spirit? On the one hand, Sobrino argues, "this spirit was defined and so became real, through a practice, because it was within that practice, and not in his pure inwardness, that Jesus was challenged and empowered." Thus, Sobrino contends that the historical reality of the spirit of Jesus was observed and remembered in his practice. "On the other hand," however, Sobrino argues, "this spirit was not merely the necessary accompaniment of Jesus' practice, but shaped it, gave it a direction and even empowered it to be historically effective."[39] Thus, the "spirit" that Sobrino says suffuses Jesus' practice is not exhausted by "what is simply debatable in space and time."[40] Rather, it is a historical force, or what Ellacuría would call a historical reality wherein "the *historical* is . . . what sets history in motion." And Sobrino asserts this is precisely what has been "handed down to us as a trust . . . [in] the New Testament . . . as narratives published to keep alive through history a reality started off by Jesus." Thus, he concludes, the New Testament should not be treated as an empirical catalogue of Jesus' activities, but rather as a narrative that captures and passes on the spirit of Jesus to his disciples, when this "spirit" is understood as the fundamental relationships, loves, commitments, and self-understanding that defined the historical reality of his life.[41]

Following these introductory remarks on method the remainder of Volume I comprises two large sections on factors that define the historical reality of Jesus. Sobrino begins by asserting, "The first thing that strikes one in beginning to analyze the reality of Jesus of Nazareth" and what "emerges incontrovertibly

---

36. Rahner, "Two Basic Types," 214.
37. Sobrino, *Jesus the Liberator*, 50-52, esp. 50.
38. Ibid., 52.
39. Ibid.
40. Ibid., 51.
41. Ibid.

from the Gospels" are that "Jesus' life was an outward-directed one, directed to something . . . expressed by two terms: 'Kingdom of God' and 'Father.'"[42] Both terms, Sobrino asserts, "are authentic words of Jesus" and "all-embracing realities." On the one hand, the "Kingdom of God" defines for Jesus "all of [historical] reality and what must be done," and on the other, "by *'Father'* Jesus names the personal reality that lends ultimate meaning to his life."[43] So he says, "we begin with Jesus' relationship to the Kingdom, because this is how the Gospels begin . . . and because, I think, one gains better access to the whole reality of Jesus by starting from his external activities on behalf of the Kingdom and by moving from there to his inner relationship with God."[44]

Building on Ellacuría's three dimensions of historicization, Sobrino then outlines how Jesus (1) understands and announces the Reign of God, (2) takes responsibility for the Reign of God, and (3) carries out transformative activities on behalf of the Reign of God. Each of these moments is summarized below, including what each contributes to Sobrino's understanding of the "spirit" or defining commitments historicized in the practice of Jesus wherein the Word of God is made flesh.

### Jesus Announces the Reign of God as a Hoped-for Utopia Addressed to the Suffering Poor

Sobrino begins by examining the "concept" of the Reign of God articulated by Jesus, which presents God's Reign as primarily addressed to the poor.[45] He says the Synoptic Jesus understands the Reign as a "hoped-for utopia in the midst of the sufferings of history,"[46] a view that he claims Jesus shares with the Hebrew Scriptures and John the Baptist. He says that Jesus believes the Reign is "possible" and "something good and liberative,"[47] which he argues reflects both the common "expectation" of country folk from first-century Galilee and the hopes and aspirations of oppressed people throughout the ages.

Sobrino asserts, however, that Jesus breaks with John the Baptist and the Hebrew prophets in three important ways. First, he says "Jesus not only hopes for the Kingdom of God, [but] he affirms that it is at hand, that its arrival is imminent, [and] that the Kingdom should be not only an object of hope, but of certainty."[48] Second, Jesus insists that, while the Reign is God's initiative, gift, and grace, its actual coming "demands a conversion, [or] *metanoia*." Sobrino says this call to conversion creates "a task for the listener" that differs according to their location in the cycle of oppression. Thus, it is imperative we not confuse "the hope the poor must come to feel" with "the radical change of

---

42. Ibid., 67.

43. Sobrino, *Jesucristo liberador,* 121; *Jesus the Liberator,* 67.

44. Sobrino, *Jesucristo liberador,* 122; *Jesus the Liberator,* 67.

45. Sobrino, *Jesus the Liberator,* 69.

46. Ibid., 70.

47. Ibid., 75.

48. Ibid., 76.

conduct required of the oppressors," while at the same time acknowledging that "demands [are] made on all to live a life worthy of the Kingdom."[49] Third, while the Reign embodies a "crisis" and/or "judgment on the world and history,"[50] Jesus insists that it is "good news" for the poor, and must therefore "be proclaimed with joy and must produce joy."[51] Indeed, Sobrino asserts that this spirit of joy and hope "is why Jesus aroused undoubted popular support throughout the whole of his ministry."[52]

Fourth, Sobrino argues that, while Jesus "did not exclude anyone from the possibility of entering into the Kingdom," he primarily addressed the Reign of God to the poor.[53] Accordingly, for Jesus, "proclaiming good news *to the poor* of this world cannot be a matter of words alone," since "what the poor need and hope for" is a change in their historical reality.[54] Therefore, while Jesus' understanding of the Reign as liberating good news for the poor provoked hope and conversion, it also required a "messianic practice" capable of historicizing this spirit as a salvation in history in the context of first-century Israel.

## Jesus Assumes Responsibility for the Reign of God through His "Messianic Practice"

Having summarized the concept of the Reign of God preached by Jesus, Sobrino asserts that Jesus assumes ethical responsibility for his vision through a "messianic practice"[55] that historicizes his role as both *"proclaimer* and *initiator* of the Kingdom of God."[56] Sobrino suggests that in order to appreciate the role of Jesus' miracles in this practice, we must see them through the eyes of the poor country folk of Galilee as liberative signs of God's compassion. The miracles of Jesus arouse faith "in a God who, coming close, makes us believe in new possibilities actively denied to the poor in history." They elicit "a faith that overcomes fatalism . . . so that believers, now healed, are converted so as to become themselves principles of salvation for themselves."[57]

Reviewing examples of their restorative power, Sobrino argues that when Jesus casts out devils, his credibility is enhanced with his oppressed Galilean audience by the fact that "the Kingdom implies, of necessity, actively struggling against the anti-Kingdom."[58] Sobrino says that Jesus' welcoming and forgiving of common sinners promotes self-acceptance while overcoming their marginalization,[59] and when Jesus calls the powerful to "an active cessation

---

49. Ibid., 76-77.
50. Ibid., 77.
51. Ibid., 78.
52. Ibid.
53. Ibid., 79.
54. Ibid., 87.
55. Ibid., 161.
56. Ibid., 87.
57. Ibid., 93.
58. Ibid., 95.
59. Ibid., 95-99.

from oppressing," the poor understand "that God is not like . . . their oppressors and the ruling religious culture."[60] Likewise, Jesus' parables about the Reign, which call the oppressor to conversion, are both a way of defending the poor and a justification for action on their behalf.[61] All of this is symbolized in the way Jesus gathers his followers and others for meals and joyful events, which serve as "signs of the coming of the Reign and of the realization of its ideals: liberation, peace, universal communion."[62]

In the end, Sobrino argues that the messianic practice of Jesus embodies a courageous confrontation with oppression, a deep spirit of compassion and forgiveness, a call to personal transformation, and joy. He asserts that Latin American liberation theology "makes the Kingdom of God central for strictly christological reasons,"[63] including its defining role in the historical reality of Jesus' messianic practice, understood as a real sign of the Word made flesh. And he concludes by asserting that Jesus' messianic practice leads to a "prophetic praxis" through which he decisively alters the history of first-century Israel.

### Jesus Carries Out Transformative Activities on Behalf of the Reign of God through His "Prophetic Praxis"

In this section I will briefly summarize Sobrino's argument that Jesus carries out a prophetic ministry that goes beyond his roles of announcing the Reign as good news to the poor and enacting this message through a messianic ministry of miracles and other acts of compassion. Sobrino says that Jesus is forced to defend the first fruits of his messianic practice through a "prophetic praxis" involving "direct denunciation of the anti-Kingdom"[64] that changes Jesus and his impact on Israel. He distinguishes it from Jesus' "messianic prac-tice," which he says produces "signs" of the Reign but cannot be described as a praxis "aimed at bringing about the . . . transformation of society."[65] He associates it with the many controversies, unmaskings, and denunciations in which "Jesus denounces the scribes, the Pharisees, the rich, the priests, [and] the rulers . . . [who] represent and exercise some kind of power that structures society as a whole." And he asserts that Jesus' prophetic actions: (1) seek to reform and change the "realities (the law, the Temple) in whose name soci-ety is structured"; (2) expose structural abuses of institutional power as "an expression of the anti-Kingdom"; and (3) "show that the anti-Kingdom seeks to justify itself in God's name."[66] In this way, then, the prophetic activity of Jesus historicizes a spirit of transformative "'praxis' . . . because . . . its pur-pose [is] the transformation of society." Sobrino says this demonstrates "that

---

60. Ibid., 97.

61. Ibid., 100-101.

62. Sobrino, *Jesucristo liberador*, 182; *Jesus the Liberator*, 103.

63. Sobrino, *Jesus the Liberator*, 123.

64. Ibid., 161.

65. Ibid., 160.

66. Ibid., 161.

Jesus, objectively, faced up to the subject of society as a whole—including its structural dimension—and sought to change it."[67]

Sobrino then analyzes a whole series of controversies, unmaskings of lies and other mechanisms of oppressive religion, and denunciations of oppressors and their idols too numerous to review here. He ends with an examination of Jesus' expulsion of the traders from the Temple (Mark 11:15-19; Matthew 21:12-17; Luke 19:45-48; John 2:14-16), which he argues plays a role in the crucifixion (more about this below). He insists that in virtually all the controversies, unmaskings, and denunciations, "Jesus not only proclaims the Kingdom and proclaims a Father God; he also denounces the anti-Kingdom and unmasks its idols."[68] And he concludes that "in this praxis, Jesus can be seen to be in the line of the classic prophets of Israel, of Amos, Hosea, Isaiah, Jeremiah, Micah . . . and in that of the modern prophets, Archbishop Oscar Romero, . . . Martin Luther King, Jr." Sobrino's point is that Jesus historicizes the prophetic traditions of Israel through a praxis designed to confront, reform, and transform the abuse of his people's ancient institutions and practices by contemporary first-century elites.

With this claim, then, Sobrino concludes his argument that (1) Jesus understands and announces the Reign of God as justice, forgiveness, and mercy for the suffering poor and marginated people; (2) Jesus' "messianic practice" responds in a liberating manner to this suffering; and (3) Jesus' "prophetic praxis" models social transformations that are both good news for the poor and lead inevitably to his crucifixion. Sobrino argues that the merciful, liberating, and prophetic spirit that suffuses Jesus' proclamation and initiation of the Reign of God as good news for the poor also provokes resistance by the forces of the anti-Reign. And the awful logic of the anti-Reign willingly sacrifices the poor and their defenders in order to preserve its treasures. Unfortunately, the same logic of crucifixion and disposal applies to those who share Jesus' spirit of service to the Reign of God as good news to the poor.

### Doing the Will of the Father: Jesus as Faithful Son

This brings us, then, to what Sobrino calls the second "*historical dimension of Jesus* in Latin American Christology,"[69] his relationship with God as Father. Sobrino argues that Jesus' role as messenger and agent of the Reign of God as good news for the poor (his "practice with spirit" which includes his prophetic praxis) leads directly to his crucifixion, the defining moment of the life and "the *person* of Jesus."[70] Praising this dimension of Sobrino's work, biblical scholar Daniel Harrington argues that "Sobrino's 'historical-theological' reading of Jesus of Nazareth offers important methodological contributions to

---

67. Ibid.
68. Ibid., 179.
69. Ibid., 50.
70. Ibid., 52-54.

both the historical and theological study of Jesus and his death."[71] Harrington argues that Sobrino correctly eschews the "narrow version of historical criticism" found in many authors and formulates a "more adequate and fruitful way of treating ancient sources," which "involves taking seriously the historical data about Jesus and trying to do theology on the basis of and in light of these data."[72]

Harrington agrees with Sobrino that "Jesus' death was not a mistake, tragic or otherwise," and that "what got Jesus killed . . . was the fact that he was a radical threat to the religious and political powers of his time."[73] He agrees with Sobrino that Jesus "got in the way" by defending the victims of these elites in the name of the Kingdom of God.[74] As evidence, Harrington cites the fact that "the four Gospels are united in presenting Jesus as the victim of persecution and in suggesting that his death was . . . the logical consequence of who Jesus was and the circumstances in which he lived and worked."[75]

Harrington then asks, "Did Jesus know beforehand that he was going to suffer and die in Jerusalem?"[76] Noting that biblical scholars generally view the three passion predictions (Mark 8:31; 9:31; 10:33-34) as later insertions, Harrington says that Sobrino "wisely points to the fate of John the Baptist" to argue that Jesus likely went to Jerusalem cognizant of John's fate and ready to accept death "out of fidelity to the cause of the Kingdom of God, out of confidence in the one whom he called 'Father,' and out of loyalty to his prophetic calling."[77] With this move, he argues, Sobrino correctly situates "the link between the historical Jesus and the Christ of faith" precisely at "the root of Jesus' resolve to go to Jerusalem . . . [and] his understanding of his life as service on behalf of others, even to the point of sacrificial service."[78] Harrington insists, "This is the link between the historical Jesus and the Christ of faith, between Jesus of Nazareth and the early church's interpretations of him (Christology)." And Sobrino himself notes that the Gospels portray it as a defining moment for the historical reality of Jesus: his decision to accept suffering and death in order to fulfill his messianic, prophetic, and priestly mission from the Father to bring the Reign of God as good news for the poor.

Harrington cites the Temple incident (Mark 11:15-19) and Jesus' prophecy of the destruction of the temple (Mark 13:2) to argue (in support of Sobrino) that "it is reasonable to conclude that at the 'religious trial' [before the Sanhedrin] Jesus was accused of wanting to destroy the Temple not only because he criti-

71. Daniel J. Harrington, S.J., "What Got Jesus Killed? Sobrino's Historical-Theological Reading of Scripture," in Stephen J. Pope, ed., *Hope and Solidarity: Sobrino's Challenge to Christian Theology* (Maryknoll, NY: Orbis Books, 2008), 79-89, at 81.

72. Ibid.

73. Ibid.

74. Ibid., 82.

75. Ibid.

76. Ibid.

77. Ibid., 82-83.

78. Ibid., 83.

cized certain aspects of it but also because he offered an alternative (the Reign of God) that implied that the Temple would no longer be the core of the political, social, and economic life of the Jewish people."[79] Similarly, Harrington endorses Sobrino's acceptance of Luke's charges in the "political trial" before the Roman governor, Pontius Pilate (Luke 23:2), as very likely historical: "We found this man perverting our nation, forbidding them to pay taxes to the emperor, and saying that he himself is the Messiah, a king."[80] Harrington asserts, "The charge that Jesus made himself 'the Messiah, a king,' would have been especially incendiary in this context. And the Roman policy for dealing with such 'messianic' figures was swift and brutal execution."[81] Thus, in Harrington's view, the evangelists' description of the inscription on the cross, "The King of the Jews" (Mark 15:26), not to mention the public torture itself, would have served as brutal public warnings to "would-be Messiahs . . . tempted to lead an uprising against the Roman occupiers."[82]

Here it is crucial to understand that Sobrino is arguing that it is Jesus' relationship with the Father that guides and motivates both his obedient response to what he sees as God's call to initiate the Reign and the liberative prophetic practice that leads to his faith-filled death on the cross. Harrington notes appreciatively that Sobrino identifies "strong analogies between first-century Palestine and late-twentieth-century El Salvador," which he says open up new insights "that other interpreters in other circumstances may miss."[83] Sobrino concedes, "I have nothing to contribute to the exegetical elucidation" of scriptural accounts of the death of Jesus, but he says "the point I want to make is that the cross that dominates the Third World greatly illuminates the coherence with which the passion and death of Jesus—as a whole—are described."[84] Thus, the received tradition remains normative in Sobrino's analogical approach. But he rises to the challenge of Vatican II by trying to read the terrifying sign of the crucified people of Latin America in light of the historical reality of Jesus embodied in his "praxis with spirit, his crucifixion, and his resurrection."[85] Harrington suggests it is this perspective that defines Sobrino's primary contribution to the interpretation of the New Testament crucifixion narratives.

79. Ibid.
80. Ibid.
81. Ibid., 83-84.
82. Ibid., 84.
83. Ibid., 85.
84. Sobrino, *Jesus the Liberator*, 196.
85. Sobrino clearly insists on the normativity of the received tradition (*Christ the Liberator*, 36), while illustrating David Tracy's widely accepted definition of systematic theology as "the discipline that articulates mutually critical correlations between the meaning and truth of an interpretation of the Christian fact, and the meaning and truth of an interpretation of the contemporary situation." See David Tracy, "The Foundations of Practical Theology," in Don S. Browning, ed., *Practical Theology: The Emerging Field in Theology, Church and World* (New York: Harper & Row, 1983), 61-82, at 62.

## "Rising Up" from the Historical Reality of Jesus
## to the Christ of Faith

How, then, is the historical reality of Jesus continued in the crucified people, and how is the historical reality of the disciples' encounter with the risen Christ continued in new disciples whom God "raises up" to take the crucified people down from the cross? I will first examine what Sobrino means by the "historical" reality of the disciples' encounter with the risen Jesus. Second, I will scrutinize his argument that the crucified people are a historical sign of God's self-offer in Jesus Christ. Third, I will conclude with a consideration of Sobrino's assertion that God raises up disciples who become living signs of the resurrection by taking the crucified people down from the cross. And finally, I will examine Sobrino's conviction that each step (the encounter with the risen Jesus, the crucified people as a continuation of God's self-offer in Jesus, and the disciples who take them down from the cross) must be understood, at least in part, as "an act proper to God himself."[86]

### *The Historical Reality of the Encounter with the Risen Jesus:*
### *An Experience of God That Demands a Response*

This brings us, then, to the second volume of Sobrino's Christology, *La fe en Jesucristo* (*Faith in Jesus Christ*), where he deals with the resurrection as a final element of what he calls *the historical dimension of Jesus*, moving "from the historical Jesus to the whole Christ."[87] The perceptive reader will note that Sobrino's saving history approach, which interprets the historical reality of Jesus as the living sacrament of the Word of God, leads him far beyond the usual approach to the historical Jesus (that is, he speaks of "the whole Christ," and includes the resurrection).

Sobrino's approach is marked by the historical reality he attributes to the New Testament "paschal experience" and to its interpretation and acceptance in faith. This emphasis on the historical dimension of the resurrection emblemizes how Sobrino's Christian historical realism is expressed in his saving history approach to the historical reality of Jesus. His analysis is driven by what he aptly calls the "reality principle,"[88] which he says is "the central presupposition of the Christologies of the New Testament." The reality principle is a kind of scribal exegetical standard that works to limit the addition of various titles and other elements to the story of Jesus in the New Testament so that "the real and historical subject is still Jesus of Nazareth."[89] His point is that the reality principle allows the New Testament authors to credibly claim—given first-century scribal standards—that "Faith . . . is referred back to 'what we have heard, what we

---

86. Rahner, "Two Basic Types," 214.

87. Sobrino, *Jesucristo liberador* 102-4; *Jesus the Liberator*, 54-55.

88. Sobrino, *Christ the Liberator*, 225.

89. Ibid., 225.

have seen with our eyes, what we have looked at and touched with our hands'
(1 John 1:1)."[90]

Sobrino convincingly argues that New Testament witnesses to the resurrection of Jesus are presented as firsthand accounts of a "paschal experience,"
which "claims to be based in a *reality* that happened to Jesus and was, in some
way, observable."[91] But what exactly does he mean when Sobrino asserts that
"the New Testament builds its reflection on this *reality of the historical Jesus
and his resurrection*"?[92] Sobrino argues,

> The resurrection of Jesus is not presented in the New Testament as
> the return of a dead body to everyday life or as being caught up into
> heaven but as the action of God by which the eschatological irrupts
> into history and in which the true reality of Jesus begins to be made
> plain. In this sense it is narrated in the New Testament as an event
> without precedent in any other historical event. Therefore, it is not and
> cannot be described as an *intrahistorical* event, but it is nevertheless
> described as an event perceived *in history* and one that—decisively—
> affects history.[93]

In this section, then, having outlined the defining elements of Sobrino's
understanding of the historical reality of Jesus above, I will focus on Sobrino's
answer to the question "What is historical in Jesus' resurrection?"[94]

Sobrino's observation that the canonical Gospels "never describe Jesus' resurrection" leads him to assert that "in order to know what happened to Jesus,
we are of necessity referred to what happened to the disciples," which he calls
"the Easter experience."[95] He then examines the pre-Pauline gospel message (or
*kerygma*) that scholars place among the earliest summaries of what Christians
believed (1 Corinthians 15:3b-5): "that Christ died for our sins in accordance
with the scriptures, and that he was buried, and that he was raised on the third
day in accordance with the scriptures, and that he appeared to Cephas, then to
the twelve."

From this material Sobrino draws three properly historical claims. First, the
kerygmatic texts "affirm that something happened to Jesus' disciples, something
they attribute to *their encounter with Jesus*, whom they call the risen Lord."[96]
Second, "a change was worked in the disciples . . . before and after Easter." The
texts describe changes in "the places in which they were (from Galilee to Jerusalem); their behavior (from fear to bravery); [and] their faith (from 'We were

---

90. Ibid.

91. Sobrino, *Jesucristo liberador,* 413; this sentence is part of a paragraph not translated
in the English edition.

92. Sobrino, *Christ the Liberator,* 226, emphasis added.

93. Ibid., 17.

94. Ibid., 64, emphasis added.

95. Ibid., 55.

96. Ibid., 64, emphasis added.

waiting, but it is now the third day' to 'The Lord is risen indeed')." Third, the kerygma does not reflect the impact of Jesus on his followers during his life and death, but emerges from the disciples' experience of the resurrection. Sobrino asserts, "The *objective* conclusion, therefore, has to be . . . [that] for them there was no doubt that this subjective faith had a corresponding reality that happened to Jesus himself."[97] He concludes, however, "From a historical point of view, I do not think one can go further than this."

This brings Sobrino face to face with the problem of the exact nature of the relationship of history and faith, the resolution of which ultimately defines his interpretation of the historical reality of the resurrection of Jesus from a Latin American context. Sobrino argues that "the proclamation of the message that 'God raised Jesus from the dead'" presents Christians with a historical "invitation" to a "reasonable faith."[98] Drawing an analogy between the claims of the resurrection and the Exodus, Sobrino argues that both accounts confront readers with historical events that some have believed can be reasonably interpreted as actions of the transcendent God. Sobrino agrees with John Henry Newman that the faith that God has acted in history through such events can in fact be seen as a "reasonable response" to the "sum total of [historical] indicators," which he says include credible texts, personal experiences, and the long-lasting impact on believers of faith. In the present case, Sobrino argues that Scripture first confronts the reader/hearer with testimonies to "the presence of the eschatological in history," from witnesses that "appear to be honest people." Second, readers/hearers judge these claims in part through the prism of their own "present-day" historical encounters with "something ultimate." And third, readers/hearers will generally take into account that believing acceptance of these claims consistently (but not always) generates "greater personal humanization" and the creation of "more and better history."

These factors lead Sobrino to conclude "that understanding Jesus' resurrection as an eschatological event is an analogous problem to that of knowing God through any divine action."[99] The underlying idea, grounded in Ellacuría's Christian historical realism, is that history and faith are not opposites but are inextricably intertwined in historical reality, understood as that human reality that must take a stand on its historical reality in the world. Adapting the three questions that Immanuel Kant famously said every person must face,[100] Sobrino asks what historical *knowledge,* what historical *praxis,* and what historical *hope* "are needed today in order to understand what is being said when we hear that Jesus has been raised from the dead"? As we will see below, Sobrino argues that "the replies will above all take account of what the scriptural texts themselves

97. Ibid., 64-65.
98. Ibid.
99. Ibid., 35.
100. Immanuel Kant, *Critique of Pure Reason,* trans. Norman Kemp Smith (New York: St. Martin's Press, 1965), 635.

require" while at the same time reflecting what emerges when the story of Jesus is "reread from the Latin American situation."[101]

In this section, then, I have outlined key aspects of what Sobrino means by the "historical reality" of Jesus Christ and have begun to suggest the role of his answer in his approach to Latin American Christology. Sobrino builds on the concept of "historical reality" developed by Ellacuría and his vision of a Latin American Christology guided by a historical logos capable of recovering the salvific significance of the historical reality of Jesus. Ellacuría's notion of historical reality as that reality that must take a stance on its history in the world is exemplified in Sobrino's claim that Jesus defines his life, his person, and the salvation he brings through his fundamental historical stance toward the Father and his people Israel, the mission the Father gives Jesus to initiate the Reign of God, and his action of raising Jesus from the dead. In Sobrino's view, these are the defining elements of the historical reality of Jesus Christ as witnessed by the Gospels, and they guide his contextualized rereading of the tradition.

I have only begun, however, to suggest the place of the historical reality of Jesus in Sobrino's overall reading of the christological tradition from a Latin American perspective. In what follows I will suggest how Sobrino builds on Ellacuría's Rahnerian theology of sign, the trinitarian spirituality of Ignatius Loyola, and most especially Archbishop Romero's vision of the poor as the crucified image of Christ to argue that it is the "victims of history" who both help us understand and historicize (in the analogous way of a sign) the historical reality of Jesus as the "real symbol" of the Word made flesh.[102]

### The Crucified People: Historical Continuation of God's Self-Offer in Jesus Christ

The unique perspective that Sobrino brings to Christology as both witness and interpreter of the unexpected grace that is the crucified people and the faith of people who love them, such as Archbishop Oscar Romero and the UCA martyrs, is reflected in the question he adds to those of Kant: "What can we celebrate in history?"[103] Sobrino insists that "however scandalous this may seem" we should remember to ask, What is there to celebrate in the blood-stained history of "the Latin American situation"? His answer includes three "hermeneutical principles," which he portrays as gifts "from the victims" of history opening a path to understanding acceptance of the resurrection of Jesus in a Latin American context.[104]

---

101. Sobrino, *Christ the Liberator,* 36.

102. Ibid., 319.

103. Ibid.

104. Ibid., 35-36. Matthew Ashley asserts that Sobrino's principles are formulated in reference to "a hope that hopes first . . . for the raising to full life of the poor; a praxis devoted to raising them up now by striving for justice for the poor and . . . a knowing that is open to the surprise of finding God revealed in the poor" (J. Matthew Ashley, "The Resurrection of Jesus and Resurrection Discipleship in the Systematic Theology of Jon Sobrino," summarized

## Hope of the "Victims"

Sobrino's first principle is the scandalous claim that the historical *hope of the crucified* in the victory of life over death is "the most essential hermeneutical requirement for understanding what happened to Jesus."[105] He argues that "if human beings were not by nature 'beings of hope' or were unable to fulfill this hope over the course of history with its ups and downs, the resurrection texts would . . . be incomprehensible. It would be like trying to explain colors to a blind person."[106] Historicizing this claim, he says the Hebrew scriptures call Israel to faith and hope in the God of life and justice who has been revealed through Israel's history of oppression and liberation. Likewise, New Testament accounts of the resurrection of Jesus call for "hope in the power of God over the injustice that produces victims"[107] and over the many forms of crucifixion and death used to defeat the promises of the Reign. He concludes, therefore, that "human transcendental hope is a necessary but [still] insufficient condition for understanding Jesus' resurrection."[108]

So where in history do we actually find this hope, and how do we make it our own? Sobrino says the answer "is difficult; [for] it requires us to make the hope of victims, and with it their situation, our own."[109] Thus, like a parable of Jesus that turns the world on its head, Sobrino says that hope is "a gift the victims themselves make to us." The risk, however, is that in order to make it our own "we have to slot ourselves into this hope," so that "by doing so we can rebuild—with different, through ultimately similar, mediations—the process followed by Israel's faith in a God of resurrection." Sobrino's point, therefore, is that only by making the historical hope of history's victims into our own hope can "we progress in finding a God who is loving and on the side of the victims, so we can respond to this God with radical love for them." The disciple, then, is confronted with a two-edged sword. On the one hand, adopting the hope of the victims "makes the question of the ultimate fate of these victims more acute," which is uncomfortable. On the other, however, it means both that "we can . . . 'hope' that the executioner will not triumph over them" and that we are offered the possibility of "a final and fulfilling hope."[110]

## Praxis of Love

Sobrino's second principle is that the hope of the victims in God's victory over death is only truly understood through a *praxis of love* that takes the crucified people down from the cross. This controversial claim reflects Sobrino's convic-

---

in Tatha Wiley, "Christology," Catholic Theological Society of America, *Proceedings of the Sixtieth Annual Convention* 60 [2005]: 104).

105. Sobrino, *Christ the Liberator*, 45.
106. Ibid., 36.
107. Ibid., 42.
108. Ibid., 45.
109. Ibid.
110. Ibid.

tion that if "the ultimate root of all hope is . . . always love," then "the Kingdom cannot be understood only as what is hoped for . . . but also . . . as what has to be built."[111] Thus, just as love leads Jesus to initiate the Reign and to accept suffering and death on its behalf, so when he appears to his followers "the risen Lord sends them out to preach, baptize, forgive sins, feed the faithful, and . . . (Matthew 28:19-20; John 20:23; 21:15, 17) . . . like the earthly Jesus, to heal and cast out demons (Mark 16:17-18)."[112] Sobrino's point is that love of neighbor is made real (or historicized) through action on behalf of the beloved.

Sobrino then argues that "understanding today that Jesus has been raised by God entails [not just] the hope that we can be *raised*, but . . . also that we have to be, in some way, *raisers*."[113] And here the mystery of salvation and historical soteriology again converge with the Mystery of God and *theōsis*. Or to put it another way, Sobrino's trinitarian theology of sign merges with his claim that the *analogatum princeps* of the life, death, and resurrection of Jesus is to be found among the crucified people and those who take them down from the cross. Sobrino says that, just as in due course God's "justice was done to the crucified Jesus, . . . so the course of action called for is [for us] to take the crucified people down from the cross."[114] Viewed as a way of following Jesus in light of his second principle, Sobrino concludes with the startling claim, "This is action on behalf of the victims, of those crucified in history, that tries in a small way— with of course no hubris—to do what God himself does: to take the victim Jesus down from the cross."[115]

The significance and potentially controversial nature of this claim is highlighted in a private letter leaked and published in 1984, where Joseph Ratzinger, then head of the Congregation for the Doctrine of the Faith (CDF), criticizes "the impressive, but ultimately shocking interpretation of the death and resurrection of Jesus made by J. Sobrino . . . that God's gesture in raising Jesus is repeated in history . . . through giving life to the crucified."[116] Responding to what he sees as a misstatement of his claim, however, Sobrino cautions, "I hope it is clear that I am not talking of repeating God's action, any more than I talked of bringing in the Kingdom of God in the previous volume of this work." He replies, however, "What I do insist on is giving signs—analogously—of resurrection and coming of the Kingdom. And this is also what Ignacio Ellacuría

---

111. Ibid.
112. Ibid., 46.
113. Ibid., 47.
114. Ibid., 48.
115. Ibid.
116. Originally published in *30 Giorni* 3, no. 3 (1984): 48-55; republished in *Il Regno: Documenti* 21 (1984): 220-23; cited in Sobrino, *Christ the Liberator,* 48. Ratzinger's comments are made in reference to Sobrino's first Christology, published twenty-three years earlier (see Jon Sobrino, *Cristología desde américa latina [esbozo a partir del seguimiento del Jesús histórico]* [Rio Hondo, Mexico: Centro de Reflección Teológica, 1976; trans. from *Christology at the Crossroads: A Latin American Approach* (Maryknoll, NY: Orbis Books, 1978)]).

meant when he . . . used the expression 'taking the crucified people down from the cross' as a formulation of the Christian mission."[117]

Sobrino's reply provides a window on the spirituality of the UCA martyrs from his perspective as witness and interpreter, and could hardly be more relevant to the topic of this book. But it is difficult, if not impossible, to understand Sobrino's claim (and Ellacuría's as well) without reference to our earlier discussion of Ignatian spirituality, Ellacuría's Rahnerian and trinitarian theology of sign, and Sobrino's Zubirian understanding of the historical reality of Jesus.[118] In the famous meditation on the Trinity from the *Spiritual Exercises* Ignatius Loyola calls the retreatant to direct collaboration with the work of the Trinity in the world.[119] This meditation is cited by the Thirty-second General Congregation of the Society of Jesus (1974-1975) as one of the defining elements of the mission and spirituality of Jesuits today in a document[120] inspired by a *postulata* first drafted by the Central American Jesuits during the very years in which Sobrino composed the text cited by Ratzinger. And as we saw earlier, Miguel Elizondo, who gave the *Spiritual Exercises* as novices to both Ellacuría and Sobrino, cites this same meditation in his key talk at the 1969 retreat where the Central American Jesuits embraced the option for the poor. Outlining the vocation of a Jesuit (and the spirituality behind Sobrino's thesis), Miguel Elizondo says:

> The Ignatian vocational experience consists in a trinitarian experience, of the Trinity present and operative in this world, in all things . . . realizing its plan for the salvation of the whole world. In this expe-

---

117. Sobrino, *Christ the Liberator,* 48. The first instance of this metaphor is cited as Ignacio Ellacuría, "Las Iglesias latinoamericanas interpelan a la Iglesia de España," *Sal Terrae* 3 (1983): 230.

118. In his important essay on Ignacio Ellacuría as an interpreter of Ignatian spirituality, Ashley asserts that Ellacuría's "philosophy and theology had as their goal the communication of a powerful 'fundamental intuition' from the *Spiritual Exercises,*" which he later describes as a "mysticism of the historical event." In a related article, Ashley asserts that Ellacuría tried to put this spirituality "at the service of the church in Latin America . . . by seeking philosophical and theological language and arguments to articulate the encounter with Christ that is structured by Ignatius Loyola's *Spiritual Exercises,*" and which is embodied in the Ignatian tradition of "contemplation in action." While I agree with and build upon Ashley's insights in this regard, my article places more emphasis on the trinitarian dimensions of Ignatian spirituality (which Ashley recognizes) and their influence on Ellacuría's theology of sign. See J. Matthew Ashley, "Ignacio Ellacuría and the *Spiritual Exercises* of Ignatius Loyola," *Theological Studies* 61 (2000): 16-39, at 37, 39; also J. Matthew Ashley, "Contemplation in the Action of Justice: Ignacio Ellacuría and Ignatian Spirituality," in Kevin Burke and Robert Lassalle-Klein, eds., *Love That Produces Hope: The Thought of Ignacio Ellacuría* (Collegeville, MN: Liturgical Press, 2006), 144, 145, 164 n. 54.

119. David L. Fleming, S.J., *The Spiritual Exercises of Saint Ignatius: A Literal Translation and a Contemporary Reading* (St. Louis: The Institute of Jesuit Sources, 1978), 70-74, 102-9.

120. "Our Mission Today: The Service of Faith and the Promotion of Justice," no. 14, *Documents of the 31st and 32nd General Congregations of the Society of Jesus* (St. Louis: Institute of Jesuit Sources, 1977), 414.

rience Ignatius sees that all things are born from God and return to God through the presence and operation of God's self. And not only by means of the presence and operation of God, but through the insertion of humanity in history. Into this history of salvation comes the human "par excellence," Christ, and with him all persons chosen to actively cooperate in the operation of the Trinity, to realize the salvific plan of God.[121]

Here, then, are the Ignatian roots of Sobrino's claim, which provides a window on the self-understanding of the UCA martyrs, that Christians are called "to do what God himself does: to take the victim Jesus down from the cross." The disciple is called to collaborate with the work of the Trinity in the world. And the initiative for this call comes from God through the incarnation of the Word in Jesus Christ and the call by the Holy Spirit to join him in discipleship and service. As a result, Elizondo says, "the definitive God of Ignatius is going to be the God of this world." And for both Ignatius's and Elizondo's colleagues, "Action becomes a totally different category. . . . Love will not be principally affective or contemplative, but a love that is realized in works, that translates into service, that is realized in this cooperation with God." Thus, Elizondo argues, "action will be for St. Ignatius the response to this trinitarian God and the sign of the active presence of the Trinity in Ignatius and in the life of his Society."[122]

Sobrino's point, then, is that when the disciple responds to the grace-filled call by Jesus Christ to take the crucified people down from the cross, he or she is caught up in what I have said the Greek Fathers called *theōsis*, becoming a living sign of God's work (including the resurrection) in Jesus Christ. Unfortunately, however, just as Jesus' prophetic praxis leads inevitably to his crucifixion, so "action on behalf of the crucified . . . is also automatically against the executioners and . . . conflictive."[123] Sobrino says this flows from the fact that, on the one hand, "action at the service of the resurrection of the *dead* [and] . . . the *many* . . . should also be social, political, seeking to transform structures, *to raise them up*."[124] On the other hand, however, such action inevitably brings persecution and suffering to the disciples of Jesus, transforming them into living signs of his life, death, and resurrection. Thus, the disciple who responds to the call embodied in the historical reality of Jesus to loving action on behalf of the poor is destined to become, analogously, a living sign of how the Reign of God brings both joy and suffering, and how the economy of salvation is carried out in the historical reality of Jesus Christ.

---

121. Miguel Elizondo, "La Primera Semana como comienzo indispensable de conversión," 3, in "Reunión-Ejercicios de la viceprovincia Jesuitica de Centroamérica, Diciembre 1969," 4-8, *Reflexion teológico-espiritual de la Compañía de Jesús en Centroamérica, II* (San Salvador: Archives of the Society of Jesus, Central American Province, Survey S.J. de Centroamérica).

122. Ibid., 3, 4.

123. Sobrino, *Christ the Liberator,* 48.

124. Ibid.

## Reality as Mystery

The third hermeneutical principle that Sobrino calls a gift from the victims of history is that "in the final analysis, to know Jesus' resurrection we have to accept that *reality is a mystery* that is being shown to us gratuitously."[125] Sobrino's point is that "if . . . one confesses [the resurrection] . . . as something real, then it is necessary to have . . . faith in God's possibilities for intervening in history." He says this implies "an understanding of reality as that which bears within itself and points to an eschatological future."[126]

As we have already seen, this conjunction of "history" and "reality" reflects Ellacuría's understanding of historical reality and his rejection of "nineteenth-century positivism"[127] with its view of history as empirical events that do not admit the possibility of radical historical discontinuity. Sobrino argues instead, however, that the claim that transcendence is known through history, like the more specific Christian claim that "the resurrection is the appearance of the eschatological in history,"[128] presupposes that historical reality comprises "more" than simply empirical events. This capacity for the "more" is the dimension of human historical reality specifically addressed by the *Spiritual Exercises* of St. Ignatius. It defines the notion of transcendence in history found in the writings and speeches of Sobrino, Ellacuría, Archbishop Romero, Rahner, and Zubiri, and it provides the basis for their insistence on the historicity of salvation and the Mystery of God.

Sobrino therefore concludes his reflection on *faith in Jesus Christ* by asserting again that Christian soteriology is driven by the fact that Christianity is first a religion of *theōsis* and the encounter with Holy Mystery historicized in God's self-offer through the crucified people of today. Thus, Sobrino concludes, "On this journey through history, not going outside history but taking flesh and delving deep into history, it can happen that reality gives more of itself, and the conviction can grow (or decrease) that . . . the journey is enveloped in the mystery of the beginning and the end, a mystery that antedates us, from which we come, which moves us to good and leads us to hope for eternal life."[129] Here Sobrino historicizes for a Latin American context the spirituality of the *Spiritual Exercises*, the Zuburian idea of the theologal dimension of reality as the "more" that calls us to growth and *deiformación*, and the trinitarian theology of Ellacuría and Rahner. But the originality of Sobrino's work springs less from these sources than from his efforts with Ellacuría to articulate the experience of the Latin American church in living with the option for the poor, and as interpreter and witness to the unexpected grace of the crucified people and the martyrs who loved them.

---

125. Ibid., 53.
126. Ibid.
127. Sobrino, *Jesucristo liberador*, 50.
128. Ibid., 52.
129. Sobrino, *Christ the Liberator*, 340.

It is not surprising, then, that we would find the voice of the UCA martyrs in Sobrino's scandalous claim, "This mystery is grace, and the victims of this world, the crucified peoples, can be, and in my view are, the mediation of this grace. [For] the victims provide the dynamism—the quasi-physical 'shove'—for carrying out the task of journeying that involves taking the crucified peoples down from their cross."[130] Sobrino confesses that for him, "the greatest encouragement comes from those who inspire with their actual lives, those who today resemble Jesus by living and dying as he did" (no matter who they are). These are the people who, like Archbishop Oscar Romero, pick up this hope, take responsibility for it, and carry out Jesus' compassionate, loving, and transformative "practice with spirit." At the end of the day, however, whether through liberation or solidarity, Sobrino concludes, "This is God's journey to this world of victims and martyrs, . . . it is the way to the Father and the way to human beings, [and] above all [it is the way] to the poor and the victims of this world."[131]

## "Raising Up" Living Signs to the Resurrection:
## "An Act Proper to God Himself"

We are now finally in position to summarize how Sobrino's Christology embodies Rahner's notion that saving history Christology makes the "process of 'rising up'" from the historical reality of Jesus to the Christ of faith "an act proper to God himself."[132]

Sobrino's trinitarian (and Ignatian) approach leads him to situate Chalcedon's teaching on the unity of humanity and divinity in the person of Jesus Christ within the larger, more "holistic" framework of the divine economy of salvation (the ongoing work of the Trinity in the world). Sobrino rejects the tendency "to understand the unity of the divine and the human in Jesus Christ as . . . the union of two realities that . . . could exist independently of one another." He argues instead for "the sacramentality of the real," endorsing Rahner's claim that "the human, Jesus, is the real symbol of the Word."[133] For Sobrino and Rahner this claim implies a dynamic understanding of the role of human nature in the economy of salvation, which Rahner places under the heading of theological anthropology. Sobrino argues, "The Word . . . took on human nature in creating it and created it in taking it on." His point is that "the humanity of Christ is . . . that created reality which becomes the Word when the Word alienates itself, goes outward from itself." The historical reality of Jesus Christ ultimately "remains the symbol of the Word for always, including in the beatific vision."[134] And he insists that the historical reality of the life, death, and resurrection of Jesus must be understood as the real symbol, and the definitive revelatory sign

---

130. Ibid., 340.

131. Ibid.

132. Rahner, "Two Basic Types," 214.

133. Sobrino, *Christ the Liberator,* 319.

134. Sobrino, "Jesus, Real Symbol of the Word," in ibid., 319.

of the Word of God in history. Ellacuría makes this point with his claim that "the historical life of Jesus is the fullest revelation of the Christian God."[135]

The key idea in all this is that the initiative in Sobrino's saving history approach to Christology originates with the work of the Trinity in the world. Ellacuría makes the point clearly when he states, "It is in the incarnation where one appreciates up to what point God has interiorized himself in history." Thus, Ellacuría insists,

> Following St. Augustine and with greater truth than in his formula-tion—*nolite foras ire, in interiore hominis habitat veritas* [do not go outside, truth resides within humanity]—it should be said: *nolite foras ire, in interiore historiae habitat Verbum trinitarium* [do not go outside, the Word of the Trinity resides within history]. That is, the Word personally resides in history, and the historical incarnation of the Word makes the Father and the Holy Spirit present . . . in history in a radi-cally distinct manner.[136]

The key point, then, is that the self-revelation and self-offer of the Word of God achieved in the historical reality of Jesus Christ and continued through the historical sign of the crucified people is an action of the Trinity!

Sobrino then insists that christological and trinitarian doctrine requires that "the presence of God in the mediation of Jesus does not take place like a momentary docetist step."[137] Accordingly, God's self-offer in Jesus must be understood as "a real continuing presence, whose full reality will be given in the Second Coming." And "the resurrection and the exaltation [of Jesus] in heaven manifest transcendence, but they are not a negation of history." Thus, the res-urrection means "that [Jesus] sends the Spirit, who is his Spirit, the Spirit of Christ, precisely in order to continue dwelling among humanity until the end of the ages."[138] And this spirit raises up historical witnesses and living signs of the resurrection, such as Archbishop Oscar Romero and the many thousands who have followed his example.

In the end, therefore, Sobrino argues that the historical reality of Jesus Christ is the sacrament of God's self-revelation and self-offer, and that the acceptance of this offer raises up witnesses to the resurrection and living signs of the work of the Trinity in the world. Thus, Sobrino concludes (in agreement with Rahner) that the "process of 'rising up'" from the historical reality of Jesus to the Christ of faith must be seen as "an act proper to God himself."[139] For it is the Holy Spirit who empowers the disciple to respond in faith to the call to follow Jesus

---

135. Ignacio Ellacuría, *Freedom Made Flesh* (Maryknoll, NY: Orbis Books, 1976), 27.

136. Ignacio Ellacuría, "Fe y justicia," *Escritos teológicos*, III (San Salvador: UCA, 2002), 307-73, at 319-20; reprinted from *Christus* 42 (August 1977): 26-33; and (October 1977): 19-34.

137. Ibid.

138. Ibid.

139. Rahner, "Two Basic Types," 214.

Christ by taking the crucified people down from the cross, thereby fulfilling the will of the Father by saying *yes* to the historical self-revelation of the Mystery of God.

## Conclusion

In concluding, I return to the question with which I began: How do Ignacio Ellacuría and Jon Sobrino make sense from the perspective of faith in Jesus Christ of the suffering, death, and apparent defeat of the hopes and aspirations of so many Salvadorans and the people who loved them, including Archbishop Oscar Romero and the UCA martyrs? I suggested the answer was to be found in the image of the crucified people inspired by Oscar Romero's homily to the terrified peasants of Aguilares, which Ellacuría extends to the notion that followers of Jesus are called to take them down from cross. Accordingly, in Part III I have examined the contextual Christology of these Jesuit collaborators, showing how it formalizes Romero's statement of faith in two christological affirmations: (1) the historical reality of Jesus Christ is the real sign of the Word made flesh and the divine economy of salvation; and (2) the *analogatum princeps* of God's unrepeatable self-offer in the life, death, and resurrection of Jesus and the divine economy of salvation is to be found today among the crucified peoples and the invitation to take them down from the cross.

In Chapter 8 I examined the contribution of four assertions from the fundamental theology of Ignacio Ellacuría (thematizing his Christian historical realism) to Sobrino's christological argument for the aforementioned assertions. First, history and salvation are complementary elements of the great history of God (which includes all history). Second, salvation history is a salvation in history, which means the historical reality of Jesus and his followers must have been experienced as such (as a salvation in history). Third, the historical reality of Jesus is the defining sign of the Word made flesh and the starting point for a truly Latin American Christology with its historical *logos*. And fourth, this Christology correlates the saving historical reality of Jesus with the crucified people as the victims of the sin of the world and bearers of its salvation.

In Chapter 9 I then explored how Sobrino's two-volume Latin American Christology appropriates and develops these and other insights in support of the two theses above. First, he argues that "the historical reality of Jesus"[140] is "the fullest revelation of the Christian God,"[141] and he examines its defining aspects (the Reign of God as good news to the poor, his relationship with the Father, and his crucifixion) as salvation in history. Second, he treats the "Easter experience"[142] as God's eschatological confirmation of the ministry of Jesus, which changes the historical reality of his followers and draws them to become more like him in a process Sobrino describes as *theōsis*. Third, he says crucified

---

140. Ellacuría, *Freedom Made Flesh*, 27; cited in Sobrino, *Jesus the Liberator*, 46-47.

141. Ibid.; cited by Sobrino in *Jesus the Liberator*, 47.

142. Sobrino, *Christ the Liberator*, 226.

people are the *analogatum princeps* of God's historical self-offer in Jesus Christ
and that when we take the crucified people down from the cross, we are drawn
into the work of the Trinity in the world and the living Mystery of God.

These affirmations give voice to the faith, hope, and love of the UCA martyrs
and remind us of Romero's prophecy: "If I am killed, I shall arise in the Salvadoran people."[143] Romero's statement is an act of faith in the God of Jesus whose
resurrection Sobrino says "cannot be described as an *intrahistorial* event,"
though it is certainly "an event perceived *in history* and one that—decisively—
affects history."[144] So how, then, does the resurrection of Jesus affect the history
of El Salvador? As we have seen, Sobrino argues that whatever happened to
Jesus in the resurrection (the New Testament is silent on this point), he is risen
and his appearances lead to faith in a Father-God who empowers us to historicize the Reign of God by taking the crucified people down from the cross. Here,
then, is the theological meaning of Romero's prophecy that through his death,
God would bring life to him and to the Salvadoran people, raising up witnesses
to the resurrection and living signs of the compassion of God. Romero's prophecy is an invitation to accept God's self-offer by embracing the Spirit of Jesus
who empowers his followers (of whatever faith) to bring life from death, and joy
from sorrow. This is the story of the UCA martyrs.

143. Brockman, *Romero, A Life*, 248
144. Ibid., 17.

# Conclusion

# *Living Signs of the Resurrection*

## THE TRINITARIAN SPIRITUALITY
## OF THE UCA MARTYRS

These men were also believers, Christians. I do not mention this here as something obvious or to be taken for granted, but as something central in their lives, something that really ruled all their lives. . . . When we spoke about matters of faith in the community, our words were sparing but really meant. We spoke about God's Kingdom and the God of the Kingdom, of Christian life as a following of Jesus, the historical Jesus, Jesus of Nazareth, because there is no other. In the university—in teaching and theological writings, of course—but also in solemn moments and public acts we recalled our Christian inspiration as something central, as what gave life, direction, force, and meaning to all our work, and explained the risks the university very consciously incurred. There was plain speaking about God's Kingdom and the option for the poor, sin and the following of Jesus. This Christian inspiration of the university was never just rhetoric when these Jesuits talked about it, and people understood that this was really the university's inspiration.

Jon Sobrino[1]

### Where We Have Been?

Jon Sobrino says the University of Central America (UCA) martyrs and their colleagues were transformed by the historical reality of El Salvador and their encounter with the risen Jesus in its suffering people. The UCA, Ellacuría's Christian historical realism, and Sobrino's contextual Christology developed with Ellacuría's help bear the marks of this experience, which can be seen as university-style efforts to take the crucified people down from the cross.

---

1. Jon Sobrino, "Companions of Jesus," in *Companions of Jesus: The Jesuit Martyrs of El Salvador* (New York: Orbis Books, 1990), 16.

The story of the awakening of the UCA Jesuits and their colleagues to God's self-offer in the crucified people and to Medellín's call to take them down from the cross was told in Part I.. It was a story of U.S. funded state-sponsored violence against Salvadoran civil society and later against the UCA for its university-style support of El Salvador's poor majorities and their mobilization for economic, military, and social reform. Ellacuría says the UCA simply tried "to do in our university way what [Archbishop Romero] did in his pastoral way"[2] guided by Medellín's discernment that God was calling the church to a preferential option for the poor. This led them to confront violent, powerful, and dehumanizing forces with a reasoned and compassionate plea for negotiations and peace. But the sanity and humanity of this approach proved a threat to U.S. congressional support for an immoral foreign policy financing a corrupt ally in a brutal and unnecessary civil war. This led to the senseless deaths of the UCA martyrs for their university-style efforts to take El Salvador's crucified people down from the cross. Ironically, however, the assassinations (combined with the 1989 National Liberation Party [FMLN] offensive) helped bring about the very thing they were meant to avoid, crippling congressional support and setting the stage for the 1992 peace accords, the *sine qua non* of the UCA's calls for a society in which all would have a chance for a future where dignity, compassion, and sanity might prevail.

I then argued that it was Oscar Romero more than anyone else who taught Ellacuría to trust the crucified people as a political barometer and a theological source for the fundamental theology described in Part II. In Chapter 4 I said that Ellacuría sought to historicize the discernment of the 1969 *Spiritual Exercises* retreat in the work of the UCA, which he saw as an apostolic collaboration with the ongoing work of the Trinity in the world. In Chapter 5 I examined Ellacuría's interpretation of Zubiri's post-Newtonian concept of reality and neuroscientifically astute model of sentient intelligence. I examined their role in his argument that historical reality is the primary object of human intelligence and the locus for the encounter with God, which made it the *locus intellectus* of the university and the *locus theologicus* of the UCA's theological work. In Chapter 6 I argued, with Jon Sobrino, that Archbishop Romero shaped Ellacuría's faith and the sense of vocation that guided the final decade of his life. I asserted that Romero taught Ellacuría to love, to trust, and to find Christ in the common people of El Salvador. And I said that Romero lit the prophetic torch and passed it to Ellacuria, inspiring him to bring God close to the suffering poor and to leaven their struggle for liberation and the future of El Salvador with the message of Jesus.

In Chapter 7 I then examined Karl Rahner's contributions to *the philosophical-theological* and strictly *theological fundamenta* developed by Ellacuria to interpret the human face of God revealed to him by Archbishop Romero in the suffering people of El Salvador. I said first that while Ellacuría insists (with Zubiri) that *historical reality* rather than *being* is the proper object of a truly

---

2. Ignacio Ellacuría, "La UCA ante el doctorado concedido a Monseñor Romero," *Escritos teológicos*, III (San Salvador: UCA Editores, 2002), 104.

Latin American theology, he agrees with Rahner that it is permeated by an absolute (or *theologal*) dimension that provides a privileged locus for the human encounter with God. Second, I said Ellacuría argues that the human person is a sentient intelligence-in-the-world (partially inspired by Rahner's concept of a spirit-in-the-world), which apprehends and therefore must take a stance in everyday life on his or her encounters with the absolute dimension of reality. Thus, he says, sentient intelligence (which incorporates but sublimates aspects of Rahner's "conversion to the phantasm") provides the most adequate model for the role for human knowing in Latin American theological method. Third, I asserted that Ellacuría develops a theological anthropology (or model of the human person before God) rooted in the notion that *historical reality has been transformed by grace*, which draws upon and historicizes aspects of Rahner's concept of the supernatural existential. And fourth, I argued that Ellacuría develops a *theology of sign* that echoes the trinitarian pattern of Rahner's "theology of symbol" while switching the focus to the crucified people as the historical sign of the sin of the world and a continuation of God's self-offer in Jesus Christ (Matthew 25:40, 45).

Finally in Part III I examined how Ellacuría's fundamental theology and Sobrino's Christology form a sustained contextual theological reflection on the historical reality of El Salvador unified by two (by now familiar) fundamental claims: the saving historical reality of Jesus is the real sign of the Word made flesh; and the *analogatum princeps* of God's self-offer in the life, death, and resurrection of Jesus is to be found today among the crucified peoples. In Chapter 8 I discussed the contribution to this Christology of four claims by Ignacio Ellacuría regarding the historicity of salvation. First, history and salvation are complementary aspects of the larger unity that he calls the great history of God. Second, if salvation history is genuinely historical, it must be experienced as a salvation in history. Third, the historical reality of Jesus is the defining sign of the Word made flesh and the starting point for a genuinely Latin American Christology (which must be guided by a historical *logos*). Fourth, Latin American Christology correlates the saving historical reality of Jesus with the crucified people as the victims of the sin of the world and bearers of its salvation. This then leads him to the conclusion that the saving power of the encounter with Jesus Christ in the crucified people lies in its power to draw us to become more like Jesus, which makes Christianity "prior to being a religion of salvation . . . and precisely in order to be such,"[3] a religion of becoming like God by becoming like Jesus.

In Chapter 9 I then explored how Sobrino's two-volume Christology appropriates and develops these and other insights in support of its two unifying theses noted above. First, he says that Latin American Christology starts with "the historical reality of Jesus" as "the fullest revelation of the Christian God."[4]

---

3. Xavier Zubiri, *El hombre y Dios* (Madrid: Alianza Editorial, 1984), 381.

4. Ignacio Ellacuría, *Freedom Made Flesh: The Mission of Christ and His Church* (Maryknoll, NY: Orbis, 1976), 27; cited in Jon Sobrino, *Jesus the Liberator: A Historical-Theological View* (Maryknoll, NY: Orbis Books, 1993), 47.

He argues that Jesus' historical reality is defined by his relationship as Son to the Father, his mission from God to announce the Reign of God as good news to the poor, and his crucifixion by those who fight against the Reign. Second, he treats the "Easter experience"[5] as God's eschatological confirmation of the historical reality of Jesus (defined in his ministry and message), which draws those who follow him to become more like Jesus in a process Sobrino describes as *theōsis*. Third, he says the crucified people are the *analogatum princeps* of God's historical self-offer in Jesus Christ and that when we take the crucified people down from the cross we are drawn like (or analogously to) Jesus into the work of the Trinity in the world and the living Mystery of God.

This review, then, provides ample evidence for the claim that the fundamental theology of Ignacio Ellacuría and the allied Christology of Jon Sobrino form perhaps the most fully developed Catholic contextual theology since Vatican II and a model for contextual theologies in a globalized church. And this claim would have provided a worthy *raison d'être* had it been the central argument of this book. Yet our primary interest has never been in making this point, though I have provided ample evidence for its defense: Instead, my interest has always been to capture and confront with the reader a glimpse of the God of the UCA martyrs. But this is a much more difficult and subtle undertaking, which one might consider beyond our reach twenty-five years from their deaths (it is worth noting that the Gospel of Mark lies farther from the death of Jesus). Fortunately, however, this is simply another version of the task that Jon Sobrino and Ignacio Ellacuría set for themselves. Sobrino says in the introduction to his two-volume Christology, "I have done nothing more than—starting from Jesus—to elevate the reality we are living to the level of a theological concept; to theorize about a christological faith that we see as real faith; to present Christ, the great witness to God, starting of course from the theological sources, . . . but also from the cloud of witnesses who illumine that testimony *par excellence*. For this reason, in spite of everything, this book is written with hope and joy."[6] Thus, Sobrino's Christology and Ellacuría's fundamental theology should be seen as opening a window on the joy and hope of their encounter with the Mystery of God dwelling at the heart of the historical reality of El Salvador. This is where we began and where we will end.

## Whom Did They See?

In what remains I will briefly explore the God revealed to the UCA martyrs by Archbishop Romero and the suffering people of El Salvador. My goal is to catch a glimpse of the God revealed to these fallible companions of Jesus through

---

5. Jon Sobrino, *Christ the Liberator: A View from the Victims* (Maryknoll, NY: Orbis Books, 2001), 226.

6. Jon Sobrino, *Jesucristo liberador: Lectura histórica-teológica de Jesús de Nazaret* (San Salvador: UCA, 1991), 30, my translation. See Sobrino, *Jesus the Liberator*, 8.

their Christian faith, their spirituality, and their praxis. As we have seen, its trinitarian cast reflects the depth of their sources and the popular religiosity of the Salvadoran people.

The latter is captured by ubiquitous crosses painted in bright colors with smiling images of the risen Jesus below a dove in flight and surrounded by campesino families reaping a bountiful harvest from the fruits of a new creation. At memorial Masses, then and now, a chorus of voices may call the names of victims or of Archbishop Romero to which the congregation responds, affirming the person's resurrection, *"Presente!"* This trinitarian habit, encouraged by Romero and most especially by his prophecy, found its way into the UCA Jesuit community where Ellacuría and Sobrino provided theological foundations grounded in the *Spiritual Exercises*, Zubiri's philosophy of God, Romero's homilies and pastoral letters, and Rahner's theology of symbol (among others). Sobrino recalls Ellacuría's "fascination" with Jesus and how, "following his admired teacher Rahner, he used to speak of Jesus as the sacrament of God."[7] For these and other reasons I will begin where Sobrino says Latin American Christology must begin, with the historical reality of Jesus of Nazareth and his role in the trinitarian spirituality of the UCA martyrs.

To state it clearly from the outset, then, the UCA Jesuits recognized the risen Jesus, vibrant and alive, in the crucified people of El Salvador. And through the years of service and solidarity as Christians, priests, and university professors they became bearers of Jesus' Holy Spirit to this crucified people and living signs of his resurrection. In the end the executioners came as they always do. But the Salvadoran people did not forget, and interest in the work of the martyrs continues to grow. Salvadorans and travelers from around the world come to see the roses in the garden where they died and soldiers' boots, with brutal symbolism, spread their brains. Communities and projects, both from rural areas where the martyrs worked and around the globe, have taken their names (Segundo Montes, Ignacio Ellacuría, Ignacio Martín-Baró, etc.). And most importantly for many of the people they so loved, the UCA martyrs have become tangible signs (with Oscar Romero, Rutilio Grande, the American women, and their sons and daughters) of the mysterious presence of God, still faithful to their crucified hopes for a just and peaceful future.

We ask now, therefore, in the pages that follow: What was the transformative character of their relationship with Jesus of Nazareth whose memory fanned the flame of love that led the UCA martyrs to a life for others? And, for the U.S. reader, what does it mean to be his disciples twenty-one centuries after his death, citizens of a country more powerful than the Rome that killed him and the nation that paid the bill for the UCA assassins?

---

7. Jon Sobrino, "Ignacio Ellacuría, the Human Being and the Christian: 'Taking the Crucified People Down From the Cross,'" in Kevin Burke and Robert Lassalle-Klein, eds., *Love That Produces Hope: The Thought of Ignacio Ellacuría* (Collegeville, MN: Liturgical Press, 2006), 1-67 (43-44).

## Their Christological Spirituality:
## Recognizing Jesus in the Crucified People

During the 1970s and '80s Ellacuria, Sobrino, Martín-Baró, Montes, and many others in the UCA community shared a spirituality that framed their work at the university and that they spoke about in community meetings and communicated to employees such as Julia Elba Ramos who began cooking for the Jesuit seminarians in 1985. This very christological spirituality was grounded in the recognition and experience of the risen Jesus in what Ellacuría called the crucified people of El Salvador. It is rooted in the words of Jesus in Matthew 25:40: "Truly I tell you, as you did it to one of the least of these my brethren, you did it to me"; it appears in the 1968 documents of Medellín ("Document on Peace," 14c); and it shapes Ellacuría's most important talk of the December 1969 retreat. Indeed, it became characteristic of the Central American Jesuits after Medellín and the 1969 option for the poor as seen in the life and ministry of Rutilio Grande and others.

### *Historicizing the Reign of God*

The thesis of Ellacuría's pivotal talk at the 1969 retreat is captured in its title: "The Third World as the Optimal Place for the Christian to Live the *Exercises*."[8] As we saw in Chapter 1, Ellacuría's startling conclusion that the poorest countries provide the best possible place to live out the call of the *Exercises* and the vocation of a Jesuit revolves around Ellacuría's assertion that "Christ is in the poor."[9] Surprising his listeners he insists, "This is a powerful idea because then it is not us who have to save the poor, but rather it is the poor who are going to save us." And to this he adds the stunning conclusion that the *Spiritual Exercises* are leading the Jesuits of Central America not only to embrace Medellín's call, but to share the fate of the crucified Christ.

   Here Ellacuría anticipates his later work on historical soteriology by correlating the fate of Jesus in preaching the Reign of God to the future of the province with the option for the poor. On the one hand, he says, "It is not true . . . that Christ loved the cross, and that he went looking for pain, poverty, and the rest. Christ was only seeking to fulfill his mission . . . and consequently what he did was say, 'I will fulfill my mission even though I know I am going to die.'" On the other hand, he warns (drawing the parallel to the present), "We are in the same situation. . . . [And] what is it they will say to us priests or Jesuits when we dedicate ourselves to this task? First of all [they will say] . . . 'these priests are communists or Marxists, we can't help them anymore. Let's find other priests,

---

   8. Ignacio Ellacuría, "El tercer mundo como lugar óptimo de la vivencia Cristiana de los Ejercicios" (Dia 29:1), 1-12, in "Reunión-Ejercicios de la viceprovincia Jesuitica de Centroamérica, Diciembre 1969," 127-38, in *Reflexión teológico-espiritual de la Compañía de Jesús en Centroamerica, II* (San Salvador: Archives of the Society of Jesus, Central American Province, Survey S.J. de Centroamérica, December 1969).
   9. Ibid., 4.

because there is always a need for priests that support us in our situation, since these Jesuits are not helping us.'" He predicts, however, that if we "stay with the mission of the Old Testament prophets . . . everything else will be given to us besides: the pain we spoke of yesterday and the beatitude which this pain gives."[10]

Here, then, is a historical snapshot of the spirituality embraced by Ellacuría and the UCA martyrs, which I argued in Chapter 9 shapes the contextual Christology he develops with Sobrino. Ellacuría's Jesus-centric approach to fundamental theology and soteriology builds on Rahner's christocentric notion that salvation is the divinizing acceptance of God's eternal self-offer expressed in creation, which Christians see as part of God's definitive self-offer in Jesus Christ. Rahner argues that we are saved by becoming like Christ, which draws us into the inner life of God (or *theōsis*). Ellacuría historicizes this approach, arguing that God's self-offer is definitively mediated through the historical reality of Jesus of Nazareth and that we are drawn into the inner life of God by following the historical reality of Jesus. It is appropriate, then, that Ellacuría explicitly describes his 1969 talk as a "small attempt" to go beyond the work of Rahner by historicizing discipleship in the "worldly reality [of Central America], and conceiving of it in theological terms."[11] And in a glimpse of the future, he predicts that while the option for the poor leads inevitably to false accusations, suffering, and death for the Jesuits of Central America, it also promises "the beatitude which this pain gives."[12] His point is that by embracing the historical reality of the poor, where Christ is present, the Jesuits of Central America can expect to share both the fate and the future of Jesus of Nazareth and to discover the unexpected joys and blessings of his love for the poor.

As noted in Chapter 5, Ellacuría and the UCA martyrs embraced the option for the poor long before Oscar Romero, including its link to the spirituality of Jesus eloquently expressed in Matthew 25 and the beatitudes of Jesus (Matthew 5:3-12; Luke 6:20-23). Ellacuría insists, however, that Romero ultimately "went ahead" of him and his colleagues in following the path of Jesus and becoming like him. For Sobrino this path is defined by (1) Jesus' sense of mission as having been sent to initiate the Reign of God as good news for the poor; (2) his relationship as beloved Son sent by the Father to bring salvation to Israel as a light to the nations; and (3) his death on the cross at the hands of those opposed to that mission. Thus Ellacuría insists (with Sobrino) that Romero "went ahead" of them by discovering in the example of Rutilio Grande concrete ways to historicize these elements for the people of El Salvador. How, then, were these elements historicized in the ministry of Archbishop Romero?

First, as we saw earlier, Ellacuría says that Romero was illumined by the "light of a priest who had dedicated himself to evangelizing the poor" with the Reign of God as liberation from poverty, military rule, and state-sponsored

---

10. Ibid., 8, 9.
11. Ibid., 2.
12. Ibid., 9.

violence. And Rutilio's death "revealed to him what it meant to be apostle in El Salvador today; it meant being a prophet and a martyr."[13] Second, once Romero caught a glimpse of "the historical Jesus in this oppressed people," he followed the path "to its ultimate consequences . . . [where] he saw in the crucified people, the God of Salvation."[14] And third, Romero's response transformed both him and his people so that both could say, "I do not believe in death without resurrection. If I am killed, I shall arise in the Salvadoran people. . . . Let my blood be a seed of freedom and the sign that hope will soon be reality. Let my death, if it is accepted by God, be for my people liberation and as a witness of hope in the future."[15] Thus, Archbishop Romeo historicized the defining aspects of the ministry of Jesus and serves as a model for the Jesus-centered trinitarian spirituality of the UCA martyrs. A bishop may die, but God will raise up new witnesses, signs of the resurrection and messengers for the Reign of God, which cannot be defeated.

### The UCA as Historical Mirror

How, then, was this historicized by the UCA martyrs? Like many realities that inhabit the heart, the spirituality of the UCA martyrs is perhaps most clearly reflected in the historical mirror of their corporate activity: their life and work at the UCA. An important article by Jon Sobrino, which appears in the official 1989 collection of university documents published months before the assassinations, clarifies how this spirituality was historicized in their work at the UCA. Sobrino asserts, "The Christian Inspiration of the University"[16] is founded on two key principles: first, the New Testament recollection of Jesus' proclamation of the Kingdom of God, which is the guiding inspiration, horizon, or goal of the UCA;[17] and second, the church's preferential option for the poor, which serves as a "hermeneutical principle" guiding the UCA's efforts to promote the Kingdom of God in El Salvador and throughout the Third World.[18] The article, therefore, provides historical evidence that, for these Jesuits, the poor majorities of El Salvador and the planet itself had become "a *locus theologicus,* a place of discernment of God's active presence in the world, and a place generating a faith response to that presence."[19]

---

13. Ellacuría, "Monseñor Romero, un enviado de Dios para salvar a su pueblo," *Escritos teológicos,* III, 96; reprinted from *Sal Terrae: Revista de teología pastoral* 811 (1980): 825-32.

14. Ibid., 97.

15. Words of Oscar Romero to José Calderón Salazar published in *Orientación* (April 13, 1980); cited in James Brockman, *Romero, A Life* (Maryknoll, NY: Orbis Books, 1989), 248.

16. Jon Sobrino, "Inspiración cristiana de la universidad," in *Planteamiento,* 390-405; translated as "The University's Christian Inspiration," in Sobrino, *Companions of Jesus,* 152-73.

17. Sobrino, *Companions of Jesus,* 158.

18. Ibid., 161, 162.

19. Ibid., 164.

But Sobrino insists that a spirituality that looks for God among the poor does not exclude the rest of humanity. This allows us to see that, for the UCA martyrs, "the option for the poor does not mean to focus on a part of the whole [of humanity] in order to ignore the rest, but rather to reach out to the whole from one part."[20] His point is that the specificity of the claim from Matthew 25 that Christ is in the poor does not limit the salvific potential of this Christ-experience for the rest of humanity. Thus, the UCA martyrs believed that God was reaching out to all of humanity by revealing God's self-offer in the rejected majority of humanity. This in no way limits the universality of that self-revelation or its salvific implications for humanity, but it does reveal the importance of solidarity with the poor for salvation history, as can be seen in the New Testament emphasis on the Reign of God as good news to the poor.

This background, therefore, puts us in a position to take seriously the claim that the UCA martyrs recognized and experienced the risen Jesus in the crucified people of El Salvador.[21] These were not empty words, spoken for strategic effect, but rather the articulation of a spirituality with deep christological and trinitarian implications. As we have seen, in 1978 Ellacuria argued that the crucified people are the "continuation . . . of Jesus and his work,"[22] the "victim of the sin of the world," and the "bearer of the world's savation."[23] And in 1981 he described them as the defining sign of the times "by whose light all the others should be discerned and interpreted."[24] My thesis, then, is that from the 1970s forward, Ellacuría, Sobrino, and the others shared this spirituality and its emphasis on the presence of the risen Christ in the crucified people of El Salvador. While there are clearly variations (the case of Fr. Juaquín López y López merits further study) this was clearly the case for Ellacuría and Sobrino, and there is strong anecdotal,[25] historical,[26] and documentary[27] evidence that this

---

20. Ibid., 162.

21. Ellacuría, "Discernir *el signo* de los tiempos," *Escritos teológicos,* II (San Salvador: UCA Editores, 2000), 58.

22. Ignacio Ellacuría, "The Crucified People: An Essay in Historical Soteriology," in Michael Lee, ed., *Ignacio Ellacuría: Essays on History, Liberation, and Salvation* (Maryknoll, NY: Orbis Books, 2013), 196; "El pueblo crucificado, ensayo de soteriología histórica," *Escritos teológicos,* II, 138.

23. Ellacuría, "El pueblo crucificado," 166, 169-70; Ellacuría, "The Crucified People," 221, 223.

24. Ellacuría, "Discernir *el signo* de los tiempos," 134.

25. Sobrino, "Companions of Jesus," 3-56; Salvador Carranza, ed., *Martires de la UCA, 16 de noviembre de 1989* (San Salvador: UCA Editores, 1990).

26. Rodolfo Cardenal, "Ser jesuita hoy en El Salvador," *ECA* nos. 493-494 (November-December 1989): 1013-39; Teresa Whitfield, *Paying the Price: Ignacio Ellacuría and the Murdered Jesuits of El Salvador* (Philadelphia: Temple University Press, 1995).

27. See the writings of the martyrs in Jon Sobrino, Ignacio Ellacuría, and others, *Companions of Jesus: The Jesuit Martyrs of El Salvador* (Maryknoll, NY: Orbis Books, 1990); and John Hassett and Hugh Lacy, *Towards a Society That Serves Its People: The Intellectual Contribution of El Salvador's Murdered Jesuits* (Washington, DC: Georgetown University Press, 1991).

spirituality permeated their life and prayer as a community, and their understanding of the UCA as a university-style effort "to take the crucified people down from the cross."[28]

## Companions of Jesus: Bearers of Jesus' Holy Spirit to the People of El Salvador

> If the university had not suffered, we would not have performed our duty. In a world where injustice reigns, a university that fights for justice must necessarily be persecuted.
>
> I should like to think—and this is the meaning I give to this honorary degree—that you understand our efforts, our mission, something of the tragic reality of El Salvador.
>
> And how do you help us? That is not for me to say. Only open your human heart, your Christian heart, and ask yourselves the three questions Ignatius of Loyola put to himself as he stood in front of a crucified world: What have I done for Christ in this world? What am I doing now? And above all, what should I do? The answers lie both in your academic responsibility and in your personal responsibility. . . .
>
> Ignacio Ellacuria at the University of Santa Clara, June 12, 1982[29]

Shortly after the assassinations Jon Sobrino wrote a piece that is full of details gathered during two decades of living together about the everyday life and vision of the UCA Jesuits. He remembers community retreats, liturgies, courses, conversations about "trying to follow Archbishop Romero,"[30] and their immersion "in the essentials of the Spiritual Exercises."[31] He recalls the importance for the community of Ellacuría's "original and extremely relevant" interpretation of Ignatius's three questions before the crucified Christ from the meditation on sin (the colloquy of the First Exercise of the First Week, #53).[32] And he suggests that the community consider their "reply to these questions" to be their response to "the conversion demanded by St. Ignatius," both in the *Spiritual Exercises* and in Jesuit life. We turn, therefore, to examine a few of the changes produced by their struggle as UCA Jesuits to answer the questions of Ignatius that Ignacio Ellacuría posed to the students and faculty of the University of Santa Clara in 1982.[33]

---

28. Sobrino, "Ignacio Ellacuría, the Human Being and the Christian," 5.

29. Ignacio Ellacuría, "The Task of a Christian University," in *Companions of Jesus*, 150, 151.

30. Sobrino, "Companions of Jesus," 17.

31. Ibid., 18.

32. See David L. Fleming, S.J., *The Spiritual Exercises of Saint Ignatius: A Literal Translation and a Contemporary Reading* (St. Louis: The Institute of Jesuit Sources, 1978, 1980 rev., 1982, 1985, 1989, 1991), 36.

33. Sobrino, "Companions of Jesus," 19.

### *"What Are We Going to Do?"*

What did it mean to be companions of Jesus (the original name given by St. Ignatius to the Jesuits) in a society where the historical reality of the crucified people was a daily sign of the passion of Christ? Sobrino says that Ellacuría asked in liturgies and retreats at the UCA the same questions he posed at Santa Clara: "What have we done to cause all these people to be crucified, what are we doing about their crosses [now] and what are we going to do to bring them down from the cross?"[34] He says, "We also reinterpreted St. Ignatius' ideal of *contemplatives in action* as *contemplatives in action for justice*" as a way of embracing the newly formulated Jesuit commitment to "'service of the faith and promotion of justice' (32nd General Congregation, 1975) . . . [which takes] the form of an 'option for the poor' (33rd General Congregation, 1983)." As a result, he recalls, the UCA Jesuits underwent a "very radical" change, one that "entailed conversion, abandoning many things and many ways of behaving, losing friendships with the powerful and their benefits, and gaining the affection of the poor."[35] In the end, however, it "meant above all returning to Jesus' gospel, . . . and to the poor [for] whom Jesus preached." Thus, while "normally it was left to us two and Juan Ramón Moreno to put into words what was Ignatian in our lives and work," he says "I believe the rest of them accepted and heartily shared this vision."[36] He insists, therefore, "These were the Ignatian ideals that moved this group. They put them into practice, . . . and they bore outstanding witness to them . . . [which] gives us a clue to understanding how they saw themselves as Jesuits in the world today."[37]

Thus, the UCA Jesuits interpreted Ignatius's three questions as a call to become companions of the Jesus present in the crucified people and to play a university-style role in taking them down from the cross. They believed this required a deep familiarity and expertise regarding the national reality of El Salvador informed by a special interest in the poor and their place in Salvadoran civil society, politics, economics, culture, history, arts, etc. Their goal, therefore, was that no other university in the world should surpass the UCA in its expertise regarding the historical reality of El Salvador. But what exactly did this mean to them as Jesuits, university professors, and administrators?

The reader will recall from Chapter 5 that Ellacuría and Zubiri use the term *intellection* to emphasize that intelligence must be understood as an action rather than as a faculty or a thing. And Ellacuría argues that the "formal structure of intelligence and its differentiating function within . . . the permanently biological character of the human. . . [is] that of apprehending reality and facing up to it."[38] Thus, the exercise of intelligence is fundamentally practical (though

---

34. Ibid., 19.
35. Ibid., 19-20.
36. Ibid., 18.
37. Ibid., 19.
38. Ellacuría, "Hacia una fundamentación del método teológico latinoamericano," *Escritos teológicos,* I (San Salvador: UCA Editores, 2000), 207.

of course it is much more), which he insists implies an ethical obligation to assume responsibility for its practical ends or purposes. And this they did by stating clearly that the university and its intellectual activity exists to serve society, that every course should address the national reality, and that the university should promote the active participation of the country's poor majorities in the national reality as a *sine qua non* for a truly rational and humane future.

As we saw, however, Ellacuría insists that this process of "facing up to real things as real has a triple dimension,"[39] comprising (1) "becoming aware of," "realizing about," or "grasping what is at stake in reality" (*hacerse cargo de la realidad*); (2) an ethical demand "to pick up" or "assume responsibility for reality" (*cargar con la realidad*); and (3) a praxis-related demand to change or "to take charge of reality" (*encargarse de la realidad*). Thus, faculty and students were asked to design and participate in university-style efforts intended to produce not just (1) awareness but also (2) practical ways of taking responsibility for the historical reality of El Salvador that (3) produce tangible results and positive outcomes for the country and its crucified people. The center of the university was to be outside of itself with a purpose of serving the whole country, not just the few entitled to study there. Thus Sobrino concludes, "What kind of university did they leave us? Above all, they left us a new idea of the Christian university for our time, comparable in importance to that of John Henry Newman a century ago. . . . In a word, what they left us was the belief that academic and Christian knowledge must be and can be at the service of the poor."[40]

U.S. readers again pay the tax for the Military High Command that silenced the martyrs in 1989 when we do not take seriously the Christian historical realism and the spirituality that inform this model. Some will insist that a university committed to the preferential option for the poor cannot succeed in the "developed" world or that it responds to publics we do not serve. Suffice to say, however, the spirituality of the UCA martyrs and their model of the university raise unsettling and transformative questions for those who take them seriously.[41]

### New Vision of the University: Taking the Crucified People Down from the Cross

How, then, did the UCA Jesuits and their colleagues historicize in their work at the university this spirituality of national service and integral development with its commitment to the liberating struggles of the crucified people?

First, they made great efforts to "become aware of," "realize about," and "grasp what is at stake in the reality" (*hacerse cargo de la realidad*)[42] of El Salvador as mediated through its crucifixion of the poor. Part I told the story of

---

39. Ibid., 208.

40. Sobrino, "Companions of Jesus," 38.

41. See the story of the rich young man (Matthew 19:16-22; Mark 10:17-22; Luke 18:18-23).

42. Ellacuría, "Hacia una fundamentación," 208.

their conversion to Medellín's preferential option for the poor and their efforts to follow Archbishop Romero and Rutilio Grande through university-style projects and programs designed to take the crucified people down from the cross. This brought Segundo Montes to the refugee camps, where tens of thousands of desperate Salvadorans had fled. Oddly enough, as they returned from exile to face further persecution at home, Montes discovered in them only months before his death the flourishing foundations for real democracy[43] of which he had previously dispaired.[44]

Ignacio Martín-Baró gained international fame for his work on post-traumatic stress after immersing himself in the national mental health epidemic produced by U.S. counterinsurgency and its doctrine of psychological war.[45] Jon Sobrino walked with Archbishop Romero as he "retook Aguilares" after the assassination of Rutilio Grande,[46] and he wrote various pieces that Romero used in his pastoral work, including the first draft of the archbishop's second pastoral letter and the text of his acceptance of an honorary doctorate at Louvain seven weeks before his death.[47] And Ellacuria gave himself, his presidency, and the prestige of the UCA to El Salvador's grassroots organizations that were demanding peace when the mere mention of dialogue was treason.

In pursuit of this goal Ellacuria met with leaders from all over the political spectrum. Two months before his death, in a published interview he described a no-win situation in responding to criticism for his support of the newly elected president, Alfredo Cristiani, the candidate of the right-wing ARENA party (who would be implicated in Ellacuría's assassination): "If you say things in favor of Cristiani . . . you have gone over to his side; if you say things in favor of the FMLN it's because you're always defending the FMLN."[48] Whitfield notes that even Jon Sobrino "made a formal appointment to see the rector and suggest that perhaps he *appeared* to be going a little far" in his engagement with the new president. But Ellacuría's agenda was peace, and as he told his assistant,

---

43. V. Compher, L. Jackson, and B. Morgan, *Going Home. Building Peace in El Salvador: The Story of Repatriation* (New York: Apex Press, 1991); Segundo Montes, "Salvadoran Refugees in Honduras," foreword to B. and S. Cagan, *This Promised Land, El Salvador* (New Brunswick, NJ: Rutgers University Press, 1991).

44. "¿Es posible la *democracía* en un país subdesarrollado?" in *Democracía y lucha de clases en América Latina* (Centro de Informatición y documentación de Bolivia, 1980). Reprinted as "Is Democracy Possible in an Underdeveloped Country?" in Hassett and Lacey, *Towards a Society That Serves Its People.*

45. Ignacio Martín-Baró, "Guerra y trauma psicosocial," *Revista de psicología de El Salvador* 28 (April-June 1988): 12-141; Adrianne Aron and Shawn Corne, eds., *Writings for a Liberation Psychology* (Cambridge, MA: Harvard University Press, 1996); Ignacio Martín-Baró, ed., *Psicología social de la guerra: trauma y terapía* (San Salvador: UCA Editores, 1990); Ignacio Martín-Baró, *Acción e ideología: psicología social desde centroamérica* (San Salvador: UCA Editores, 1983, 1985);

46. Jon Sobrino, "Some Personal Recollections," in *Archbishop Romero: Memories and Reflections* (Maryknoll, NY: Orbis Books, 1990), 1-58, esp. 26-29.

47. Ibid., 30-31; Brockman, *Romero: A Life*, 80; 226.

48. *El Mundo*, September 16, 1989; cited in Whitfield, *Paying the Price*, 338.

"I'd negotiate with the devil himself" if it would end the war! So the "Chair for the National Reality" brought leaders from all sides of the political spectrum to the university to present and debate their visions for the country in one of the few national forums representing the perspective of the poor. All proposals for faculty research, as well as master's theses and senior projects, were expected to address the national reality; projects were reviewed in terms of the university's mission of solidarity with the poor, and university students were required to do community service oriented toward the dispossessed.[49]

At the personal level, Martín-Baró spent most weekends in a very poor parish in the coffee-growing region of Jayaque. Segundo Montes regularly visited the refugee camps at Colomancagua, Honduras, and elsewhere. Ellacuria made visits to embattled communities in Chalatenango. Amando López worked at Tierra Virgen, a poor semi-rural area near Soyapango. Juaquin López y López led "Fe y Alegria" with its thirteen schools and twelve workshops (eight thousand students in all), plus two clinics (with fifty thousand clients) for Salvador's poor. Juan Ramón Moreno worked tirelessly with El Salvador's religious who served in the front lines with the poor. And as landless campesinos who came to the city for work, Elba Ramos, her husband, and their daughter Celina belonged to El Salvador's poor. Thus, as academics, Christians, and human beings the UCA martyrs were deeply immersed in the reality of El Salvador and its poor majorities.[50]

Second, to the best of their ability, they tried "to pick up" or "assume responsibility for" the reality (*cargar con la realidad*)[51] of El Salvador and its suffering people by speaking out about the ongoing suffering of the crucified poor. Segundo Montes directed the UCA Institute for Human Rights (IDHUCA) and bravely documented hundreds of political assassinations through the year of his death.[52] He brought the attention of El Salvador and the world to the suffering and the promise embodied in the historical reality that at least 20 percent of the country had become refugees during a decade of war.[53] He demonstrated that the small quantities of money sent by refugees to their families back home (or *remesas*) comprised the largest source of foreign capital in El Salvador, larger

---

49. Robert Lassalle-Klein, unpublished interview with Mario Dimas, director of the UCA's program of student social service (San Salvador, January 27, 1992), taped. See Charles J. Beirne, S.J., *Jesuit Education and Social Change in El Salvador* (New York: Garland Publishing, 1996), 184-87.

50. Rodolfo Cardenal, "Ser jesuita hoy en El Salvador," *ECA* nos. 493-494 (November-December 1989): 1013-39.

51. Ellacuría, "Hacia una fundamentación," 208.

52. IDHUCA (Instituto de Derechos Humanos Universidad Centroamericana), *José Simeón Cañas, Los derechos humanos en El Salvador en 1989* (San Salvador: UCA Editores, 1990).

53. Instituto de Investigaciónes and IDHUCA, *El Salvador 1985: Desplazados y refugiados* (San Salvador: UCA Editores, 1985); Instituto de Investigaciónes and IDHUCA, *El Salvador 1986: En busca de soluciónes para los desplazados* (San Salvador: UCA Editores, 1986); Instituto de Investigacions and IDHUCA, *El Salvador 1987: Salvadoreños refugiados en los Estados Unidos* (San Salvador: UCA Editores, 1987);

than all U.S. foreign aid and export income! This was explosive information because it placed refugees and low-income wage earners ahead of the U.S. government and Salvadoran business elites as the country's primary source of foreign capital and a key to its future.[54] And he worked tirelessly with his students to support the repopulation of the country's rural areas in the mid to late 1980s.

As we saw, Ignacio Martín-Baró directed the university's national opinion poll, which provided one of the very few sources of documentation during the 1980s regarding the wishes of El Salvador's poor majority. These polls helped to clarify the political reality by reflecting it back to those who were in the process of creating it, energizing the push for a negotiated settlement to the war when those who espoused this view were subject to severe persecution. And his writings on the psychological trauma inflicted by U.S.-sponsored "low-intensity conflict" helped its intended victims to defend themselves while exposing the psychological war to criticism in the United States.

Ignacio Ellacuria helped turn *ECA* and the UCA's Chair for the National Reality into the country's leading forums for analyzing virtually every major event and policy proposal from the perspective of its effect on the country's poor majority. He gathered a team that produced literally hundreds of articles and dozens of books analyzing El Salvador's situation in light of the gospel. He led the creation of a university dedicated to the option for the poor and was a leading figure in its embrace by the Central American Jesuits. And finally, his was one of the first, and perhaps the most persistent and prominent, voices calling for a negotiated end to the war and legal protections for civil society (its "third forces") as vehicles for the participation of the country's poor majorities in shaping the future of El Salvador.

All of these efforts, then, should be seen as historicizations of the spirituality expressed in the seminal May 1979 statement of the UCA's new self-understanding as a Christian university. Synthesized by Jon Sobrino from a broad consultation of faculty, staff, and administration, the document concludes with the remarkable claim:

> The most explicit testimony of the Christian inspiration of the UCA will be truly putting itself at the service of the people in such a way that . . . it allows itself to be oriented by oppressed people themselves. This will make the University see and denounce what there is of sin in our reality; it will impel it to create models that historically correspond better to the Reign of God; and it will make it develop typically Christian attitudes, such as . . . hope, the passion for justice, the generous self-giving to others, the rejection of violent means, etc.[55]

---

54. Segundo Montes, *El Salvador 1989: Las remesas que envían los salvadoreños de Estados Unidos: Consecuencias sociales y econónomicas* (San Salvador: UCA Editores, 1990), 130.

55. Universidad Centroamericana José Simeón Cañas, "Las funciónes fundamentales de la universidad y su operativización," in *Planteamiento universitário 1989* (San Salvador: Universidad Centroamericana José Simeón Cañas, 1989): 53.

Here, then, is an explicit statement of the link between the spirituality of the UCA martyrs and their vision of the Christian university as one reooted in the preferential option for the poor.

Third, and finally, they attempted to transform and to "take charge of" the reality of El Salvador[56] by bringing about real changes that would take this crucified people down from their cross. In Part I, I reviewed the myriad ways in which the UCA martyrs and their colleagues worked with many organizations to end the worst excesses of the political repression of the 1970s and 1980s and to promote policies consistent with "the fullest realization possible of the Kingdom of God."[57] In Chapter 3 I argued that a coherence emerged during the mid-1980s in the work of Ellacuria, Martín-Baró, and Montes in support of the political mobilization of the country's "third forces." For example, Ella-curia successfully promoted the 1988 National Debate, a forum in which the country's poor majorities could express their desire for a negotiated end to the war through an emergent civil society, a perspective not shared by the government, ARENA, or the FMLN. And the previously mentioned IUDOP polls, run by Martín-Baró, fostered the national awareness (or collective consciousness) needed to make the goal of peace a political force, while Montes and IDHUCA played an important role in the organization of El Salvador's rural majority behind refugee return, a key factor in this sector's emergence as a democratizing force.

The net result of these and a host of other activities was a powerful contribution to the emergence of El Salvador's poor majorities as a political, economic, and social force through the sundry vehicles of civil society. The autonomy, integrity, and appropriateness of the average Salvadoran's insistence on a negotiated end to the war was not enough, however, to change the minds of the military, the government, or even the FMLN (because they still believed victory was possible). It is ironic, therefore, that the Salvadoran government's brutal attempt to silence the voice of the university and civil society helped bring about the very outcome it was designed to prevent.

### The "Marrow" and the "Bones": Honesty, Fidelity, and Love

We have been looking, then, at the spirituality of the UCA martyrs reflected in the historical mirror of their work at the university. I have argued that it was a spirituality dedicated to taking the crucified people down from the cross through university-style efforts to support their hopes and aspirations for liberation from military rule and generations of social, political, and economic oppression. We turn now, however, to a more direct description of its content in a 1979 article by Jon Sobrino. He describes what he calls the "spirituality of

---

56. Ellacuría, "Hacia una fundamentación," 208.
57. Ignacio Ellacuría, "La teología como momento ideológico de la praxis eclesia," *Escritos teológicos,* I, 163-85.

liberation," which he says "we have rediscovered . . . or at least . . . clarified . . . in the practice of liberation."[58]

Sobrino asserts that the "spirituality of liberation" discovered by the martyrs comprises three moments, which we should note correspond to Ellacuría's afore-mentioned threefold process of "facing up to real things as real":[59] "(1) honesty about the real, (2) fidelity to the real, and (3) a certain *correspondence* by which we permit ourselves to be carried along by the *more* of the real."[60] Here I would argue that "the real" refers to the encounter of the UCA martyrs with the historical reality of God embodied in the crucified people.

First, then, Sobrino says that honesty, fidelity, and correspondence to the encounter with the crucified people became "mediations for our relationship with God."[61] And he says the UCA martyrs discovered that while scripture and tradition call for solidarity with the poor, "deep down, there is an even more profound logic in our insistence on active solidarity with the poor of this world, which proceeds, at bottom, from a profound *honesty* about Latin American reality."[62] Second, "*fidelity* to the real, the second prerequisite . . . is simply and solely perseverance in our original honesty," even when threatened by "the negative element in history.[63] He says "this fidelity to the real is exemplified in Jesus," who continues to preach the Reign of God "in the history he seeks to transform, though that history now be his cross." And third, honesty with and fidelity to the crucified people turn out to be "our positive response to . . . God's [self-]revelation" in the crucified people,[64] something that was not entirely clear at the time. Fortunately, he says, honesty and fidelity *carried us along* to "go about doing good," thereby fulfilling the love command of Jesus (John 13:34-35; 15:17; Matthew 22:39; Mark 12:31; Luke 10:27). And this is what draws them into "the *for* with which Jesus' life is suffused . . . the *sine qua non* of all future Christian soteriologies . . . [and] the affirmation of what it actually means to be alive . . . [and] attuned to God's creation."[65] Sobrino's argument, then, is that the honesty and fidelity of the UCA martyrs to the crucified people turned out to be their "yes" to God's saving self-offer in the crucified people.

Sobrino insists, "here . . . we touch the very marrow of Jesus' personal spirituality." In systematic terms Jesus devoted himself to the humanizing of human beings. "His point of departure was the *pauper vivens* [the poor person alive], the living indigent, and the life that he offered flowed from this starting point to all other human beings . . . (in the case of oppressors, by calling them to

---

58. Jon Sobrino, *Spirituality of Liberation: Toward Political Holiness*, trans. Robert R. Barr (New York: Orbis Books, 1990), 13-22, originally published as Jon Sobrino, "Espiritualidad de Jesús y de la liberación," *Christus* (December 1979–January 1980): 59-63.

59. Ellacuría, "Hacia una fundamentación," 208.

60. Sobrino, *Spirituality of Liberation*, 14.

61. Ibid.

62. Ibid., 17.

63. Ibid., 18.

64. Ibid., 21.

65. Ibid., 20.

conversion)."[66] Here, we find the core of the spirituality of the UCA martyrs, which Sobrino insists is also "the marrow of liberation theology. . . . The cruci-fied people themselves are bearers of salvation. The one chosen by God to bring salvation is the servant, which increases the scandal."[67] Here again, as we saw in Chapter 8, soteriology converges with *theōsis*; honesty, fidelity, and love for the poor transforms the martyrs to become like Jesus, collaborators with the saving work of the Trinity in the world and bearers of Jesus' Holy Spirit to a suffering people.

On February 2, 1980, seven weeks before his assassination, Archbishop Romero claimed this spirituality as his own. In words written for him by Jon Sobrino and delivered at the University of Louvain in Belgium, Romero states, "We believe that this is the way to sustain the identity and the very transcen-dence of the Church: by inserting ourselves in the real socio-political process of our people, evaluating it from the perspective of the poor, and promoting those liberation movements that really lead to justice and peace for the majority of our people. We believe that this is the way . . . because this is how we sustain faith in God."[68] Then turning to the heart of the matter he concludes, "The ancient Christians said, '*Gloria Dei, vivens homo*' (the glory of God is the person who lives). But I would concretize this by saying: '*Gloria Dei, vivens pauper*' (the glory of God is the poor person who lives). For . . . by putting ourselves on the side of the poor and by giving them life we will know the eternal truth of the Gospel."

Here, therefore, are the *marrow* and the *bones* of the spirituality of Oscar Romero and his followers, including the UCA martyrs, Rutilio Grande, the four American women, and thousands of Salvadorans as witnessed by their colorful crosses and their faith-filled struggle for life. It is a trinitarian spirituality that believes that God acts in history through Jesus' Holy Spirit, transforming the public lives and innermost existences of his followers, and making them holy through their "yes" to God's historical self-offer in the crucified people. Here also is the claim of this book: that the honesty, fidelity, and love of the UCA martyrs for the crucified people of El Salvador transformed them into living signs and bearers of Jesus' Holy Spirit to them and to us.

### An Easter Event: Sacrament of the Mystery of God Transforming the Historical Reality of the Americas

It is well known that the martyrdom of Ellacuría and his companions, because of its magnitude and international repercussions, and the his-

---

66. Ibid., 19-20

67. Jon Sobrino, *The Principle of Mercy: Taking the Crucified People from the Cross* (Maryknoll, NY: Orbis Books, 1994), 53.

68. Archbishop Oscar Romero, "Una experiencia eclesial en El Salvador, Centro América," *La voz de los sin voz: La palabra viva de Monseñor Oscar Arnulfo Romero* (San Salvador: UCA Editores, 1980, 1996), 193.

torical moment when it occurred, undoubtedly helped bring about a negotiated end to the war. In addition to this, however, we must think about the salvation that Ellacuría and the martyrs leave us over time. This salvation is real. And it consists, I believe, in having generated an historical and real tradition, which is both supremely necessary and constructive. This means that by their life and death, these martyrs have opened a track in history along which it easier to travel[:] . . . hunger and thirst for justice for the crucified people, . . . tireless analysis and condemnation of the truth about their crucifixion, and . . . steadiness and fidelity . . . in seeing them taken down from the cross.[69]

I have suggested, therefore, that the lives of the UCA martyrs and their work at the university can be understood as their answer as humans and Christians to the three questions posed by Ignatius Loyola in the First Week of the *Spiritual Exercises*. Or to put it more clearly, as Sobrino suggests, "Though the human person may be questioning God, God is also asking something and one must respond to that question . . . through action."[70] He argues, therefore, that the life of Ignacio Ellacuría, and by extension his colleagues, "can be interpreted as a praxis responding to the question put by God," a question posed in the form of the crucified people.

We have focused thus far, then, on the honesty, fidelity, and love of UCA martyrs for crucified people. And I have argued these made them more like Jesus of Nazareth, whose memory fed the flame of love, transforming them into "men for others,"[71] drawing them into the work of the Trinity and the Mystery of God. But the question of Ignacio Ellacuria at Santa Clara University remains unanswered. What does it mean *for us* to be disciples of Jesus twentyone centuries after his death, living in a country that trained the assassins and paid their salaries? Speaking to a university audience Ellacuría asserted, "The answers lie in your academic responsibility and in your personal responsibility."[72] Implied here is a question: Will we allow ourselves to be addressed by the Holy Mystery that finally permeated the lives of the UCA martyrs? And here we return to the trinitarian dimensions of the role of Jesus in the spirituality that animated their life and work.

Words fail in the attempt to thematize a Holy Mystery, but it permeates the reverence and the unstated invitation in the claim of Ignacio Ellacuría: "With

---

69. Sobrino, "Ignacio Ellacuría, the Human Being and the Christian," 56.

70. Ibid., 49.

71. This was a favorite expression of the German theologian Dietrich Bonhoeffer to describe the ideal of Christian discipleship. It was borrowed by the Jesuit general, Fr. Pedro Arrupe, S.J., to describe the goal of Jesuit education.

72. Ignacio Ellacuría, "The Task of a Christian University," in *Jon Sobrino, Ignacio Ellacuría and Others: Companions of Jesus* (Maryknoll, NY: Orbis Books, 1990), 150-51; translated from "Discurso de graduación en la Universidad de Santa Clara," in Ignacio Ellacuría, *Escritos universitarios* (San Salvador: UCA Editores, 1989), 228.

Monseñor Romero God visited El Salvador."[73] Shortly after the assassination Ellacuría wrote that the archbishop was "an exceptional example of how the power of the gospel can become a transformative historical force. This is why he continues living after his death, . . . because there are many who are disposed to follow his steps, knowing that Monseñor Romero was an exemplary follower of Jesus of Nazareth in the last three years of his public life."[74] Following Sobrino's example, then, what can be said about the God of UCA martyrs?

In answering this question it is exceedingly important to stay firmly grounded in the historical reality of their lives in order to preserve what Sobrino calls the "hermeneutical circularity between Jesus the martyr and the present-day martyrs of Latin America due to the horizon of the Reign of God that is common to both."[75] We have seen that Ellacuría and his colleagues allowed themselves to be addressed by the Mystery of God historicized in Oscar Romero's faith that God's self-offer was unfolding in the real history of El Salvador, and most especially in its crucified people. Here, then, is the historical grace that mediated their encounter with the risen Christ in the crucified people.

Sobrino demonstrates the seriousness with which the UCA Jesuits took what may seem to us like poetic references when he suggests that, just as Jesus' public ministry began with his "hearing that they had assassinated the Baptist," so "we can say this is something like what happened in El Salvador."[76] The discipleship of Archbishop Romero emerged from the assassination of Rutilio Grande, S.J., and what it revealed about Grande's small efforts to take the crucified people of Aguilares down from their crosses. And the prophetic discipleship of Ignacio Ellacuría, along with that of the other martyrs, emerged from the assassination of Archbishop Romero for having taught the entire archdiocese of San Salvador to do the same. We may wonder, then, what will be the fruit of Ignacio Ellacuría's questions from the *Spiritual Exercises* to us at Santa Clara University? What will come of what we have seen and heard about God from the UCA martyrs reflected in the historical mirror of an American Christian university taking the Salvadoran people down from the cross?

The UCA martyrs recognized and experienced Jesus in the crucified poor of El Salvador. They responded as university professors, Jesuits, (and, yes, as a mother and a cook), as humans, and as Christians to the agony of this people. And in so doing they were transformed into bearers of Jesus' Holy Spirit to both sides of the civil war (as epitomized in the story of Captain Francisco Mena Sandoval), finally playing a critical role in promoting the fragile beginnings of a process of national reconciliation. In the process, having faced the terrible yet beneficent realities of a life for others, their innermost lives were caught up in a holy transformation, a transformation incarnated by (and inseparable from) their positive response to God's self-offer through the history and people of El

---

73. Sobrino, "Ignacio Ellacuría, the Human Being and the Christian," 43.
74. Ellacuría, "Monseñor Romero, un enviado de Dios para salvar a su pueblo," 100.
75. Ibid., 66-67 n. 100.
76. Ibid., 53.

Salvador. They bequeath to us, therefore, a flawed icon of their discipleship, a university whose Christian character was (and is) embodied by its efforts to humanize the national reality of El Salvador guided by the values of the Reign of God and to insure a place at the table for the poor. For it is finally through their lives and their deaths at the UCA that the UCA martyrs were transformed into tangible signs of God-with-us, sacraments of a Holy Mystery offered to all by the crucified people of El Salvador.

They leave us, then, with many things. Ellacuría's Christian historical realism holds untapped promise for a new generation of contextual theologies. We have a new model of the Christian university; a trove of social-scientific, philosophical, historical, and theological analyses and prophetic writings about El Salvador, Central America, and the tragic role of the U.S. foreign policy; and numerous ideas of interest for theologians, social ethicists, social scientists, educators, historians, and spiritual writers (including the historical reality of Jesus and the Kingdom of God; human rights as the historicization of the common good; the reality of idols; historicization, neuroscience, and theological method; the *Spiritual Exercises* and political discernment; liturgy and justice; civil society and the option for the poor; social sin; tradition and culture as historical realities, etc.). We also have the outstanding example of their ministry and their love for the poor. Finally, however, I believe it was their encounter with the historical reality of the Mystery of God on the back roads of our world, far from the centers of power, that most embodies who they were.

In conclusion, I would simply suggest that it is not without reason that the lives and deaths of the UCA martyrs have come to share the quality of their mentor, Jesus of Nazareth. For with all their human flaws, they have become events of the tangible presence of a Holy Mystery dwelling at the heart of and transforming both El Salvador and the United States, both the Galilees and the capitals of our world. These companions of Jesus died for their attempt to take the Nazarene's crucified people down from their cross. The cries and hopes of the suffering majorities that populate our planet reach us through the lives of the martyrs. And the trinitarian spirituality of the UCA martyrs, historicized in their encounter with the risen Jesus vibrant and alive in the crucified people, offers a grace-filled invitation to a new generation years after their faith-filled martyrdom on an American cross.

At the end of the day, then, I am left to wonder by the blood and ink mingled on the pages of Jürgen Moltmann's book, *The Crucified God*, which fell from Jon Sobrino's shelf by the body of Juan Ramón Moreno: What is the mysterious quality of suffering and failure born in love that releases life and grace into the human community in the face of crucifixion? Perhaps what is most true is that the perception of the Mystery is an invitation to be transformed by it.

# Index

Agrarian Transformation Institute (ISTA), 76, 102
Alliance for Progress, 14, 15, 45, 51
*analogatum princeps*
  crucified people as, 309-36
  of God's self-offer in Jesus Christ, 312, 313, 329, 335, 336, 339, 340
  of the historical reality of Jesus, 309-36
  of the life, death, and resurrection of Jesus, 254, 287
*An Analysis of a National Experience*, 68, 69, 80
Anselm of Canterbury, 23
apprehension
  primordial, 209, 210, 214, 215, 262, 266
  of reality, 213, 216, 262
Aquinas, Thomas, 260, 267, 269-71, 275
  being, 260, 267, 270, 275
  *exitus–reditus,* 277, 300
  prime matter, 267
Arias Plan (for peace in Central America), 169
Aristotle, 210, 266, 269, 291
Arnson, Cynthia, on U.S. policy in Central America, 174
Arrupe, Pedro, S.J., 30, 36, 40, 41, 51, 52, 56, 63, 83, 86, 103, 118, 119, 203, 355
Ashley, J. Matthew, on writings of Ellacuría, 195-99, 327, 330
assassins (of UCA Jesuits)
  Atlacatl Battalion: Espinoza Guerra (*Bull*), Lt. José Ricardo, xvii, xix, xx, 100, 130, 179; Guevara Cerritos, Second Lt. Gonzalo, 130; Avalos Vargas (*Toad* or *Satan*), Sub-sergeant Antonio Ramiro, 179;

Amaya Grimaldi (Pilijay), Pvt. Oscar Mariano, 179
  Military Academy, 177, 178: Benavides Moreno, Col. Guíllermo Alfredo, xvii, xix, xx, 130, 177, 178; Mendoza Vallecillos, Lt. Yusshy René, xx
  Salvadoran Armed Forces: Avilés Buitrago, Col. Carlos Armando, 177, 178; Bustillo, Col. Guillermo, xix; Fuentes, Col. Francisco Elena, xix; Larios López, Gen. Rafael Humberto, xix, xx, 177; Montano, Col. Inocente Orlando, xix; Ponce, Col René Emilio, Chief of Staff (1989), xvii, xviii, xx, 177, 178; Zepeda, Col. Juan Orlando, xix, 100, 175
  Salvadoran Officials: Cristiani, President Alfredo Félix, xix, xx, 349. *See also under* Cristiani
Atlacatl Battalion, 138, 139, 146, 147, 178
  El Mozote massacre, 135, 138, 139
Augustine of Hippo, 247, 248, 258, 282, 334
Azcue, Fr. Segundo, 27, 28, 32, 33, 49, 63, 88, 226

Being
  act of, 216, 261
  Aquinas and, 260, 267, 270, 275
  comprehension as a mode of being, 210
  Ellacuría and, 216, 217, 218, 259-66
  *en propio,* 209, 214, 217, 262
  *ens,* 210
  *esse, esse real,* 210
  *ente* or being-as-an-entity, 210, 261
  Heidegger and, 259-62

and meaning, 212
  philosophies of, 208
  Rahner and, 256, 259-66
  *ser* or being-itself, 210, 261
  space, time, consciousness, and, 217
  in Western philosophy, 216
  will-to-being, 219
  Zubiri and, 210-12, 216-18, 256, 259-
    63, 265
Benedict XVI, Pope, 4, 18, 22, 303. *See
    also* Ratzinger, Joseph
bondedness/*religación* to reality, 218, 265
Bonhoeffer, Dietrich, 355
Brockman, James, S.J., on Archbishop
    Romero, 111, 237, 242
Buckland, Major Erik Warren, 177, 178,
    181
Byrne, Hugh, on El Salvador civil war, 77,
    78, 117, 118, 125, 129, 180

capitalism
  in Catholic Social Teaching, 18, 19
  Ellacuría's critique of, 102, 103
  laissez-faire, 18
  Medellín's critique of, 18, 19
Cardenal, Rodolfo, S.J., 55, 64, 69-72, 75,
    76, 83-89, 92, 98, 99, 100, 102, 104-
    8, 112, 114, 123, 128, 202-3, 255
Cardoso, Fernando Henrique, 15, 16
Carpio, Salvador Cayetano, 72, 73
Catholic Church
  and civil society, 101-20
  corporatism, 18, 231, 239
  in Latin America, 16, 17, 20, 30, 32,
    35, 41, 59, 65, 83, 104, 109, 188,
    190, 191, 231, 272, 286, 287, 310,
    323, 340
  and Vatican II, 4, 12, 23, 30
Catholic Social Teaching
  Chávez y González, Archbishop Luis,
    23, 24, 71, 240
  civil society in, 170
  corporatist vs. rights-based
    approaches, 18
  development in, 12, 13, 14, 23
  in El Salvador, 59, 72, 120
  evolution of Oscar Romero, 242
  integral development in, 4, 13, 20, 25,
    30, 60, 61, 62, 79, 348

in Latin America, 17, 18
  liberation in, 4, 5, 16, 17, 18, 19, 20,
    26, 29, 340, 31
  Medellín, 18, 242
  Pope Benedict XVI, 18
  Pope John Paul II, 17
  Pope John XXIII, 17, 23
  Pope Paul VI, 17, 23
  preferential option for the poor, 4, 17,
    18
  Vatican II, 23
CELAM (Conference of Latin American
    bishops), 16-19
  church in civil society, 236
  corporatism, 18
  and development, 25
  Medellín, Colombia, 4, 16-19, 25, 29,
    54, 62, 97, 107, 281
  preferential option for the poor, 22,
    107
  Puebla, Mexico, 17, 247
  Aparecida, Brazil, 18, 22
Center for Social Outreach, 69
Center for Theological Reflection, 63, 70,
    88, 107, 178, 231
Christian-Democratic Party, and UCA, 55
Christian Federation of Salvadoran Farm
    Workers (FECCAS), 106, 107, 165
Christology
  of Ellacuría, 316-18, 334-35, 343, 345
  "from above, 314
  "from below," 288, 314, 316
  of Rahner, 313, 314, 315, 316
  "rising up," 324-33
  of Sobrino, 313-35
church
  carrying forward Jesus' mission
  and civil society, 15, 18, 101-20
  in El Salvador, 24, 25, 71, 103, 153,
    101-16
  as historical sign of Reign of God, 281
  historicizing the reign of God
  of the poor, 285, 287
  role in promoting justice, 12, 13, 17, 18
  as sacrament, 194, 283, 303
civil society
  and body of Christ, 114-16
  Catholic Church as part of, 15, 18
  corporatism, 231, 239

civil society (*continued*)
  Medellín, 18
  mobilization of, 14, 18, 82, 101, 131
  Romero as prophetic defender of,
      108-14
  and social agency
  and state-sponsored violence, 121-57
civil war, in El Salvador, 73, 91, 103, 119,
      132-36, 142, 151, 155, 162, 163,
      167, 183, 338, 356
cognition
  intellection as, 210-17
  neuroscience and, 201, 205, 206, 208,
      212, 213, 215, 216, 272
  perception and, 205-9, 212, 213, 215,
      217, 269, 272
  sentient intelligence, 209, 212-21, 224,
      256, 262-64, 266, 269, 272, 273,
      284, 289, 338, 339
  unity of sensing and intellection, 205,
      208, 209, 213
cognitive neuroscience, 201, 205, 206,
      208, 212, 213, 215, 216, 272
  Joel Nigg, 207
  perception and cognition, 206, 209
  sentient intelligence and, 209, 212-21,
      224, 256, 262-64, 266, 269, 272,
      273, 284, 289, 338, 339
  Zubiri anticipates aspects of, 205, 206,
      215
Cold War
  counterinsurgency doctrine and
      program, 119, 120, 125, 129, 137,
      138, 139, 140-43, 146-51, 183
  Kennan, George C., 6
  low intensity conflict doctrine, 137
  Marshall Plan, 6, 7, 14
  Soviet containment, 6, 7, 14
  Truman Doctrine, 6, 7, 14
colonialism, 6, 9, 10, 11, 18
confrontation with reality, 186, 193, 219,
      225
conversion
  called for by crucified people, 156
  of Central American Jesuits, 3, 4, 23-
      52, 54, 91, 309
  Gelpi, Donald, 111
  as move from one horizon to another,
      3, 4

  personal, 111
  to the phantasm, 262-64, 266, 270-72,
      277, 278, 339
  political, 111, 112, 114, 244
  of Romero, 110, 111, 237, 244, 246,
      252
  Sobrino and, 318, 319, 320
Congregation for the Doctrine of the
      Faith (CDF), 237, 314, 329
consciousness, 208, 209, 217, 218
  collective, 99, 162, 352
Copeland, Shawn, 10
Coreth, Emerich, 94
creation
  Ellacuría and, 277, 343
  economic Trinity, 279
  *exitus-reditus*, 277, 300
  as grafting *ad extra* of the divine life,
      277, 300
  and Logos, 279, 280, 295
  Rahner and, 277, 279, 280, 295, 343
  Zubiri and, 300
Cristiani, President Alfredo Félix, 147,
      173-77, 181, 349
crucified people
  bearing of world's salvation, 293, 306,
      307
  continuing historical presence of
      Jesus, 305, 306
  continuing the historical reality of
      Jesus, 324-35
  continuing the work of God, 304
  as defining sign of the times, 187, 257,
      284
  Ellacuría's idea of, as vocation, 200,
      246, 252, 254, 283, 289, 307
  and historical soteriology, 303-8
  as principle of salvation, 2
  recognition of Jesus in, 342
  Romero's homily at Aguilares, 115,
      248, 285, 297, 303, 335
  sign of God's self-offer in Jesus, 293
  sign of sin and salvation, 305-7
  as suffering servant, 305, 306
  taking down from the cross, 329
crucifixion of Jesus
  *analogatum princeps* of, 254, 287, 312,
      313, 329, 335, 336, 339
  Daniel Harrington on, 321-23

Sobrino on, 321-23
why, 40, 322

D'Abuisson, Roberto, 119, 124-33, 145-52, 168, 174, 240, 246
  and assassination of Archbishop Romero, xvii, 131, 146, 174
  and National Salvation, 124-32
*Dasein*, 208, 224, 261, 274, 275, 276
death
  of the crucified people, 254, 282, 305, 307, 312, 323, 328, 329, 331, 333, 339
  of Ellacuría, 177-80, 225
  historical necessity of, 295
  of Jesus, 46, 96, 250, 254, 282, 285, 287, 288, 294, 295, 297, 298, 302, 303-5, 307, 312, 314-16, 321, 322, 323, 329, 331, 333, 339, 343
  of the poor, 305
  of Romero, 130, 131, 136, 249, 250, 251, 336, 344, 356
  of Rutilio Grande, 108, 109, 111, 113, 244, 245, 248, 344
  of suffering servant, 305
death squads, 107, 114, 116, 121, 125-30, 138, 140, 146, 147, 174
*deiformación* (deification), 301, 307, 313, 332
Delgado, Monsignor Freddy. 235, 239, 240
*Deliberatio primorum patrum*, 36
DeLubac, Henri, 196
dependency
  Andre Gunder Frank and, 15
  Fernando Henrique Cardoso and, 15, 16
  Gustavo Gutiérrez and, 15
  ideology for liberation movements, 9, 10, 11
  liberation theology and, 15
  Paul Prebisch and, 15
  theory of, 14, 15, 16
de Sebastián, Luis, S.J., 57, 64, 85, 116
*de suyo*, 209, 217, 218, 262, 263, 274
Dezza, Paolo, S.J., 26, 86, 165, 166, 226
development
  Catholic Social Teaching and, 12-14, 17, 18

church in El Salvador and, 24, 25
colonization and underdevelopment, 7, 8
developmentalism, 20, 30, 32, 50, 52, 57, 61
discontent with, 4-14
Edward Said and, 9, 10
Frantz Fanon and, 9, 10
integral development, 4, 13, 20, 25, 30, 60, 61, 62, 79, 348
Latin American critics of, 14-16
liberation and, 5, 14, 17, 18
non-aligned nations and, 11-12
post-colonial critiques, 8, 9, 10, 11
quasi-corporatist, 18
Truman Doctrine and, 6, 7
UCA and, 24, 25, 26
United Nations and, 8, 11, 12, 15
Diez, Fr. Zacarias, 241
discernment
  1969 Jesuit retreat, 36, 37, 45
  *Deliberatio primorum patrum*, 36
  of God's preferential option for the poor, 30, 185, 201, 204, 243, 244, 277, 281, 288, 338
  recovery of early Jesuit group discernment, 36
  *Spiritual Exercises*, 36, 37
disciples
  encounter with risen Jesus, 324-27
  living signs of Reign of God, 330, 331
discipleship
  of Archbishop Romero, 253, 356
  Bonhoeffer's ideal of Christian, 355
  collaboration with Trinity, 331
  God raises up, 324
  historicized in worldly reality of Central America, 343
  as living sign of the resurrection, 324, 331, 333, 334
  and option for the poor, 22, 287
  prophetic, 356
  as taking the crucified people down from the cross, 224, 307, 324, 329, 330, 331
  UCA as icon of, 357
dualism
  church and reign of God among humanity, 281

dualism (*continued*)
  cosmic, 223
  Ellacuría's critique of, 223, 224, 281
  grace vs. sin, 223, 224
  history vs. transcendence, 291, 292,
    293
  natural vs. supernatural, 258, 274, 291
  Parmenides and, 205
  sensation vs. intellection, 208, 209,
    264, 268, 271, 278
  theological, 291
  Western thought, 291
Duarte, José Napoleon, 75, 77, 101, 132,
  133, 146, 151, 168, 169, 174, 233

*ECA. See Estudios centroamericanos*
economy of Salvation, 294, 314, 331, 333,
  335
  economic Trinity, 279, 282, 307
  historicity of salvation, 289-301
  Karl Rahner, 279, 280, 291, 293, 294,
    295, 296, 298, 300, 333, 334
Einstein, Albert, 201
Ellacuría, Fr. Ignacio, S.J.
  1969 retreat, 41-43, 45-48, 190, 191
  academic background, 254, 255, 256
  assassination of, xvii-xxii, 177-80
  background, 188, 189
  challenge to Central American Jesuits,
    37-43, 45-48
  Christian historical realism, 219-27,
    289-308
  Christology, 303-8, 315-35
  and Cristiani, 176, 177, 349
  and correlation between Jesus and
    crucified people, 303-8
  criticism of apostolic nuncio, 296
  critique of FMLN, 154, 155, 171
  and D'Abuisson, 129, 130, 131
  dissertation, 35, 94, 202, 203
  distinction of salvation and soteriology,
    293-98
  editor of *Estudios centroamericanos*,
    76, 77, 82, 89
  exile, 132, 158, 161
  on grace and sin, 300
  and historical reality of Jesus, 313-23
  historical soteriology, 296-98, 303-8
  on historicity of salvation, 293-301

  historicization of the *Spiritual
    Exercises*, 197, 198, 199
  history and transcendence, 292, 293
  influence of Aurelio Pólit, S.J., 35, 254
  influence of Elizondo, 35, 188, 189,
    190, 192
  influence of Rahner, 35, 95, 96, 255,
    293, 294, 296, 343, 344
  influence of Romero, 35, 229, 243,
    244-52
  influence of Zubiri, 35, 94, 95, 201-27
  and Inter-American Bank loan, 57, 58
  Jesus-centric approach to fundamental
    theology and soteriology, 297, 298,
    300, 301, 304, 312, 313, 343
  Latin American interpreter of Rahner,
    256
  mentors, 35, 176, 196, 202-4
  mission to Central America, 33, 34,
    189
  negotiations, and, 152, 154, 155, 161-
    64, 167, 175
  peace proposal of, 169, 170, 171
  philosophy of historical reality, 201-27;
    and *Spiritual Exercises*, 196-200
  removal from Jesuit government, 86,
    87
  renewal of Jesuit formation, 35, 36
  revelation and history in, 222, 223
  role in *An Analysis of a National
    Experience*, 80, 81
  salvation, 293-301, 303-8
  Sobrino, collaboration with, 289, 290,
    293, 294, 307
  as target of death squads, 129, 130,
    131
  tension with Salvadoran hierarchy,
    165, 166
  *Teología politica*, 66, 194, 197, 231,
    237, 239, 256, 277, 280-83, 290-93,
    296, 298, 299, 301, 302, 306, 313
  theologian of the *Spiritual Exercises*,
    190-200
  theology of sign, 299, 305, 306; and
    *Spiritual Exercises*, 199, 200
  thinking as action oriented, 66
  third forces, 170-73
  Third World as optimal place to live
    the *Exercises*, 45, 46

and *theōsis*, 300, 301
on salvation in history, 293-301
on transcendence, 292, 293
and UCA commitment to poor, 54
UCA president, 87, 127, 158, 161, 162
vocation to take the crucified people
down from the cross, 252, 254, 307
Elizondo, Miguel, S.J., 26, 30, 33-41, 43-
45, 188-92, 199, 230, 256, 277, 286,
310, 330, 331
as Latin America's retreat master, 188-
95
and *Spiritual Exercises*, 191, 192
El Salvador
1979 coup, 55, 56, 91, 117, 124, 126,
127, 129, 134, 151, 154, 165, 182
agrarian reforms, 71, 72
Catholic Church, 24, 25, 71, 103, 153,
101-16
civil society, 172, 173, 174
civil war, 73, 91, 103, 119, 132-36, 142,
151, 155, 162, 163, 167, 183, 338,
356; peace talks at Ayagualo, 167,
168; peace talks at La Palma, 167
conscienticization of people of, 61
corruption in public life, 73, 74, 75
dirty war, 160
electoral fraud, 74, 75, 76, 103, 104,
116, 231, 233
elite and public policy, 71-76
land reform, 72, 79, 80, 97, 102, 119,
124, 140, 143, 146, 148-50, 175,
230
military alliance with oligarchy, 74, 75
military control of, 102-3
National Debate, 170-74, 179, 352
National Salvation and, 124-32
psychological war, 160, 349, 351
state-sponsored violence, 121-57
UCA expertise in national reality of,
347, 348, 349, 350
U.S. foreign policy and, 136-54; and
land reform, 148-49; and military
reform, 140-42; and political
reform, 150-52
and war with Honduras, 77, 78
*El Salvador: The Political Year of 1971-
1972*, 82, 83
empiricism, 205, 207, 208, 214, 216

entification of reality, 205, 210, 211, 212,
217, 218, 249
ERP (Revolutionary Army of the People),
73, 139
Estrada, Fr. Miguel Francisco, S.J., 36,
42, 49, 50, 51, 63, 64, 82, 83, 84,
86, 87, 104, 158, 165, 234, 235
*Estudios centroamericanos*, 64, 76-79, 82,
89, 102, 158, 173, 230
Ellacuría, as editor of *ECA*, 351
and land reform, 79, 80, 102, 103
and national reality of El Salvador, 351
and university and public affairs, 76,
77, 78, 79
and war of El Salvador with Honduras,
77, 78
*Evangelii nuntiandi*, 243
existentialism, 201, 208
*Externado* (Jesuit high school), 56, 63, 83,
84, 85, 89, 234, 235, 238

faith
of the crucified people, 200, 327
as decision to live by one's intellections
of the absolute dimension of
reality, 264
Ellacuría's carried by Romero's, 243,
244, 247, 252, 253, 338
and history, 23, 96, 98, 290, 291, 298,
300, 302, 303, 304, 324, 326, 327,
332, 333, 334, 356
and liberation theology, 287, 312, 313
and politics, 186, 232
reality, 226
of Romero, 206, 243, 244, 247, 248,
249, 250, 253, 286, 356
Fanon, Frantz
*Black Skins, White Masks* (1952), 9
*The Wretched of the Earth* (1962), 9
Farabundo Martí, Augustín, 123
FARN (Armed Forces of the National
Resistance), 73, 139
Feuerbach, Ludwig, 247, 299
*Filosofía de la realidad histórica*, 60, 196,
203, 204, 220, 221, 263, 276, 280,
307
FMLN (Farbundo Martí National
Liberation Front), xvii, xviii, xix, xx,
xxi, 52, 63, 72, 81, 121, 122, 127,

FMLN (*continued*)
129, 133-37, 139, 147, 148, 150,
152-55, 157, 161, 162, 167-77, 180-
83, 338, 349, 252
FPL (Popular Forces of Liberation), 52,
72, 73, 117, 132, 139
Frank, Andre Gunder, 15
*Freedom Made Flesh* (Ellacuría), 66, 67
Freire, Paolo, and conscientization of the
poor, 30
fundamental theology, 185-87, 201, 254,
256, 277, 286, 289, 296, 306, 335,
338, 339, 340, 343

Gadamer, Hans-Georg, 68, 94
*Gaudium et spes*, 4, 12, 13, 22, 58, 280,
287
Gelpi, Donald, 111
General Conference of Latin American
Bishops *See* CELAM, Medellín,
Puebla, Aparecida
General Congregation XXXII of the
Society of Jesus, 37, 85, 86, 191,
286, 287, 330, 347
God
apprehension of reality of, 256, 259,
260, 264, 265, 266, 271
and crucified people, 329, 344
economic Trinity, 279, 282, 307
as Father of Jesus, 321-23
historical reality of, 292, 353
historical self-communication of, 274,
276, 277
and history, 292
Holy Spirit, 309, 314, 331, 334, 341,
354, 356
knowing, through divine action, 326
love of neighbor and love of, 329
Mystery, 229, 254, 257, 275, 278, 279,
290, 291, 299, 311, 313, 329, 332,
335, 336, 340, 354-57
ongoing self-revelation, 289
presence in natural and historical
reality, 299
as raising up living signs to the
resurrection, 333-35
reality of, 265, 292, 353
as revealed to the UCA martyrs, 340-
57

salvation history and salvation-in-
history, 293-301
self-communication, 274, 276, 277,
279, 294, 296
self-offer, 96, 187, 274, 293, 295, 297,
298, 301, 303, 306, 312-14, 324,
332, 334, 335, 336, 338, 339, 340,
343, 345, 353, 356
transcendence in history, 292, 293
of UCA martyrs, 356
Zubiri's theology of, 203, 218, 265, 266
*See also* Reign of God; Trinity; Jesus
Christ; *theōsis*
Gondra, Fr. José Maria, S.J., 25, 56, 57,
58, 62, 64, 107, 230
Gospels
death of Jesus, 305, 322
as faithful witness, 303
historical reality of Jesus as subject of,
302, 303, 327
inspiration of the UCA, 97-101
Jesus, Reign of God, and the Father,
305, 318
life and ministry of Jesus, 303
resurrection accounts, 313, 325
grace
Archbishop Romero as, 243, 244
and Christian historical realism, 224,
293
and the crucified people, 254, 307,
311, 327, 331-33, 356
Ellacuría's theology of, 187, 197, 281,
294, 300
God's self-offer as, 274, 276, 296
historical account of, 274
historical reality as transformed by,
257, 273-77, 284, 339
nature and, 281, 293
Rahner's supernatural existential and
Ellacuría's theology of, 197, 257,
273-77, 284, 294, 339
reign of, 259, 292
and sin, 223, 258, 259, 274, 289, 292,
293, 300
structural, 259
Gracia, Diego, 205, 207, 208, 209, 218,
224
Grande, Rutilio, S.J., 35, 63, 64, 73, 83,
101-17, 156, 186, 212, 219, 229,

231, 238, 244-46, 248, 250, 253,
280, 341-43, 349, 354, 356
Greece, U.S. intervention in, 6
Greek philosophy, 206, 291
Gutiérrez, Gustavo
agency of the poor, 20
Anselm of Canterbury and theological
method, 23
background, 19, 20
Chimbote, Peru, 20, 31
and Ellacuría, 224, 225, 226
hermeneutical circle, 23
and ideology of modernization, 20
irruption of the poor as agents in
history, 20, 21, 290
liberation theology, 19-23
priority of option for poor, 22, 23, 30
renunciation of dependency theory,
20, 21
and social revolution, 21
theological method, 22, 23

Haig, Alexander, 153
Heidegger, Martin
being, 259, 260, 261
*Dasein,* 208, 224, 261, 274-76
ontology of being, 210, 261, 276
Rahner as student of, 274, 275
subordination of *Dasein* to reality, 276
Zubiri as student of, 196
hermeneutical circle
Emerich Coreth, 94
Gustavo Gutiérrez, 23
Jesus the martyr and present-day
martyrs, 356
Sobrino and, 287, 288, 356
Hernández Pico, Juan, S.J., 30-34, 36, 37,
41, 42, 49, 50-55, 63, 64, 81-88, 91,
105-8, 110, 155, 191, 194, 199, 232,
233, 235
historical Jesus, 313-23
John P. Meier on, 302
*See also* Jesus of Nazareth
historical logos, 292, 302, 308, 327, 335,
339
historical realism, 201, 203, 212, 222, 223,
228, 273, 277, 283, 283, 288, 289,
292, 293, 300, 302, 306, 307, 316,
324, 326, 335, 337, 348, 357

historical reality
of the crucified people, 193, 277, 288,
291, 306, 308, 314, 339, 347, 353
of El Salvador. *See* reality, national
Ellacuría's philosophy of, 195-200;
based on Zubiri, 201-27, 276; and
historical reality of Jesus, 302, 303
of Jesus, 313-23
of Latin America, 4, 5, 45, 46, 49, 58,
59, 65-70, 95, 97, 99, 184, 185, 219,
220, 225, 227, 254, 256, 347, 348
of the poor majorities, 5, 193, 201,
213, 220, 255, 348, 350
proper object of philosophy and
theology, 197, 203, 204, 220, 263,
276, 280
of the Reign of God, 224, 257, 313
*theologal* dimension of, 259, 264
historical soteriology
based on a historical correlation, 304,
305
and Christology, 303-8
and the crucified people, 291, 293,
303-8, 313
and Ellacuría's theology of sign, 299,
306
and the historicity of salvation, 297-98
and the meta-historical character of
salvation, 294, 296, 298
and saving work of Jesus, 297, 304
historical transcendence, 222, 257, 259,
292, 294, 299
and salvation history, 294, 295
historicity of salvation, 289-301, 307, 332,
339
historicization
actualization of human subject
through, 224
of the Christ of the San Salvador
retreat, 45-48
meaning in Ellacuría, 60, 198
method for verifying truth claims, 197,
211, 222, 283
of the mission and ministry of Jesus,
304, 344
of option for the poor, 182, 183, 230
of Rahner's theology of symbol to
theology of sign, 197, 198, 257,
273-83, 306

historicization (*continued*)
    *Spiritual Exercises* and, 197, 198, 199,
      200, 332
    transcendence and, 301
    Zubiri vs. Ellacuría, 197, 221
history and salvation, 292, 293
    and great history of God, 291-93
history, and faith, 326
Ho Chi Minh, 11
hope
    gift of the crucified people, 328
    Sobrino and, 328
    of the victims, 311, 328-31
horizon (philosophical concept), 94, 260,
    261, 271, 276, 278, 279
humanization, 13, 227, 309, 326, 353, 357
human being
    bonded to reality, 218, 265
    grace and, 274, 275, 276, 295
    humanization of, 353, 354
    reality of God *ad extra*, 265
    as relative absolute, 300
    self-definition of, 221
    as a small God, 300

idealism
    neuroscience and, 205-16
    Parmenides and, 205, 210, 291
    reductionist, 205, 207, 208, 212, 219,
      221
    transcendental, 208
    Western, 216, 291
    Zubiri's critique of, 205-12
Idoate, Fr. Florentino, S.J., 25, 27, 28, 29,
    33, 48, 49, 56
idolatry, 301, 312, 321, 357
Ignatius of Loyola, 34-40, 43, 44-48, 186,
    188, 198-93, 195-202, 228, 231,
    232, 251, 277, 282, 283, 286, 289,
    307, 327, 330-32, 346, 347, 355
    and ideal of contemplatives in action,
      347
    spirituality of, 36, 44, 59, 186, 188,
      189, 191, 195, 196, 197, 200, 330
imperialism, 6, 8, 9, 10, 11, 14, 29
impression of reality, 213, 214
*Inteligencia sentiente* (Zubiri), 205, 206,
    209, 210, 211, 212, 213, 214, 216,
    261, 262, 263, 276

*Inteligencia y logos* (Zubiri), 209, 215
*Inteligencia y razón* (Zubiri), 215
intellection
    as act of the *logos*/reason, 215
    and perception, 257, 266, 284
    and sensing, 205, 213-16
intelligence
    as action, 347
    apprehension, 215-218
    cognitive neuroscience, 201, 205, 206,
      208, 212, 213-16
    intellection, 205, 213-16, 257, 266, 284
    logification of, 205, 206, 207, 208, 211,
      212, 215
    as perception, 205, 206, 207, 209, 213,
      215, 216, 217
    sentient, 186, 187, 201, 209, 212-19,
      221, 224, 256, 262-64, 266, 269,
      272, 273, 284, 289, 338, 339
intramundane reality, 203, 263

Jesuits
    1968 meeting in Rio, Brazil, 29-32
    1969 Central American retreat, 36-52
    accused of being Marxists and com-
      munists, 342, 343
    Central-Americanization of province,
      34, 190
    conflict in provincial leadership, 86, 87
    contemplation in action, 44, 192, 195,
      198, 199, 330
    conversion to preferential option for
      the poor, 23-52
    dismissal from diocesan seminary, 82,
      83, 233, 235
    expectation to share the fate and
      future of Jesus, 343
    General Congregation XXXII of the
      Society of Jesus, 37, 85, 86, 191,
      286, 287, 330, 347
    gradualists and liberationists, 44, 54,
      63, 64, 65, 87
    Ignatius Loyola, 34-38, 40, 44, 46,
      188-200, 286, 347
    meditation on the Trinity, 330
    as objectification of the *Exercises*, 45
    and option for the poor in apostolic
      planning, 63-65
    prayer in religious life, 44, 45

province vs. vice-province, 30, 86
reaction to murders of, 180-84
rural evangelization, 103-8
seminary education in El Salvador, 63, 64
*Spiritual Exercises*, 34-39, 43, 45, 46, 48, 188-200, 342, 346
subordination of Central American province to Spain, 33, 34
as targets of death squads, 129-31
Trinitarian mysticism, 40, 307
and UCA Coup, 118, 119
Vatican II, 30-33, 35, 37, 41, 51
Jesus of Nazareth
controversies, 320, 321
correlated with crucified people, 304, 305
as culmination of salvation history, 301
defining sign of the Word made flesh, 291, 308, 335, 339
as faithful son of the Father, 321-23
historical Jesus, 246, 287, 301-3, 315-17, 322-25, 337, 344
historical reality of, 301-3, 313-25; continued in crucified people, 324-33, 344; as starting point for Latin American Christology, 301-3
importance for Christology, 302
as liberator, 287
messianic practice of, 319, 320
miracles, 319
mission and message, 317-21
option for the poor
personal spirituality of, 353, 354
proclamation of the Reign of God, 43-45, 316-21, 342, 344, 353
prophetic acts, 320-23
Reign of God as good news for the poor, 316, 318-20
Sobrino on, 315-17, 325, 344
solidarity with the martyrs, 292, 293
spirit of, 317
as suffering servant, 305, 306
unity with Christ of faith, 315, 322
Jesus Christ
absolute symbol of God, 280, 306
crucifixion, 292, 316, 321-23, 331, 340
as divine and human, 333
divinity, 281, 291, 314, 333

living sacrament of the Word of God, 324
resurrection, 303, 307, 311-17, 323-29, 331-34
salvation in, 302
Son of the Father, 316
why he was killed, 321, 331
Word made flesh, 277, 287, 291, 308, 312, 320, 327, 335, 339
*See also* Jesus of Nazareth
John Paul II, Pope, 4, 17, 113
John XXIII, Pope, 12, 13, 17, 23
justice
General Congregation XXIII of the Society of Jesus, 346, 347
Medellín, 5, 18, 19, 41, 52, 97, 231, 236
in ministry of Archbishop Romero, 245, 248-51, 354
ministry of Jesus, 321
and option for the poor, 5, 18, 29, 52, 67, 93, 97, 321, 327
role of church in promoting, 12, 13, 17, 18
Vatican II, 13, 41

Kant, Immanuel, 217, 326, 327
Kennan, George F., 6
Kennedy, President John F., 14
Khrushchev, Nikita, 11
Kissinger Commission, 138, 146, 147, 181
knowing. *See* intellection; cognition; cognitive neuroscience; sentient intelligence; Zubiri
Kolvenbach, Fr. Peter Hans, S.J., 166

Latin America
bishops, 4, 5, 15-17, 25, 29-32, 54, 62, 97, 192, 231, 237, 247, 281, 287, 290
Cardoso, Fernando Henrique, 15, 16
civil society, 18, 172-74
dependency theory, 14, 15, 16
historical reality of, 4, 5, 45, 46, 49, 58, 59, 65, 66, 67, 69, 70, 95, 97, 99, 184, 185, 219, 220, 225, 227, 254, 256, 347, 348
military rule, 5, 14, 21, 30, 83, 170, 230, 232, 245, 285, 343, 352

Latin America (*continued*)
　Nicaragua, 14, 26, 35, 39, 64, 72, 106,
　　107, 117, 132, 137, 166
Lee, Michael, 297, 298, 304
LeoGrande, William M., 77, 117, 119,
　153
liberation
　as critique of development, 9, 11, 14
　as historicizing the mystery of
　　salvation, 293, 294
　from military rule, 5, 20, 31, 285, 321
　post-WWII national movements for, 9,
　　10, 11, 14, 15, 20
　role in mobilization of civil society, 18,
　　129
　spirituality of, 352, 353, 354
　as theological category, 17, 18, 19
liberation theology
　agency of the poor and, 62, 63
　and Central American Jesuits, 23-52
　contribution to universal church, 22
　Ellacuría and, 32-36, 41-43, 45-52
　emerged from small Christian
　　communities, 232, 238
　Gustavo Gutiérrez and, 20-23, 30
　historical reality and, 23
　Medellín, 4, 5, 16-20, 22, 26, 30-32
　as number one enemy of El Salvador,
　　108
　poor as *locus theologicus* for, 344
　poor majorities and, 245
　preferential option for the poor as
　　essential insight/defining concept,
　　19, 20, 22
　and Romero, 245
　Sobrino and, 290, 320, 352, 353, 354
logification of intelligence, 205, 206, 207,
　208, 210, 211, 212, 215
Logos/logos
　historical, 298, 302, 308, 327, 335, 339
　intelligence and, 206, 210, 215
　of nature, 302
　as *realsymbol* of the Father, 278, 279
　Zubiri's analysis of, 206, 209, 210, 215
Lonergan, Bernard, S.J., 3
López, Fr. Amando, S.J., xxi, 179, 233,
　238, 350
López Vigíl, María, 104, 232, 233, 234,
　236

López y López, Fr. Joaquín, S.J., xxii, 27,
　56, 64, 179, 345, 350
love
　of Archbishop Romero for people of
　　El Salvador, 136, 230, 245, 247,
　　250, 252, 254, 273, 286, 289, 327
　"Contemplation to Attain Divine
　　Love," 48
　for the crucified people, 200, 354, 355
　and discipleship, 329, 331
　for poverty, 38
　praxis of, 328-31
　produces hope, 328, 329
　realized in works, 40, 192, 193
*Lumen gentium*, 13

MacArthur, Gen. Douglas, 11
Macho, Fr. Juan, 241, 242, 243
Magaña, A. Jerez, 129
Maier, Martin, S.J., 228, 231, 255, 273,
　280
Marshall, George C., 6, 7, 14
Martín-Baró, Fr. Ignacio, S.J., xxi, 102,
　158, 159, 160, 161, 166, 170, 179,
　341, 342, 350, 351, 352
martyrdom/martyrs
　of Archbishop Romero, 130, 131, 136,
　　249, 250, 251, 336, 344, 356
　El Salvador, 103, 245, 250
　of Ellacuría, 177-80, 225
　of Rutilio Grande, 103-8
　UCA, 3, 5, 34, 139, 166, 180, 181, 183,
　　184, 240, 327, 330-33, 335-38, 340-
　　57; as signs of transcendence and
　　hope, 292, 293; recognition of Jesus
　　in crucified people of El Salvador,
　　345, 346, 356, 357; as signs of God-
　　with-us, 341, 357; spirituality of,
　　330, 331, 340-57
Marx, Karl, 10, 247, 299
Marxism
　accusation against Jesuits, 47, 107
　Andre Gunder Frank, 15
　Christian alternative, 24
　D'Aubuisson's General Framework
　　for Anti-Marxist Struggle in El
　　Salvador, 125, 131
　Ellacuría: critique of Marx's reduc-
　　tionist materialism, 299; defense of
　　Jesuit high school, 84, 85

Medellín avoids laissez-faire capitalism and Marxism, 18

National University and, 24, 55

post-colonial critiques by Fanon and Said, 9, 10

Report for Conference of American Armies, 100

La Matanza, 72, 121, 123

Mayorga, Dr. Román

blueprint for UCA, 92-96

presidency of UCA, 85-101

role in institutional formation of the university, 55, 56, 57

Medellín, 16-19

Meier, John, on historical and real Jesus, 302, 303

Menendez, Fr. Valentin, S.J., 166

mercy, 306, 312, 317, 321

mind and brain, 213-16

Molina, Col. Arturo Armando, 75, 76, 82, 83, 85, 89, 101, 102, 103, 104, 107, 133, 163, 233, 234, 241

Moltmann, Jürgen, *The Crucified God,* xxii, 179, 310, 357

Montes, Fr. Segundo, S.J., xx, xxi, 34, 64, 100, 119, 158, 159, 175, 179, 341, 342, 349, 350, 351, 352

Montgomery, Tommie Sue, 72, 74, 75, 77, 124, 126, 128, 148, 168

Moreno, Fr. Juan Ramón, S.J., xxii, 49, 179, 310, 347, 350, 357

Mothers of the Disappeared, 112-14, 117, 241

Municipalities in Action, 150

*Mysterium liberationis,* 289-308

*Mysterium salutis,* 290, 293, 294

National Agrarian Reform Congress, 71, 72, 75, 102

National Campaign Plan, 146, 150

*Naturaleza, historia y Dios* (Zubiri), 217

nature

and grace, 274, 281, 293

human, 300, 333; of Christ, 295

as system, 263

negation

*excessus* in Aquinas and Rahner, 270, 271

of history, 334

neuroscience. *See* cognitive neuroscience

Newman, John Henry, 326, 348

faith as "reasonable response," 326

idea of the university, 348

Nietzsche, Friedrich, 221

Nigg, Joel, 207

Nyerere, Julius K., 8

openness, transcendental, 274

Operation Rescate, 135

oppression

context for liberation movements, 5, 14, 19

denunciation in *Evangelii nuntiandi* and documents of Medellín, 30, 243

oppression-liberation axis, 21

socio-political and personal, 223, 247

the UCA and, 70, 90

papal nuncio (El Salvador), 165, 233, 240, 242

Parmenides, 205, 210, 291

Paul VI, Pope, 4, 12, 13, 17, 18, 20, 23, 29, 60, 62, 86, 243

PCS (Community Party), 72, 73, 139

peasant training centers, 242

Peirce, C.S., 209, 222, 280

perception, 205-9, 213, 215-17

phenomenology

*epoche,* 210

formal reality, 209, 210, 217, 218

Gracia, Diego, 205, 207, 208, 209, 218, 224

Heidegger, Martin, 94, 196, 201, 208, 210, 224, 259-62, 270, 274-76, 278

Husserl, Edmund, 196, 201, 208, 209, 210, 217, 261, 262

*noema,* 209, 215

*noesis,* 209

*reity,* 209, 210, 276

philosophy of liberation, 228

Pius XI, Pope, 29

Pius XII Institute, 23

Pólit, Aurelio, S.J., 35, 254

poor

agency of, 20, 62, 63

as Christ (Matthew 25), 342, 343, 345

church of the, 285, 287

poor (*continued*)
  crucifixion of the, 348
  God's preferential option for the, 4-14
  historical reality of, 5, 67, 68, 225, 332,
    343
  irruption of, 5, 19-23, 96, 290
  as *locus theologicus*, 344
  as majority in Latin America, 67
  as participants in shaping the future of
    El Salvador, 351, 352
  Romero's love for, 229, 245
  salvation through the, 46, 342
  as victims of history, 316, 327
*Populorum progressio*, 13, 18, 20, 29, 31,
  61, 62
post-colonialism
  Edward Said, 9, 10
  Frantz Fanon, 9, 10
  and liberation movements, 9, 10, 11,
    14, 19
  underdevelopment, 4, 13, 17
poverty
  document on (Medellín), 4, 16, 30,
    290
  God's preferential option for the poor,
    4, 16, 19, 156, 188, 219, 251
  Ignatian desire for, 38
  Romero and issue of
  spirit of, 13
  vow of, 42, 86
power of the real, 218, 219, 263-66, 299
  directional presence, 265
  encounter with God, 262-66
  foundation of our personal being, 265
  primordial apprehension of, 209, 210,
    214, 262, 266, 272
praxis
  ecclesial, 244, 254, 286
  as historical reality, 197, 221, 307, 348
  of Jesus: prophetic, 320-23, 331; with
    spirit, 323
  of love, 328, 329, 330, 331
  and nature of intelligence, 226
  noetic, ethical, and praxical
    dimensions of intelligence, 95
Prebisch, Paul, 15
preferential option for the poor
  1969 Jesuit retreat
  Catholic Social Teaching, 4, 17, 18

Central American Jesuits: apostolic
    planning and, 63-65; conversion to,
    23-52
  discernment of, 30, 185, 201, 204, 243,
    244, 277, 281, 288, 338
  discipleship and, 22, 287
  God's, 4, 16, 19, 156, 188, 219, 251
  of Jesus, 318, 319, 320
  and justice, 5, 18, 29, 52, 67, 93, 97,
    321, 327
  Latin American bishops, 4, 5, 16-19,
    22, 107
  and liberation theology, 19, 20, 22
  priority of, 22
primordial apprehension of reality, 214,
  262
Private School Law, 26
*Proceso*, 158, 164
Puebla, 17, 247

Rahner, Karl
  agent intellect, 187, 256, 269-72, 278,
    284
  Being/being, 259-66, 267, 270, 271;
    Absolute, 259, 260; metaphysics of,
    259-66; as symbol, 267, 268
  christocentric approach to soteriology,
    295, 296
  connatural transcendence, 275
  conversion to the phantasm, 262, 263,
    264, 266, 270, 271, 272, 278, 339
  Ellacuría and, 35, 95, 96, 253, 255,
    293, 294, 296, 343, 344
  *excessus*, 270, 271
  hearer of the Word, 274
  Heidegger and, 260, 262, 270, 274,
    275
  hylomorphic theory, 187, 256, 259,
    266-73, 278, 284
  influence on Sobrino, 311, 313-16,
    327, 330-34
  meta-historical character of salvation,
    282, 294-99, 301, 306
  *Mysterium salutis*, 293, 294
  Mystery, Absolute, 260, 275
  obediential potency, 274
  preapprehension of Absolute Being,
    256, 259, 264, 265, 266, 271
  *realsymbol*, 267, 268, 278

on salvation, 294, 295, 296
on salvation history, 294
Sheehan, Thomas, 260, 275
on soteriology, 294-98
*Spirit in the World*, 260, 262, 263, 264
supernatural existential, 187, 197, 257,
    273, 274, 275, 276, 284, 339
symbol, theology of the, 277-83
theory of knowing, 262-65, 266-73
Thomas Aquinas and, 260, 265-72,
    275, 277, 278
transcendental Christology of, 295
Ramos, Celina Mariceth, xxii, 179, 350
Ramos, Julia Elba, xxii, 179, 342, 350
Ratzinger, Joseph, 329, 330. *See also*
    Benedict XVI, Pope
Reagan, Ronald, 126, 137, 153, 154, 168,
    172
realism, post-Newtonian, 187, 216-19,
    256, 284, 289, 338
reality
    actualization of, 209, 214, 217, 218,
        224, 227, 262
    apprehension of, 209, 213-18, 256,
        259-66, 271, 272
    assumed into social realm of freedom,
        197
    of the cosmos, 204, 220
    *de suyo,* 209, 217, 218, 262, 263, 274
    Ellacuría's dimensions of facing up to:
        pick up or assume responsibility for
        (*cargar con la*), 94, 221, 225, 244,
        348, 350; realize about or grasp
        what is at stake in (*hacerse cargo
        de la*), 94, 221, 224, 244, 348; take
        charge of or change (*encargarse de
        la*), 94, 221, 244, 348
    entification of, 205, 210-12, 217, 218
    evasion of, 204-6, 212
    as formality, 209, 217, 218
    as fundamentality, 209, 218
    historical. *See* historical reality
    of historical Jesus and resurrection,
        324, 325
    impression of, 213, 214
    intelligence and, 214, 215
    intramundane, 203, 262, 263
    material, biological, sentient, and
        historical dimensions of, 217, 263

as mystery, 332-33
national, 65, 68-71, 80, 81, 90, 95, 98,
    158, 160-64, 194, 213, 347-52, 357
phenomenological definition of, 209
primacy of, 186, 212, 217, 218, 219,
    256, 259, 284
primordial apprehension of, 209, 210,
    214, 215, 262, 266, 272
of qualities, 206, 215, 216
*reity,* 209, 210, 276
as subcategory of being, 210, 216
of the subject, 218
theologal dimension, 187, 256, 259,
    264, 266, 273, 284, 301, 332, 339
transcendental march toward, 215
reason, 215
redemption, objective and subjective,
    295, 296
reductionism, 205, 206, 210
    Ellacuría's critique of, 186, 205
    entification of reality, 210-12
    logification of intelligence, 206-8
reductionist
    empiricism, 207, 208, 214, 216
    idealism, 186, 205-8, 212, 219, 221
Reign of God (Kingdom of God)
    already/not yet realized, 223
    church as historical sign of, 281
    and the crucified people, 257, 293, 336
    as good news to the poor, 317-22, 340,
        343, 344
    historicizing the, 317-24, 342-44
    Jesus of Nazareth and, 43-48, 257,
        303, 305, 315-22, 327
    as liberation from poverty, military
        rule, and state-sponsored violence,
        343, 344
    vs. sin, 39, 40, 305
    *Spiritual Exercises* and, 43-48
    UCA creating models that better
        correspond to, 98
reity, 209, 210, 276
*religación*/bondedness to reality, 218,
    265
resurrection
    as eschatological event, 326
    as historical dimension of Jesus, 325-
        27
    historical witness, 325-27

resurrection (*continued*)
  Newman's notion of faith as
    "reasonable response," 326
  paschal experience, 324, 325
  raising up living signs of the, 333-35
  as something real, 324, 325
  viewed from Latin American context,
    326, 327
  what is historical in Jesus', 325, 326,
    327
revelation
  crucified people as, 335, 353
  God's self-revelation, 67, 97, 289, 294,
    303, 334, 335, 345
  historical reality of Jesus as, 301-3,
    313, 334, 335, 339
  and history, 67, 97, 222, 289, 298-301,
    304
  as ongoing, 298, 299
rich, troubling questions for, 348
Rist, Gilbert, 207, 211, 215, 216
Rivera Damas, Archbishop Arturo, 23, 24,
    71, 101, 105, 145, 152, 153, 161,
    168, 170, 171, 172, 235, 236, 240
Rivera, Jorge Eduardo, 276
Rivera, Julio, 28, 101
Romero, Archbishop Oscar
  assassination of, xvii, 130-32, 136, 249,
    250
  auxiliary in San Salvador, 230-36
  church as unifier and social glue, 231
  civil society and the body of Christ,
    114, 115, 116
  conflicts with the Jesuits, 232-35, 237
  conversion, 109, 110-13, 237
  critique of Jesuit high school, 84, 234
  defender of civil society, 108-16
  and dismissal of Jesuits from diocesan
    seminary, 82, 83
  editor of *Orientación*, 231-37
  encounter with suffering/crucified
    people, 240, 241, 242, 246, 247
  evolution in relations with priests, 109,
    239, 242, 243
  good relations with government, 233,
    234
  ideological warrior, 237, 238, 239
  influence of assassination of Rutilio
    Grande, 109-11, 229, 244-46

  influence on Ellacuría, 229, 243-52,
    343, 344
  and peasant training centers, 242
  prophet of Salvadoran state, 246-49
  salvation in the history of El Salvador,
    248, 249
  in Santiago de María, 236-43
  seminary closed under, 235
  and Sobrino, 116, 312, 321, 327, 332-
    36
  spirituality of, 354
  as teacher of the UCA, 155-57, 250-51
Rosa Chávez, Bishop Gregorio, 110, 111,
    112, 114

sacrament
  body of Christ, 115, 281
  church as, 194, 283, 303
  crucified people as, 194, 195, 254, 303
  historical reality of Jesus as, 287, 324,
    334
  Romero's procession in Aguilares, 115
  UCA martyrs as, 357
Said, Edward
  *Orientalism* (1978), 10
  post-colonialism, 9
Salvadoran Communal Union (UCS), 76
salvation
  crucified people as sign of, 273-84
  Ellacuría's concept of, 257-59, 274,
    277, 282, 283, 290-301
  historicity of, 257, 258, 290, 291-93
  history and, 291-93, 335, 339
  meta-historical character of, 282, 294,
    295-301, 306
  *Mysterium salutis*, 290, 293, 294
  mystery of, 290, 294, 297, 299, 313,
    329
  objective and subjective dimensions
    of, 295, 296
  poor as sacrament of, 303
  Rahner's influence on Ellacuría's
    concept of, 257-59, 274, 283, 291,
    294-98, 300
  as salvation in history, 228, 249-50,
    257, 258, 277, 282, 283, 290, 291,
    293-301
  vs. soteriology, 294, 295, 296, 300
  in suffering and death of Jesus, 297

second coming, and self-offer of Jesus, 334

self-communication of God, 274, 276, 277, 279, 294, 296

self-determination (and historicization), 264

self-revelation of God, 97, 289, 294, 303, 334, 335, 345

semiotics, 208, 280, 282

sensing
 formal unity of intellection and, 213
 and intellection, 205, 213-16

sentient intelligence, 209, 212-21, 224, 256, 262-64, 266, 269, 272, 273, 284, 289, 338, 339

servant, suffering, 305, 306

Sheehan, Thomas, 260, 275

sign
 Ellacuría's theology of, 197, 257, 277-84, 289, 296, 299, 305, 306, 330, 339; influence of Rahner's theology of symbol, 197, 257, 268, 277-84, 327, 330, 339
 of salvation, 273-77
 of the *Spiritual Exercises*, 195-200
 vs. symbol, 277-83, 289
 of the times, 187, 193-95, 198, 204, 247, 257, 281, 283, 284, 306, 345

sin
 Archbishop Romero's fourth pastoral letter and, 301
 Ellacuría's 1969 challenge to Central American Jesuits, 41, 42, 43
 and grace, 223, 258, 259, 274, 283, 289, 292, 293, 300, 312
 history of, 223, 258, 283, 292, 293
 social, 357
 *Spiritual Exercises,* first week, 39-43; meditation on sin, 346
 structural, 98, 259

*Sobre el hombre* (Zubiri), 208

*Sobre la esencia* (Zubiri), 210, 221, 261, 262, 275, 276

Sobrino, Jon
 and Archbishop Romero, 116, 312, 321, 327, 332-36; *gloria Dei, vivens homo,* 228, 354; *gloria Dei, vivens pauper,* 28, 353, 354; second pastoral letter, 116, 349

background, 310, 311
and CDF, 314, 329
Christian university, 53, 348, 351, 355
Christology, 286, 287, 288, 312-35
collaboration with Ellacuría, 286-88
critique of Joseph Ratzinger, 329
Easter experience, 313, 325, 335, 340
evangelist of Medellín's option for the poor, 309
and historical reality of Jesus, 313-23
history and faith, 326
hope, 328
influence of Rahner, 314-16, 330, 333-35
reality principle, 324
and Reign of God, 318, 319
"rising up" from the historical reality of Jesus to the Christ of faith, 324-33
and spirituality of liberation, 352-54
target of death squads, 129
whole Christ, 316, 324
as witness to the crucified people and those who love them, 311, 312

Society of Jesus. *See* Jesuits

solidarity with the poor and oppressed, 20-23, 30, 32, 46, 67, 68, 76, 86, 98, 182, 184, 186, 193, 194, 223, 225, 245, 249, 284, 286, 288, 292, 295, 307, 333, 341, 345, 350, 353

*Sollicitudo rei socialis,* 4, 17

soteriology
 doctrine of grace, not confused with, 296, 298
 Ellacuría on, 296, 297, 298, 300, 303, 304, 305, 306, 308, 313
 and grace, 298
 historical, 291, 293, 297, 300, 303, 304, 305, 306, 308, 313
 Jesus Christ, focused on saving work of, 297, 298
 and Michael Lee, 297, 298
 Rahner and, 294-98
 salvation: not confused with, 294-96, 300; and historicity of, 289-91, 293, 294, 297-98, 301, 307, 332, 339

Soviet Union, 5, 7, 8, 11, 12, 172, 239

Spirit
 handed down in New Testament, 317

Spirit (*continued*)
   as historical force/reality, 317
   Holy, 9, 14, 331, 334, 341, 346, 354,
      356
   human person as spirit-in-the-world,
      266, 268, 272, 274, 279, 339
   Jesus' practice with, 316, 317, 321,
      323, 333
   of Medellín and Rio, 42, 84, 85, 193,
      231, 289
   poor with, 316
spirituality
   of Archbishop Romero, 286, 354
   Jesuit/Ignatian/of *Spiritual Exercises*,
      34, 36-38, 44, 59, 186, 188-91, 195-
      97, 200, 286, 327, 330, 332
   of liberation, 352-54
   Sobrino and, 352-54
   Trinitarian, 192, 354
   of UCA martyrs, 330, 331, 336
suffering
   caused by sin and idolatry, 312
   liberating praxis brings, 321
   miracles of Jesus addressed to, 319,
      320
   Reign of God address to suffering
      poor, 318, 319, 321

*Teología politica* (Ellacuría), 66, 194, 197,
      231, 237, 239, 256, 277, 280-83,
      290-93, 296, 298-302, 306, 313
theologal dimension
   of historical reality, 259
   influence of Rahner (Absolute)
   of reality, 187, 256, 259, 264, 266, 273,
      284, 301, 332, 339
theology of sign
   of Ellacuría, 197, 257, 277-84, 289,
      296, 299, 305, 306, 330, 339; and
      *Spiritual Exercises*, 199, 200
   Rahner's theology of symbol, influence
      of, 197, 198, 257, 273-83, 306
*theōsis*, 282, 300, 301, 307, 313, 329, 331,
      332, 335, 340, 343, 354
   as *deiformación* (deification), 301, 307,
      313, 332
Third World, 11-13, 24, 32, 46-51, 93, 99,
      104, 107, 116, 138, 153, 192, 193,
      219, 247, 256, 323, 342, 344

   as optimal place to live the *Exercises*,
      342
Tracy, David, 323
tradition
   Catholic Social Teaching, 12, 22, 23
   Jesuit spirituality, 330
   prophetic, 22, 23, 321
   *Spiritual Exercises*, 35, 36, 37
   Western philosophical, 200, 210
transcendence
   of God, 300, 326
   historical, 222, 257, 259, 292, 294, 299
   in history, 292, 293
   as known through history, 332
Trinity
   economic, 279, 282, 307
   Elizondo and, 40, 43, 192, 277, 294,
      295, 296, 299, 300, 307, 330, 331
   Ellacuría's theology of the, 254
   Rahner: economic Trinity is the
      immanent Trinity, 279; influence
      on Ellacuría, 254, 294, 307;
      influence on Sobrino, 307, 313,
      334; and theology of symbol, 279,
      280
   and self-revelation and self-offer of
      God, 334
   in Sobrino, 307, 313, 333, 334
   and *Spiritual Exercises*, 192, 330, 331
Truman, Harry, 5, 6, 7, 12, 14, 20

UCA. *See* University of Central America
UCA Coup, 53, 56, 73, 116-20, 133
Ungo, Guillermo, 69, 101, 102, 118, 127,
      128, 129, 133, 165, 233
United for Reconstruction, 150
United Nations
   Commission on the Truth for El
      Salvador, xvii, xviii, xix, xx, xxi, 122,
      124, 125, 127, 129, 130, 132, 135,
      140, 143, 146, 177, 178
   Decade of Development, 4, 12, 13, 20,
      29
United States
   Cold War politics, and El Salvador,
      152-54
   counterinsurgency policy, 136-52
   and human rights in El Salvador, 142-
      48

nation building in El Salvador, 136-52
Reagan administration, 126, 137, 153,
    154, 168
unity
    of history, 223, 258, 291, 292, 316
    of history and transcendence, 292, 293
    of human history and salvation history,
        257, 258
    in-difference between matter and
        form (hylomorphism), 267, 278
    and intramundane reality, 203, 263
    of mind and brain, 213-16
    of self-transcending systems
        comprising the cosmos, 263
    of sensing and intellection, 213, 216,
        262, 272
University of Central America (UCA)
    accusation of Marxist tendencies, 164,
        165
    and agrarian reform, 71, 72, 79, 80,
        102, 103
    blueprint of Mayorga and Ellacuría,
        92-96
    Center for Information, Documen-
        tation, and Research Support
        (CIDAI), 158, 162
    Center for Political and Social
        Documentation, 157, 158
    Chair for the National Reality, 161,
        350, 351
    Christian character of, 65, 66, 96-101,
        344, 345, 357
    as conscience for Salvadoran reality,
        61, 62
    and conscienticization of El Salva-
        dorans, 61
    contributions of lay faculty, 53, 55, 56,
        91
    critical conscience, 27, 81
    development and, 24, 25, 60
    Ellacuría's vision for, 94-96
    *Estudios centroamericanos,* and public
        affairs, 76, 77, 78, 79
    eviction from Salesian property, 28, 29
    and expertise in national reality of El
        Salvador, 347, 348, 349, 350
    founding and early years, 24, 25, 26,
        27, 28, 29, 53-85
    funding for, 56-58

and historical reality of Central
    America, 59
Human Rights Institute (IDHUCA),
    158
Institute for Public Opinion (IUDOP),
    158, 159, 160
and integral development, 60, 61
Inter-American Bank, speech to, 56-
    58, 2, 97
Jesuits: as bearers of Jesus' Holy Spirit
    to the people of El Salvador, 346-
    56; as contemplatives in action for
    justice, 347, 348, 349; and option
    for the poor, 347, 348; recognition
    of risen Jesus in crucified people,
    341
"Justifying and Clarifying Considera-
    tions for the Salary Scale of the
    University," 69, 70
land reform. *See* UCA, and agrarian
    reform
martyrs, 174-80
Mayorga's vision for, 85-101
as negotiators, 167
as new kind of Christian university,
    157-67, 348-52
obligation to pursue truth and liberty,
    60, 67, 68
and option for the poor, 65, 66, 344,
    347, 348
Organizational Handbook, 69
as place of discernment of God's
    presence in the world, 344
position in political debates, 71-76
presidency of Dr. Román Mayorga,
    85-101
presidency of Fr. Florentino Idoate,
    25, 27, 28, 29, 33, 48, 49, 56
presidency of Fr. Luis Achaerandio,
    56-85
presidency of Fr. Ignacio Ellacuría, 87,
    127, 158, 161, 162
and promotion of liberty, 62
role in negotiations for peace in El
    Salvador, 161-64
role of lay faculty and staff, 91, 92
role in El Salvador civil society, 167-80
self-understanding as university, 351,
    352

University of Central America (*continued*)
  and solidarity with the poor, 67, 68
  synthetic statement of 1979, 96-101
  target of violence, 131, 132, 167, 175
  tension with Salvadoran hierarchy, 165, 166
  *theoria* of self-understanding, 88-101
  truth in mission of, 61, 62
  and values of Reign of God, 59
  and Vatican II, 58, 59
utopia, Reign of God as, 318, 319

Vatican II (Second Vatican Council), 4, 12, 13, 16, 17, 20, 23, 30, 31, 32, 33, 35, 37, 41, 83, 104, 109, 188, 190, 191, 197, 228, 231, 255, 272, 286, 293, 323, 340
  and UCA, 58, 59, 65, 310
Vietnam War, 11, 137, 142, 143
Von Balthasar, Hans Urs, 294

Weber, Max, 19, 21
White, Robert, 126, 152, 153, 154
White Warriors Union, 103, 114, 117
Whitfield, Teresa, 81-84, 86, 105, 106, 176, 349
World War II, 5, 7, 190

Young Officers' Coup, 73, 120, 128, 132, 152

Zamora Rivas, Mario, 132
Zubiri, Xavier
  anticipation of aspects of cognitive neuroscience, 205, 206, 215
  bondedness (*religación*) to reality, 218, 265

critique of evasion of reality, 204-12
critique of reductionist idealism, 205-8, 212, 214, 216, 219, 221
deification (*deiformación*), 300, 301, 307, 313, 332
*de suyo*, 209, 217, 218
*El hombre y Dios* (Zubiri)
entification of reality, 205, 210-12, 217, 218
formal definition of reality, 276
human intelligence model, 66
influence of Edmund Husserl, 207, 208
influence of Martin Heidegger, 275, 276
influence of Rahner, 202, 203, 261, 275, 276
influence on Ellacuría, 35, 94, 95, 201-27, 276
intellection, knowing, 205-17, 347
logification of intelligence, 206-10
natural sciences, influence of, 201
*noema* and reality, 209, 215
*noesis* and reity, 209
reality, 206-20
sentient intelligence, 209, 212-16, 218, 219, 221, 224, 256, 262-64, 266, 269, 272, 273, 284, 289, 338, 339
structural unity of sensing and intellection, 213, 216, 262, 272
systems theory, 201, 263
theologal dimension of reality, 187, 256, 259, 264, 266, 273, 284, 301, 332, 339